北京外国语大学中华文化国际传播研究院

"十四五"规划项目资助

A SOURCEBOOK IN CLASSICAL CONFUCIAN PHILOSOPHY

先秦儒家哲学文献译解

〔美〕安乐哲 著
Roger T. Ames

商务印书馆
创于1897　The Commercial Press

图书在版编目(CIP)数据

先秦儒家哲学文献译解 = A Sourcebook in Classical Confucian Philosophy：英文/(美)安乐哲(Roger T. Ames)著.—北京：商务印书馆，2023(2024.4 重印)
ISBN 978-7-100-21434-6

Ⅰ.①先… Ⅱ.①安… Ⅲ.①先秦哲学—文献—研究—英文 Ⅳ.① B220.5

中国版本图书馆 CIP 数据核字（2022）第 152902 号

权利保留，侵权必究。

A Sourcebook in Classical
Confucian Philosophy
先秦儒家哲学文献译解
Roger T. Ames
〔美〕安乐哲　著

商 务 印 书 馆 出 版
(北京王府井大街36号　邮政编码100710)
商 务 印 书 馆 发 行
三河市春园印刷有限公司印刷
ISBN 978-7-100-21434-6

2023 年 4 月第 1 版　　开本 880×1230　1/32
2024 年 4 月第 2 次印刷　印张 25 1/2

定价：168.00 元

TABLE OF CONTENTS

INTRODUCTION ... vii

CONFUCIAN NATURAL COSMOLOGY: AN INTERPRETIVE CONTEXT ... 001
    Interpretive Assumptions ... 001
    Philosophy of Culture: Change and Persistence ... 005
    Distinguishing Confucian Cosmology from Greek Transcendentalism ... 007
    Power and Creativity ... 011
    Contrasting Confucian Zoetology with Greek Ontology ... 015
    A Chinese Cosmology with "Its Own Causality and Its Own Logic" ... 019
    Shi 勢: An Aesthetic Alternative to the Logic of "Things" and to an "External Causality" ... 027
    Genealogical Cosmogony and Its "Epistemogony" ... 029
    Qi 氣 as a Moral Cosmology ... 033
    A Thick Generalization: Distinguishing "Events" from "Objects" ... 038
    A Thick Generalization: Distinguishing "Phases" from "Elements" ... 041
    Vital *Qi* 氣 as Functional Structure and Structured Function ... 044
    A Human "Being" or Human "Becomings"? ... 048
    Defining a World by Association ... 057
    The *Book of Changes* 易經: A Cosmological Vocabulary ... 063
    Tang Junyi 唐君毅 and the Philosophical Implications of a *Qi* 氣 Cosmology ... 071

THE CANONICAL TEXTS: SELECTED PASSAGES 090
I. THE *BOOK OF CHANGES* (*YIJING* 易經): A PROCESS COSMOLOGY 090
II. THE *EXPANSIVE LEARNING* (*DAXUE* 大學): SETTING THE CONFUCIAN PROJECT 120
The *Expansive Learning*: Part 1 124
The *Expansive Learning*: Part 2 128
The *Expansive Learning*: Part 3 131
III. THE *ANALECTS* (*LUNYU* 論語): A BASIC CONFUCIAN VOCABULARY 133
Cultivating One's Person (*xiushen* 修身) 137
III.1 Cherishing Learning (*haoxue* 好學): A Confucian Philosophy of Education 142
III.2 A Joyful Wisdom (*zhi* 知) 160
III.3 Virtuosity (*de* 德) 170
III.4 Doing Your Utmost (*zhong* 忠) and Making Good on Your Word (*xin* 信) 178
III.5 Putting Oneself in the Other's Place Through Dramatic Rehearsal (*shu* 恕) 185
Setting the Family Right (*qijia* 齊家) 190
III.6 Reverencing Family (*xiao* 孝) 196
III.7 Consummate Conduct/Persons in Roles and Relations (*ren* 仁) 211
III.8 Seeking Optimal Appropriateness in Roles and Relations (*yi* 義) 230
III.9 Aspiring to Ritual Propriety in Roles and Relations (*li* 禮) 240
III.10 The Making of Music (*yue* 樂) 254
Bringing Proper Order to the State (*zhiguo* 治國) 263
III.11 Using Names Properly (*zhengming* 正名) 268
III.12 Exemplary Persons (*junzi* 君子) and Scholar-Officials (*shi* 士) 286

III.13 Harmony as an Optimizing Symbiosis (*he* 和)	310
III.14 Making Friends (*you* 友)	314
III.15 Governing Properly (*zheng* 政)	322
Effecting Peace in the World (*pingtianxia* 平天下)	339
III.16 Human Way-Making (*rendao* 人道)	345
III.17 Confucius: One Special Person Extending the Proper Way (*dao* 道)	360
III.18 A Family-Centered Religiousness (*tian* 天)	384

IV. THE *MENCIUS* (*MENGZI* 孟子): EXTENDING THE VOCABULARY — 395

IV.1 An Interpretive Context for Reading the *Mencius*	402
IV.2 Continuing on the Way of Confucius	413
IV.3 The Vocabulary of Mencius's Moral Sensorium	433
IV.4 Role Politics and Consummate Governing (*renzheng* 仁政)	507
IV.5 Maintaining *Tian's* Mandate (*tianming* 天命)	551

V. THE *FOCUSING THE FAMILIAR* (*ZHONGYONG* 中庸): THE HIGHEST EXPRESSION OF THE CONFUCIAN PROJECT — 556

V.1 Chapter 1: The Confucian Project: "The Continuity Between and Inseparability of the Human and the Cosmic Orders" (*tianrenheyi* 天人合一)	564
V.2 Chapters 2, 3, 5, 8: Explaining the Term *zhongyong* 中庸	569
V.3 Chapter 12: The Proper Way of Exemplary Persons (*junzi* 君子)	572
V.4 Chapter 15: Family as the Trailhead of the Proper Way (*dao* 道)	573
V.5 Chapter 17: The Cosmic and the Human as a Contrapuntal Dynamic	574
V.6 Chapter 19: Effecting Order Through Family Reverence (*xiao* 孝)	575

    V.7 Chapter 21: The Foundational and the Creative Aspects of Education   577

    V.8 Chapter 25: Resolve (*cheng* 誠) as a Collaborative and Reflexive Creativity   578

    V.9 Chapter 30: Confucius as a Force of Nature   581

    V.10 Chapter 31: Optimal Sagacity (*zhisheng* 至聖)   583

    V.11 Chapter 32: Optimal Resolve (*zhicheng* 至誠)   585

    V.12 Chapter 33: The *Book of Songs* (*Shijing* 詩經) as a Confucian "Ode to Joy"   586

VI. THE *CLASSIC OF FAMILY REVERENCE* (*XIAOJING* 孝經): THE PRIME CONFUCIAN MORAL IMPERATIVE   590

    VI.1 Chapter 1: Setting the Theme and Illuminating Its Meaning (開宗明義章)   594

    VI.2 Chapter 2: The Emperor as Son of *Tian* (天子章)   596

    VI.3 Chapter 6: The Common People (庶人章)   597

    VI.4 Chapter 7: The Three Powers and Resources (三才章)   597

    VI.5 Chapter 8: Effecting Sociopolitical Order Through Family Reverence (孝治章)   599

    VI.6 Chapter 9: Sagely Governance (聖治章)   600

    VI.7 Chapter 12: Expanding upon the Essential Way (廣要道章)   603

    VI.8 Chapter 13: Expanding on the Utmost Moral Virtuosity (廣至德章)   604

    VI.9 Chapter 15: On Remonstrance (諫諍章)   605

    VI.10 Chapter 18: Mourning for Parents (喪親章)   607

VII. THE *FIVE MODES OF VIRTUOSIC CONDUCT* (*WUXINGPIAN* 五行篇): THE INTERIM BETWEEN CONFUCIUS AND MENCIUS   608

    VII.1: Habituating Moral Virtuosity   619

    VII.2: Humans Can Broaden the Way and Sages Can Continue and Carry Out the Workings of *Tian* 人能弘道, 聖人能繼天立極   621

VII.3: The Authentication of Moral Virtuosity in Action   626
VII.4: Consummate Conduct (*ren* 仁), Wisdom (*zhi* 智), and Sagacity (*sheng* 聖) as Necessary Conditions for Moral Suasion   627
VII.5-7: The Thinking of Consummate, Wise, and Sagacious Persons   630
VII.8: Consolidating Virtuosic Habits as an Inner Disposition for Action   632
VII.9: The Inexhaustibility of the Habitude of Moral Virtuosity (*de* 德)   635
VII.10: Opening with Bells and Rallying Others with Jade Tubes   635
VII.11-14: Vocabulary Clusters for Modes of Virtuosic Conduct   637
VII.15-16: The Need for Sagacity and Wisdom in Recognizing the Way of Exemplary Persons   638
VII.17: A Perceived Logic Among the Five Modes of Virtuosic Conduct   639
VII.18: Efficacy (*shan* 善) as the Symbiosis of Four Modes of Virtuosic Conduct   641
VII.19: Consummate Conduct (*ren* 仁) and the Power of Human Feelings   641
VII.20: Appropriateness (*yi* 義) Is Being Steadfast in Walking the Walk   642
VII.21: Propriety (*li* 禮) Is Deference in Broad Compass   643
VII.22-23: Seeing the Big Picture and Making Allowances   644
VII.24: Consolidating Great Accomplishments and Promoting the Worthy   645
VII.25: A Symbiosis Among the Heartmind's (*xin* 心) Attendants   647
VII.26: Correlative Methods for Advancing Knowledge   649

    VII.27: Tian 天 as a Guide in the Tian-Human (tianren 天人) Relation   650

    VII.28: The Different Modes of Virtuosic Conduct as Different Responses to the Proper Way (dao 道)   651

VIII. THE *MOZI* 墨子: ON DENOUNCING THE CONFUCIANS AND THEIR DOCTRINES   651

    VIII.1 Gongmeng (公孟)   656

    VIII.2 Denouncing the Confucians (feiruxia 非儒下)   658

IX. THE *XUNZI* 荀子: A SYNCRETIC CONFUCIAN PHILOSOPHY   666

    IX.1 Chapter 1: Exhortation to Learning (quanxue 勸學)   681

    IX.2 Chapter 2: Personal Cultivation (xiushen 修身)   689

    IX.3 Chapter 8: Confucian Achievements (ruxiao 儒效)   695

    IX.4 Chapter 9: Regulations of a True King (wangzhi 王制)   697

    IX.5 Chapter 12: The Way of the Ruler (jundao 君道)   714

    IX.6 Chapter 15: Debating Military Affairs (yibing 議兵)   723

    IX.7 Chapter 17: On Nature (tianlun 天論)   735

    IX.8 Chapter 19: On Ritual Practices (lilun 禮論)   744

    IX.9 Chapter 21: Dispelling Obsessions (jiebi 解蔽)   756

    IX.10 Chapter 22: On Using Names Properly (zhengming 正名)   763

    IX.11 Chapter 23: Native Human Propensities Are Base (xing'e 性惡)   777

BIBLIOGRAPHY OF WORKS CITED   791

INTRODUCTION

The last generation of sourcebooks for Chinese philosophy consists primarily of original translations of excerpts from selected, representative texts, with an attempt by the editors at a sufficiently broad coverage of each of the several philosophical lineages under review. In Wing-tsit Chan's 陳榮捷 ground-breaking contribution to this important initiative, *A Source Book in Chinese Philosophy* (Princeton, 1963), his choice was to provide his readers with a considerable volume of translated textual materials organized chronologically, with a minimum of philosophical commentary or interpretive context. This Chan *Source Book* has been foundational in several senses. In what it includes and what it excludes, it circumscribed the parameters of the philosophical corpus for a generation of students of Chinese philosophy. For example, "original" pre-Qin texts and figures of "orthodox" schools are much emphasized while Han dynasty philosophy is underrepresented, being described as merely eclectic and "miscellaneous" (*za* 雜). Again, this Chan anthology has set a high bar in the quality of its translations. In this respect, it has galvanized a specific formula of translations for key philosophical terms, promoting what scholars have since come to regard as the standard if not "literal" rendering of the classical Chinese philosophical vocabulary. For its time, it was a quantum advance on what had rather serendipitously been translated previously from the Chinese philosophical canons both in its coverage and in its quality.

In the decades that have ensued since the initial publication of Chan's *Source Book*, substantial and sometimes complete translations of many of the traditional philosophical works included in its pages have appeared. Although these new publications are usually more comprehensive than the sometimes brief excerpts found in Chan's *Source Book*, the fuller translations with some notable exceptions have in many respects provided the student of Chinese philosophy with more of the same. That is, many of the more recent publications have expanded the coverage of this philosophical corpus through either setting their own chronological limits or focusing selectively on one tradition or another. And they have, with varying degrees of success, aspired to match the quality of the translations found in Chan's *Source Book*.

In my efforts to compile this new *Sourcebook*, while highly appreciative of the progress that has been made, I have had two closely related concerns about the limitations of what has come before. First, many of these new translations have uncritically perpetuated the same formula for rendering key philosophical terms proffered in the earlier efforts. Secondly, there has been insufficient attention paid to locating these philosophical classics within their own interpretive contexts as a precondition for allowing these texts to speak on their own terms. Indeed, I will argue that by default, we have in some important degree inadvertently transplanted these texts into a worldview and a commonsense not their own. And the consequence of uncritically preserving the same formula for rendering key philosophical terms is that this now "standard" vocabulary has encouraged a sense of confidence in the literalness of what is taken to be an erstwhile "Chinese" philosophical vocabulary.

To be fair to the important new translations that have appeared over the past few generations, we must ask the question: At the end of the day, can European languages, freighted as they are with a historical commitment to substance ontology—what Jacque Derrida has called "logocentrism" and "the language of presence"—actually "speak" the processual worldview that grounds these early Confucian texts? Can canonical texts such as the *Book of Changes* (*Yijing* 易經) and the *Expansive Learning* (*Daxue* 大學) be translated into English and still communicate the worldview that has been invested in them? And more to the point, given the project presently at hand, how does this new *Sourcebook* address the challenge of trying to provide a translation of these Chinese texts that would respect their own implicit worldviews?

It is in this effort to take Chinese philosophy on its own terms then, that the first section of this *Sourcebook* is an extended essay, "Confucian Natural Cosmology: An Interpretive Context." This introductory section is an attempt to excavate and make explicit the tradition's own indigenous presuppositions and its own evolving self-understanding. A careful reading of it will hopefully sensitize the reader to some of the ambient and persistent assumptions that have given the evolving Confucian philosophical narrative its unique identity over time. It is these same presuppositions that inform the philosophical vocabulary and set the parameters within this cosmological context from which their meanings must be parsed. As I have argued in setting out this interpretive context for classical Confucian philosophy, making cultural comparisons without the hermeneutical sensitivity necessary to guard against cultural reductionism is undertaken at the risk of overwriting these same texts with our own cultural importances. In this insufficiently critical process, we inadvertently make a world familiar to us that is not familiar at all, and in this specious familiarity, effectively surrender much of the substance of the tradition's own uniqueness and value.

As its point of departure, the *Sourcebook* includes a critical version of the original classical Chinese text for both the expert and generalist alike as a basis for making whatever comparisons with, and evaluations of, the translations they might choose. Informing this comparative exercise, I and my collaborators D.C. Lau, David Hall, and Henry Rosemont have over the years in our earlier translations of the canonical texts compiled a rather substantial glossary of philosophical terms describing the implications and the nuanced evolution of this extended cluster of key philosophical concepts. Just as the introductory essay on the interpretive context is a self-conscious attempt to be as cognizant as we can about our uncommon assumptions, I think it equally important to say up front why we have translated particular terms in the way we do, and what reasons we have for abandoning many of the earlier formulations. This abiding concern to provide the context and an explanation for the central vocabulary has prompted me not only to revise but to expand substantially upon this rather extensive lexicon and produce a companion volume for this *Sourcebook* entitled *A Conceptual Lexicon for Classical Confucian Philosophy*. In my best efforts to encourage readers to become familiar with this *Conceptual Lexicon*, I have in the *Sourcebook* within the translated texts themselves included along with their "placeholder" translations, the romanization and the Chinese characters for these key terms: for example, "exemplary persons" (*junzi* 君子). Again, sometimes the same Chinese term in a different context is better served by a different English translation. For example, in alternative contexts, *junzi* should quite properly be translated as "lord" or "prince" or "ruler" rather than as "exemplary persons."

Respecting the fact that there are no real equivalencies for the key philosophical terms in our European languages, the project here is not to replace one set of problematic translations with yet another contestable set of renderings. The goal instead is to encourage students of Chinese philosophy in their reading of the translated texts to consult this *Conceptual Lexicon* of key philosophical terms with the expectation that in the fullness of time they will appropriate the key Chinese terminologies themselves and make them their own—*tian* 天, *dao* 道, *ren* 仁, *yi* 義, and so on. In thus developing their own increasingly robust insight into these philosophical terms, the students will be able to carry this nuanced understanding over to inform a critical reading of other currently available translations. Ultimately for students who would understand Chinese philosophy, *tian* 天 must be understood as *tian* 天, and *dao* 道 must be *dao* 道.

In the philosophical introduction, "Chinese Natural Cosmology: An Interpretive Context," I have argued for what I take to be the evolving worldview within which these Chinese philosophical terms of art must be understood. With this in mind, I have organized the readings thematically in a way that seeks to be consistent with the living tradition itself. This is necessary because Chinese philosophy does not parse comfortably into the standard Western philosophical categories such as metaphysics, epistemology, ethics, and so on. To take just one example, in a culture where there is a presumed continuity between "knowing" as "realizing" and thus as a productive "doing" (*zhixingheyi* 知行合一), what is erstwhile epistemology very quickly spills over into ethics and into social and political philosophy as well.

Again, Chinese philosophy cannot be accommodated wholesale by appeal to the formal disciplines and areas of cultural interest that have come to define the Western academy: philosophy, religion, psychology, and so on. In the case of religion, for example, the well-intended attempt of some recent interpreters to rescue Chinese philosophy from the overlay of a Judeo-Christian worldview fails utterly if, in the process, this rehabilitation serves to secularize Chinese philosophy by robbing it of its importantly distinctive religious dimension. After all, there are many different ways of being religious, and while the Abrahamic traditions might assume uncritically that religion necessarily entails an appeal to a concept of God to the extent that an erstwhile "a-theistic religiousness" sounds like an oxymoron, this should not disqualify the entertainment of an alternative family-centered Chinese religiousness that has never subscribed to this same presupposition.

Without denying that our familiar disciplines and their categorical and theoretical structures can be qualified, expanded upon, and reshaped in sufficient degree to permit their application to the Chinese tradition, I have proceeded on the premise that to invoke these existing taxonomies as principles of organization would, on balance, be a source of more loss than gain. Indeed, the technical vocabularies and categories that define these familiar academic disciplines would only be a persistent and compounding source of equivocation. Of course, the important exception to this decision to abjure most of our formal categories is to retain reference to the discipline of "philosophy" itself. And this is not just a semantic quibble. First, philosophy is curious in the sense that it is the only intellectual discipline that takes the definition of its subject matter itself as a basic element in its subject matter. Again, this allowance is made because the use of "philosophy" as opposed to "thought" or "culture" is not neutral—it is a normative term that bestows high value on the object of its discourse. The designation "philosophy" in the academy is an acknowledgment awarded to profound and serious thinking to the extent that many if not most of professional philosophers are disinclined to refer to themselves directly as "philosophers," usually preferring some more modest variant of "doing philosophy" or of being a "professor of philosophy." This entire *Sourcebook*, then, is an attempt to extend the synoptic term "philosophy" and to bring it into clearer definition when applied to the Chinese tradition broadly and to Confucian philosophy in particular. It is at the same time an argument for the depth and quality of Chinese thinking with respect to some of the most perennial and important issues that confront us as human beings.

In exploring early Chinese cosmology as the relevant interpretive context for this *Sourcebook*, I have tried to find the language necessary to distinguish it from the reductive single-ordered, "One-behind-the-many" model more familiar in classical Greek idealism in which we seek to understand the "many" by coming to know the "one" ideal that lies behind them. Instead, I have argued for the persistence of a more holistic focus-field model perhaps most succinctly illustrated in the *Expansive Learning* (*Daxue* 大學), one of the canons of Confucian philosophy that is included below as seminal in setting the Confucian project of an optimizing symbiosis sought through personal and thus cosmic cultivation.

As an organizing strategy then, I appeal to the ecological project of an unrelenting regimen of personal cultivation as the pervasive preoccupation of Confucian philosophy, where this process is radically embedded and symbiotic to the extent that not only the family and community, but the very cosmos is perceived as expanding in meaning by virtue of this continuing human enterprise. A personal commitment to achieving virtuosity within one's own relationships is thus both the starting point and the ultimate source of personal, social, and indeed cosmic meaning. In cultivating one's own person through achieving and extending robust relations in one's family and beyond, one not only enlarges the cosmos by adding meaning to it, but in turn, this increasingly meaningful cosmos provides a fertile context for the project of one's own continuing personal cultivation.

To take a concrete example, the modest and always self-effacing Confucius not only allows but endorses with enthusiasm one description of himself—that he is a person who "cherishes learning" (*haoxue* 好學). Confucius is adamant that true "learning" is coincident with moral cultivation as a commitment to growth in relations. And for Confucius, such learning means specifically to have the unrelenting resolve to become increasingly consummate in the way one lives one's roles and relations (*ren* 仁). Becoming consummate in one's conduct is a lifelong project that quite literally begins at home, and that through the refined and elegant expression of a relational virtuosity in all one does, is irreducibly collateral and transactional. I have selected the most representative passages and assembled them thematically in a way that replicates this process of meaning-making, beginning with personal cultivation and expanding radially outward to constitute a distinctively Confucian form of human and family-centered religiousness.

In deliberating on what to include in this *Sourcebook*, I have begun from what is close at hand: that is, the vocabulary most immediately necessary to the project of personal cultivation. I have then extended this terminology radially to include the cultivation of one's person within the context of the family, the community, the polity, and ultimately, the cosmos. Surrendering any pretense at being able to represent this rich classical tradition in any comprehensive way, I have simply sought to choose those illustrative passages that define both the terms of art and the problems they address. I want to highlight some of the philosophical issues that have been important to this culture's story as it has, and as it continues, to unfold. It is hoped that students by developing their own understanding of the vocabulary and the issues defining the classical Confucian philosophical narrative, will thus be inspired to read other available, fuller translations of Chinese philosophy with a greater degree of nuance and insight.

Reflecting on the actual use of this *Sourcebook* in the classroom, I have followed the *Expansive Learning* and tried to think in terms of its guiding metaphor, the root and branches. I have limited myself to the formative and foundational pre-Buddhist Confucian thinkers who in the course of time became the orthodoxy of a continuing and evolving philosophical discourse. I have tried to treat the philosophers included as disparate members of sometimes interconnected but loosely defined lineages rather than as members of erstwhile "schools" of thought. I have read them both ecologically and as evolutionary in deference to the cosmological postulates that are acknowledged to be defining assumptions within this early Confucian narrative: "continuity in change" (*biantong* 變通), "the inseparability of continuity and multiplicity, of particular uniqueness and vital context" (*yiduobufen* 一多不分), "the mutuality of forming and functioning" (*tiyong* 體用), and "the continuity between and inseparability of the human and the cosmic orders" (*tianrenheyi* 天人合一).

In my translations I have tried wherever possible to use the plural form ("exemplary persons") with the pronoun "their" to avoid the sexist language of "his" and "her." Neither gender nor the distinction between singular and plural is marked in the classical Chinese language. In avoiding sexist language, I am not concealing and thus excusing gender discrimination as an integral aspect of Chinese culture predating and certainly reinforced by the Confucian tradition. On the contrary, I want to acknowledge the didactic and programmatic function of these Confucian texts as they are reinterpreted and reauthorized to serve the needs and enhance the possibilities of succeeding generations. To this end, a progressive and evolutionary Confucian philosophy as a living tradition must in our time be reconfigured to prompt a future free of gender prejudice. Confucianism is not a dogma, and there is nothing in the language that requires the gender bias.

CONFUCIAN NATURAL COSMOLOGY: AN INTERPRETIVE CONTEXT

Interpretive Assumptions

Nathan Sivin has famously observed that "man's prodigious creativity seems to be based on the permutations and recastings of a rather small stock of ideas."[1] I will argue that the correlative mode of thinking first described by Marcel Granet in and as *La pensée chinoise* seems to belong to this small but fertile inventory, and that it has had a long evolution in the Chinese cultural tradition that parallels the defining force of metaphysical realism in shaping the categories and the grammar of the Western philosophical narrative.[2] Historian Wang Aihe 王愛和 appeals to prominent scholars such as Li Ling 李零, Robin Yates, and Mark Lewis who argue that these correlative cosmologies, far from being a marginal, esoteric interest to a few court adepts, in fact constituted a shared symbolic discourse through which "both intellectuals and ordinary people spoke and thought."[3] Certainly, recent Warring States archaeological discoveries reinforce this judgment, demonstrating as they do the pervasiveness of correlative cosmological presuppositions entailed in everything from the regimens for personal cultivation and strategies for prosecuting effective warfare to the mantic practices that directed the daily lives of the people.

---

[1] Nathan Sivin, Forward to Manfred Porkert, *The Theoretical Foundations of Chinese Medicine*, Cambridge, MA: MIT Press, 1974, p. xi.
[2] Marcel Granet, *La pensée chinoise*, Paris: Editions Albin Michel, 1934.
[3] Wang Aihe, *Cosmology and Political Culture in Early China*, Cambridge: Cambridge University Press, 2000, p. 76.

What then is the "commonsense"—the deep cultural stratum, the uncommon assumptions—of this persistent and yet always evolving ancient Chinese worldview expressed through this correlative mode of thinking? David Keightley in his lifetime study of the Shang dynasty (c. 1600-c. 1046 BCE) and its divination practices claims that "the origins of much that is thought to be characteristically Chinese may be identified in the ethos and world view of its Bronze Age diviners."[1] The highly cultured Shang people had a much-developed written language that provides us with the earliest recorded history of life in ancient China. Beginning in the Shang and continuing in the subsequent Zhou dynasty (1046-256 BCE), descriptions of significant events of the court were sometimes inscribed for posterity on the inner walls of commemorative bronze vessels as a medium for this writing and thus called the bronze inscriptions (jinwen 金文). In the early twentieth century, this same script written on the physical medium of bovid scapula and turtle plastrons was recovered on what are called "the oracle bones" (jiaguwen 甲骨文) used much earlier for divinatory practices. The oracle bones inscriptions themselves contain a rich vocabulary of over five thousand characters that are unintelligible to most contemporary people. Indeed, even trained paleographers have now after a century of painstaking analysis only been able to decipher a quarter of these ancient inscriptions.[2]

Reflecting on what these early writings reveal about this early high culture, Keightley opines that

> ... it is possible for the modern historian to infer from the archaeological, artistic, and written records of the Shang some of the theoretical strategies and presuppositions by which the Bronze Age elite of the closing

---

[1] David Keightley, "Shang Divination and Metaphysics," *Philosophy East and West* 38 (1988), p. 389. Keightley here is positing a position shared by several of our most distinguished interpreters of the Shang dynasty, including Kwang-chih Chang, "Some Dualistic Phenomena in Shang Society," *Journal of Asian Studies* 24, No. 1 (1964), and Marcel Granet, "Right and Left in China," *Right and Left: Essays on Dual Symbolic Classification*, ed. Rodney Needham, Chicago: University of Chicago Press, 1977.

[2] The complexity and scope of this early language are startling when we consider that educated Chinese persons today might have a reading vocabulary of about four to five thousand characters with a writing competency of something less.

centuries of the second millennium BC ordered their existence.①

Keightley would insist that certain cosmological presuppositions sedimented into the Shang culture evolved to become further elaborated in what we take to be the formative period of classical Chinese philosophy:

> The glimpse that the oracle-bones inscriptions afford us of metaphysical conceptions in the eleventh and tenth centuries B.C. suggests that the philosophical tensions that we associate primarily with the Taoism [Daoism] and Confucianism of Eastern Chou [Zhou] had already appeared, in different form, in the intellectual history of China, half a millennium earlier.②

Keightley perceives the syntactical structure of the language itself to be a resource that can be mined to reveal a vein of cultural assumptions and importances:

> Without necessarily invoking the Sapir-Whorf hypothesis of linguistic relativity, one can still imagine that the grammar of the Shang inscriptions has much to tell us about Shang conceptions of reality, particularly about the forces of nature.③

What, then, specifically are these underlying assumptions that Keightley has identified and recovered in his archaeology of Shang dynasty culture? Keightley contrasts a Chinese cosmology of ceaseless process with a classical Greek worldview in which a metaphysical transcendentalism guarantees an ideal reality:

> Put crudely, we find in classical Greece a Platonic metaphysics of certainties, ideal forms, and right answers, accompanied by complex, tragic, and insoluble tensions in the realm of ethics. The metaphysical foundations being firm, the moral problems were intensely real, and as inexplicable as reality itself. To the early Chinese, however, if reality was forever changeable,

---

① Keightley, "Shang Divination and Metaphysics," p. 367.
② Keightley, "Shang Divination and Metaphysics," p. 388.
③ Keightley, "Shang Divination and Metaphysics," p. 389 n1.

man could not assume a position of tragic grandeur and maintain his footing for long. The moral heroism of the Confucians of Eastern Chou [Zhou] was not articulated in terms of any tragic flaw in the nature of the world or man. This lack of articulation, I believe, may be related to a significant indifference to the metaphysical foundation of Confucian ethics.[1]

Positively speaking, Keightley ascribes to these divinatory sources what is today being described by interpreters of classical China as a distinctively Chinese mode of "correlative thinking." According to his reading, oracle-bone divination subscribed to

> ... a theology and metaphysics that conceived of a world of alternating modes, pessimistic at times, optimistic at others, but with the germs of one mode always inherent in the other. Shang metaphysics, at least as revealed in the complementary forms of the Wu Ting [Ding] inscriptions, was a metaphysics of yin and yang.[2]

Keightley appeals to a rhythm of "alternation and transformation" (*bianhua* 變化) as a modality of change already present in Shang dynasty metaphysics. This conception of change is elaborated upon in the aspectual language of symbiotic bipolar opposites that entail each other, and that together, constitute the whole.[3] For example, it is captured in the language of "persistence and flux" or "persistence within change" (*tongbian* 通變) when it is later made explicit in the "Great Commentary" (*Dazhuan* 大傳) fascicle of the *Book of Changes* (*Yijing* 易經).

The origins of correlative thinking, dating back at least into the Shang dynasty, is a modality of reflection that advances in both complexity and explanatory force through a proliferation and aggregation of productive dyadic associations, novel metaphors, suggestive images, and evocative patterns, all of which are weighed, measured, and tested in ordinary experience. It is my assumption in this survey of the formative period of Confucian philosophy that the correlative process cosmology omnipresent in the cultural practices and the philosophical literature of Warring States China

---

[1] Keightley, "Shang Divination and Metaphysics," p. 376.
[2] Keightley, "Shang Divination and Metaphysics," pp. 376-377.
[3] Keightley, "Shang Divination and Metaphysics," pp. 374-375.

was evolving *pari passu* with the philosophical themes, and that exploring the central issues and arguments of the early texts within the framework of this cosmology provides our best access to their philosophical significance. Stated conversely, a failure to correlate the content of the philosophical corpus with this evolving cosmology would by default locate the early developments of Chinese philosophy within a worldview not its own, thereby precluding an appreciation of how these philosophical concerns belong to a distinctively Confucian culture.

There is a second assumption that informs my interpretation of philosophical themes and issues as they unfold within and throughout the narrative of early Confucian culture. I embrace the basic idea that culture is an ongoing evolving process that entails both novelty and persistence, both crises and continuities, both idealities and realities, both transformation and resistance. Although Alfred North Whitehead's claim that "the safest general characterization of the European philosophical tradition is that it consists of a series of footnotes to Plato"[1] illustrates all too well what John Dewey has impatiently criticized as Whitehead's "excessive piety toward those historic philosophers from whom he has derived valuable suggestions,"[2] still Whitehead's basic point that the ideas of Plato were not only formative but indeed continue to have real relevance in understanding the trajectory of contemporary Western culture is well made. Continuing Dewey's qualification here, and consistent with the postulate of "persistence in change," we might further observe that rather than taking the seminal ideas of our ancient philosophers Greek and Chinese alike to be the exclusive product of singularly great minds, it might be better to see these same philosophers more as archaeologists quarrying and making explicit the wisdom of the ages as it has over millennia been sedimented into their natural languages.

Philosophy of Culture: Change and Persistence

Philosophy of culture requires us to attempt to identify and articulate generalizations that distinguish different cultural narratives. It is only in

---

[1] A.N. Whitehead, *Process and Reality: An Essay in Cosmology*, Donald Sherburne Corrected Edition, New York: Free Press, 1985, p. 39.
[2] Paul Schilpp (ed.), *The Philosophy of Alfred North Whitehead*, New York: Tudor, 1941, pp. 659-660.

being cognizant of these uncommon cultural assumptions that, in some degree at least, we are able to respect the differences as well as the commonalities, and to locate the philosophical discussion within its own alternative worldview. Just as with the classical Greek philosophers in the Western cultural narrative, certain enduring commitments were made in the formative period of Confucian philosophy that are more persistent than others, and that allow us to make useful generalizations about its evolving configuration. In fact, one of the premises that allows for such generalizations is the importance of reading and understanding persistent assumptions as the history of an organic process unfolds.

Edward Said in his influential book, *Orientalism*, published in 1978, made the claim that largely for political reasons, the discipline of "Oriental Studies" in the Western academy has constructed a distorted description of Islamic cultures in service to its own self-image and understanding. In the decades since Said announced these cautions against the projection of "orientalist" prejudices in the study and teaching of other cultures, the tendency in academic circles has been to steer clear of what has come to be understood as "essentialist" constructions of culture. This concern has resulted in valuable efforts to peel back layers of exotic and universalizing veneer that previous generations of scholarship had effectively laid over cultural realities, and to bring to light the often complex and convoluted strata that form the ground of living cultures. In this process, a genuine endeavor has been made to try with imagination to take other cultures on their own terms. However, this important attempt to rethink and get past the naïve constructions of cultural others now runs the risk of obscuring the crucial and still vital role played by persistent values and ideals as they inspire and sustain cultural change—what Charles Taylor has called cultural "hypergoods."①

Are we then to understand what we would call "an interpretive context"

---

① "Hypergoods" is a useful neologism introduced by Charles Taylor in his *Sources of the Self: The Making of the Modern Identity*, Cambridge, MA: Harvard University Press, 1989, pp. 62-63:
  Most of us not only live with many goods but find that we have to rank them, and in some cases, this ranking makes one of them of supreme importance relative to the others. . . . Let me call higher-order goods of this kind "hypergoods," i.e. goods which not only are incomparably more important than others but provide the standpoint from which these must be weighed, judged, decided about.

as the generic and persistent cultural assumptions that distinguish this early Confucian worldview as "essential" and thus unchanging conditions? Of course not. We have to unload this familiar "essentialism" charge that elides the important distinction between an impoverishing orientalism and responsible generalizations, between an exclusionary relativism and an open, inclusive pluralism, between incommensurability and the mutual accommodation of cultures that provides for the possibility of hybridic growth.[①]

Thus, my defense against the familiar charge directed against philosophy of culture that it "essentializes" the other, is first to acknowledge cultural narratives are both historical and contingent. Further, the entertainment of other cultures is always reflexive. If we allow that alternative cultural experiences are expressed as different, often mutually shaping stories, then perhaps the only strategy more dangerous than trying to make generalizations about these narratives is the naïve realism with its "view from nowhere" that would defend an unwillingness to make them. After all, without struggling with imagination to identify, refine, and ultimately argue for the persistence of such characterizations, the default position is an uncritical cultural assimilation. Such pernicious cultural reductionism follows from the seemingly respectful and inclusive assumption that we are all the same, a claim that, far from being innocent, is in fact asserting that "they" are the same as "us." And in the cautionary language of Richard Rorty, such forced redefinition is condescending and humiliating.

Distinguishing Confucian Cosmology from Greek Transcendentalism

The distinguished French sinologist Marcel Granet observes rather starkly that "Chinese wisdom has no need of the idea of God."[②] This characterization of classical Chinese philosophy is a premise that underlies the correlative mode of thinking, and that has had many iterations albeit in different formulations by many of our most prominent sinologists, both Chinese

---

[①] See my essay "Unloading the Essentialism Charge: Reflections on Methodology in Doing Philosophy of Culture," *Comparative Philosophy and Method: Contemporary Practices and Future Possibilities*, ed. Steven Burik, Robert Smid, and Ralph Weber, London: Bloomsbury Academic Press, 2022.

[②] Granet, *La pensée chinoise*, p. 478.

and Western alike. Contemporary New Confucian philosopher (*xinruxuejia* 新儒學家) Tang Junyi 唐君毅 for example states unequivocally that

> ... the Chinese as a people have not embraced a concept of "Heaven" (*tian* 天) that has transcendent meaning. The pervasive idea among Chinese with respect to *tian* is that it is inseparable from the world.①

Joseph Needham would also disassociate Chinese cosmology from assumptions about some underlying permanent structure when he claims that

> ... Chinese ideals involved neither God nor Law. ... Thus the mechanical and the quantitative, the forced and the externally imposed, were all absent. The notion of Order excluded the notion of Law.②

Indeed, our best interpreters of classical Chinese philosophy are explicit in rejecting the idea that Chinese cosmology begins from some independent, transcendent principle and thus entails the ontological reality/appearance distinction followed by the plethora of dualistic categories that arise within such a worldview.③ The philosophical implications of this seemingly off-hand observation are fundamental and profound. One consequence of taking this insight into Chinese cosmology seriously is that it enables us to disambiguate some of the central philosophical vocabulary of classical Chinese philosophy by identifying equivocations that emerge when we elide the distinction between classical Greek cosmological assumptions and those indigenous to the classical Chinese worldview. Angus Graham cautions us about such equivocations, insisting that

---

① Tang Junyi 唐君毅, *The Complete Works of Tang Junyi* 唐君毅全集, Vol. 11, Taipei: Xuesheng Shuju, p. 241: 中國民族無含超絕意義的天的觀念。中國人對天有個普遍的觀念，就是天與地是分不開的。
② Joseph Needham, *Science and Civilisation in China,* Vol. II, Cambridge: Cambridge University Press, 1956, p. 290.
③ For the argument I have made against the relevance of strict philosophical transcendence for classical Confucian cosmology that includes a survey of similar characterizations of early Chinese cosmology in both Chinese and Western sources, see Roger T. Ames, *Confucian Role Ethics: A Vocabulary,* Albany: State University of New York Press, 2020, Chapter 5.

... in the Chinese cosmos all things are interdependent, without transcendent principles by which to explain them or a transcendent origin from which they derive.... A novelty in this position which greatly impresses me is that it exposes a preconception of Western interpreters that such concepts as *Tian* "Heaven" and *Dao* "Way" must have the transcendence of our own ultimate principles; it is hard for us to grasp that even the Way is interdependent with man.①

We will find that an important corollary to the absence of "God" in Chinese cosmology is the need for a different language in thinking about issues as basic as cosmic origins, the source of meaning in the world, and the nature of creativity itself.

Trying to be self-conscious about the cultural assumptions that we willy-nilly bring to our attempt to translate and understand the Chinese philosophical tradition raises an important issue: What is the distinction between a literal and an expository interpretation? If by "literal" we mean to accord with the exact or at least the primary meanings of terms without our own embellishment of them, then to translate *dao* 道 conventionally as "the Way" or *tian* 天 as "Heaven," far from being "literal" as many would claim, is a case of naïve exposition of the most egregious kind. After all, we must allow that in terms of both sense and reference, "the Way" and "Heaven" as understood within our own linguistic universe not only infer, but are indeed metonymic for the Abrahamic conception of "God" and all that it entails, a theological concept that has little relevance for traditional Chinese cosmology.② Again, a failure of translators to be self-conscious and to take fair account of their own Gadamerian "prejudices" with the excuse that they are relying on an existing "objective" dictionary that gives us this equation between *tian* 天 and "Heaven," is to fail to acknowledge that in the case of China at least, this lexical resource given its missionary origins, is itself so heavily colored with cultural biases that Chinese

---

① A.C. Graham, "Replies" in Henry Rosemont Jr. (ed.), *Chinese Texts and Philosophical Contexts: Essays Dedicated to Angus C. Graham*, La Salle, IL: Open Court, 1991, p. 287.

② Metonymy is a figure of speech in which a word or phrase is substituted for another word or phrase with which it is closely associated, such as in the use of *Peking* for *the Chinese government* or of *the throne* for *the sovereign ruler*.

philosophy is for the most part taught in religion or Asian studies departments in our universities, and shelved in the religion or literature sections of our libraries.① To fail to be self-conscious as translators is to betray our readers not once, but twice. That is, not only do we fail to provide the "objective" reading of the text we have promised, but we also neglect to warn our unsuspecting readers of the cultural assumptions we willy-nilly insinuate into our translations.

If, as the dominant classical Greek metaphysical views would have it, unity and permanence are fundamental, then the phenomenal world experienced as unbounded change cannot be finally real. In this classical Greek worldview, of which A.N. Whitehead's interpretation of Plato as a metaphysical realist is a fair representative, "reality" must refer to that which *grounds* the world of appearances, while changing phenomena as *mere appearances* are at best misleading and illusory.② By contrast, there is little recourse to anything like this reality/appearance "two world" distinction in classical Chinese thought.③ The early Confucian thinkers showed little interest in the search for an ontological ground for phenomena. Tang

---

① Hans-Georg Gadamer uses "prejudices" not in the sense of blind prejudice, but on the contrary, in the sense that our prejudgments can facilitate rather than obstruct our understanding. Our assumptions can positively condition our experience. For Gadamer, we must always entertain these assumptions critically, being aware that the hermeneutical circle in which understanding is always situated requires of us that we continually strive to be conscious of what we are bringing to our experience. In thus being self-conscious in our interpretation of experience, we must pursue increasingly felicitous prejudgments that can inform our behaviors in better and more productive ways.

② Much good research is being done to rescue the artist Plato from the received idealist Plato, dominated as this latter interpretation has been by systematic metaphysics. But it is this received Plato filtered through the Church fathers and 20th century scientism that has exercised such important influence on the evolution of the Western cultural narrative.

③ For a discussion of this issue in some detail see David L. Hall and Roger T. Ames, *Thinking from the Han: Self, Truth, and Transcendence in Chinese and Western Culture,* Albany: State University of New York Press, 1998, pp. 123-146. Nathan Sivin, a most cautious interpreter of the classical Chinese world, has recently stated unequivocally that the "fundamental claim, which we usually refer to as appearance vs. reality, has no counterpart in China." See Nathan Sivin, *Medicine, Philosophy and Religion in Ancient China: Researches and Reflections,* Aldershot: Variorum, 1995, p. 3.

Junyi insists that

> ... when Chinese philosophers speak of the world, they are thinking of the world that we are living in. There is no world beyond or outside of the one we are experiencing.... They are not referencing "*a* world" or "*the* world," but are simply saying "worlding" or "world as such" without putting any indefinite or definite article in front of it.①

It is this assumption of metaphysical realists that they can make an object of the world and thereby decontextualize themselves that allows such deracinated philosophers to entertain an erstwhile "view from nowhere." And it is indeed this view from nowhere that stands as guarantor for the possibility of apodictic truth and certainty.

The intellectual milieu for early Chinese thinkers as it is captured in the vocabulary of the "Great Commentary" fascicle of the *Book of Changes* was a phenomenal world of process and change construed simply as *dao* 道: "the unfolding of the boundless field of experience," or *wanwu* 萬物: "the ten thousand processes or events," or more simply put, "everything that is happening." Importantly, without any subject/object dualism, *dao* 道 as "experiencing" far from providing a view from nowhere, is always being construed from one particular perspective or another. These early thinkers were less inclined to ask *what* makes something real or *why* things exist, and more interested in *how* the complex relationships among the changing phenomena of their surroundings could be correlated to negotiate an optimum productivity. It is an achieved personal, social, and ultimately cosmic harmony more than teleological assumptions about origins or design that served these early thinkers as a fundamental guiding value.

Power and Creativity

David Hall introduces the distinction between the notions of "power"

---

① Tang Junyi, *Complete Works*, Vol. 11, p. 101-103: 中國哲人言世界，只想着我們所處的世界。我們所處的世界以外有無其他的世界……中國的哲人說世界，不說我們的世界是一世界 A World, 亦不說是這世界 The World, 而只是說世界，天地，World as Such 前面不加冠詞，實是有非常重大的意義的。

and "creativity" as one way of clarifying the meaning of such transactional and inclusive events, observing that

> ... "creativity" is a notion that can be characterized only in terms of self-actualization. Unlike power relationships that require that tensions among component elements be resolved in favor of one of the components, in relations defined by creativity there is no otherness, no separation or distancing, nothing to be overcome.[1]

Such a definition of creativity—or better, co-creativity between persons and their natural, social, and cultural environments—cannot be reconciled with notions of external causation that appeal to determination by some external agency. In fact, there is a persisting confusion regarding "creativity" that has attended all but the most recent thinking about religious experience within the *creatio ex nihilo* doctrines familiar in the Abrahamic religious culture.[2] Hall further avers that

> ... *creatio ex nihilo*, as it is normally understood, is in fact the paradigm of all power relationships since the "creative" element of the relation is completely in control of its "other," which is in itself literally *nothing*.[3]

The traditional theological all-*power*ful "Creator" God *determines* things, *makes* things. God, as Omnipotent Other who commands the world into being, is *Maker* of the world, but is not in any interesting sense its "Creator" because nothing novel emerges in the process. The aseity or self-sufficiency of God ascribes "Perfection" itself to Godhead, and hence nothing can be added to Him or taken away. Indeed, in such a world there is

---

[1] See David L. Hall, *Eros and Irony: A Prelude to Philosophical Anarchism*, Albany: State University of New York, 1982, p. 249.

[2] A.N. Whitehead has identified and attempted to address what he takes to be a serious incoherence in the relationship between world, God, and creativity in the Abrahamic tradition by making creativity itself more fundamental than God. This challenge is perhaps acknowledged by the fact that the *Oxford English Dictionary* introduces a new entry for "creativity" into its pages in a 1971 supplement with two of its three references to Whitehead's own *Religion in the Making*.

[3] Hall, *Eros and Irony*, p. 249.

nothing new under the sun, and in Friedrich Schleiermacher's terms, gives us a religion of absolute dependence.① Any subsequent human acts of "creativity" that by definition ought to entail the spontaneous emergence of novelty can in fact only be secondary and derivative exercises of power.

Creativity understood in terms of the spontaneous emergence of novelty can only make sense in a world with ontological parity among things. Either everything shares in creativity, or the world is sharply divided into *creators* and their shadows, into Being and its mere appearances. In the latter world, the elements of novelty and spontaneity are fatally threatened. Such concerns are precisely what are at issue in the process understanding of creativity.

Power is to be construed as the production of intended effects determined by external causation. Creativity, on the other hand, is the spontaneous production of novelty, and is thus irreducible to an exhaustive causal analysis. Power is exercised with respect to and over others. Creativity is always reflexive and is exercised over and with respect to radically embedded "persons" who are inclusive of themselves and their environing others. And since persons in a processive world are always social, such creativity is a transactional and multi-dimensional undertaking.

Stated the other way around, it is the transactional, co-creative character of all creative processes that renders personal cultivation irreducibly social. In "creating" oneself as a committed and effective teacher, one is producing extraordinary students. And the standards in teaching demanded by exceptional students produce a committed and effective teacher. Both teacher and student are the cause and the effect in their transactional relationship. Since all persons are constituted by their relationships, self-creation means being trustworthy and true in one's associations. It is effectively integrating oneself within one's social, natural, and cultural contexts, the ground from which one's person as simultaneously self and other arise together to maximum benefit. Self-creation is not ultimately *what* things are, but *how well* and *how productively* they are able to fare in their synergistic alliances.

---

① Friedrich Schleiermacher in *The Christian Faith* uses this language of "absolute dependence"—a self-abnegating deference to a self-sufficient, independent Deity—as a positive expression of religious humility. See *The Christian Faith,* ed. H.R. Mackintosh and J.S. Stewart, London: T & T Clark, 1999, p. 132.

Focusing the Familiar (*Zhongyong* 中庸) provides us with a dramatic account of precisely this contextualized understanding of self-consummation:

> Resolve (*cheng* 誠) is self-consummating and its way-making is self-directing. Resolve is the beginning and the end of things, and without this resolve, there would be nothing. It is thus that, for exemplary persons, it is resolve that is prized. But resolve is not simply the self-consummating of one's own person; it is what consummates everything. Completing oneself is achieving virtuosity in one's roles and relations (*ren* 仁); completing all things is advancing wisdom in the world (*zhi* 知). Such is the virtuosity achieved in one's natural propensities and the way-making that integrates what is more internal and what is more external. Thus when and wherever one applies this virtuosity, it is fitting.[①]

What does *cheng* 誠 —translated here as "resolve" but conventionally rendered "sincerity" or "integrity" mean as a technical cosmological term? The Song dynasty scholar Xu Zhongche 徐中車 emphasizes the dynamic aspect of *cheng* 誠 by alluding to the phrase in *Zhongyong* 26 "the utmost creativity is ceaseless" (*zhichengwuxi* 至誠無息), thus defining *cheng* as "ceaseless" (*buxi* 不息). Similarly, Tang Junyi understands the *Zhongyong's* use of *cheng* 誠 as "continuity itself" (*jixubenshen* 繼續本身).

Wing-tsit Chan in translating the *Zhongyong* for a Western audience insists that *cheng* 誠 in this text "is not just a state of mind, but an active force that is always transforming things and completing things, and drawing man and Heaven together in the same current."[②] Tu Wei-ming takes this reflection further in observing that the term *cheng* 誠 as it appears in *Zhongyong* "has been somewhat unjustifiably translated as 'sincerity'" since "the last thirteen chapters deal mainly with the metaphysical concept of ch'eng [cheng] (sincerity, reality, and truth)."[③] In his monograph length

---

① *Focusing the Familiar* 中庸 25: 誠者自成也，而道自道也。誠者物之終始，不誠無物。是故君子誠之爲貴。誠者非自成己而已也，所以成物也。成己，仁也；成物，知也。性之德也，合外內之道也，故時措之宜也。

② Wing-tsit Chan, *A Source Book in Chinese Philosophy*, Princeton: Princeton University Press, 1963, p. 96.

③ Tu Wei-ming, *Centrality and Commonality: An Essay on Confucian Religiousness*, Albany: State University of New York Press, 1989, pp. 16-17.

study of this text, Tu collates earlier commentarial exegesis and insists that *cheng* 誠 must be understood as "creativity." In his own words, *cheng* 誠

> ... can be conceived as a form of creativity. ... it is that which brings about the transforming and nourishing processes of heaven and earth. As creativity, *ch'eng* [*cheng*] is "ceaseless" (*pu-hsi* [*buxi* 不息]). Because of its ceaselessness it does not create in a single act beyond the spatiotemporal sequence. Rather, it creates in a continuous and unending process in time and space. ... it is simultaneously a self-subsistent and self-fulfilling process of creation that produces life unceasingly.①

Contrasting Confucian Zoetology with Greek Ontology

The classical Greeks have given us a substance ontology grounded in "being *qua* being" or "being *per se*" (*to on he on*) that guarantees a permanent and unchanging subject as the substratum for the human experience. With the combination of *eidos* and *telos* as the formal and final cause of independent things such as persons, this "sub-stance" necessarily persists through change. In this ontology, "to exist" and "to be" are implicated in one term. The same copula verb answers the two-fold questions of first *why* something exists, that is, its origins and its goal, and then *what* it is, its substance. This substratum or essence includes its purpose for being, and is defining of the "what-it-means-to-be-a-thing-of-this-kind" of any particular thing in setting a closed, exclusive boundary and the strict identity necessary for it to be this, and not that.

The question of *why* something exists is answered by an appeal to determinative, originative, and undemonstrable first principles (Gk. *arche*, L. *principium*), and provides the metaphysical separation between creator and creature. The question of *what* something is, is answered by its limitation and definition, and provides the ontological distinction between substance and accident, between its essence and its contingent attributes. In expressing the necessity, self-sufficiency, and independence of things, this substance or essence as the subject of predication is also the object of

---

① Tu Wei-ming, *Centrality and Commonality*, pp. 81-82.

knowledge. It tells us, as a matter of logical necessity, what is what, and is the source of truth in revealing to us with certainty, what is real and what is not. As the contemporary philosopher Zhao Tingyang 趙汀陽 avers, this kind of substance ontology in defining the real things that constitute the content of an orderly and structured cosmos

> ... provides a "dictionary" kind of explanation of the world, seeking to set up an accurate understanding of the limits of all things. In simple terms, it determines "what is what" and all concepts are footnotes to "being" or "is."[①]

In the *Book of Changes* we find a vocabulary making explicit cosmological assumptions that are a stark alternative to this substance ontology, providing the interpretive context for the Confucian canons by locating them within a holistic, organic, and ecological worldview. This cosmology begins from "living" (*sheng* 生) itself as the motive force behind a continuing process of change, and gives us a world of boundless "becomings." Rather than "things" that *are*, it gives us "events" that *are happening*. The intuition that "only Being is" at the core of Parmenides's *On Nature* with its contrast between "The Way of Truth" (*aletheia*) and "The Way of Opinion" (*doxa*) is the basis of the ontology that follows from it: reality versus mere appearance. As a way of expressing this process cosmology's alternative to this fundamental assumption of *on* or "being," we might borrow the Greek notion of *zoe* or "life" and create the neologism "*zoe*-tology" as "the art of living." The *Book of Changes* "Great Commentary" B1 states that 天地之大德曰生 "the greatest capacity of the cosmos is life itself." Again, in A5 in describing the unfolding confluence of vital "way-making" (*dao* 道) it observes that 生生之謂易 "it is because of its ceaseless procreating we call it 'the changes' (*yi* 易)." Change itself is defined denotatively and thus specifically as procreative living. Zoetology as an underlying cosmological assumption then stands in contrast to Greek "ontology," and borrowing from the *Changes* might be translated into modern Chinese as 生生論 *shengshenglun*, "the art of living."

[①] Zhao Tingyang, 惠此中國 (*The Making and Becoming of China*), Beijing: CITIC Press Group, 2016, p. 147: ……是對世界的"字典式"解釋，試圖建立界定萬物的確定理解，簡單地説，就是斷定"什麼是什麼"，一切觀念皆爲"在/是"(being/is)的注脚。

What recommends the conventional translation of *Yijing* 易經 as the "*Book of Changes*" is the ambiguity of the word "changes" itself. That is, "change" is ambiguous to the extent that there are many different modalities of change referenced in this early process cosmology. Indeed, there is a rather extensive vocabulary of terms that can and often have been translated as "change," beginning with "changing places, exchanging, ease, ceaseless procreating" *yi* 易, and then "transforming" *hua* 化, "being in flux" *bian* 變, "removing" *qian* 遷, "replacing" *geng* 更, "taking away" *ti* 替, "transferring, altering" *yi* 移, "reforming" *gai* 改, "exchanging" *huan* 換, "peeling away" *ge* 革, "increasing, adding, profiting" *yi* 益, and many more. The early commentaries parse the specifically *yi* 易 modality of change paronomastically (that is, by phonetic and semantic association) as *yi* 益 "increasing, gaining, adding to, profiting," a kind of change that is consistent with the declared and self-conscious claim of the text to provide its sagely counsel in getting the most out of the human experience reflected in the cognate character *ci* 賜: the "gifting, transacting, exchanging" that leads to such increase.

We can thus infer that in this ecological cosmology made explicit in the *Book of Changes*, such autopoietic, transactional change occurs synchronically *in situ* and diachronically *in medias res* as expansive and advantageous growth in the vital, situated relations that constitute our experience. While the zoetological term *sheng* 生 certainly means "birthing," it is a birthing that takes place not antecedent to but within the continuing process of "living" and "growing." What is "born" is not the beginning of a discrete and independent "life," but rather the emergence of an incipient, embedded, and relationally-constituted lifeform within the vital ecology that provides it its context. The mutual interest and interactions expressed among persons and things in their constitutive relations grows and "appreciates" them in the sense of adding value to both themselves and their worlds.

And just as human flourishing arises from positive growth in the relations of family and community, cosmic flourishing is isomorphic as an extension of this same kind of transactional growth, only on a more expansive scale. Indeed, human values and a moral cosmic order are both grounded in life and its productive growth, and are thus continuous with each other as coterminous and mutually entailing. In canonical texts such as *Focusing the Familiar* (*Zhongyong* 中庸) and the *Classic of Family Reverence* (*Xiaojing* 孝經), for example, human values such as "sincerity, resolution" (*cheng* 誠) and "family reverence" (*xiao* 孝) are elevated to cosmic status, asserting that human beings with their intense feelings have normative force as co-creators of a cosmic order that is at once natural and moral. At the same time, these human values are imbricated in erstwhile cosmic ideas such as "way-making" (*dao* 道) and "coherence" (*li* 理) as themselves being inclusive of a decidedly human aspect. Far from any nature/nurture dualism, human values and natural order are two aspects of the same thing: "the continuity between and inseparability of the human and the cosmic orders" (*tianrenheyi* 天人合一).

The starting point in this zoetological cosmology then is that nothing does anything by itself; association is a fact. Since the very nature of living is associative and transactional, the vocabulary appealed to in defining Confucian cosmology is irreducibly collateral: always multiple, never one. Everything is at once what it is for itself, for its specific context, and for the unsummed totality. Thus there are always the correlative and generative *yinyang* 陰陽 aspects within any process of change, describing the focus and resolution that makes something uniquely what it is, and what by virtue of its vital relations, it is continually becoming. Important to an understanding of this vocabulary is the gestalt shift from the Greek noun-dominated thinking with its world of essential "things" and thus human "beings," to the Confucian gerundive assumptions about "events" and the always eventful nature of human "becomings" living out their lives within their natural ecology. Such is the difference between a leg and walking, between a brain and minding, between a body and person-ing, where the latter far from being a discrete "thing," is a focal, vital, and thus unbounded event taking place in the world.

Referring to the contrast Confucian cosmology has with Aristotle's doctrine of "things" and their external relations, Angus Graham opines that in Chinese thought

> ... things appear not as independent but as interdependent ... and the questions that isolate things from each other have no primacy over those which relate them.[①]

Graham is saying here that in Confucian cosmology the *what* question

---

① A.C. Graham, *Studies in Chinese Philosophy and Philosophical Literature*, Albany: State University of New York Press, 1990, p. 395.

that would tell you what something "is" and the other questions that would reveal how it is correlated with its environing others, are two first-order aspects of the same phenomenon. Said another way, the individuality of something, far from being exclusive of its relationships, is constituted by those first-order relations, and the degree of its uniqueness is a function of the quality achieved in these same relations. This is but to say that the difference between personal identities and their narratives is simply a matter of foregrounding this focus or that field. Our persons and our narratives, rather than entailing some means and end distinction between a given potential and its actualization, between an innate nature and its reduplication in practice, are in fact one and the same thing.

Turning to the human experience specifically, persons are not defined in terms of limitation, self-sufficiency, and independence, but ecologically by the growth they experience and initiate in their intercourse with other persons and their worlds. Since any one thing exists at the pleasure of everything else, the question of why things exist is explained by how they can exist most productively for each other. And the necessity of defining what is what, is replaced by the possibilities each thing affords everything else for growth, revision, and redefinition. Zhao Tingyang suggests that in contrast to the dictionary definition of the cosmos afforded by Greek ontology, the Confucian cosmology provides

> ... an explanation of the "grammar" of the world, striving for a coordinated understanding of the relationships—between heaven and humankind, humankind and things, and humans and humans—by which all doings are generated, with a special emphasis on the mutuality of relationships, and the compatibility of all things.①

A Chinese Cosmology with "Its Own Causality and Its Own Logic"

Marcel Granet in his study of the early Chinese canons finds what he

---

① Zhao Tingyang, 惠此中國 (*The Making and Becoming of China*), pp. 147-148: ……是對世界的"語法式"解釋，力求對萬事所生成的關係（天與人，人與物，人與人）的協調理解，尤其重視關係的相互性或萬事的合宜性。

takes to be just such a distinctive way of thinking—what some sinologists and comparative philosophers have come to call variously "correlative," "analogical," "associative," or "coordinative" thinking. Joseph Needham, much influenced by what he defers to as the "genius" of Granet, takes the organic wholeness and ecological nature of experience together with the correlative way of thinking that attends it, to be a persistent and defining presupposition in the process cosmology of classical China.① I cite Needham here at some length, relying heavily as he does upon Granet, to provide us with an entry point for further reflection on what this notion of "correlative thinking" might mean. Needham observes that

> ... a number of modern students—H. Wilhelm, Eberhard, Jablonski, and above all, Granet—have named the kind of thinking with which we have here to do, "coordinative thinking" or "associative thinking." This intuitive-associative system has its own causality and its own logic. It is not either superstition or primitive superstition, but a characteristic thought-form of its own. H. Wilhelm contrasts it with the "subordinative" thinking characteristic of European science, which laid such emphasis on external causation. In coordinative thinking, conceptions are not subsumed under one another, but placed side by side in a pattern, and things influence one another not by acts of mechanical causation, but by a kind of "inductance."②

Needham describes this correlative thinking as having "its own causality

---

① Although Needham takes Marcel Granet's *La pensée chinoise* to be "a work of genius," he criticizes Granet along with other major commentators on Chinese cosmology such as Alfred Forke and H.G. Creel for having "the serious defect of assuming that the cosmism and phenomenalism of the Han was ancient." The scientist Needham chooses instead to attribute the emergence of this correlative worldview to the School of Naturalists—Zou Yan 鄒衍 (305-240 BCE) and the *Yinyang* lineage 陰陽家—a special company of thinkers who had the marked advantage of having "a mind trained in the natural sciences." See Joseph Needham, *Science and Civilisation in China*, Vol. II, pp. 216-217. On this matter, as rehearsed above, I side with scholars such as David Keightley who in his many publications wants to ascribe correlative thinking to intellectuals as far back as the Shang dynasty as a characteristic and evolving pattern of thinking.
② Joseph Needham, *Science and Civilisation in China*, Vol. II, p. 280.

and its own logic" and as being "a characteristic thought-form of its own."[1] It is on this basis that Needham invites us down a portal that would seem to take us, like Alice, to the other side of the looking glass where he shares with us his encounter with a somewhat wonky world that has left the reassuring stability of our own rational structures behind:

> The key-word in Chinese thought is *Order* and above all *Pattern* (and if I may whisper it for the first time, *Organism*). The symbolic correlations or correspondences all formed part of one colossal pattern. Things behaved in particular ways not necessarily because of prior actions or impulsions of other things, but because their position in the ever-moving cyclical universe was such that they were endowed with intrinsic natures which made their behaviour inevitable for them. If they did not behave in those particular ways they would lose their relational position in the whole (which made them what they were), and turn into something other than themselves. They were thus parts in existential dependence upon the whole world-organism. And they reacted upon one another not so much by mechanical impulsion or causation as by a kind of mysterious resonance.[2]

Needham again draws on Granet to provide what is a vivid description of the unfamiliar cosmological vision we need as our interpretive context for understanding Confucian philosophy, alerting us not only to what this cosmology is, but perhaps more importantly, to what it is not:

---

[1] In a chapter I wrote on "methodology" in Chinese philosophy, I tried to temper the claim by Granet and Needham about the uniqueness of this associative way of thinking. I have sought to demystify it by building on the example of "abductive reasoning" as perhaps a more familiar form of correlative thinking developed by C.S. Peirce, the reputed founder of American pragmatism. Indeed, when his fellow pragmatist William James characterizes the pragmatic method as simply asking "What difference does it make?" he is requiring that "doing philosophy" be an imaginative and experimental way of thinking directed at enhancing the human experience by making productive and open-ended correlations in the best effort to live life intelligently—a demand that resonates immediately with these Chinese canons. See "Philosophizing with Canonical Chinese Texts: Seeking an Interpretive Context," in Sor-hoon Tan (ed.). *The Bloomsbury Research Handbook of Chinese Philosophy Methodologies*, London: Bloomsbury Press, 2016.

[2] Joseph Needham, *Science and Civilisation in China*, Vol. II, pp. 280-281.

Social and world order rested, not on an ideal of authority, but on a conception of rotational responsibility. The Tao [*dao*] was the all-inclusive name for this order, an efficacious sum-total, a reactive neural medium; it was not a creator, for nothing is created in the world, and the world was not created. The sum of wisdom consisted in adding to the number of intuited analogical correspondences in the repertory of correlations. Chinese ideals involved neither God nor Law. The uncreated universal organism, whose every part, by a compulsion internal to itself and arising out of its own nature, willingly performed its functions in the cyclical recurrences of the whole, was mirrored in human society by a universal ideal of mutual good understanding, a supple regime of interdependences and solidarities which could never be based on unconditional ordinances, in other words, on laws.①

Needham says in explanation of *dao* 道, "the universal uncreated organism" often described as the "source" of all things, that it "was not a creator, for nothing is created in the world, and the world was not created." What he means here is that this cosmology brings with it an alternative understanding of creativity: that is, creativity as a generative procreativity and a continuing *in situ* or "situated" increase in meaning that would defy any *ex nihilo* separation between creator and creature. The furniture of the world is not created in the sense of emerging out of nothing, and it does not suffer annihilation in the sense of returning to nothing.② *Dao* 道 and the

---

① Needham, *Science and Civilisation in China*, Vol. II, p. 290.
② The counterexample that immediately comes to mind is *Daodejing* 40:
天下萬物生於有，有生於無。
The myriad happenings of the world arise from the determinate,
And what is determinate arises from the indeterminate.
Importantly, the determinate and indeterminate are correlative categories that entail each other, so that each exists only within the context of the other. *Wu* is not void in any absolute sense, but the functional emptiness within a cup or within the hub of a wheel. And the process, rather than being "creation" in the *ex nihilo* sense that separates creator from creature, is the holistic process of transformation. The first two lines of this same chapter state:
反者道之动，弱者道之用。
"Returning" is how way-making proceeds,
And "weakening" is how it functions.
(Continued on next page)

myriad things (*wanwu* 萬物), rather than referencing distinct, separate realities, are two aspectual ways of looking at the same always transforming phenomenal world and our continuing experience within it.

Granet appeals to precisely this language of "aspect" to express the way in which erstwhile "things" are in fact dynamic matrices of productive relations that constitute continuous, extended events:

> Instead of observing successions of phenomena, the Chinese registered alternations of aspects. If two aspects seemed to them to be connected, it was not by means of a cause and effect relationship, but rather "paired" like the obverse and converse of something, or to use a metaphor from the *Book of Changes*, like echo and sound, or shadow and light.①

Granet is here reflecting on the resonant "pairing" among alternations of aspect defining of all events denoted by the familiar dyadic vocabulary of the *yinyang* tension (陰陽), "field" and "focus" (*daode* 道德), "determinacy" and "indeterminacy" (*youwu* 有無), "change" and "continuity" (*biantong* 變通), "the heavens" and "the earth" (*tiandi* 天地), "the world" and "the human experience" (*tianren* 天人), "forming" and "functioning" (*tiyong* 體用), "the social grammar" and its "musicality" (*liyue* 禮樂), "heartminding" and "spirituality" (*xinshen* 心神), "intensity" and "extensiveness" (*jingshen* 精神), "the lived body" and "heartminding" (*shenxin* 身心), "the consummatory" and "the optimally appropriate" (*renyi* 仁義), and so on.

To take "determinacy" and "indeterminacy" (*youwu* 有無) as an example, these terms are a nonanalytic, descriptive vocabulary of "aspects" that we must appeal to in giving a fair account of the ceaseless emergence

---

(Continued from previous page) Looking at the ecological process from the perspective of any particular focal "thing" or "event," the swinging gates open and this event embarks upon its initial phase of determinacy, and emerges nested within its already determinate context. Culminating in its full maturation, the event then begins a gradual process of decline, and in transforming into something else, returns as this particular event, to indeterminacy. Looking at the particular thing from the perspective of the process or field within which it emerges, erstwhile "things" are simply shifting horizons within its ecology.

① Granet, *La pensée chinoise*, p. 329; cited in Joseph Needham, *Science and Civilisation in China*, Vol. II, pp. 290-291.

of any of the things and events that come to constitute the continuing human experience. An ineluctable process of transformation requires a gerundive, explanatory language such as "determinacy" (*you* 有) and "indeterminacy" (*wu* 無), and "forming" (*ti* 體) and "functioning" (*yong* 用), to report on the mutuality of structuring and performing as the world turns.

The alternating deployments of aspectual and analytic language serve the processual cosmology, requiring as it does a strategy for denoting both the continuity of process and the punctuating of this process as particular events. In this process cosmology, the notions of "time" and "place" can only serve functionally as separate dimensions that can be parsed respectively as discrete moments, and as the simple locations of individuated things. Indeed, in this cosmology, time and place (or perhaps better, "timing" and "taking place") are more importantly to be understood as inseparable "aspects" of the whence and whither of the diverse currents of events within the ceaseless flow of the human experience. At the same time, as with the relationship between continuous process and determinate event, there is also an important role for our analytic and discriminating sensibilities that allows for the punctuating of the lived experience, and in so doing, to thus appreciate both its cadence and its multivalence.

In invoking "aspectual" language to "speak" this cosmology, we are identifying different yet mutually entailing ways to talk about what is in fact the same phenomenon. For example, we can use the aspectual language of "forming and functioning" (*tiyong* 體用) to describe different perspectives on living persons, where the persistently formal and determinate aspects (body, language, ritual observances, institutions, life patterns, roles) can be distinguished from the vital, informal, and indeterminate ones (growth, creativity, passion, shame, skill, taste, insight, spirit). Such differences can be readily observed and experienced, but as different perceptions of the same phenomenon—this particular person—they cannot be isolated and separated analytically. Human persons are at once determinate and vital. At the same time, however, although these aspects cannot be separated out, the very different perspectives are integral to the meaning of the phenomenon itself, providing complexity and intensity to the same unique and continuous quantum of human experience.

This aspectual nature of language is revealed in the structure of many Chinese linguistic expressions themselves. As an example, the binomial that denotes our human "worlding" (*shijie* 世界) is constructed by combining a diachronic aspect, *shi* 世 "worlding-as-intergenerational-temporal-succession," with a synchronic aspect, *jie* 界 "worlding-as-the-traversing-of-spatial-boundaries." Similarly, the binomial for "cosmos" (*yuzhou* 宇宙) combines a synchronic aspect, *yu* 宇 "cosmos-as-eaves-extending," and a diachronic aspect, *zhou* 宙 "cosmos-as-temporally-enduring." Importantly, each of these aspects is altered by both its dyadic relationship with the other, and the vitality of a process cosmology. The inseparability of time and place, of form and flow, becomes the measured cadence and musicality of the human experience. Flow that cannot be separated from place becomes events as "taking place," and form that cannot be separated from time becomes the rhythm of life.

In understanding what Needham means here by "rotational responsibility" with each thing having "a compulsion internal to itself," we will have to appeal to the doctrine of internal, constitutive relations and the alternative, holistic "causality" it entails in which everything is the cause of anything, and anything is the cause of everything. In this classical cosmology, the animating and transforming *qi* 氣 is conceptualized in terms of what in modern parlance we might call a "vital energy field" in which "things" are sometimes more and sometimes less persistent perturbations or foci within this field. Having arisen, these intertwined "events" continue in the fullness of time to transform into other things. The vital field is not only pervasive as a condition of all things, but consistent with Needham's description of this field as "a reactive neural medium," it is also the "neural" or felt, existential medium through which all situated things emerge in their relations to both negotiate and to constitute what they are becoming. There is neither animating *qi* 氣 without structuring form, nor form without *qi* 氣. Indeed, as we have seen, "form" and "animating *qi* 氣" are two nonanalytic aspects of the same transforming reality, where "transitivity" and "form" are both implicit ways of understanding the transformative "functioning and forming" (*tiyong* 體用) process. As such, "animating *qi* 氣" and the various ways we have of saying "forming" are an explanatory rather than an ontological vocabulary; we need both terms to give an adequate account of what it is that we are experiencing.

The focus-field cosmology that Granet and Needham are ascribing to this Chinese worldview, and the aspectual language needed to give it voice are revealing of what Needham is referring to as "the universal uncreated organism" with "its own causality and its own logic." With respect to causality then, given the vital, internal, and constitutive nature of the relations that underlies the focus-field holography, causality does not reference some agency outside and temporally prior to the perceived configuration of the things that are happening, but rather speaks to the creative, interdependent, and causal nature of the relations themselves.

When we posit the problem: Which comes first, the chicken or the egg? we have to allow that chicken and egg must evolve together, or not at all. In fact, the problem arises from the categorical thinking that would make them independent entities in the first place. From the perspective of classical Greek metaphysics, we might say this Chinese cosmology shaves with Ockham's razor not once, but twice. Chinese cosmology begins from what is happening within the autogenerative world itself (*ziran* 自然) rather than appealing to the notion of a transcendent and independent First Mover as the cause and architect of the world. And with respect to persons, Chinese cosmology begins from a phenomenology of what unfolds and compounds as moral habits within the human narrative itself rather than appealing to an independent and reduplicative nature or soul as the source of human conduct.

If, as Peter Hershock has observed, we see "relationality as first order (or ultimate) reality and all individual actors as (conventionally) abstracted or derived from them,"[①] then we must understand causality in a cosmos described as autogenerative (*ziran* 自然) to be the backgrounding or foregrounding of particular foci and their unbounded fields, where anything is the cause of everything, and everything is the cause of anything. First, this *ziran* 自然 causality means that the "self" (*zi* 自) in the "self-so-ing" process is certainly uniquely what it is, one of a kind; it is a continuing, specific identity. Secondly, this *zi* 自 identity has both an objective and subjective dimension to it, perceived from the outside, but also lived from the inside. It is this existential self-awareness that is prospectively negotiating its *zi* 自 identity from within, having some projective influence in setting and fusing its horizons within its environing conditions. And thirdly, since this *zi* 自 identity is constituted by an unbounded field of relations, the *zi* 自 is what it is by virtue of the quality of the coalescence it has achieved within the manifold of relations that conspire together to make it insistently so (*ran* 然). Said simply, everything together conspires to cause

---

[①] Peter D. Hershock, *Buddhism in the Public Sphere: Reorienting Global Interdependence*, New York: Routledge, 2006, p. 147.

anything, and thus any particular thing is both the cause and the effect of everything else.

Shi 勢: An Aesthetic Alternative to the Logic of "Things" and to an "External Causality"

There is another complex term that might be helpful in thinking through a cosmology described above by Needham as having "its own causality and its own logic," a claim that "human becomings" with importantly different cosmological assumptions, think in an importantly different way from a "human being." *Shi* 勢 is a generic term that expresses the complex, holistic, and dynamic process of "trans-*form*-ing" (*tiyong* 體用) as it occurs within the evolution and consummation of any particular "thing" or situation. There is an aesthetic to the cultivating and refining of things that is captured in the etymology of this term *shi* 勢 as "sowing and cultivating" (*yi* 蓺) along with its cognate term, the "performing arts" (*yi* 藝). Such associations suggest that situations do not just happen; they emerge in their complexity as a growing pattern of changing relations that are vital, and that display the possibilities of incremental design as well as an achieved, aesthetic virtuosity. At the same time, situations by definition are "situated" and as such, have a formal morphology or "habituated" aspect—a localized "taking place" with its insistent particularity and its own persistent yet always changing configuration.

We might be initially overwhelmed when we rehearse what is in fact a non-exhaustive list of the possible English translations given for this term *shi* 勢. At the same time, we might look for an organizational logic in this glossary of terms by subsuming the list of various translations under four closely related rubrics:

Embodiment: terrain, configuration, situation, circumstances, disposition, shape, appearance
Relationality: leverage, differential, advantage, purchase
Vitality: potential, momentum, timing, tendency, propensity
Virtuosity: influence, power, force, style, dignity, status

Such a range of renderings used to translate *shi* 勢 as it is found in different contexts is revealing of the extraordinarily broad compass of meaning implicated in this one term. On reflection and with imagination, we can recover a perhaps unfamiliar, alternative logic and a sense of causality from a survey of these seemingly disparate meanings. We might observe that *shi* 勢 is holistic, denoting "thing," "action," "attribute," and "modality" all at once. Hence, it is translated in different contexts as a noun, verb, adjective, and adverb. In lifting coherence out of this pattern of seemingly disjunctive associations, we might begin from the matrix of relations that constitute any particular situation and register the vital and thus changing pattern or structure that emerges from them. This dynamic structure—from its first-order relationality and vitality to its achieved virtuosity as it bodies forth—can be drawn upon to answer some of our basic cosmological questions.

An ostensive "thing" is first a specific focus or matrix or configuration within an expansive context of always changing, constitutive relations. Importantly, it can be cultivated and shaped to achieve insistent focus and resolution in its interdependent relations with the "other" things that constitute it. The dynamics of *shi* 勢 explains what it means for something that is at once unique and yet continuous with other things to act and to move, and to be acted upon and to be moved, where its shaping and being shaped is one continuous process.

This reflection on *shi* 勢 provides an alternative vocabulary for thinking through the dynamics of our field of continuing experience and the multiplicity of its content. *Shi* 勢 provides a centered, 'from-field-to-focus' conception of the principle of how we come to individuate things and set horizons upon them. That is, beginning from the wholeness of experience, we divide up, conceptualize, foreground, and thus make determinate an eventful "thing" within an otherwise continuous flow of relations by bringing focus and meaningful resolution to its horizons as it is entertained from one perspective or another. The primacy of vital relations means that situation will always have priority over agency, and that no putative agent does anything by itself.

Shi 勢 as thus one and many—as unique foci within their respective fields—provides some insight into the logic of a more fluid sense of continuity within diversity, and of an internal and spontaneous *ziran* 自然 causality in which everything "causes" anything, and anything is implicated as a cause of everything. Indeed, the inseparability of continuity and diversity not only problematizes any notion of strict identity, but also guarantees the uniqueness of each situation, and means at the very least that there can be no single dominant order, but only many interdependent and interpenetrating sites of order.

When this term *shi* 勢 with its alternative logic and causality is used to reflect on the human condition specifically, it explains the emerging individuality of unique, potentially large-souled "persons" situated within the evolving circumstances of their extended families and communities, and within the changing conditions of their natural and cultural environments. *Shi* 勢 suggests how the persisting habits and the specific habitudes that constitute human identities can be cultivated from originating impulses into the definite and significant activities of always unique persons. Such persons are irreducibly transactional, ingesting and embodying their environs as uniquely focused fields of roles and relations. The cultivated distinctiveness of such persons far from being exclusive of their relationships, is rather the immediate product of the quality that is being achieved in them. To the extent that we are able to thrive within productive relations, we can emerge as distinctive and sometimes even distinguished persons, thereby bringing distinction to the nexus of relations to which we belong. The holographic reversibility of inner and outer means that in searching inwardly for a unique, lived identity we are in fact exploring the web of outward relations that make us who we are. And in projecting outward to register most fully the unbounded web of relations that give us context we are discovering our innermost selves.

Since the entire world is implicated within each of us as persons, it is only appropriate that we regard ourselves with the same esteem that we would extend to the world. Or said more simply, to love ourselves is to love the world. It is only those who by fully realizing this interpenetration between world and things, and the interpenetration among things themselves, can extend themselves to the full compass of experience as a precondition for making their own distinctive contribution to it and exercising their influence upon it.

Genealogical Cosmogony and Its "Epistemogony"

In a metaphysical cosmogony, the originative and determinative principle is independent of its creature—the Judeo-Christian God or Plato's Forms—and imposes a preassigned design on chaos. Natural change is then driven by a linear teleology that takes us from origination to the realization of the given design. There is a plan, a beginning, and an end. Some ahistorical, acultural Agent—some Being behind the beings, some Creator behind the creatures—must be asserted in order to explain why things *are* rather than *are not*, and are changing rather than remaining the same. Metaphysical cosmogony is very ambitious. It promises us that if we are able to trace "the many" back to "the ordering One," all will be intelligible.

As stated above, *dao* 道 is not a superordinated metaphysical principle, but the ongoing and always contingent genealogical unfolding of the world itself as our field of experience. If order is truly inherent and emergent rather than existing as an independent, determinative principle, then the language that describes all aspects of it—*yin* and *yang*, time and space, heaven and earth—must be historicized as a contingent vocabulary for the world order *as we know it*. These categories cannot stand as first "principles," as *necessary*, *apriori* conditions that give us a Greek *Kosmos*. Instead, the sense of "beginning" in these narratives is *shi* 始—a natal beginning associated with a "fetus" (*tai* 胎) that inherits a world "passed on" (*yi* 貽) and "bequeathed" (*yi* 詒) to it from progenitors who have come before. The language is pervasively genealogical and ancestral (*zong* 宗), including within this vocabulary expressions such as "thearch" (*di* 帝) and the often anthropomorphic *tian* 天 that is probably a pictograph of a large and important person.

Again, *dao* 道 has as much to do with the subjects of knowing and their quality of understanding as it does with the object of knowledge. *Dao* 道 references an emergent and always reflexive cosmic order, but it also means "to speak" that order, and as the order changes, so must its terms of art. That is, the cosmogonic narrative is also an "epistemogonic" account that at once recounts an emerging interpretation of world order, negotiates and anticipates an order that will become, and sets historical horizons upon what is boundless experience. Our relatively clear understanding of our present, always provisional situation, cannot be universalized and relied upon to explain all other situations, past or future. Unlike the metaphysical cosmogony that promises light at the source, the further we go back in the genealogical cosmogony—the birthing tunnel of the cosmos—the darker it gets. The cosmogonic narrative takes us back to an earlier set of conditions that, requiring its own terms of understanding, cannot be explained by the application of our current philosophical vocabulary.

Summarizing cosmological speculations from a significantly earlier period, the second century BCE "cosmological" section of the *Huainanzi* 淮南子 contains these words:

> When the heavens and the earth had yet to take shape,
> There was soaring, gliding, plunging, sinking,
> And as such it is known as the Great Natal Beginning.
> The Great Natal Beginning gave rise to the empty and transparent,
> The empty and transparent gave rise to space-time,
> And space-time gave rise to *qi* 氣.
> There are horizons and limits within *qi* 氣,
> So that the pure and radiant expanded outward to become the heavens
> And the heavy and turbid congealed to become the earth.[①]

In the process cosmology described here, determinacy and indeterminacy together with the change and the novelty that accompanies it, are conditions of a continuing present. In the fullness of time, whether viewing the cosmos retrospectively or prospectively, any rationalizing vocabulary we might appeal to as an interpretive grid for explaining our experience is ultimately outrun by process itself. Hence while our present language of interpretation—the heavens and the earth, *dao* 道, space-time, *qi* 氣—

---

① 天墬未形，馮馮翼翼，洞洞灟灟，故曰太始。太始生虛廓，虛廓生宇宙，宇宙生氣。氣有涯垠，清陽者薄靡而爲天，重濁者凝滯而爲地。Text emended according to Lau, D.C. and Chen Fong Ching, *A Concordance to the Huainanzi*, Hong Kong: Commercial Press, 1992, 3/18/18; compare John Major, *Heaven and Earth in Early Han Thought*, Albany: State University of New York Press, 1993, p. 62. The "empty" (*xu* 虛) is to be understood contextually as a positive ellipsis within shaped, determinate things that makes things functional—the empty cup that is available for filling. This space is further the pregnant source of the as-yet unmanifested determinacy that makes the next moment different from this one. An important distinction has often been elided between *xu* 虛 thus understood as a correlative indeterminacy within the bounds of determinacy and the primordial Chaos familiar in Western cosmogonies as a gaping emptiness, a dark formless void. There is no void as such in the classical Confucian cosmology and, thus, no final emptiness. Both shaped and unshaped things have, by default, only a phenomenological reference. This fact helps to account for the absence in the early Chinese tradition of anything like "Not-Being" as the putative absence of existing things and hence for the irrelevance of *creatio ex nihilo* thinking.

has explanatory force in the present moment, these terms of art too were "born" as a theoretical and conceptual structure emerging out of concrete experience, and will in the fullness of time, expire.

The "cosmogony" is natal or genealogical as opposed to metaphysical: a birthing from an inchoate, incipient life-form that presupposes progenitors and genealogy rather than originative principles, and a pattern of always situated and cultivated growth rather than the actualization of some given, intrinsic potential. Taking this cosmogony a step further, many of our most prominent commentators have noted that cosmogonic myths did not feature in classical Chinese cosmology, and only begin to appear in China during the Han period (202 BCE-220 CE).[1] For example, Angus Graham states:

> The past to which Confucius looks back is not the beginning of things; there is no cosmogonic myth in pre-Han literature, merely a blank of pre-history before the first Emperors...[2]

John Major in his interpretation of the technical chapters of the Han dynasty text, *Huainanzi*, discusses in detail the various versions of cosmogony found in this work. Indeed, we might join the conversation between John Major and Hal Roth about the almost antithetical point being made when we compare a passage first presented in the pre-Han *Zhuangzi* 莊子 and then later repeated in the Han dynasty *Huainanzi* 淮南子.[3] Here I translate the later *Huainanzi* version:

> There is that which had a beginning.[4] There was that which had not yet had "that which had a beginning." And there was that which had not yet

---

[1] See for example Michael Loewe, *Chinese Ideas of Life and Death: Faith, Myth, and Reason in the Han Period (202 BC-220 AD)*, London: Allen and Unwin. Loewe, 1982, p. 63; Kristofer Schipper, "The Taoist Body" in *History of Religions* 17, No. 3/4 (1978), p. 371; Frederick Mote, "The Cosmological Gulf Between China and the West," *Transition and Permanence: Chinese History and Culture*, ed. David C. Buxbaum and Frederick W. Mote, Hong Kong: Cathay Press, 1972, p. 7.

[2] A.C. Graham, *Disputers of the Tao*, La Salle, IL: Open Court, 1989, p. 12.

[3] See Major, *Heaven and Earth in Early Han Thought*, pp. 326-327.

[4] Note that the phrase that precedes is always embedded in the phrase which follows.

had "that which had not yet had that which had a beginning." There is that which had something; there is that which had nothing. There was that which had not yet had something or nothing. There was that which had not yet had "that which had not yet had something or nothing."①

While the intent of the author of the *Zhuangzi* in a similarly worded passage is to reject the possibility of an initial beginning on the basis of an infinite regress, the author of this *Huainanzi* version wants instead to describe the various increasingly obscure stages in a cosmogonic birthing of the world that we presently know. While the point being made in these two versions is clearly different, they still share an important assumption that would distinguish both of them from what might be taken to be seemingly resonant accounts in classical Western cosmology. That is, we must resist a possible equivocation between two very different senses of cosmogony—genealogical and metaphysical—where both the *Zhuangzi* and the *Huainanzi*, as different as they are, come down on the genealogical side. We must distinguish a world that *emerges* historically and genealogically in the Chinese texts from a world *derived* from some transcendent principle or metaphysical intervention so familiar in the classical Western accounts: *Genesis*, *Timaeus*, and the *Theogony*, for example.② Such a genealogical understanding of cosmogony puts a euhemeristic spin on the kinds of mythical stories, fabulous creatures, and geological anomalies remembered in classical texts such as the gazetteer *Classic of Mountains and Seas* (*Shanhaijing* 山海經), setting real temporal limits as it does on our powers of understanding and explanation.

Qi 氣 as a Moral Cosmology

One of the terms of art developed to give expression to this alternative

---

① *Huainanzi* 2/10/14-15: 有始者，有未始有有始者，有未始有夫未始有有始者；有有者，有無者，有未始有有無者，有未始有夫未始有有無者. Cf. *Zhuangzi* 5/2/49: 有始也者，有未始有始也者，有未始有夫未始有始也者。有有也者，有無也者，有未始有無也者，有未始有夫未始有無也者。

② See François Jullien, *The Book of Beginnings*, trans. Jody Gladding, New Haven: Yale University Press, 2016 in which Jullien makes comparisons that underscore this fundamental difference.

process cosmology is the notion of *qi* 氣 that so defies definition that it has become an English word instead. Kwong-loi Shun in the preamble to his discussion of the references to *qi* 氣 found in the *Mencius* 孟子, rehearses passages from the classical anthologies of historical stories, the *Zuozhuan* 左傳 and *Guoyu* 國語, that expound upon *qi* 氣 as the vital energies making up and animating the natural world around us.[1] In the several discourses in which Mencius himself invokes *qi* 氣, he is not, as suggested by some, waxing mystical.[2] On the contrary, he is making explicit the commonsense of his own time and place in pre-Qin China. Indeed, to make sense of the *qi* 氣 worldview in our own times, we might consider it the classical Chinese analog of the now largely unconscious quantitative, genetic, and atomistic assumptions that began for Western culture in classical Greece, and that continue to inform our own commonsense.

From the *Expansive Learning* (*Daxue* 大學) that sets the Confucian project we learn the most persistent and pervasive theme in shaping the Confucian philosophy is our capacity and responsibility for personal cultivation. Mencius interprets the field of *qi* 氣 in terms of specifically moral energy and offers advice on the attainment of human excellence. He speaks of his ability to nourish his "flood-like *qi* 氣" (*haoranzhiqi* 浩然之氣), describing this *qi* 氣 as that which is "most vast" (*zhida* 至大) and "most firm" (*zhigang* 至剛).[3] Restated in the cosmological language of focus and field, Mencius is saying that his "flood-like *qi* 氣" achieves the greatest "extensive" (most vast) and "intensive" (most firm) magnitudes when properly nurtured and cultivated. This language of extensive field and intensive focus suggests that when one nourishes one's *qi* 氣 most successfully, one achieves the greatest degree of meaningful resolution and coalescence within the most extensive field of *qi* 氣. In this manner, one gains the greatest virtuosity (*de* 德) in relation to the most far-reaching elements of one's environments (*dao* 道). In fact, this isomorphic relationship between personal resolution and the reach of one's influence is the explicit message of *Mencius*:

---

[1] Kwong-loi Shun, *Mencius and Early Chinese Thought,* Stanford: Stanford University Press, 1997, pp. 67-68.
[2] Chad Hansen, *A Daoist Theory of Chinese Thought,* Hong Kong: Oxford University Press, 1992, p. 175 is not alone among commentators who would describe Mencius on *qi* as a "moral mysticism."
[3] *Mencius* 2A2.

Mencius said, "Is there any enjoyment greater than, with the myriad things of the world all implicated here in me, to turn personally inward and to thus find resolution with these things? Is there any way of seeking to become consummate in my person more immediate than making every effort to act empathetically by deferring to the interests of others?"[①]

The character *cheng* 誠 that is translated here as "to find resolution with these things" is conventionally translated as "sincerity" or "integrity." However, as discussed above, in this processional world of classical Confucianism "integrity" is not simply retaining what you "have" or "are;" it is also what you "do" and "become" in your relations with other things. *Cheng* is thus an *integrative and creative process*. It is not simply "being whole," but also "becoming whole" through achieving resolution in the roles and relationships that comes to constitute one's personal identity. This inseparability of integration and creativity is reinforced explicitly in this *Mencius* passage by appeal to *ren* 仁, the correlative, consummatory notion of "relationally constituted persons" in which the realization of oneself and others in the roles of family and community are mutually entailing in one's own person. The *Analects* defines the project of becoming *ren* 仁 in precisely these terms:

> Consummatory persons (*ren* 仁) establish others in seeking to establish themselves and promote others in seeking to get there themselves.[②]

In the *Mencius* passage cited above, perhaps a clearer rendering of the phrase "with the myriad happenings of the world all implicated here in me" that expresses the holographic relationship of persons as foci within their fields of experience, might be: "My field of *qi* 氣 is brought into intense and meaningful resolution in my person, and thus the entire field is brought into focus here in me." Restated in more familiar language, it is asserting that my life has cosmic consequences. I am in my ecological relations continuous with the entire world as experienced, and since in cultivating my own person, I have been able to construe my life in a meaningful

---

① *Mencius* 7A4: 孟子曰："萬物皆備於我矣。反身而誠，樂莫大焉，強恕而行，求仁莫近焉。"
② *Analects* 6.30: 夫仁者，己欲立而立人，己欲達而達人。

and resolute way, I am in fact able to bring focus to the entire cosmos and make it more meaningful.

There is no external vantage point outside the flow of *qi* 氣. The world is necessarily entertained from one particular perspective or another, and hence this insistently particular field of *qi* 氣 is always construed perspectivally—from a continuing here or from a continuing there, from a persistent you or from a persistent me. Further, each particular perspective is holographic in the sense that it contains within its own compass the extensive field of relations that contextualizes it and that is made more or less meaningful by its own intensity of focus. When understood in light of this pervasive notion of *qi* 氣, the phenomenal world as the way things are, is the site of process and becoming. In such a world, human experience is a *field* both focused by and bringing into focus the myriad items comprising it. Indeed, in addition to the *extensive* field of *qi* 氣 that registers the reach of one's influence, the *Mencius* passage places equal emphasis upon the *intensive* "me"—*this* unique and particular focus—as an active and creative participant in the emerging world order.

If we translate this rather abstract Mencian language into the vocabulary of the human community, we might say that exemplary persons (*junzi* 君子) are intensive as loci of rigorous cultivation and personal articulation. What makes them exemplary is the assiduous effort that has enabled their personal growth. By virtue of this personal intensity and discerned worth, they are celebrated as objects of emulation within the community, thereby extending their influence through patterns of deference both within their own generational boundaries, and for generations yet to come. In the words of the *Mencius*, they have become "most vast" as persons of intensive and enduring influence, and "most firm" as resolute beacons that guide others toward human virtuosity.

Particular exemplars provide the "heading" (*dao* 道 understood as *dao* 導) for the continuing community, and it is the project of much of the Confucian philosophical tradition to provide guidance as to how to become such a person. In lieu of an otherworldly God or gods as a separate order of being, the Confucian tradition has seen fit to elevate ancestral figures, cultural heroes, and supreme personalities to cosmic status, and to continue to celebrate them over its long career. Although profoundly religious in its nature, such deference to exemplary persons as a human-centered religiousness is better conceived of as the reverence that inspires emulation rather than the adoration and supplication we associate with worship.

This need for models to emulate, then, late and soon, has required the philosophers to become paradigmatic individuals—scouts to reconnoiter and provide the bearings for a "way" forward for the generations to come. This analogical appeal to models as the basis of moral reasoning is captured succinctly in the *Analects*:

> Correlating one's conduct with those near at hand can be said to be the method of becoming consummate in one's person (*ren* 仁).[①]

This process of "correlating one's conduct" is bidirectional. Personal cultivation requires deference to worthy exemplars available as social and cultural leaders within one's own world. At the same time, the growth made possible by such emulation allows one to aspire personally to a quality of conduct that will, in the fullness of time, make one a moral paragon for one's own family, community, and in the exceptional cases, for one's cultural tradition.

The interpretation of a world of processes and events eschews any notion of final discreteness. It is for this reason that *qi* 氣 requires the use of a focus and field rather than a part-whole vocabulary for its explication. One of the implications of the shift from a part-whole to a focus-field sensibility involves the manner in which one characterizes the interactive dynamics of the human experience, of its "ten thousand" processes and events. To the extent that notions such as action and reaction, and cause and effect are grounded in the assumption that things are externally related to each other, they lose their relevance. Essentialistic ideas of potential and actualization and the notion of a linear causality driven by strong teleological assumptions do not apply. Instead, all such interactions are to be regarded in terms of mutual growth and creative advance in the "doings and undergoings" of interdependent, transactional events. We shape and are shaped by the other participants in the shared, interdependent ecology in which we live our lives. All creativity is reflexive: in acting upon the world, we are acting upon ourselves.

---

① *Analects* 6.30: 能近取譬,可謂仁之方也已。

A Thick Generalization: Distinguishing "Events" from "Objects"

Perhaps the most fundamental difference between these two contrasting classical cosmologies is the prominence of "substance" as ontological ground in the classical Greek tradition and the fluid "process" orientation of the classical Chinese narrative, defining us as either discrete human "beings" or as eventful human "becomings" respectively. The irrelevance of the familiar ontological reality-appearance dichotomy in its various forms that would separate the objective from what is subjective has broad consequences for the way in which the human experience has been understood and the manner in which the Confucian cultural sensibilities have been shaped. The realist notion of the "real" as what is exclusively *objective*—that is, the "object" of true knowledge—is one immediate implication of the reality-appearance distinction and the dualistic worldview that issues from it. Such dualistic thinking is simply anathema to Confucian process cosmology.

A corollary to the privileging of a formal, unchanging reality over the flux of appearances in the dominant classical Greek worldview is the tendency to again give privilege to the discrete and quantitative over the continuous and qualitative.① The identity of "things" or persons tends to be atomistic: a function of quantitative discreteness that parses identity in terms of essential and accidental properties. Wholes are constructed out of discrete yet coherent parts. Families and communities are collections of individual persons who, because each of them has their own integrity, are externally conjoined. The priority of discreteness and quantity follows from the priority of stasis and permanence, and of the substantial over the processual. Because each person in the community is defined by some self-same identical characteristic, they have some pre-social, pre-cultural, and enduring warrant for their membership. Further, this priority given to discreteness and quantity in turn disposes toward a concern for the clarity

---

① See Jean-Paul Reding, "Words for Atoms, Atoms for Words—Comparative Considerations on the Origins of Atomism in Ancient Greece and the Absence of Atomism in Ancient China," *Comparative Essays in Greek and Chinese Rational Thinking*, Aldershot: Ashgate, *passim*. See also Nathan Sivin, *Medicine, Philosophy and Religion in Ancient China*, pp. 2-3.

of formally defined concepts and the necessity of unchanging truths—both of which are more congenial to a quantitatively discrete and measurable world.①

What Tang Junyi in describing Chinese cosmology refers to as the "world as such," is a unique and boundless "world-ing," and we observers always live our lives within it. Without an external standpoint for asserting objective truths about the world, persons are always reflexively implicated in the way in which they understand and organize their experience of it. And the values of the always interested viewer are thus necessarily implicated in any observation they make about it. As a consequence, saying something about the world is always a matter of selected interest that says something about one's own person and perspective. The absence of an abstract basis for making objective statements about our experience means that erstwhile objective definition and simple description are problematic, making fact and value interdependent and mutually entailing. Thus, any ultimate line that would purport to divide and then elevate science from culture, chemistry from alchemy, astronomy from astrology, geology from geomancy, and psychology from physiognomy, would be tenuous. Indeed, the distance between description and prescription is ultimately dependent upon the degree of self-consciousness in what is done, where a greater awareness of who one is and the prejudgments one brings to the experience would presumably reduce one's own footprint. William James provides some insight here into the inescapability of the subjective point of view that we find assumed in the Confucian understanding of an alternative, holistic notion of objectivity. For James he would define a holistic "fact" in the following terms:

> A conscious field *plus* its object as felt or thought of *plus* an attitude towards the object *plus* the sense of self to whom the attitude belongs ... is a *full* fact, even though it be an insignificant fact; it is of the *kind* to which

---

① It is the priority given to the quantitatively discrete that is the target of William James when, in the *Principles of Psychology*, he argues for the equal reality of "conjunctions and transitions" in the stream of consciousness. See *William James: The Essential Writings*, ed. Bruce W. Wilshire, Albany: State University of New York Press, 1984, pp. 47-81.

all realities whatsoever must belong...①

This alternative sense of a holistic, inclusive, and emergent objectivity captured in the language of "one is many, many one" (*yiduobufenguan* 一多不分觀) has a prominent role in the Confucian process cosmology. When we go to the Confucian texts, the sense made of an "objective" standard is not some antecedent, abstract principle that can be applied as a norm to any particular situation exclusive of subjective concerns. Indeed, perhaps it is the ambitiousness of the realist notion of objectivity that has given the term a seemingly derivative meaning: that is, of some undertaking having its "objective" in the sense of a goal or purpose that has been set for it. It is this holistic and productive understanding of objectivity that is primary in the Confucian tradition. Such an understanding is suggested by the Chinese loanwords appropriated from the modern Japanese *kanji* 漢字 translation of "subjective" and "objective" as *zhuguan* 主觀 and *keguan* 客觀 respectively: literally, the perspective of the host and the guest as they defer to each other in service to the best possible outcomes. Even though these perspectives are different, *zhuke* 主客 is a gerundive *yinyang* 陰陽 correlative dyad rather than a dualism with each aspectual term deferring to and being integral to the other as the relationship unfolds. Applying this to the "objective" in "taking Chinese philosophy on its own turns," for example, is allowing this tradition full participation in the conversation for the "growth" of an optimizing symbiosis (*gongsheng* 共生) within the global discipline of philosophy. With an optimizing symbiosis (*gongsheng* 共生) being its "objective" and highest value, the proper measure (*du* 度) of the quality of such deferential objectivity is an optimizing

---

① William James, *The Varieties of Religious Experience: A Study in Human Nature*, New York: Penguin, 1981, p. 499. One unresolved incoherence in James is that he wants to hold on to this holistic understanding of experience and at the same time, as a scientist, to assert the possibility and desirability of pure description, of descriptive neutrality that would bracket out subjectivity. Perhaps one way of resolving this issue would be to distinguish phenomenal description from interpretive description. What does it mean to give a good account of something? For James, genius lies with what Emerson called "seeing-into" things and taking them all in—being a good visualizer. Again, perhaps for James it is just a matter of psychological motivation. It makes a difference for us to try to be neutral in our descriptions because we then get more out of things.

symbiosis (*gongsheng* 共生) that is inclusive of all relevant interests.

In the early Confucian cosmology, absent the assumed dualistic and decontextualized notion of *objectivity*, there can only be the flux of passing circumstances. Without *objectivity*, erstwhile objects dissolve into the flux and flow—into the changefulness of their surround. Indeed, they are not "objects" as such, but *events,* continuous with all other events. What are perceived as persistent "things" that sustain an identity across time from birth, maturation, and eventual decline are in fact horizons of relationships that have relative yet transitory stability within a manifold of constant change. The identity of any "thing" thus conceived, though persistent, is analogic in the sense of being constituted by and a function of its range of dynamic associations. It is what it is, by virtue of its location and role within a boundless pattern of vital relations. The language of process is an eventful discourse without discrete objects or erstwhile objective facts, and to speak and hear this language is to experience and be inspired by the flow of things.

As human beings, the notion of the real as *objective* gives privilege to the analytic and dialectical mode of engagement by promising a single truth that allows discrete parties to "protest" in the sense of first standing apart from, "objecting" to, and thus dissenting on behalf of, this single truth. An alternative mode of discourse to this exclusionary dialectic available for human "becomings" is captured in the positive sense of "protest" that we find in the common expression, "I protest my innocence." To protest thusly, far from taking exception and objecting to something, is "to testify on behalf of" and to thus affirm with solemnity one's allegiance to an interpretation of a particular situation. Here the guiding assumption is an awareness that our transactions are always relational and reflexive, implicating us in one way or another in whatever depositions we might choose to make.

A Thick Generalization: Distinguishing "Phases" from "Elements"

The distinction between human beings and human becomings is further brought into focus by another contrast we find between substance ontology and process cosmology. Elemental theory is a prominent theme in classical Greek thought paradigmatic of substance ontology in privileging both discreteness and quantity. According to Nathan Sivin, such elemental theories "claim that things are made up of minute ultimate parts that usually do not look like the parts that are big enough for us to see."[1] Early on, the Chinese *wuxing* 五行 were in fact translated as "the five elements," associating this cosmology with the various Greek elemental theories. But several prominent scholars such as Sivin himself, Angus Graham, and John Major have, in their interpretive studies, sought to correct this earlier misleading understanding of the *wuxing* cosmology. According to Major,

> ... the problem with "five elements" is that the Chinese concept of *wu-hsing* [*wuxing*] ... has none of the sense of "basic ingredient" or "irreducible essence" of the Latin *elementum* nor of that term's various Greek conceptual ancestors. ... In contrast, the translation Five Phases, which now is rapidly gaining acceptance, clearly has connotations of change consistent with the Chinese concept of cyclical transformation.[2]

Wang Aihe has provided a cogent summary of this sinological debate about the proper translation of this term, *wuxing* 五行:

> The traditional translation is "Five Elements," a term most convenient for comparative studies of Chinese thought and thought in other civilizations. Yet "elements" does not fully represent the Chinese term *Wuxing*, which is literally five "goings," "conducts," or "doings," nor does it convey the basic nature of *Wuxing* as a cosmology of interaction and change. Many scholars have proposed alternatives, including five forces, agents, entities, activities, or stages of change. Of these, "Five Phases" has acquired a wide

---

[1] Sivin, *Medicine, Philosophy and Religion in Ancient China*, pp. 2-3.
[2] John Major, "A Note on the Translation of Two Technical Terms in Chinese Science: *wu-hsing* and *hsiu*," *Early China* 2 (1976), pp. 1-2. I would, however, disassociate myself from Major's initial claim that "the Chinese concept *wu-hsing* is one of function rather than constituent matter." Major in a subsequent exchange with Richard Kunst then clarifies what he means by "function" as "categories of relations." See his "Reply to Richard Kunst's Comments on *hsiu* and *wu hsing*," *Early China* 3, pp. 69-70. My understanding is that *wuxing* 五行, like *qi* 氣 or *dao* 道 or *yinyang* 陰陽, would resist any severe function-structure distinction, and that the relations are themselves constitutive.

acceptance among specialists.①

These recent elucidations of *wuxing* 五行 as "five phases" have permitted a much more productive approach to the important and pervasive notion of *qi* 氣 that becomes explicit among cosmologists in the late fourth and early third centuries BCE.

The Greek elemental theories are one familiar version of the reality-appearance distinction that is markedly absent in Chinese cosmological explanations. That is, in the Chinese sensibility, there is no putative Being behind the beings, no unchanging formal aspect behind the changing world, no One behind the many, no atomic level where unchanging "real" atoms rearrange themselves to constitute an apparent world. The Chinese counterpart to Greek "elemental" theories that, as we have seen, was initially confused with them is the phasal understanding of the animated, autogenerative process of *qi* 氣 transformation. The *yinyang* 陰陽 driven transformations that occur in *qi* 氣 are described metaphorically as the "five phases" (*wuxing* 五行). *Qi* 氣 is both *what* experience is and *how* it is, as it persists and yet is constantly changing in its formal aspect. The five phases are quite literally a "functional" equivalent of the Greek elements in that, rather than referring to ultimate "parts," they reference both the functioning and the reforming of the various phases of the changing world itself as such transformation is captured in the metaphorical and imagistic language of "shade and light" (*yinyang* 陰陽) and of metal, wood, water, fire, and earth (*jinmushuihuotu* 金木水火土). The bipolar opposition and temporality symbolized by *yinyang* 陰陽 tensions generates a vitality that drives the ongoing processes of change. These creative processes are parsed into the distinctive though continuous, transitional five phases that provide an account of both continuity and flux, persistence and change, similarities and differences, associations and contrasts. It is the application of the imagistic notion of "phases" to the manifold of processes that allows for these processes to be punctuated into distinctive, consummatory "events" that can then be correlated with each other in meaningful ways. Even though summer is a transition between spring and autumn, we can still treat it as a distinctive period of time in any given year, with each summer being continuous with and yet different from the summer of

---

① Wang Aihe, *Cosmology and Political Culture in Early China*, p. 3.

the year before. And similarly, although persons are transitional between progenitor and progeny, they are also uniquely particular persons. Such distinct "events"—narratives nested within narratives—then serve conceptually as the functional and structural equivalent of the quantitatively discrete "things" that we find in a substance ontology.

In Wang Aihe's work on the relationship between this evolving cosmology and political change, she cautions us that such *wuxing* 五行 "theorizing" has to be understood within the holistic process cosmology. This cosmology begins from the primacy of practice and takes theorizing as an intrinsic feature of practical activity itself that tries to make practices more productive and intelligent within the context of the practices themselves. Such theorizing is an effort to influence the always evolving circumstances to their best advantage. Wang observes that

> ... *wuxing* is not simply a set of concepts, a school of philosophy, a mode of thinking, or a commonly agreed-upon representation; instead, it is a cultural phenomenon that changes through history, a discourse for political argument and power struggle, and above all, an art of action in a world of conflict and change.[1]

This inseparability of the theoretical and the practical, the functional and the structural defining of this cosmology reflects a profoundly different way of thinking about what things are, and how they arise in the human experience.

Vital *Qi* 氣 as Functional Structure and Structured Function

Today we are most familiar with *qi* 氣 as a vital energy field in the areas of health, medicine, and the exercises leading to bodily well-being. Traditional Chinese Medicine (TCM) is quite properly to be understood as a practical application of this early process cosmology, and thus exploring its underlying assumptions can be instructive. Understanding body as *qi* 氣 can be helpful. But in this classical correlative cosmology, the term "body" like any predication of *qi* 氣 must of course be used advisedly; everything is a continuous

---

[1] Wang Aihe, *Cosmology and Political Culture in Early China*, p. 3.

field of *qi* 氣 manifesting itself at once as "body" and as "environing context," as "lived, existential body" and "body-as-corpse," as "physical" and "spiritual," as "forming" (*ti* 體) and "functioning" (*yong* 用), as "temporal" (*shi* 世) and "spatial" (*jie* 界). It is because of just such assumptions about "body" that TCM can provide us with a useful explanatory window on *qi* 氣 cosmology and a very different way of understanding the myriad "things" that constitute this world. As medical anthropologist Judith Farquhar observes,

> *Qi* is both structural and functional, a unification of material and temporal forms that loses all coherence when reduced to one or the other "aspect."[①]

It is thus that physiological, systemic functions have parity if not privilege over the enduring yet changing anatomical structures in TCM sensibilities. In fact, the purpose of the self-cultivating regimens that have been the persistent focus of Confucian philosophical inquiry, whether predominantly physical or spiritual, has been to achieve an equanimity and balance that allows for a productively continuous flow of *qi* 氣 without it suffering stagnation or obstruction.

Pursuing her observation that structure and function are two aspects of the same thing, Farquhar searches for an appropriate language that will provide the necessary contrast between TCM's very different processual understanding of the body, and the formal anatomical assumptions of biomedicine:

> Chinese medicine most classically envisions embodiment as a dynamic complex of interwoven processes, as a physiology that must be understood in the living through analysis of signs, symptoms, and a subjective sensorium.[②]

This functional understanding of formal structures in *qi* 氣 cosmology is radically contextual, locating "things" such as the "lived body" or "the

---

[①] Judith Farquhar, *Knowing Practice: The Clinical Encounter of Chinese Medicine*, Boulder: Westview Press, 1994, p. 34.
[②] Judith Farquhar, "Technologies of Everyday Life: The Economy of Impotence in Reform China," *Cultural Anthropology* 14, No. 2 (1999), p. 162.

body as experienced" within its ever-changing circumstances. Body is understood from the inside and the outside, as more or less subjective and more or less objective. If we are to overcome "our commonsense commitment to a materialism which must reduce phenomena to synchronically observable collections of objects," we must understand "things" as both existing in time, and as entailing a subjective dimension. That is, the temporality and reflexivity of "things" must be considered in any and all attempts at understanding them. Because "body" must be understood diachronically or "through time,"

> ... it is signs and symptoms, experiences and perceptions, which are the material foundation of medical perception. They are not less concrete than anatomical organs, but they are not conceivable outside of lived time.[1]

Thus, any attempt to treat "body" as simply a physical object would violate the contextual and processional sensibilities of the *qi* 氣 cosmology in which TCM is grounded. Unsurprisingly, the personal narrative is of enormous importance in traditional Chinese medical practices where

> ... the evidence here suggests ... that Chinese medicine accords a certain importance to quotidian self-perception; while never denying the object-nature of bodies, it privileges processes of change that take place in personal time, which can only be entered into medical consideration via the patient's own narrative.[2]

The inseparable subjectivity of "lived body" and the abstracted "body as object" in TCM—the body as at once "me" and as my corpse for other subjects—provides one way of making sense of ourselves as organisms. But how can we then apply this insight into body cosmologically to our understanding of "things" more generally? One consequence of this unwillingness in the tradition to separate time from matter is that there is no warrant, in Aristotle's language, to distinguish an active, efficient cause

---

[1] Judith Farquhar, "Objects, Processes, and Female Infertility in Chinese Medicine," *Medical Anthropology Quarterly* (NS) 5, No. 4 (1991), p. 386.
[2] Farquhar, "Objects, Processes, and Female Infertility in Chinese Medicine," p. 386.

from a passive material cause. In fact, expressions such as *ziran* 自然 and *tiandi* 天地, conventionally translated "nature" and "the world" do not simply refer to *a* world or *the* world; they refer to an active, ongoing, autogenerative process as experienced from within the process itself—what Tang Junyi above has called "world as such." A corollary to this notion of an invigorated world is the absence of any final boundary between the sentient and insentient, animate and inanimate, living and lifeless. *Qi* 氣 cosmology is thus "hylozoistic"—that is, life and matter are inseparable aspects of the same reality, two ways of looking at the same thing. It is a commonplace in classical Greek interpretations of the vital and spiritual character of things to appeal to a physical and spiritual dichotomy, assuming that the animating principle is distinguishable from the things it animates.

In classical China, the animating, transforming *qi* 氣, was thought of in terms of what in modern parlance we might call a "vital energy field" that is at once objective and existential. This field is not only pervasive as a condition of all things, but is also the medium through which all things are constituted. There is neither *qi* 氣 without form nor form without *qi* 氣. Indeed, "form" and "animating *qi* 氣" are two nonanalytic aspects of the same transforming reality, where "transitivity" and "form" are both implicit ways of understanding the transformative process. By nonanalytic, I mean that form and animation are aspectual—that is, simply two ways of looking at the same phenomenon. And they are separable only by foregrounding one as opposed to the other. As such, "animating *qi* 氣" and the various ways of saying "forming" or "constructing" are a descriptive and explanatory rather than an ontological vocabulary. We need both terms to give a coherent account of what we experience.

Qi 氣 is an image rather than a concept that, like water, is deliberate and provocative, defying the Aristotelian categories that structure and discipline our language and our thinking. That is, *qi* 氣 is at once one and many. When it accumulates, it can have a formal coherence by taking on a shape inspired by its context that is persistent and yet changing too. Axiologically, *qi* 氣 is again both noble and base. It is conceived of through the analogy of water, where water is life-giving and purifying, irrigating our world and cleansing our bodies and spirits. At the same time, water is destructive and contaminating, working its way down through the bowels and into the sewers to offend against polite human sensibilities. And further, just as water can be a "thing" (water) and an "action" (watering) and an "attribute" (moist) and a "modality" (cascading) all at the same time, so *qi* 氣 too will not be resolved into categories that would separate forming from functioning, agent from action, psychic from physical, things or actions from their properties or qualities.

"Time" (*shi* 時) then is the abstracted description used to denote this active, processual, and transformative nature of experience, the quantum of change that when optimally productive, evidences "good timing," and is indeed, "timely." *Qi* 氣 as energizing field is expressed as the unique and always changing foci of everything that constitutes our experience. The division of the world into correlative *yinyang* 陰陽 images, while arguably implicit in the natural cosmology of a proto-Chinese worldview documented at least as far back as the Shang dynasty, was in the course of time formalized, systematized, and made explicit in the complex Han dynasty cosmological charts and the "*yinyang* and five phases" (*yinyangwuxing* 陰陽五行) doctrines.[1]

The resolute uniqueness of these always situated "things," the "myriad of phenomena" (*wanwu* 萬物), precludes the existence of forms or ideas or categories or principles or inviolate species that would provide a basis for "natural kinds." Thus, things are individuated in the field of *qi* 氣 by analogy. Discriminations are made in terms of observed and conventionalized classifications associated with diurnal and seasonal changes, directions, deities, colors, tastes, sounds, numbers, smells, body parts and so forth. Such discriminations, far from being final in any sense, are described by Needham as processive and diffusive, "patterns simultaneously appearing in a vast field of force, the dynamic structure of which we do not yet understand."[2] As Needham goes on to report, it is the aggregation of these productive correlations or associations that enables us to act effectively, where "the sum of wisdom consisted in adding to the number of intuited analogical correspondences in the repertory of correlations."[3]

A Human "Being" or Human "Becomings"?

What is a human "being"? This was a perennial Greek question asked

---

[1] Major, *Heaven and Earth in Early Han Thought*.
[2] Needham, *Science and Civilisation in China*, Vol. II, p. 291.
[3] Needham, *Science and Civilisation in China*, Vol. II, p. 290.

in Plato's *Phaedo* and in his *Republic*, and in Aristotle's *Categories* as well. And there were many different answers, two of which are pointed at metonymically in Raphael's famous "School of Athens" fresco by the pointing "up" and "down" gestures of Plato and his student Aristotle respectively. One persistent answer to this question was an ontological one, predating Plato's psyche with the Egyptian transfiguration of the *ka* and *ba* life-forces animating the spiritual entity *akh* in the afterlife, and with the Pythagorean doctrine of the reincarnation of an immortal soul that anticipates and informs Plato's *Phaedo*.

Aristotle's ontology allows for a notion of simple location and of discrete individuality, and favors the noun form grammatically—the "man" in the market-place—as the ground for the attributes that can then be ascribed to him. In Aristotle's search for a complete description in the *Categories*, the "What?" question has primacy because it provides us with the necessary essence or substance of the subject (Gk. *ousia*, L. *substantia*): that is, it identifies the underlying substance of what the specific man as subject *is*. The various other questions that are prompted by the remaining secondary conditions—quantity, quality, relation, place, time, position, state, action, and affection—seek to provide us with the full complement of attributes that are "in" a subject or can be said "of" a subject that describe it as contingent and conditional predicates, none of which can exist without supervening on this subject. In Aristotle's own language:

> All the other things are either said of the primary substances as subjects or in them as subjects.... So if the primary substances did not exist it would be impossible for any of the other things to exist.[1]

From these deep historical roots, the "being" of a human being has come to be understood popularly in Christian doctrine as some variation on a permanent, ready-made, and self-sufficient soul. Early on in the narrative, "know thyself," as the signature exhortation of Socrates doctrine of "recollection" (*anamnesis*), is an exhortation to remember, recover, and thus know this soul fully. Each of us *is* a person, and from conception, has the integrity of *being* an individual person.

---

[1] Aristotle, *The Complete Works of Aristotle: The Revised Oxford Translation*, ed. Jonathan Barnes, Princeton: Princeton University Press, 1984, 2a35-2b7.

How, or in what "way" (*dao* 道), can persons through a cultivated and critical self-awareness in their various roles and relations *become* consummately human (*ren* 仁)? This then was the perennial Confucian question asked explicitly in all of the *Four Books*: in the *Expansive Learning* (*Daxue* 大學), in the *Analects of Confucius* (*Lunyu* 論語), in the *Mencius* (*Mengzi* 孟子), and again in *Focusing the Familiar* (*Zhongyong* 中庸). And the answer by the *ru* 儒 literati long before the time of Confucius himself was a moral, aesthetic, and ultimately religious one. Persons (always and necessarily plural) *become* humans by cultivating those thick relations that constitute our native conditions and that shape the trajectory of our life narratives: that is, that guide the whence and whither of our life's journey within family, community, and cosmos.[①] In this Confucian tradition, because we emerge in our associated lives lived in the roles of family and community to become persons, our assertive "I" is always a "we," and our socialized "me" is always an "us." "Cultivate your persons" (*xiushen* 修身) as the signature exhortation of the Confucian canons is described in *Expansive Learning* as the root of the Confucian project: that is, the project of becoming the distinctively unique persons we aspire to be (*ren* 仁). We are to cultivate our conduct assiduously as it is expressed in the activities of the specific family, community, and cosmic roles and relations we live together.

Perhaps the single most important common denominator within the interpretation of Confucian philosophy rehearsed in this *Sourcebook*, from education to ethics, from family to cosmology, is the relationally-constituted conception of persons. Persons or "human becomings" is necessarily plural because no one can become a person by themselves. Herbert Fingarette has famously opined that "for Confucius, unless there are at least two human beings, there can be no human beings."[②] In making this claim, Fingarette is suggesting that "person" in the singular as a discrete individual has little relevance for the relational and irreducibly social notion of persons at play in Confucian philosophy. Persons either come together or not at all.

Although this is a *Sourcebook* in classical Confucian philosophy, I

---

① See *Analects* 12.1: "Through self-discipline and achieving propriety in one's roles and relations one becomes consummate in one's conduct" 克己復禮爲仁 .

② Herbert Fingarette, "The Music of Humanity in the *Conversations of Confucius*," *Journal of Chinese Philosophy* 10 (1983), p. 217.

want to argue that the value of this way of thinking about persons is by no means simply antiquarian. I have elsewhere joined my collaborator Henry Rosemont in making the argument that perhaps the most important contribution Confucian philosophy has to offer our contemporary world is precisely its own elaborate, sophisticated, and ethically compelling conception of relationally-constituted persons that can be drawn upon to challenge and critique the entrenched ideology of a foundational individualism.[①] We must locate this notion of a relationally-constituted conception of "human becomings" within the generic features of an early Chinese process or "event" zoetology in which putative "things" and their contexts are interdependent and thus inseparable. What it means to become human, far from referencing an antecedent given that takes us back to our origins (*eidos*) or forward to some given, pre-determined end (*telos*), is in fact an always provisional and emergent process embedded within the context of an evolving cosmic order. It is just such a worldview that I and my collaborators, following Marcel Granet, Tang Junyi 唐君毅, Fei Xiaotong 費孝通, K.C. Zhang 張光直, Frederick Mote, Joseph Needham, and Angus Graham as our intellectual heroes, have argued for at length as the most appropriate interpretive context for understanding classical Confucianism.

The contemporary philosopher Li Zehou 李澤厚 makes a distinction between "morality" (*daode* 道德) and "ethics" (*lunlixue* 倫理學) by appealing to Kant and Hegel respectively. For Li, Kant's philosophical psychology makes "morality" a function of comporting oneself according to the dictates of our innate reason and its moral imperatives, while Hegel takes a philosophy of history perspective and locates "ethics" within the parameters of the relationships that obtain within family, community, and country. The important question for Li then is whether human "beings" are born with some universal moral faculty that makes them good, or instead that human "becomings" become morally good over time as the product of their personal cultivation. While many if not most of the contemporary interpreters of the debate between Mencius and Xunzi might ascribe the

---

[①] See Henry Rosemont, Jr., *Against Individualism: A Confucian Rethinking of the Foundations of Morality, Politics, Family, and Religion*, Idaho Falls: Lexington Books, 2015, and Roger T. Ames, *Human Becomings: Theorizing Persons for Confucian Role Ethics*, Albany: State University of New York Press, 2021.

former innatist, psychological position to Mencius, and the latter appeal to personal cultivation and refinement to Xunzi, I am glad to have the corroboration of Li Zehou who also sees both Mencius and Xunzi as advocating for the latter position. Li insists that

> ... Mencius and Xunzi are consistent with Confucius in both advocating for "education." The first chapter of *Xunzi* is "Exhortation to Learning." And Mencius says that "what distinguishes people from the brutes is ever so slight, and while the common run of people might lose this difference, exemplary persons preserve and develop it." Hence this distinguishing human characteristic has to be sought after or it will be lost. Both Mencius and Xunzi emphasize *aposteriori* cultivation and learning. The distinguishing characteristic of Confucianism is that what is fundamental to the human experience is not some fixed nature but a process of ceaseless change and growth. Learning to become human is a key precept in Confucianism.①

Of course, to insist on a narrative understanding of persons does not preclude the necessary generalizations about persons and our evolving cultural values that we need to describe, analyze, evaluate, and ultimately to use as a guide for the human experience. As Borges's "Funes the Memorius" and Plato before him would insist, such generalizations are necessary for the thinking process itself; after all, we cannot think particularity. In the Confucian texts we find frequent reference to the values of courage (*yong* 勇), living up to one's word (*xin* 信), family reverence (*xiao* 孝), conscientiousness (*zhong* 忠), empathetic deference and dramatic rehearsal (*shu* 恕), cherishing learning (*haoxue* 好學), an optimizing, superlative harmony (*he* 和), achieving propriety in one's roles and relations (*li* 禮), living wisely (*zhi* 知), and many more such normative abstractions.

What we must understand, however, is that such generalizations about

---

① Li Zehou in his "An Explanation of the Summary Chart on Ethics" (關於 "倫理學總覽表" 的說明)《中國文化》Spring 2018: 所以我說孟、荀統一于孔, 即 "學"。荀子有《勸學》作爲首篇, 孟子也講 "人之所以異於禽獸者幾希, 庶民去之, 君子存之", 所以要 "求放心", "求則得之, 捨則失之"。孟荀雙方都重視後天的培養和學習。孔學的特點就是認爲人的本性並不是固定的 nature, 而是一個總在不斷成長、變化的過程。從而 "學做人" 始終是孔學要義之一。

the human experience ultimately emerge from human lives lived, and that the general emerges from specific rather than the other way around. Far from beginning from some teleological notion of a fixed human nature with antecedent, determinative principles to guide our conduct, such functional generalizations that are to be made about persons and their values, are importantly post hoc abstractions from the continuing confluence of particular narratives and the patterns of conduct expressed therein. As such, these modal generalizations describing human conduct in general terms are always provisional and revisionist, being constantly theorized out of our practices to make these practices more productive and intelligent. The "journey or way-making we have undertaken together"—our *dao* 道—is the classical Chinese expression of personal narratives, where the *genus* of this term that purports to describe humans in a general way (*rendao* 人道) is emerging continuously out of the history of a confluence of the specific and always unique lives lived. It is thus "the way of becoming human" rather than "the way of being human." Again, and by extension, it is analogy with the lives of exemplary models remote and near at hand that provides the concrete guidelines for a consummate human life as "the way of becoming consummately human" (*rendao* 仁道).

The important adjustment in thinking that a narrative understanding of persons requires is that we must abjure what John Dewey has called *the* philosophical fallacy: the abstracting of one element out of the continuing process of experience, reifying it, and then turning this second order "principle" into first order by claiming that it is antecedent, causal, and determinative. Dewey references this fallacy specifically with reference to the notion of "good:"

> There is no morality in my ethics i.e., there is no apart morality. Good conduct (once conduct is defined as activity which is an end to itself) seems to me a pleonasm. Conduct, full activity, is the good.... Now the usual idea of the Good seems to be an abstraction which has been frozen. It denotes full activity, but then it [is] abstracted and put over by itself and then frozen in its isolated apart from the content of specific activities which first gave it meaning.[①]

[①] *The Correspondence of John Dewey, 1871-2007 (I-IV)*, Electronic Edition, Vol. 1, 1871-1918, 1891.03.14 (00453), John Dewey to Thomas Davidson, ed. Larry Hickman, Virginia: Intelex Corporation, 2009.

We are guilty of this fallacy of "pleonasm" or redundancy when the notion of "potential" as cause, root, source, or nature is reduced to some antecedent teleological principle that is then reduplicated in the process of growth. We first dissect the human experience and then try to splice it back together by making causal and idealist claims about some isolated source. Again, when Dewey claims that "full activity" is itself what is meant by good and that there is "no apart morality," he is simply making the point that morality is nothing other than a continuing robust growth in our relationships.

In turning to the Confucian notion of "good" (*shan* 善) specifically, rather than referencing some antecedent, generic "virtue" or some far-off end, it actually means first and foremost, the growth achieved in one's roles and relations through the critical self-awareness that enables effective communication. Good is not some qualitatively superior action or a character trait derived from some prior and higher virtue of "goodness" that inheres "in" a person, or some general principle of "goodness" that informs and supervenes on an action as it is "done" by a person. Indeed, *shan* 善 is most concretely imputed to the shared narrative rather than to the traits of person as the efficacious life-path one is walking together with others (*zhishanzhidao* 至善之道), contrasting this way with the paths of those whose narratives are less so. "Good" in the first instance is "good with," "good to," "good in," "good for," "good at," and then only abstractly and in summary, "good." "Good" in this sense of moral growth begins from discursive activities within the continuing life story and only then can serve as a description of a person or action. *Shan* 善 is the gregarious activity of growing our relations and making them "meaningful" by communicating effectively and thus "relating" to each other. This discursive source of *shan* 善 is made evident in the graph as it is found on the bronzes and in the small seal script 䡤 where it is written with at least two and occasionally three "speech" (*yan* 言) radicals, prompting philosopher-philologist Kwan Tze-wan 關子尹 to suggest that

> ... this kind of repetition might reflect the fact that when the ancients talked about *shan* 善 they were not referring to "good" in itself, but "good" as it obtains in the relations among people. Thus, putting the auspicious sheep and multiple speech components together gives us the meaning of

two persons speaking face-to-face with warmth and affection.①

Of course, the identities of persons are certainly grounded in their thick native beginnings as they emerge within the environing relationships of family and community. As a received and thus retrospective inheritance integral to who they are, these native, prosocial tendencies need to be both nurtured and protected from loss or injury. And further, the conduct of such persons is certainly guided by the normative generalizations that a cultural tradition has best remembered as the substance of its customs and institutions. But identities of persons and the realization of their highest aspirations only emerge prospectively as these initial relationships are cultivated, grown, and consummated over their particular lifetimes. The potential of persons far from being an antecedent given, in fact emerges most significantly in the always transactional events that in sum constitute lives lived together in the world.

Again, the "potential" for becoming human is not some causal "beginning" or teleological "end"—that is, some inborn, latent and essential potential that lies outside of context and of family relations, or some potential that is actualized as the ineluctable process of growth toward some predetermined ideal. To begin with, in this Chinese natural cosmology, there are no such deracinated, individual persons who could possibly be described as living outside of the context of family relations. Persons do not live their lives inside their skins; they live and grow in their associations, and only in their associations. And since persons in their nested, narratives-within-narratives are constituted by these evolving, eventful relations, the "potential" of persons and their achieved identities in fact emerge *pari passu* from out of the specific, contingent transactions of their lives. Thus, the best sense we can make of "potential" is that while it certainly has a retrospective reference to important native conditions within an evolving narrative, rather than being understood as wholly antecedent as a set of given, defining factors, such potential is most significantly prospective and contingent, evolving and compounding within the ever-changing ebb and flow of circumstances. Rather than being generic or universal, such potential is

---

① Kwan Tze-wan, "Multi-function Character Database," 善夫吉父鬲（西周晚期） CHANT 704. 凡此種種，可能反映古代談 "善" 都不指獨善，而指人際關係中的 "善"，故 "羊"、"誩" 合起來意會二人好言相向（關子尹）。

unique to the career of specific, self-aware and irreducibly relational persons; and rather than existing simply as an inherent and defining endowment, the full measure of such potential can only be known post hoc after the unfolding of the particular narrative, a shared narrative that usually continues long beyond the putative demise of specific persons.[①]

In our own contemporary world, where variations on a foundational "individualism" have become an ideology without any seemingly robust alternatives, it behooves us to ask whether the "vocabulary cluster" of agents, acts, generic virtues, character traits, autonomy, motivation, reasons, choice, freedom, principles, consequences, and so on, that gives expression to our own default, commonsense assumptions about the human experience and the discrete human "beings" that populate it, makes sense within the Confucian project of human "becomings."

Indeed, the Confucian conception of persons as "human becomings" was developed within the natural process cosmology that has served this tradition as the context for such personal growth. Confucian ethics is formulated by invoking its own radically different focus-field cluster of terms and distinctions: "aspiring to become consummate in our roles and relations" (ren 仁), "optimizing appropriateness in our roles and relations" (yi 義), "seeking relational virtuosity" (de 德), "aspiring to propriety in our roles and relations" (li 禮), "embodying the tradition through its intergenerational transmission in our roles and relations" (ti 體), "bodyheartminding" (xin 心), "cultivating and growing our human propensities" (xing 性), "resolve and commitment in what we do in our roles and relations" (cheng 誠), "pursuing an optimizing symbiosis within the diversity of our relations" (he 和), and so on. Confucian ethics begins from fundamentally different assumptions about how personal identities emerge in our human narratives, and how moral competence is expressed as a habituated

---

① For Dewey too, "the idea that potentialities are inherent and fixed by relation to a predetermined end was a product of a highly restricted state of technology." *Later Works*, Vol. 14, p. 110. In Dewey's process thinking, "potentialities cannot be known till after the interactions have occurred. There are at a given time unactualized potentialities in an individual because and in as far as there are in existence other things with which it has not as yet interacted." *Later Works*, Vol. 14, p. 109. Lincoln is not Lincoln independent of the circumstances of history, nor are the circumstances of history the making of Lincoln. Indeed, Lincoln is a collaboration between person and circumstances expressed as thick habits of conduct.

virtuosity in the roles and relationships that come to constitute us. It is thus that, within this holographic process cosmology, our familiar dualistic understanding of not only "potential" but of concepts closely related to it such as "root," "cause," "source," and "human nature" have to be reconsidered, and reinterpreted in a holistic way.

Defining a World by Association

Another way of illustrating Needham's claim that in contrast with the Greeks, this early Chinese cosmology has "its own causality and its own logic" is to look at assumptions about the very nature of the language through which these traditions have been transmitted. For example, we can find a ready contrast between two different models of definition. There is the analytical approach to defining terms in the pursuit of the *whatness* of things and events: the reality behind appearance, the univocal aspect behind the many instances, the objective behind the subjective, the essential behind the contingent, the literal behind the metaphorical, the root meaning behind the history of a term's usage, the "one" behind the many. We might refer to this analytic approach as the search for literal definitions that we associate with Plato and Aristotle, each in their own different way. It is this analytic understanding of definition that gives us the language of concepts and theories and literal translation. Indeed, the history of "concept" as it is understood in Plato gives us hypostatized ideas (*eide*), and although Aristotle abandons this reification of concepts, he still insists that conceptual *eidos* is the universal of predication and the subject of definition.[①]

An alternative to analytic definition is the processional or narrative approach to defining specific terms that attempts to locate them within an evolving web of semantic and phonetic associations, and to thus define them by appeal to their most relevant relationships: an allusive, historicist, evocative, "one and many at the same time" notion of definition. Since the technical term for defining and in fact redefining expressions by using words that sound alike or that have a similar meaning is "paronomasia," we might refer to this notion of defining a term by its associations

---

① See the entry for *eidos* in F.E. Peters, *Greek Philosophical Terms: A Historical Lexicon*, New York: New York University Press, 1967, pp. 46-51.

as paronomastic "definition." I put the word "definition" in scare quotes because paronomasia as a rhetorical device is directed at the open-ended disclosing of additional meaning through association rather than closure in the sense of the clarity that would be achieved by setting a boundary on such meaning. Indeed, we find in the practice of "defining" terms, instead of seeking to set limits on them, the invoking of a combination of the semantic and phonetic associations they might stimulate and bring to mind. Of course, these two models of definition—literal and paronomastic— need not be exclusive, but a particular emphasis does emerge when we consider the weight given to each within their respective substance and processual worldviews.

To illustrate the former sense of "literal definition," in Plato's *Euthyphro*, we find Socrates in search of the real definition of "piety:" not the definition of the term or the concept, but what piety really *is*. He asks Euthyphro, his would-be teacher

> ... isn't it true that in every action piety is self-identical, and similarly impiety is in every instance the opposite of piety, but consistent with itself; in other words that everything that is to be regarded as impious has a single definite characteristic [Gk. *eidos*] in respect of its impiety? ... Then explain to me what this characteristic is in itself, so that by fixing my eyes upon it and using it as a pattern I may be able to describe any action, yours or anyone else's, as pious if it corresponds to the pattern and impious if it doesn't.[①]

This notion of strict identity, fundamental to Aristotelian logic, means that each thing is one of a "kind" by virtue of a single, self-identical and reduplicative characteristic. What is true of the "kinds" that make up the world is also assumed to be true of the language that describes them and the subjective ideas through which they are known. That is, as corollary to an abstract and essentialist definition of moral law and natural kinds, words themselves—our repositories of cultural interests—are a currency that, upon investigation, are expected to yield up etymologies that not only reveal their particular historical careers, but more fundamentally, bring

---

① H. Tredennick (trans.), *The Last Days of Socrates*, New York: Penguin, 1954, pp. 24-26.

to light their ostensive root meanings—their essential, literal definitions. Such literal definitions are a window on reality, providing access to a secure ground of unchanging principles from which we can construct our univocal concepts and theories. It is a short move for Plato, having committed to natural kinds in respect of both natural and moral laws, to discover the soul in positing an essential defining condition for each "kind" of thing, including human beings themselves.

When the philosopher Confucius, like Plato, attempts to formulate a basis for human morality, he is seemingly less ambitious than his Athenian cousin. He is not interested in positing the existence of some divinely sanctioned, independent, universal, and objective standard beyond our empirical experience that can be appealed to for adjudication and justification of moral decisions. On the contrary, Confucius allows that morality is invariably a function of the interface between the conservative inertia of a cultural tradition that, in its past efficacy, has achieved a religious status, and those present, specific, and always fluid circumstances that are defining of each unique situation. Moral competence requires that the most efficacious response to any situation be consistent with both precedent and contextually site-specific circumstances at the same time. This then is the interdependence of reforming and functioning (*tiyong* 體用), of continuity and flux (*biantong* 變通):

> Exemplary persons in making their way in the world, are neither bent on nor against anything; rather, they go with what is most appropriate (*yi* 義).①

The classical Chinese term translated here as "appropriate" (*yi* 義) has conventionally been translated into English as "righteous" or "righteousness," a palpably biblical term suggesting compliance with some external ethical standard, some Divine Will. However, this classical Chinese notion viewed both etymologically and in context suggests that it is better rendered "appropriateness"—L. *proprius*>proper>property, "making something one's own." Morality, then, is the effort to negotiate what is best in one's circumstances, where one's own interests and the interests of one's natural, social, and cultural environments must all be considered. *Yi* 義 is

---

① *Analects* 4.10: 子曰："君子之於天下也，無適也，無莫也，義之與比。"

thus resolutely situational, reflexive, inclusive, and pragmatic.

Also included within *yi*'s 義 domain of meaning as it appears in the classical literature is the notion of "meaning" itself, acknowledging as it does the fact that the most appropriate relationships are the most productive of meaning. Indeed, when we look for the paronomastic definition of *yi* 義 in the classical literature, we find it defined by the similar sounding *yi* 宜 that means "fitting, proper, suitable." Interestingly, *yi* 宜 is a character that like *yi* 義 itself is closely associated with sacrifice, in this case, to the altar to the soil. There are no events in the human experience in which appropriate protocols and decorum are more necessary and more culturally meaningful than in the ritualized observances of ancestral sacrifices.

When we consult the second century *Shuowen* 説文 lexicon or survey the Chinese philosophical literature that purports to explain such a world, we discover that the meanings of other philosophical terms are also often brought into focus "paronomastically:" that is, they are defined by their evolving web of semantic and phonetic associations. Such paronyms are most obvious as a family of cognate terms that, derived from the same root, have semantic overlap in their range of meaning. For example, in English, as we have seen, the words "proper," "propriety," "appropriate," "to appropriate," and "property" are all derived from the Latin, *proprius*, meaning "making something one's own." A less obvious form of paronym is when different words are associated by virtue of the same or similar pronunciation, evoking a kind of punning among their several meanings.

Paronomastic definition is to be found everywhere in the classical Chinese philosophical literature as a familiar trope. When we consult traditional dictionaries that themselves chronicle the cultural associations of this world—the *Shuowen*, for example—we discover that terms are not as much defined analytically and etymologically by appeal to essential, literal, putatively "root" meanings, as they are explained metaphorically by semantic and phonetic associations. The term "exemplary persons" or "ruler" (*jun* 君), for example, is defined by its cognate and phonetically similar term, "gathering" (*qun* 群), an association between two words that arises because of the underlying assumption people will "gather round" and defer to exemplary persons or rulers. After all, the *Analects* insists that: "Excellent persons do not dwell alone; they are sure to have neighbors."[1]

---

[1] *Analects* 4.25: 子曰："德不孤，必有鄰。"

"Mirror" (*jing* 鏡 or *jian* 鑒) is defined as "shining radiantly" (*jing* 景) or "looking into, overseeing" (*jian* 監) respectively: a mirror is a source of illumination that enables one to oversee a situation with clarity. "Battle formation" (*zhen* 陣) is defined as "arraying and displaying" (*chen* 陳). Perhaps the most important service provided by a battle formation rather than being to kill efficiently is to a display strength that will deter an enemy from fighting in the first place. "To die" (*si* 死) is "draining away" (*si* 澌): dying is the dispersal of one's *qi*. In the *Analects* 12.3, "consummate person or conduct" (*ren* 仁) is defined as "being circumspect in speech" (*ren* 訒): one's words must not outstrip one's deeds. "*Tian* 天" (conventionally translated as "Heaven") is "*dian* 顛" (the crown of the head, the highest point): we look up to the sky, to ancestors, and to cultural heroes who have shaped our identity and bequeathed to us our legacy. A "ghost or spirit" (*gui* 鬼) is defined as "returning" (*gui* 歸): the *qi* 氣 of the deceased person disperses to find its way back to some more primordial condition. "Way-making" (*dao* 道) is defined as "treading" (*dao* 蹈): as the *Zhuangzi* says so eloquently, "The way is made in the walking" (*daoxingzhiercheng* 道行之而成).① "King" (*wang* 王) is defined as "going to" (*wang* 往): the people repair to the True King. Such examples of paronomastic definition are legion.

Sometimes this association is reinforced by a semantically driven choice of the phonetic element in the construction of a graph. For example, the graph "harmony" (*xie* 諧) contains the phonetic, "being in accord" (*jie* 皆), and the graph "deceiving, false" (*wu* 誣) contains the phonetic "sorcery, magician, shaman" (*wu* 巫). Sometimes the association is made ideographically: *xiao* 孝 meaning "family reverence," is constructed by combining the characters for "old" (*lao* 老) and "child" (*zi* 子).

And the association among a range of different ideas can be a shared meaning that defines a broad cognate set of characters as we saw above with L. *proprius*. For example, the character-stem *jian* 戔 means "small, little." From it comes *qian* 錢 "(small money =) coins," *qian* 淺 "shallow," *jian* 賤 "(small shells used for currency =) cheap, lowly," *jian* 俴 "shallow," *can* 殘 "(small and wicked =) a fragment, cruel," *jian* 踐 "trample underfoot," *jian* 箋 "(small bamboo chip =) a note," *jian* 諓 "(shallow words =) insincere," *zhan* 盞 "a shallow cup," *zhan* 棧 "a small wooded pathway,"

---

① *Zhuangzi* 4/2/33.

and so on.

From a classical Greek perspective where literal, formal meanings of terms are presupposed as the expected norm, paronomastic definition seems at best random and playful if not even capricious. Significantly however, in this paronomastic process, the assumption is not that we are just "discovering" definitions about an existing world, but are rather actively delineating a world and bringing it into being. What is remarkable about this paronomastic way of constructing meaning is that a term is defined non-referentially by mining relevant and yet seemingly random phonetic and semantic associations implicated in the word itself. Another second term becomes relevant as a source of redefinition by simply being a homophone or a rhyme or a cognate expression. Meaning continues to emerge between and among the words that constitute the language as it is used in different ways to express and to extend the culture. There is real poesy and imagination in such expectations.

A further observation can be made that would underscore the primacy of process over form as a grounding presupposition in this cosmology. The terms chosen to define erstwhile nominal expressions ("nouns" or "things") are frequently if not usually verbal, gerundive expressions (or "events"). For example, as we have seen, "battle formation" (*zhen* 陣) is defined as "arraying and displaying" (*chen* 陳), *junzi* 君子 ("exemplary person") is defined as *qun* 群 ("gathering"), and so on. The implication is that in a process cosmology, "something" is primarily an abstraction from the "*doing*" of something.

Where literal definitions in a Platonic world provide us access to principles as the ultimate source and proper object of knowledge, paronomastic associations compound correlations among things in our experience and enable us to produce those meaningful relationships that increase significance and value as a source of practical wisdom. Simply put, "insightful" associations "incites" growth in meaning. We have called this *ars contextualis*: the art of productive contexualization.[①] Through this process of analogical thinking and doing, we expand upon existing resources that enable

---

[①] See David L. Hall and Roger T. Ames, *Thinking Through Confucius*, Albany: State University of New York Press, 1987, pp. 246-249; *Anticipating China: Thinking Through the Narratives of Chinese and Western Culture*, Albany: State University of New York Press, 1995, pp. 273-275; *Thinking from the Han*, Albany: State University of New York Press, 1998, pp. 39-43, 111-112.

intelligent practice and that is called wisdom. For this classical cosmology, it is metaphor rather than metaphysics that makes the world real.

Above using the *Euthyphro* we extrapolated from the assumption that literal language defines reality to the positing of an essential soul or *psyche* as defining of what is most real about persons. In this Confucian cosmology, we find that instead of assuming some essential feature of the discrete human being, persons, like words, are to be understood by exploring their specific patterns of meaningful associations. Persons are not perceived as superordinated ready-made individuals—as agents who stand independent of their actions. Rather, persons (*ren* 人) are complex, ongoing relational "events" that emerge qualitatively as "consummate co-persons" (*ren* 仁) by conducting themselves appropriately (*yi* 義) in always shared narratives (*dao* 道) expressed through their ritualized roles and relationships (*li* 禮) in their specific families and communities. Persons are *constituted* by their web of relationships.

The classical Chinese tradition begins from the assumption that the human being is something that one *does* rather than what one *is*; it is *how* one behaves and achieves a personal identity within the associations of the human community rather than some essential endowment that inheres within one as a potential ready to be actualized. For Confucius, to "know thyself" is to cultivate and thus "realize oneself" within the roles and relationships that locate one within family and community.

The argument herein is that in the world of classical China, the images and institutions being devised to express its culture, the language that reports on this culture, the relational conception of persons that embodies the culture, and the ways of thinking and living that are defining of and expanding upon the culture, are most fruitfully accessed by tracing relevant associations available within the fabric of the narrative itself. Knowing a world is not only a process of mapping and reconnoitering it, but also activating those meaningful resources that enable one to forge a way forward in it most effectively.

The *Book of Changes* 易經: A Cosmological Vocabulary

The contemporary philosopher Zhang Xianglong 張祥龍 draws upon the philosophy of the *Book of Changes* to make a useful distinction between what he calls "image thinking" (*xiangsiwei* 象思維) and the more familiar "concept or conceptualizing thinking" (*gainiansiwei* 概念思維 or *gainianhuasiwei* 概念化思維).① Above we saw Zhao Tingyang ascribe a kind of "dictionary knowledge" to dualistic, ontological thinking that seeks to know what is what. In the same vein, Zhang Xianglong describes five characteristics he would associate with "conceptual thinking." (1) It is a universalizing or generalizing way of thinking (*pubianhua* 普遍化 or *yibanhua* 一般化) that would abstract out the shared features of things rather than dealing with them concretely and specifically. (2) In seeking out the erstwhile unchanging essences of things rather than dealing with the changing things themselves, conceptual thinking provides thought with a stabilizing function (*jingtaihua* 靜態化) by taking as its subject matter what is most dependable, foundational, static, and logical. (3) Conceptual thinking is a form of higher order objectification (*gaojieduixianghua* 高階對象化) that takes abstract, objective principles as the substance of reality and as the subject of its intellectual reflection: beauty-in-itself, the principle of justice, and so on. (4) Conceptual thinking belongs to a specifically conceptual understanding of philosophy that takes as its subject matter the content of retrospective reflection (*shihoufansi* 事後反思) rather than immediate empirical experience. In explaining his philosophy of history, G.W.F. Hegel writes, "The owl of Minerva spreads its wings only with the falling of dusk." What he means is that the objects of all philosophical understanding are, by necessity, only those things which we have already experienced, and have rationally deduced from principles we already know. (5) Conceptual thinking is non-meaning generating (*bushengchengyiyide* 不生成意義的) in the sense that it arranges, organizes, and systematizes meaning but does not produce it.

Zhao Tingyang contrasts the dictionary knowledge offered by ontological thinking with Confucian cosmology that provides a grammar of the world in seeking a coordinated understanding of the relations among things behind all of their doings. As "image thinking" (象思維), Zhang Xianglong sees it as (1) an originative and generative source of meaning (*yuanfaxing* 原發性) in the sense of being a "doing" that constitutes the doer, what is being done, and what is initiated within the continuing process itself. Unlike conceptual thinking that would abandon phenomena

---

① Zhang Xianglong 張祥龍, 概念化思維與象思維 (Conceptualizing Thinking and Imagistic Thinking), *Journal of Hangzhou Normal University*, No. 5 (2008).

and their concrete process of growth, image thinking invests itself in this same empirical process to repair, make adjustments, and reconstruct the content of experience. (2) Image thinking is non-objectifying (*feiduixiang* 非對象) in the sense that it does not objectify experience that would allow for its definition as in the bureaucratic structure of conceptual thinking, but instead makes meaning, determines meaning, and makes clear the pathway through which meaning and its structure is manifested, thereby distinguishing its levels and functions. More than other ways of thinking, the office of imagistic thinking without itself having any fixed mode of expression is image-enabling with the capacity of images to induce meaning and to activate the first stages in the growth of meaning. (3) Image thinking functions to bring insights and alternative perspectives with it that will have a complementary "repairing and elaborating" (*bu* 補) function in the growth of meaning (*buduiershengcheng* 補對而生成), making those adjustments and modifications that will reinstate equilibrium and balance. (4) Since images do not resolve to the form and formless distinction nor do they entail some native stuff, we can only think of them in terms of a pure tendency or state of emerging and dissipating (*chunshitai* 純勢態), a rising and falling wave, the distinction between a living image and one that is dying. (5) There is a holographic latency or potentiality (*qianzaiquanxi* 潛在全息) in images that resists definition or boundary. With an image, one seems to not know and yet to understand more expansively and more deeply. On encountering an image, there is a beginning for understanding that then sets off a surge of meaning. (6) Images are vital and temporalizing (*shihua* 時化), and have a life of their own that contrasts with the hardening and reifying of the conceptual. They necessarily arise suddenly, and yet seem to be long anticipated. (7) Human beings live in a world of images, and their language is imagistic, riding as it does upon waves of underlying images (*yuanchudeyuyanhua* 原初地語言化): the metaphors we live by. Images are neither universalistic nor particular, and what gives expression to an image is neither a proper name nor a concept. Images change and grow according to the linguistic context, and activate the growth of new meaning.

In the *Book of Changes*, the notion of both cosmic and human change is described in the aspectual and processual images of symbiotic bipolar opposites such as "flux and continuity" (*biantong* 變通), "alternating succession" (*yinyang* 陰陽) and "penetration and receptivity" (*qiankun* 乾坤) within the vital context of "the heavens and the earth" (*tiandi* 天地). Such images complement each other, and together provide an account of the ongoing process of transformation that continues without respite within an unbounded totality.[①] It is within this flux and flow that the transactional human life unfolds, with the challenge for human beings to fathom these cosmic operations and correlate the events of their experience to optimum effect.

The intellectual milieu for early Chinese thinkers as it is captured in the vocabulary of the "Great Commentary" fascicle of the *Book of Changes* was a phenomenal world of process and change construed both as continuity, *dao* 道 : "the unfolding of the boundless field of experience," and as multiplicity, *wanwu* 萬物: "the ten thousand processes or events," or perhaps more simply put, "everything that is happening." A familiar metaphor in the early corpus for the novel arising and subsiding of the always unique phenomena of the world is the "swinging gates of *tian*" (*tianmen* 天門):

> Thus the closing of the swinging gates is called receptivity (*kun* 坤); the opening of the gates is called penetration (*qian* 乾). The ongoing alternation of openings and closings is called flux (*bian* 變), and the inexhaustibility of the comings and goings is called continuity (*tong* 通). When something is manifest, it is called an image (*xiang* 象), and taking on physical form it is called a phenomenon (*qi* 器). To get a grasp of these things and apply them is called emulation (*fa* 法). Putting them to good use so that all of the people can take advantage of them is called insight into the mysteries of the world (*shen* 神).[②]

The process of change imaged here provides us with insight into how change was conceived, and what vocabulary was used to think about it. The generative opening and closing of the swinging gates is an image that resists our default assumptions about the primacy of casual agency. As in so many passages in the "Great Commentary," this text begins with observations about the form and functioning of the natural processes, and then concludes with advice on how effective collaboration with this changing world

---

① Keightley, "Shang Divination and Metaphysics," pp. 374-375.
② "Great Commentary" A11: 是故，闔戶謂之坤；闢戶謂之乾；一闔一闢謂之變；往來不窮謂之通；見乃謂之象；形乃謂之器；制而用之，謂之法；利用出入，民咸用之，謂之神。

can inspire the human experience:

> Thus, that which goes beyond form is called *dao* 道; those things that have form are called phenomena. The transforming and tailoring that goes on among things is called their flux, while their advance and application is called their continuity. To take up this understanding and bring it into the lives of the common people is called the grand undertaking.①

The coordination of the relationship between the changing world and the human experience in pursuit of optimal effect is the main axis of the *Book of Changes*. The purpose of this text is fundamentally normative and prescriptive. It purports to address what is perhaps life's most pressing question: What kind of human participation in the natural processes can optimize the possibilities of this world in which natural and human events are its two inseparable, mutually shaping aspects? This *Book of Changes* describes life itself—a generative procreativity—as the most generic characteristic of our experience:

> The greatest capacity (*dade* 大德) of the cosmos is life itself. The greatest treasure of the sages is said to be the attainment of standing (*wei* 位). The means of maintaining standing is aspiring to become consummate in one's conduct (*ren* 仁). The means of attracting and mobilizing others is the use of the available resources. Regulating these resources effectively, insuring that language is used properly, and preventing the people from doing what is undesirable is called optimal appropriateness (*yi* 義).②

Human spirituality as "inspired living" arises from a penetrating understanding of the workings of change, and then "aspiring" to a quality of appropriate conduct that such an understanding can occasion. We must read the initial natural conditions while they are still inchoate, anticipate the possibilities of these stirrings, and then aspire to make the most of the productive indeterminacy that is the ever-present penumbra of the

---

① "Great Commentary" A12: 是故，形而上者謂之道，形而下者謂之器。化而裁之謂之變，推而行之謂之通，舉而錯之天下之民，謂之事業。
② "Great Commentary" B1: 天地之大德曰生，聖人之大寶曰位。何以守位曰仁，何以聚人曰財。理財正辭，禁民爲非曰義。

phenomenal world. The "intensive" conduct of the exemplary person becomes "extensive" as it serves as a model for and is deferred to by the people:

> Understanding the incipient (*ji* 幾) gives insight into the mysteries of the world (*shen* 神). That exemplary persons (*junzi* 君子) are not obsequious with respect to what is above nor condescending to what is below is because they understand the incipient. The incipient is a hint of movement from which one can see in advance impending fortune. Exemplary persons having seen the incipient are aroused to action without waiting to see what transpires.... Exemplary persons in their understanding of both the inchoate and the obvious, of both the soft and the hard, make such paragons a beacon for the myriad people.[①]

In fact, it is a spirituality emerging from always appropriate and productive conduct that is the highest achievement humanity can aspire to:

> It is because making the most of the mysteries of the world (*shen* 神) in our understanding of the processes of transformation is the fullness of human virtuosity (*de* 德) that no one has yet to figure out how to go beyond this.[②]

This "Great Commentary" in telling the story of its own inspired origins explains how a human responsiveness to context has in the past, and continues now, to enchant the cosmos. The remote ancestors Fu Xi and Shen Nong established a rhythm in the human experience, enabling them to chime in with the cadence of the "flux and continuity" (*biantong* 變通) they perceived to be enduring characteristics of the world around them. Inspired by the efficacy of their insights into the workings of the cosmos, these early progenitors then represented their interpretation of life in the world in a hexagramatic language of images, models, and patterns for the benefit of the generations yet to come. Importantly, these hoary sages, far

---

① "Great Commentary" B4: 知幾其神乎？君子上交不諂，下交不瀆，其知幾乎，幾者動之微，吉之先見者也，君子見幾而作，不俟終日。……君子知微知彰，知柔知剛，萬夫之望。

② "Great Commentary" B5: 過此以往，未之或知也。窮神知化，德之盛也。

from pursuing some disinterested interrogation of nature, were engaged in a project of human articulation, refinement, and enculturation (*wenhua* 文化) that reflexively incorporates within itself the world around them:

> According to the *Book of Changes*, with everything running its course, there is flux (*bian* 變), where there is such flux, there is continuity (*tong* 通), and where there is such continuity, it is enduring.①

In their efforts at *ars contextualis*—at "the art of contextualizing"— Fu Xi and Shen Nong sought to effectively coordinate the experience of the human being with the processes of nature, and in so doing, to optimize the creative possibilities of the cosmos. There is a perceived continuity between the human experience and the natural world within which it takes place: between human-inscribed petroglyphs and the natural striations found in stone, between the changing modalities of human thought and the turning array of terrestrial and celestial patterns, between human expressions of moral imperatives and a fundamentally moral cosmos. The sage kings cultivated a thick continuity between nurture and nature that is expressed through the evocative images that constitute the *Book of Changes*. This continuity is then captured and made explicit in expressions such as "the continuity between and inseparability of the human and cosmic orders" (*tianrenheyi* 天人合一), the "mutual responsiveness of the human and cosmic orders" (*tianrenxiangying* 天人相應), and "the resonance between the human and cosmic orders" (*tianrenganying* 天人感應). Importantly, such expressions are not reporting on two originally separate elements being reconciled after the fact, but rather on the symbiotic mutuality and interpenetration of these aspectual dimensions of the human experience.

In this co-creative relationship with the world around us, there is no initial or originative *logos*. Language and its significance emerge *pari passu* with a world that is continually being spoken into being by what Charles Taylor has called "the language animal," with the important qualification that these early progenitors were able to "read" the natural world and discern a shared and evolving cosmic language in the images they captured

---

① "Great Commentary" B2: 易窮則變，變則通，通則久。

in the hexagrams.① Within this cosmic context, the collaborative process of making meaning was first activated in the imagination of the earliest ancestors, and then applied semiotically to "figure out" and give expression to their experience of the world. In the fullness of time, this discursive process has come to configure and express reality, the cultural *imaginaire*.

Building on this auspicious beginning, the sage kings who were later descendants of Fu Xi and Shen Nong—first the Yellow Emperor, then Yao and Shun—continued to construct human technologies, modes of transportation, social institutions and customs, and the written language as innovations that were inspired by particular hexagrams, with each hexagram providing a dynamic image of some natural process. The *Changes* reports on this continuing symbiotic collaboration:

> The sages had the capacity to see the way the world operates, and perceiving the way things come together and commune, they put into practice their statutes and codes of propriety.②

It has been this gradual and ongoing process of structuring and ritualizing the human experience thus remembered in and inspired by the "Great Commentary" that has enchanted life in the world, and that continues to produce its mystery and spirituality:

> When Shen Nong had passed, the Yellow Emperor, Yao, and Shun continued his innovations. They fathomed the flux and flow of the world around them and saved the people from exhaustion. Through spiritual insight (*shen* 神) they transformed the human experience, and enabled the people to find what was most fitting in their lives.③

The productive symbiosis that can be achieved between the human and the natural world is a practical inspiration for effective human living, lifting the human experience out of its base animality and elevating it to

---

① Charles Taylor, *The Language Animal: The Full Shape of the Human Linguistic Capacity,* Cambridge, MA: Harvard University Press, 2016.
② "Great Commentary" A8: 聖人有以見天下之動，而觀其會通，以行其典禮。
③ "Great Commentary" B2: 神農氏沒，黃帝、堯、舜氏作，通其變，使民不倦，神而化之，使民宜之。

become the magic and magnetism of high culture. Human culture has transformed the markings on the backs of turtles into awe-inspiring calligraphy and pottery designs; feeding at the trough has been elevated into haute cuisine and the elegance of the tea house rituals; raw natural ore has been smelted and cast as sacred bronze ceremonial vessels; extracted plant matter has been transmuted into exquisite paintings and architectural designs; the cacophony of life has been focused and refined into the magic of sublime music; the animal heat of random copulation has been transformed into the warmth of hearth and home; mere associations have become the institutions of family, true fellowship, and the flourishing community.

In addition to enabling human beings to live moral and aesthetic lives, this understanding of the processes of change and productivity revealed by the *Book of Changes* has given humankind access to the very mysteries of the cosmos:

> The Master asked rhetorically, "Does not the person who understands the course of flux and transformation in fact have insight into the mysterious workings of the world?"①

Of significance in the nature and function of religiousness in this tradition is that the enchanted, numinous dimension of the human experience and its many mysteries (*shen* 神) does not belong to some other world. Far from it, such spirituality is the inexhaustible product of efficacious living and refinement within this world, and the boundless penumbra that emanates out from always contexualized human activities to suffuse the cosmos.

Tang Junyi 唐君毅 and the Philosophical Implications of a *Qi* 氣 Cosmology

The philosopher, Tang Junyi, has captured the coherence of this *qi* 氣 worldview in identifying what he takes to be several distinctive and persistent features of Chinese natural cosmology. For Tang, "natural"

---

① "Great Commentary" A10: 子曰：「知變化之道者，其知神之所爲乎。」

cosmology stands in contrast to the "supernatural" or "metaphysical" cosmology of classical Greece. In fact, the generic traits referenced in Tang Junyi's own language express in a different vocabulary many of the characteristics of the *qi* 氣 process cosmology I have attempted to describe above. We can use Tang's terminology to further explore and elaborate upon these distinguishing generalizations as a way of testing my own best efforts to describe Chinese cosmology, hoping in so doing to bring something of his insight and authority to this interpretive summary. Tang Junyi derives several organically related and mutually entailing postulates from the *Book of Changes* that can be used to reveal underlying assumptions about the human experience, and more specifically, about how human becomings are to be conceptualized within this process cosmology.[1] A claim the *Book of Changes* itself makes explicitly is that its way of characterizing the "holographic" cosmos can in turn be used to characterize any particular thing within it as the unbounded totality to be found in every graph:

> As a document, the *Book of Changes* is vast and far-ranging, and has everything complete within it. It contains the way of the heavens, the way of human beings, and the way of the earth.[2]

Such a macro characterization of the cosmos is consistent with how

---

[1] It should be noted that Tang Junyi himself in his preface to *The Spiritual Value of Chinese Culture* 中國文化之精神價值 (1953) repudiated some of the ideas he had developed in his earlier work *Collected Studies on a Comparison of Chinese and Western Philosophical Thinking* 中西哲學思想之比較研究集 (1943) from which these cosmological propositions are drawn. Although Tang is less than clear on his reasons for doing so, my own understanding of Tang's contribution is that there is indeed a greater profundity in this later volume that supersedes his earlier writings. I depend heavily upon this second volume in appealing to Tang's understanding of what it means to become consummately human within Chinese natural cosmology. A speculation we might make regarding the reservations he expressed about his own earlier work might be the seemingly exclusive nature of his comparisons, and his failure to appreciate the possibilities of bringing these traditions together productively. Whatever Tang's motivation, the criticism is certainly not directed at his appeal to the *Book of Changes* as ground for reflecting upon Chinese natural cosmology.

[2] "Great Commentary" B8:《易》之爲書也，廣大悉備，有天道焉，有人道焉，有地道焉。

micro relationally-constituted persons and the possibilities for the human experience have been conceptualized in this Confucian tradition. For example, Angus Graham arrived over time at an understanding of the term "human propensities" (*xing* 性) that is consistent with this open-ended and emergent conception of cosmic order. Rejecting the assumption that *xing* 性 references some predetermined and innate human nature—what he describes as a "transcendent origin" that would anticipate a "transcendent end"—Graham came to a narrative understanding of *xing* 性 as the capacity of always unique relationally-constituted "human becomings" to pursue an optimal symbiosis within their ever-changing world. Such an emergent conception of cosmic order is consistent with the notions of life and death as these events occur and are understood within the context of a continuing family lineage and the intergenerational transmission of culture. Again, there is an understanding of culture that, rather than requiring the teleologically-informed regulating and stewarding of nature's spontaneous growth, is instead a contrapuntal responsiveness to nature's bounty that allows human beings to elaborate upon it, to elevate it, and through this collaboration, to live a decidedly aesthetic if not profoundly spiritual life.

In his reflections on the cosmology underwritten by the *Book of Changes*, Tang Junyi begins from its affirmation of the reality and sufficiency of our empirical experience without any need to go beyond it. Indeed with his first postulate, the proposition that "there is no fixed substance" (*wudingtiguan* 無定體觀), Tang rejects outright the relevance of any notion of ontological substance or substratum. For Tang

> ... the cosmos in the minds of Chinese people has always been nothing more than a continuous stream, a kind of moving flow. All of the things and events of the cosmos are just a continuing process. And beyond this process there is no fixed substratum that supports it.[1]

When understood with respect to the conceptualization of persons then, such a characterization immediately suggests the irrelevance of any

---

[1] Tang Junyi, *Complete Works*, Vol. 11, p. 9: 中國人心目中之宇宙恒只爲一種流行，一種動態；一切宇宙中之事物均只爲一種過程，此過程以外別無固定之體以爲其支持者（substratum）。

foundational and superordinate notion of self, soul, mind, nature, and so on. With this postulate, Tang is acknowledging both the fluidity and the coagulating of *qi* 氣 as it animates the world in its ceaseless flux and flow.① The absence of any essentializing substratum—"what-it-means-to-be-this-kind of a thing"—means that experience, rather than being constituted by "things" that can be parsed as indivisibles into a taxonomy of natural kinds, is a flow of resolutely unique perturbations of and transactions among foci of *qi* 氣—"the myriad events" (*wanwu* 萬物) and "all that is happening" (*wanyou* 萬有). Given the intrinsic and constitutive nature of relations, persons are in fact understood to be narrative streams of unique, mutually conditioning and interpenetrating events. And the web of always shifting relationships that constitutes each person as an "event"—as *this* particular focus within *this* expansive field of experience—is itself a novel and unique construal of the totality. Entailed by the uniqueness of all persons as matrixes of relations is the absence of any notion of strict identity, and the categorical "law of non-contradiction" logic that would follow from it. There is no appeal in this cosmology to some self-same shared characteristic that would make any two "different" persons in fact essentially the same.

Another proposition offered by Tang Junyi that is a corollary to the absence of any appeal to substratum is "the inseparability of the one and the many" (*yiduobufenguan* 一多不分觀).② This *yiduobufen* 一多不分 proposition can be read in many different ways, as it speaks at once to the inseparability of the one and the many, to the continuity between particular identity and context, to the co-presence of uniqueness and multivalence, to the mutuality of continuity and multiplicity, to the inclusiveness of integrity and integration, to the dynamics of a shared harmony emerging out of relational tensions, to the expression of the specific details in the totality of the effect, and so on. In the *Book of Changes* cosmology, the identity of anything and everything, far from having ontological self-sufficiency, can only be understood by reference to context. What Tang means by this claim is that if we begin our reflection on the emergence of cosmic order from the wholeness of lived experience, we can view experience in terms of both its dynamic continuities and its manifold multiplicity, as both a

---

① Tang Junyi, *Complete Works*, Vol. 11, pp. 9-11.
② Tang Junyi, *Complete Works*, Vol. 11, pp. 16-17.

ceaseless processual flow and as distinctive, consummatory events. This postulate is one more example of the mutual implication of binaries that characterizes all phenomena in the natural world—in this case, particularity and the totality, self and other, this and that.

Any particular phenomenon in our field of experience can be focused in different ways: on the one hand, it is a unique and persistent particular; on the other, since it is constituted by the full complement of its relationships, it has the entire cosmos and all that is happening implicated within it. How this is reflected in the understanding of persons is that they are uniquely who they are as distinct from all others, and yet in their magnitude, to give a full account of the social, natural, and cultural relationships that constitute any one of them, we must exhaust the cosmic totality.

We begin from the ambiguity of "one," meaning something quite different in a process worldview than it does when we appeal to substance ontology. Sorting out which of the following connotations of "one" are properly in play in the *qi* 氣 cosmology will enable us to begin to distinguish between a more apposite vocabulary for Chinese cosmology, and language that might be misleading. We might parse these connotations of "one" into two different ranges of meaning that are distinguishable by the way in which things are thought to be related. One familiar range of meaning we might associate with Aristotle entails a kind of extrinsic relatedness that allows things to stand independent of each other, while at the same time having some essential and universal defining characteristic that allow them to be subsumed into some single whole: a species or genera. All individual human beings are alike rational creatures which allow them to be summed as the species, "*homo sapien*." Humanity shares the characteristic of being a warm-blooded species that allows it to be summed into the genera, "mammals." Such an understanding of things makes them discrete and quantifiable. Things are individually exclusive and yet sortable into natural kinds by appeal to essential characteristics. The tree of these species and genera ultimately yields up a universe—a single ordered cosmos of parts and the whole. This discrete and quantifiable understanding of "one" is most relevant to the substance worldview that has had privilege in the philosophical narrative informed by classical Greek thinking. In this ontological model, many are derivative of the one identical form.

The vocabulary of a single-ordered cosmos—the *uni-* of universal, universe, uniformity, unity, univocality—is helpful only by contrast in understanding *qi* 氣 cosmology. In early Greek philosophy, the term "*kosmos*" connotes a clustered range of meanings, including *arche* (originative, material and efficient cause/ultimate undemonstrable principle), *logos* (underlying organizational principle), *theoria* (contemplation), *nomos* (law), *theios* (divinity), and *nous* (intelligibility). In combination, this cluster of terms conjures forth some notion of a single-ordered Divine universe governed by natural and moral laws ultimately intelligible to the human mind.① But these essentializing connotations of "one" that would allow for strict identity and a decontextualizing discreteness—a final atomistic separation between the one and the many, and among the many themselves—would not be appropriate to what is ultimately an unsummed and thus "acosmotic" Confucian cosmology.② That is, the classical Confucian worldview will not accommodate a cosmos in which the "many" are determined by and thus reducible to a transcendent, independent "One." It will not allow for the dissolution of the myriad particulars—the *kosmoi*—into some higher reality.

In this Confucian cosmology, the certainly less familiar range of meaning of "one" begins from intrinsic and constitutive relations within an ecology that would explain the interdependence of things. In this cosmological model, it is the holographic entailment of the context within each always unique particular that requires an entertainment of the full complexity of particular things. To really know any particular person is to know the entire cosmos in a unique way and from a unique point of view.

In their irreducibly communal identity, human beings are each a particular locus and a nexus of more or less meaningful roles and relationships that collaborate to constitute them as meaningful persons. Each person is in fact a "field of selves." When persons step up, the whole web of their relationships—family, friends, mentors, colleagues, compatriots, progenitors—step up with them. Personal "integrity" then is consummatory: the ongoing creative process of "becoming productively one" with other persons within these constitutive relationships. In so doing, one aspires to become *ren* 仁, or a "consummate person" (L. *com-* "together" and *summa* "the highest") by optimizing the possibilities made available by these same

---

① For most of the Presocratics, *kosmos* was divine, and for both Plato and early Aristotle, *kosmos* was the "visible God" (*horatos theos*).

② In *Anticipating China*, David Hall and I coined the expression "acosmotic" in claiming that "the Chinese tradition ... does not depend upon the belief that the totality of things constitutes a single-ordered world" (pp. 11-12).

relations. *Yiduobufen* 一多不分 also restates in a different language the focus-field conception of persons, where each self-conscious person, and each impulse in the life of each person, has implicated within it the boundless "many." This defining feature of Chinese natural cosmology is fundamental to our understanding of the relationally-constituted, focus-field conception of persons; again, as Mencius says, "the myriad things of the world are all implicated here in me."①

This sense of "one" also entails a principle of individuation that is an alternative to the familiar idea of things of a kind sharing some self-same identical characteristic, some formal identity that would define each of them as an individual human "being." Instead, in Confucian philosophy persons with effort aspire to achieve meaningful relationships within their families and communities, and as they emerge in their relations to become an object of increasing deference for others, they become a "distinctive" and indeed "distinguished" member of the family and community. Tang Junyi's postulate asserts not only that any phenomenon in our field of experience has implicated within it the contextualizing, unbounded many, but further that as a unique "one" it can find self-conscious resolution and purpose, and be focused in many different ways according to the multiplicity of roles that come to be defining of its narrative. Importantly, any claim to uniqueness and individuality, far from excluding a person's relations with others, is a function of the quality that this person has been able to achieve within the unique configuration of these same relations.

"One" certainly connotes the quality of being uniquely authentic and genuine. But one and many are inseparable in the sense that "one" in this cosmology also means continuity, and integrity means "becoming one together." This relational, interdependent, and qualitative understanding of "one" is more relevant to the process worldview in which one and many are two ways of looking at the same reality. A process worldview is one of radical contextuality, where the embedded particular and its context are at once continuous and distinct.

In the *Book of Changes*, this sense of the mutuality of oneness and manyness is reflected in the image of the four seasons that are each certainly distinctive and yet at the same time continuous with, and implicated in, each other:

---

① *Mencius* 7A4: 孟子曰：萬物皆備於我矣。

In their magnitude and scale, the processes of nature are a counterpart to the heavens and the earth; in their flux (*bian* 變) and in their continuity (*tong* 通), they are a counterpart to the four seasons.[1]

This notion of the inseparability of continuity and multiplicity is necessary to understand the familiar claim we find throughout the early philosophical canons about the "oneness" of things, or of humans becoming "one" with all things, often stated as a kind of personal, even religious, achievement.

This persistent *yiduobufen* 一多不分 characteristic of Confucian cosmology provides us with yet another way of conceiving this dynamic process of personal identity formation. Tang Junyi would insist that this protean expression is a distinctive, generic feature of the Chinese processual cosmology locating our persons as vital and specific foci that have implicated within each of us an unbounded field of relations. Importantly, "one is many, many one" is another way of describing the doctrine of intrinsic, constitutive relationality that stands in contrast to the second-order external relations of a substance ontology. It is, simply put, the assumption that in the compositing of any "one," there is implicated within it the contextualizing "many."

Bringing the discussion of *yiduobufen* 一多不分 back to how Confucian philosophy conceptualizes self-conscious and purposeful persons, to know someone is to know their story and to be able to locate them in their continuing, always transactional narrative. It is to know their whence, and to know their whither. One need only reflect on the metaphor of "family" and family relatedness pervasive in the Confucian worldview to find a concrete example that would illustrate Tang Junyi's insight into the inseparability of one and many. It is because unique human beings emerge in the world within the context of multivalent family relationships that family is taken as the basic human unit, making any particular person in the family a conceptual abstraction from it.

The meaning of family as one locus of resolution, is emergent and constantly being negotiated out of the continuing needs and contributions of the members that constitute it. And its value is disclosed in the quality of meaningful relations they are able to achieve together. The family and the

---

[1] "Great Commentary" A6: 廣大配天地，變通配四時。

quality of life available to its members is the invariably evolving and provisional consequence of associated living contingent upon the quality of the conduct of those particular persons that come to constitute it. Each of the individual members of the family from his or her own unique perspective expresses the full complement of relations with all of the family members in what they do and who they become. Being neither rigidly linear nor teleologically disciplined toward some given, rationalizing end, this family—and it is always a *this*—is fundamentally and ideally too, an inclusive, always inimitable, aesthetic achievement.

Another way of "imaging" what Tang Junyi calls "the inseparability of one and many" is to appeal the defining icon of the Chinese cosmological tradition, the *long* 龍—conventionally translated as the "dragon."① This image of the *long* 龍 is pervasive as an early, persistent, and dominant theme in Chinese art and cosmology. Now undulating, sprawling, wriggling, coiling, spiraling, thrusting, and ultimately soaring through the clouds, this embodied moving line combines the totemic notions of aggregation and diversity on the one hand, and the continuity of a single stroke (*yihua* 一劃) on the other. This *long* 龍 is unrestricted transformation and articulation across the axes of time and space.

Where does the moving line as the continuous yet always changing cultural horizon begin in the Chinese tradition? Fu Xi and Nü Wa, the ancestors to whom the fundaments of Chinese culture such as farming, fishing, and abstract symbols are sometimes ascribed, are represented in the earliest texts as human figures with the bodies of snakes. In fact, this representation is typical of many of the gods, supernaturals, and cultural heroes remembered in ancient Chinese legends. Over time, this snake-like figure, now swallowing creatures whole, now shedding its skin, accumulated the features of "every animal" to become the generative and transformative symbol of Chinese culture. Probably the most substantial presentation of the *long* 龍 image is the Great Wall, composite of many walls, as it peaks and lunges, dances and glides, meandering across thousands of miles and

---

① A caution is needed here. To translate this iconic *long* 龍 as "dragon" as is conventionally done reflects the difficulties encountered in cultural translation. *Long* 龍 needs to be clearly distinguished from its Anglo-Saxon cousin that quite properly meets its end under the Christian foot of St. George. See John Hay, "The Persistent Dragon (*lung* [*long*])," *The Power of Culture*, ed. W. Peterson, A. Plaks, and Y.S. Yü, Hong Kong: Chinese University Press, 1994.

countless generations to give expression to the cadence of time as it meets space on the Chinese landscape.

Tu Wei-ming sees this *long* 龍 icon as a symbol of the process of cultural accumulation and integration defining of the Chinese cultural, social, and political sensibility:

> As a composite totem, the dragon possesses at least the head of a tiger, the horns of a ram, the body of a snake, the claws of an eagle and the scales of a fish. Its ability to cross totemic boundaries and its lack of verisimilitude to any living creature strongly suggest that from the very beginning the dragon was a deliberate cultural construction. The danger of anachronism notwithstanding, the modern Chinese ethnic self-definition as the "dragon race" indicates a deep-rooted sense that Chineseness may derive from many sources.[1]

When this totemic processual sensibility of the "dragon"—the mutuality and interdependence of foci and fields (events and their environments)—is translated into the world of intellectual engagement and politics, it becomes the valorization of the "one and many" model of inclusive, consensual orthodoxy over exclusive, dialectical disputation in the search for some putative single truth,[2] it becomes the valorization of the "one and many" model of canonically driven commentary over dialectically competing philosophical systems committed to an exclusive certainty, it becomes the valorization of "one and many" model of remonstrating "institutional intellectuals" over an excluded loyal opposition in competition for the one seat of power, it becomes the valorization of the "one and many" model of attaining an inclusive "right thinking" consensus over every individual's exclusive "right-to-think" as the best guarantee for discovering the unconstrained truth.[3]

That the *Book of Changes* has traditionally been given pride of place as

---

[1] Tu Wei-ming, "Chinese Philosophy: A Synopsis," *A Companion to World Philosophies*, ed. Eliot Deutsch and Ron Bontekoe, Oxford: Blackwell, 1997, p. 4.
[2] Nathan Sivin, *Medicine, Philosophy and Religion in Ancient China*, p. 9.
[3] See Randell P. Peerenboom, "Confucian Harmony and Freedom of Thought: The Right to Think Versus Right Thinking," *Confucianism and Human Rights*, ed. Wm. T. de Bary and Tu Wei-ming, New York: Columbia University Press, 1998.

first among the classics is revelatory of the primacy invested in process and change in Chinese cosmology, contrasting rather starkly with the ontological intuitions of classical Greece. Tang Junyi's postulate acknowledging the fact that the processual flow of experience is without initial beginning or final end is captured in his third postulate: "ceaseless procreating" (*shengshengbuyiguan* 生生不已觀) that echoes the observation in the *Book of Changes* that "it is because of its ceaseless procreating we call it 'the changes' (*yi* 易)" (*shengshengzhiweiyi* 生生之謂易). We might get further clarification on the nature of such "change" by remembering the commentary above that associates the character for "change" (*yi* 易) with its cognate *ci* 賜, "exchanging, transacting, gifting." Cosmic meaning is emergent in the vital transactions and exchanges among the unique events that constitute our world of experience. And experience so understood is continuous, is genealogical, and is naturalistic in the sense of making no appeal to any metaphysical or supernatural source.

The phenomenal world in classical China is an endless flow, evidencing its formal character only as "trans-*form*-ation" in which the formal aspect, always attended by temporality, is the cadence of change, and when properly cultivated, the musicality of life itself. In fact, the *Book of Changes* says explicitly that "the mysteries of the world have no squareness and change has no shape" (*shenwufang'eryiwuti* 神無方而易無體).[1] Insight into the mysteries of the world must transcend all rationalizations made about it because the process of change can never be contained or arrested by any formal structure. Putative "things" are in fact a processive and hence always provisional flux of "events."[2]

The contemporary philosopher, Pang Pu 龐樸, in explaining the notion of "procreating" (*sheng* 生) provides us with an illuminating distinction. He contrasts procreating as "derivation" (*paisheng* 派生) in the sense of one thing being the source or origin in giving birth to an independent existent, like a hen producing an egg or an oak tree producing an acorn, with procreating as "transmutation" (*huasheng* 化生) in which one thing continuously transforms into something else, like summer becoming autumn,

---

[1] "Great Commentary" A4.
[2] In fact, at least as early as the Ming dynasty, the Chinese expression for "thing," *dongxi* 東西, is literally "east-west," referencing the location of town markets and underscoring the relational and contextual understanding that attends Chinese phenomenological perceptions.

and autumn becoming winter.① These two senses of "procreating" are profoundly asymmetrical. In the *paisheng* 派生 "derivative of" modality of growth, it is only the rare egg that is incubated to become another hen, and it is only the rare acorn that takes root to become another oak tree. In the predominant *huasheng* 化生 "transmutating into" modality of change, most eggs in fact become omelets and most acorns, squirrels. And even in the rare cases where a hen's egg actually becomes another chicken, the erstwhile discreteness of this "independent existent" is qualified by a genealogical continuity with both its progenitor and its progeny.

Both of these senses of "procreating"—derivation and transmutation—are relevant to Chinese cosmology. Importantly, as we have seen with the hen and her egg, the discreteness and independence entailed by *paisheng* 派生 is qualified by the processual and contextual assumptions of *huasheng* 化生. And the processual continuity of *huasheng* 化生 is punctuated as unique "events" by the consummatory nature of *paisheng* 派生. Hence Pang Pu's distinction is another way of saying "one is many, many one" (*yiduobufen* 一多不分). Neither uniqueness nor continuity will yield to the other; both are implicated in one another. The notion of intrinsic relationality that allows for the uniqueness and distinctiveness of particular things on the one hand, and for the continuity that obtains among them on the other, disqualifies part-whole analysis and requires instead a gestalt shift to focus-field thinking in which "particular" and "totality" are two non-analytic foregrounding and backgrounding perspectives on the same phenomenon.

In pursuing this distinction between "derivation" and "transmutation," Pang Pu is alerting us to a further refinement in our understanding of the relationship between what comes before and what follows in the ongoing cosmological process. Taking the human experience specifically, while we might be inclined to understand the progenitor and progeny genealogy as a series in which there is an independence of the latter from the former, early Chinese cosmology on reflection sees genealogy as clearly a combination of both *paisheng* 派生 as "derivative of" and *huasheng* 化生 as "transmutating into." *This* progenitor in one sense gives way to *this* unique progeny, but at the same time, the progenitor physically and culturally

---

① Pang Pu 龐樸, "Yizhong Youjide Yuzhou Shengcheng Tushi: Jieshao Chujian *Taiyi Shengshui*" 一種有機的宇宙生成圖式：介紹楚簡《太一生水》, *Daojia Wenhua Yanjiu* 道家文化研究 17 (1999), p. 303.

lives on within the same progeny in a continuing family lineage. The child is certainly "independent" of the parents, and yet the parents in so many ways beyond their obvious physicality, live on in their child, and in their children's children too.

In Confucianism, with the emphasis on history, on ancestor reverence, on intergenerational transmission, and on a continuing cultural identity, there is traditionally a powerful sense of genealogical continuity where the progeny is to be understood as the foregrounding of this particular person in a continuing lineage. One's family surname (*xing* 姓) is the first and continuing source of identity, while one's given name (*ming* 名) within the course of one's lifetime is complemented by a proliferation of assumed style names (*zi* 字), sobriquets (*hao* 號), and a web of specific family designations such as "uncle number two" (*ershu* 二叔) and "auntie number three" (*sanshen* 三嬸), with a series of professional titles such as "teacher" (*laoshi* 老師) and "director" (*zhuren* 主任), and then when all is done, with a usually celebratory posthumous title (*shi* 謚). Each one of these different names is a role one lives within a complex "one is many" narrative, and at the same time, is a reflection of one's unique contribution to the meaning of family and community. Philosophically speaking, "meaning" as "sense," or "making sense" of something, requires that we acknowledge the narrative function of language wherein the social and political context is always integral to the meaning of what is being said. The application of such correlative pragmatics that relate persons to the events of their lives and that amplify the meaning of these episodes is not only retrospective, but is importantly prospective and programmatic as well, constantly being deployed to anticipate new situations and to extend our complex, continuous and evolving narratives.

From this excursus on the cosmological postulate of "ceaseless procreating," we can see how this description of cosmic order reflects the resolutely familial source of Confucian values, with both its genealogical assumptions and its commitment to the intergenerational transmission of culture. As corollary to this "ceaseless procreating" and the narrative understanding of persons that follows from it, Tang Junyi's fourth characterization of the *Book of Changes* natural cosmology is "the postulate of non-determinism" (*feidingmingguan* 非定命觀).[1] At some point *ming* 命

---

[1] Tang Junyi, *Complete Works*, Vol. 11, pp. 17-19.

came to designate those specific conditions that define a person's existence in the world: one's lifespan, one's social and economic status, one's physical health—not only one's "lot" in life, but one's life itself. It is in this sense that *ming* 命 refers to the propensity of things, the force of circumstances. In any case, *ming* 命 identifies those factors in a life over which human beings seem to have the least control. Tang wants to qualify such factors by asserting the irrelevance of a strong fatalism for both Confucian cosmology and the human experience as well.

It is certainly true that there is a preoccupation with *ming* 命 in this culture, but *ming* 命 is not "fate" or "destiny" in the sense of some irrevocable predestined future, some prophetic "doom of the gods." Rather, *ming* 命 is an always negotiated and, in greater or lesser degree, contingent future that emerges out of the interface between the forces of circumstance and the self-directing habits and spontaneous impulses of particular things or persons. That all things in the fullness of time are "fated" to expire is certainly true, but when and how and under what circumstances this comes to pass is a matter of always contingent, emerging conditions. This *dao* 道, always focused as one particular *de* 德 or another, is the unfolding of a corridor of experience that reflects the collaboration of interrelated and interactive participants who through their conduct, influence its outcomes. A strict fatalism is not an option in a cosmology in which one and many are inseparable, since each unique particular shapes and is shaped by its contextualizing "many." In a world in which one and its context are mutually forming, no single aspect can have some unconditioned and determinative power over all others. "Cause" and "effect" in this ecological worldview are simply a matter of perspective rather than being determined by temporal priority.

For Tang Junyi in his reading of the *Changes*, the vitality of "ceaseless procreating" precludes the kind of determinism we associate with strong teleology because for him, there can be no real temporality or history or change in a universe that is predetermined and has a fixed end. The human experience then, is the bottomless unfolding of an emergent, contingent narrative according to the rhythm of its own internal creative processes without any fixed or final pattern, or any external guiding hand. Importantly, in this transformative process, a lifetime is understood as inseparable from the quantum of change that attends the underdetermined and emerging narratives of always unique persons. Indeed, genuine change is just another way of saying genuine time. Time in the human experience is nothing other than the capacity of persons to change and to be changed in their associations, and as such, describes their propensity for transformation and renewal within their specific family and communal ecologies. In this open-ended cosmology, neither time nor the fecundity of our relationality will be denied.

Tang Junyi also restates this "non-deterministic" characterization of Chinese natural cosmology in a positive way with his fifth postulate, "the notion that there is a continuity and inseparability that obtains between determinacy and indeterminacy, between motion and equilibrium, and all other such correlative binomials" (*heyouwudongjingguan* 合有無動靜 觀).[①] Rather than being driven by any kind of a necessary, deterministic teleology, the *Book of Changes* cosmology assumes the possibility for full human collaboration in a contingent and negotiated optimizing symbiosis (*he* 和) at a cosmic scale. This is but to say that human flourishing is the consequence of our best attempt to make the most out of the creative possibilities of the human experience. The penumbra of indeterminacy that honeycombs an always provisional cosmic order means that the erstwhile forms and functions that define the events of our lives are mutually entailing. All form is constantly undergoing adjustment to maintain functional equilibrium, and is vulnerable to and ultimately outrun by the process itself. At the same time, all functioning is made intelligible, shaped, refined, and made more efficient by evolving formal structures, and is constantly being reformed to meet changing demands. There is nothing and thus no one that does not give way to the process of trans-*form*-ation.

Given that the world is without beginning or end, the goal for human beings in each and every moment is to achieve that kind of productive coordination that optimizes the creative possibilities of the always unique situation. The achievement of an optimally productive harmony is an aesthetic rather than being driven by some predetermined mechanical process, divine design, or rational blueprint. While the articulation and stabilizing regularity in the narrative of any particular person anticipates the way in which the events will continue to unfold, the indeterminate aspect within this story defeats any notion of formal necessity or absolute predictability. The combination of pattern and uncertainty precludes the possibility of universal claims about the human experience and renders precarious any

---

① Tang Junyi, *Complete Works,* Vol. 11, pp. 11-16.

globalizing generalizations. All we can depend upon is the *relative* stability provided by the confluence of always site-specific and particular expressions of order, with the need for vigilant attention to those variables at every level that might well amplify into larger scale changes. Order so conceived is thus emergent and unique, and its ultimate source is local.

The omnipresent feature that underscores the contingent nature of any emerging order—human or otherwise—is its underdeterminacy. That is, there is an indeterminate aspect (*ji* 幾) that follows from the uniqueness of each participant, making any pattern of order novel and site-specific, irreversible, reflexive, and in degree, unpredictable. Taking persons as an example, all human beings might be similar enough to justify certain generalizations, yet each person is at the same time a unique, *one* of a kind. It is this uniqueness of each person that precludes the possibility of any logarithmic understanding of human conduct, and that keeps the definition of humanity an open-ended and ongoing proposition.

What follows from this interface between continuity and multiplicity is the cyclical and recursive nature of this processual cosmological order. This feature of the cosmology is described by Tang Junyi with a sixth proposition: "the notion that nothing advances but to return" (*wuwangbufuguan* 無往不復觀). This characteristic in the human experience registers the reflexivity of all conduct as it turns back to reshape its source. Since all participants in any particular event are correlational, the unique particular cannot be separated from its context—focus cannot be separated from its field. Again, looking at this feature of cosmic order from a human perspective, any personal construal of order is recursive, a coming back upon itself. Personal conduct begins from a cultivated, critical, and purposeful self-awareness, shapes the world in what it accomplishes, and then returns back to reconfigure the source of the conduct itself. Quite literally, what goes around comes around. To pollute the world is to pollute one's own body; to enchant the world is to enchant one's own life; to serve the best values of one's community is to serve one's own best interests. Great persons produce great worlds. It is this recursion that punctuates process, distinguishing and consummating the particular "events" of a life lived within it.

The flowering of this particular orchid is a unique life, while in its withering it produces the compost necessary to nourish the roots of the new life it has invested in its seeds. Such generative procreativity is the observed cadence and regularity of the world around us as it expresses its inherent capacity for self-transformation. The human experience also has its flowering with the turning of the seasons, where sixty years completes one full cycle, from the refulgent spring of life to the depths of winter, only to produce out of itself yet another cycle. Importantly, the "cyclical" process, while passing through familiar phases, is not replication. Each day is a new day. It is the unfolding of an endless spiral that evidences on the one hand persistent and continuing life patterns, and on the other, novelty, with each moment having its own unique character. The human experience unfolds as always unique persons through the discursive activities that command their specific worlds of meaning into being, advance together to shape their shared narratives.

A corollary that follows from this notion of the consummating of particular life stories is that there is a priority of a dynamic, radial center over any putative boundaries. Order begins here and goes there, only to return. Perhaps these several postulates proffered by Tang Junyi can be summed up in the claim that, in Confucian natural cosmology, everything is at once local and global, and the more intense and resolved the local, the greater its reach and influence at the global level. Hence, we can describe person, family, community, and world, in terms of the dynamics of being at once centripetal, and centrifugal centers that extend outward as radial circles, in degree subjective and objective, and in degree local and global. But these centers radiate outward only to draw back into themselves an energy that intensifies their own foci by having deferred to and appropriated what is most extended. Through these patterns of deference one can experience what is distant (*yuan* 遠) and even what is at the furthermost reaches (*taiji* 太極), but one can never extricate oneself from one's particular perspective to discover some ultimate boundary on experience. The particularity and the temporality of experience precludes the very possibility of such fixed, ultimate boundaries. Experience is always entertained from some particular perspective within the experience itself.

Tang Junyi has a final cosmological proposition derived from the *Book of Changes* that again expresses the idea that we are born into and extend out from a particular and specific context: "our natural propensities are in fact the way of *tian*" (*xingjitiandaoguan* 性即天道觀).[1] This last of Tang's seven cosmological presuppositions seeks to characterize the collaboration

---

[1] Tang Junyi, *Complete Works,* Vol. 11, p.22.

of cultivated human beings and their environments as a source of cosmic meaning. This proposition states specifically that human propensities are nothing but the unfolding of the natural and cultural processes themselves. This claim is really only a more complex way of acknowledging the holographic interpenetration between particular human beings and the cosmos referenced in "the continuity between and inseparability of the human and the cosmic orders" (tianrenheyi 天人合一), a continuity that is always centered, genealogical, historicist, and boundless.

Persons begin their careers inchoately as both one and many. That is, persons at their inception although unique have little to distinguish themselves as individuals. Yet such persons are born into a matrix of relations thick with culture and values made available to them initially through the care of a small circle of family intimates. The natural and cultural context provides the nourishment for persons who will, in the fullness of time, make their own contribution to a world that has sponsored their own growth. Importantly, the relationship between person and environment is symbiotic and collaborative rather than unilateral and derivative. While Confucius can say: "It is the natural and cultural environment (tian 天) that has engendered the virtuosity in me," we can also say that it is Confucius who has made a substantial contribution to the character of Chinese culture.[1]

Using the Confucian vocabulary, we might describe the evolving careers of members of the community from beginning as a mere persons (ren 人) to becoming exemplary in their conduct for their community (junzi 君子) through achieving a consummate relational virtuosity with other people (ren 仁). For only a few, by coordinating and embodying in themselves the values and the meaning that distinguish some historical epoch of human flourishing, they have the ultimate distinction of becoming sages (shengren 聖人), and as such, sources of enduring cosmic meaning. In Confucian philosophy, the expectation is that human beings and the natural, social, and cultural worlds they inhabit must be full collaborators in a flourishing cosmos. At the very heart of Confucian role ethics, distinguishing it fundamentally from more familiar Western ethical "theories," is a concept of relationally-constituted persons who realize their vision of the moral life through a kind of moral artistry.

---

[1] Analects 7.23: 天生德於予。

As we can see from this set of seven propositions, the cosmology that Tang Junyi derives from the *Book of Changes* and appeals to as the ground for the "idea" of Confucianism, is resolutely genealogical, meliorative, particularist, and emergent. Tang's Confucianism is a pragmatic naturalism directed at achieving the highest integrated cultural, moral, and spiritual growth for persons-in-family-and-community as they coordinate the human experience within its cosmic context. In Tang's understanding of harmony as an optimizing symbiosis that starts here and goes there, the Confucian sages are no more than ordinary persons who, through commitment and assiduous discipline in cultivating their relations, are able to carry out the most ordinary of things in extraordinary ways. Those persons who in their own lives achieve *real* significance are our sages. And all of us, given the conditions the human experience in its wholeness provides, have the opportunity to live just such significant lives.

THE CANONICAL TEXTS: SELECTED PASSAGES

I. THE *BOOK OF CHANGES* (*YIJING* 易經): A PROCESS COSMOLOGY

The Confucian canons have certainly been of central importance in the articulation of Chinese intellectual history. But as much as they can be appealed to as textual evidence for claims about early Chinese cosmology, perhaps no single text can compete with the *Yijing* 易經 or *Book of Changes* in terms of the sustained interest it has garnered from succeeding generations of China's lettered classes, and the influence it has had on a continuing Confucian self-understanding. The *Book of Changes* has been and still remains, in every sense of the term, the first among the Confucian classics.

The *Changes* as a text is itself an object lesson in the ecological worldview it attempts to present. That is, when we reflect on the nature of "events" (rather than "things") within this process worldview, the relationship of these particular foci to their fields lends itself to a holographic understanding of world systems. The totality or field is both adumbrated in and construed from the unique perspective of each particular focus. As Willard Peterson suggests, the text of the *Changes* itself is a particular focus within a field and thus "duplicates relationships and processes at work in the realm of heaven-and-earth," providing those who understand it with a window on the workings of the cosmos. For it is the timely application of an embodied understanding of these same relationships and processes that "is the basis for efficacious action in the realm of human society."① As Peterson continues, "the *Change* [*Yijing*] is not separate from but equal to the cosmos, and it is in virtue of that relationship that it 'works.'"② The commentary on the *Changes* announces its own importance in no uncertain terms:

B10:《易》之爲書也，廣大悉備。有天道焉，有人道焉，有地道焉。
As a document, the *Changes* is vast and far-ranging, and has everything complete within it. It contains the way of the heavens, the way of human beings, and the way of the earth.

Indeed, it is this open-ended classic with its centuries of accruing commentaries that has set the terms of art for an evolving cosmology and a cultural commonsense, and has served as a shared interpretive context for the Confucian, Daoist, and Buddhist philosophies, and most recently, for their engagement with the Western philosophical traditions.

The *Changes* is a complex text that includes both a prognostication manual used as a heuristic for thinking through problems, and a subsequent set of seven appended commentaries that make its wisdom explicit. Its declared purpose is to "figure out" the human experience by using a vocabulary of "figures" or images (*xiang* 象) to conjure forth analogies and make productive correlations about the way things work in the transactional relations between the human world and its cosmic context.③ The

---

① Willard J. Peterson, "Making Connections: Commentary on the Attached Verbalizations of the *Book of Change*," *Harvard Journal of Asiatic Studies* 42:1 (1982), p. 85. Peterson in response to the question, "how can a divination text 'connect' with the cosmos?" allows that the term "duplicated" is "my feeble attempt to provide a necessarily inadequate name for the relationship." He goes on to describe in rather clear language what I have called the holographic, focus-field relationship between the cosmos and the *Changes*:
  They are each "one of two things" exactly alike, each a double of the other, each "has in it" the other. (p. 91)
  Adumbrated in the *Changes* is the entire cosmos, and its capacity to reveal the workings of this cosmos are dependent upon the insights and applications of the persons who have taken it up and engaged it.
② Peterson, "Making Connections," p. 91.
③ Since three of these commentaries are divided into two sections each, they are usually in sum referred to as the "Ten Wings." The manual itself, used traditionally as an instrument for pursuing productive correlations, is of a much earlier vintage than the commentaries.

commentaries are themselves composite and sometimes fragmentary, and were certainly produced subsequent to the manual itself, in some cases dating to as late as the early Han dynasty. Whatever their provenance, portions of these commentaries have been hugely important as a summary statement on an early cosmology that has had a persisting influence on Chinese culture and its sense of its world. One of these documents, the "Xici" 繫辭, or "Appended Sayings," often referred to more simply as the "Dazhuan" 大傳 or "Great Commentary," is perhaps the most important source we presently have for thinking through the assumptions of early Chinese cosmology. Given that a silk manuscript version of this text dating from 168 BCE was recovered at the Mawangdui archaeological site in Changsha in 1973, we have at least a *terminus ad quem* for its compilation.

Peterson in analyzing this profound, protean, and frustratingly opaque document—the "Great Commentary"—insists that it "has been for some two thousand years one of the most important statements in the Chinese tradition on knowing how the cosmos works and how humans might relate to that working. Especially from the Sung [Song] through the Ch'ing [Qing] periods, the 'Great Commentary' ('Ta chuan [Dazhuan]'), as it was called, provided the *locus classicus* for vocabulary and concepts in nearly every major abstract discussion of the physical world and man's place in it."①

Edward Shaughnessy in his translation of the "Great Commentary" based on the newly recovered Mawangdui materials echoes Peterson's evaluation of the importance of this text in observing that "the worldview of its *Xici* or *Appended Statements* Commentary—integrating man and nature through the medium of the *Yijing*—is arguably the most sophisticated (it is certainly the most subtle) statement of the correlative thought that has been so fundamental to all of China's philosophical systems."② Shaughnessy is not exaggerating when he says that "indeed, so central has the *Yijing* been to Chinese thought over these two millennia that a history of its exegetical traditions would require almost a history of Chinese thought."③

The *Changes* has functioned over the centuries and now millennia as

---

① Peterson, "Making Connections," p. 67.
② Edward L. Shaughnessy (trans.), *I Ching: The Classic of Changes*, New York: Ballantine, 1997, p. 1.
③ Shaughnessy, *I Ching*, p. 1.

a heuristic guide for ordering the Chinese world, providing a language of imagistic analogies for reflection on the ceaseless processes of transformation. That is, we do best to abjure seeing the *Changes* as either a book of revelation or as a systematic cosmology that, in providing us with a language to describe the sum of all possible situations we might encounter, instructs us as to what we ought to do. Rather the text provides a capacious vocabulary of familiar images that might inspire us to draw meaningful correlations and to thus think through and articulate appropriate responses to the changing conditions of our lives.

David Keightley sees the rhythm of "alternation and transformation" (*bianhua* 變化) in this ceaseless process of "continuity in change" made explicit in this "Great Commentary" fascicle as a later elaboration on a modality of change already recognized in Shang dynasty metaphysics.① In order to bring this alternating modality of change into sharper focus, we might begin from the observation that our conventional translation of the title of the *Yijing* 易經 as the "*Book of Changes*" is ambiguous to the extent that there are many different modalities of "change" referenced in this early process cosmology, and that this term defined as a "ceaseless pro-creating" (*shengsheng* 生生) references them all at once. The earliest philological commentaries parse this specifically *yi* 易 modality of "change" paronomastically (that is, through semantic and phonetic association) with the homophone *yi* 益 "increasing, adding, gaining, profiting," thus stipulating a kind of change that is consistent with the declared and self-conscious claim of the text that within its pages can be found the wisdom necessary to grow and to make the most of the human experience. The contemporary commentator Guo Moruo 郭沫若 argues that the term *yi* 易 in fact should be read as an ancient abbreviated form of the cognate graph *ci* 賜 meaning "gifting," "transacting," "exchanging." Given that the transactional "ex-changing" modality of "change" is itself the ultimate source of both increased meaning and value in a cosmology that gives primacy to vital relationality, Guo's suggestion is compelling.②

If Greek ontology is grounded in an unchanging and self-sufficient

---

① David Keightley, "Shang Divination and Metaphysics," *Philosophy East and West* 38 (1988), p. 377.
② See the entry for 易 in Kwan Tze-wan, "Multi-function Character Database" at http://humanum.arts.cuhk.edu.hk/Lexis/lexi-mf/.

"substance" (*ousia*) or "being *per se*" as its starting point, the cosmology of the *Changes* takes as the most generic characteristic of experience "the generative procreativity of life itself" (*shengsheng* 生生), stating 天地之大德曰生 "The greatest capacity of the cosmos is life itself." If Greek "ontology" is the study of the nature of being in itself (*on*), then its counterpart in the cosmology of the *Changes* would be a kind of "zoology" and "zoogony:" an attempt to best understand the function of "life" (*zoe*) and the evolution of living things (*zoon*) as this process unfolds through the condensing and dispersing of *qi* 氣. Perhaps as a functional equivalent of the Greek "*on*-tology" as "the science of being" we might introduce the neologism "*zoe*-tology" (*shengshenglun* 生生論) as "the art of living."

Dao 道 then, as the counterpart perhaps of the inclusive Greek *kosmos*, does not reference some pre-existing and external originative principle that, according to its own formal perfection and self-sufficiency, would rationalize the human experience. In this sense, *dao* 道 is an inside without an outside. It is the totality of experience as it is informed by the procreative vitality inherent in the unceasing processes of transformation that is continuously filling in the gap between determinacy and indeterminacy to produce its own emergent order. *Dao* 道 is not the actualization of an inherent, teleological design determined by some external agency. Rather, it is the boundless unfolding of an always provisional and evolving pattern wherein all of the various interpenetrating events have their own unique and creative role in making the indeterminate aspect of the process determinate. *Dao* 道 as it is described in the *Changes* explicitly denotes an efficacious continuity in the correlative relations that constitute all things and events as they collaborate in the animated cosmic process of transforming what already is, into what it will become. In the *Changes*, the phenomenon of cosmic life is described in the aspectual and processual language of symbiotic bipolar dyads such as "flux and continuity" (*biantong* 變通), "alternating succession" (*yinyang* 陰陽), and "penetration and receptivity" (*qiankun* 乾坤). Life is always happening within a context, a shaping and being shaped, a doing and an undergoing. Within the unbounded totality of the heavens and the earth (*tiandi* 天地), these transactional tensions in their complementarity, describe the processes of transformation that continue without respite—the ceaseless and always creative rhythm of *yin* 陰 and *yang* 陽 alternations.

Below I have selected and translated a substantial portion of this "Great Commentary" as both a historical and conceptual framework that can be

I. THE *BOOK OF CHANGES* (*YIJING* 易經): A PROCESS COSMOLOGY

used by readers to help locate the early Confucian discourse within its own interpretive context and its hard-won commonsense.

A1 天尊地卑，乾坤定矣。卑高以陳，貴賤位矣。動靜有常，剛柔斷矣。方以類聚，物以群分，吉凶生矣。在天成象，在地成形，變化見矣。是故剛柔相摩，八卦相盪，鼓之以雷霆，潤之以風雨。日月運行，一寒一暑。乾道成男，坤道成女，乾知大始，坤作成物。

The heavens being revered and the earth being humble, *qian* 乾 and *kun* 坤 are thus defined. The lofty and low having been set out, the noble and the mean each have their place. Action and equilibrium have their rhythms determined in the encounter with firmness and what is yielding. Entities gather together according to their tendencies, things divide themselves up into their groupings, and thus the distinction between the auspicious and the inauspicious arises.

In the heavens, images are formed, and on the earth things take shape, thus giving expression to the changes and transformations. It is thus that the firm and the yielding rub against each other and the eight trigrams move against and activate each other. These processes are urged on by thunder and lightning and nourished by wind and rain. The sun and the moon follow their cycles, alternating hot and cold. The path *qian* 乾 takes gives shape to the male, and the path *kun* 坤 takes gives shape to the female. *Qian* 乾 occasions the great birthing of things and *kun* 坤 brings about their consummation.

Comment: What images and distinctions can we conjure forth to describe the human experience, both in its phenomenal and its moral aspects? These images are always dyadic because they are describing the vital *yin-yang* 陰陽 transactional tensions characteristic of all living organisms as they are constantly interacting with, shaping and being shaped by, their environing others. And built into descriptions such as high and low are the prescriptive values of noble and base. In offering a sequencing of these distinctions, the text both describes and valorizes these images as they are revealed to us in experience.

The term *Kosmos* in classical Greek is not simply a single, rational order, but is also being valorized aesthetically as "elegant" as is evidenced in its cognate term, "cosmetic." In a similar way here in the *Changes*, we are certainly given a cosmology where aspects of it are rationalized and described by these distinctions, but we are also introduced to how such operations carry with them important aesthetic and moral implications.

The text begins with the most generic, abstract, and remote categories we use to parse our experience, making what we do both intelligible and expressive of our values. It then introduces familiar environmental images such as thunder and lightning, wind and rain, sun and moon that serve as concrete, everyday manifestations of such abstract categories. Again, the text brings these images into the specifically human world with male and female, birthing and making.

This sequencing from abstract to particular, from cosmos to the human world seems to reflect the logical order of understanding the particular by reference to the universal, but in fact when read that way, it reverses the process through which our cosmologies are actually formulated. The satirist Xenophanes, impatient with the Olympian pantheon of anthropomorphic gods, famously observes that Ethiopians see their gods as snub-nosed and black, and that Thracians insist their gods are blue-eyed and red-haired. Xenophanes then extends this same thought to how oxen, horses, and lions would likely conceive of their deities, with the idea that we make gods in our own image rather than the other way around.[1] The point is that a worldview and its commonsense is negotiated over time by first identifying the particular values and metaphors that inform the everyday experience of a particular population, and then extending them to the operations of the world broadly that gives such experience its context. The ordinary experience of love and strife, of pleasure and pain, of law and chaos, of life and death, are elevated as cosmic principles. Cosmological speculation takes us from here to there.

乾以易知，坤以簡能。易則易知，簡則易從。易知則有親，易從則有功。有親則可久，有功則可大。可久則賢人之德，可大則賢人之業。易簡而天下之理得矣。天下之理得，而成位乎其中矣。

It is through ease that *qian* 乾 makes things known; it is through simplicity that *kun* 坤 makes things doable. Given such ease, things are easy to understand, and given such simplicity, it is a simple matter to follow them. Being easily understood, they attract a kindred kind, and being simple to follow, there are accomplishments. Having such kin, they are long enduring; having accomplishments, they grow increasingly in stature. To be thus enduring is the virtuosity of worthy persons, and to grow increasingly in stature is their

---

[1] Xenophanes Fragments B15 and B16.

occupation. It is through ease and simplicity that the patterns of the world are made their own, having grasped the patterns of the world, they assume their proper status in between the heavens and the earth.

Comment: The *Book of Changes* brings simplicity and facility to the human experience. The project of the *Changes* with its vocabulary of images, distinctions, and familiar illustrations is not only to make the human experience understandable, but also to make it productive. This "inseparability of knowing and doing, of understanding and accomplishing" expressed herein, is captured in the expression *zhixingheyi* 知行合一 that from earliest times is a persistent philosophical assumption in the tradition. Indeed, it is the symbiotic relationship between understanding and productivity that is the substance of living wisely. The worthy persons who understand the ease and simplicity imparted by the *Changes* attract those of a kindred spirit, and thus become both enduring and a source of growth. The worthy achieve their status as moral exemplars by understanding the workings of the cosmos and coordinating human institutions and conduct with their natural context. It is the growth occasioned by living wisely that learning and morality find their congruence. The *Changes* is not only instrumental in the ease and comfort it brings to the human world, but when properly engaged, it is a source of cosmic flourishing. Humanity has the capacity to become one of the "three forces" (*sancai* 三才)—the heavens, the earth, and mankind—but it is an achievement rather than a given. Indeed, the earliest oracle bones version of *cai* 才 is a depiction of plant life breaking through the ground ✝, emphasizing the centrality of the life-force and its vitality in this "zoetological" cosmology.①

A2 聖人設卦觀象，繫辭焉而明吉凶。剛柔相推而生變化。是故吉凶者，失得之象也；悔吝者，憂虞之象也；變化者，進退之象也；剛柔者，晝夜之象也。六爻之動，三極之道也。

The sages set out the hexagrams and observed the images. Attaching their commentaries to them, they made clear what is auspicious and inauspicious. The firm and the yielding lines displacing each other produces the changes and transformations. It is thus that auspiciousness and inauspiciousness are the image of gaining and losing, regret and care are the image of anxiety and

---

① Kwan, "Database," 甲骨文合集 CHANT 3332A.

concern, change and transformation are the image of advancing and withdrawing, and firm and yielding are the image of day and night. The movement of the six lines is the progression (*dao* 道) of the three ultimates: the heavens, the earth, and humankind.

Comment: The sages have created a dynamic, imagistic discourse drawn from their understanding of the generative procreativity of the cosmos to communicate their insights into how we might guide the human experience deliberately, enabling it to unfold within the context of the heavens and the earth in the most auspicious way. Contemporary philosophers such as Mark Johnson and John Dewey before him are making an argument similar to the one we find here in the *Changes*. The imagistic discourse of the sages is not only descriptive of the physical operations of the cosmos, but through promoting benign growth it also provides a resource for the human being to create the higher order concepts that make the human experience increasingly moral and intelligent.

The subtitle of Johnson's *The Body in the Mind* is *The Bodily Basis of Meaning, Imagination, and Reason*.[1] In this work, Johnson has done much to argue for the bodily basis of human meaning-formation, and also for the ultimately aesthetic ground of human flourishing. Johnson maps the way in which the barest of physical image-schemata are extended through the metaphorical projections and elaborations of our imagination to generate complex cognitive and affective patterns of meaning:

> Our world radiates out from our bodies as perceptual centers from which we see, hear, touch, taste, and smell our world.[2]

For Johnson, the formal, logical structures of human understanding are a direct extension of the activities of our lived bodies as such intelligence is fashioned through the exercise of our seemingly boundless imagination. Such is the human capacity to produce complex culture. Johnson identifies his basic image-schemata as "containment," "force," "balance," "cycles,"

---

[1] In many ways Johnson is following the project we find in John Dewey's earlier work, *Experience and Nature*.

[2] Mark Johnson, *The Body in the Mind: The Bodily Basis of Meaning, Imagination, and Reason*, Chicago: University of Chicago Press, 1987, p. 124.

"scales," "links," and "center-periphery." In his own words, Johnson has urged the view

> ... that understanding is never merely a matter of holding beliefs, either consciously or unconsciously. More basically, one's understanding is one's way of being in, or having, a world. This is very much a matter of one's embodiment, that is, of perceptual mechanisms, patterns of discrimination, motor programs, and various bodily skills. And it is equally a matter of our embeddedness within culture, language, institutions, and historical traditions.[①]

In appreciating this emergent process of human understanding, we have to be wary of simple epiphenominal language that would separate root from tree as cause and effect. Rather root and tree are a holistic, symbiotic process where they grow together or not at all. Similarly, lived bodies and embodied living are two aspectual ways of looking at the same process of growth.

The image-schemata we find here in the *Changes* is captured in the correlative images as the early sages have described them, and are reflective of the primacy given to vital relationality in the classical Chinese process cosmology. That is, these always situated images are understood in fundamentally and irreducibly relational terms with agency being a second-order consideration. Such images describe the transactional relationships that locate the activities of organisms within their human and natural ecologies. To give just one example of how higher order thinking might be the extension of bodily actions, it is not difficult to conceive of how recurrent, habituated physical patterns such as giving and getting, rising and falling, agitation and equilibrium could be transformed and metaphorically extended to produce higher order economic and political concepts defining of a mature culture such as "relational equity" and "social justice." Again, such higher order but still zoetological concepts in turn are internalized to become integral to our body consciousness.

是故君子所居而安者，《易》之序也；所樂而玩者，爻之辭也。是故君子居則觀其象而玩其辭，動則觀其變而玩其占，是以自天祐之，吉无不利。

---

① Johnson, *The Body in the Mind*, p. 137.

Thus, what allows exemplary persons to find amity anywhere they dwell is following the succession of the lines in the hexagrams of the *Changes*, and what gives them pleasure is musing over the commentaries on the hexagram lines. It is for this reason that when exemplary persons (*junzi* 君子) are abiding in any situation, they observe the images and ruminate on the commentaries, and when they take action, they observe the changes and ruminate on the prognostications. It is in this way that, being assisted by *tian*, their actions are auspicious and yield only what is advantageous.

Comment: We might take the ubiquitous Confucian metaphor "way" or "way-making" (*dao* 道) and use it to trace out how meaning evolves from the simplest image to higher order concepts. In all of the early Confucian writings, the theme perhaps most persistent and pervasive in shaping the philosophical tradition broadly is the project of making our proper "way" in the world through a regimen of personal cultivation in our roles and relations. The earliest form of this character *dao* 道 is comprised of the coiffured human head (*shou* 首) with a full head of hair, and the signific that indicates walking (*chuo* 辶), providing a physical portrait of human beings resolutely forging a path forward. We can see with the linked polysemy of this term *dao* how meaning is extended from our physical to our more complex cognitive experience—that is, from the physicality of "way-making" to "showing the way" to the "pathway" we have made. The meaning of this character *dao* 道 is then further extended to the cognitively and affectively informed actions of "speaking" and "explaining" that eventuate in proposing the deliberate "method" we have devised for doing things. Indeed, this one term takes us from the physical process of treading and thus laying a pathway, to the intellectual challenge of extending the cultural vector within the continuing human experience, our *daotong* 道統. Our potential as human "becomings" is not a predetermined given, but rather emerges as a function of our collaboration with the various circumstances of our lives that have their beginnings in our embeddedness within our embodied experience.

A4《易》與天地準，故能彌綸天地之道。仰以觀於天文，俯以察於地理，是故知幽明之故。原始反終，故知死生之説。精氣爲物，遊魂爲變，是故知鬼神之情狀。

It is because the *Changes* is modeled on the heavens and earth that it is able to cover the full complement of their operations (*dao* 道). Looking upward, the sages observed the constellations in the heavens, and looking downward, they discerned the topography of the earth. It is thus that they came to understand the source of both what is apparent and what is obscure. In tracing things back to their origins and then following them to their end, they came to understand what can be said about life and death. The condensing of *qi* 氣 produces things, and the wanderings of their life-force animate change. It is thus that the sages came to understand the actual circumstances of the gods and spirits.

Comment: There is a cluster of key philosophical terms around which this "Great Commentary" is constructed that reveal the world as it is immediately experienced, providing us with a proliferation of correlated dyadic terms: the high and the low, the moving and the still, the hard and the soft, the full and the empty, the large and the small, the bright and the dark, the hot and the cold, and so on. Rather than appealing to an Unmoved Mover or some other external source of change, it is the correlative, bipolar, and dynamic tensions inherent in a life-world so defined, that produce the energy of transformation. As this text reports: "The greatest capacity (*dade* 大德) of the cosmos is life itself."[①] And it is these same tensions between the determinate and the indeterminate that are the source from which the novelty that always attends these processes is produced. Important here is a description of how things and events, from the most ordinary and every day to the non-corporeal world of gods and spirits, are formed and eventually dissipate, taking shape through perturbations in the hylozoistic *qi*, and animated by motive life-forces. Importantly, the correlative relationship in dyadic pairs such as "life and death" (*sisheng* 死生) and "gods and spirits" (*guishen* 鬼神) reflects the porousness of such classifications and the absence of the categorical thinking that would set any final and exclusive limits on them.

與天地相似，故不違。知周乎萬物，而道濟天下，故不過。旁行而不流，樂天知命，故不憂。安土敦乎仁，故能愛。範圍天地之化而不過，曲成萬物而不遺，通乎晝夜之道而知，故神无方而易无體。

Because the sages are comparable to the heavens and the earth, they do not run contrary to them. Because they have a comprehensive understanding of

---

① B1: 天地之大德曰生.

all that is, and a way that gives the world what it needs, they do not overstep the boundaries. Because they act circumspectly without getting carried away, find pleasure in *tian* 天, and are aware of the propensity of circumstances (*ming* 命), they are free of all anxieties. Because they are at ease in their place and genuine in their consummatory conduct, they are able to be loving. It is because they embrace the transformations of the heavens and earth without going beyond them, because everywhere they bring all there is to fruition without leaving anything behind, and because their understanding comes from penetrating the course of day and night, that in their mysterious progresses they remain undefined, and in their changes they have no set structure.

Comment: Throughout the *Changes*, the language cluster used to express the various modalities of human virtuosity—"consummatory conduct in roles and relations" (*ren* 仁), "love" (*ai* 愛), "awareness, wisdom, understanding" (*zhi* 知), and so on—is naturalized to be integral to the workings of the cosmos. Love for example, is not only a feeling shared by people, but is also facilitated by stable, external conditions. Such a common vocabulary suggests the isomorphism we find between the human and the natural worlds. There are the "five modes of virtuosic conduct" (*wuxing* 五行) in the human world—"consummatory conduct in roles and relations" (*ren* 仁), "aspiring to an optimal appropriateness" (*yi* 義), "propriety in roles and relations" (*li* 禮), "living wisely" (*zhi* 知), and "sagacity" (*sheng* 聖). The "five cosmic phases" are described by the same term, *wuxing* 五行—that is, "water" (*shui* 水), "fire" (*huo* 火), "metal" (*jin* 金), "wood" (*mu* 木), and "earth" (*tu* 土). The *Changes* is a normative text that reports on a shared moral cosmos. There is a mysterious aspect of cosmic unfolding that is not determinate or intelligible. As the sages come to embody these transformations in what they do, their insight into such workings and their influence on behalf of all things that make up the cosmos is unbounded and beyond rationalization.

A5 一陰一陽之謂道，繼之者善也，成之者性也。仁者見之謂之仁，知者見之謂之知，百姓日用而不知，故君子之道鮮矣。顯諸仁，藏諸用，鼓萬物而不與聖人同憂，盛德大業至矣哉！

It is the alternating of *yin* 陰 and *yang* 陽 that is the meaning of the proper way (*dao* 道). What continues the proper way is its efficacy, and what brings it to fruition are the natural propensities of things. Those who are consummate in their conduct (*ren* 仁) see the proper way and call it "consummatory conduct," and those who are living wisely (*zhi* 知) see it and call it "wisdom." The common people routinely make use of it, yet are unaware. It is thus that the proper way of exemplary persons (*junzi* 君子) is rarely noticed. It is made manifest in consummate conduct (*ren* 仁), and lies stored up in its possible applications. The proper way urges on all things yet does not share the same anxieties as the sages. How sublime is the grand working of its copious virtuosity (*de* 德).

Comment: *Dao* 道, the "proper way," or "way-making" as described herein is animated by the transactional nature of life itself, and is a collaboration between the human and natural worlds. Holographically, we find ourselves adumbrated in this way-making, as a more or less focal particular within our field of experience. Consummatory persons are self-consciously able to find themselves in this proper way, and the wise as well. While the common people derive great benefit from the way, they do so without knowing why. It is thus that the proper way, far from being merely an object of knowledge, is a function of the achieved quality realized in the relations of those things that participate in the process itself.

To know *dao* 道 says as much about the knower as the known. The reason that the way-making of exemplary persons is rarely noticed is not only because such persons are rare, but because most people do not have the wherewithal to recognize them. And while the sages in their wisdom are properly concerned about the welfare of their people, the proper way as the unfolding of the cosmic order in all of its profusion and abundance moves forward unconstrained and without respite.

There is an important grammatical distinction in this passage that we find throughout the text. Sometimes the text uses the denotative "is what is meant by" (*zhiwei* 之謂) and sometimes the conative "is termed" (*weizhi* 謂之). The former expression defines its antecedent explicitly, while the latter connotes or references one "aspect" of some greater whole.

富有之謂大業，日新之謂盛德。生生之謂易，成象之謂乾，效法之謂坤，極數知來之謂占，通變之謂事，陰陽不測之謂神。

It is because of the proper way's sheer abundance we call it "the grand workings;" it is because of its daily renewal we call it "copious virtuosity;" it is because of its ceaseless procreating we call it "the changes" (*yi* 易). The forming of images we call *qian* 乾; the bringing about of their specific contours we call *kun* 坤. Providing foreknowledge of what has yet to come through exhaustive calculations we call prognostication. The continuity in flux we call events. And what cannot be fathomed by appeal to *yin* 陰 and *yang* 陽 is what we call the truly mysterious (*shen* 神).

Comment: Each phrase in this passage provides one specific way of looking at the same thing, one denotative aspect of *dao* 道 as "way-making," or "the proper way," or less metaphorically, as the unfolding of the cosmic order. The last line of this passage takes us back to the first one, reminding us of the open-endedness and boundlessness of the processes of change captured in the language of *yinyang* 陰陽 correlations. Whatever "things" in this cosmos might be, they must ultimately be understood as uniquely centered foci of eventful relations within a boundless field that gives them their always changing definition and identity. It recalls the concluding phrase in A4 that states in similar terms: "in their mystery they remain undefined, and in their changes there is no set structure" 神无方而易无體.

A6 夫《易》，廣矣大矣，以言乎遠則不禦，以言乎邇則靜而正，以言乎天地之間則備矣。夫乾，其靜也專，其動也直，是以大生焉。夫坤，其靜也翕，其動也闢，是以廣生焉。廣大配天地，變通配四時，陰陽之義配日月，易簡之善配至德。

The *Changes*, so capacious in its compass and so great in its parts! In speaking to what is distant, it is unconstrained; in speaking to what is close at hand, it is unwavering in its accuracy; in speaking to what goes on in the world, it is comprehensive. For *qian* 乾, at rest it is concentrated, and aroused it moves straight ahead. This is how its greatness comes to life. As for *kun* 坤, at rest its gates are closed, and aroused they open wide. This is how its capaciousness comes to life.

In its capacious compass and in its greatness, the *Changes* is a complement to the heavens and the earth; in its flux and persistence it is a complement to the four seasons; in the appropriateness of *yin* 陰 and *yang* 陽 it is a complement to the sun and moon; in the efficacy of change and simplicity it is a complement to the highest potency (*de* 德).

Comment: In this seminal text, the tensions within both cosmic and human transformation as they are manifested within the vital context of "the heavens and the earth" (*tiandi* 天地) are described in the processual language of symbiotic bipolar opposites such as "flux and continuity" (*biantong* 變通), "alternating succession" (*yinyang* 陰陽) and "penetration and receptivity" (*qiankun* 乾坤), with each term connoting one aspect of the same event. These modalities of change complement each other, and together describe the ongoing processes of transformation within an unbounded cosmic ecology.[①] It is within this contextual flux and flow that the always transactional human life unfolds, with the challenge for humankind being to correlate the events of their experience with the environing cosmos to optimum effect.

A7 子曰:"《易》,其至矣乎! 夫《易》,聖人所以崇德而廣業也。知崇禮卑,崇效天,卑法地。天地設位,而《易》行乎其中矣。成性存存,道義之門。"
　　The Master said: "How superb is the *Changes*! It was by appeal to the *Changes* that the sages were able to venerate virtuosity and broaden the compass of their endeavors. In their wisdom, they aspired to be lofty; in their performance of ritual propriety they were properly humble. In aspiring to the lofty, they emulate the heavens; in their humility, they emulate the earth. With the heavens and the earth assuming their proper stations, the *Changes* operates within their midst. It is the process in which the natural propensities of things come to fruition and are sustained, and is the gateway to the meaningfulness of the proper way (*dao* 道)."

Comment: This is a succinct account of the correlative, analogical, first problematic thinking that early on became a dominant modality of thought within the Confucian philosophical tradition. It is a holistic way of thinking that stands in immediate contrast with Greek rationalism—systematic, conceptual, theoretical thinking—that became mainstream early in the Western philosophical narrative. We might find resonances between this Confucian analogical thinking and the counterculture within the Western narrative: the trope of Anglo-Saxon kenning, for example, or Giambattista Vico's anti-Cartesian philosophy of history and imagination, or more recently, with the abductive reasoning of C.S. Peirce.
　　There is a threefold correlation here between 1) the structure and operations of the cosmos itself, 2) the capacity of the *Changes* as a heuristic manual that reveals the vital patterns of nature to the sages, and 3) the aspiration of the sages to "figure out" and emulate these same processes in their own conduct and in developing those human institutions that can

---

[①] Keightley, "Shang Divination and Metaphysics," pp. 374-375.

serve as the complement to nature. Important here is the assumption that the very configuration of the cosmos is consistent with the highest human values, and the coordination of human conduct within these patterns is the way to optimize the human experience. The last phrase in this passage echoes *Focusing the Familiar* 25 in which it celebrates radical, ecological contextualism: that is, how the full realization of the natural propensities of things and their possibilities emerges from coordinating the growth of all things with their environments to optimal effect: 性之德也，合内外之道也，故時措之宜也 "Such is the virtuosity achieved in one's natural propensities and the way-making that integrates what is more internal and what is more external. Thus, when and wherever one applies this virtuosity, it is fitting." The possibilities of the "natural propensities" (*xing* 性) of all things, and of human beings in particular, far from being the actualization of some essential, inherent nature, in fact emerge *pari passu* as they grow and optimize their relations with their environing others to expand the meaning of the cosmos. When in this Confucian cosmology we ask the question "Where does meaning come from?" there is always a correlation between what is most fitting (*yi* 宜) in the vital roles and relations that constitute things and events, and the production of meaning (*yi* 義). Indeed, the coincidence of "optimal appropriateness" and the "production of meaning" is captured in the polysemy of the character *yi* 義. Said another way, what makes a cosmology grounded in procreation and life (*sheng-sheng* 生生) irreducibly moral, is that morality itself is nothing other than that quality of activity that conduces to productive growth in relations.

A8 聖人有以見天下之賾，而擬諸其形容，象其物宜，是故謂之象。聖人有以見天下之動，而觀其會通，以行其典禮，繫辭焉以斷其吉凶，是故謂之爻，言天下之至賾而不可惡也，言天下之至動而不可亂也。

The sages, having the capacity to survey the complexities of the world, found correlations among the vital shapes and the appearances of things, and thus conjured up suitable images for them. It is for this reason they are called "images" (*xiang* 象). The sages, having the capacity to survey the activities of the world, and perceiving how things come together and commune, put into practice their statutes and their codes of propriety. They appended their commentary to these codes in order to distinguish what is auspicious from the inauspicious. It is for this reason they are called "lines." Though these commentaries speak to the most profound complexities of the world, they do not provoke aversion; though they speak to the most complicated activities

I. THE *BOOK OF CHANGES* (*YIJING* 易經): A PROCESS COSMOLOGY

of the world, they do not give rise to any confusion.

Comment: In their efforts at *ars contextualis*—at "the art of contextualizing"—the early sages, Fu Xi and Shen Nong, sought to coordinate the experience of humankind within the processes of nature, and in so doing, to optimize the creative possibilities of the cosmos. We are provided with an account of how the sages in consulting the *Changes*, added their several kinds of supplementary commentary to the text to provide future readers with a clear explanation of how to make the best use of this canonical text. The sage kings cultivated a thick continuity between nurture and nature that is expressed in the evocative images that constitute the *Changes*. This vital cosmic continuity comes to be made explicit in the mantra, "the continuity between and inseparability of the human and the cosmic orders" (*tianrenheyi* 天人合一), where such an expression is not reporting on two originally separate elements of the world that are being reconciled after the fact, but rather on the symbiotic mutuality and interpenetration of these aspectual dimensions of the human experience. Rather than aspiring to the conjoining of two separate domains, the emphasis is on the depth and quality (*du* 度) achieved in the first-order, constitutive relationship between two inseparable aspects of what is a shared experience. Human beings are integral to the natural world, and the human experience cannot occur save within its natural context.

擬之而後言，議之而後動，擬議以成其變化。"鳴鶴在陰，其子和之。我有好爵，吾與爾靡之。"
They spoke about such things only after having found their correlations, and acted upon them only after having deliberated at length. Through making correlations and by thorough deliberation, they could respond effectively to the flux and transformations. "A crane cries from the shadows, and her young cries back in response. I have a goblet of fine wine that I would share with you."

Comment: The sages thought through the many resonances between the human experience and the cosmic operations that give it context, enabling them to respond effectively to the always changing world around them. The poem cited here describes the most intimate kind of relationship between a crane and her young, and how such natural conditions resonate with the most cherished shared experiences among friends. Throughout this text, there is this perceived symbiosis between the natural and the human worlds.

子曰：" 君子居其室，出其言善，則千里之外應之，况其邇者乎？居其室，出其言不善，則千里之外違之，况其邇者乎？言出乎身，加乎民；行發乎邇，見乎遠。言行，君子之樞機。樞機之發，榮辱之主也；言行，君子之所以動天地也。可不慎乎！"

The Master said, "Though exemplary persons might be at home in their quarters, if they say something felicitous, even those a thousand miles away will respond to them—how much more so those close at hand. If in dwelling at home what they have to say is infelicitous, those a thousand miles away will oppose them—how much more so those close at hand. Words are uttered by one's person and affect the common people; actions arise near at hand and have their impact at great distances. Words and actions are the pivot and trigger of exemplary persons, where their release governs both honor and disgrace. Since words and actions are how exemplary persons move the heavens and the earth, how can they be anything but circumspect in their deployment?"

Comment: Confucius gives an account of how the power of discourse—of felicitous language and targeted actions—elicits responses even from the most distant quarters, and in so doing, precipitates profound changes in the lives of the people. Given the enormous sway exemplary persons and their spoken words have in transforming the cosmos, and the consequences these exemplars have for the fortunes of everyone, it behooves them to be most judicious in the way in which they choose to use this influence.

A10 子曰："知變化之道者，其知神之所爲乎。"

The Master asked rhetorically, "Does not the person who understands the course of flux and transformation in fact have insight into the mysterious workings of the world?"

Comment: An understanding of the processes of change and productivity revealed by the *Changes*, in addition to enabling human beings to live moral and aesthetic lives, has given them access to the very mysteries of the cosmos. This passage has to be read together with A5 陰陽不測之謂神 "what cannot be fathomed by appeal to *yin* 陰 and *yang* 陽 is what we call the truly mysterious (*shen* 神)," and B4 知幾其神乎 "understanding the incipient (*ji* 幾) gives insight into the mysteries of the world (*shen* 神)." At the end of the day, this eventful and fluid cosmology cannot be fully rationalized and contained. And insight into its workings and the opportunities to make a difference begin from a sensitivity to what is as yet embryonic and indeterminate. In the opening chapter of *Focusing the Familiar*, it states:

> 是故君子戒慎乎其所不睹，恐懼乎其所不聞。莫見乎隱，莫顯乎微。故君子慎其獨也。
> It is for this reason that exemplary persons are so concerned about what is not seen, and so anxious about what is not heard. There is nothing more present than what is imminent, and nothing more manifest than what is inchoate. Thus, exemplary persons are ever concerned to consolidate their virtuosic habits as an inner disposition for action.

We human beings are integral to the creative cosmic process, and as we cultivate ourselves as meaning-makers, we have a recursive relationship within the context of a generative cosmic order, shaping and being shaped at the same time. And we cannot extricate ourselves from this responsibility. Importantly, it is the imminent, inchoate, and thus underdetermined penumbra of the emerging cosmic order that provides cultivated persons with the opening and the opportunity to function as co-creators and to collaborate fully with the heavens and the earth in achieving a flourishing world. Moreover, through the internalization and consolidation of this virtuosic conduct in their own persons, they come to have the entire flourishing cosmos implicated in their project of becoming fully who they are. We must be able to read the initial natural conditions while they are still incipient, anticipate the possibilities of these stirrings, and then aspire to get the most out of our collaboration with the productive indeterminacy that honeycombs the phenomenal world.

A10 夫《易》，聖人之所以極深而研幾也。唯深也，故能通天下之志；唯幾也，故能成天下之務；唯神也，故不疾而速，不行而至。

The *Changes* is the sage's means of probing what is profound to its very limits, and of examining thoroughly what is still incipient (*ji* 幾). It is only through having reached such depths the sages can discern the purposes of the world; it is only through the incipient they can consummate the business of the world; it is only through insight into the mysteries of the world they can be quick without haste and can arrive without even going.

Comment: Such high expectations of the possibilities of the human experience have produced what I have referred to as an "a-theistic" religiousness—a religiousness that makes no appeal to an independent, transcendent Deity as the source of spirituality and order. It is this human and family-centered religiousness that elevates the cultivated human experience into what *Focusing the Familiar* describes as human beings becoming a complement to *tian* 天 and co-creators with the heavens and the earth. Human beings, without the limiting assumptions about religious transcendentalism and supernaturalism that would set boundaries on their experience, become a source of profound meaning in their own boundless world, a human-inspired world that is the only world. Cosmic creativity as described in the *Changes* is fully a collaboration between human beings and their environing context, positing a natural cosmology that reverses the gravity of theistic religiousness to convey what John Berthrong has aptly called "the world-dependent nature of divine reality."[1]

A11 是故闔戶謂之坤，闢戶謂之乾，一闔一闢謂之變，往來不窮謂之通，見乃謂之象，形乃謂之器，制而用之謂之法，利用出入，民咸用之謂之神。

Thus, the closing of the swinging gate is called receptivity (*kun* 坤); the opening of it is called penetration (*qian* 乾). The ongoing alternation of openings and closings is called flux (*bian* 變), and the inexhaustibility of the comings and goings is called continuity (*tong* 通). When something is manifest, it is called an image (*xiang* 象), and taking on physical form it is called a phenomenon (*qi* 器). To get a grasp of these things and apply them is called emulation (*fa* 法). Putting them to good use so that all of the common people can take advantage of them is called insight into the mysteries of the world (*shen* 神).

Comment: The intellectual milieu for early Chinese thinkers as it is captured in the vocabulary of the "Great Commentary" is a phenomenal world of process and change construed alternatively as *dao* 道 : "the unfolding

---

[1] John Berthrong, *Concerning Creativity: A Comparison of Chu Hsi, Whitehead, and Neville*, Albany: State University of New York Press, 1998, p. 1.

of the boundless field of experience," a world that emphasizes continuity and persistence. An alternative way of describing experience is *wanwu* 萬物 : "the ten thousand processes or events," or perhaps even more simply put, "everything that is happening" that emphasizes the multiplicity of things. *Dao* 道 and *wanwu* 萬物 as continuity and multiplicity are simply two ways of entertaining the same phenomenon. A familiar metaphor in the early corpus for the novel arising and subsiding of the always unique phenomena of the world is the "swinging gates of *tian*" (*tianmen* 天門). The process of change imaged here as the opening and closing of the gates provides us with a vocabulary used to think about it, and insight into how creative change was conceived as a kind of presencing rather than the product of an efficient cause. One obvious association is human sexuality and procreation as an image of how new life is consummated and emerges in the world. Perhaps the most vivid application of this metaphor comes in passages such as *Daodejing* 6:

谷神不死，是謂玄牝。玄牝之門，是謂天地之根。綿綿呵若存，用之不勤。
The mystery of the valley never dies—this is called the dark female.
The gateway of the dark female—this is called the root of the world.
Wispy and delicate, it only seems to be there, and yet in its use, it is inexhaustible.

A13 是故形而上者謂之道，形而下者謂之器。化而裁之謂之變，推而行之謂之通，舉而錯之天下之民謂之事業。
Thus, that which goes beyond form is called *dao* 道; those things that have form are called phenomena. The transforming and tailoring that goes on among things is called their flux, while their advance and application is called their continuity. To take up this understanding and bring it into the lives of the common people is called the grand undertaking.

Comment: As in so many passages in the "Great Commentary," this text begins with observations about the form and functioning of the natural processes, and then concludes with advice on how contrapuntal collaboration with this changing world can inspire the human experience. We should note that the text is using the grammatically conative "is called" (*weizhi* 謂之) in this passage rather than the denotative "is what is meant by" (*zhiwei* 之謂), connoting or referencing some "aspect" of its referent. Here, each of these expressions reports on some aspect of the same experience, and indicates what term we conventionally use as our descriptor for it. Such clarification offered by the process of naming should not be confused with a realist "labeling" of the furniture of the world. Rather, human beings as the language animal with their performative and perlocutionary naming practices are participating and doing their part in bringing a particular world into being.

The coordination of the relationship between the changing world and the human experience to optimal effect is the main axis of the *Changes*. The purpose of this text is fundamentally normative and prescriptive. It purports to address what is perhaps life's most pressing question: What kind of human participation in the natural processes can optimize the possibilities of this world in which natural and human events are its two inseparable, mutually shaping aspects? These early Confucian philosophers were less inclined to ask *what* makes something real or *why* things exist, and more interested in *how* the complex relationships that obtain among the changing phenomena of their surroundings could be negotiated for optimum productivity and value. Rather than any predetermined necessity in teleologically-derived assumptions about origins, or causal speculations about some grand design, it is the pursuit of the highest quality in an achieved personal, social, and ultimately cosmic harmony, and the creative possibilities of aestheticizing experience (*wenhua* 文化) that serves as a fundamental guiding value for these seminal thinkers.

B1 天地之大德曰生，聖人之大寶曰位。何以守位曰仁，何以聚人曰財，理財正辭，禁民爲非曰義。

The greatest capacity (*dade* 大德) of the cosmos is life itself. The greatest treasure of the sages is the attainment of standing (*wei* 位). The means of maintaining standing is aspiring to become consummate in one's conduct (*ren* 仁). The means of attracting and mobilizing others is the use of the available resources. Regulating these resources effectively, insuring that language is used properly, and preventing the common people from doing what is undesirable is what is optimally appropriate and most meaningful (*yi* 義).

Comment: Life as growth in relations is the magic of a fundamentally moral cosmos. In the human world, such growth and effective living is the substance of morality, education, and the production of knowledge. Meaning is not available to us from putative metaphysical foundations—what David Keightley has described as "a Platonic metaphysics of certainties, ideal forms, and right answers."① Instead, guidance for leading the most meaningful lives must be formulated and passed on within the historical narrative by the most sagacious of our progenitors coordinating the human experience with the changing cosmic processes. Confucian morality itself is a cosmic phenomenon emerging out of the symbiotic and synergistic transactions that take place between the operations of nature and our concerted human efforts.

B2 古者包犧氏之王天下也，仰則觀象於天，俯則觀法於地，觀鳥獸之文與地之宜，近取諸身，遠取諸物，於是始作八卦，以通神明之德，以類萬物之情。作結繩而爲罔罟，以佃以漁，蓋取諸《離》。包犧氏沒，神農氏作，斲木爲耜，揉木爲耒，耒耨之利，以教天下，蓋取諸《益》。日中爲市，致天下之民，聚天下之貨，交易而退，各得其所，蓋取諸《噬嗑》。

In ancient times when Fu Xi ruled the world as its king, he looked up to contemplate the images and omens in the heavens above, and looked down to contemplate the patterned regularities of the earth below. He contemplated the ornate designs on the feathers and furs on the fauna, and how the flora was at one with its topography. Close at hand, he discerned the regularities of his own body and then extended his gaze to meditate on all of the various things. From this meditation, he formulated the eight trigrams to capture the mysterious potency of the natural world and to catalogue the dispositions of all things and events. He plaited cord to make nets and traps for fishing and hunting. Such innovation was probably inspired by the "cord" hexagram *li* 《離》.②

When Fu Xi had passed, Shen Nong carried on his work. Chiseling wood to shape the plowshare and steaming wood to bend it into a plow handle, he then taught the benefits of this farming technology to the world. Such innovation was probably inspired by the "wood moving" hexagram *yi*《益》. He further initiated the mid-day market to gather together the various wares of the world in one place. They traded together, with each person returning

---

① Keightley, "Shang Divination and Metaphysics," p. 376.
② I am taking the imagistic meanings of the several hexagrams mentioned in this passage from the analysis provided by Gao Heng 高亨. See his 周易大傳今注，濟南：齊魯書社，1979, pp. 560-568.

home after getting what they needed. Such innovation was probably inspired by the "moving under the sun" hexagram *shihe* 《噬嗑》.

神農氏沒，黃帝、堯、舜氏作，通其變，使民不倦，神而化之，使民宜之。《易》，窮則變，變則通，通則久。是以自天祐之，吉无不利。黃帝、堯、舜垂衣裳而天下治，蓋取諸《乾》《坤》。刳木爲舟，剡木爲楫，舟楫之利，以濟不通，致遠以利天下，蓋取諸《渙》。服牛乘馬，引重致遠，以利天下，蓋取諸《隨》。重門擊柝，以待暴客，蓋取諸《豫》。

When Shen Nong had passed, the Yellow Emperor, Yao, and Shun carried on with his work. They fathomed the flux and flow of the world around them and saved the common people from exhaustion. Through spiritual insight (*shen* 神) they transformed the human experience, and enabled the common people to find what was most fitting in their lives. According to the *Changes*, with everything running its course, there is flux (*bian* 變), where there is such flux, there is continuity (*tong* 通), and where there is such continuity, the process is enduring. This transformation was described in the *Changes* as: "with the assistance of *tian* 天, they had good fortune with everything working to their advantage." With the emperors Huang, Yao, and Shun doing nothing more than wearing the garments of state, the world was properly governed. Such innovation was probably inspired by the "clothed above and below" hexagrams *qian*《乾》 and *kun*《坤》.

They hollowed out trees to make boats and split lumber to make the oars. With the benefit of boats and oars they were able to traverse the lakes and the rivers to their farthest reaches for the benefit of the peoples of the world. Such innovation was probably inspired by the "wood on water" hexagram *huan*《渙》. Yoking oxen to their carts and riding their horses, they were able to transport heavy cargo to the distant quarters for the benefit of the peoples of the world. This was probably inspired by the "domesticated animal in front of the vehicle" hexagram *sui*《隨》. They built double doors and established night patrols with warning clappers to secure themselves against marauding bandits. Such innovation was probably inspired by the "moving and making noise on the ground" hexagram *yu*《豫》.

斷木爲杵，掘地爲臼，臼、杵之利，萬民以濟，蓋取諸《小過》。弦木爲弧，剡木爲矢，弧、矢之利，以威天下，蓋取諸《睽》。上古穴居而野處，後世聖人易之以宮室，上棟下宇，以待風雨，蓋取諸《大壯》。古之葬者，厚衣之以薪，葬之中野，不封不樹，喪期无數。後世聖人易之以棺椁，蓋取諸《大過》。上古結繩而治，後世聖人易之以書契，百官以治，萬民以察，蓋取

I. THE *BOOK OF CHANGES* (*YIJING* 易經): A PROCESS COSMOLOGY

諸《夬》。
They carved wood into pestles and hollowed out the ground for mortars, providing their people with the benefit of the mortar and pestle technology for preparing their food. Such innovation was probably inspired by the "moving and making noise with foodstuffs" hexagram *xiaoguo*《小過》. They steamed and bent shafts of wood to string as bows and split wood to make their arrows, and with the benefit of this bow and arrow technology were able to bring the world under their sway. Such innovation was probably inspired by the "cord strung on wood or bamboo" hexagram *kui*《睽》. While in high antiquity the people lived in caves and on the wild grasslands, subsequent sages replaced this way of dwelling with housing technology. With the ridge beam above and eaves below they were able to shield the people from wind and rain. Such innovation was probably inspired by the "rain and thunder above and a vaulted roof covering below" hexagram *dazhuang*《大壯》. For burial in ancient times the corpse was wrapped up in thick foliage and buried in the grasslands, with no raised mound or planted trees, and with no set mourning period. Subsequent sages replaced this practice with the custom of using inner and outer coffins. Such innovation was probably inspired by the "wood inside a hollowed pit" hexagram *daguo*《大過》. While in high antiquity governance was effected with the use of knotted string to keep records, the subsequent sages introduced writing and documents. The various offices of government used this literacy in carrying out their duties and provided oversight for the common people. Such innovation was probably inspired by the "bamboo and knife" hexagram *jue*《夬》.

Comment: The remote ancestors Fu Xi and Shen Nong established a rhythm in the human experience that enabled them to chime into the cadence of the "flux" and "continuity" (*biantong* 變通) that they perceived as persistent characteristics of the world around them. Inspired by the efficacy of their insights into the workings of the cosmos, they then represented their interpretation of life in the world in a hexagramic language of images, models, and patterns for the benefit of generations yet to come. Importantly, these antique sages were engaged in a reflexive project of personal understanding and articulation rather than some disinterested interrogation of nature. By their efforts at *ars contextualis*—the art of effectively contextualizing the experience of the human being within the processes of nature in an effort to optimize the creative possibilities of the cosmos—Fu Xi and Shen Nong cultivated a thick continuity between nurture and nature expressed in the evocative images that constitute the *Changes*.

There is a perceived continuity between the human experience and the natural world within which it takes place, between human-inscribed petroglyphs and the natural striations found in stone, between the changing modalities of human thought and the turning array of terrestrial and celestial patterns. It has been this incremental and continuing process of structuring and ritualizing the human experience thus remembered in and further inspired by the "Great Commentary" that has enchanted life in the world, and that continues to produce its mystery and spirituality.

The sage kings who were the later descendants of Fu Xi and Shen Nong—first the Yellow Emperor, then Yao and Shun—continued to innovate and construct human technologies, modes of transportation, social institutions, and customs that were inspired by the dynamic images derived from particular hexagrams. Indeed, this assumed symbiotic continuity between nature and nurture is reflected in the fact that the same vocabulary is used to express the creative advance in both the human and the natural ecologies. For example, the vocabulary of "the proper way" or "way-making" (*dao* 道), "vital energies" (*qi* 氣), "patterned inscribing" (*wen* 文), "patterning" (*li* 理), "alternating" (*yinyang* 陰陽), and the perpetual interface between "flux and continuity" (*biantong* 變通) are all used to reference both the human and the natural worlds. In this co-creative relationship with the contexualizing world, there is no initial and originative *logos*.

This historical record has immediate relevance today with our revolution in artificial intelligence and new technologies. The difference is that, to the extent that new technologies as an extension of these early innovations are consistent with the values that ground a moral cosmos, they ought to be described as the product of a "natural" rather than "artificial" intelligence. The culture that is expressed through human insight into the workings of the cosmos is itself integral to the natural processes themselves, not an exception to it.

B5 易曰："憧憧往來，朋從爾思。"子曰："天下何思何慮？天下同歸而殊塗，一致而百慮，天下何思何慮？日往則月來，月往則日來，日月相推而明生焉。寒往則暑來，暑往則寒來，寒暑相推而歲成焉。往者屈也，來者信也，屈信相感而利生焉。尺蠖之屈，以求信也。龍蛇之蟄，以存身也。精義入神，以致用也。利用安身，以崇德也。過此以往，未之或知也。窮神知化，德之盛也。"

The *Changes* says: "Coming and going and wholly distracted, only friends can follow your train of thought." The Master said: "What in the world is the use of ruminating on this and calculating that? Everything under the heavens takes different paths but gets to the same place; everything in spite of myriad calculations happens as it should. When the sun sets, the moon comes up, and when the moon sets, the sun returns. The sun and moon take their turns and their illumination is born therefrom. When the cold comes, warmth recedes, and when warmth comes the cold recedes. Cold and warm take their turns, and the yearly cycle finds its completion.

"That which goes forward suffers contraction, and that which is coming is being extended. It is in the resonances between contracting and extending that benefits are born. Caterpillars coil up in order to straighten themselves out again. Dragons and snakes go into deep hibernation in order to keep themselves alive. We get into the mystery of things in the most nuanced and meaningful ways in order to make the greatest use of them. We benefit from their usefulness and facility in celebrating the virtuosity of our lives. It is because making the most of the mysteries of the world (*shen* 神) in our understanding of the processes of transformation is the fullness of human virtuosity (*de* 德) that no one has yet to figure out how to go beyond this."

Comment: Confucius avers how insight into the natural pattern of life that can be discerned in the world around us gives us a breadth of understanding that precludes the fretting and fussing that arises in its absence. The productive symbiosis that can be achieved between the human and the natural worlds is practical inspiration for effective human living, thereby lifting humankind out of its animality to celebrate a virtuosity that can be achieved in the various dimensions of the human experience. Importantly, Confucius is not recommending that humankind "follow" the principles that govern nature. Rather he is recommending that we coordinate the uniquely human experience with the world around us to optimize a shared flourishing expressed by humans as a distinctively human virtuosity.

子曰:"危者,安其位者也;亡者,保其存者也;亂者,有其治者也。是故,君子安而不忘危,存而不忘亡,治而不忘亂;是以身安而國家可保也。易曰:'其亡其亡,繫于苞桑。'"

The Master said: "Those in danger are so because they felt secure in their positions; those who perish do so because they felt their lives to be safe; those suffering from disorder do so because they felt themselves to be well-ordered. It is for this reason that exemplary persons although secure do not forget the possibility of danger; although alive do not forget the possibility of perishing; although properly ordered do not forget the possibility of disorder. This was the way that they were secure in their persons and their states could be kept safe. The *Changes* says: 'Will we perish? Will we perish? Let's tie ourselves to a stout mulberry bush.'"

Comment: Exemplary persons while secure in their place and their persons are anything but complacent. They always see the big picture constituted as it is by dyadic opposites: security and danger, life and death, order and disorder. They are circumspect in their thinking, and are thus proactive in anchoring themselves securely in the world and in warding off any possible turn circumstances might take for the worse. The mulberry bush is a metaphor for grasping a trunk that is firm and secure.

子曰：「德薄而位尊，知小而謀大，力小而任重，鮮不及矣，易曰：'鼎折足，覆公餗，其形渥，凶。'言不勝其任也。」

The Master said: "It is rare for those to escape peril who are wanting in character yet occupy high stations, who are shallow in wisdom yet undertake grand schemes, and who are lacking in fortitude yet have weighty responsibilities. The *Changes* says: 'The foot of the bronze tripod being broken the ceremonial feast has spilled over; their punishment is grave. Most inauspicious.' The reference here is to those who cannot live up to their responsibilities."

Comment: High station, grand schemes, and weighty responsibilities might be noble goals, but for those who are unqualified in character, intellect, and fortitude, they are a source of grave and imminent danger. The three legs of the bronze tripod used to prepare the communal offerings in ancestral sacrifices is a symbol of both physical balance and cosmic stability.

子曰：「知幾其神乎？君子上交不諂，下交不瀆，其知幾乎，幾者動之微，吉之先見者也，君子見幾而作，不俟終日。易曰：'介于石，不終日，貞吉。'介如石焉，寧用終日，斷可識矣，君子知微知彰，知柔知剛，萬夫之望。」

The Master said: "Understanding the incipient (*ji* 幾) gives insight into the mysteries of the world (*shen* 神). That exemplary persons (*junzi* 君子) are not obsequious with respect to what is above nor condescending to what is below is because they understand the incipient. The incipient is a hint of movement from which one can see in advance impending fortune. "Exemplary persons having discerned the incipient are aroused to action without waiting a single day to see what transpires. The *Changes* says: 'Solid as a rock and without loss of a single day, doing what is proper ensures good fortune.' Being solid as a rock in what is being done, why would a single day be needed for the judgment to be known? Exemplary persons in their understanding of both the inchoate and the obvious, of both the soft and the hard, are a beacon for the myriad people."

Comment: This passage follows from what has gone before in encouraging us to understand the human experience in its fullest measure, from the incipient stirrings to the celebration of cosmic flourishing. It is only in being responsive to every aspect of this dramatic cycle from beginning to end that we can maximize its worth. We must read the initial conditions while they are still inchoate, anticipate the possibilities of these stirrings, and then aspire to make the most of them. Human spirituality as "inspiration" arises from a penetrating understanding of the workings of change, and from the quality of appropriate conduct that such an understanding can occasion. Simply put, human spirituality is the product of inspired living. The "intensive" conduct of the exemplary person becomes "extensive" as it serves as a model for and is deferred to by the people. In fact, it is this spirituality emerging from always appropriate and productive conduct that is the highest achievement to which humanity can aspire.

"天地絪縕，萬物化醇，男女構精，萬物化生，易曰：'三人行，則損一人；一人行，則得其友。'言致一也。"
"The heavens and the earth are intimately entangled, the myriad things collaborate with each other, male and female combine their fluids, and the myriad things proliferate. The *Changes* says: 'If three persons travel together one is sure to turn away, but if one person travels alone, it is easy to find a companion.' The reference here is to the unifying of things."

Comment: It is the nature of all particular things to couple with another and to seek out intimacy in a monogamous relationship. Such is the way of the world in producing the new life needed to continually inspire the process of transformation. The wisdom of the *Changes* is that while three is a crowd and thus often a source of conflict, the promise of two is intimacy and affection.

子曰:"君子安其身而後動,易其心而後語,定其交而後求,君子修此三者,故全也。危以動,則民不與也;懼以語,則民不應也;无交而求,則民不與也。莫之與,則傷之者至矣。易曰:'莫益之,或擊之,立心勿恒,凶。'"

The Master said: "Exemplary persons only take action when they are fully composed; they only speak when they are at their ease, and they only make demands on others when they are confident in their relations. It is because exemplary persons have cultivated these three dispositions that they are whole. Where there is risk in what is undertaken, the people will not join you. Where there is trepidation in what is said, the people will not be responsive. And where demands are made without good relations, the people will have nothing to do with you. When no one will join you, those who mean you harm are sure to appear. The *Changes* says: 'When none are there to lend a hand and some are there to strike you down, such a lack of steadfastness can only lead to misfortune.'"

Comment: The characteristic disposition of exemplary persons in everything that is said and done is confidence and composure. Such a disposition reflects the quality of those fiduciary relations that have elevated them within their families and communities to be an object of emulation. Absent such trust, there is no one who will be willing to take their part, and those who are thus lacking support quickly become the target of misfortune.

II. THE *EXPANSIVE LEARNING* (*DAXUE* 大學): SETTING THE CONFUCIAN PROJECT

The *Five Classics* (*wujing* 五經) that constituted the core of early Confucian learning included the canonical text, the *Record of Rituals* (*Liji* 禮記) probably compiled in the early Han dynasty but including at least some fascicles from Warring States vintage. *Expansive Learning* (conventionally translated as the *Great Learning*) is a document that was first canonized as a chapter in this early classic. More than a millennium later, the Southern Song philosopher Zhu Xi 朱熹 (1130-1200) canonized *Expansive Learning* a second time in selecting it to be first and foundational among his *Four Books* (*Sishu* 四書). Already included in the Confucian corpus as early as the Han dynasty, from the Song dynasty on this text and its appended commentaries became one important element within the standard curriculum for the civil service examinations. Zhu Xi endorsed the judgment of the Cheng brothers who proclaimed that

> ... as a text handed down from Confucius, it is the gateway into virtuosity for those beginning their studies. The fact that we can see today how the ancients thus prioritized their learning lies solely with the transmission of this work. The *Analects* and the *Mencius* come after it. It is only if students are committed to following this sequence in their studies that they will not go astray.①

Expansive Learning is frequently paired in the curriculum with a second chapter on pedagogy in the *Record of Rituals*, "On Teaching and Learning" (*Xueji* 學記). "On Teaching and Learning" is primarily focused on defining the conduct and decorum proper to life within the National Academy (*Taixue* 太學), a state institution that goes back into the mists of history. Indeed, it was this institution that became the basis for the imperial examination system when it was expanded dramatically in the Han dynasty under Emperor Wu.

Expansive Learning, on the other hand, provides us with deeper insight into what is meant by education itself as a transformative disciplining of the human experience. Although I have followed convention in translating the character *xue* 學 in the title as "learning," the original meaning of this graph is a regimen of personal cultivation that provides ample justification for Andrew Plaks to translate this same *Daxue* 大學 title as *The Highest Order of Cultivation*. Elsewhere I have made much of the fact that the earliest meaning of *xue* 學 is "teaching and learning," illustrating as it does the inseparability of these two occupations in the process of learning.②

I have followed Kim Jung-Yeup in translating the character *da* 大 in the

---

① Cf. *Daxue and Zhongyong: Bilingual Edition*, ed. Ian Johnston and Wang Ping, Hong Kong: Chinese University Press, 2012, p. 132: 子程子曰:《大學》, 孔氏之遺書而初學入德之門也。於今可見古人爲學次第者獨賴此篇之存, 而《論》《孟》次之。學者必由是而學焉, 則庶乎其不差矣。

② See my essay "On Teaching and Learning (*Xueji* 學記): Setting the Root in Confucian Education" in *Chinese Philosophy on Teaching and Learning: Xueji* (學記) *in the Twenty-First Century*, ed. Xu Di and Hunter McEwan, Albany: State University of New York Press, 2016.

title as "expansive" to capture the centered and radial nature of personal growth that makes morality and education two aspects of the same project in the classical Confucian tradition. I have translated excerpts of this short but influential text below as a starting point for considering at least one particular strategy developed in the Confucian philosophical tradition to organize the human experience. *Expansive Learning* provides this *Sourcebook* and the student of Chinese philosophy who would use it, with an organizing structure that expresses this focus and field, root and branches, and radial sensibility.

The central message of this canonical document is that while personal, familial, social, political, and cosmic cultivation is isomorphic, and thus ultimately coterminous and mutually entailing, it must always begin from the Confucian project of personal cultivation (*xiushen* 修身). "Human becomings," interdependent and thus always plural, stand as unique, relationally-constituted projects within their family, community, polity, and cosmos. Through a commitment to deliberate growth and articulation, they are able to bring the resolution of the relationships that locate and constitute them within family and community into clearer resolution and more meaningful focus. That is, cultivating one's own person enlarges the cosmos by adding meaning to it, and in turn, this increasingly meaningful cosmos provides a flourishing environment for the project of one's own personal cultivation.

In *Analects* 14.35, Confucius insists that order starts here and goes there: 下學而上達 "I study what is near at hand and aspire to what is lofty." In *Analects* 6.30, Confucius captures the gist of personal articulation in one sentence: 能近取譬, 可謂仁之方也已 "being able to correlate one's conduct with those close at hand can be said to be the method of becoming consummate as a person." This same point is again made in *Analects* 12.1: 爲仁由己, 而由人乎哉? "Becoming consummate in one's conduct is self-originating—how could it originate with others?" The *Expansive Learning*, the seminal, foundational canon that sets and anchors this Confucian project from early in the tradition, exhorts its readers to get their priorities right in their commitment to becoming consummately human. The text insists that it is only through binding oneself to a resolute, practical regimen of personal cultivation that one can achieve the comprehensive intellectual and moral growth necessary to optimize the human experience for both persons and their world.

I have used the *Record of Rituals* version of *Expansive Learning* rather than Zhu Xi's heavily edited version, dividing it here into Parts 1, 2, and 3.

II. THE *EXPANSIVE LEARNING* (*DAXUE* 大學): SETTING THE CONFUCIAN PROJECT

Zhu Xi attributes Part 1 (minus the last sentence) to Confucius himself as a summary statement of the Confucian project. What I have labeled Parts 2 and 3 are selections from the commentary on Part 1 included within the text itself that Zhu Xi attributes to Confucius's student, Zeng Shen 曾參 (505-436 BCE, usually called Master Zeng 曾子).① Although Zhu Xi is adamant in his attributions of authorship, and with his authority they have

---

① Zeng Shen 曾參, was born in 505 BCE and survived his teacher Confucius by more than four decades, dying in 436 BCE. In the "Biography of the Disciples of Confucius" in the *Shiji* (*Records of the Grand Historian*), it states that "Confucius regarded Zeng Shen as a person able to truly penetrate the way of family reverence, and accordingly passed on his teachings to him. Zeng Shen compiled the *Classic of Family Reverence*, and later died in the state of Lu." He is most commonly known to us honorifically as Zeng Zi, or Master Zeng, indicating that he was a much-revered teacher in his own right. He is one of only two disciples regularly accorded the "Master" title in the *Analects*, wherein he appears in 15 sections, occasionally quoting Confucius, but more usually making a philosophical remark of his own. These remarks are, for the most part, highly incisive. Master Zeng is best remembered in the tradition as the paragon of family reverence (*xiao* 孝)—devotion and service to one's family in the intergenerational transmission of a living cultural tradition. A natural extension of this affection for one's family is friendship, and Master Zeng is portrayed as being able to distinguish between the sincerity of Yan Hui, and the rashness of Zizhang.

In addition to Master Zeng's reputation for family reverence, another noteworthy aspect of his life is that he was the teacher of the grandson of Confucius, Zisi 子思 (or Kong Ji 孔伋), a role that later led to Master Zeng being given the title Zong Sheng 宗聖, "Ancestral Sage." Indeed, Zisi shared with Confucius and with his teacher, Master Zeng, a reputation for being expert in the details of ritual practices and propriety. However, while Master Zeng was not particularly interested in achieving a position of political influence, Confucius and Zisi both expressed considerable frustration in frequently being sought out for counsel by persons of high political station, but then being ignored when it came time for political appointments.

It is odd that in a passage without attribution to Confucius himself or anyone else for that matter, several of Confucius's disciples are criticized rather unkindly, with Master Zeng being described as "thick" (*lu* 魯). Traditional commentaries, making the most they can of this passage, allow that such candor was "tough love" meant for the edification and positive improvement of those being gently cudgeled (11.18). In the *Classic of Family Reverence* purportedly compiled by Master Zeng, Confucius has given Master Zeng a sustained tutorial in the meaning of family reverence (*xiao* 孝). But Confucius expresses real exasperation with Master Zeng when in chapter 15 he equates the complexities of family reverence to a blind obedience to one's elders.

thus become standard assumptions, there is no real textual evidence to support them. The alternative attribution of authorship is to the grandson of Confucius, Kong Ji 孔伋 (better known as Zisi 子思), a student of Master Zeng, and also the putative author of another of the *Four Books, Focusing the Familiar* (*Zhongyong* 中庸). This traditional claim about authorship is also a matter of conjecture.

Part 3 is important in rehearsing a fundamental ethical distinction ubiquitous in these classical Confucian texts between seeking an exclusive "personal advantage or profit" (*li* 利) or making the inclusive choice of "doing what is most appropriate for all concerned" (*yi* 義).

The *Expansive Learning*: Part 1

大學之道，在明明德，在親民，在止於至善。知止而后有定，定而后能靜，靜而后能安，安而后能慮，慮而后能得。

The proper way (*dao* 道) of becoming expansive in our learning lies in displaying a brilliant personal virtuosity for all to see, in cherishing the common people, and in dedicating ourselves to doing our very best. Such a regimen for learning can only be set once we have made such a commitment. Only in having set such a regimen are we able to find equilibrium, only in having found equilibrium are we able to be composed, only in being composed are we able to be deliberate in what we do, and only in being deliberate in what we do are we able to become the persons we want to be.

Comment: Each person stands as a unique, relationally-constituted perspective on family, community, polity, and cosmos, and through a dedication to deliberate growth and articulation, everyone has the possibility of bringing the resolution of the relationships that constitute them within family and community, into clearer and more meaningful focus. Given the organic, ecological sensibilities of the *Expansive Learning*, there is a symbiotic and holistic focus-field model of order where "learning" itself is nothing other than the cultivation of virtuosity in the transactional events that come to constitute one's narrative. The meaning of the family is implicated in and dependent upon the productive cultivation of each of its members that begins from a critical and purposeful self-awareness. And by extension, the meaning of the entire cosmos is in turn implicated in and dependent upon the productive cultivation of each person within family

II. THE *EXPANSIVE LEARNING* (*DAXUE* 大學): SETTING THE CONFUCIAN PROJECT

and community. Importantly, while existential narratives themselves are certainly the lived lives of particular persons, they are also unbounded and interpenetrating stories within their natural, social, and cultural ecologies.

物有本末，事有終始，知所先後，則近道矣。
There is the important and the incidental in things and a beginning and an end in what we do. It is in realizing what should have priority that we approach the proper way (*dao* 道).

Comment: The "learning" (*xue* 學) of the *Expansive Learning* is the cultivation of virtuosic, intrapersonal habits of conduct, and the "expansiveness" (*da* 大) of this learning lies in its extension from resolute personal cultivation to familial, political, and ultimately, cosmic growth. As the *Expansive Learning* enjoins us, in the singularly important project of becoming consummate persons, we must get our priorities right. In this eventful process cosmology, the notions of timing, of setting priorities, and of taking root are familiar themes.

The *Expansive Learning* then goes on to locate such personal cultivation holographically within the process of an expanding cosmic order. Since each person shapes and is shaped by the entire cosmos, the whole cosmos is implicated in each moment of a person's narrative. Such assiduous personal cultivation thus extends outward radially, ripple by ripple, to ultimately contribute one's own growth to the attainment of a sustained equanimity in the world. Having endorsed the priority of making a resolute commitment to personal cultivation, the text then continues by turning to the example of the ancient sage-kings and rehearsing the cosmic reach and influence they were able to achieve when they dedicated themselves to this Confucian project.

古之欲明明德於天下者先治其國；欲治其國者先齊其家；欲齊其家者先修其身；欲修其身者先正其心；欲正其心者先誠其意；欲誠其意者先致其知；致知在格物。
The ancients who sought to display their brilliant virtuosity to the whole world first effected proper order in their states; in seeking to effect proper order in their states, they first set their families right; in seeking to set their families right, they first cultivated their own persons; in seeking to cultivate their persons, they first became proper in their own thinking and feeling; in seeking to become proper in their thinking and feeling, they first became

resolute in their own purposes; in seeking to become resolute in their purposes, they first expanded their wisdom. And the most expansive wisdom lies in understanding how things fit together most productively.

Comment: In thus cultivating themselves, the ancients contribute to the most efficacious environment not only for their own continuing personal growth, but also by extension, for a flourishing cosmos. The symbiotic and mutually entailing relationship between achieved persons and a felicitous context, between the project of personal cultivation and the quality achieved in the social and geopolitical order of the world, between the cultivation of a critical and purposeful self-awareness and the coalescence of a person's relations with their environing others, is made clear as the text then reverses the order of this radical process.

物格而后知至，知至而后意誠，意誠而后心正，心正而后身修，身修而后家齊，家齊而后國治，國治而后天下平。

Once they understood how things fit together most productively, their wisdom reached its heights; once their wisdom reached its heights, they were resolved in purpose; once resolved in purpose, they were proper in their thinking and feeling; once proper in their thinking and feeling, their persons were cultivated; once their persons were cultivated, their families were set right; once their families were set right, their states were properly ordered; and once their states were properly ordered, there was peace in the world.

Comment: The *Expansive Learning*, in emphasizing the holistic, radial, and organic character of education, and in stressing the role of personal cultivation as both the root and ultimate goal of learning, provides much of the broader interpretive context we need for understanding the substance of Confucian education. In the account of the Confucian project provided here, it is personal cultivation that is the ultimate source of meaningful growth in relations, and it is the fertile context provided by a harmonious cosmos and an increasingly robust culture that facilitates this project of personal articulation. In particular this canonical text enables us to locate the personal development we associate with the Confucian understanding of education within the unique and evolving nexus of family and community roles that come to constitute the narrative of each person.

To be clear on this point, education so conceived, far from being the search for apodictic knowledge by solitary knowers exclusive of immediate

II. THE *EXPANSIVE LEARNING* (*DAXUE* 大學): SETTING THE CONFUCIAN PROJECT

relations, is in fact only achieved and expressed through virtuosity in those same roles and relationships that we live as family members, and ultimately as denizens of the world. Education is the situated reception, embodiment, and deliberate reauthorization of the living culture as it has been inherited by one generation that in turn has the responsibility of transmitting it not only intact but with dividends to the next generation and to the subsequent generations that succeed it.

自天子以至於庶人，壹是皆以修身爲本。其本亂而末治者否矣，其所厚者薄而其所薄者厚，未之有也！此謂知本，此謂知之至也。

From the emperor down to the common folk, everything is rooted in personal cultivation. There can be no healthy canopy when the roots are not properly set, and it would never do for priorities to be reversed between what should be invested with importance and what should be treated more lightly. This commitment to personal cultivation is called both the root and the height of wisdom.

Comment: It is a commonplace that personal cultivation is certainly the root of the Confucian philosophy of education. But I also want to observe that any root not properly set and that is lacking a fertile context will soon wither and die. To continue this metaphor, Confucian education must be understood as a process that is "radically" embedded in and grows within the roles and relations that constitute us as persons and thus provides us with the culturally rich context of our families and communities. The metaphor is that, in these ongoing transactional processes of associated living, cultivation of one's unique person within one's specific and often changing relations is the "root" from which a full canopy of interdependent personal bonds grows. These bonds define the various radial spheres of family lineage, neighborhood, community, village, polity, and ultimately, cosmos, with each of these mutually implicated dimensions making its own contribution to the prevailing social ethic. The close link between education and Confucian morality lies in the fact that they are both grounded in deliberate growth in our roles and relations. Education and morality so conceived are not instrumental as a means to some desired end, but is a process that is an end in itself. We get educated to live intelligent lives, and become moral to act morally. The ultimate goal of personal cultivation is a practical wisdom that produces a flourishing world in all of its parts. It is important to understand that both the "root" and the fruit of "wisdom" are to be perceived as an organic whole that either grow together, or not at all. The Confucian philosophical narrative from earliest times has seen a direct and immediate correlation between personal cultivation as the ultimate source of meaning, and a world inspired by a joyful wisdom.

The *Expansive Learning*: Part 2

所謂誠其意者，毋自欺也，如惡惡臭，如好好色，此之謂自謙，故君子必慎其獨也！小人閑居爲不善，無所不至，見君子而後厭然，掩其不善，而著其善。人之視己，如見其肺肝然，則何益矣！此謂誠於中，形於外，故君子必慎其獨也。曾子曰："十目所視，十手所指，其嚴乎！" 富潤屋，德潤身，心廣體胖，故君子必誠其意。

What is meant by "being resolved in purpose" is this: Be free of self-deception, loathe a bad smell, and appreciate a beautiful face. This is what is called being unaffected in one's person. It is for this reason that exemplary persons consolidate their virtuosic habits as a resolute disposition for action. Petty persons dwell happily in their vices, and there is nothing they would not do. On encountering an exemplary person, they dissimulate, concealing their vices and making a show of their assets. Since others on looking at them see right through them, what is the use? This is what is meant when it is said that resolve on the inside is expressed without. And it is why exemplary persons consolidate their virtuosic habits as a resolute disposition for action. Master Zeng said: "It is what all eyes see and what all fingers point at: how awesome!" Just as wealth enriches the home, virtuosity enriches the person; a sound mind makes a sound body. It is thus that exemplary persons are resolved in their purposes.

所謂修身在正其心者：身有所忿懥，則不得其正；有所恐懼，則不得其正；有所好樂，則不得其正；有所憂患，則不得其正。心不在焉，視而不見，聽而不聞，食而不知其味。此謂修身在正其心。

What is meant by "in seeking to cultivate their persons, they first became proper in their own thinking and feeling" is this: If one's person is consumed by hatred or rage, they are not proper in their thinking and feeling; if they are consumed by fear and anxiety, they are not proper in their thinking and feeling; if they are consumed by likings and pleasures, they are not proper in their thinking and feeling; if they are consumed by worry and grief, they are not proper in their thinking and feeling. If they are not there in their thinking and feeling, they look but do not see, they listen but do not hear, they eat but do not taste. This is what the text means in its saying that cultivating their persons lies in being proper in their thinking and feeling.

所謂齊其家在修其身者：人之其所親愛而辟焉，之其所賤惡而辟焉，之其所畏敬而辟焉，之其所哀矜而辟焉，之其所敖惰而辟焉。故好而知其惡，惡而知其美者，天下鮮矣！故諺有之曰："人莫知其子之惡，莫知其苗之碩。" 此謂身不修不可以齊其家。

What is meant by "getting their families right lies in the cultivation of their persons" is this: Persons are inclined to approach and compare themselves with those they love dearly, to approach and compare themselves with those they despise, to approach and compare themselves with those they hold in awe, to approach and compare themselves with those they pity, to approach and compare themselves with those they disdain. It is a rare thing in the world indeed for persons to approve of someone in knowing his faults, or to disapprove of someone in knowing his merits. Hence there is the old saying: "There is no one who knows the faults of their son or the bountifulness of their crops." This is what it means to say that if they are not cultivated in their persons they cannot get their families right.

所謂治國必先齊其家者，其家不可教而能教人者，無之。故君子不出家而成教於國：孝者，所以事君也；弟者，所以事長也；慈者，所以使衆也。《康誥》曰："如保赤子"，心誠求之，雖不中不遠矣。未有學養子而後嫁者也！一家仁，一國興仁；一家讓，一國興讓；一人貪戾，一國作亂。其機如此。此謂一言僨事，一人定國。堯、舜率天下以仁，而民從之；桀、紂率天下以暴，而民從之。其所令反其所好，而民不從。是故君子有諸己而後求諸人，無諸己而後非諸人。所藏乎身不恕，而能喻諸人者，未之有也。故治國在齊其家。《詩》云："桃之夭夭，其葉蓁蓁。之子于歸，宜其家人。" 宜其家人，而後可以教國人。《詩》云："宜兄宜弟。" 宜兄宜弟，而後可以教國人。《詩》云："其儀不忒，正是四國。" 其爲父子兄弟足法，而後民法之也。此謂治國在齊其家。

What is meant by "to order their states properly they must first set their families right" is this: There is no one who is able to teach others when they cannot teach their own family. It is for this reason that exemplary persons are able to teach the whole country without leaving their homes. Family reverence is how they serve their ruler; fraternal respect is how they serve their elders; maternal commiseration is how they serve the multitude.

The Proclamation of Kang says: "It is like carrying for an infant" where if you are truly sincere in your feelings, even if you fall short of the mark, you will still be close. No young women first learned how to raise a child and then got married. If the first family is consummate in their conduct, the whole state will be inspired to do the same. If the first family is courteous (*rang* 讓), the whole state will be inspired to be the same. If the ruler as a single person is greedy and ruthless, it will throw the whole state into disorder. This is how such actions are triggered off. This is what it means in saying a single word can bring ruin upon an undertaking, but a single person can secure a state.

The sage-kings Yao and Shun led the world with their consummate conduct, and the people all followed them; the tyrants Jie and Zhou led the world with their violence, and the people all followed them. If what is commanded of them is contrary to what they like, the people will not follow. This is why rulers seek such conduct from others only when they behave in such a way themselves, and condemn such conduct in others only when they will have none of it for themselves. There has never been anyone who without being the embodiment of deference (*shu* 恕) has been able to make this modality of action clear to others. Thus it is that ordering the state lies in getting the family right.

The *Book of Songs* 6 says: "The peach tree so young and its leaves so lush; the young woman in her new married home is a fitting match for the family." It is only when you are a fitting match for your family that you can teach the people of a state.

The *Book of Songs* 173 says: "Fitting as an older brother, and as a younger brother too." It is only when you are fitting as an older brother and as a younger brother too that you can teach the people of a state.

The *Book of Songs* 152 says: "In his comportment, he is beyond reproach, and he makes proper the entire state." It is only when the ruler is worthy of being emulated as a father, a son, and a brother, that the common people will emulate him. This is what it means to say that ordering the state lies in getting the family right.

所謂平天下在治其國者：上老老而民興孝，上長長而民興弟，上恤孤而民不倍，是以君子有絜矩之道也。所惡於上，毋以使下；所惡於下，毋以事上；所惡於前，毋以先後；所惡於後，毋以從前；所惡於右，毋以交於左；所惡於左，毋以交於右。此之謂絜矩之道。《詩》云："樂只君子，民之父母。"民之所好好之，民之所惡惡之，此之謂民之父母。《詩》云："節彼南山，維石巖巖。赫赫師尹，民具爾瞻。"有國者不可以不慎，辟則爲天下僇矣。

II. THE *EXPANSIVE LEARNING* (*DAXUE* 大學): SETTING THE CONFUCIAN PROJECT

What is meant by "securing peace for the world lies in bringing proper order to the state" is this: When those above treat the aged as they should be treated, the common people are inspired to family reverence; when they treat the elders as they should be treated, they are inspired to fraternal deference; when they give relief to the orphaned, the common people are not contrary. This is because the ruler has a way of taking the proper measure of things.

What is disliked in those above is that they do not delegate to those below; what is disliked in those below is that they do not serve those above. Do not promote those who follow on the basis of what you dislike about those in front; do not follow those in front on the basis of what you dislike about those who follow; do not engage those on the left on the basis of what you dislike on the right; do not engage those on the right on the basis of what you dislike on the left. This is what is meant by the way of taking the proper measure of things.

The *Book of Songs* 172 says: "So happy is the lord; he is father and mother to the people." For the lord to love what the people love and to hate what they hate, is what is meant by being the father and mother to the people.

The *Book of Songs* 191 says: "So lofty is the Southern mountain, with its steep rocky crags; so illustrious Grand Tutor Yin, the people all look up to you." The ruler of a state must be ever so careful; to be otherwise is to suffer the contempt of the world.

The *Expansive Learning*: Part 3

生財有大道。生之者衆，食之者寡，爲之者疾，用之者舒，則財恒足矣。仁者以財發身，不仁者以身發財。未有上好仁而下不好義者也，未有好義其事不終者也，未有府庫財非其財者也。

There is a grand thoroughfare to the production of wealth. If those who produce wealth are many while those who consume it are few, and if those who make it do so with some urgency while those who make use of it do so slowly, then the wealth will always be enough. Those rulers who are consummate in their persons (*ren* 仁) use wealth in raising their own image, while those rulers who are not consummate persons exert themselves in raising the wealth. It never happens that when rulers cherish consummate conduct, their subordinates do other than cherish conduct that is most appropriate for all concerned (*yi* 義). It never happens that subordinates who thus cherish conduct that is most appropriate for all concerned do other than make good on their affairs. And it never happens that the wealth stored up in the warehouses and granaries belongs to someone other than the ruler.

孟獻子曰:"畜馬乘,不察於雞豚;伐冰之家,不畜牛羊;百乘之家,不畜聚斂之臣。與其有聚斂之臣,寧有盜臣。"此謂國不以利爲利,以義爲利也。長國家而務財用者,必自小人矣。彼爲善之,小人之使爲國家,災害并至。雖有善者,亦無如之何矣!此謂國不以利爲利,以義爲利也。

Meng Xianzi said: "Those who maintain horses and carriages do not bother with chickens and pigs; a household responsible for the accoutrements of ritual ceremonies does not bother with cows and sheep. A household of a hundred chariots does not employ a tax-collector. If they are going to make use of a tax-collector, they would be better off hiring a thief."

This passage means that a state does not take what is of profit exclusively to it as beneficial, but instead takes what is most appropriate for all concerned to be beneficial. When the head of state or of a household are devoted to wealth and its consumption, they are certainly acting on the advice of petty persons. If they promote such advisors as being good persons and employ them in the service of their state or households, they will bring calamity down on their heads. Even though they might in fact have good subjects, of what use would these subjects be to them? This is but to say that a state should not take what is of profit exclusively to it as beneficial, but instead should take what is most appropriate for all concerned to be beneficial.

Comment: In both of these passages, a familiar and important distinction is being made between seeking "personal advantage, benefit, or profit" (*li* 利) that is exclusive of the interests of others, and "doing what is most appropriate for all concerned" (*yi* 義) that is inclusive of everyone. As this distinction relates to governance, there is the underlying assumption that when rulers are consummate in their conduct (*ren* 仁), the officials who carry out the business of the state will exercise themselves in pursuing policies that serve the interests of all concerned (*yi* 義).

In the Confucian tradition, modalities of action that promote growth in vital relations that are holistic and inclusive are positive, but when such dispositions are defined in partial and exclusive terms, they take on a negative cast. Love (*ai* 愛), for example, in describing one's relationships with others, is inclusive of both self and other, and is thus a positive quality of action. But when the same affection is directed exclusively to oneself, it becomes negative as a kind of narcissism. The same is true of "benefit, profit" (*li* 利). When the concern for benefit is directed exclusively towards one's own interests, it has the negative value of seeking after "personal advantage," and as such, stands in opposition to "doing what serves the interests of all concerned" (*yi* 義). The contrast is between dedication to the furtherance of private interests as opposed to an effort to extend one's moral compass to "do what is most appropriate for all concerned" in each unique situation. On the other hand, when this concern to benefit is unbounded and inclusive, it is positive, and in fact becomes coincident with "doing what is most appropriate for all concerned" (*yi* 義). The term "benefitting the people" (*limin* 利民), for example, is a positive term found throughout the Confucian canons. In this positive sense, *li* 利 frequently occurs together with (in the ancient pronunciation) its rhyming antithesis "harm" (*hai* 害) (in the ancient pronunciation): "the bringing about of benefit or harm" (*lihai* 利害).

In the first passage of the *Mencius*, King Hui of Liang asks Mencius, 亦將有以利吾國？ "How do you plan to benefit my kingdom?" Mencius replies: 王何必曰利？亦有仁義而已矣。"Why must your Majesty raise the issue of 'benefit' (*li* 利) when we should in fact be talking about you 'being consummate in your conduct' (*ren* 仁) and 'doing what is most appropriate for all concerned' (*yi* 義), and nothing else."

III. THE *ANALECTS* (*LUNYU* 論語): A BASIC CONFUCIAN VOCABULARY

If influence is measured by the sheer number of people who have lived their lives and died in accordance with the thinker's vision of how people ought to live and die, a fair argument can be made that Master Kong 孔子 latinized as "Confucius" (551-479 BCE) is probably the most influential thinker in human history. Like many epochal figures of the ancient world—Socrates, Buddha, Jesus, and so on—Confucius does not seem to have written anything that can be clearly attributed to him. All we know of him and his vision of the moral life must be pieced together from accounts of his teachings, and reports on his life found in the *Analects* and other collateral but perhaps less reliable sources.

Confucius was born in the ancient state of Lu (in modern Shandong province), during one of the most formative periods in the evolution of Chinese culture. Two centuries before his birth, scores of city-states owing their allegiance to the imperial House of Zhou filled the Yellow River basin. This was the Zhou dynasty (traditionally 1046-256 BCE) out of which the empire of China was later to emerge. By the time of Confucius's birth, only fourteen independent states remained, with seven of the strongest contending militarily with each other for hegemony over the Central Plain. It was a period of escalating internecine violence, driven by the knowledge that all comers were competing in a zero-sum game, and no state was exempt. To fail to win was to perish. The accelerating ferocity of battle was like the increasing frequency and severity of labor pains, anticipating the eventual birth of the imperial Chinese state.

Designated China's first great teacher both chronologically and in importance, Confucius's ideas have been the fertile soil in which the Chinese cultural tradition has been cultivated and has flourished. In fact, whatever we might mean by "Chineseness" today, some two and a half millennia after Confucius's death, is inseparable from the example of personal virtuosity that Confucius provided for posterity. All of the Sinitic cultures—China, Korea, Japan, Vietnam—have evolved around ways of thinking and living derived in significant measure from his ideas as set down and transmitted by his students and others after his death, ideas that are by no means irrelevant to contemporary social, political, moral, and religious concerns.

As a teacher, Confucius expected a high degree of commitment to learning from his students. On the one hand, he was tolerant and inclusive. He did not make distinctions among economic classes in selecting his students (15.39), and would take whatever they could afford in payment for his services (7.7). His favorite student, Yan Hui, was desperately poor, a fact that simply added to Confucius's admiration for him (6.11). On the other hand, Confucius set the highest of standards, and if students did not approach their lessons with seriousness and enthusiasm, he would not suffer them (7.8).

Although Confucius enjoyed great popularity as a teacher and many of his students found their way into political office, his enduring frustration was that he personally achieved only marginal influence in the practical politics of the day. He was a *philosophe* rather than a theoretical philosopher; he wanted to be actively involved in the intellectual and social trends of his times, and to improve upon the quality of the human experience

III. THE *ANALECTS* (*LUNYU* 論語): A BASIC CONFUCIAN VOCABULARY

that was dependent upon these real-world events. Late in his life he left his home state of Lu and traveled throughout the Central States, but was no more successful in securing preferment abroad than he had been at home. He eventually returned to Lu, lived out his last few years as a counselor of the lower rank, and according to later accounts, continued his editing and compilation of the classics.

Shortly after the death of Confucius, recognizing that someone extraordinary had walked among them, some of Confucius's first-generation students began setting down what they remembered of their conversations with the Master. This process continued, as the story goes, and within a century of the founder's demise, there were at least ten such little "books" about his life and teachings in circulation. Another dozen or more were compiled by we-know-not-whom during the following century, and it was to be yet another hundred years before a number of these books were gathered together to make up the volume we now know as the *Analects*, or "sayings" of Confucius.

There are different stories told on the compilation of the *Analects*. D.C. Lau stands with the traditional wisdom: this text was compiled shortly after the death of Confucius. He suggests the first fifteen books were assembled relatively soon after the death of the Master, and the last five books containing mostly reports of his now mature students came together towards the end of their lives a generation later. More recently, John Makeham has insisted upon the fluidity of the resources that would ultimately provide the content of our received text, dating its relatively fixed status to about 150 BCE.[①] The question of "when" might well be answered in due course by the accelerating number of texts being recovered in the exciting archaeological finds that continue in China today.[②] But however this mystery plays out, the enormous influence the received *Analects* has had on defining Chinese culture can never be in question.

According to the ecological Confucian moral sensibility, human beings

---

[①] John Makeham, "The Formation of *Lunyu* as a Book," *Monumenta Serica* 44 (1996), pp.1-25.

[②] In our translation of the *Analects*, we were able to take advantage of a partial manuscript of this text recovered in 1973 called the Dingzhou *Analects* dating to 55 BCE. For a discussion of this find, see Roger T. Ames and Henry Rosemont, Jr., *The Analects of Confucius: A Philosophical Translation*, New York: Ballantine, 1998, Appendix 1.

are radically situated. We can say that persons are defined and thus known paronomastically—that is, by those associations they have that require us to call them by another name. They are constituted by the relationships that locate them in community in their roles as a daughter, a teacher, a neighbor, and indeed, an ancestor. Personal growth is expressed through the cultivation and deepening of these constitutive relations. And to get to know such people then, is to learn and register the quality of their associations with others they have cultivated within family and community, and to acknowledge the distinguished name they have made for both themselves and their family lineage in doing so.

The meaning to be found in Confucian texts functions much the same way as we learn and register the quality of other persons through their associations. That is, passages like persons are not discrete and do not stand alone. One passage will bring to mind an association with another, and as students ponder the meaning of this second passage, a third is remembered. Familiarity with a Confucian text is being able to trace out a web of interpenetrating connections that extends the meaning organically, and on this basis, to grow an increasingly comprehensive interpretation. Key philosophical terms and explanatory themes also resonate with each other, and with the personal experience of readers as well. This meaning-making process is always reflexive. As readers make sense of, and appropriate the meaning of the text, the text also transforms its readers. It provides a vocabulary for organizing experience, and thereby makes their lives increasingly significant. In the tradition, texts such as the *Analects* would often be memorized during childhood as a framework that would gradually gain its substance as it comes to be informed by the many events of a human life. Over time the Confucian project of personal cultivation rooted in a deliberate regimen of reading becomes a person's world-making, where such a process of learning is transformative of both person and world (*jiaohua* 教化).

I am adhering to Zhu Xi's admonition to read the *Analects* as the second text in the *Four Books* following the *Expansive Learning*, thereby acknowledging the singular importance of the *Analects* in providing the terms of art that serve as a foundation for the Confucian project of learning, a project that is properly described as expansive in every sense. Again, the *Expansive Learning* provides what has become a mantra for the Confucian project. The process of cultivating and producing meaningful relations that starts here and goes there is radial and recursive: "cultivate your person" (*xiushen*

修身), "set the family right" (*qijia* 齊家), "bring proper order to the state" (*zhiguo* 治國), and "effect peace in the world" (*pingtianxia* 平天下).

Following the exhortation of the *Expansive Learning* to set the root properly, I have provided substantial portions of this text organized paronomasically around key terms and shared themes. These many threads are again woven through the lives of specific human "becomings" and the radial environments within which they live out their lives as unique persons, and cultivate themselves in family, community, polity, and cosmos. It is the growth of these symbiotic and synergistic relationships that extends and transforms human beings, and in the process, makes their lives significant.

Cultivating One's Person (*xiushen* 修身)

In Confucian China, the traditional assumption has been that there is a symbiosis between personal order and the order of community and state, with the broader configuration always emerging out of what is more immediate and concrete. When the state succumbs to disorder, exemplary persons return to the more immediate and substantive precincts of home and community to begin again to shape an appropriate social and political order (5.2, 5.21, 8.3, 11.14, 15.7).

On being asked by a rather unkind second party why Confucius was not given a formal office in government, Confucius replies that the achievement of order in the home is itself the basis on which any broader attainment of social and political order depends (2.21). The central doctrine of graduated love and ritually-ordered community in which family plays such a vital role—in fact, where all roles are reduced to the familial—is predicated on the priority of participation in the immediate and concrete over more general principles and ideals. Even when a higher order of social or political organization is deferred to, it is often given definition and represented in the concrete embodiment of a particular role model—a specific ruler or leader with whom one can assume a personal relationship.

Given the emphasis on a ritually constituted family and community, what then is the value of the individual? A pertinent contrast can be developed between the Western liberal commitment to many voices (the right to think) and the traditional Confucian concern for a communitarian consensus as a social good (right thinking).[1] It is this dialectical commitment to freedom of thought that underlies a Western sense of a healthy pluralism, deep suspicions about rigid conservatism and orthodoxy, and the persistent respect for a loyal opposition. It is the Confucian commitment to emergent harmony that underlies the sense of a centripetal center evidenced in notions such as familial hierarchy, institutional intellectuals, commentary on defining canonical texts, and the singularly inviolable continuity of the Confucian tradition itself. At the same time, it is this same concern for communal solidarity that, on the Confucian side, encourages the perception of excess in individual freedom as license, and exaggerated concern for individual choice as selfishness.

Following perhaps from this assumption about "right thinking," there is an equivocation that has plagued our understanding of persons in the Confucian tradition. In much of the interpretive literature, there is the unfortunate assumption that community interest and self-interest are mutually exclusive, and hence, to be a viable member of family and community, one must become selfless.[2] This attribution of "selflessness" to the Confucian tradition, both ancient and modern, seems to arise out of an unfortunate equivocation between "selfish" and "selfless" when in fact to eschew exclusively selfish concerns does not necessarily lead to self-abnegation.

The classical Confucian position contends that, because personal realization is fundamentally a social undertaking, exclusively "selfish" concerns are to be rejected as an impediment to one's own growth and realization. Stated positively, shared new year's celebrations and the fireworks on the national holidays have a different order of magnitude than how a particular

---

[1] See Randell Peerenboom, "Confucian Harmony and Freedom of Thought: The Right to Think Versus Right Thinking," *Confucianism and Human Rights*, ed. Wm. Theodore de Bary and Tu Weiming, New York: Columbia University Press, 1998.

[2] See for example Donald J. Munro who observes that "selflessness . . . is one of the oldest values in China, present in various forms in Taoism and Buddhism, but especially in Confucianism." "The Shape of Chinese Values in the Eye of an American Philosopher," in *The China Difference*, ed. Ross Terrill, New York: Harper & Row, 1979, p. 40. Again, there is Mark Elvin who concludes: "The individual remains of significance only as the locus of an ever-renewed moral struggle whose aim is the extinction of individuality." "Between Earth and Heaven: Conceptions of the Self in China," in *The Category of the Person: Anthropology, Philosophy, History*, ed. Michael Carrithers, Steven Collins, and Steven Lukas, Cambridge: Cambridge University Press, 1985, p. 185.

III. THE *ANALECTS* (*LUNYU* 論語): A BASIC CONFUCIAN VOCABULARY

person's birthday is remembered. A perennial issue in Confucian philosophy that has spanned the centuries has been the likelihood of conflict between the pursuit of exclusive personal advantage (*li* 利) and the negotiation of an inclusive way forward that is appropriate and meaningful to all concerned (*yi* 義), including oneself. Concern for selfish personal advantage is associated with the stunted moral development of "petty persons" (*xiaoren* 小人) while the pursuit of what is optimally "appropriate" for everyone—including one's own interests—is the mainstay of consummate conduct (*ren* 仁) and is what it means to become exemplary as a person (*junzi* 君子).

It is certainly the case then, that the Confucian tradition has been largely persuaded by a relational and hence social definition of persons rather than by any notion of discrete individuality. It must be further allowed that there does not seem to be an adequate philosophical basis to justify person as a locus of interests independent of or prior to society. Under the sway of this relational understanding of human beings, the mutuality and interdependence of personal, familial, societal, and political realization in the classical Confucian model can and has been generally conceded. But it certainly does not follow that the consequence of this interdependence is selflessness. Under scrutiny, the consequence of attributing "selflessness" as an ideal to the Confucian tradition is to insinuate both the public/private and the individual/society dichotomies in by the back door when the Confucian model is one of persons embedded within a social ecology. To be "selfless" requires that an individual self first exist, and that it then be sacrificed for some higher public interest. And the suggestion that there are "higher interests" on the part of either person or society covertly establishes a boundary between them that justifies an adversarial relationship. The "selfless" interpretation of the Confucian person does not support the claim that "person" is irreducibly social; ironically, it vitiates it.

The "selfless" ideal ultimately entails a contest between state and individual—the struggle between advocates of group interests over the priority of individual interests—that has in large measure separated collectivist thinkers from the liberals in the Western experience, but has little relevance for the Confucian tradition. While it is true that for the traditional Confucian philosophy, personal realization does not require a high degree of individual autonomy, it does not follow that the alternative to such autonomy is capitulation to the general will. Rather, becoming a Confucian person involves benefiting and being benefitted by membership in a world of reciprocal loyalties and obligations which surround and stimulate one, and which define one's own worth. The coterminous relationship between strong family and strong state presumed in the Confucian world contrasts with the liberal Western concern to limit state powers as a precondition for individual autonomy.

It is commonly noticed that in Confucian China, from ancient times to the present, conflicts are generally dealt with through informal mechanisms for mediation and conciliation as close to the dispute as possible. Society has largely been regulated through ritually defined relationships, and thus has required relatively minimal government. It is this same communal harmony that defines and dispenses order at the most immediate level that is also relied upon to define and express authoritative consensus without more obvious formal provisions for effecting popular sovereignty. Clearly, to the extent that the Confucian model is a project of cultivation directed at personal realization, the social and political order is derived from the participants themselves who thus cannot be fairly construed as self-abnegating.

It can be argued that person does necessarily entail a notion of discrete individuality. But, exposed in the differences we have discovered between being "unselfish" and being "selfless," there is a further unnoticed conceptual equivocation on the term "individual." Individual can mean either one-of-a-*kind*, like one human being as a member of a class of human beings, or *one*-of-a-kind, like Turner's unique "Snow Storm." That is, "individual" can refer to a single, separate and indivisible thing that, by virtue of some essential property or properties, qualifies it as a member of a class. By virtue of its membership in a "kind," it is substitutable—"equal before the law," "entitled to equal opportunity," "a locus of unalienable rights," "one of God's children," and so on. It is this definition of individual that generates notions like autonomy, equality, liberty, freedom, will, and so on. By virtue of both its separability and its indivisibility, it relates to its world only extrinsically, and hence, where animate, has dominion over its own interiority.

Individuality can alternatively also mean uniqueness: the character of a single and unsubstitutable particular, such as a work of art, where its own value is a function of its contextualizing associations: a particular oeuvre, genealogy, movement, period. Under this definition of individuality, an alternative, qualitative understanding of equality can only mean relational equity—a comparable degree of excellence. In this model of the

III. THE *ANALECTS* (*LUNYU* 論語): A BASIC CONFUCIAN VOCABULARY

unique individual, determinacy, far from serving to individuate, lies in the achieved quality of a person's relationships. Persons emerge to become "recognized," "distinguished," or even "renowned" by virtue of the quality achieved in their relations. Much of the effort in coming to an understanding of the traditional Confucian conception of person has to do with clarifying this distinction, and re-instating the unique individual in the Confucian picture. While the definition of person as "irreducibly social" certainly precludes the autonomous individual, it does not rule out the second, less familiar notion of unique individuality.

In understanding the Confucian person in this way, we resist the familiar move to separate agents from actions: *that which orders* (the self, rationality, volition) from *that which is ordered* (specific thoughts, desires, experiences). We abandon notions of a unitary person that makes our many experiences our own in favor of a more underdetermined range and locus of experiences expressed through specific focal roles and relationships. And we really must go further to question the appropriateness of using "concept" rather than "narrative" language to discuss the Confucian person. Concept in a strict pre-Wittgensteinian sense belongs to the "one-many" model where person can be understood categorically as having some univocal and hence formal definition, where such a concept reifies or entifies self as an ego or an ideal. Concept understood in this way is dependent upon formal abstraction: a formal and a final cause.

Given the dependency of the Confucian notion of person on the particular narrative without appeal to some self-same defining characteristic or essence, we might have to allow that the Confucian person is best understood in terms of that particular and detailed portrait of Confucius found in the middle books of the *Analects*, where each passage is a remembered detail contributed by one of the students who belonged to the conversation. And this portrait, as it attracts the deference of more adherents in the continuing tradition, plays a role in shaping both their own unique self-images, and the shared communal life-forms.

It is this propensity for personal growth and extension—Confucius as a living corporate person—that is the basis for traditional Confucian religious practices in which the objects of religious veneration are the past makers of culture and value: the ancestors and cultural heroes. These euhemerized persons are precisely how the idea of a "god" as an object of reverence has to be reconceived within the Confucian world.

III.1 Cherishing Learning (*haoxue* 好學): A Confucian Philosophy of Education

1.6 子曰：" 弟子入則孝，出則悌，謹而信，汎愛眾，而親仁。行有餘力，則以學文。"

The Master said: "As a younger brother and son,[1] be filial (*xiao* 孝) at home and deferential to elders in the community (*ti* 悌); be cautious in what you say and then make good on your word (*xin* 信); love the multitude broadly and be intimate with those who are consummate in their conduct (*ren* 仁). If in so behaving you still have energy left, use it to improve yourself through more scholarly pursuits (*xuewen* 學文)."

Comment: This passage illustrates the reflexive "radiality" pervasive in these *Analects* passages, where the cultivating of one's person is the ecological starting point and center. Personal cultivation then ripples outward centrifugally into family, community, polity, and cosmos, only to then reverse direction as an increasingly meaningful cosmos provides the centripetal center with its enhanced significance. This organic structure immediately brings to mind the first chapter of *Expansive Learning*.

Such personal cultivation is never a solitary or unilateral affair, and is always *in medias res* as a matter of narratives nested within narratives, contexts within contexts, a shared symbiosis that is the ultimate source of meaning. There seems to be a contrast here between an emphasis on the cultivation of personal virtuosity over application to more scholarly pursuits. At the same time, throughout the text, there is the celebration of the production of culture (*wen* 文) as the highest defining capacity of what it means to become human. One point being made that is repeated in the following passage, is that the ultimate product of education is the quality of one's own person.

On the first encounter, the *Analects* seems random in the ordering of its content, but over time, a paronomastic reading of the passages—that is, the continuing process of associating one passage with another—brings a highly personalized structure to the text, that through the gradual correlation of resonant ideas, terms, and images, produces an organic

---

[1] An alternative reading of the first two characters is "My young students," an affectionate term that Confucius sometimes uses in addressing his followers.

understanding of it. A suggestion for reading each passage that arises from the assumption that there might be a suppressed logic behind the editing of the text is to check the passages that precede and follow it for further resonances. For example, we find at this location in the text that 1.5 on one side as advice to a ruler also references "making good on your word" and taking care of the people. And 1.7 that follows it insists that the ultimate measure of education rather than being formal schooling, is the quality of one's person achieved through cultivating one's roles and relations.

14.24 子曰: "古之學者爲己, 今之學者爲人。"
The Master said, "Scholars of old would pursue learning (*xue* 學) for their own betterment, while those of today do so only to impress others."

Comment: The Confucian project as described in *Expansive Learning* takes as its starting point one's own commitment to personal cultivation. As stated in 12.1: 爲仁由己, 而由人乎哉? "Becoming consummate in one's conduct is self-originating—how could it originate with others?" And again in 15.15: 躬自厚而薄責於人, 則遠怨矣。"To demand much from oneself and not overmuch from others will keep ill-will at bay." Cf. *Xunzi* 2/1/32.

9.11 顏淵喟然嘆曰: "仰之彌高, 鑽之彌堅; 瞻之在前, 忽焉在後。夫子循循然善誘人, 博我以文, 約我以禮。欲罷不能, 既竭吾才, 如有所立卓爾。雖欲從之, 末由也已。"
Yan Hui, with a deep sigh, said, "The more I look up at it, the higher it soars; the more I penetrate into it, the harder it becomes. I am looking at it in front of me, and suddenly it is behind me. The Master is good at drawing me forward one step at a time; he broadens me with culture and disciplines my behavior through the aspiration to ritual propriety. Even if I wanted to quit, I could not. And when I have exhausted my abilities, it is as though something rises up right in front of me, and even though I want to follow it, there is no road to take."

Comment: This passage is a good example of *dao* 道 or "way-making" as the governing metaphor of the text. The standard reading of this passage is that the "it" here refers to the way-making (*dao* 道) of Confucius. The passage gives an account of how difficult it is for even the best student of Confucius—Yan Hui—to find his way forward on the road of personal cultivation inspired by the model of his Master. While this reading from the perspective of Yan Hui celebrates the steep heights one must climb on the road to personal consummation, less obvious is the collaborative nature of Confucian education, and the concomitant growth of the teacher in the relationship with students. A perhaps complementary interpretation would emphasize the collaboration in way-making that has Confucius and Yan Hui moving ahead together.

The Latin roots of "education" are *educare* and *educere*, a distinction between education by transmission from teacher to student, and education by the teacher "educing" new knowledge out of the student respectively. Yan Hui provides us an image here of the best kind of education by the best kind of educator for the best kind of student. With Yan Hui exhausting his formidable abilities and Confucius in his role as mentor struggling to move the process forward, it is still only possible for teacher and student together, to take "one step at a time."

Education so construed is fundamentally aesthetic and open-ended, allowing for the spontaneous emergence of novelty in the production of new knowledge that enriches both teacher and student. *Educere* is a transactional process that is always particular and specific, providing an opportunity for growth in both *this* able teacher and *that* able student. While retrospective in building upon the quality of the teacher-student relationship, it is also decidedly prospective in the sense that it reaches for, shapes, and addresses issues that have heretofore been unknown by both. Indeed, in this phase of education, the distinction between student and teacher is blurred and sometimes reversed as both participants through the exercise of their insight and imagination break through the boundaries of existing knowledge.

19.5 子夏曰:"日知其所亡,月無忘其所能,可謂好學也已矣。"
Zixia said, "A person can be said to truly cherish learning (*haoxue* 好學) who on a daily basis is aware of what is yet to be learned and who from month to month does not forget what has already been mastered."

Comment: In the *Analects* that walks us along the narrative road of Confucius, it is imperative to follow Confucius in treating the persons encountered as unique individuals. Who is Zixia? Zixia was a man of letters, and is remembered by tradition as having had an important role in establishing the Confucian canon. He has a major place in the last five chapters of the

Analects where he underscores the importance of learning. Confucius allows that he himself has gotten a great deal from his conversations with Zixia. Although Zixia tries to compensate for his image as a pedant by insisting virtuous conduct in one's personal relationships is what learning is all about, Confucius criticizes him at times for being petty and narrow in his aspirations. Witness the contrast set between pragmatic application in 19.6 and repetitive training in 19.7.

Knowing who specifically is speaking is essential to understanding any passage in the text. For example, there is the importance of distinguishing the speaker in the contrast between Zixia and Zizhang in 19.3. The expression "one who cherishes learning" (*haoxue* 好學) is Confucius's preferred description of himself. The definition given of this commitment to learning here underscores the perceived synergistic relationship between being steeped in the tradition and initiating innovative advance.

1.7 子夏曰:"賢賢易色；事父母，能竭其力；事君，能致其身；與朋友交，言而有信。雖曰未學，吾必謂之學矣。"

Zixia said: "As for persons who care for personal worth (*xian* 賢) more than beauty, who in serving their parents are able to exert themselves utterly, who give of their whole person in the service to their ruler, and who in their interactions with their colleagues and friends, make good on their word (*xin* 信)—even if it were said of such persons they are unschooled (*weixue* 未學), I would insist they are well educated (*xue* 學) indeed."

Comment: This passage is again radial in its structure, and provides a definition of what Zixia takes to be the content of real education: the noble regard for personal worth above physical beauty, a commitment to family reverence, dedicated service to one's ruler, and integrity in relations with friends. There is a direct correlation between education as it is described here and the prime moral imperative, "family reverence" (*xiao* 孝) announced in the opening chapter of the *Classic of Family Reverence* (*Xiaojing* 孝經): 子曰:夫孝，德之本也，教之所由生也。"It is familial reverence (*xiao* 孝)," said the Master, "that is the root of virtuosity (*de* 德), and whence education (*jiao* 教) itself is born."

Again, the prominence given personal integrity defined here as "making good on one's word" highlights the largely aesthetic rather than principled nature of moral judgments. Given that what one actually should do in any particular situation is always situation-specific, the emphasis in the

Confucian texts is on the modality of action, not on the *what* but the *how*. Presumably if one acts from a habituated commitment to credibility (*xin* 信), to resolve (*cheng* 誠), to earnestness (*hao* 好), to conscientiousness (*zhong* 忠), to optimal appropriateness (*yi* 義), to fraternal deference (*ti* 悌), and so on, the specific action appropriate to the situation will present itself. Conduct is not judged so much as being right or wrong, good or bad, but rather on being reliable not only in the degree of one's commitment but also in being able to accomplish what one says one will do. That is, making good on one's word (*xin* 信) requires authentication in action. It is this notion of "trust" that does much of the work of "truth" in Confucian philosophy in the sense that "true" friends acting "truly" engenders "trust" and thus provides social and political solidarity. There is a parallel in this relational and emergent understanding of "truth" (*xin* 信) and the irreducibly social source of "good" (*shan* 善) in its various expressions.

7.24 子曰: "二三子以我爲隱乎？吾無隱乎爾。吾無行而不與二三子者，是丘也。"

The Master said, "My young friends, you think I have something hidden away from you, but I do not. There is nothing I do that I do not share with you—this is the person I am."

Comment: Perhaps the most persistent quality of Confucius that comes through the profile of him sketched in the *Analects* is his self-effacing modesty. It is this same personal humility that drives him to "cherish learning" more than anyone else, and yet at the same time, to have a humble assessment of his own worth and accomplishments (see 5.28 and 5.9). It is again such modesty that is an encouragement for him to elevate the modality of actions above what is specifically done as his basis for judgment.

5.28 子曰: "十室之邑，必有忠信如丘者焉，不如丘之好學也。"

The Master said, "There are, in a town of ten households, bound to be people who are better than me in doing their utmost (*zhong* 忠) and making good on their word (*xin* 信), but there will be none who can compare with me in cherishing learning (*haoxue* 好學)."

2.15 子曰: "學而不思則罔，思而不學則殆。"

The Master said: "Learning (*xue* 學) without due reflection (*si* 思) leads to perplexity; reflection without learning leads to perilous circumstances."

III. THE *ANALECTS* (*LUNYU* 論語):
A BASIC CONFUCIAN VOCABULARY

Comment: Learning (*xue* 學) can be understood as the embodiment of a shared set of values, institutions, and commonsense necessary to integrate persons within family and community. Writ large and in the long term, such *xue* 學 is the substance of civilization itself. A common discourse is certainly a necessary condition for communal solidarity, but is not in itself sufficient. We should recall Ralph Waldo Emerson's exhortation on behalf of personal reflection and deliberation captured in his observation that "a foolish consistency is the hobgoblin of little minds." Given identity politics, without critical engagement, these same shared values can easily become a kind of divisive parochialism that draws the lines between "us" and "them."

But perhaps even more threatening for community than the prejudices arising from indoctrination are the idiosyncratic outliers who are lacking in the socialization necessary to participate effectively in the lives of their families and communities. Solitary sociopaths in standing outside of society do not develop the sense of shame that would move them to care about what others think, and as a consequence, they couldn't care less. As such, these shameless, aberrant individuals are a danger both to themselves and to the community.

Both of these images—learning without refection and reflection without learning—isolate persons from full participation in and contribution to inclusive and civilized humanity. Emerson again in his essay "American Civilization" gives us the image of a carpenter perched at the top of his ladder, using his broad-axe to clumsily hack away at a wooden beam. He then conjures up a picture of the same carpenter with the beam on the ground lifting his axe over his head to dress the timber with the full weight of the cosmos behind his shoulders. These two images provide a vivid contrast between a solitary and thus impotent figure so awkwardly and ineffectively going it alone, and persons who are animated by the *gravitas* of a continuing civilization making their incremental and compounding contributions to a living community.[①]

15.31 子曰："吾嘗終日不食,終夜不寢,以思,無益,不如學也。"
The Master said, "Once, lost in my thoughts (*si* 思), I went a whole day

---

① Ralph Waldo Emerson, "American Civilization," *Atlantic Monthly* 9 (1862), pp. 502-511.

without eating and a whole night without sleeping. I got nothing out of it, and would have been better off devoting the time to learning (*xue* 學)."

Comment: This passage sets a contrast with 2.15 above that underscores a necessary balance between learning and reflection. Hence, the expectation is that we should read the text as "making a point" rather than being expository or categorical. The expression "a watched pot never boils" is empirically false, but to a sympathetic ear it does make an important point. While cultivating a habit of critical reflection is a necessary condition for education, reflection alone without the complement of a disciplined regimen of learning (*xue* 學) is not sufficient.

2.11 子曰："溫故而知新，可以爲師矣。"
The Master said: "Reviewing the old as a means of realizing (*zhi* 知) the new—such a person can be considered a teacher."

Comment: This same phrase occurs in *Focusing the Familiar* 27, associating this attitude with the conduct of exemplary persons (*junzi* 君子), and emphasizing the progressive, evolutionary, and ultimately hybridic nature of the Confucian tradition. Dogmatism in any of the dimensions of the human experience is the anti-Christ of learning. Persons can only function as teachers if, while grounded in their best efforts to embody the traditional culture, they simultaneously have a capacity for collaboration and deliberate innovation. The familiar expression 君子不器 "exemplary persons are not functionaries" found in 2.12 makes a similar point in contrasting the innovative teacher with the negative image of a mere pedant.

17.2 子曰："性相近也，習相遠也。"
The Master said, "Human beings are similar in their natural propensities (*xing* 性) but vary greatly by virtue of their habits."

Comment: Angus Graham warns us that when we translate *xing* 性 as "human nature," we are insinuating some "transcendent origin" that "would also be a transcendent end;" that is, with the term "human nature" we willy-nilly introduce a formal and a final cause.[①] Tang Junyi is also offering a caution

---

[①] A.C. Graham, "Replies," *Chinese Texts and Contexts: Essays Dedicated to Angus C. Graham*, ed. Henry Rosemont, Jr., La Salle, IL: Open Court, 1991, p. 287.

III. THE *ANALECTS* (*LUNYU* 論語):
A BASIC CONFUCIAN VOCABULARY

in observing that

> ... this passage does not mean Confucius is asserting "human nature" (*xing* 性) is something fixed and given, but rather implies that "similar in their natural propensities to each other" refers to the human capacity for personal growth and transformation without any fixed limit to its possibilities.①

Confucius is emphasizing the transformative possibilities that come with cultivation and education. By "similar in their natural propensities" (*xingxiangjin* 性相近), Confucius means that human beings are alike in having the capacity to apply themselves to the project of personal cultivation and articulation. We humans are alike in being educable, and in fact, the wide-ranging variance we have in our personal habitudes is a function of our shared, unbounded capacity for education. Such a liberating capacity takes us in many different directions. In this sense, productive habits (*xi* 習), far from being divergent dispositions that stand in contrast to some ostensibly shared, fixed nature, are in fact the expression and realization of this shared yet always particular capacity for creative change.

13.5 子曰: "誦詩三百, 授之以政, 不達; 使於四方, 不能專對; 雖多, 亦奚以爲?"
The Master said, "If some persons can recite all of the three hundred *Songs* and yet when given official responsibility, fail to perform effectively, or when sent to distant quarters, are unable to act on their own initiative, then even though they know so many of the *Songs*, what use is it to them?"

Comment: The fact that the *Book of Songs* is the most cited classic in most of the early Confucian texts is fair indication of its perceived importance. Tradition has it that three thousand songs were collected from all levels of society, from court dirges to ritual liturgy to popular ballads sung to celebrate the harvest season. Three hundred and five of these songs were edited by Confucius to become the compelling voice of the *Book of Songs*. It is the *Book of Songs* as the anonymous and commonly shared repertoire

---

① Tang Junyi, *Complete Works*, Vol. 13, p. 32: 此即孔子不重人性之爲固定之性之旨, 而隱含一相近之人性, 爲能自生長而變化, 而具無限之可能之旨者也。

of the people that, in having both powerful affective force and absolute veracity, serves typically as the ultimate Q.E.D. endorsement for claims made within many if not most of the Confucian canonical texts.

The *Songs* as a shared vocabulary of anecdotes, images, metaphors, and allusions has an immediate relationship with professional administrative and diplomatic responsibilities. Dexterity in using this text provides both nuance and elegance in what is said, and can serve as an intervention on the basis of which important decisions are made.

A persistent theme in the *Analects* is this contrast between mere book-learning and the practicable application of what is learned. The expression, "the inseparability of knowing and doing" (*zhixingheyi* 知行合一), is usually associated with the prominent Ming dynasty Confucian philosopher, Wang Yangming 王陽明 (1472-1529), but this precept is a pervasive assumption in the early canonical texts.

8.17 子曰: "學如不及，猶恐失之。"
The Master said, "Study (*xue* 學) as though you cannot catch up to it, and as though you are afraid you are going to lose it."

Comment: In our reading and appropriation of the *Analects*, we must respect the governing metaphor of the entire text: the repeated exhortation to commit ourselves to "way-making" (*dao* 道) in forging our way forward together. This is an appeal to make keenness in learning and a constant review of what has been learned, into a way of life. See also 8.16.

19.6 子夏曰: "博學而篤志，切問而近思，仁在其中矣。"
Zixia said, "Learn (*xue* 學) broadly yet be focused in your purposes; be earnest in your inquiry yet reflect (*si* 思) on its immediate relevance—becoming consummate in your conduct (*ren* 仁) lies in doing this."

Comment: The parallel structure between "broad" and "focused" is key to understanding "earnest inquiry" and "immediate relevance." There is a parallel with 6.30 which states 能近取譬，可謂仁之方也已 "being able to correlate one's conduct with those near at hand can be said to be the method of becoming consummate in one's person." This passage likewise suggests correlating broad learning with what is immediately at hand and reflecting on the immediate relevance of one's inquiries is the method for becoming consummate. The broader the field, the greater is the focal resolution achieved.

Much is made of the fact that the graph for "consummate person" (*ren* 仁) is a combination of the character for "person" (*ren* 人) and the number "two" (*er* 二), suggesting as it does the irreducibly relational nature of becoming consummate as a person. But while the "twoness" of *ren* 仁 is descriptive in denoting relationality as the site of personal growth, it is also prescriptive in advocating for the "twoness" of the dynamic correlative method that transforms first-order relationships into productive advance. Friendships for example can be described in terms of relationships, but friendships grow in strength and become consummate when both parties with earnestness and imagination coordinate their interactions to serve the best interests of the relationship.

19.7 子夏曰："百工居肆以成其事，君子學以致其道。"

Zixia said, "The various craftsmen labor away in their shops so that they may master their trades; exemplary persons (*junzi* 君子) abide in their teaching and learning (*xue* 學) that they might promote their proper way (*dao* 道)."

Comment: The parallel here seems to be between the time craftsmen spend in their shops (*jusi* 居肆) and that exemplary persons spend in study. Grammatically the graph *xue* 學 taken in its earliest meaning as the "academy" in which teaching and learning takes place might do the work of "dwelling." Confucius himself in other passages seems to resist any immediate parallel between "training or skill" (*neng* 能) and real "education" (*xue* 學) (2.12, 9.2, 9.6, 9.7, 13.4). Perhaps Zixia's correlation between the assiduous on-the-job work needed to become a master craftsman and the way-making of exemplary persons who "effect" their proper way is the unrelenting attention required for the task at hand. Again, such a correlation might also be the reason Zixia is sometimes criticized as emphasizing the pedantic labor of book-learning over the more aesthetic cultivation of personal virtuosity.

9.6 大宰問於子貢曰："夫子聖者與？何其多能也？"子貢曰："固天縱之將聖，又多能也。"子聞之，曰："大宰知我乎！吾少也賤，故多能鄙事。君子多乎哉？不多也。"

The Grand Minister asked Zigong, "Your Master is a sage, is he not? Then how is it he is skilled in so many things?"

Zigong replied, "*Tian* 天 certainly set him on course to become a sage

(*sheng* 聖), but again he does have many skills."
On hearing of this, the Master said, "The Grand Minister certainly knows me! We were poor when I was young, so I learned many a menial skill. Do exemplary persons (*junzi* 君子) have so many skills? I think not."

Comment: What is the content of education? In the tradition from earliest times down to the present there has been a clear distinction between the cultivated conduct of exemplary persons (*junzi* 君子) needed to effect a flourishing community, and those technical, professional skills (*neng* 能) needed to build the structures that facilitate its flourishing, with the emphasis clearly placed on the former. The pervasive distinction in contemporary Chinese governance between the role of the party secretary and the executive office of any institution is a reflection of this persistent value. The assumption is that the quality of personal conduct is the necessary catalyst for accomplishing all things. Said another way, exemplary persons are defined by the virtuosity of their conduct rather than by any particular skill-set (2.12).

9.7 牢曰："子云：'吾不試，故藝。'"
Lao remarked, "The Master says of himself, 'It is because I have never been appointed to office that I have learned these many arts.'"

Comment: Perhaps the distinction here between political office and education in the arts says a lot. We know that one description of the Confucian curriculum is the "six arts" (*liuyi* 六藝): ritual performance (*li* 禮), the making of music (*yue* 樂), archery (*she* 射), charioteering (*yu* 御), calligraphy (*shu* 書), and logistics or calculations (*shu* 數). In this passage and the one that follows, Confucius seems to be saying that as important as these "arts" are for the refinement of a person, real education cannot be pursed independent of the social and political responsibility that comes with holding office. He believes he would have been better off in his career had there been a proper balance between learning and application.

What was Confucius seeking to impart to his many students? And is his answer different from Plato's purpose at his Academy? While personal refinement is certainly important if not indeed necessary, statesmen are ultimately to be measured by appeal to the reach and influence their persons have over others in changing the world for the better.

III. THE *ANALECTS* (*LUNYU* 論語):
A BASIC CONFUCIAN VOCABULARY

9.2 達巷黨人曰: "大哉孔子! 博學而無所成名。" 子聞之, 謂門弟子曰: "吾何執? 執御乎? 執射乎? 吾執御矣。"

A villager from Daxiang said, "How grand is Confucius! But although broad in his learning, he has not really made a name for himself in any particular area."

The Master on hearing of this, said to his disciples, "What should I specialize in? Perhaps charioteering? Or maybe archery? No, I think I'll take charioteering."

Comment: This is one of several examples in the text of Confucius's levity. See also 17.4 for example. Although charioteering and archery are numbered among the six arts as the desired training of exemplary persons, until they are authenticated in practice, they are merely learned "skills." There seems to be a parallel in the contrast between skill and real practical learning on the one hand, and knowledge and wisdom on the other Cf. 6.20, 6.23. We do best to understand the idea of "making a name" for oneself through the dyadic pair of "name" and "fruition" (*mingshi* 名實). When read within the process cosmology of early Confucianism, this would mean something like "bringing what is said to fruition," and amounts to accountability in what one has been able to accomplish. The concern with reputation is only to the extent that it reflects one's contribution, and how one has given the best account of oneself that one can. This theme of being concerned over one's own merit rather than public approbation features prominently in the *Analects*. See 1.2, 1.16, 4.14, 15.19, 15.20.

17.8 子曰: "由也, 女聞六言六蔽矣乎?" 對曰: "未也。" "居! 吾語女。好仁不好學, 其蔽也愚; 好知不好學, 其蔽也蕩; 好信不好學, 其蔽也賊; 好直不好學, 其蔽也絞; 好勇不好學, 其蔽也亂; 好剛不好學, 其蔽也狂。"

The Master said, "Zilu, have you heard of what have been termed the six desired qualities and the six faults that can come with them?"

"No, I have not." replied Zilu.

"Sit down," said the Master, "and I'll tell you about them. The fault that arises from trying to act consummately (*ren* 仁) without sufficient regard for learning (*xue* 學) is that you will be easily duped; the fault in trying to act wisely (*zhi* 知) without sufficient regard for learning is that it will lead to license; the fault in trying to making good on your word (*xin* 信) without sufficient regard for learning is that it will lead you into harm's way; the fault in trying to be straightforward (*zhi* 直) without sufficient regard for learning is that it will lead to rudeness; the fault in trying to be courageous (*yong* 勇) without sufficient regard for learning is that it will lead to belligerence; the fault in trying to be firm without equal regard for learning is that it will lead to recklessness."

Comment: Zilu is one of Confucius's best-known and favorite protégés. He was a military person of courage and action who was sometimes upbraided by Confucius for being too bold and impetuous. When he asked Confucius if courage was indeed the highest virtue, Confucius tried to rein him in by replying that a person who has courage without a sense of appropriateness will be a troublemaker, and a lesser person will be a thief. Confucius's feelings for Zilu were mixed. On the one hand, he was constantly critical of Zilu's rashness and immodesty, and impatient with his seeming indifference to book-learning. On the other hand, Confucius appreciated Zilu's unswerving loyalty and directness—he never delayed on fulfilling his commitments. But being nearer Confucius in age, Zilu with his military temper was not one to take criticism without giving it back. On several occasions, especially in the apocryphal literature, Zilu challenges Confucius's judgment in associating with political figures of questionable character and immodest reputation where Confucius is left defending himself—the wife of Duke Ling of Wei, for example. At the end of the day, Confucius's enormous affection for the irrepressible Zilu comes through the text.

This passage is a good example of the theme fitting the interlocutor. Confucius is trying to persuade the reluctant Zilu that not paying attention to learning comes at a real cost. To begin with, when we ask the fundamental question, what is Confucius referring to when he advocates for "learning," we have to allow that it is primarily the personal growth and refinement that comes with aspiring to ritual propriety in our relations in family and community. Cf. 1.12, 8.2, and 12.1.

These various pairings of desired qualities and possible faults are carefully correlated. Confucius lays out the standard formula of desirable personal qualities, making the argument that they can only be achieved through the discipline that comes with a proper regimen of learning. Even when committed to pursuing such habits of conduct, unless these qualities are cultivated in tandem with the kind of sound education that conduces to personal growth, not only will they be much less than desired, they will in fact be morally problematic. In the moral aesthetic, there is an ascendance from baseness to elegance, from rudeness to refinement.① More specifically, unschooled persons who are properly sincere in pursuing the best possible relations with others are, in their naivety, put at risk. For the "sophomore," literally the "wise fool," a little wisdom is a dangerous thing.

15.39 子曰："有教無類。"
The Master said, "I teach (*jiao* 教) everyone, regardless of class distinctions or other such discriminations."

Comment: As pointed out in detail by Ni Peimin, numbered among Confucius's many students were rulers and commoners, people of noble birth and peasants, rich people and poor, northerners and southerners, young and old, lifetime students and mere advice-seekers.② When Confucius asks rhetorically "Isn't having friends and colleagues coming from afar a source of great enjoyment!" (1.1 有朋自遠方來不亦樂乎) he is certainly expressing the enjoyment—that is, a joy shared by all—that comes with the diversity achieved by accommodating all different kinds of people and their different perspectives. Such a declaration tells us about the world of Confucius during the Spring and Autumn period in which many different ethnicities surrounded the Central Plain. In addition, Confucius is perhaps also conveying the sense of satisfaction felt in being able to attract persons who would travel a great distance to receive his instruction. While certainly being inclusive and accommodating in his reception of students, a very critical Confucius makes it clear elsewhere that he has high expectations for assiduous application on the part of these students, and that he will not suffer layabouts or fools.

7.7 子曰："自行束脩以上，吾未嘗無誨焉。"
The Master said, "I have never failed to instruct students who, using their own resources, could only afford a gift of dried meat."

6.11 子曰："賢哉回也！一簞食，一瓢飲，在陋巷。人不堪其憂，回也不改

---

① See Amy Olberding, *The Wrong of Rudeness: Learning Modern Civility from Ancient Chinese Philosophy*, New York: Oxford University Press, 2019.
② Ni Peimin, *Understanding the Analects of Confucius: A New Translation of* Lunyu *with Annotations*, Albany: State University of New York, 2017, pp. 372-373.

其樂。賢哉回也！"

The Master said, "An exceptional person is this Yan Hui! He has a bamboo bowl of rice to eat, a gourd of water to drink, and a dirty little hovel in which to live. Other people would not be able to endure his hardships, yet for Hui it has no effect on his enjoyment. An exceptional person indeed is this Yan Hui!"

Comment: A prime example that illustrates the inclusiveness of Confucius's teaching announced in 15.39 is that his favorite protégé, Yan Hui, was a pauper. The relationship that Confucius had with this very special student is one of the strongest themes in the *Analects*. Not only is Confucius glad to have Yan Hui as his apprentice, but he goes on to describe this one young man alone among all of his students in the same terms as he does of himself—that is, as being singularly motivated in his commitment to education (*haoxue* 好學). Cf. 6.3, 9.20,11.7. Indeed, Confucius ascribes to Yan Hui abilities that not only go far beyond those of his other students, but far beyond his own as well. Cf. 5.9, 6.11, 11.19. And at the end of the day, it is not always clear in the student-teacher relationship between Confucius and Yan Hui, who is teacher, who is student, and who is learning from whom. Cf. 2.9, 6.11, 9.21.

It is the mutually transformative relationship between Confucius and Yan Hui that provides clear insight into a kind of "relational autonomy" in the coordinated purpose of teacher and student. Education here is not the teacher presiding over the students to instruct them morally as to what is right and what is wrong, but rather the non-coercive growth that teachers as the most advanced learners in the classroom are able to experience in their collaborative interactions with their best students. I suspect most educators have had just such a learning experience in the teaching of our students, where in our classrooms we share in purposive growth together with these students, and become keenly aware of ourselves as relationally-constituted "teacher-learners."

6.3 哀公問："弟子孰爲好學？" 孔子對曰："有顏回者好學，不遷怒，不貳過。不幸短命死矣！今也則亡，未聞好學者也。"

Duke Ai inquired, "Which of your protégés truly cherishes learning (*haoxue* 好學)?"

Confucius replied, "There was one Yan Hui who truly cherished learning. He did not take his anger out on others; he did not make the same mistake twice. Unfortunately, he was to die young. Nowadays, there is no one—at least, I haven't come across anyone—who truly cherishes learning."

Comment: Yan Hui is the only student that Confucius describes in the same terms that he uses to characterize himself—and it is only after Yan Hui's early passing. We might look to Confucius's emphasis upon the modalities of acting rather than the specifics of what is done as an explanation for why the teacher is reluctant to describe any of his students in categorical terms like "cherishing learning" and "being consummate in their conduct" (*ren* 仁). Within this process cosmology, moral conduct is always a work-in-progress rather than a done deal. While an established habitude might be one answer, the text maintains healthy fallibilism where even those among the highest order of humanity have their lapses. In 19.21, for example:

> 君子之過也，如日月之食焉：過也，人皆見之；更也，人皆仰之。
> When exemplary persons (*junzi* 君子) go astray, it is like an eclipse of the sun and moon. When they stray, everyone sees it, and when they correct their course, everyone looks up to them.

5.9 子謂子貢曰："女與回也孰愈？" 對曰："賜也何敢望回。回也聞一以知十，賜也聞一以知二。" 子曰："弗如也！吾與女弗如也。"
> The Master asked Zigong, "Comparing yourself with Yan Hui, who is the better person?"
> He replied, "How dare I have such expectations. With Yan Hui, learning one thing he will know ten; with me, learning one thing I will know two."
> The Master said, "You are not his match. Neither you nor I am a match for him."

Comment: Zigong excelled as a statesman and as a merchant, and was perhaps second only to Yan Hui in Confucius's affections. Confucius was respectful of Zigong's abilities, and in particular, his intellect, but was far less impressed with his use of this intellect to amass a personal fortune. Putting the many references to Zigong together, it is clear that Confucius was not entirely comfortable with his lack of commitment to the well-being of others, choosing to increase his own wealth rather than taking on the responsibilities of government office. Zigong was aloof, and not a generous spirit. And in his readiness to pass judgment on others, he acted superior. Coming from an affluent, educated home, Zigong was well-spoken, and being such, Confucius's most persistent criticism of him is that his deeds could not keep pace with his words. Even so, much of the flattering profile of Confucius collected in the *Analects* is cast in the words of the eloquent Zigong.

In this passage, we have evidence of how the modesty of Confucius himself was carried over into the self-appraisal of his students. Again, excelling as a person is understood to be a matter of being able to make productive correlations in what is learned.

7.8 子曰：『不憤不啟，不悱不發，舉一隅不以三隅反，則不復也。』

The Master said, "I do not open the way for students who are not driven with eagerness; I do not supply a vocabulary for students who are not trying desperately to find the language for their ideas. If on instructing students on one corner they do not come back to me with the other three, I will not repeat myself."

Comment: This passage reflects the other side of an inclusive and accommodating Confucius. While he did not make economic or political discriminations among the students he would teach, he was impatient with anything less than hard work and full diligence from them. Confucius had the highest expectations of his students to be self-motivated and to strive assiduously in their learning. He required that they reflect long and hard on what he had to say, and come back with much more than he had given them. There is an emphasis here on the inseparability of the *how* and the *what*, the rhetoric and the substance of what is being said. Students must themselves not only find what to say, but also how to say it. Again, with the metaphorical language of one corner and the other three, we are given the sense that meaningful learning arises out of the making of productive correlations.

15.17 子曰：『群居終日，言不及義，好行小慧，難矣哉！』

The Master said, "Those who would get together all day long, occupying themselves with witty banter and never once getting to the topic of appropriate conduct (*yi* 義)—such persons are insufferable."

Comment: This passage can be interpreted as Confucius the teacher being impatient with students who would in their associations spend their time trying to impress each other with displays of their cleverness without ever getting to the real task at hand—that is figuring out how education can serve the project of personal moral growth. The term *yi* 義 meaning both "optimal appropriateness" and "meaning" captures the coincidence between appropriate conduct and meaningful growth. Throughout the text, while keenly aware of the power of the aesthetic in moral artistry, Confucius at the same time is unrelentingly critical of the glib and eloquent use of language that is specious, and lacking in moral substance.

1.14 子曰："君子食無求飽，居無求安，敏於事而慎於言，就有道而正焉，可謂好學也已。"
　　The Master said: "In eating, exemplary persons do not look for a full stomach, nor in their lodgings for comfort and ease. They are persons of action yet cautious in what they say. They repair to those who know the proper way (*dao* 道), and find improvement in their company. Such persons can indeed be said to cherish learning (*haoxue* 好學)."

8.12 子曰："三年學，不至於穀，不易得也。"
　　The Master said, "It is not easy to find students who will study (*xue* 學) for three years without their thoughts turning to an official salary."

Comment: For Confucius, the love of learning and the personal growth that comes with it is an end in itself, not a means to an official post or a comfortable salary. One gets educated to be educated; one learns to be learned. John Dewey once famously said that education is not preparation for life, it is life itself. The two important factors in education emphasized here are accountability in word and deed, and the importance of associating with persons who in their actions conduce to one's own moral growth.

9.23 子曰："後生可畏，焉知來者之不如今也？四十、五十而無聞焉，斯亦不足畏也已。"
　　The Master said, "The young should be held in high esteem. After all, how do we know that those yet to come will not surpass our contemporaries? It is only when a person reaches forty or fifty years of age and yet has done nothing of note that we should withhold our esteem."

Comment: This passage is a corrective on the uncritical assumption that age in itself makes a person the object of reverence. Allowing that real accomplishment often takes time, it is one's contribution much more than seniority that is to be respected. Taking sixty years to be the human cycle, to reach forty or fifty years and to have accomplished nothing becomes one's identity, and a fair reason for family and community to pause in according any deference. Said another way, it is the narrative itself as it is embodied in the person that either earns respect or not.

14.43 原壤夷俟。子曰："幼而不孫弟，長而無述焉，老而不死，是爲賊！"以杖叩其脛。

Yuanrang was sitting on the floor with his legs akimbo, waiting. The Master scolded him, saying, "In one's youth to be neither modest nor respectful to one's elders, to grow up without having accomplished anything at all to pass on, and on growing old, to not have the courtesy to die—such a person is a thief." He then rapped Yuanrang on the shin with his cane.

Comment: Yuanrang was a contemporary of Confucius. There is a story in the *Record of Rituals* (*Liji* 禮記) 4.69/30/6 about Yuanrang. On the death of Yuanrang's mother, Confucius went to help with the funeral arrangements and, finding Yuanrang singing by the coffin, pretended not to hear him. Here as a senior Yuanrang again shows a lack of manners in waiting for Confucius with his legs haphazardly splayed. Confucius gives him a severe dressing down, even to the point of rapping him on one of his impolite legs. Getting past the familiar stereotype of reverence for age, Confucius reinforces the point that it is accomplishment rather than seniority that is deserving of respect. In a Confucian culture in which morality is growth in relations, a lack of proper manners across a lifetime is not simply crudeness, but a gross moral failing, and thus incurs Confucius's contempt.

III.2 A Joyful Wisdom (*zhi* 知)

2.17 子曰："由！誨女知之乎！知之爲知之，不知爲不知，是知也。"

The Master said: "Zilu, shall I teach you what wisdom (*zhi* 知) means? To know what you know and know what you do not know—this then is wisdom."

Comment: It is not surprising that Zilu is Confucius's interlocutor in this passage. The profile we have of Zilu as an older, retired military person is that he is brash and impulsive, and does not have the patience to accrue the full information necessary to act wisely. The Master is simply advising Zilu to be aware of his own limitations (which for Zilu are major).

We find a version of this definition of wisdom in many of the early philosophical texts. In Plato's *Apology*, for example, we read: "The wisest of you men is he who has realized, like Socrates, that in respect of wisdom he is really worthless."[①] For Socrates like Confucius, a positive value is attached both to the knowledge one has acquired and to recognition of the limitations of such knowledge. In classical Chinese, the character *zhi* 知 can be read as either "knowing" or "wisdom" (or perhaps better, "wise-*ing*" or "acting wisely"). For this tradition, the distance between "knowing" and "wisdom" is the authentication in practice that is captured in the familiar mantra: *zhixingheyi* 知行合一, "the inseparability of knowing and doing."

There is another example of this formulation in the standard version of *Daodejing* 71 that is often emended in one way or another to bring it in line with the Confucian concern for acknowledging the limits of one's understanding. In the *Daodejing* we read 知不知上，不知知病. Unemended it states "Knowing that one does not know is knowing at its best, but not knowing that one 'knows' is suffering from a disease." If instead of changing the text, we take it on its own terms, we might understand it to be making quite a different point from Confucius. Perhaps it is asserting that achieving the positive state of *wuzhi* 無知 as literally "not knowing" comes from the stubborn effort to know the particularity of our environing others utterly and without remainder without bringing some assumptions about them with us in the encounter. For this Daoist sensibility, the greatest obstacle for "appreciating" experience in the sense of optimizing its value, is a failure to both acknowledge and to suspend those generic presuppositions that overwrite the uniqueness of things, and that we then pass off as "knowing." The starting point for "seeing" (rather than "knowing") and engaging the world fully in all of its particular detail, seems to require an act of forgetting. In traditional Chinese medicine, disease (*bing* 病) usually references some kind of blockage. In this instance, the remedy for the epistemic disease of "knowing" the world would seem to require the

---

① Hugh Tredennick and Harold Tarrant (trans.), *Plato: The Last Days of Socrates*, London: Penguin, 1993, p. 44.

dissolution of that set of assumptions blocking our access to the "hadness" of immediate experience.

6.20 子曰："知之者不如好之者，好之者不如樂之者。"

The Master said, "To truly cherish something (*hao* 好) is better than just to know it (*zhi* 知), and to find enjoyment in it (*yao* 樂) is better than to simply cherish it."

Comment: This passage introduces three distinctive modalities of "knowing," suggesting that knowing is best understood as a cumulative process rather than the either/or binary where you either know it or you don't. The first, lowest, but necessary mode of knowing seems to be an abstract, cognitive knowing. Such knowing is basic but is also a limited condition of what is possible. In fact, it is our commonsense understanding of "knowing" as a binary that precludes its use in a gerundive form as an on-going process. While we say I am running or jumping, we do not say "I am knowing."

The affective, modal aspect of knowing comes into the picture with the "cherishing" (*hao* 好) of what we know. The use of "cherishing" here evokes the expression "cherishing learning" (*haoxue* 好學) that Confucius uses as his preferred description of himself. Presumably the product of "cherishing learning" is the quality of purposeful, practicable knowing that enables us to live wisely in the world.

But the highest and optimally effective level of knowing must wait upon the third quality of "finding enjoyment" in our experience of the world captured with the term *le* 樂 (but read *yao* in this transitive context): what we might call a truly joyful wisdom. Since "knowing" as "realizing" is a "doing," it has immediate ethical as well as epistemic import. The value or worth of knowledge is a direct consequence of its efficacy. To what degree does such awareness and mindfulness conduce to human flourishing? In the *Conceptual Lexicon*, I have rehearsed the related musical and therapeutic connotations of this term "enjoyment" (*le* 樂).

17.3 子曰："唯上知與下愚不移。"

The Master said, "Only the wisest and the most obtuse do not change."

Comment: "Change" here is ambiguous to the extent that it can mean to move or to be moved. That is, it can mean to change of one's own accord or to be altered by some external force, or perhaps both. That obtuse persons do not change seems rather straightforward. Such persons unaware of the limitation of their own knowledge, are resistant to the intellectual and moral growth that elevates human beings above their animality, or in this case, their *animal* obtuseness. That is, the term translated as "obtuse" combines the character for a primate (*yu* 禺) as an element that has both a phonetic and semantic reference, with *xin* 心 meaning "thinking and feeling." That obtuse persons do not grow has to be understood as a function of their failing to cultivate their relations; they think they have little or nothing to learn from others. Of course, such obtuse persons are seldom aware of their own plight, leaving their obtuseness to be a judgment made on them by others.

That the wisest persons do not change must likewise be understood relationally. In this Confucian tradition, wisdom is life, and life is growth, and it never stops. But the wisest of persons, even while continuing to live and grow in their relations with others, when viewed from the perspective of other people, are stout and unwavering beacons that light the way. The wisest are exemplary in providing role models that inspire others and give them their bearings. Just as the North Star certainly moves and yet is a stable point of reference, the wisest among us guide the passage of others as they navigate the complexities of a human life. Cf. 2.1.

2.1 子曰:"爲政以德,譬如北辰,居其所而衆星共之。"

The Master said: "Governing with virtuosity (*de* 德) can be compared to the North Star; the North Star dwells in its place, and the multitude of stars circumambulate to pay it homage."

Comment: In 17.3 the wisest are described as being "unchanging" in the sense that they serve as a constant and steadfast beacon for their communities. Effective governance is similar. The most effective rulers as role models are a source of stability and direction that enable others to carry out their own responsibilities effectively. Of course, the North Star does in fact "move," but from the perspective of those persons who depend upon it to find their bearings, it provides humankind in its relationship to the turning firmament that constant point of reference necessary to secure them on their way.

6.23 子曰:"知者樂水,仁者樂山。知者動,仁者靜。知者樂,仁者壽。"

The Master said, "The wise enjoy water; those consummate in their conduct enjoy mountains. The wise are active; consummate persons are still. The wise find enjoyment; consummate persons are long-enduring."

Comment: The many metaphorical correlations between acting wisely and water are instructive. As a metaphor, water like wisdom is a dynamic "doing" that makes a difference: it provides life, nutrition, and growth to all living things. Said the other way round, the world absent either water or wisdom is barren and lifeless. The communal aspect is also highlighted in this passage where both water and wisdom are a source not of joy, but of enjoyment (*en-* as the relational "making or giving" joy). The harvest to be reaped and the wisdom to be sown benefits all. Water is sacred as a source of purification, and at the same time, is humble, finding its way into the bowels of the earth. Water is checked only at our peril, assuming its shape according to each particular context only to take on another shape as it flows along. It is fluid, challenging not only natural boundaries, but linguistic categories such as the distinction between noun and verb, and the natural states such as solid, liquid, and gas. It is because of these many life-giving, fluid, and unbounded associations that water is frequently used as a metaphor for *dao* 道 or cosmic way-making itself.

The mountain metaphor is also revealing. Mountains in their relationship to the human world are prominent, defining the landscape, and giving us a sense of permanence and place. We take our bearings from them. They are holy in being the closest to the heavens, and awesome in the sense of being stately, uniquely dignified, and majestic. They lend us their lofty heights, and with their collaboration, we are able to view our world in its broadest compass. In all of these senses, mountains can be associated with persons who are consummate in their conduct.

The familiar felicitous combination of "mountains" and "water" is the term *shanshui* 山水 that means the highest mode of natural scenic beauty, and thus has come to refer to landscape painting as an art form. This binomial would suggest this passage is not describing two distinct things, but the relationship between them. There is a perceived symbiosis between mountain and water, between wisdom and consummate conduct. It is clouds against the mountains that produce rain, and it is the streams and waterfalls produced by such precipitation that in turn give shape to the mountains. This same symbiotic association between acting wisely (*zhi* 知) and being consummate in our conduct (*ren* 仁) is a connection that we find recurrent throughout the *Analects* and the philosophical literature more broadly.

15.12 子曰: "人無遠慮，必有近憂。"
The Master said, "Those who fail to concern themselves about the long-term are certain to have more immediate worries."

6.22 樊遲問知。子曰: "務民之義，敬鬼神而遠之，可謂知矣。" 問仁。曰: "仁者先難而後獲，可謂仁矣。"
   Fan Chi asked about wisdom (*zhi* 知).
   The Master replied, "Devoting yourself to what is optimally appropriate (*yi* 義) for the common people, and showing respect for the ghosts and spirits while keeping them at a distance can be called wisdom."
   He then asked about consummate conduct (*ren* 仁).
   The Master responded, "As for consummate conduct—to reap one's successes only after having dealt with difficulties can be called becoming consummate."

Comment: In this passage we find the frequent correlating of acting wisely (*zhi* 知) and consummate conduct (*ren* 仁), where at least one connection is the assiduous effort needed in serving the community to achieve either one of them. Becoming intelligently moral is irreducibly social, and is hard work. And it would seem that the ultimate measure of wisdom is the communal flourishing achieved in promoting what is optimally appropriate for the people (*yi* 義).

Given the speculative assumptions that commonly attend our own religious beliefs, this counsel to pursue a practical efficacy in one's relations with others while keeping ghosts and spirits at a distance has persuaded many commentators that Confucius is at least a-religious if not anti-religious. On this reading, Confucius is seen as expressing at the very least a lack of interest in, if not an aversion to, the demands of a cultivated religiousness. For these interpreters, Confucius's reticence in seeking intimacy with the spiritual world is a clear indication of his commitment to a kind of secular humanism. Confucius focuses on who we are, and what we have achieved as our cultural accomplishments, but seems reluctant to venture speculation upon what we and our world might become.

While some would ascribe this kind of a disenchanted humanism to Confucius, we might also look for a reading more consistent with his own emphasis upon the family-centered life in community. Can we find an interpretation that reflects the correlation Confucius sees between wisdom (*zhi* 知) and consummate conduct (*ren* 仁) in this passage? Given the primacy of vital relationality exemplified by the centrality of family reverence (*xiao* 孝) as the Confucian prime moral imperative, if *religare*, the Latin root of "religious," does mean "binding tightly" (as reflected in cognates such as "ligament," "obligation," "league," and "ally"), then we can see that "family reverence" (*xiao* 孝) so described has a profoundly religious import as well, referencing as it does binding tightly through those familial, communal, and ancestral bonds that together produce a resilient and enduring social fabric.① It would be this profoundly religious sense of "binding tightly" in the strengthening of family and communal bonds we would appeal to in interpreting the Master's autobiographical response to Zilu's question about what he would most like to do: "I would like to bring peace and contentment to the aged, share relationships of trust and confidence with friends, and to love and protect the young."②

We might conclude that for Confucius real religiousness, rather than lying in reverence for and supplication to remote supernatural entities, is to be found in those bonds much nearer to home. To the extent that communal flourishing is a source of meaning, serving the people by promoting what is optimally appropriate for them is itself a kind of religiousness. Such an alternative religiousness is manifested as a shared, family and community-centered spirituality in aspiring to live truly inspired lives within our families and communities. We have seen that Confucius has a sense of growth centered in a commitment to personal cultivation within intimate family and community relations that is then extended outward radially and reflexively to the cosmic totality. There is a synergistic and interpenetrating center and periphery—a focus and its field. What is most extensive is reflected back to fortify what is most intensive, and what is most intensive has the greatest extensive reach and influence.

More concretely, we might infer that for Confucius, there is a direct and inseparable link between the self-conscious deference, veneration,

---

① Sarah F. Hoyt, "The Etymology of Religion," *Journal of the American Oriental Society*, Vol. 32, No. 2 (1912), pp. 126-129 provides some interesting textual evidence for this very old and sometimes disputed etymology.
② *Analects* 5.26: 子路曰："願聞子之志。" 子曰："老者安之，朋友信之，少者懷之。"

and gratitude expressed within the moral life at home, and the quiet, reassuring spirituality we associate with ancestor reverence and natural piety. Or said more simply, such Confucian religiousness is nothing other than the sense of cosmic belonging inspired by our achieved sense of felt worth within our most immediate and intimate relations. And while these relations constitute the current center, they reach back genealogically and are informed by the uninterrupted legacy of a living culture, and again anticipate its transmission to those generations yet to come.

9.8 子曰："吾有知乎哉？無知也。有鄙夫問於我，空空如也。我叩其兩端而竭焉。"
　　The Master said, "Do I possess wisdom (*zhi* 知)? No, I do not. But if a simple farmer puts a question to me, and I come up empty, I then attack the question from both ends until I have gotten to the bottom of it."

Comment: We begin from the familiar expression of Confucius's modesty. Even so, education as it is reported on in the *Analects* is in important measure dialectical as the correlation between questions posed and answers given. And it is thus the social and discursive nature of wisdom that is at issue. Wisdom as it is referenced here does not seem to be a quantum of knowledge, but facility in providing the most effective answers to whatever questions might be asked of one. Wisdom is intellectual dexterity certainly, but perhaps more importantly, requires the insight into one's interlocutors that enables a morally informed responsiveness in serving their particular needs. The emphasis here seems to be on the modality of acting wisely rather than on providing any specific details. Rather than making some claim about the quality of the answers he is able to offer, Confucius is most interested in communicating to his students his pedagogical habit of investing the effort necessary to answer even the most inconsequential of the questions asked of him, never mind those of real consequence.

7.20 子曰："我非生而知之者，好古，敏以求之者也。"
　　The Master said, "I am not someone who is precocious and has wisdom (*zhi* 知) from the outset. Rather I am someone who, loving antiquity and its culture, is most earnest in seeking after it."

Comment: How do we make sense of the description here literally of someone "who has wisdom at birth" (生而知之者)? Is this a disclaimer about not having a kind of *apriori* knowledge independent of our experience? What would such a statement mean in a process cosmology that takes as a primary assumption the inseparability of knowing and doing, and in fact, rejects all such dualisms that would separate knowledge from wisdom, fact from value, and so on? As we have seen, acting wisely (*zhi* 知) is irreducibly social, and is the product of a discursive, communal process.

First, we should observe that the term *sheng* 生 is not limited to the moment of "birth," but rather describes the continuing process of "life, growth, and birth," where birthing occurs *in medias res* within the narrative itself. What makes a Mozart or a Wang Bi 王弼 (226-249) precocious? Mozart was born into a musical family at the court of Salzburg renowned for its contribution to the musical culture of the European royalty. Wang Bi wrote among the most influential commentaries on the *Daodejing* and the *Book of Changes,* and then died at the age of twenty-three. He was the scion of a clan from which some eighty scholars made their way to the heights of power during the Han dynasty, and was part of a government reform movement headed by the great scholar He Yan 何晏 (d. 249).

Confucianism is a tradition that assumes a continuing intergenerational embodiment of the cultural and familial lineage in which ancestors and their culture live on in their progeny. This being so, we must register the assumption that infants are born as a narrative nested within a narrative, with their tentacles reaching into and drawing upon the resources of family, community, and the mature culture for their growth and sustenance. Mencius's "four inclinations" (*siduan* 四端) as a moral sensorium that describes the native conditions of this relationally constituted infant includes "wisdom" (*zhi* 智) as the native disposition of newborns within their initial matrix of relations that enables them to be deliberative and discriminating (*shifeizhixin* 是非之心) in their response to circumstances.

Rather than taking the allusion here to be referencing some Kantian-like dualism that posits an innate, *apriori* knowledge as a condition of birth, then, we might observe that in education, complex and substantial genealogical factors expressed as native ability as well as the circumstances of one's birth such as family and community have a direct bearing on one's performance. To translate *zhi* 知 here as a quantum of "knowledge" and to embrace a metaphysics of the mind is to vitiate Confucius's insistence that knowledge and wisdom come together or not at all. In addition, such an interpretation would endorse the persistent dualism distinguishing knowledge and truth from wisdom still alive and well in professional philosophy today. After all, in academic philosophy, we still offer our courses in epistemology rather than "sophiology," and any instructor with the temerity to include "wisdom" as a desired "student-learning-outcome" (SLO) might raise an eyebrow.

16.9 孔子曰: "生而知之者上也，學而知之者次也；困而學之，又其次也；困而不學，民斯爲下矣。"
Confucius said, "Those who are precocious and have wisdom (*zhi* 知) from the start are the best among us, while those who come to wisdom through application and study (*xue* 學) are the next. Those who learn in response to difficulties encountered are again the next, while the common people who will not learn even when vexed with difficulties—they are at the bottom of the heap."

Comment: A modest Confucius does not want to preclude the possibility that there are undoubtedly people who, for reasons of birth and family circumstances, have had an easier time with their intellectual and moral growth than he has had. His emphasis as always is on seriousness and assiduous effort in addressing the project of personal cultivation. Confucius does use the expression "common people" (*min* 民) here. At the same time what we learn from the text as a whole is that Confucius teaches everyone, regardless of social or political status or other such discriminations (6.11, 7.7, 15.39). What makes people "common" then, are not the uncritical economic and social prejudices that are all too familiar, but a world in which there is a decided lack of opportunity and resources for some, and sometimes a failure on the part of some people to set the proper priorities in the human experience required for applying themselves in earnest to the project of personal cultivation.

15.8 子曰: "可與言而不與言，失人；不可與言而與之言，失言。知者不失人，亦不失言。"
The Master said, "To fail to speak with people who are worth talking with is to let them go to waste; to speak with people who are not worth the effort is to waste your words. The wise (*zhi* 知) do not let people go to waste, but they do not waste their words either."

Comment: Here again wisdom is defined discursively and relationally as the outcome of effective communication. Wisdom is the product of communicating effectively with people who have the substance to be collaborators in finding the best way forward. This same attitude is expressed in Confucius's seemingly stern recommendation found in 1.8 and 9.25 that one only befriends those who are better than oneself, a recommendation that takes advantage of the freedom to be critical and selective in choosing one's interlocutors.

III.3 Virtuosity (*de* 德)

4.25 子曰: "德不孤，必有鄰。"
The Master said, "Persons who are virtuosic in their conduct (*de* 德) do not dwell alone; they are sure to have neighbors."

Comment: Virtuosity (*de* 德) is frequently glossed paronomastically with its homophone "getting and gaining" (*de* 得). The Latin *virtus* as a Roman virtue means courage, strength, power, virility, character, worth. Understood relationally, one achieves "virtuosity" and thus influence in the world through "gaining" or perhaps better "winning over" the deference of others in one's interactions with them. Role models become such because others defer to and are inspired by what they do. Being thus elevated as an exemplar leads to continuing growth in the sense of being sought out by others as an authoritative source of cultural meaning. Such virtuosic conduct is "gaining" in the sense of producing the magnetism that attracts the company of others and extends the scope of one's influence.

The increase in such virtuosity entails both an act of intending and the attraction of the support necessary to effect what is intended; such persons draw communal support towards their ideals. A particular person is thus understood as a configuration of patterns of deference within a community and world, where the direction and volition of the contextualizing "others" are integrated into one's own field of construal, giving one charisma and influence. One is able to interpret, extend, and display the local culture as it is implicated in oneself. As an artist, as a communal leader, as a teacher, one is able to organize and guide one's natural, social and cultural environments to disclose their shared possibilities for a sustained and productive harmony.

III. THE *ANALECTS* (*LUNYU* 論語): A BASIC CONFUCIAN VOCABULARY

9.14 子欲居九夷。或曰:"陋。如之何?" 子曰:"君子居之,何陋之有?"

The Master wanted to go and live amongst the nine clans of the Eastern Yi barbarians. Someone said to him, "What would you do about their baseness?" The Master replied, "Were exemplary persons (*junzi* 君子) to live among them, what baseness could there be?"

Comment: For Confucius, *yi* 義 or "rightness" in the sense of "doing what is optimally appropriate for all concerned" is certainly the standard he would invoke as the ultimate determining factor in the situation of living among the Eastern Yi or any other people. But for him, the idea of rightness is not some remote, antecedent principle that, by virtue of its ostensive objectivity and universality, can be applied globally to all cases. Instead, it is not only inclusive but also reflexive, having a transformative effect on oneself as well as others. I think Confucius is suggesting that in living among the "barbarians," those persons who would aspire to be exemplary and the barbarians as well, through a process of mutual accommodation and the pursuit of optimal appropriateness in their relations, would become increasingly "significant" (*yi* 義) for each other. The barbarians, being inspired to learn from Confucius and to emulate him as a role model, would certainly be transformed in their conduct, enabling them to rise above any habitual baseness. At the same time, Confucius too would expand in compass to have implicated in him, the now increasingly virtuosic and yet still resolutely unique conduct of the Eastern Yi people. Importantly, Confucius and the Eastern Yi have a collateral relationship that can work together for mutual accommodation.

What is important here is that, far from occasioning the unilateral imposition of a given standard on the Eastern Yi, living among them would be a process of shared growth. Confucius's sense of what is appropriate and meaningful (*yi* 義) would become more capacious by being exposed to and learning from an alternative cultural source. Models certainly inspire those who would emulate them, but they cannot become exemplary models absent such emulation, and such deference effects important changes upon the models as well as upon the people who would defer to them. Indeed, the stature and influence of Confucius himself would appreciate in value to the extent that his teachings are adopted by and adapted to the different ways of thinking and living of a new population.

As a concrete, historical way of understanding this passage, we might think of the extension of Confucian culture to the "Eastern Yi:" that is, the East Asian peoples of Korea, Japan, and Vietnam. Confucian culture in different ways and in different degree has over the centuries been appropriated voluntarily by these alternative cultures, and in the process, has been transformative of not just three, but indeed all four, of these Sinitic cultural traditions. The unique cultures of Korea, Japan, and Vietnam, and the substance of Chinese Confucian culture itself, have all been made different and made richer because of this holographic focus-field process wherein each cultural site has come to be implicated in the others.

13.18 葉公語孔子曰："吾黨有直躬者，其父攘羊，而子證之。"孔子曰："吾黨之直者異於是。父爲子隱，子爲父隱，直在其中矣。"

The Governor of She in conversation with Confucius said, "In our village there is this young man, 'True Goody.' When his father stole a sheep, he reported him to the authorities."

Confucius replied, "Those who are 'true' (*zhi* 直) in my village conduct themselves differently. A father would cover for his son, and a son for his father, and being 'true' lies in doing so."

Comment: While on tour late in his life, Confucius travels from the state of Cai to visit the region of She in the state of Chu. The governor of the local county is aware of Confucius's reputation as a well-known moralist and teacher, and wants to impress Confucius with the high ethical standards of the people under his jurisdiction and moral sway. The governor relates an incident that involves one particularly upright young man in his district known revealingly as "True Goody." The name of this young man speaks volumes. *Zhi* 直 means "true" in the sense of being "true, upright, honest." *Gong* 躬 is a term for one's body that specifically references a deliberate public display of one's personal merits. As Deborah Sommer in her analysis of the various designations for "body" in classical Chinese reports, *gong* 躬 "most often signifies a body in the process of personally and consciously performing an action, usually in a ritual context before an audience, that demonstrates visually the virtuous character of the actor. . . . The conduct of the *gong* 躬 body is ritualized, stylized, nonspontaneous, and guided by traditional mores and social obligations."[1] In this particular context, *gong*

---

[1] Deborah Sommer, "Boundaries of the *Ti* Body." *Asia Major* Third Series, Vol. XXI, Part I (2008), p. 307.

III. THE *ANALECTS* (*LUNYU* 論語): A BASIC CONFUCIAN VOCABULARY

躬 conveys a sense of piousness—a sanctimonious person making a conscious display of his virtues for all to see. It recalls Confucius's antipathy to anything and anyone that is duplicitous.

A first impression on reading this passage might be that it sets up a contrast between an objective principle of justice and a perhaps understandable but illegitimate impulse to protect family members from justice, a contrast between impartiality and partiality. But at the end of the day, the notion of justice in this Confucian tradition is holistic rather than simply principled, and requires a consideration of both higher level norms and particular historical circumstances: "the inseparability of one and many" (*yiduobufen* 一多不分). The question at issue is how to best achieve an inclusive balance between impartiality and partiality.

This same Duke of She also appears in *Analects* 13.16 that records an occasion during the 26th year of King Zhao of Chu (490 BCE) when the Duke asks the itinerant Confucius about governing properly. Confucius replies: 近者悦，遠者來 "If those near at hand are pleased, those at a distance will repair to you." This is a much-cited passage from the *Analects* that suggests the pressing need to continue to cultivate virtuosity in family relations close to home as the ultimate ground of all familial, communal, and political morality. The position that Confucius is advocating here is that a true and trusting relationship among members of a family is the fabric from which the norms of community and society and ultimately polity draw their tensile strength.

Confucius's reaction suggests quite plausibly that calling in the authorities is *not* what any of us would do in the first instance in response to such a lapse on the part of a family member, but is something we might have to do only as a last resort. Initially at least we would almost certainly try other means to remedy the situation. As far as our family is concerned, and very probably our neighbors and friends as well, there are priorities in our response to circumstances that require ingenuity and imagination.① In 1.2, the *Analects* insists that "family reverence" (*xiao* 孝) when properly understood, far from being a source of nepotistic corruption that would

---

① See Henry Rosemont, Jr. and Roger T. Ames, "Family Reverence (*xiao*) as the Source of Consummatory Conduct (*ren*)," *Dao: A Journal of Comparative Philosophy*, Vol. VII, No. 1 (March 2008) for an extended discussion of this and similar cases in which a seeming tension between loyalty to the family and to the state is at issue.

compromise social morality, is itself the ultimate source of "consummate conduct" (*ren* 仁) that is respectful of proper authority:

其爲人也孝弟，而好犯上者，鮮矣；不好犯上，而好作亂者，未之有也。
It is a rare thing for someone who has a sense of family reverence and fraternal responsibility (*xiaoti* 孝弟) to have a taste for defying authority. And it is unheard of for those who have no taste for defying authority to be keen on initiating rebellion.

What sheds light on this case while at the same time making the situation somewhat more complex is the internal demand in Confucian role ethics to make the situation right by achieving optimal appropriateness in the particular situation (*yi* 義). To this end, "remonstrance" (*jian* 諫)—that is, the obligation that a child has to remonstrate with and to rectify the conduct of an erring parent—has a prominent and crucial role in the Confucian literature on family reverence (*xiao* 孝). Importantly, the sense of protest here would be to affirm with solemnity in an inclusive way ("I protest my innocence") rather than directing some exclusive indictment towards a parent. Not "you" but "we." With this in mind, we would have to assume that the expectation of Confucius in his evaluation of this case would be the concerned son in "covering for his father" would necessarily do his best to set the ledger right with any members of the community who have suffered loss on account of the conduct of his wayward parent, and further, would do what is needed to return his father to the straight and narrow.

There has been much in ethical theorizing late and soon that ignores or excludes the consideration of the kind of partiality evidenced in family roles as being relevant to moral conduct. But Confucian role ethics begins from family feeling. It is not an abstract theory that provides principled moral judgments for hard cases we might encounter along the way, nor does it give primacy to developing a deliberate, rational means to achieve some moral end. Rather than appealing to some set of objective principles then, Confucianism offers a way of trying to live consummately in family and community through achieving relational virtuosity (*ren* 仁) in one's conduct that is preemptive of moral transgressions. Such a holistic vision of life within roles and relationships requires the ongoing cultivation of an aesthetic, moral, and religious imagination that will enable one to pursue an optimal appropriateness in all that one does (*yi* 義). It is an attempt to use moral artistry in one's roles and relations to live life most significantly.

There are interesting and amusing parodies on this specific anecdote found in several of the other early canonical texts critical of Confucius's position. They give an account in which the clever young man "True Goody" goes on to petition the magistrate to replace his aged and ailing father in detention, and thus receives much public praise as a model son. After the magistrate allows the son to take his father's place in jail, the young man then again petitions the magistrate, wondering what effect it might have on the moral fiber of the community if the magistrate continues to incarcerate what he himself has praised as a model son. The magistrate on reflection has no choice but to release the son as a clear gesture of the magistrate's own high moral standards.①

On Zhu Xi's reading, the father is in dire straits, taking *rang* 攘 to mean "stealing when in difficult circumstances." Zhu Xi would have it that the father is stealing out of the need to feed his starving children. But on such an interpretation, the putative "crime" of the father evaporates, and the son is just rotten. Perhaps Confucius has a more complex situation in mind. Cf. 2.21.

14.4 子曰："有德者必有言，有言者不必有德。仁者必有勇，勇者不必有仁。"

The Master said, "Virtuosic persons (*de* 德) are certain to have something to say, but someone who merely has something to say is not necessarily a virtuosic person. Consummate persons (*ren* 仁) are certain to have courage (*yong* 勇), but someone who is merely brave is not necessarily a consummate person."

Comment: Although memorable words are indeed a mark of excellence, it takes more than just an occasion or two of offering such words to be virtuosic in personal conduct. Virtuosity is a consistent habitude of optimally appropriate behavior as a way of being in the world. Because *de* 德 is what we accrue through a life of service to others, Confucius in *Analects* 12.21

---

① *Hanfeizi Suoyin* 韓非子索引, ed. Zhou Zhongling 周鍾靈, Shi Xiaoshi 施孝適, and Xu Weixian 許惟賢, Beijing: Zhonghua Shuju, 1982, 49.9.2; *Lüshichunqiu* 呂氏春秋, ed. Xu Weiyu 許維遹, Beijing: Wenxue Guji Kanxingshe, 1955, p. 449; *Huainanzi Zhuzi Suoyin* 淮南子逐字索引, trans. D.C. Lau, Hong Kong: The Commercial Press, 1992, 13/125/14.

defines the accumulating of such virtuosity (*chongde* 崇德) explicitly in terms of 先事後得，非崇德與 "getting only after having given of oneself—is this not the accumulating of virtuosity?" The getting comes in the giving. In this passage, Confucius is playing on the paronomastic definition of "virtuosity" (*de* 德) with its homophone, "getting and gaining" (*de* 得).

Again, courage is certainly a mark of consummate conduct, but it takes more than a few instances of bravery to become consummate as a person. The *Analects* makes much of the fact that while being consummate in one's actions is as easy as doing it (4.6, 7.30, 12.1), the difficulty lies in sustaining it as consistent pattern in all that one does (5.8, 5.19, 6.7, 6.22, 8.7). Consummate persons are consummate in their conduct in order to be consummate in their conduct.

A sustained theme throughout the Confucian canons is the distinction between merely doing those things that occasion public approbation, and acting out of a sustained habit of moral conduct. Of course the question is whether one can actually habituate conduct without beginning from emulating particular instances of actions approved by others.

15.27 子曰："巧言亂德。小不忍，則亂大謀。"

The Master said, "Clever words confound virtuosity (*de* 德). And a lack of forbearance in minor details will undo the greatest of plans."

Comment: The parallel structure of the two phrases suggests that something seemingly incidental can undo something really important—virtuosity in conduct as well as great plans. And that is perhaps why a repeated refrain throughout these passages is the exhortation to be vigilant in what one says. The frequent coupling of language and action as being complementary "aspects" of experience underscores the inseparability in conduct of saying and doing. Stated another way, saying is doing, and as with the relationship between what is said and what can be accomplished, the former is anything but incidental to the latter.

14.33 子曰："驥不稱其力，稱其德也。"

The Master said, "A fine steed is praised for its quality as a horse (*de* 德) rather than for its strength."

Comment: Horses like persons are to be measured on demonstrated excellence in what they do in their specific roles rather than by the quantum of force they are able to exert in different situations. While strength might be admirable, it is what it is used to accomplish that transforms it into virtuosity.

9.18 子曰：＂吾未見好德如好色者也。＂
The Master said, "I have yet to meet the person who is fonder of demonstrated virtuosity (*de* 德) than of physical beauty."

Comment: Remembering the paronomastic relationship between *de* 德 as "virtuosity" and *de* 得 as "getting and gaining," in the ranking of Confucian priorities, the cultivation of those qualities of conduct that draw others to one's vision of the moral life is to be esteemed over the mere allure of physical beauty. An important consideration here is that while virtuosity is a higher-level aesthetic than physical beauty, it in itself has its own charisma and powers of attraction.

6.29 子曰：＂中庸之爲德也，其至矣乎！民鮮久矣。＂
The Master said, "The virtuosity (*de* 德) required to bring the familiar affairs of the day into proper focus is of the highest order. That it is rare among the common people is an old story."[①]

Comment: This is the single occurrence of the term "focusing the familiar" or "hitting the mark in the every day" (*zhongyong* 中庸) in the Confucian literature prior to the compilation of the canonical text that takes this term as its title. Again, the *Zhongyong*, translated herein as *Focusing the Familiar*, is a celebration of the capacity of humankind to confront and overturn this old story by taking responsibility themselves as a profound source of meaning to become co-creator with the cosmos.

15.4 子曰：＂由！知德者鮮矣。＂
The Master said, "Zilu, those who realize (*zhi* 知) virtuosity (*de* 德) in their conduct are rare indeed."

Comment: Confucius is consistent throughout the *Analects* in his reluctance to use the terms such as "virtuosity" (*de* 德) as the highest quality of

---

① Compare *Focusing the Familiar* 3.

exemplary conduct to describe any particular persons, historical or otherwise. Such a reticence suggests that these qualitative terms best suit his purposes as never-to-be-realized exhortative ideals to which we must aspire without ever expecting to achieve them. At the same time and of note, in *Focusing the Familiar* and other canonical texts, it is precisely these same terms that are readily ascribed to the conduct of Confucius himself.

III.4 Doing Your Utmost (*zhong* 忠) and Making Good on Your Word (*xin* 信)

2.22 子曰："人而無信，不知其可也。大車無輗，小車無軏，其何以行之哉？"

The Master said, "I am not sure that anyone lacking credibility (*xin* 信) is viable as a person. If a large carriage is without the linchpin for its yoke, or a small carriage is without its cross-bar, how can they go anywhere?"

Comment: Morality in Confucian philosophy, simply put, is conduct that conduces to growth in relations. Human "becomings" come together or not at all. If there is no connecting linchpin, there is no carriage; if there is just one person, there are no persons. Thus, making good on one's word is the modality of conduct that gives one the credibility as a person (*xin* 信) that other people can trust. I have translated it as "making good on your word" rather than as simply "trust" to emphasize the fact that it must be an accomplished action rather than simply a matter of good intentions. It is only in finding the proper fit between word and deed that persons can function effectively in family and society. As with the image of the carriage, such credibility serves as the linchpin necessary to make relationships work and thus carry us along the proper way.

4.22 子曰："古者言之不出，恥躬之不逮也。"

The Master said, "The ancients were loath to speak because they would be ashamed if they themselves did not live up to what they said."

14.20 子曰："其言之不怍，則爲之也難。"

The Master said, "When people hold forth with no sense of shame, it will be hard indeed for them to live up to their word."

5.10 宰予晝寢。子曰："朽木不可雕也，糞土之墻不可杇也；於予與何誅？"子曰："始吾於人也，聽其言而信其行；今吾於人也，聽其言而觀其行。於予與改是。"
Zaiwo was still sleeping in the middle of the day. The Master said, "You cannot carve rotten wood, and you cannot trowel over a wall of manure. As for Zaiwo, what is the point of upbraiding him?"
The Master said further, "There was a time in my dealings with others when on hearing what they had to say, I assumed they would live up to their word (*xin* 信). Nowadays in such dealings, on hearing what they have to say, I then watch what they do. It is Zaiwo that has taught me as much."

Comment: Zaiwo was devoted to the Master, yet on numerous occasions, Confucius criticizes him roundly for the lethargy in his thinking and the kind of behavior that reflects it, making his name Zaiwo emblematic of Confucius's very worst student. In this passage, we have an example of Confucius's droll humor. In reference to his own best attempts to educate Zaiwo, he says "you cannot carve rotten wood, and you cannot trowel over a wall of manure." Confucius offers the negative example of Zaiwo, a marginal student and also a morally "perverse" person (*buren* 不仁 in 17.21) who with his many deficiencies, seems beyond all remedy. Perhaps the most serious personal fault that makes Zaiwo hopeless is his failing to live up to his word. Relatedly, the name of Zaiwo is elsewhere included in a list of students described as "eloquent" (11.3), alluding perhaps to Confucius's aversion to speakers who are deemed "glib." For Confucius, glibness reflects a lack of sincerity in what one says, and eventuates in a crippling gap between word and deed.

1.13 有子曰："信近於義，言可復也。恭近於禮，遠恥辱也。因不失其親，亦可宗也。"
Master You said: "When making good on your word (*xin* 信) is done in tandem with optimal appropriateness in your conduct (*yi* 義), your words will bear repeating. When showing deference is done in tandem with living with ritual propriety (*li* 禮), disgrace and insult will be kept at bay. To accord with those who have good relations with their kinfolk is also a reliable course to follow."

Comment: Master You along with Master Zeng were almost always referred to with the honorific "Master" (*zi* 子) by Confucius's inner circle.

And as in this passage, Master You has the status of making his own always important statements rather than just asking questions. In the *Mencius* 3A4, Master You is given the honor of being described as resembling Confucius to the extent that three of the most prominent students 子夏、子張、子游以有若似聖人，欲以所事孔子事之 "Zixia, Zizhang, and Ziyou all wanted to serve Master You in the same way as they served Confucius." High praise indeed. Again, in the *Record of Rituals* 3.70/18/8 Ziyou says "Amazing! Master You in what he says resembles the Master." 子游曰：甚哉。有子之言似夫子也。

The positive value of making good on one's word, deferring to others, and according with one's neighbors is dependent upon context. A thief might make good on his word or defer to his partners in crime, but when the circumstances served are less than inclusive of everyone's interests, such behavior does not rise to the level of proper conduct. Again, deference is given context by locating it as a value within the patterns of ritual propriety. In fact, the three proper modes of conduct aspired to here—trustworthiness, deference, and social accord—can only be achieved within webs of relations in which the interests of all those affected are properly respected. When such interests are served—living with optimal appropriateness, observing the demands of ritual propriety, and according with proper kinship relations, they bring tensile strength to the social fabric of family and community.

7.25 子以四教：文、行、忠、信。

The Master taught under four rubrics: culture (*wen* 文), proper conduct (*xing* 行), doing one's utmost (*zhong* 忠), and making good on one's word (*xin* 信).

Comment: Does the order of these four rubrics tell us anything? Perhaps "culture" that might be ambiguously understood in the language of arts or skills must be qualified by the kind of authentication in practice that would require the other behaviors. It is for this reason the modern Chinese term for "culture" is the elevating and transformative process of "enculturation" and "becoming cultured" (*wenhua* 文化). It is because modalities of practice such as "making good on one's word" (*xin* 信) and "doing one's utmost" (*zhong* 忠) are coterminous and mutually entailing that we find them repeatedly paired in the text.

Confucian philosophy offers a holistic vision of the moral life that begins from the primacy of practice and takes theorizing as an intrinsic,

III. THE *ANALECTS* (*LUNYU* 論語):
A BASIC CONFUCIAN VOCABULARY

nonanalytic aspect of practical activity. Erstwhile theoretical tools arise for philosophers in this tradition *in medias res* from the need to make our human practices more intelligent and productive within the context of the practices themselves. Such a way of thinking about the moral life stands in contrast to rule-based morality by attempting to give full measure to the indeterminacy and the open-ended transitivity that attends what are always unique activities. In serving as a holistic alternative to such abstract theorizing, it trades off a degree of clarity and rigor achieved at the unacceptable expense of simplifying circumstances that are always more complex. Another way in which Confucian role ethics departs from ethical theory is that, far from being simply expository, it relies on and is in important measure dependent upon the existentially derived insights of persons themselves in their various activities.

15.6 子張問行。子曰：＂言忠信，行篤敬，雖蠻貊之邦，行矣。言不忠信，行不篤敬，雖州里，行乎哉？立則見其參於前也，在輿則見其倚於衡也，夫然後行。＂子張書諸紳。

Zizhang asked about proper conduct. The Master replied, "It is to do your utmost (*zhong* 忠) and make good on your word (*xin* 信), and to be earnest and respectful in your conduct. Even if you are living in the barbarian territories of the Man or Mo tribes, your conduct will be as it should be. But if you fail to maintain this standard, even if you have never left your own neighborhood, how could your conduct be appropriate? Your conduct will only be as it should be when in standing, you see right in front of you the phrase: 'do your utmost and make good on your word, and be earnest and respectful in your conduct,' and when riding in your carriage, you see this same phrase propped up against the stanchion."

Zizhang wrote the characters down on his sash.

Comment: The profile we have of Zizhang is that he seems to be rash without taking in a situation in its entirety (2.18), caring more for ingratiating appearances than for substance. He is sometimes criticized by other prominent protégés such as Master Zeng and Ziyou (19.15, 19.16), and Confucius himself describes Zizhang as someone who will not find access to the inner sanctum (11.20). In any case, Confucius finds it necessary to repeat the same counsel to Zizhang about doing his utmost and making good on his word in other passages in the text (12.6, 12.10, 12.14). The fact that Zizhang so obviously takes to writing the characters down on his sash might reflect his own sense that Confucius is becoming impatient with him on this particular topic.

Here again we find both "saying" and "doing" categorized as a continuous practice. There is no formula for moral conduct, with people always doing different things in always unique situations, but the modalities that inform such conduct remain a constant.

1.8 子曰: "君子不重則不威; 學則不固。主忠信。無友不如己者。過則勿憚改。"

The Master said: "Exemplary persons lacking in gravity would have no dignity, yet in their studies they remain flexible. Take doing your utmost (*zhong* 忠) and making good on your word (*xin* 信) as your mainstay. Do not have as a friend anyone who is not as good as you are. And where you have erred, do not hesitate to mend your ways."

Comment: In the *Analects* and the *Mencius* 5B1 as well, Confucius is repeatedly celebrated for his flexibility in responding differently to different situations (4.10, 9.4, 15.16, 18.8). The point being made here is that the kind of gravity and dignity necessary to be exemplary as a person does not preclude flexibility in what is done. Even though Confucius is open and accommodating in what he takes to be the best response, he is at the same time resolute in his commitment to doing his utmost and living up to his word.

In the Confucian process cosmology that eschews any strong sense of teleology or idealism, the focus is on making the most of the "very now." As a personal regimen, this cosmology locates conduct relationally, and focuses on shaping a habitual disposition that functions most effectively in responding to what are always changing circumstances. Such flexibility is required from persons who, being keenly aware of the transactional and associated nature of the human experience, acknowledge their own imbricated identities as variable and yet resolute foci within the contextualizing fields of their environing others. Such focus-field agents are irreducibly transactional, consciously shaping and being shaped in the vital patterns of their relations as they unfold.

At the end of the day, such agency can only be negotiated through established habits of commitment and deference. That is, while such agency is necessarily passive in the archaic sense of invariably "suffering" the actions of others, it must at the same time find the right balance in also being self-conscious, animated, purposeful, and projective. Simply put, morally responsible lives can only be lived through flexible responsiveness in the give and take of those activities that in aggregate come to define our narrative identities. On the important theme of friendship achieved through the personal growth made possible by activating differences, see Hall and Ames, *Thinking from the Han* section 10 and Ames, *Confucian Role Ethics*, pp. 114-121. This passage is repeated in 9.25.

1.4 曾子曰："吾日三省吾身：爲人謀而不忠乎？與朋友交而不信乎？傳不習乎？"

Master Zeng said: "Daily I repeatedly examine my own person: In my undertakings on behalf of others have I failed to do my utmost (*zhong* 忠)? In my interactions with colleagues and friends have I failed to make good on my word (*xin* 信)? In the instruction I have received have I failed to carry it into practice?"

Comment: Master Zeng is the paragon of "family reverence" (*xiao* 孝) in the tradition, and one of Confucius's most important students credited with continuing his teachings after his death. In the text Master Zeng comes across as a serious proponent of what he takes as the truly arduous task of aspiring to consummate conduct (*ren* 仁), described by him as carrying a heavy burden on a long road that comes to an end only with one's death (8.7). And the report of Master Zeng's last moments before his own death describes a person relieved that he can depart this world having kept his body free of desecration, the first announced precept in the code of "family reverence" (*xiao* 孝). See also footnote 1, page 123, on Master Zeng.

In this passage, Master Zeng is recommending a regimen of daily reflection in which he examines "his own person." As we should anticipate in this Confucian tradition, his person is located in the activities he undertakes on behalf of others and in the interactions he has with colleagues and friends. And his introspection, far from a turning inwards, requires an assessment of his own resolution in growing meaning in these constitutive relations. Moral responsibility for Master Zeng is a matter of his unwavering commitment to practicing what he has learned to the extent that, in the fullness of time, such responsive practices become the habitude of who he is.

12.10 子張問崇德、辨惑。子曰:"主忠信、徙義,崇德也。愛之欲其生,惡之欲其死。既欲其生,又欲其死,是惑也。'誠不以富,亦祇以異。'"

Zizhang inquired about accumulating virtuosity (*de* 德) and resolving perplexity.

The Master replied, "To take doing your utmost (*zhong* 忠) and making good on your word (*xin* 信) as your mainstay, and to seek out what is optimally appropriate in your roles and relations (*yi* 義), is to accumulate virtuosity. In loving someone you want them to live; in hating someone you want them to die. To simultaneously want a person to live and to die is to be of two minds. 'If you are not doing it to gain in fortune, you must be doing it just for the sake of difference.'"

Comment: Commentators have struggled with this passage, and have suggested that the quote from the *Book of Songs* is likely out of place here. But perhaps the key lies in the person of the interlocutor, Zizhang. In the question, Zizhang sets the contrast between accumulating virtue and overcoming the uncertainty of being of two minds. And Confucius's answer seems to be that the former resolves the latter.

In his teacher-student relationship, Confucius has found it necessary to repeat the same counsel to Zizhang. In his regimen of personal cultivation, Zizhang must do his utmost and make good on his word (12.6, 12.14, 15.6). Such repetition suggests that Zizhang is lacking in this kind of commitment. In this passage, Confucius adds to this counsel the need for Zizhang to find optimal appropriateness in his conduct (*yi* 義) as being integral to achieving real virtuosity.

For Confucius, virtuosity is what we accrue through a life of service to others. In 12.21, Confucius defines the accumulating of such virtuosity (*chongde* 崇德) explicitly as 先事後得,非崇德與 "getting only after having given of oneself—is this not the accumulating of virtuosity?" The getting comes in the giving. A contrast is set between conduct that has been fully habituated on the one hand, and occasional instances of admirable behavior on the other (14.4). With such accumulated virtuosity, one's actions are consistently and without deviation deployed in the optimizing of relationships. As such, it obviates any indecision that might arise from being unsure of what to do. The passage from the *Songs* 188 tells the story of a forsaken wife who says to her husband that in taking up with a new mate, he gains not in fortune, but only in difference. While a decent husband would have the constancy that comes with virtuosity described herein, the marriage has become the victim of a wayward husband who is under the sway of mere difference rather than improvement. With such a husband who is inclined to be of two minds, there is little guarantee for the second wife as well.

III.5 Putting Oneself in the Other's Place Through Dramatic Rehearsal (*shu* 恕)

4.15 子曰:"參乎！吾道一以貫之。"曾子曰:"唯。"子出，門人問曰:"何謂也？"曾子曰:"夫子之道，忠恕而已矣。"

The Master said, "Zeng, my friend! My way (*dao* 道) is bound together with one continuous thread."

Master Zeng replied, "It is as you say."

When the Master had left, the other protégés asked, "What does he mean in saying this?"

Master Zeng replied, "The way of the Master is simply putting oneself in the other's place (*shu* 恕), and then doing one's utmost (*zhong* 忠), nothing more."

Comment: D.C. Lau 劉殿爵 makes the compelling argument that *zhong* 忠 and *shu* 恕 can be fairly described as "one" continuous thread because they are in fact two aspects integral to the same decision-making process. *Shu* 恕 is the imaginative reflection through a process of scenario rehearsals whereby one tries to determine the best thing to do, and *zhong* 忠 is then the commitment to doing one's best in accomplishing the outcome of such a determination.[①]

The need for *shu* 恕 begins from moral perplexity and requires the creative search for the most appropriate response by rehearsing alternatives. It then culminates in investing the assiduous effort necessary to realize what is determined to be the best course of action. The important question is what does "putting oneself in the other's place" mean in the Confucian tradition? If the underlying assumption is the inseparability of knowing and doing, there is a warrant for understanding *shu* 恕 as not only arriving at a determination of the most felicitous response to a particular situation,

---

[①] See Confucius, *The Analects* (*Lunyu*), trans. D.C. Lau, Hong Kong: The Chinese University Press, 2nd edition, 1983, pp. xv-xvi.

but also acting on one's best judgment. It would require a "dramatic rehearsal" of alternative possibilities and then doing one's utmost to implement the insights derived from this process.

It is not surprising that *shu* 恕 in the classical texts and in the *Shuowen* lexicon is frequently associated with "consummate conduct" (*ren* 仁) as the desired outcome of this method of deliberation: that is, *shu* 恕 is dramatic rehearsal of alternatives as a method for achieving consummate conduct in one's roles and relations. Just as *shu* 恕 is the method of reflectively coordinating one's own conduct with the behavior of others to optimum effect, *ren* 仁 is the product of such analogical deliberation and growth. *Ren* 仁 is making the most of the commonalities, and in particular the differences, that one has with others in achieving a focal personal identity. Importantly, *shu* 恕 as a method of deliberation and *ren* 仁 as consummate conduct are at once both means and ends. One deliberates in order to be deliberate, and one aspires to act consummately in order to be consummate.

Shu 恕 is the moral application of correlative or analogical thinking. The centrality given to *shu* 恕 in the *Analects* alerts us to the unparalleled importance that imagination plays in correlating one's conduct with others and in refining our moral judgment through deliberation. Moral imagination is not invoked as supplemental or subsidiary or remedial. Indeed, it is necessary for the continuous education and refinement of our empathetic capacity to understand and respond effectively to the interests of others. As in any aesthetic judgment, imagination is the motive effort to read the specific details and correlate them within the big picture of what is occurring. In so doing, one expands the context of moral consideration and enhances the quality of one's response.

Shu 恕 is a fundamentally aesthetic disposition initially shaped within family bonds where one's "person" emerges in the process of striving to optimize the concrete roles and relations one lives. *Shu* 恕 is this particular grandson responding to this grandmother, taking her both as an object of his deference and, with her response to his regard, as a resource for his own personal growth. Both grandson and grandmother grow in the appreciation of each other. In the fullness of time, *shu* 恕 is extended as a quality of responsiveness in shaping and deepening relations outside of the home. "Putting oneself in the other's place" (*shu* 恕) is thus an omnipresent and indispensable disposition for living life deliberately and responsively. It requires a keen memory that recalls analogous situations, a penetrating intelligence that is able to make the most of felicitous correlations, and a creative imagination that can provide a serial rehearsal of possible scenarios in always particular situations in anticipation of their consequences.

Shu 恕 contrasts sharply with more abstract and calculative analytic or theoretical strategies for determining moral conduct. Understood as "putting oneself in the other's place," it is the most fundamental gesture of a concrete, contextualizing moral disposition. It entails a recognition of the importance of "deference" both in the sense of giving full consideration to the interests of others, and in the sense of deferring action until we can overcome uncertainty through sound deliberation in our moral inquiry. *Shu* 恕 is a contextualized doubt in search of a guiding idea to stabilize and then set in motion one's best response.

15.24 子貢問曰："有一言而可以終身行之者乎？" 子曰："其恕乎！己所不欲，勿施於人。"

Zigong asked, "Is there one expression that can be acted upon until the end of one's days?"

The Master replied, "It is probably *shu* 恕: do not impose on others what you yourself do not want."

Comment: According to the *Analects*, effective communication is so fundamental in the flourishing of our communal lives that we are exhorted by Zigong, perhaps the most eloquent of Confucius's students, to realize the high stakes at issue in the choice of each and every word. In another context, Zigong allows that a word well-chosen elevates one in the eyes of others, while an inopportune word can lead to their contempt:

Analects 19.25: 君子一言以爲知，一言以爲不知，言不可不慎也。
Exemplary persons must be ever so careful about what they say. On the strength of a single word others can deem them either wise (*zhi* 知) or foolish.[1]

In this passage, Zigong is prompted to ask if there is a single word that can be practiced with profit until the end of one's days. And Confucius replies emphatically that it must be this word "putting oneself in the place of others" (*shu* 恕), or more broadly, "deference." For Confucius, this one

---

[1] See also 1.6, 1.14, and 2.18.

protean word captures in summary everything he has been trying to convey to his students about the immediate correlation between exercising an educated moral imagination and the possibility of optimizing their relations with others.

There is a further point with regard to deference that can be inferred from the *Analects*, where *shu* 恕, "putting oneself in the other's place," in this passage is given a second, alternative definition. *Shu* 恕 is defined negatively here as "do not impose on others what you yourself do not want." In using the reflective strategy of dramatic rehearsal as the basis for the decision-making process in determining what is best to do, an obvious principle of exclusion is to avoid doing to others what we ourselves do not like. In deliberating on the best response, doing to someone else what we do not want done to us would at the very least contaminate our own motivation. Indeed, what is required in "putting oneself in the other's place" is a keen awareness that they are indeed in a different place, and that we must respect this. A good starting point then, would be to discount those actions that we find undesirable. At the same time, we must recognize that beyond this beginning, there is a world of contingencies that requires thoughtful and imaginative exploration.

This "negative" version of the Golden Rule recommends itself because it does not begin from the assumption that one has access to some objective and universal standard that can serve as warrant for "doing unto others as you would have them do to you." Indeed, to begin from the assumption that there is such a universal standard, to further presume one has ownership of it, and that on that basis, to take it for granted one knows what is the right thing to do to someone else, is at the very least condescending if not disrespectful. Instead, in assuming this negative version of the rule, one remains open and provisional in one's response, allowing that that deliberation on how to best grow a relationship can only be pursued through careful consideration of the needs of this specific person within the possibilities of these specific circumstances.

5.12 子貢曰："我不欲人之加諸我也，吾亦欲無加諸人。" 子曰："賜也，非爾所及也。"

Zigong said, "I do not want others to impose on me, nor do I want to impose on others."

Confucius replied, "Zigong, this is quite beyond your reach."

III. THE *ANALECTS* (*LUNYU* 論語): A BASIC CONFUCIAN VOCABULARY

Comment: This passage is important in highlighting the impositional implications of the positive version of the Golden Rule: "Do unto others as you would have them do unto you." The presumption that persons can, on the basis of what they themselves want, make a determination as to what to do to others amounts to such persons imposing on each other. Avoiding such an imposition on other people requires a keen interest in and understanding of their specific needs. We see elsewhere that Confucius's twofold criticism of the well-bred and eloquent Zigong is that he often falls short of living up to his word. He is judgmental, and insufficiently concerned about the well-being of his fellows. How can a person with such self-absorbed conduct avoid imposing on others?

6.30 子貢曰:"如有博施於民而能濟眾,何如? 可謂仁乎?" 子曰:"何事於仁! 必也聖乎! 堯、舜其猶病諸! 夫仁者,己欲立而立人,己欲達而達人。能近取譬,可謂仁之方也已。"

Zigong said, "What about someone who is broadly generous with the common people and is able to help the multitude—is this who we could call a consummate person (*ren* 仁)?"

The Master replied, "Why stop at consummate person? Such a person is certainly a sage (*sheng* 聖). Even a Yao or a Shun would find such a task daunting. Consummate persons establish others in seeking to establish themselves and promote others in seeking to get there themselves. Being able to correlate one's conduct with those near at hand can be said to be the method of becoming consummate as a person."

Comment: The *shu* 恕 method of deference and deliberation in search of consummate conduct (*ren* 仁) is prompted by moral uncertainty—the need to find the best way to respond in a particular situation. It requires an imaginative rehearsal of the alternative possibilities, and an assessment of their probable outcomes. Having determined the most productive response, it requires one act earnestly upon this judgment. The response is shaped through a process of analogical thinking, taking the present situation and associating it with other remembered or imagined scenarios. In this important passage, we see this same *shu* 恕 method of deliberation only in a different language: "Correlating one's conduct with those near at hand can be said to be the way of becoming consummate in one's conduct."

In putting oneself in the other's place (*shu* 恕), the role of deliberation and the cognitive understanding that follows from it is very important, but there is more. Since *shu* 恕 requires holistic responsiveness, we do well to avoid overly rationalizing the process. Beyond the cognitive there is perhaps an even more central role for an affective inquiry—an epistemology of feeling—that requires a weighing of the circumstances with empathy and concern. Just as critical skepticism can become a matter of intelligent habit, so too empathetic responsiveness to others can result in a sedimented, spontaneous pattern of compassionate concern. In fact, the evolution of a *shu* 恕 habitude lies in its potential to grow from what is at first a more deliberative exercise to become a kind of extemporaneous moral artistry in one's interpersonal activities. As Ni Peimin argues, such refinement in one's dispositions becomes morally empowering by expanding one's range of options for intervention beyond conventional expectations:

> Once a person becomes a master artist, he or she would be able to use discretion and respond appropriately even when the situation demands deviation from well-established protocols (cf. 9.30).[1]

When in 4.15 Confucius insists that 吾道一以貫之 "my way is bound together by one continuous thread" and again in 15.24 that 有一言而可以終身行之 "there is one expression that can be acted upon until the end of one's days," we can glean a sense of the importance he invests in the moral method of "putting oneself in the other's place" (*shu* 恕). It is not surprising then that there are several alternative statements of this same strategy for becoming consummate in one's conduct. For example, again in 12.1: 克己復禮爲仁 "Persons through self-discipline and achieving propriety in their roles and relations become consummate in their conduct." The method of becoming consummate in one's conduct is the deference required to achieve propriety and full participation in those personal relations near at hand.

Setting the Family Right (*qijia* 齊家)

From its origins in the prehistoric past, an ever-evolving Chinese culture has been unique among the world's civilizations, both in terms of its

---

[1] Ni, *Understanding the Analects of Confucius*, p. 67.

III. THE *ANALECTS* (*LUNYU* 論語): A BASIC CONFUCIAN VOCABULARY

unbroken continuity, and in the rich and varied institutional, material, and conceptual artifacts its peoples have produced. Upon entering into China's past, certain major themes emerge as they are repeatedly expressed in different facets of Chinese life. One of these themes is the centrality of the family that has thoroughly permeated the socio-political, economic, metaphysical, moral, and religious dimensions of Chinese history since at least the early Neolithic period. A fair argument can be made that all relationships within a Chinese world—social, political, and indeed cosmic relations—are conceived of as familial. Physical evidence of ancestral sacrifices has been found in archaeological remains from as early as the fifth millennium BCE. It should therefore come as no surprise that family reverence (*xiao* 孝) was one of the most basic and defining values of the Chinese people, especially the early Confucians. Indeed, one may even go so far as to say that for them, filial reverence was a *necessary* condition for developing any of the other human qualities of excellence. In the Confucian tradition, human morality and the personal realization it inspires is grounded in the cultivation of family feeling.

From earliest times then, "family reverence" (*xiao* 孝) has served the Confucian tradition as its prime moral imperative. I would argue that Confucian role ethics not only takes the cluster of terms surrounding "family reverence" (*xiao* 孝) as the prime moral imperative that has made family feeling the explanation of its minimalist morality, but also continues today as the root and the substance of the living Confucian social, political, and global order.

In reflecting on Confucian philosophy as offering an alternative concept of the political, we must begin from and give full weight to the perceived isomorphism that obtains among the familial, political, and global orders as they are rooted in and emerge from a regimen of cultivation among relationally-constituted persons. This organic symbiosis is described in the *Mencius* as a concept of the political in which the state and the world are simulacra of the family in serving as the expanding and reflexive locus of personal cultivation:

Mencius 4A5: 人有恒言，皆曰"天下國家"。天下之本在國，國之本在家，家之本在身。
There is a popular maxim heard among the people who all say: "The world, the state, the family." The world is rooted in the state, the state in the family, and the family in one's own person.

Morality as it is cultivated through the commitment to "consummate conduct in one's roles and relations" (ren 仁) is thus an extension and expression of immediate family feeling. In the *Analects* we read:

Analects 1.2: 君子務本，本立而道生。孝弟也者，其爲仁之本與。
Exemplary persons concentrate their efforts on the root, for the root having been properly set, the vision of the moral life will grow therefrom. As for family reverence and fraternal deference, they are I suspect, the root of consummate conduct (ren 仁).

In this Confucian process of world-making, persons are imbricated as unique, relationally-constituted perspectives rooted within an ecology of family, polity, and cosmos. Through dedication to the cultivation of deliberate growth in their own relations, every person has the capacity for bringing resolution and more distinctive, meaningful focus to the roles and relations that constitute them. At the center of this personal project, the meaning of the family is implicated in and dependent upon the productive cultivation of each of its members. Then by radial extension, the meaning of the community, polity, and the entire cosmos is in turn implicated in and ultimately derived from the cultivation of each person as a family member.

To clarify this organic, ecological root metaphor, while allowing that all levels of order are ultimately derived from personal cultivation, we must avoid the inveterate habit of separating root as cause from the order as effect. Rather, root and canopy grow together symbiotically, with the tree spreading its roots outward beneath the earth and simultaneously stretching its branches upward towards the sky. While the root is certainly growing the tree, the tree is also in turn growing its roots. The root and its flourishing canopy are two aspects of an interactive and organic whole that grow together symbiotically, or not at all. Importantly, while existential narratives themselves are certainly rooted in the lived lives of particular persons in particular families, they are also the unbounded and interpenetrating stories that in sum constitute their natural, social, and cultural ecologies. The isomorphism means that order at every level is inflected symbiotically in every other, where personal cultivation expands the meaning of the cosmos, and a more meaningful cosmos in turn provides an important resource for personal cultivation.

III. THE *ANALECTS* (*LUNYU* 論語): A BASIC CONFUCIAN VOCABULARY

The ecological language often used to characterize Confucian social, political and cosmic order is itself grounded in the institution of family. The term "ecology" was coined by the German zoologist, Ernst Haeckel, in 1866 to describe the "economies" of living forms. The etymology of "ecology" is *eco* from the Gk. *oikos* meaning "household, habitat," and *logia* meaning "the study of." More generally, ecology means our best efforts to understand the vital, interdependent relations that obtain among organisms within their environments. Given the primacy of relationality in this alternative, eventful way of thinking about ostensive "things," I and my several collaborators have over time introduced a holographic, "focus-field" language as a way of giving expression to such an "eventful" world as well as of distinguishing it clearly from our default ontological "thing" and "part-whole" way of thinking.

The etymology of "focus" is L. *focus* meaning "hearth, fireplace" (figuratively, "home, family") as the area or point of convergence that can be resolved into a clear image and thus be seen distinctly. Such a focus thus made "familiar" is the nucleus around which life in the home has traditionally taken place. And "field" is another term that like focus, has a domestic, agrarian reference as the land that is farmed and grazed, and that supplies the family with the provisions to be prepared at the fireplace. From this core idea of hearth and home, focus has come to mean the "locus of divergence and convergence" of persons as organisms within a "field" environment—that is, the distinctive, continuing identity of a particular family that emerges from what members carry off from the home, and what they are able to bring back to it.

In applying this ecological way of thinking, we have to be self-consciously aware of our own ontologically-informed commonsense that defaults to construing the furniture of the world as self-sufficient "things" rather than as interpenetrating events. A limitation of our own application of this holographic, focus-field language then is that it seems insufficiently dynamic to capture the process of ceaseless change and growth that attends the eventful lives of organisms always evolving and transforming in their environments. And again, in making use of the organic metaphor, we have to absolve it of its heavily freighted teleological assumptions as it is rooted in classical Greek ontology. On the other hand, this holographic focus-field language is particularly felicitous in explaining Confucian values where family is the governing cultural metaphor, and the notion of "family reverence" (*xiao* 孝) is the prime moral imperative. These terms that constitute the language of ecology become normative in taking the discussion back to an achieved resolution and propriety in the flourishing of family roles and relations.

Within Confucian China, family has been and continues to be the pervasive metaphor for social, political, and cosmic order. In all aspects of life such as communal bonds, politics, one's religiousness, it is the family rather than the individual that constitutes the lowest denominator. Persons have traditionally lived within the interstices of the changing associations and hierarchical patterns of deference that define family and lineage, and the quality of their personal realization is a function of the deepening significance of these same relationships. Familial relatedness is fundamental in understanding the Confucian sense of person and world. The bureaucratic structure, the state, and even the cosmos itself are radial extensions of familial order.

The family is the primary model of order because it functions to optimize the possibilities of human relationships. Confucianism begins from the profound insight that persons if anywhere are most inclined to dedicate themselves to the institution of family utterly and without remainder. If in fact the family provides a structure that enables the community to get the most out of its constituent members, then one does best to construe the world broadly as an extended family. It is proper family relationships that are the basis of proper government, and proper government is isomorphic with the natural order. It is for this reason that one must return to the familial source of order when the affairs of government go awry.

Confucius himself is making an astute observation when he asserts that within this cultural tradition, since the family is the ultimate source of governance, the proper functioning of the institution of family is integral to the production of the socio-political order of the state:

Analects 2.21: 或謂孔子曰:"子奚不爲政?" 子曰:"《書》云:'孝乎惟孝, 友于兄弟, 施於有政.' 是亦爲政, 奚其爲爲政?"
Someone asked Confucius, "Why are you not employed in government?" The Master replied, "The *Book of Documents* says: 'It all lies in family reverence (*xiao* 孝). Being filial to your parents and finding fraternity with your brothers is in fact carrying out the work of governing.' In doing these things I am participating in governing. Why must I be employed in government?"

III. THE *ANALECTS* (*LUNYU* 論語):
A BASIC CONFUCIAN VOCABULARY

More recently, but in the same vein, the distinguished late-Qing scholar Yan Fu 嚴復 (1854-1921) who translated and introduced Western liberalism and evolutionary theory into the Chinese academy through the works of Adam Smith, John Stuart Mill, T.H. Huxley, Herbert Spencer and others, once remarked that if we ask after the source of social and political order in imperial China over the past two millennia, thirty percent can be attributed to emperor, and seventy percent to family lineage.① Yan Fu is remarking here on the fact that almost all aspects of the human experience in pre-Republican China—economic, political, ethical, religious, and so on—took place within the life of distinctive, extended family and clan lineages (*jiazu* 家族 or *shizu* 氏族).②

This dependence upon the institution of family as the primary source of social and political order has not been given full shrift except by a few of our most astute observers. Today as we anticipate the continuing rise of Chinese economic, political, and cultural influence, we might remember that centuries ago, G.W. Leibniz, a comparative philosopher in an earlier age, attempted to make productive sense of Confucian China for the Europe of his own time and place. Comparing China with Europe, Leibniz asks

> ... who would have believed that there is on earth a people who, though we are in our view so very advanced in every branch of behavior, still surpass us in comprehending the precepts of civil life, ... the precepts of ethics and politics adapted to the present life and use of mortals.③

Leibniz goes on in this comparison to express in language that would seem to preempt Hegel's later caricature of China as an oriental despotism defined as a top-down, unilateral imposition from the emperor as Law. On

---

① Zhou Yiqun cites Yan Fu as claiming that social and political order in the two millennia of imperial China was from its beginnings "seventy percent a lineage organization and thirty percent an empire." Yiqun Zhou, *Festival, Feasts, and Gender Relations in Ancient China and Greece,* New York: Cambridge University Press, 2010, p. 19n55.

② The Chinese experience might prompt us to ask ourselves whether the center of our own political lives lies in fact in those thick relations in the workplace and home rather than in our relation to some distant potentate.

③ See G.W. Leibniz, *Writings on China,* trans. Daniel J. Cook and Henry Rosemont Jr., La Salle, IL: Open Court, 1998, p. 46. See also Franklin Perkins, *Leibniz and China,* Cambridge: Cambridge University Press, 2004.

Leibniz's reading, the social and political order in China emerges importantly from within. In the very words Leibniz chooses we can hear clear reverberations of the specific Confucian moral imperatives of "family reverence" (*xiao* 孝) and "ritual propriety" (*li* 禮):

> In a vast multitude of men they [the Chinese] have virtually accomplished more than the founders of religious orders among us have achieved within their own narrow ranks. So great is obedience toward superiors and reverence toward elders, so religious, almost, is the relation of children toward parents, that for children to contrive anything violent against their parents, even by word, is almost unheard of.... Moreover, there is among equals, or those having little obligation to one another, a marvelous respect, and an established order of duties.... Neighbors and even members of a family are so held back by a hedge of custom that they are able to maintain a kind of perpetual courtesy.①

In advancing his own generalizations about European and Chinese cultures, Leibniz saw a clear contrast between the value invested in those abstract, theoretical disciplines in the European academy that are in search of axiomatic-deductive demonstration, and the more aesthetic and pragmatic applications of the Chinese tradition—a distinction that broadly distinguishes European confidence in the disciplining dividends of the rational sciences and formal institutions, from those alternative rewards that can be derived from virtuosity in the art of living within the activities of family and community life.

III.6 Reverencing Family (*xiao* 孝)

1.2 有子曰："其爲人也孝弟，而好犯上者，鮮矣；不好犯上，而好作亂者，未之有也。君子務本，本立而道生。孝弟也者，其爲仁之本與！"

Master You said: "It is a rare thing for someone who has a sense of family reverence and fraternal responsibility (*xiaoti* 孝弟) to have a taste for defying authority. And it is unheard of for those who have no taste for defying authority to be keen on initiating rebellion. Exemplary persons (*junzi* 君

---

① Leibniz, *Writings on China*, pp. 47–48.

III. THE *ANALECTS* (*LUNYU* 論語): A BASIC CONFUCIAN VOCABULARY

子) concentrate their efforts on the root (*ben* 本), for the root having been properly set, the vision of the moral life (*dao* 道) will grow therefrom. As for family reverence and fraternal deference, these are, I suspect, the root of becoming consummate in one's conduct (*ren* 仁)."

Comment: Henry Rosemont and I in our translation of the *Classic of Family Reverence* chose to translate the term *xiao* 孝 as "familial reverence" or "reverencing family" rather than following the convention of "filial piety." The virtue of "family reverence" as a translation is it disassociates *xiao* 孝 from the duty to God implied by "piety" and from the top-down, blind obedience assumed in *paterfamilias*. "Family reverence" is collateral, with the elder generation receiving appropriate deference from their younger members within their family lineages, and the younger generation deriving pleasure from deferring to those who have provided both meaning and substance to their lives. Family "reverence" also has the virtue of retaining the sacred connotations of *xiao* 孝 that are certainly at play in the ritualized culture of ancestral sacrifice.

Given the reference to authority in this passage, we must resist any simplistic equation between family reverence (*xiao* 孝) and blind obedience. *Xiao* 孝 that is focused on the intergenerational transmission of culture must be distinguished clearly from the *paterfamilias* we associate with Roman law as the juridical *patria potestas* or power and privilege of the father. Indeed, there are times when being truly filial within the family as well as being a loyal minister within the family simulacra of the court, requires courageous remonstrance (*jian* 諫) rather than automatic compliance. And indeed, such remonstrance is not perceived merely as a possibility or an option one might choose, but as a stern if not sacred obligation.

Another way in which authority is qualified here is the active, creative role human beings have in extending the proper path (*dao* 道). *Dao* 道 certainly has authority as a historically composite and cumulative way of being in the world, but far from being an end in itself, the received *dao* 道 is described as a gateway that provides exemplary persons with access and direction:

Analects 6.17: 誰能出不由戶？何莫由斯道也？
Since none can go out except through a gateway, how is it that no one is going out from this proper way (*dao* 道)?

What does it mean to take the practical activities of revering family members (*xiao* 孝) and of deferring appropriately to elders (*ti* 弟) as the root (*ben* 本) of becoming consummate in one's conduct (*ren* 仁)? Should we not rather regard such *xiao* and *ti* activities as a practical expression of *ren* that itself is taken to be integral to "human nature?" In making the erstwhile product of human nature the source, are we not putting the cart before the horse? Zhu Xi 朱熹 seems to worry over this possible inversion, and cites the interpretation of his philosophical predecessors, the Cheng brothers 二程, for clarification:

> Some have wondered whether or not identifying *xiao* 孝 and *ti* 弟 as the root of *ren* 仁 is because *xiao* 孝 and *ti* 弟 can bring about *ren* 仁. I think not. Saying that practicing *ren* 仁 commences from *xiao* 孝 and *ti* 弟 means that *xiao* 孝 and *ti* 弟 are expressions of *ren* 仁; saying that they are the root of practicing *ren* 仁 is fine, but saying that they are the root of *ren* 仁 itself will not do. As for *ren* 仁, it is human nature (*xing* 性); *xiao* 孝 and *ti* 弟 are its applications (*yong* 用). Within human nature, there are only the four components: *ren* 仁, *yi* 義, *li* 禮, *zhi* 智. How would *xiao* 孝 and *ti* 弟 factor into it? Now the main import of *ren* 仁 is love, and there is no love greater than that for one's kin. Hence the text reads: "As for family reverence (*xiao* 孝) and fraternal deference (*ti* 弟), these are, I suspect, the root of becoming consummate in one's conduct (*ren* 仁)."①

The Cheng brothers argue that the problematic expression in this *Analects* passage is "*becoming ren*" (*weiren* 爲仁), and that it should in fact be read as "*practicing ren*" (*xingren* 行仁). But if we understand the notion of "human nature" (perhaps better, "human propensities") at play here as the "root" (*ben* 本) that nourishes our human behavior, this root cannot in any way be conceived of as independent of the other elements that together constitute the organic process of becoming human. Such an interpretation would take nature and nurture as interdependent and correlative categories, rendering them symbiotic and mutually entailing.

---

① Zhu Xi (1969 rep.), *Lunyu Jizhu* 1:2a: 或問孝弟爲仁之本，此是由孝弟可以至仁否？曰非。謂行仁自孝弟始，孝弟是仁之一事；謂之行仁之本則可，謂是仁之本則不可。蓋仁是性也，孝弟是用也。性中只有個仁義禮智四者而已，曷嘗有孝弟來？然仁主於愛，愛莫大於愛親。故曰：孝弟也者其爲仁之本與。

III. THE *ANALECTS* (*LUNYU* 論語): A BASIC CONFUCIAN VOCABULARY

In order to appreciate the importance of family reverence (*xiao* 孝), we need to locate this prime moral imperative within the early process cosmology. Relationally-constituted persons are born into the broadest swath of family, community, and cosmic relations. They cannot exist exclusive of these relations, nor can they grow without them. Such an alternative understanding of the project of the civilizing of experience is immediately relevant in thinking through the intergenerational, genealogical, and holographic implications of family reverence (*xiao* 孝) that would construe persons as radial centers within an unbounded cosmic ecology.

In the ecological cosmology that gives this passage context, one must understand the root in terms of the whole process of becoming a tree, and must reflect on the nature of a person or any particular thing as the ongoing outcome of the total dynamic pattern of its relationships. Rather than understanding persons as a reduplication of some given, essential nature, persons and the unfolding of their narratives are the same thing. By locating the notion of human nature within this relational *qi* 氣 cosmology, we discover that what are sometimes taken to be unilateral and exclusive terms generally associated with human nature such as "root," "potential," "cause," and "source" have to be reconceived as collateral, transactional, and reflexive. The tree is an organic whole, and while the root may be thought to grow the tree, the tree in turn grows its roots.

The association between *ren* 仁 and "family" is clear in the alternative graphic form of the character *ren* 仁 found on the bamboo strips, with the character *ren* 𫮃 being the combination of a woman's pregnant body coupled with "heartmind" 心 below it.[①] Clearly, any conception of family must begin from woman with child. Allowing that human narratives are always *in medias res* as narratives nested within narratives, *ren* 仁 as "consummate person/conduct" cannot be taken to be descriptive of the content of some essential, *ab initio* notion of "human nature" (*xing* 性). Indeed, we must resist any means-end reduction that would introduce a severe separation between "practicing" what it means to be consummate, and "becoming" consummate as a person. Getting an education and being educated have the same content. Thus, *ren* 仁 has no meaning or possibility independent of our family and community relations.

---

① Kwan, "Database," 上博竹書五, 君子爲豊 1.

1.11 子曰:"父在,觀其志;父沒,觀其行;三年無改於父之道,可謂孝矣。"

The Master said: "While a person's father is still alive, observe what he intends; when his father dies, observe what he does. A person who for three years refrains from reforming the ways of his late father can be called a filial son (*xiao* 孝)."

Comment: Important in this passage is how the relationship between father and son is a microcosm of that between the present generation and the living tradition that has come before. On the one hand, the transmission is conservative in the sense that the son must give full consideration and respect to the ways of the father. On the other hand, the transmission is evolutionary in the sense that having demonstrated appropriate deference, it is incumbent upon the son to reform the ways of the father, and for each generation to reauthorize the tradition for their own time and place.

While *xiao* 孝 certainly references the aid and comfort that older generations can enjoy as it is provided by the progeny that succeeds them, the complement flows in the other direction as well. In addition to young deferring to their elders, *xiao* 孝 is also the vital process whereby the members of the younger generation are transformed into and become a novel yet persistent embodiment of those elders to whom they have deferred. The older generation is a reservoir of culture from whom the succeeding generation can draw sustenance and meaning, and in so doing, this younger generation provides those who have gone before them with a conduit to live on in the bodies and in the lived, cultural experience of a continuing lineage.

As with the term *ren* 仁 that resists any formulaic understanding, *xiao* 孝 requires us to access and to build upon our own existential sense of what it means to optimize our specific roles within family and community: what does it mean for me to be a father and an older brother? *Xiao* 孝 has immediate reference to our lived experience within the narrative of succeeding generations as we remember our own parents and grandparents, and as we attend to our own children and grandchildren. *Xiao* 孝 quite literally describes and makes normative the lived roles and relationships that constitute the communities of elders and youth across successive generations, and the thick relations that obtain between the present generation and those that have gone before. It references the continuing process of physical and cultural embodiment from one generation to the next, and thus the inseparability of grandparents and grandchildren, of fathers and

III. THE *ANALECTS* (*LUNYU* 論語): A BASIC CONFUCIAN VOCABULARY

daughters, of progenitors and progeny, and how such familial roles can only be learned and lived together.

We can also read "the ways of the father" here in a more general sense. To ground a vision of the consummate human life in "family reverence" is to assert that each succeeding generation is the teacher of the generation that is to follow. It is important to keep this idea of generational continuities and changes *via* lineages in mind when reading the *Analects*, for (at least) two reasons. First, while Confucius regularly cites the *Songs* (*Shijing* 詩經) and the *History* (*Shujing* 書經), and urges his disciples to read and re-read them, he lived when oral instruction was still the norm in education. As Michael Nylan has argued, China did not become a true "manuscript culture" until many centuries after the death of Confucius during the Han dynasty (202 BCE-220CE) with the appearance of libraries, archives, book shops, and other signs of such a culture.[①] Thus, just as with other schools of thought in early China, Confucianism as a "school" is probably best understood in terms of lineages transmitted orally, beginning with the Master himself and his own disciples, some of whom later took on disciples of their own. The dominant pattern of education was probably formal and informal discussions among a group of learners centering around a talented teacher and remembered passages from the classics rather than the study of the books themselves.

8.3 曾子有疾，召門弟子曰："啟予足！啟予手！《詩》云'戰戰兢兢，如臨深淵，如履薄冰。'而今而後，吾知免夫！小子！"

Master Zeng was ill, and summoned his students to him, saying, "Look at my feet! Look at my hands! The *Book of Songs* says:

Fearful, fearful! Trembling, trembling!
As if peering over a deep abyss,
As if walking across thin ice.

It is only from this moment hence, my young friends, that I can be sure I have avoided the desecration of my body."

Comment: Master Zeng is Zeng Shen 曾參, born in 505 BCE. He survived his teacher Confucius by more than four decades, dying in 436 BCE. It is with the cultivation of "family reverence" (*xiao* 孝) that Master Zeng's

---

① See Michael Nylan, *Yang Xiong and the Pleasures of Reading and Classical Learning in China*, New Haven: American Oriental Society, 2011.

name is most closely associated in early Chinese thought. There are a number of stories, some of them very probably apocryphal, narrating an extreme concern and reverence for his parents. Indeed the fact that he also receives mention for such sentiments in the canonical texts of non-Confucian schools of thought such as Daoism (in the *Zhuangzi* 莊子), and Legalism (in the *Hanfeizi* 韓非子) as well is sure testimony to his commitment to family reverence. This persistent association of the name of Master Zeng with family reverence has been undoubtedly reinforced by his appearance in the *Classic of Family Reverence* even if, *contra* tradition, it is unlikely he authored this text. Many of the other disciples of Confucius either had political careers, or at least aspired to such; Master Zeng is one of the few who does not seem to have had such goals himself, focusing instead on personal cultivation. For Master Zeng, see also footnote 1, page 123.

Master Zeng is alluding here to one of the basic precepts found in the *Classic of Family Reverence*: having inherited one's physical body from one's ancestors, one is obliged to return it intact. In this early tradition, amputory punishments and facial branding were commonly used on criminals not only to alert the community of a ne'er-do-well in their midst, but also to shame such miscreants before their ancestors in the world beyond. Thus it is only on his deathbed that Master Zeng can at last relax his vigilance.

It is perhaps important to note that respecting one's own physicality is respecting one's continuity with one's ancestors, and in a deeper cultural sense, respecting one's responsibility for embodying a living tradition. Even so, it is not physical disability in itself that is considered shameful. Witness *Analects* 15.42 in which Confucius is most solicitous in attending to the blind Music Master Mian:

> The blind Master of Music, Mian, had an interview with Confucius, and, on reaching the steps, the Master said, "Here are the steps" and on reaching the mat, the Master said, "Here is the mat." When they had all sat down together, the Master informed him of who was present: "So-and-so is here, and so-and-so is there."
>
> When Master of Music Mian had departed, Zizhang asked Confucius, "Is this the way that one should speak with a blind music master?"
>
> Confucius replied, "Indeed, this has been the way of helping a music master."

On Confucius's affordances towards the blind, see also 9.10 and 10.25.

2.6 孟武伯問孝。子曰:"父母唯其疾之憂。"
   Meng Wubo asked about family reverence (*xiao* 孝). The Master replied: "Give your mother and father nothing to worry about beyond your physical well-being."

Comment: It seems that perhaps the only two things many if not most parents really want from their children is that they survive, and that they find their own happiness. And it is the first of these concerns that never goes away regardless of age, and that parents simply cannot escape. There is a proper sequence to be respected in living and dying, and there is real tragedy when it is broken.

4.21 子曰:"父母之年,不可不知也。一則以喜,一則以懼。"
   The Master said, "Children must know the age of their father and mother. On the one hand, it is a source of joy; on the other, of trepidation."

Comment: The *Changes* cosmology is grounded in the concept of "life" (*sheng* 生) rather than "being" (*ousia*), "zoetology" (*shengshenglun* 生生論) as the "art of living" rather than ontology as "the science of being." It is thus that primary human occupations such as education and morality are defined in terms of productive "growth." This value is expressed in family and community by the younger generation with the conspicuous celebration of the good fortune and longevity (*fushou* 福壽) of their elders. While the longevity of parents is a source of joy, long life also means that as seniors they are also becoming increasingly vulnerable to the ineluctable consequences of time, and this then becomes a cause for worry.

2.7 子游問孝。子曰:"今之孝者,是謂能養。至於犬馬,皆能有養;不敬,何以別乎?"
   Ziyou asked about family reverence (*xiao* 孝). The Master replied: "Those today who are filial are considered so because they are able to provide sustenance for their parents. But even dogs and horses are given that much care. If you do not show respect for your parents, is there any difference?"

Comment: Certainly, providing the material comforts for one's parents is a necessary condition for family reverence. But given the isomorphism assumed between family and state, "family reverence" (*xiao* 孝) also entails sincere deference to one's elders and to one's ruler. Confucius repeatedly insists on the importance of duty and compliance when the young are serving in an official capacity, and again on the continuing weight of deferential conduct as a cultivated habit throughout one's life at home. While Confucius is surely claiming these patterns of interpersonal behavior are necessary for family flourishing and societal harmony, he is at the same time guiding his protégés toward such deference as a path of spiritual cultivation. Appropriate conduct expressed through a respectful if not reverential attitude to family elders and political authority is an opportunity to galvanize one's own identity as a contemporary member of a continuing genealogical and cultural lineage with its roots deep in history. Of course, as we see throughout the Confucian canons, such reverence must always be qualified by the stern obligation to remonstrate with both parents and ruler when circumstances demand we do so.

2.8 子夏問孝。子曰："色難。有事弟子服其勞，有酒食先生饌，曾是以爲孝乎？"

Zixia asked about family reverence (*xiao* 孝). The Master replied: "It all lies in showing the proper countenance. As for the young contributing their energies when there is work to be done, and deferring to their elders when there is wine and food to be had—how can merely doing this be considered family reverence?"

Comment: On being asked about family reverence (*xiao* 孝), Confucius would insist that this moral imperative cannot be satisfied by some set of formally prescribed, reduplicative activities that would resolve to a binary right or wrong. Rather, true family reverence is a function of the specific attitude expressed as appropriate actions are being carried out. It is the bounce in one's step and the warmth in one's smile that is catalytic in turning duty into pleasure. The proper attitude not only personalizes such actions, but elevates them from the mere satisfaction of what is expected to become a source of pleasure for both the young and the old alike.[1]

---

[1] For an indepth study of the importance of pleasure as a value in this Confucian tradition, see Michael Nylan, *The Chinese Pleasure Book*, Princeton: Zone Books, 2018.

III. THE *ANALECTS* (*LUNYU* 論語): A BASIC CONFUCIAN VOCABULARY

4.18 子曰: "事父母幾諫。見志不從，又敬不違，勞而不怨。"

The Master said, "In serving your father and mother, remonstrate (*jian* 諫) with them gently. On seeing that they do not heed your suggestions, remain respectful and do not act contrary. Although concerned, voice no resentment."

Comment: It is not just an option for children to remonstrate (*jian* 諫) with their elders; it is a stern obligation. Indeed, the concept of family reverence can only be understood when *xiao* 孝 is qualified by this solemn duty on the part of the younger generation. The word "protest" in the English language has two rather distinct meanings. The literal and yet less familiar meaning is (Latin *pro* forth + *testari* to affirm =) "to affirm with solemnity." For example, "I protest my innocence." A second, derivative, and yet more common use of protest is "to object to," "to speak strongly against," "to dissent." "I protest against going to war."[1] The first meaning of protest is centripetal and inclusive, with the object being to draw everyone together into a consensus or literally, "shared feeling". The second is dialectical and exclusive, an attempt to resolve a logical contradiction by affirming the truth of one side as opposed to the other. Even though examples can certainly be marshaled from both traditions to lay claim to both meanings, the inseparability of one and many in early Chinese cosmology gives privilege to consensus, while the privileging of a single order in classical Greece makes the second dialectical model most familiar.

Nathan Sivin makes an important distinction between the dialectical versus consensual expectations of philosophical engagement in the classical Greek and Chinese worlds respectively:

> Greek culture in the period that concerns us encouraged disagreement and disputation in natural philosophy and science as in every other field; in China the emphasis remained on consensus.[2]

The contrast herein is between Greek dialogue and its assumption that rational analysis will provide access to some exclusive *logos* on the one hand, and

---

[1] See Roger T. Ames, "Pluralism and Protest: The Chinese Experience," *China Report* 27:2 (1991).

[2] Nathan Sivin, *Medicine, Philosophy and Religion in Ancient China: Researches and Reflections*, Aldershot: Variorum, 1995, p. 8.

a Chinese conversation that requires the ongoing negotiation of an open and inclusive consensus on the other. While the pursuit of apodictic truth drove the Greek dialogue, the continuing need to negotiate and sustain order within the assumed processual experience of Chinese cosmology had far-reaching ramifications. Such ongoing inclusive negotiation would explain why the continuing pursuit of an achieved consensus in its many forms was regarded as having high value in the classical Chinese world: a continuing reauthorization of a moral orthodoxy, a continuing commentary on a shared canonical core, "the art of accommodation" *jianshu* 兼術 in philosophical deliberation, and so on.[1]

This contrast between dialectic and consensus carries over and is important in understanding the role of earnest remonstrance in Confucian doctrine, where the value invested in consensus makes suspect contrary actions on the part of the remonstrator (see also 2.5). There is an important difference between censuring a parent's conduct, and the genuine assertion that "we can do better." While children must remonstrate with their parents when they deem it necessary, such actions should be done with tact and sensitivity. Again, remonstrance on the part of the children while sincere does not guarantee that their concerns are in fact warranted or will ultimately be vindicated. And to have one's concerns rebuffed by a parent is certainly not a license for resentment.

Is the role of the younger generation simply limited to their personal and political remonstrance?

Analects 1.11: 三年無改於父之道，可謂孝矣。
A person who for three years refrains from reforming the ways of his late father can be called a filial son.

The point is first that in the fullness of time, the cultural tradition as it comes to be embodied in this younger generation, will be theirs to reform and perpetuate with the complement of remonstrance coming from their

---

[1] Angus Graham, *Disputers of the Tao*, La Salle, IL: Open Court, 1989, p. 3 develops this same contrast when he observes that dialectical dispute is characteristic of people who would ask, "What is the Truth?" as opposed to those who would ask "Where is the Way?" See also David L. Hall and Roger T. Ames, *Thinking from the Han*, part II.

own juniors. And secondly, that ultimately deference is due to accomplishment rather than mere seniority.

Analects 9.23: 後生可畏，焉知來者之不如今也？
The young should be held in high esteem. After all, how do we know that those yet to come will not surpass our contemporaries?

In a cosmology in which we are human "becomings" rather than human "beings," becoming human is having an evolving narrative integral to a genealogical lineage in which we are beneficiaries and benefactors in different ways over time.

17.21 宰我問："三年之喪，期已久矣。君子三年不爲禮，禮必壞；三年不爲樂，樂必崩。舊穀既沒，新穀既升，鑽燧改火，期可已矣。"子曰："食夫稻，衣夫錦，於女安乎？"曰："安。""女安則爲之！夫君子之居喪，食旨不甘，聞樂不樂，居處不安，故不爲也。今女安，則爲之！"宰我出。子曰："予之不仁也！子生三年，然後免於父母之懷。夫三年之喪，天下之通喪也。予也，有三年之愛於其父母乎？"

Zaiwo inquired of Confucius, "The period of three years mourning on the death of one's parents is already too long. If exemplary persons (*junzi* 君子) were to give up observing ritual propriety (*li* 禮) for three years, the rites would certainly go to ruin. And if for three years, they were to give up the performance of music (*yue* 樂), such practices would certainly collapse. Over the duration of one year, the old grain has been used up, the new crop is ready for harvest, and the kindling of the fires marking each of the seasons has gone through its full cycle[1]—surely a year is good enough."

The Master replied, "Would you at that time be comfortable eating fine rice and wearing robes of fine brocade?"

"I would indeed," responded Zaiwo.

"If you are comfortable in doing so, then do it." said the Master. "When exemplary persons (*junzi* 君子) are in the mourning shed, they can find no relish in fine-tasting fare, no pleasure in the sound of music, and no comfort in their usual lodgings. It is for this reason they give up these things. Now if you can find comfort in them, then by all means, enjoy them."

---

[1] Different kinds of woods were used ceremonially as drills to kindle fire at the beginning of each season.

When Zaiwo had left, the Master remarked, "Zaiwo is really perverse (*buren* 不仁)! It is only after being tended by parents for three years that infants can finally leave their bosom. The ritual of three years of mourning for one's parents is practiced throughout the world. Didn't Zaiwo receive this three years of loving care from his parents?"

Comment: The imperfect Zaiwo is a constant source of disappointment for Confucius. With "family reverence" (*xiao* 孝) being the prime moral imperative in this Confucian culture, Confucius takes maintaining the heavily choreographed social practices that express this high value very seriously. Zaiwo, in making his rather clever argument that a single year's mourning should be sufficient, has two points. First, three year's abstinence from the daily practices that punctuate the ritually ordered lives of exemplary persons would certainly take a toll on the quality of their future performances. And secondly, given the isomorphism assumed between the natural and the human worlds, the cycle of the turning seasons provides us with a clear conception of what is most natural in the beginnings and endings of things that should define our social practices.

Confucius's response is to test Zaiwo's own sense of what is appropriate under such circumstances by asking him to reflect on his own feelings. Could your mourning for your own parents be comfortably completed with just this one-year period? Zaiwo responding perhaps too quickly and cleverly, prompts Confucius to draw a contrast between Zaiwo's shallowness and those moral exemplars whose proper feelings have set the traditional standard. Confucius contrasts the casual if not cavalier way Zaiwo is able to anticipate such abstentions with the profound feelings that naturally attend the practices of better persons. After Zaiwo has departed, Confucius is rather harsh in berating him as being a perverse person who is incapable of appreciating the balance observed within family relations: that is, the three years of unremitting attention given to infants by parents necessary to secure their well-being, and the natural gratitude these now grown infants should feel towards their deceased parents.

Cf. 14.40 in which Confucius argues for the antiquity and pervasiveness of such mourning practices and *Mencius* 3A2 in which the genuine respect for the three-year mourning period shown by a once wayward prince recommends this prince to his court and his people.

14.22 子路問事君。子曰："勿欺也而犯之。"

III. THE *ANALECTS* (*LUNYU* 論語): A BASIC CONFUCIAN VOCABULARY

Zilu asked how to serve one's lord properly. The Master replied, "Let there be no deceit even while taking a stand against him."

Comment: The prime moral imperative in the Confucian culture is "family reverence" (*xiao* 孝), a doctrine that has both familial and political reference. This passage speaks to the political application of the obligation of remonstrance (*jian* 諫) as what those in service owe to those in power. Just as children are obliged to remonstrate with their parents when persuaded they are following the wrong course, so too must the ministers remonstrate with their ruler when they believe the ruler has strayed (2.14, 13.15, 13.23, 15.22). Of course, to be effective such remonstrance whether in family or the court must be attended by the utmost sincerity uncontaminated by any semblance of deceit. Cf. *Classic of Family Reverence* 15.

14.21 陳成子弒簡公。孔子沐浴而朝，告於哀公曰：「陳恒弒其君，請討之。」公曰：「告夫三子！」孔子曰：「以吾從大夫之後，不敢不告也。君曰『告夫三子』者。」之三子告，不可。孔子曰：「以吾從大夫之後，不敢不告也。」

Chen Chengzi assassinated Duke Jian. Confucius having performed a ritual cleansing went to court and reported the event to Duke Ai, saying, "Chen Chengzi has assassinated his lord. I implore you to send an army to punish him."

The Duke replied, "Report this to the heads of the Three Families."

The Master on withdrawing said, "Ranking below the high ministers, I had no choice but to report this event. And the Duke says to me 'Report this to the heads of the Three Families.'"

In going to the heads of the Three Families and reporting this event, they refused Confucius's petition. He said, "Ranking below the high ministers, I had no choice but to report it."

Comment: For this event, see the *Zuo Commentary to the Spring and Autumn Annals* 春秋左傳 Ai 14.

甲午，齊陳恒弒其君壬于舒州。孔丘三日齊，而請伐齊，三。公曰：「魯爲齊弱久矣，子之伐之，將若之何？」對曰：「陳恒弒其君，民之不與者半。以魯之衆，加齊之半，可克也。」公曰：「子告季孫。」孔子辭，退而告人曰：「吾以從大夫之後也，故不敢不言。」

On the day *jiawu*, Chen Heng of Qi assassinated his ruler Ren at Shuzhou. Confucius fasted for three days, and then petitioned three times that Qi be attacked. The Duke replied to him, "That Lu is weaker than Qi is an old story. If we were to attack them, what do you think would be the outcome?"

"Chen Heng has assassinated his ruler," responded Confucius, "and half of the people of Qi are disaffected. With the Lu forces augmenting this half of the Qi population, Lu could take the victory."

"You go and report this to the Ji Sun clan," said the Duke. Confucius took his leave, and then said to someone, "Having held rank below the high officials at court, I had no choice but to speak up." Cf. James Legge (trans.), *The Chinese Classics*, 5 Volumes, Hong Kong: University of Hong Kong Press, 1960 rep., Vol. 5, p. 840.

We are herein given a historical example of Confucius himself remonstrating with both his ruler Duke Ai and the Three Families who had usurped the Duke's power. It is clear from the beginning that Confucius 是知其不可而爲之者 "is the one who keeps trying even though he knows it is in vain" (14.38). What is important here, however, is that Confucius's own conduct, from the ritual bathing and fasting to remonstrances made (*jian* 諫), is consistent with both ritual propriety (*li* 禮) and his obligation as minister to the moral imperative of "family reverence" (*xiao* 孝) as it applies at the political level. Confucius is quite right that, according to his own teachings, he simply has no choice but to speak up.

8.4 曾子有疾，孟敬子問之。曾子言曰："鳥之將死，其鳴也哀；人之將死，其言也善。君子所貴乎道者三：動容貌，斯遠暴慢矣；正顏色，斯近信矣；出辭氣，斯遠鄙倍矣。籩豆之事，則有司存。"

Master Zeng was gravely ill, and when Meng Jingzi asked after him, Master Zeng replied, "Baleful is the cry of a dying bird; felicitous are the words of a dying person. There are three habits that exemplary persons consider of the utmost importance in their vision of the moral life. By maintaining a dignified demeanor, such persons keep violent and rancorous conduct at a distance; by maintaining a proper countenance, they keep trust and confidence near at hand; by taking care in their choice of language and their mode of expression, they keep vulgarity and impropriety at a distance. As for the details in the arrangement of ritual vessels, there are minor functionaries to take care of such things."

III. THE *ANALECTS* (*LUNYU* 論語): A BASIC CONFUCIAN VOCABULARY

Comment: An important *dramatis persona* in the *Analects* who in his own conduct underscores this primacy of relationality is Confucius' protégé, Master Zeng 曾子. He is the paradigmatic figure most closely associated with the fullest expression of "family reverence" (*xiao* 孝). See footnote 1, page 123.

In this passage, Master Zeng, plainly aware of his own impending demise, begins by exhorting his listener to pay serious attention to what he is about to say, for Master Zeng on his deathbed believes his last words as he will give them utterance are of real consequence. Master Zeng's message then is that all three of the habits of deportment considered by exemplary persons to be vital to the moral life—that is, a dignified demeanor, a proper countenance, and a commitment to effective communication—are essential to the productive growth of interpersonal relations. And it is such growth in relations that is the substance of Confucian morality. On the other hand, a failure to cultivate such dispositions precipitates vulgarity, impropriety, and violent, rancorous actions. Such untoward behavior is an immediate source of diminution and disintegration in one's relations, and as such is for the Confucian the substance of immoral conduct.

While Master Zeng with his last breath would express this vital concern for the cultivation of personal familial and communal relations, he regards the formal and material trappings of the refined life to be of relatively marginal significance. The example given here is the arrangement of ritual vessels that can be taken care of by minor attendants. It is thus that in the Confucian ethic, the familial and social roles are seen to have normative force, serving us as concrete guidelines for how we ought to proceed, and quite felicitously, for determining what we ought to do next. Indeed, it is this continuing process of elevating, refining, and deepening our lived roles and relations to make the most of our associated lives that prompts us to describe Confucian morality as an ethics of roles, and to claim that Confucian role ethics is a *sui generis* vision of the moral life.

III.7 Consummate Conduct/Persons in Roles and Relations (*ren* 仁)

12.1 顏淵問仁。子曰："克己復禮爲仁。一日克己復禮，天下歸仁焉。爲仁由己，而由人乎哉？"顏淵曰："請問其目。"子曰："非禮勿視，非禮勿聽，非禮勿言，非禮勿動。"顏淵曰："回雖不敏，請事斯語矣。"

Yan Hui inquired about consummate conduct (*ren* 仁). The Master replied, "Persons through self-discipline and achieving propriety in their roles and relations (*li* 禮) become consummate in their conduct.[①] If for the space of a single day they were able to accomplish this, the whole world would defer to them as consummate models. Becoming consummate in one's conduct is self-originating—how could it originate with others?"

Yan Hui said, "Could I ask what becoming consummate entails?" The Master replied, "Do not look at anything that offends against ritual propriety; do not listen to anything that offends against ritual propriety; do not speak about anything that offends against ritual propriety; do not do anything that offends against ritual propriety."

"Though I am not clever," said Yan Hui, "allow me to act upon what you have said."

Comment: When we reflect on *ren* 仁 as it is used in the *Analects* and take it to be one way of "saying" role ethics, we must acknowledge the substance of *ren* 仁 is different for different people in different roles and contexts. For example, in the *Analects* it is recorded that, Yan Hui, puzzled by the Confucius's frequent use of his *ren* 仁 neologism, asks after its meaning: "Yan Hui inquired about *ren* 仁." In comparing the Master's answer to Yan Hui with the responses he gives to precisely the same question when it

---

① This passage occurs in the *Zuo Commentary to the Spring and Autumn Annals* Zhao 12 (cf. Legge, *Chinese Classics*, Vol. 5, p. 641) where Confucius says,

仲尼曰，古也有志，克己復禮，仁也，信善哉，楚靈王若能如是，豈其辱於乾谿。

There is an ancient record that states, "Through self-discipline and observing ritual propriety one becomes authoritative in one's person." This is well-said indeed. If King Ling of Chu had been able to live up to this, how could he have come to such disgrace at Ganqi?"

The context is a king who comes to a bad end because he has no "self-control" (*zike* 自克). Arthur Waley in *The Book of Songs*, London: Grove Press, 1937, p. 162 notes that *ke* can also mean "able," but the *Zuo* passage is rather clear evidence that in this context it is best translated as "self-discipline." It is important not to "naturalize" a notion of "ego-self" that then has to be overcome. Rather, those as yet inchoate and incipient persons nested within their relations need cultivation, discipline, and extension.

is asked by equally nonplussed Zhonggong, Sima Niu, Fan Chi, and Zigong in other passages, we might begin by reflecting on the form of the question itself—the interrogative term.① That is, rather than uncritically assuming his protégés are asking "What does *ren* 仁 mean?" and thus that they are expecting a generic answer or a formal definition, we might infer they are instead asking "How given my particular narrative do I become *ren* 仁?" This would explain why the Master has very different answers for each of them. Indeed, even when the "same" Fan Chi on a second occasion asks the same question, he gets a significantly different answer.

This passage reinforces the close relationship between family roles and becoming consummate as a person. *Ren* 仁 does not describe persons independent of their family relations, but instead references specific persons who are being defined by the cultivated relationality in their specific family roles. The *Analects* links *ren* 仁 with aspiring to ritual propriety first within one's roles in family and then by radial extension, within those roles one occupies in the community more broadly construed. What it says most clearly here is that the disciplining of one's person and the refinement made possible by aspiring to propriety in one's roles and relations is the substance of becoming consummate in what one does.

The distinguished sociologist Fei Xiaotong 費孝通 insists that Confucian ethics must be conceived of as always unique "centers fanning out into a web-like network"② that are "composed of webs woven out of countless personal relationships."③ Fei would further claim that this predominant pattern of kinship relations with its hierarchically-defined roles and relations produces its own distinctive kind of morality in which "no ethical concepts . . . transcend specific types of human relationships."④ That is, kinship as the root of human relations is defined by the values of "family reverence" (*xiao* 孝) and "fraternal deference" (*ti* 悌). And friendship as the way of extending this pattern of kinship relations to include non-relatives is pursued through an ethic of "commitment and resolve" (*cheng* 誠),

---

① Yan Hui 12.1, Zhonggong 12.2, Sima Niu 12.3, Fan Chi 12.22 and 13.19, and Zigong 15.10.
② Fei Xiaotong, *From the Soil: The Foundations of Chinese Society*, A Translation of *Xiangtu Zhongguo* 鄉土中國 by Gary G. Hamilton and Wang Zheng, Berkeley: University of California Press, 1992, p. 68.
③ Fei, *From the Soil*, p. 78.
④ Fei, *From the Soil*, p. 74.

of "doing one's utmost" (*zhong* 忠), and of "making good on one's word" (*xin* 信).① All such ethical modalities of action are aspired to as the way of reconciling the tensions that obtain among, and promoting the affordances made within, the specific personal relationships of family members and community. The function of ritual propriety (*li* 禮) as that moral medium necessary for transforming the looking, listening, speaking and doing of all human activity from mere actions into consummate conduct is a constant theme in the text. Cf. 1.12, 8.2, and 17.8.

12.2 仲弓問仁。子曰："出門如見大賓，使民如承大祭。己所不欲，勿施於人。在邦無怨，在家無怨。"仲弓曰："雍雖不敏，請事斯語矣。"

Zhonggong inquired about consummate conduct (*ren* 仁).

The Master replied, "In your public life, behave as though you are receiving honored guests; employ the common people as though you are overseeing a great sacrifice. Do not impose upon others what you yourself do not want, and you will not incur personal or political ill-will."

"Though I am not clever," said Zhonggong, "allow me to act on what you have said."

Comment: Zhonggong, like Yan Hui, was three decades younger than Confucius. In another passage that echoes this one, Confucius allows himself to be corrected by Zhonggong when, in response to Confucius's praise of a colleague's simplicity and candor, Zhonggong insists that such candor is not enough; those in office must truly respect the people they govern (6.2). Although Zhonggong like Yan Hui was of humble origins, Confucius thought so highly of him and of his refinement he said that in spite of his low birth, Zhonggong would make a fine ruler (6.1, 6.6). Allowing that Zhonggong is quite happily without eloquence, Confucius leaves open the question of whether or not he is a consummate person—a designation

---

① See for example *Analects* 1.4 and 1.8. There is an ambiguity in the expression "associates and friends" (*pengyou* 朋友) as it is used in the documents of the Western Zhou and Spring and Autumn period where these texts do not distinguish non-related friends from agnatic male relatives—that is, paternal relatives such as brothers, uncles, nephews, cousins, and so on. Some scholars have argued that *pengyou* 朋友 becomes a term commonly used to specifically denote non-kin friends only in the Warring States period. See Zhou Yiqun, *Festival, Feasts, and Gender Relations in Ancient China and Greece*, pp. 110-111 and 137-139.

he is loath to give anyone except the brothers Bo Yi and Shu Qi (7.15), a perhaps deceased Yan Hui (6.7), three victims of the Shang dynasty tyrant Zhou (18.1), and maybe the historical figure, Guan Zhong (14.16, 14.17).

Confucius in responding to Zhonggong's question on consummate conduct seems to be aware of this otherwise able student's lack of experience as an official at court and in the practices of governance. At the same time, he expresses the highest expectations for what Zhonggong would look like in such roles. In Confucian role ethics, the entry point for consummate conduct is certainly family relations (1.2). But while such visceral family feelings might begin at home, when they are extended radially into all of our roles and personal relationships more broadly, they suffuse the vital bonds that come to constitute the events of everyday life with a family and community-centered religiousness. Such attentiveness to *ren* 仁 as it informs our ritualized roles and relations (*li* 禮) has the power to elevate mere associated living into a social sacrament. The important religious function of ancestral sacrifice in this culture as an opportunity to sanctify the social and political order and correlate it with the inherited tradition cannot be overstated.

The simile of employing the people as though conducting a grand sacrifice is significant. It is the function of such ceremonies to reinforce the social institutions and hierarchies within the context of the ancestral genealogy, and to thus locate everyone in their proper place. *Analects* 20.1 in describing the priorities needed for effective governance, ascribes importance to four areas of responsibility: 民、食、喪、祭 "the common people, food, mourning, and sacrifice." Again in 10.21, it states that Confucius 朋友之饋，雖車馬，非祭肉，不拜 "would not kowtow on receiving gifts from friends, even those as lavish as a horse or a carriage, with the sole exception of sacrificial meat." The responsibility of continuing sacrificial practices to ancestors has high value in an aristocratic tradition that takes "family reverence" (*xiao* 孝) expressed through intergenerational transmission of the cultural legacy as its prime moral imperative. Throughout the Confucian texts, sacrifice as a sign of deference and respect to ancestors and the cultural heroes who have come before is taken as an integral aspect of the "ritual propriety" (*li* 禮) that undergirds the continuity of the civilization itself.

This same importantly negative formulation of the Golden Rule is repeated in 15.24.

12.3 司馬牛問仁。子曰: "仁者，其言也訒。" 曰: "其言也訒，斯謂之仁已乎？" 子曰: "爲之難，言之得無訒乎？"

Sima Niu inquired about consummate conduct (*ren* 仁).

The Master replied, "Consummate persons are circumspect in what they say (*ren* 訒)."

"Does just being circumspect in what you say make you consummate?" he asked.

The Master replied, "When things are difficult to accomplish, how can you be but circumspect in what you have to say?"

Comment: According to historian Sima Qian 司馬遷, among Confucius's students, Sima Niu had the distinction of being both garrulous and impulsive.[1] Confucius is speaking to this condition in his seemingly impatient response to Sima Niu, thereby criticizing specifically those who fail to treat their words as having the force of action.

Confucius is able to make much out of the intimate association he perceives between careful attention to what one says (*ren* 訒) and the cultivation of consummate conduct (*ren* 仁). Defining terms paronomastically by invoking such semantic and phonetic associations is a familiar feature in the early philosophical literature broadly, and of the *Analects* specifically. It is perhaps the most obvious form of correlative thinking. The Confucian project of aspiring to become consummate in one's roles and relations (*ren* 仁) is defined unambiguously as "speaking with circumspection" (*ren* 訒) because, simply put, effective communication in growing relations is the source of meaning and the substance of morality. We might register a correlation between *shu* 恕 as the dramatic rehearsal of putting oneself in the place of others in determining what it is best to do, and *ren* 訒 as the deference shown to our interlocutors in determining what it is best to say. Of course, such a distinction must be qualified by appreciating the fact that saying is a performative doing, and a doing is a practical saying.

There is much to be made of the claim in this passage that, for Confucius, not only are "saying" and "doing" inseparable, but further, the more difficult the task at hand, the more care we must exercise in the use of the language that informs it. Consider the demands of diplomacy in

---

[1] See Sima Qian 司馬遷, *Shiji* 史記 (*Records of the Grand Historian*), Beijing: Zhonghua Shuju, 1959, pp. 2214-2215.

international relations, for example.

12.22 樊遲問仁。子曰:"愛人。" 問知。子曰:"知人。" 樊遲未達。子曰: "舉直錯諸枉,能使枉者直。" 樊遲退,見子夏曰:"鄉也吾見於夫子而問知, 子曰:'舉直錯諸枉,能使枉者直。' 何謂也?" 子夏曰:"富哉言乎! 舜有天 下,選於眾,舉皋陶,不仁者遠矣。湯有天下,選於眾,舉伊尹,不仁者遠 矣。"

Fan Chi inquired about consummate conduct (*ren* 仁), and the Master replied, "Love others (*airen* 愛人)."

He inquired about living wisely (*zhi* 知) and the Master said, "Realize others (*zhiren* 知人)." Fan Chi did not understand and so the Master explained, "If you promote the true into positions above the crooked you can make the crooked true."

Fan Chi withdrew, and on being received by Zixia, he asked, "Recently I was received by the Master and asked him about living wisely. The Master replied, 'If you promote the true into positions above the crooked you can make the crooked true.' What does he mean by this?"

"Profound indeed are the words of the Master!" said Zixia. "When Shun ruled the land, he selected Gao Yao from among the multitude and promoted him, thereby keeping those who are perverse at a distance. When Tang ruled the land, he selected Yi Yin from among the multitude and promoted him, thereby keeping those who are perverse at a distance."

Comment: Consummate conduct (*ren* 仁) and living wisely (*zhi* 知) are two terms we find frequently coupled in the text, reflecting the inseparability of these two ways of being in the world. And both of these terms are defined by the meaningful quality of the relations one is able to achieve with others.

In the exchange, Fan Chi "inquired about living wisely" and the Master replies "realize others." I am using "living wisely" and "realizing" (rather than "knowing") as translations for the same term, *zhi* 知. The point is that "knowing" in this tradition while certainly entailing a cognitive awareness, is more importantly not only a "doing" but a productive "doing," a "making real." Fan Chi seems truly puzzled by the response he has received, first asking the Master for clarification, and then again asking his fellow protégé Zixia what the Master means.

Confucius is saying here that those who live wisely in the world in so doing transform it, and inspire the people around them to live better. The wise "realize others" in the sense of providing the occasion and the meaningful context in which other people can flourish. Zixia then provides two historical examples of how when the right persons are promoted as social and political leaders—when the true is promoted above the crooked—the entire community is transformed by their leadership. Such role models elevate the discourse and provide the impetus for communal flourishing. Cf. 2.19.

13.19 樊遲問仁。子曰:"居處恭,執事敬,與人忠。雖之夷狄,不可棄也。"

Fan Chi inquired about consummate conduct (*ren* 仁), and the Master replied, "At home be deferential, in handling public affairs be respectful, and do your utmost (*zhong* 忠) in your relationships with others. Even living among the Yi or Di barbarians, you could not do without such conduct."

Comment: All conduct is irreducibly relational in nature. Thus, "good" is the quality to be achieved in the relations themselves rather than being some isolated character trait that consummate persons infuse into their conduct or some external principle that can be applied to particular situations. The modality of "doing your utmost" (*zhong* 忠) is the measure (*du* 度) to be aspired to in optimizing the possibilities of any situation. The distinction between living among a civilized population or barbarians is certainly relevant to the details of *what* is actually being done, but is irrelevant to the habituated modalities of *how* consummate persons would behave. Having said this, all relations are collaborative, and living among an unfamiliar population would be an opportunity to exercise one's imagination and expand one's scope of understanding. Role models must themselves be responsive, and are thus transformed in the process of modeling.

A question prompted by this passage is this: If "human becomings" emerge in their narratives as a contrapuntal collaboration between their native conditions and their environments, what happens when their environing conditions are not simply unfamiliar, but in fact toxic? The Confucian answer would again be modal. The narrative of Confucius himself tells the story of a person who lived under conditions that were vexing, discouraging him at every turn. It is quite likely that Confucius while having undiminished faith in the civilizing force of his own teachings left this world a frustrated teacher whose self-understanding was that he had accomplished little. At the same time, the model of his commitment to making the most of his difficult circumstances has served the tradition as a continuing inspiration for building upon his teachings, and in some important degree, accomplishing in his name what he could not.

While Confucius lived in trying circumstances, perhaps the story of Shun and his father the Blind Man who tried repeatedly to kill Shun is more properly described as toxic. Shun's response to such a challenge that made him "the great exemplar of family reverence" (*daxiao* 大孝) was to persevere against all odds in doing everything he could to make the relationship right, and in the end, to succeed in bringing his father around.

We might have to concede that everything is in degree a trade-off, and while an important outcome of Confucian role ethics is to preempt hard cases in the first place, in the end such an ethic might not have as much clarity and force as a rule-based ethic in addressing those hard cases that do arise.

15.10 子貢問爲仁。子曰："工欲善其事，必先利其器。居是邦也，事其大夫之賢者，友其士之仁者。"

Zigong inquired about consummate conduct (*ren* 仁).

The Master replied, "Craftsmen wanting to be good at their trades must first sharpen their tools. While dwelling in a particular state then, we should serve those ministers who are most worthy of it, and befriend those scholar-officials who are the most consummate in their conduct."

Comment: Confucius is drawing an analogy here between craftsmen "sharpening their tools" to carry out their trades, and what he and his protégés need to do to accomplish their mission of promoting moral governance. Although Zigong is a favorite student of Confucius, he is well-bred, well-spoken, financially successful, and aloof. It is thus not surprising that a persistent theme in the passages in which he appears is how he might cultivate better relationships. For Confucius, wherever he and his apprentices go, the first order of business must be to seek out those in office who are the demonstrated moral exemplars for the people in that place, and to make every effort to strengthen their relationships with them. The concrete starting point for making the world a better place is effective relationships with those who have the greatest degree of moral influence. This passage with its reference to craftsmen is reminiscent of 19.7.

4.6 子曰："我未見好仁者、惡不仁者。好仁者，無以尚之；惡不仁者，其爲仁矣，不使不仁者加乎其身。有能一日用其力於仁矣乎？我未見力不足者。蓋有之矣，我未之見也。"

The Master said, "I have yet to meet anyone who truly cherishes consummate conduct (*ren* 仁) and who abhors what is contrary to it. There are none superior to those who cherish consummate conduct. And those who abhor what is contrary to it, in acting consummately themselves, will not allow contrary conduct to be associated with their persons.

"Is there anyone who, for the space of a single day, has devoted themselves fully to consummate conduct? I have yet to meet anyone who lacks the capacity to do so. Perhaps there are persons who lack the capacity, but I at least, have yet to meet them."

Comment: For Confucius, those who cherish consummate conduct and despise conduct contrary to it are among our highest moral exemplars. It is noteworthy that Confucius is making a modal claim that speaks to commitment and resolution rather than to the actual behaviors themselves. Just as his preferred way of defining himself is as someone who "cherishes learning" (*haoxue* 好學), he is here praising persons who "cherish consummate conduct" (*haoren* 好仁). There is a dramatic tension in the text between consummate conduct being as easy as doing it, and the fact that at the same time it is profoundly difficult because no one can seem to fully habituate it and sustain such a standard of behavior. Thus it is that even though everyone has the capacity to act consummately, Confucius rues the fact that he has yet to meet anyone who can maintain this quality of conduct even for a single day. Throughout the text, Confucius makes it clear that he has set the highest bar on what in his judgment he would deem to be consummate conduct. Cf. 6.12 and 7.30.

7.30 子曰："仁遠乎哉？我欲仁，斯仁至矣。"

The Master said, "How could consummate conduct (*ren* 仁) be at all remote? No sooner do I seek it than it has arrived."

Comment: This passage seems to contradict the profile of Confucius who is most reluctant to ascribe the consummate *ren* 仁 quality of conduct to anyone, including himself (7.34). In the entire *Analects*, only a few persons—the brothers Bo Yi and Shu Qi (7.15), the ancient statesman Guan Zhong (14.16, 14.17), three martyrs of the Shang tyrant Zhou (18.1), and Confucius's student Yan Hui, perhaps after his early demise—are accorded such a characterization. But with the brothers Bo Yi and Shu Qi, Confucius makes it clear he does not agree with what he takes to be their rigid stance (18.8). And even with Guan Zhong, the attribution is qualified in both instances by two students, Zilu and Zigong, asking how Guan Zhong's conduct could possibly warrant such a description. Even with Yan Hui, he is deemed remarkable not for having become *ren* 仁, but for being able to sustain this high standard for extended periods of time longer than other students. Given that Confucius is trying to encourage a commitment to this quality of conduct, the point of this passage might best be grasped from the perspective of the inseparability of knowing and doing, of living wisely and the quality of conduct that demonstrates as much. Just as we might say that no one can be deemed wise until they authenticate such a characterization in practice, we must also say that as soon as someone is acting wisely, they have a claim on being deemed wise. Since *ren* 仁 requires a commitment to unrelenting personal cultivation, as soon as someone embarks on this project, they are on their way. At the same time, given Confucius's high standards, it is not likely that we will encounter someone who has been able to fully habituate it and sustain it in their behavior. Thus, we might say that becoming *ren* 仁 is at once the easiest and the most difficult thing to accomplish. See also 9.19.

6.7 子曰："回也，其心三月不違仁，其餘則日月至焉而已矣。"
　　The Master said, "With my one disciple, Yan Hui, he could go for several months without departing from consummate thoughts and feelings (*xin* 心) in his conduct; as for the others, only every once in a long while might consummate thoughts and feelings make their appearance."

Comment: A familiar distinction we find in the Confucian canons is between acting out of a habituated disposition for proper conduct, and merely doing something that might be deemed proper by others. For example, in *Mencius* 4B19 we read that the legendary ruler Shun 由仁義行，非行仁義 "acted from the moral habit of being consummatory and appropriate in his conduct rather than merely doing what is deemed consummate and appropriate by others." Again, in *Five Modes of Virtuosic Conduct* 五行篇 1, we have the passage:

仁形於內謂之德之行，不形於內謂之行。

Consummatory conduct (ren 仁) taking shape within is called moral virtuosity (de 德); where it does not take shape within, it is called merely doing what is deemed consummate.

In this *Analects* passage, we are given a snapshot of Yan Hui who seems well on his way to developing such a ren 仁 habitude, save for his early demise.

Although with heartmind (xin 心), the "formal" and the "functional" (tiyong 體用) are aspectual and mutually entailing, there is still a primacy of the "functional" over its "anatomical" implications. On the analogy of distinguishing the activity of "walking" from the abstracted leg that walks, xin 心 is first something done—the activities of thinking and feeling in the world—and only then it can be abstracted as a center of such activity—the heartmind. This priority of the gerundive in a process cosmology would be a warrant for translating xin 心 first as "thoughts and feelings" and then derivatively as "heartmind," depending of course upon the context.

15.36 子曰: "當仁, 不讓於師。"
The Master said, "In striving to be consummate in your conduct (ren 仁), do not defer even to your teachers."

Comment: If there is one term that captures the spirit of the Confucian vision of the moral life, it is perhaps "deference" as it is expressed in terms such as *rang* 讓 here and elsewhere as *shu* 恕: "putting oneself in the other's place" and considering a situation from their point of view. The fabric of the Confucian family and community is constituted by the patterns of deference defining of the roles of father and daughter, of friend and neighbor (*li* 禮), of uncle and shopkeeper. The need to be inclusive of the interests of all concerned (*yi* 義) means that deference is multilateral, where grandmothers must defer to the needs of their grandsons just as much as the other way around. The intergenerational transmission of the culture requires first deference in the relations of young and old within a given generation, and then deference by each generation to those that have come before.

In this Confucian tradition, deference to exemplary role models available within the historical narrative do much of the work that abstract "principles" do in serving as guidelines for proper conduct. But even with the central importance given to such exemplars, the project of habituating consummate conduct is still a uniquely personal undertaking. There is a fundamental distinction between inspiration and emulation on the one hand, and imitation and replication on the other. That is, consummate conduct (*ren* 仁), far from being reduplicated actions or generic virtues, is always a singular achievement by particular persons under particular circumstances. We can and should be properly inspired by our role models— our teachers included—but consummate conduct will not brook imitation.

One criticism that has been directed at the term "role ethics" is that "playing a role" introduces a distance if not "duplicity" into the relationship that separates the "actors" themselves from the roles they play. Duplicity from the Latin *duplicare* means first "twofold, having two parts," and then by extension within a substance ontology with the integrity and self-sufficiency of particular persons, deceit. But within a cosmology that gives primacy to vital relationality, we might use this same insight and take duplicity in its original sense of "twoness" to appreciate the necessary gap there will always be between protégés and their mentors, and between succeeding generations as each embodies the one that has come before. There is a twoness in the way that relationality functions in the growth of meaning, as the inspiration of the teacher as model is transformed into the always unique qualities of the consummate student. It is incumbent upon students to seize upon whatever inspiration they can find in their intimate relationships with their teachers, and adapt this stimulation in whatever direction will best serve the nourishing of their own personal growth. And there is deference to the cultural heroes and meaning-makers as one generation inherits the continuing tradition from the one before it. While there is deference to our teachers in the sense of being inspired by them, there must also be respect for the uniqueness and particularity defining of each and every person and situation. And one further point to be made is that there is a sense in which a "twoness" belongs to mentoring as well. Mentors can only become mentors by the deference accorded to them by those who are inspired by their conduct. Role models cannot be role models by themselves.

13.27 子曰: "剛、毅、木、訥，近仁。"
The Master said, "Being firm, resolute, genuine, and deliberate in what you say will get you close to consummate conduct (*ren* 仁)."

Comment: Insight into the nature of consummate conduct is provided in modal terms: the way, manner, or mode in which something is done. All of these modes of behaving describe discursive transactions with others. Given the uniqueness of each situation, such modalities are resistant to general prescription in defining the actual behaviors of exemplary conduct, and are thus often illustrated by appeal to specific historical examples. Throughout the text, moral behavior is usually illustrated rather than defined, alluding to such specific situations more than offering up rules of conduct or binary judgments on abstract principles.

4.4 子曰："苟志於仁矣，無惡也。"
   The Master said, "When intentions are firmly set on consummate conduct (*ren* 仁), one will be free of unseemly actions."

Comment: Resolution in living life consummately is the best way to set a high standard in what we do, and to thus fend off the possibility of unseemly conduct. Importantly, the character 惡 here is pronounced *e* in its noun and adjectival forms, and *wu* as a verb, with the former being translated as "base," "raw," "unrefined," "mean," and the latter "despising," "loathing," "hating." *E* 惡 is fundamentally an aesthetic term, denoting a judgment being made on conduct that displays a lack of cultivation or refinement. Mencius and Xunzi have been typically described as advocating the doctrines that "human nature" is "good" (*shan* 善) or "evil" (*e* 惡) respectively. Such a characterization falters in two ways. First, the notion of "human nature" that is usually read as a universal, reduplicated given introduces an ontology that is not relevant. And secondly, Xunzi's understanding of "human propensities" (*xing* 性) being "base" and "unrefined" (*e* 惡) stands in contrast to Mencius's doctrine that being born into a discursive family and community inclines us towards prosocial conduct (*shan* 善).

   Again, the commitment to the inseparability of knowing and doing means conduct is to be understood holistically. Ethical theory tends to fragment motivation from consequences, agents from actions, the right from the good, and actors from their communities. Such post hoc distinctions have little relevance here, given that as a circuit, all of these phases in what is a continuing activity are mutually implicated. Our purposes far from standing prior to or independent of our conduct, are in every way integral to it, and emerge from it. This passage is not suggesting that good intentions necessarily guarantee good outcomes, but only that purposeful and refined conduct itself precludes untoward actions.

4.3 子曰：＂唯仁者能好人，能惡人。＂

The Master said, "It is the consummate person (*ren* 仁) alone who has the wherewithal to properly discriminate in cherishing some people (*haoren* 好人) while despising others (*wuren* 惡人)."

Comment: In the Confucian tradition, persons and their narratives are one and the same thing, precluding any severe distinction between agents and their actions. You are what you do. Indignation is a familiar human response to social injustice. Far from being discouraged, when educated and informed, such outrage is seen as a necessary resource for identifying and objecting to untoward conduct. Given that perverse, disintegrative behavior on the part of immoral persons has negative consequences for everyone, consummate persons cannot stand idly by and allow such actions to go unnoticed. It is the quality of the conduct achieved by consummate persons that provides them uniquely with the moral purchase necessary to differentiate between those persons who contribute to human flourishing, and those whose conduct takes a toll on the life of the community.

4.1 子曰：＂里仁爲美。擇不處仁，焉得知？＂

The Master said, "It is consummate persons (*ren* 仁) who make a neighborhood attractive. How can anyone be deemed wise who, given the choice, does not seek to dwell among those who are consummate?"[①]

Comment: Confucius on several occasions makes the point that persons should not make friends with those who are not better than themselves (1.8, 9.25, 19.3). Of course, this advice is qualified by his acknowledgment that we all have something to learn from everyone (19.22, 7.22). His reasoning is that since it is the quality and diversity of other persons who constitute the best resource for one's own personal growth, one should do one's utmost to seek out and surround oneself with the best friends one can find (16.4). In fact, Confucius contrasts the institution of friendship with family relations, suggesting that since we can actually choose our

---

① Compare *Mencius* 2A7.

friends, we have to be more demanding and critical in our dealings with them (13.28). Such an approach to personal growth reflects the Confucian understanding of "optimal harmony" (*he* 和) as the kind of diversity achieved when those differences among people are activated to make a difference in the well-being of all.

A historical situation that immediately comes to mind is Emerson's Concord where he surrounds himself with people of intellectual and emotional substance who then became a resource integral to his own personal growth. Close friends such as Margaret Fuller, Louisa May Alcott, Henry Thoreau, and Nathanial Hawthorne were complemented by visitors such as Walt Whitman, Herman Melville, and many others.[①]

An interesting comparison can be made between Confucius and his Greek cousins Plato and Aristotle on the topic of friendship. For Aristotle, for example, the highest kind of friendship is based upon unchanging virtues, where the rare friend in virtue becomes a mirror and a "second self" that can serve as the corroboration of common ends. For Confucius, on the other hand, the substance of friendship is the growth in relationships achieved by activating differences and amplifying diversity: harmony in difference rather than moral homogeneity.

15.9 子曰:"志士仁人，無求生以害仁，有殺身以成仁。"

The Master said, "Resolute scholar-officials (*shi* 士) and consummate persons (*ren* 仁) would never compromise in the quality of their consummatory conduct, even at the cost of their own lives. Indeed, they would willingly forfeit their lives in order to sustain it."[②]

Comment: Confucius is anything but rash. He has no truck with the unnecessary risk of serving in a perverse administration that is lacking in moral vision (*dao* 道), where one is endangering one's own life (5.2, 8.13, 14.3, 15.7). He praises the prudent Yan Hui for knowing enough to remove himself from such dangers, and on more than one occasion, criticizes the bold and impulsive Zilu for being only too willing to bring trouble upon himself by

---

[①] See Susan Cheever, *American Bloomsbury: Louisa May Alcott, Ralph Waldo Emerson, Margaret Fuller, Nathaniel Hawthorne, and Henry David Thoreau: Their Lives, Their Loves, Their Work*, New York: Simon and Schuster, 2007.

[②] Compare *Mencius* 6A10.

rushing into perilous situations (7.11). For Confucius, having underscored the wisdom of avoiding unnecessary personal danger, he is still persuaded that truly moral persons live their lives in a way that gives priority to consummate conduct over everything else, including life itself. Under circumstances that would demand it, such persons will happily sacrifice their own lives rather than compromise their commitment to the highest quality of personal conduct. Cf. 14.12.

15.35 子曰："民之於仁也，甚於水火。水火，吾見蹈而死者矣，未見蹈仁而死者也。"

The Master said, "Consummate conduct (*ren* 仁) is more vital to the common people than even fire and water. I have seen persons lose their lives by walking into fire and water, but I have yet to see any casualties from walking the path of consummate conduct."①

Comment: Fire and water provide the energy needed for the making of tools. They are among the most basic resources necessary for the possibility of human civilization. Given untoward circumstances such as extreme weather events, however, these same natural elements can not only become life-threatening, but can occasion a devastating toll on life and property. As fundamental as fire and water properly harnessed are to human life, consummate conduct is even more vital. While fire and water might be necessary conditions for the possibility of civilization, consummate conduct is the substance of civilized life itself.

14.16 子路曰："桓公殺公子糾，召忽死之，管仲不死。"曰："未仁乎？"子曰："桓公九合諸侯，不以兵車，管仲之力也。如其仁，如其仁。"

Zilu said, "When Duke Huan had his elder brother Prince Jiu killed, the Prince's tutor Shao Hu took his own life, but Guan Zhong did not."② "In this case," Zilu continued, "did Guan Zhong fall short of consummate conduct (*ren* 仁)?"

---

① Compare *Mencius* 7A23.
② See the *Zuo Commentary to the Spring and Autumn Annals* Zhuang 8-9 (cf. Legge, *Chinese Classics*, Vol. 5, pp. 83-84). At Duke Huan of Qi's request the state of Lu put his elder brother Prince Jiu to death, with Prince Jiu's tutor Shao Hu taking his own life in protest. Guan Zhong on the other hand returned to Qi and eventually became prime minister to Duke Huan.

The Master said, "Many times did Duke Huan bring the various feudal lords together, and his success in doing so was always made possible by the efforts of Guan Zhong rather than by a resort to arms. Such was his consummate conduct, such was his consummate conduct."①

14.17 子貢曰:"管仲非仁者與？桓公殺公子糾，不能死，又相之。"子曰："管仲相桓公，霸諸侯，一匡天下，民到于今受其賜。微管仲，吾其被髮左衽矣。豈若匹夫匹婦之為諒也，自經於溝瀆而莫之知也？"

Zigong said, "Surely Guan Zhong was not consummate as a person (*ren* 仁). When Duke Huan had his elder brother Prince Jiu killed, not only did Guan Zhong not die with him, but he became the prime minister for Duke Huan."

The Master replied, "When Guan Zhong served as prime minister for Duke Huan, he enabled the Duke to become leader of the various feudal lords, uniting and bringing order to the world. The common people living down to today are still benefitting from his contribution. If there were no Guan Zhong, we would likely be wearing our hair loose and folding our robes to the left like barbarians. Should we expect that Guan Zhong would have the earnestness of some country yokel, managing to strangle himself in an irrigation ditch with no one the wiser?"

Comment: Passages 14.16 and 14.17 have to be read together. That they make the same reference to the person of Guan Zhong and rehearse the same story about him might be important in understanding how Confucius conceives of consummate conduct (*ren* 仁). Guan Zhong (c. 720-645 BCE) was one of the most distinguished statesmen of the Spring and Autumn period who as prime minister assisted Duke Huan of Qi in becoming the first hegemon of an alliance among the vassal Zhou states. In these passages, two of Confucius's most prominent protégés Zilu and Zigong question the appropriateness of the Master according Guan Zhong the high praise of being consummate as a person (*ren* 仁), a designation that Confucius rarely confers on anyone.

Again, elsewhere in the *Analects* (3.22), Confucius himself expresses reservations about Guan Zhong's person, describing him obliquely in an unflattering way as a "small vessel" (*xiaoqi* 小器). In 3.22, Confucius's

---

① The Ding Zhou manuscript version of the *Analects* does not repeat this phrase.

stated criticisms are very serious: Guan Zhong has offended against ritual propriety in usurping the same standards of decorum as his lord. For Confucius who is intent on promoting a renaissance of the ritualized culture of the Zhou dynasty, such conduct both in broad compass and in the case of Guan Zhong specifically is to be roundly condemned (see 3.1, 3.2, 3.6).

In characterizing Guan Zhong as a consummate person, Confucius's praise is that he was able to bring the vassal lords into alliance without resort to arms, and that across subsequent history, his model of statesmanship has had a profoundly civilizing effect on the proto-Chinese world, one that had endured down to Confucius's day. Interesting in this ascription of *ren* 仁 to Guan Zhong is Confucius's willingness to allow for consummate conduct in a non-categorical way. In spite of Guan Zhong's serious shortcomings, on balance his singular and inimitable contribution to Chinese culture has been sufficient to accord him such an attribution. Perhaps we can find an analogy in the American experience where Founding Fathers such as George Washington and Thomas Jefferson are still celebrated by many in spite of their intimate and conflicted association with human slavery.

3.3 子曰: "人而不仁，如禮何? 人而不仁，如樂何? "

The Master said: "What do persons who are not consummate in their conduct (*ren* 仁) have to do with observing ritual propriety (*li* 禮)? What do persons who are not consummate in their conduct have to do with the making of music (*yue* 樂)?"

Comment: This statement is best read together with those passages in the *Analects* (3.1, 3.2, 3.6) in which Confucius condemns the Three Houses of Lu—Meng, Shu, and Ji—who by conducting rituals and performing music belonging exclusively to the royal court were usurping the prerogatives of the Zhou house and the Duke of Lu. For Confucius, the conventions of titles and ranks provide the social and political structure for society, and thus offences against them threaten the stability and continuity of the tradition. In a cosmology that does not appeal to some permanent and unchanging principle guaranteeing cosmic order—that is, some variant on the concept of "God"—the greatest threat to humanity is its possible descent into chaos. Confucius's doctrine of "using names and titles properly" (*zhengming* 正名) when applied retrospectively has an important role in reinforcing the existing social and political order.

In addition to offering a clear rebuke to the Three Houses, Confucius has perhaps a more fundamental point to make here. Standing in contrast to the impersonal imposition of the rule of law, both ritual and musical performances require personalization, and are ultimately defined by the quality of the performers who participate in them. Music and ritual certainly provide the formalities necessary for personal refinement, but it is ultimately the consummatory status of the performers in the personalization of these forms that is the final measure of the efficacy of ritual and music.

Nietzsche in *Zarathustra* reflecting on the importance of music, famously says that "without music, life would be a mistake. I would only believe in a God who knew how to dance." At the same time, Nietzsche like Confucius correlates the making of music with the moral quality of persons when he insists that "evil men have no songs."

III.8 Seeking Optimal Appropriateness in Roles and Relations (*yi* 義)

4.10 子曰：''君子之於天下也，無適也，無莫也，義之與比。''

The Master said, "Exemplary persons (*junzi* 君子) in making their way in the world are neither bent on nor against anything; rather, they go with what is most appropriate (*yi* 義).''

Comment: With the introduction of Confucianism into the Western academy by missionaries, the conventional translation of *yi* 義 has been "righteousness" as in the translation of the Greek *dikaiosunē*: "being righteous before God" (as in Romans 1:17). Being righteous literally means to be objectively right, especially in a moral way, by comporting oneself according to the one standard set by the will of God. Hence, we have the binary of right and wrong.

In the first place, such an understanding of the basis of ethical judgments has little relevance in a tradition without a transcendent God as an absolute standard. While on the one hand a sense of social justice requires one be resolved and stand firm, *yi* 義 is still the outcome of a negotiation between relationally-constituted persons and their always specific contexts. Just as achieving consummate conduct (*ren* 仁) can be read as an alternative to the ideology of individualism, achieving optimal appropriateness (*yi* 義) is a challenge to the adequacy of objectivism and its corollary that justice must be blind.① A rationalized justice reduced to the mere application of some abstract and exclusive principle as it is applied to deracinated, generic individuals, far from achieving its ends, can as a forced uniformity become an impoverishing source of violence.

Real fairness requires a synoptic view of circumstances that includes flexibility, inclusiveness, and accommodation, dispositions associated with the person of Confucius himself (9.4, 14.32). For Confucius, it is not possible to enter into what are always novel situations with its best outcome ready to hand. While analogy with past achievements can certainly provide us with important guidance, Confucius is also resolute in respecting the particularity of the circumstances. Determining what is optimally appropriate requires unrelenting attention to the different interests at stake, and is thus hard work. And perhaps the most important asset we have in this always difficult task is an alert, educated, and dexterous imagination that would allow us to put ourselves empathetically into the place of others in search of our own most efficacious response.

15.16 子曰："不曰'如之何如之何'者，吾末如之何也已矣。"
The Master said, "There is nothing I can do for people who are not constantly asking themselves: 'What to do? What to do?'"

Comment: Throughout the early literature, *yi* 義 as "optimally appropriate" is frequently defined in terms of its homophone *yi* 誼 and its root, *yi* 宜 "right, fitting, suitable" that is sometimes used as its loan character. While these two cognate terms are reflexive in referencing "persons-in-context," the emphasis in the first case *yi* 義 would seem to be on *person* as actively seeking out what is most appropriate for all concerned within a particular context, while the emphasis in the second case *yi* 宜 would be on making adjustments to the *context* in order to become fitting or suitable to it. Both terms and their several cognates are associated with ancestral sacrifice, with *yi* 義 being constituted by a sacrificial sheep (*yang* 羊) and the dagger-axe (*ge* 戈) that is used to dispatch and bleed it for the ceremony. As found on the oracle bones, *yi* 宜 is 🔲 that depicts two pieces of meat

---

① Henry Rosemont, Jr., *Against Individualism: A Confucian Rethinking of the Foundations of Morality, Politics, Family, and Religion*, Idaho Falls: Lexington Books, 2015.

being displayed on a sacrificial stand.① The critical function of sacrifice is to galvanize the hierarchical social and political order to assure everyone is in their proper place. The association of this key moral vocabulary with sacrifice not only elevates it and makes it sacrosanct, but also brings with it a sense of proper poise and decorum captured in the cognate character *yi* 儀, underscoring the relationship between civility and morality.②

Being consummate in one's conduct is the unrelenting application of the moral imagination to find what conduces to optimal growth in always unique circumstances. The starting point is that "appropriateness" is always going to be situation specific, and thus cannot be achieved by applying some predetermined standard. Rather, appropriateness requires critical reflection—What to do? What to do?—in every case. Cf. 7.8.

2.24 子曰：“非其鬼而祭之，諂也。見義不爲，無勇也。”

The Master said, "Sacrificing to ancestral spirits other than one's own is being unctuous. Failing to act upon what is seen as most appropriate (*yi* 義) is a want of courage."

Comment: In this Confucian tradition with "family reverence" (*xiao* 孝) as its prime moral imperative, there are few things human beings do that require greater attention to propriety and decorum than the formalities developed for respecting those who have come before. Intergenerational veneration is the powerful motive force that perpetuates the cultural tradition with each generation having to build the connector for the one that follows.

How are we to understand the parallel in this passage between sacrificing to ancestral spirits and valuing appropriateness as a quality of conduct? Proper sacrificial offerings (*ji* 祭) and doing what is most appropriate (*yi* 義) are to be commended, but offering made for ulterior motives and failing to act in service to what should be done are moral deficiencies. The contrast in each phrase then, lies in the attempt to clarify what is actually entailed by appropriate *yi* 義 and inappropriate conduct. In a formal sacrifice, there is a clear lack of decorum in the gratuitous behavior of

---

① See Kwan, "Database," 甲骨文文集 CHANT 3279.
② See Amy Olberding, *The Wrong of Rudeness: Learning Modern Civility from Ancient Chinese Philosophy*, New York: Oxford, 2019 for a sustained argument on this point.

going beyond one's own family lineage in the observance of ancestral ritual performances that in fact would dilute and impoverish the ceremony and diminish the proper object of reverence. On the other hand, the stern commitment to do what is optimally appropriate regardless of the cost to one's own person is itself a clear expression of the dignity and solemnity associated with formal sacrifice. A serious commitment to stand on the right side of what should be done is not always popular or easy, and often demands a quantum of courage. There is certainly an attitude of flexibility and inclusiveness necessary in determining the most appropriate course of action in any particular situation, but such accommodation does not preclude the firmness and resolve needed to act upon it when required. Indeed, drawing upon such resolve is a major theme in the *Analects*.

The character *yi* 義 is composed of a sheep (*yang* 羊) and what is now the character used as the first person(s) pronoun (*wo* 我). When it is remembered that sheep were periodically sacrificed at large communal gatherings, we may gloss *yi* 義 as the solemn, dignified attitude one assumes, the proper stance one takes, when preparing the lamb for the ritual slaughter. The pronoun *wo* 我 as attested in the bronzes depicts a dagger-axe (*ge* 戈): ![char],① and it has been argued that the *wo* 我 character is long-handled weapon with serrated, saw-like teeth. At some point for phonological reasons, it came to be used as a loan character for its homophone, the first-person pronoun, *wo* 我. This association of *wo* 我 as a dagger-axe and *yi* 義 with sacrifice is consistent with their cognate *xi* 犧 "sacrificing, sacrificial animal" that in its original form on the oracle bones and bronzes was written as *xi* 羲. Again, *yi* 義 is glossed in the *Shuowen* lexicon as "dignity, majesty" (*weiyi* 威儀), where the connotation of assuming a proper demeanor can be attested by the cognate character 儀—"an *yi* person"—meaning specifically a person with dignity, decorum, courtesy, graciousness. The propriety of this ritualized disposition and its deferential attitude not only carries over to make a person a sacred representative of the community, but also purifies and consecrates the sacrificial animal.

4.16 子曰："君子喻於義，小人喻於利。"

The Master said, "Exemplary persons (*junzi* 君子) understand what is most appropriate (*yi* 義); petty persons understand what is of personal advantage (*li*

---

① See Kwan, "Database," 春秋 CHANT 102.

利)."

Comment: Throughout the *Analects* there is frequent reference to "petty or mean persons:" literally "small persons" (*xiaoren* 小人). In the repeated contrast Confucius offers us between these "petty persons" (*xiaoren* 小人) and "exemplary persons" (*junzi* 君子), petty persons are portrayed as socially and morally stunted individuals where the impact of such selfish conduct reaches beyond themselves. They are a continuing source of communal divisiveness and distress. Petty persons are properly described as "small" in a relational sense. They are aberrant "individuals" who, having failed to grow themselves in their vital family and community roles, are thus underdeveloped and devoid of meaningful relations.

By contrast, those who are "exemplary" (*junzi* 君子) in their conduct are persons who emerge as socially and politically "exemplary" by virtue of the patterns of deference they occasion from the communities in which they reside. In addition to exemplary persons, there are other designations for those who have extended themselves in the world by cultivating their relations and who are again described literally in terms of growth such as *daren* 大人, literally "big or grand persons," or *chengren* 成人 "accomplished persons."

A second frequently encountered distinction in the Confucian texts we find in *Expansive Learning* is between a sense of inclusive optimizing appropriateness that seeks to take into account the interests of all concerned including oneself (*yi* 義), and a preoccupation with personal advantage that has as its exclusive reference one's own personal benefit (*li* 利).

7.3 子曰："德之不修，學之不講，聞義不能徙，不善不能改，是吾憂也。"

The Master said: "To fail to cultivate virtuosity in my conduct (*de* 德), to fail to practice what I have learned, to fail to follow through on what I know to be the most appropriate course of action (*yi* 義), and to fail to reform my misdeeds—these are the things that give me the greatest concern."

Comment: The ever-modest Confucius, while inclined to self-deprecation when it comes to describing his own native capacities (5.9, 7.1, 7.20), prides himself unabashedly on his love of teaching and on his personal eagerness to learn. These propensities for teaching and learning are both captured in his description of himself as *haoxue* 好學—that is, as someone who truly cherishes both practical education and educated practice (5.28,

7.2, 7.3, 7.19, 7.34). The substance of such education is the assiduous cultivation of one's person as it is expressed in the moral compass of one's own conduct. Regardless of their social status or personal means, Confucius exhibits an unwavering commitment to provide able students their best opportunity for such education (7.7). And it is because Confucius makes such high demands on himself in his own personal regimen of study that, in the high expectations he has for his students and in the sometimes harsh judgments he is wont to make on their progress, it is clear that he takes their resolve and their unrelenting effort as his foremost criteria (7.8, 8.12, 8.17, 14.24).

17.23 子路曰："君子尚勇乎？" 子曰："君子義以爲上，君子有勇而無義爲亂，小人有勇而無義爲盜。"

Zilu said, "Do exemplary persons (*junzi* 君子) give first priority to courage?"

"In fact," the Master replied, "exemplary persons give first priority to being optimally appropriate in their conduct (*yi* 義). Exemplary persons who have courage yet fail in being appropriate will be unruly, while petty persons of the same cut will be thieves."

Comment: It is important to observe here that the interlocutor to whom Confucius is directing his counsel is the impulsive and undisciplined Zilu, a person given to precipitous action rather than learning. See the *Comment* on 17.8 (p. 154) for a profile of Zilu. There is a familiar pattern in the *Analects* in which otherwise unrefined action is elevated and transformed into virtuosic action by being mediated through "learning" (*xue* 學) (17.8) or "ritual propriety" (*li* 禮) (8.2, 12.1) or here through "appropriateness in conduct" (*yi* 義). The point is that erstwhile "courageous conduct" that is not in the service of doing what is most appropriate in any particular situation even when carried out by otherwise exemplary persons is mere boldness, and when done by lesser persons can be coercion if not even criminality. In neither case would such conduct, uninformed as it is by appropriateness, rise to the level of courage. An interesting point made here and elsewhere is that "exemplary persons" are given to have lapses, and are not to be taken as categorical in the sense of being exemplary in every situation (see also 19.21).

7.16 子曰："飯疏食飲水，曲肱而枕之，樂亦在其中矣。不義而富且貴，於我如浮雲。"

The Master said, "To eat coarse food, drink plain water, and pillow oneself on a bent arm—there is enjoyment (*le* 樂) to be found in these things. But wealth and position gained through inappropriate means (*buyi* 不義)—these are to me like floating clouds."

Comment: From the very first passage in the received *Analects*, "enjoyment" (*le* 樂) is a high value that goes underreported in the commentaries (see for example 1.1, 6.11, 6.23, 9.24, 16.5). There is rejoicing to be felt that has both moral and religious meaning when a morally eventful life is being consummated within the relationships of family, community, and cosmos. Such enjoyment can only arise within conduct that is beyond moral reproach. When this enjoyment is coupled with the kind of productive "knowing" (*zhi* 知) that is of service to the community for example, it elevates such knowing to the level of a joyful wisdom (6.20). The expectation is that wealth and status for most people would be perceived as a source of enjoyment far outweighing the simple comforts described herein, and yet for Confucius, if such good fortune is the reward of questionable conduct, he would have no part in it.

14.32 微生畝謂孔子曰："丘何爲是栖栖者與？無乃爲佞乎？"孔子曰："非敢爲佞也，疾固也。"

Weisheng Mu said to Confucius, "Why do you flit from perch to perch? Are you aspiring to be an eloquent speaker?"

Confucius replied, "It is not that I would aspire to be an eloquent speaker, but rather that I hate inflexibility."

Comment: We are not sure of the identity of Weisheng Mu, but since he uses Confucius's given name and his question is candid if not bordering on impolite, we can assume that he is someone who has a higher station than Confucius or at least is his elder. Again, "flitting from perch to perch" might be an allusion to Confucius's frustrating travels from court to court toward the end of his life, trying to persuade rulers to accept his counsel on how best to rule. In any case, this passage has a rather dramatic function in underscoring Confucius's basic values. Two persistent themes in the text are first that, when it comes to the use of language, Confucius has a sustained impatience with glibness and feigned eloquence (1.3, 5.5, 5.25, 11.25, 15.11, 16.4), and secondly that he has high regard for a stern commitment to doing

III. THE *ANALECTS* (*LUNYU* 論語): A BASIC CONFUCIAN VOCABULARY

one's best (*zhong* 忠) and making good on one's word (*xin* 信). At the same time, this serious and resolute person Confucius is also portrayed in the *Analects* and throughout the Confucian canons as someone who prides himself most on his flexibility and moral dexterity (1.8, 4.10, 9.4, 13.20, *Mencius* 5B1). Resolution and flexibility are not necessarily contraries.

16.11 孔子曰：" 見善如不及，見不善如探湯。吾見其人矣，吾聞其語矣。隱居以求其志，行義以達其道。吾聞其語矣，未見其人也。"

Confucius said, "'On seeing what is working well (*shan* 善), I go after it as though I cannot catch up to it; on seeing what isn't, I recoil from it as though testing boiling water.' I have seen such people and have heard such words.

"'I dwell in seclusion to pursue my purposes, and act on my sense of what is most appropriate (*yi* 義) to extend the proper way (*dao* 道).' I have heard such words, but I have yet to see such persons."

Comment: Even though Confucius seems to be citing popular sayings here, we might correlate this passage with how he describes the lives of the brothers Bo Yi 伯夷 and Shu Qi 叔齊 who as recluses died of starvation in service to what they felt to be right (16.12). Theirs is one of the most frequently alluded to stories in classical Chinese literature broadly, and in the *Analects* specifically.

As the story is recounted in the *Records of the Grand Historian* (*Shiji* 史記) 61, Bo Yi and Shu Qi had withdrawn after a dispute over legitimate rulership in their own state, and were growing old in exile. King Wen, founder of the Zhou dynasty, had a reputation for caring for the aged, and thus Bo Yi and Shu Qi sought him out. But by the time they arrived at the court, King Wen had already passed away. His son Wu, carrying his father's sacrificial tablet and honoring him as "king" (*wang* 王), had set out eastward to attack the tyrannical imperial overlord of the Shang dynasty, Zhou. Bo Yi and Shu Qi, interpreting such intentions as regicide, seized the bridle of Wu's horse and admonished him, saying "Your father is not yet buried and you are taking up arms—can this be called 'family reverence' (*xiao* 孝)? A subject assassinating his ruler—can this be called 'consummate conduct' (*ren* 仁)?"

Wu's retainers wanted to kill Bo Yi and Shu Qi on the spot, but Duke Tai intervened, saying "These are men doing what they believe to be right." He protected them and sent them on their way. When Wu had conquered the Shang empire and overthrown its dynasty, the people paid homage to him and his father as the founders of the Zhou dynasty, but Bo Yi and Shu Qi regarded his investiture as a source of shame. In accordance with their sense of what is right, they refused to eat the grain of Zhou, secluded themselves on Shouyang Mountain, and lived on wild beans. They recorded their grievances in a song that has been passed on to posterity:

> 登彼西山兮，采其薇矣。以暴易暴兮，不知其非矣。
> 神農、虞、夏忽焉沒兮，我安適歸矣？于嗟徂兮，命之衰矣！
> We have climbed Shouyang Mountain and gathered wild beans.
> They have replaced a violent ruler with a violent subject and do not realize their wrong.
> The succession of the ancient sage-kings has abruptly come to an end.
> Where can we turn? Alas! We depart.
> Such then is the unhappy tide of circumstance.

Subsequently they starved to death on Shouyang Mountain. The Grand Historian remarked: "Viewing the situation thusly, have they done anything to incur ill-will? Yet is what they call 'wrong' really wrong?"

To begin with, these two brothers are the only persons that Confucius is willing to describe without qualification as "consummate persons" (*ren* 仁). He says 求仁而得仁 "seeking to be consummate in their conduct, they achieved their ends" (7.15). Again, in 18.8, Confucius says: 不降其志，不辱其身，伯夷、叔齊與 "It was Bo Yi and Shu Qi who were unwilling to compromise their purposes or bring disgrace on their own persons."

What is it that Confucius finds so admirable about Bo Yi and Shu Qi? They refused their father's throne, they were unwilling to challenge their brother's appointment, they remonstrated fearlessly with King Wu's violations of ritual propriety, and they sacrificed their own lives as a protest against King Wu's regicide. In all of their actions, they set aside personal advantage to comport themselves in a way consistent with the established values of "family reverence" (*xiao* 孝) and "ritual propriety" (*li* 禮) while at the same time making their own personal judgments on what is most appropriate (*yi* 義). In all cases, they saw themselves as "acting on a sense of what is most appropriate to extend the proper way."

The fact that Confucius allows that Bo Yi and Shu Qi were doing what is appropriate in withholding their support for King Wu while at the same time himself reserving high praise for King Wu (8.20, 19.22) certainly suggests that for Confucius, "appropriateness" (*yi* 義) can only be the exercising of one's own best judgment rather than pronouncing on the basis of some objective standard. This understanding of "appropriateness" is underscored when Confucius distinguishes himself from Bo Yi and Shu Qi specifically in saying 我則異於是，無可無不可 "I differ from them in not having any presuppositions as to what may and may not be done" (18.8). Perhaps Confucius, given his singularly high regard for the Zhou dynasty, would under similar circumstances have arrived at judgments different from the brothers. But by conferring the high compliment of "consummate persons" (*ren* 仁) on them, he is making the point that being appropriate is not one thing, and requires deference and accommodation to the judgment of others.

11.22 子路問："聞斯行諸？"子曰："有父兄在，如之何其聞斯行之？"冉有問："聞斯行諸？"子曰："聞斯行之。"公西華曰："由也問'聞斯行諸'，子曰：'有父兄在'；求也問'聞斯行諸'，子曰：'聞斯行之'。赤也惑，敢問。"子曰："求也退，故進之；由也兼人，故退之。"

Zilu inquired, "On learning something, should I act upon it?" The Master said, "While your father and elder brothers are still alive, how could you on learning something, act upon it?"

When Ranyou asked the same question, the Master replied, "On learning something, act upon it."

Gongxi Hua said, "When Zilu posed the question about acting on what he has learned, you said not while his father and elder brothers are still alive, but when Ranyou asked you the same question, you told him to act on what he learns. I am confused, and would ask for your clarification."

The Master replied, "Ranyou is diffident, and so I urged him on. But Zilu has the energy of two, and so I sought to rein him in."

Comment: Confucius is not given to generic answers. True to his hermeneutical method of "putting oneself in the place of others" (*shu* 恕) in determining the most productive course of action, Confucius draws his different answers from his understanding of the evolving narratives of his many students. He concerns himself about where are they "coming from" and where are they going as specific persons. He is responding to the whence and whither as their narratives unfold. Seeing that his protégés are so diverse in their capacities and temperaments, the always specific answers

Confucius chooses to give each one of them must be tailored to the unique situations and challenges they face in their very different lives.

In this passage, Confucius is asked the same question by two of his students, Zilu and Ranyou: that is, "On learning something, should I act upon it?" And in reply, Confucius gives them not only a different response, but indeed precisely the opposite answer: "yes" to Ranyou and "no" to Zilu.

When Confucius is then asked by a perplexed witness why he would give clearly contradictory counsel to his two students, his response is that he must consider what is most appropriate to the habituated dispositions of the questioners: "Ranyou is diffident, and so I urged him on. But Zilu has the energy of two, and so I sought to rein him in." We know that Ranyou is younger, and has a major interest in government administration (for a profile of Ranyou, see the *Comment* on *Mencius* 4A14, p. 537). In 6.12, he admires the way of Confucius, but worries that he does not have the fortitude to follow his example. The older Zilu has a military background, and throughout the text, is presented as rash and impulsive (for a profile of Zilu, see the *Comment* on 17.8, p. 154).

III.9 Aspiring to Ritual Propriety in Roles and Relations (*li* 禮)

8.2 子曰: "恭而無禮則勞, 慎而無禮則葸, 勇而無禮則亂, 直而無禮則絞。君子篤於親, 則民興於仁; 故舊不遺, 則民不偷。"

The Master said, "Deference unmediated by aspiring to propriety in our roles and relations (*li* 禮) is lethargy; circumspection unmediated by such propriety is timidity; bravery unmediated by such propriety is rowdiness; candor unmediated by such propriety is rudeness. Where exemplary persons are earnestly committed to their parents, the common people will aspire to consummate conduct (*ren* 仁); where they do not neglect their old friends, the common people will not be indifferent to each other."

Comment: Confucius would insist that important social values such as deference, circumspection, bravery, and candor can only rise above the thin, indeed perverse dispositions of lethargy, timidity, rowdiness, and rudeness, when they are properly transformed and authenticated through aspiring to propriety in our personal relations. Such passages reflect the Confucian commitment to the aestheticized life that can be traced back to the Shang dynasty. Subsequently during the Zhou dynasty, the scope of *li* 禮 was gradually extended beyond the court into the everyday lives of the people. From earliest times, the strategy for lifting the human experience out of its animality was to refine it through ritualized institutions and practices, the first of which is the family with its tradition of ancestral reverence. The importance of this civilizing project is reflected in the extent to which *li* 禮 with all of its accoutrements has immediate relevance to every aspect of daily life.

In our understanding of *li* 禮, we must begin from the holistic and thus reflexive assumptions of the process cosmology that serves as the interpretive context for these texts. The substance and depth of *li* 禮, unlike formal regulations, is dependent upon a process of personalization—that is, it is the aspiration of this particular daughter in her unique relationship with this particular father, to make the relationship something moving and magical.

The passage concludes with its claim that exemplary persons finding propriety in their relations through the *li* 禮 are a powerful influence on the values and practices of the common people. The correlation between parents and consummate conduct reinforces the important point that family is the entry point for aspiring to moral competency and that family reverence (*xiao* 孝) is the prime moral imperative. Cf. 1.2.

3.12 祭如在，祭神如神在。子曰："吾不與祭，如不祭。"
The expression "sacrifice as though present" is taken to mean "sacrifice to the spirits as though they are present." But the Master said: "If I myself do not participate in the sacrifice, it is as though I have not sacrificed at all."

Comment: What makes ritual performance profoundly different from law or rule is this sustained effort to internalize the tradition and its institutions as integral to one's own identity. The Latin *proprius*, "making something one's own," gives us a series of reflexive cognate expressions that are useful in translating key Confucian philosophical terms to capture this sense of participation and personalization.

As a footnote to this understanding of *li* 禮 as "making something one's own," we have to be aware that an important factor that determines the quality of our understanding of these Confucian texts is a correlation between the text and our own lived experience. Theoretical explanation and cognitive insight are certainly important, but they cannot do all of the work in making the institutions and practices of *li* 禮 clear to an apprentice. That is, the expository limits of these canonical texts lie in their tacit assumption that readers will evoke their own life experience to inform and amplify the themes under discussion. While these documents will certainly provide their readers with the vocabulary necessary to reflect cogently on moral issues, their function does not end there. The further expectation is that readers in refining their own lives through a close reading of these texts as well as in exercising their best efforts to make use of them in theorizing their own practices, will do nothing less than transform their persons into morally competent human beings (*jiaohua* 教化).

17.11 子曰："禮云禮云，玉帛云乎哉？ 樂云樂云，鍾鼓云乎哉？"

The Master said, "In referring time and again to observing ritual propriety (*li* 禮), how could I just be talking about jade and silk? And in referring time and again to making music (*yue* 樂), how could I just be talking about bells and drums?"

Comment: Such passages in the *Analects* can be used as a heuristic from which to glean insights into what "ritual propriety" had come to mean by the time of Confucius at some half of a millennium remove from the fall of the Shang dynasty. One of Confucius's most consistent complaints about his own era was how decadence had set in with respect to the various institutions governed by *li* 禮. And he saw it as one of his most important responsibilities to reinstate the centrality of this way of elevating and transforming the human experience for his own time and place. For Confucius, in his time an impoverished *li* 禮 had been reduced to the formal accoutrements of such ritual practices at the expense of people using these institutions to educate and refine the human experience in their proper commitment to a higher way of life.

Li 禮 has to be understood in a holistic way covering both the formal and the informal aspects of these life forms. Importantly, ritual practices and the making of music are inseparable aspects of a lifetime regimen of personal refinement. While the ritual "forms" such as jade and silk, bells and drums have a role in such performances, there is the "idea" of ritualized practices captured in a serious commitment to the personalization and reauthorization of these institutions in every moment of our lives. Our very identities as civilized persons emerge in this process.

20.3 子曰："不知命，無以爲君子也。不知禮，無以立也。不知言，無以知人也。"

The Master said, "Someone who does not understand the propensity of circumstances (*ming* 命) has no way of becoming an exemplary person (*junzi* 君子); someone who does not understand the achievement of propriety in our roles and relations (*li* 禮) has no way of knowing where to stand; someone who does not understand human discourse (*yan* 言) has no way of knowing other people."

Comment: The parallel structure in this passage provides us with important insight into the term *ming* 命, conventionally translated as a unilateral "command," or the equally unilateral notions of "fate" or "destiny" as the doom of the gods. In a close reading of the *Analects* we find that a pervasive concern throughout this most seminal of the Confucian texts is sensitivity to the proper use of language. The communicating family and community has a central role as the locus of personal growth. Indeed, almost all of the terms that define human morality in Confucian philosophy allude to deliberate and effective communication within family and community as the source of this personal growth. For example, the characters for exemplary persons (*junzi* 君子) and for the propensity of circumstances (*ming* 命) are written with the mouth signific, the relationship of trust and credibility (*xin* 信) is written with the speech signific, the dynamics of empathetic deference (*shu* 恕) with the mouth and the heartmind (or "thinking and feeling") signific, the attainment of true sincerity and resolution (*cheng* 誠) with the speech signific, the expression of moral virtuosity (*de* 德) with the heartmind signific, and so on. In this passage, just as "words" (*yan* 言) and "ritual propriety" (*li* 禮) are modes of discourse that require personalization and negotiation among people, so "the propensity of circumstances" (*ming* 命) has to be understood analogously as discursive rather than impositional that in some degree is open to negotiation. For example, while *tianming* 天命 might properly be translated as "the command of *tian* 天," far from being a unilateral anointment establishing the divine right of kings, such a command belongs to a communication between *tian* 天 and those human rulers who in their virtuosity have come to command the respect of *tian* 天. Cf. *Mencius* 2A2 that seems to allude to this passage and the crucial role of understanding human discourse (*zhiyan* 知言) in the project of personal cultivation.

1.12 有子曰："禮之用，和爲貴。先王之道斯爲美，小大由之。有所不行，知和而和，不以禮節之，亦不可行也。"

Master You said: "An optimizing harmony (*he* 和) is the most valuable function of aspiring to propriety in our roles and relations (*li* 禮). In the ways of the Former Kings, this optimizing harmony made them refined, and was a guiding standard in all things large and small. But when things are not going well, to pursue harmony just for its own sake without regulating the situation through aspiring to propriety in our roles and relations will not work."

Comment: Morality is simply the outcome of growing, refining, and thus optimizing relations. And it is the attainment of a ritualized propriety in roles and relations that transforms mere mechanical harmony into an optimizing symbiosis. Without being properly negotiated through our roles and relations, harmony as simply the absence of dissonance can be meaningless or worse. A putative "harmony" that is achieved by imposing external mechanisms and constraints as a means of enforcing order—the application of laws, policies, and rules—is dehumanizing to the extent that such "harmony" precludes personal confirmation and participation. Historically it has been the development of the civilizing institutions and practices of *li* 禮 and their application to the human experience in all of its parts that have elevated life in this world to become something elegant and refined. Morality understood in this way describes a quality of personal conduct that makes familial and communal bonds stronger and thicker and more enduring.

3.4 林放問禮之本。子曰："大哉問！禮，與其奢也，寧儉；喪，與其易也，寧戚。"

Lin Fang asked about the root of achieving ritual propriety in roles and relations (*li* 禮). The Master replied: "What an important question! In aspiring to ritual propriety, it is better to be modest than extravagant; in mourning, it is better to express real grief than to worry over formal details."

Comment: The "root" metaphor is apposite in describing ritual propriety as it functions as a source of familial and communal growth. While the social and political forms serve as the apparatus for aspiring to such propriety in our roles and relations and have an important function, it is the modal "how" we pursue this propriety rather than formal "what" we do that is most fundamental. We only need survey our religious institutions

III. THE *ANALECTS* (*LUNYU* 論語): A BASIC CONFUCIAN VOCABULARY

to see how extravagance and opulence have been used to create awe in the hearts of the faithful. And we have also seen how modesty and sincerity have been preached as an antidote when the decadence of form has come to overwhelm substance.

On the one hand, in aspiring to a life lived through ritual propriety, refinement is impossible without the formal aspect. On the other hand, because "form" is recalcitrant and does not reform itself, in order to avoid decadence in our formal institutions, we must constantly return to the "idea" or the "root meaning" of such institutions that lie behind their formal expression. A major theme of Chapter 3 in the *Analects* in particular, is finding the right balance between the informal and the formal, between substance and its elegant ornamentation.

3.8 子夏問曰："'巧笑倩兮，美目盼兮，素以爲絢兮。'何謂也？"子曰："繪事後素。"曰："禮後乎？"子曰："起予者商也！始可與言詩已矣。"

Zixia inquired: "What does the verse mean when its says:
'Her smiling cheeks—so radiant,
Her dazzling eyes—so sharp and clear,
It is the unadorned that is then enhanced'?"

The Master replied: "The application of color is to the unadorned."

"Does this mean that ritual propriety (*li* 禮) is itself an outcome?" asked Zixia.

The Master replied: "Zixia, you have stimulated my thoughts. It is only with the likes of you that one can discuss the *Songs*."

Comment: One feature of the classical Chinese language is the ubiquitous pairing of terms: the heavens and the earth (*tiandi* 天地), forming and functioning (*tiyong* 體用), flux and persistence (*biantong* 變通), ritual and music (*liyue* 禮樂), and so on. Given the *yinyang* 陰陽 correlative and complementary nature of these dyadic pairs, each member is implicated in, and completes, the second. And again, the pairs are hierarchical, with the former usually being privileged over the latter. Given these linguistic features, the appearance of any one of these terms can usually be read as representing both of them: that is, *tian* 天 represents both the heavens and the earth (*tiandi* 天地). This characteristic of the language is certainly apparent where the appearance of the term "ritual propriety" (*li* 禮) is actually doing the work of both "ritual proprieties" and "the making of music" (*liyue* 禮樂).

Zixia is one of Confucius's most distinguished students, and has had an important role historically in how Confucius has been interpreted and received by the cultural tradition (see his profile in the *Comment* to 19.5, p.145). The first two lines of a verse in the *Book of Songs* 57 are cited here, describing as they do a handsome lady of the court. This citation is a good example of how the *Songs* is regularly being appropriated in a creative way by the philosophers to coopt the authority of this canonical text for their philosophical insights. The third line in the verse—itself an interpolation—makes the philosophical point. While we usually understand cosmetics as enhancing natural features, it is the quality of the natural features that is not only a necessary condition for, but in fact circumscribes the possibilities of the cosmetic effect. In a painting, for example, the quality of the canvas must come first. It is in this sense then, that there is the primacy of the unadorned over adornment. But even with such a priority, we must understand the relationship between the natural features and the adornment not as an essential substance being served by a contingent attribute, but rather as a *yinyang* 陰陽 collateral relationship with each being reflexively complemented by the other. The root does not "cause" the tree; rather, they are each responsible for the growth of the other. While a linen canvas that has a tight weave and a smooth surface qualifies it as a fine canvas, that Turner's *Snow Storm* has been painted on it makes what is a mere canvas into a priceless painting.

Once Confucius has drawn this insight as to the collaterality of substance and ornamentation out of the verse, Zixia then applies it to the relationship between ritualized propriety and the quality of the people who participate in these life forms, with each of these aspects of the refined life being enhanced by the other. In his response to Zixia, Confucius is delighted that an able student has come back in the conversation with much more than he has been given, reinforcing the inseparability of teaching and learning in the original meaning of the character for "learning" (*xue* 學). Cf. 7.8.

10.3 君召使擯，色勃如也，足躩如也。揖所與立，左右手。衣前後，襜如也。趨進，翼如也。賓退，必復命曰："賓不顧矣。"

When summoned by his lord to receive a guest at court, Confucius's countenance would change visibly and he would hasten his pace. He would salute the others standing in attendance, gesturing his clasped hands to the right and to the left, and as his flowing robes swayed front and back with his movements, he would glide forward briskly. When the guest retired, he would be certain to report to his lord, "Our guest no longer looks back."

Comment: From this passage and many others like it, it should be clear that achieving propriety in one's roles and relations does not reduce to generic, formally prescribed "rites" or "rituals," performed at stipulated times to announce status and to punctuate the seasons of the human life. In our reading of the *Analects*, there is a tendency to give short shrift to the middle books 9-11 as a series of intimate portraits depicting the historical person, Confucius, that themselves offer little by way of content. If such personal information is considered at all, we are inclined to pass over it quickly as insufficiently philosophical to be relevant to the Confucian project of personal cultivation. But in fact, in overlooking these personal details, we are in danger of missing the real substance of Confucius's moral vision. It is precisely passages such as this one that remember the specific moments in the exemplary life of Confucius himself, and that are defining of him as a role model for the ages.

10.4 入公門，鞠躬如也，如不容。立不中門，行不履閾。過位，色勃如也，足躩如也，其言似不足者。攝齊升堂，鞠躬如也，屏氣似不息者。出，降一等，逞顏色，怡怡如也。沒階趨進，翼如也。復其位，踧踖如也。

On passing through the entranceway to the Duke's court, Confucius would bow forward from the waist, as though the gateway were not high enough. While in attendance, he would not stand in the middle of the entrance; on going through the passageway he would not step on the raised threshold. On passing by the empty throne, his countenance would change visibly, his legs would bend, and in his speech, he would seem to be breathless. He would lift the hem of his skirts in ascending the hall, bow forward from the waist, and hold in his breath as though ceasing to breathe. On leaving and descending the first steps, he would relax his expression and regain his composure. He would then glide briskly from the bottom of the steps, and returning to his place, would resume a reverent posture.

Comment: A careful reading of the classical Confucian literature uncovers a way of life carefully choreographed down to appropriate facial expressions and physical gestures, a world in which life is a performance requiring enormous nuance and attention to detail. Importantly, this *li* 禮 -constituted performance begins from the insight that personal refinement is only possible through the discipline provided by formalized roles and behaviors. Form without personalization is the external imposition of coercive and thus dehumanizing regulation, while creative personal expression without form is randomness at best, and license at worst. It is only with the appropriate combination of form and functional personalization (*tiyong* 體用) that behavior within family and community can be self-regulating and increasingly refined.

With respect to Confucius himself, *li* 禮 is a resolutely personal performance revealing his worth to both himself and to his community. It is a public discourse through which he is able to constitute and reveal himself qualitatively as a unique individual, a whole person, doing what he does for the benefit of everyone, including himself. Importantly, there is no respite. *Li* 禮 requires the utmost attention to every detail of what Confucius does, at every moment he is doing it, from the drama of the high court to the posture he assumes in going to sleep, from the reception of different guests to the proper way to comport himself when alone, from how he behaves in formal dining situations to appropriate extemporaneous gestures when encountering friends. Such a portrait is most revealing of the extent to which the appropriate conduct of an official participating in the daily activities of the court was choreographed: the cut of his robes, the cadence of his stride, his keen sense of context and requisite proprieties, his posture and facial demeanor, his profound expression of reverent attention, his tone of voice, his gestures of deference, and even the rhythm of his breathing. And the grace and musicality of such artful living does not go without one's own delight in the performance of it.

10.5 執圭，鞠躬如也，如不勝。上如揖，下如授。勃如戰色，足蹜蹜，如有循。享禮，有容色。私覿，愉愉如也。

On grasping the jade tablet as the lord's envoy, Confucius would bow forward from the waist as though it were too heavy to lift. He would raise it as though saluting and then lower it as though offering it to someone. His countenance would change visibly as though going off to battle, and his steps were short and measured as though following a straight line. On the occasion of presenting his credentials, his demeanor was dignified, and in private audience, he was at ease.

Comment: We must not lose sight of the fact that Confucian role ethics ultimately and invariably has to do with specific persons in their specific situations who serve as role models for others. While laws and formal institutions can certainly provide important guidelines for conduct, it is ultimately analogy and correlation with family members, role models, and cultural heroes that has the greatest motive force in promoting the flourishing community. This being the case, the deferential yet authoritative life habits of Confucius himself and the emulation of this role model over succeeding generations is nothing less than an object lesson in understanding the real workings of role ethics.

9.3 子曰："麻冕，禮也；今也純，儉。吾從眾。拜下，禮也；今拜乎上，泰也。雖違眾，吾從下。"

The Master said, "The use of a hemp cap is prescribed in the observance of ritual propriety (*li* 禮). Nowadays, that a silk cap is used instead is a matter of frugality. I would follow accepted practice on this. A subject kowtowing on entering the hall at the bottom of the steps is prescribed in the performance of ritual propriety (*li* 禮). Nowadays that one only kowtows after having ascended to the top of the steps is a matter of hubris. Although it goes contrary to accepted practice, I still kowtow on entering the hall."

Comment: An important point in understanding ritualized propriety is that, in terms of form, while fundamentally conservative, it is still in degree evolutionary and emergent. Constancy comes in the serious attitude with which it is to be performed. For Confucius, the transition from making a ceremonial cap out of one fabric to an alternative material that is cheaper and more available is acceptable, especially when ideally such ritualized conduct should be practiced broadly among the people. On the other hand, for Confucius, the reverence invested in performing such ritual behaviors is a constant. To abandon the practice of kowtowing at the bottom of the stairs as well as at the top reflects a personal arrogance inconsistent with proper conduct. To thus diminish the degree of reverence expressed in making one's obeisance to the proper social and political authority as it has been invested in the structures of ranks and titles is for Confucius, a quantum diminution in the meaning of the gesture, and an unacceptable loss.

3.17 子貢欲去告朔之餼羊。子曰："賜也，爾愛其羊，我愛其禮。"

Zigong wanted to dispense with the sacrifice of a live sheep at the Declaration of the New Moon ceremony. The Master said: "Zigong! You begrudge (*ai* 愛) the sheep—for me, I love (*ai* 愛) the ritual practice (*li* 禮)."

Comment: We are remarked here of the cognate relationship between the performance of sacrifice (*xi* 犧) and the sense of what is optimally appropriate in conduct (*yi* 義). The serious decorum that attends sacrifice as a shared familial and communal event is integral to the Confucian understanding of what is most appropriate and meaningful in human behavior. Everyone at the sacrifice has their proper place, including the sheep, and everyone must conduct themselves in a way that respects the solemnity and decorum of the occasion. The term *ai* 愛 can be translated positively as the "love" of something or negatively as to "begrudge" it in the sense of being unwilling to part with something that is loved.

6.6 子謂仲弓曰："犁牛之子騂且角，雖欲勿用，山川其舍諸？"

The Master, remarking on the humble origins of Zhonggong, said, "If the calf of a plow-ox has the red coat and the nicely shaped horns of a sacrificial ox, even though some might not want to use it in the sacrifice, do you think the spirits of the mountains and rivers would turn it down?"

Comment: Zhonggong like Yan Hui is of low birth (see his profile in the *Comment* to 12.2, p. 215). Even so, Confucius confers high praise on Zhonggong and the possibilities this fine young man has for attaining the highest levels of governance, suggesting in one passage that he has the makings of a true king (6.1). The primacy of the unadorned basic stuff from which a life is to be shaped is a frequent theme throughout the text, but the relationship between substance and adornment is complementary and a matter of mutual enhancement rather than adornment being merely a second-order cosmetic enhancement. There is a contrapuntal relationship between the finest ore and a sacred bronze vessel, where the creative possibilities of each are being realized by virtue of the other, not to mention those of the artisan who is heavily invested in the project.

3.15 子入大廟，每事問。或曰："孰謂鄹人之子知禮乎？入大廟，每事問。" 子聞之曰："是禮也。"

The Master on entering the Grand Ancestral Hall dedicated to the Duke of Zhou, asked questions about everything. Someone remarked: "Who said this son of a man from the Zou village knows all about ritual propriety (*li* 禮)? On entering the Grand Ancestral Hall, he asks questions about every manner of thing."

On hearing of this, Confucius said: "To thus ask questions about everything is itself observing ritual propriety."

Comment: Confucius in his lifetime aspired to high political office and the influence on proper governance appertaining to it, but never attained it. A familiar theme in the text is for Confucius to respond to criticism directed at his lack of status by asserting that in spite of the complementarity of basic substance and ornamentation, there is still a primacy to be given to the former. When a mean-spirited question is raised about his failure to achieve political office, for example, he makes a distinction between "governing" and "government." He appeals to how good governance is first and foremost grounded in the proper management of the core family relations captured in the prime moral imperative of "family reverence" (*xiao* 孝). (2.21). However, while proper governance is "rooted" in the flourishing family, and the state is a simulacra of the institution of family, the relationship between the two is still symbiotic rather than merely derivative, with the productive synergy between family and state enhancing them both.

In this passage, Confucius reveals his understanding of ritual propriety as conducting oneself with an appropriate attitude of deference rather than in making some self-important display of one's encyclopedic knowledge of ritual detail. The reference to Zou comes from the tradition that Confucius's father was a military official from the town of Zou.

10.1 孔子於鄉黨，恂恂如也，似不能言者。其在宗廟朝廷，便便言，唯謹爾。

In Confucius's home village, he was most deferential, as though at a loss for words, and yet in the ancestral temple and at court, he spoke articulately, though with deliberation.

Comment: Throughout the text, the person of Confucius is often a ritualized performance in the sense that his way of presenting himself is determined by the disposition that has been habituated as most appropriate to the circumstances. Taking short steps, bowing forward, taking shallow breaths are all expressions of proper humility and deference in the presence of his elders and his lord. At the same time, in those professional settings that require deliberation and precision of him in his language, he is certainly up to the task.

10.27 色斯舉矣，翔而後集。曰："山梁雌雉，時哉！時哉！" 子路共之，三嗅而作。

Sensing their approach, the bird took to flight, and soared above them before alighting. The Master said, "Look at that hen-pheasant on the mountain bridge—what timing! what timing!" Zilu clasped his hands together and saluted the bird, which flapping its wings three times, once again took to the air.

Comment: In the *Analects*, we are given a detailed portrait of Confucius through a succession of images that are revealing of his unrelenting attention to the ritualized life, including proper countenance and his responsiveness to particular circumstances. The portrait discloses a pattern of refined conduct on the part of this particular human being in all of the particular circumstances of his life, from the kitchen to the court. And at the end of this series of snapshots, the text then naturalizes these ritualized behaviors by ascribing a responsive pattern of conduct to the life of the animal world as well. Throughout the Confucian texts, we are introduced to a moral cosmology in which human and cosmic values are coterminous and mutually entailing. A deferential, ritualized relationship obtains among the celestial bodies paying homage to the North Star just as it does with the officials paying tribute to their lord at court (2.1).

11.1 子曰："先進於禮樂，野人也；後進於禮樂，君子也。如用之，則吾從先進。"

The Master said, "The first to come to observing ritual propriety (*li* 禮) and to the playing of music (*yue* 樂) were the simple folk; those who came to them later were the nobility (*junzi* 君子). In putting such things into practice, I would follow those who came first."

Comment: Confucius seems to be using the term *junzi* 君子 in the political sense here, referencing those of noble birth. Under the influence of Confucius and his followers, this key term was undergoing a transition from a purely political to a moral category, and hence in the *Analects* it can sometimes mean rulers or aristocrats, but most often exemplary persons. What complicates the distinction is that becoming morally exemplary as a person can only be accomplished through social and political service.

This passage immediately calls to mind passage 3.4 in which Lin Fang asks about the "root" of ritual propriety (*lizhiben* 禮之本). In responding to this question, Confucius recommends modesty over extravagance, and sincere feeling over formal propriety. But rather than interpreting this passage as selecting one modality over the other, perhaps it is better to see the distinction as being compensatory and thus holistic and inclusive. The high ritual of the court cannot be separated from its origins in the institutions governing the lives of ordinary people, where each enhances the other. The moral influence of the ruler as role model has a transformative effect on the people, and the lives of the people thus morally transformed enables them to be self-ordering, allowing the ruler to reign rather than rule (2.3).

Compare *Mencius* 3A3 for this same contrast between modesty and extravagance. See *Analects* 6.18, 12.8, and 12.20 for the interdependence of basic substance and refinement.

11.8 顏淵死，顏路請子之車以為之椁。子曰："才不才，亦各言其子也。鯉也死，有棺而無椁。吾不徒行以為之椁。以吾從大夫之後，不可徒行也。"

When Yan Hui died, his father Yan Lu asked Confucius for his carriage to provide an outer coffin for his son. Confucius replied, "Talented or not, a son is a son. My son, Boyu, also died, and I provided him with an inner coffin, but no outer coffin because I could not go on foot in order to give him one. In my capacity as a retired official, it is not appropriate for me to travel on foot."

Comment: From Yan Hui's portrait in the *Analects*, we know that for Confucius, this young student was someone special. In 11.9 and 11.10 that reference his passing, Confucius mourns the death of Yan Hui with such extreme grief that the students worry Confucius will ruin his own health in doing so. In 11.11, Yan Hui's fellow students want to provide him with a lavish funeral, and in spite of Confucius's stern disapproval, much to his consternation they do so anyway.

The two reasons for Confucius not to oblige Yan Lu in his request to provide an outer coffin for Yan Hui are a matter of ritual protocol: Yan Hui did not have the status deserving of this honor, and at the same time, Confucius had a rank requiring of him the use of his carriage. These passages taken together certainly tell us about the high esteem Yan Hui enjoyed among his peers, but they also provide an image of Confucius who in spite of his deep and abiding affection for Yan Hui, is unwilling for Yan Hui's sake or anyone else's to forsake those social conventions that secure the ritualized order of the state. Confucius's own unremarkable son Boyu mentioned here died at age 50 when Confucius was 70. For other references to Boyu, see 16.13 and 17.10.

III.10 The Making of Music (*yue* 樂)

8.8 子曰:"興於詩,立於禮,成於樂。"

The Master said, "I find inspiration by intoning the songs (*shi* 詩), I learn where to stand from performing ritual proprieties (*li* 禮), and I find fulfillment in the playing of music (*yue* 樂)."

Comment: It is possible to read the terms, the songs (*shi* 詩), ritual proprieties (*li* 禮), and music (*yue* 樂) as either the abbreviated titles of the classical texts, the *Book of Songs*, the *Record of Rituals*, and the *Classic of Music*, or as Confucius's own personal engagement with the songs, ritual proprieties, and music. Either way, Confucius is identifying these three aspects of his own regimen as a source of inspiration, as providing an awareness of his proper place, and as giving him a sense of personal fulfillment. Confucius regards music as an activity that provides enhanced possibilities for disclosing personal style, spirit, and consequence. In musical performances, especially those in which composition, execution, and appreciation are not separated, there is an emphasis on personal disclosure in a manner meaningful to one's audience. The fact that the *Classic of Music* (*Yuejing* 樂經) has been lost utterly bears testimony to the fact that the musical mode of discourse is heavily dependent upon concrete enactment more than abstract symbol for its preservation and transmission.

We need to understand these distinctive practices as "aspects" of a ritualized life in the sense that each of them is imbricated in, and enables the others. The goal is the aestheticization and civilization of the human experience expressed through poesy, ritual, and music. And the grace, elegance, and refinement embodied through these practices inspire growth in human relations, and thus become the substance of morality.

The "making of music" is not limited to music as such but is used in the more general sense of all aesthetic experience. There is the musicality of growth in the human experience that moves in step with the rhythmical changes of the natural world. When we reflect on how the human being expresses the aesthetic, we can see that the sequential movement of images in a particular story and the tonal cadence in a line of poetry are themselves a kind of musicality. We can see that the brush strokes as they are applied in a piece of calligraphy, and the detailed depiction of the wandering footpaths in a landscape painting have their own rhythm. And the rise and fall of dynasties in history echo the natural turning of the seasons. Indeed, all significant experience seeks after a musical rhythm in its growth and consummation.

7.32 子與人歌而善，必使反之，而後和之。

When the Master was in the company of others who were singing and who sang well, he would invariably ask them to sing the piece again before joining in and harmonizing (*he* 和) with them.

Comment: This passage is a good example of how the dyadic pair, "performing ritual propriety" (*li* 禮) and "making music" (*yue* 樂) overlap and are synergistic. There is a prescription here for how, in optimizing the quality of relationships through deliberate patterns of deference, we can achieve a social musicality. This passage might serve as commentary on the "one thread" that runs through the *Analects* alluded to in 4.15: that is, the combination of "putting oneself in the other's place" (*shu* 恕) and "doing one's utmost" (*zhong* 忠). On experiencing musicality in the conduct of others, we must defer to it twice. We must resist any immediate, insufficiently informed response to it. And again, in order to appreciate it fully, we must allow space for its own full rehearsal. Only when we can take it fully on its own terms are we in a position to improvise and contribute our own personalized response to the continuing progression.

3.23 子語魯大師樂。曰：「樂其可知也：始作，翕如也；從之，純如也，皦如也，繹如也，以成。」

The Master was in conversation about music with the Grand Master of Lu, and said: "Much can be realized with music if one begins by playing in unison, then goes on to improvise with purity of tone, contributing distinctiveness and continuity, and thereby bringing all to completion."

Comment: As with all ritual proprieties (*li* 禮), music begins as a repository through which meaning can be transmitted and appropriated. At the same time, just as ritual proprieties are by definition personalized—this daughter to this father—so music too is open-ended, and serves as a medium through which to improvise, and to display one's own unique contribution.

Music requires both continuity and innovation. The capacity of music to sustain its inherited value as well as to grow with the personal significance of its conveyer is always a function of the quality of the persons to whom it has been entrusted (3.3). The pattern revealed in the musical life of ritualized propriety is to draw upon the meaning sedimented into the tradition to inform one's own circumstances, and then to expand upon this meaning to optimize the always unique conditions of one's own time and place. In this passage, and elsewhere (8.8), there is the repeated association between music and "completion" (*cheng* 成), where it is the nature of musical performances like all real experience to be consummatory, having a beginning and an end, only to begin again. The continuing process of experience can only be parsed into meaningful events by finding closure, even while such endings are always only provisional.

9.15 子曰："吾自衛反魯，然後樂正，雅頌各得其所。"

The Master said, "It was only after my return to Lu from Wei that I revised the *Book of Music*, and put the 'Songs of the Kingdom' and the 'Ceremonial Hymns' in proper order."

Comment: After spending many years abroad, Confucius in 484 BCE late in his life returned to the state of Lu. Tradition has it that Confucius at this time continued to edit the *Book of Songs*, reducing the existing three thousand songs to the three hundred and five contained in the received text. The *Book of Songs* is the most cited of the *Five Classics* in the *Analects* and most other Confucian writings, and we know from other passages that Confucius saw this canonical text as being fundamental to his curriculum and his conception of a proper education.

1.15 子貢曰："貧而無諂，富而無驕，何如？"子曰："可也。未若貧而樂道，富而好禮者也。"子貢曰："《詩》云：'如切如磋，如琢如磨'其斯之謂與？"子曰："賜也，始可與言詩已矣！告諸往而知來者。"

Zigong said: "What do you think of the saying: 'Poor but not unctuous; wealthy but not arrogant'?"

The Master replied: "Not bad, but not as good as: 'Poor but rejoicing in the proper way (*dao* 道); wealthy but cherishing ritual propriety (*li* 禮).'"

Zigong said: "In the *Book of Songs* it says:

Like bone carved and polished,

Like jade cut and ground.

Is this not what you have in mind?

The Master said: "Zigong, it is only with the likes of you that I can discuss the *Songs*! Having just been told one thing, you already know the rest."

Comment: In a resonant passage in 3.8, Zixia cites the *Songs* 57 that describes a handsome lady of the court, using this verse to make a philosophical point about the primacy of natural substance in the collateral relationship between persons and ritual propriety. Similarly, in this passage from the *Songs* 55, Zigong translates a lover's praise of the physical elegance of the lord into how best to understand the project of personal cultivation. In such cases, the original intention of the song is adapted to render it appropriate to the discussion at hand. We have here an illustration of the dynamics involved in "learning" (*xue* 學), "reflecting" (*si* 思), and "realizing" (*zhi* 知). There is an appropriate familiarity with the received text, a creative manipulation of its original meaning to make a relevant point, and thus a refining of the given circumstances to realize a desired enhancement of them.

The extent to which Confucius is willing to manipulate the original meaning of such passages from the *Songs* can be more fully appreciated by a repeated worry that Confucius expresses about our human proclivities: 已矣乎！吾未見好德如好色者也 "I have yet to meet the person fonder of virtuosity in conduct (*de* 德) than of physical beauty (*se* 色), and I fear I never will." (15.13, 9.18). With Zixia and Zigong, Confucius is effectively translating classical verses that express this fondness for physical beauty to communicate the importance he invests in the personal cultivation of virtuosic conduct. For Confucius and his students, they are deepening these descriptions of physical beauty with their own scale of values to advocate for a world in which virtuosic conduct does take precedence over physical attraction.

These examples of deploying the cultural legacy in a creative way make a more general point about the nature of communication in both diplomatic and interpersonal relations in this tradition. By invoking an allusion to some element within the cultural legacy, one introduces into a situation both the authority of the historical record and a prompting to perpetuate its wisdom by application to novel situations. The ambiguity of the allusion provides the flexibility for renegotiation and disclosure. The more productive the allusion is in prompting new possibilities for the current situation, the more powerful is the correlation as a source of meaning. One clear and distinctive example of this strategy for making meaning is the pervasiveness in the modern Chinese language of the use of four character (or two couplets of four character) sayings (*chengyu* 成語) usually drawn from classical sources.

Many of the redactions, including the Dingzhou strips, have "poor but rejoicing" (*le* 樂) but some also have "poor but rejoicing in the proper way" (*yaodao* 樂道). Parallel structure with the phrase "cherishing ritual propriety" (*haoli* 好禮) would recommend the latter.

7.14 子在齊聞韶，三月不知肉味。曰："不圖爲樂之至於斯也！"

When the Master was in the state of Qi he heard the *shao* 韶 court music, and for several months he did not know the taste of meat. He said, "I had no idea that music could achieve such heights!"

Comment: Confucius loved the *shao* 韶 music imbued with the moral qualities of its creator Shun, a commoner who by virtue of his exemplary conduct was elevated as successor to the Emperor Yao. Music as a discourse has the power to recall, to register, and to convey meaning in a most powerful and personal way. Confucius's intense feeling for this music was so strong that it monopolized his entire physical sensorium for an extended period of time.

3.25 子謂韶，"盡美矣，又盡善也"。謂武，"盡美矣，未盡善也"。

The Master said of the *shao* 韶 court music it is both superbly beautiful (*mei* 美) and conduces to what is good (*shan* 善). Of the *wu* 武 martial music he said it is superbly beautiful but is not conducive to what is good.

Comment: Confucius allows that the *shao* 韶 court music associated with the sage-ruler Shun is so powerful that it overwhelms his senses utterly (7.14), being both exquisite to listen to and inspiring of good conduct on the part of its listeners. The character *shan* 善 that is conventionally translated as "good" is primarily relational—"good to, good for, good at, good in"—and then only derivatively "good" as a generalization from such conduct. It is a social discourse that conduces to good consequences. *Shao* 韶 music is not only superb, it has edifying consequences for the moral quality of its listeners.

The *wu* 武 martial music, on the other hand, establishes the familiar contrast between *wen* 文 as civil order achieved through literary and cultural means, and *wu* 武 as order achieved through military prowess. The *wu* 武 music is associated with King Wu who overthrew the Shang dynasty, and who then posthumously honored his father Wen as the founder of the Zhou. The name "Wen" means "culture," and is celebrated throughout the early literature as a metonym for the intergenerational transmission of the cultural legacy.

In fact, the historical records are clear on the military conquest of Shang by King Wen, where his second son Wu simply won the final battle after the death of his father. Still, it is King Wu who is associated with the military force used to effect the dynastic change. For Confucius, as is reflected in this passage, the choice is not a binary either-or because both kinds of music have their place. Resort to military arms like invoking penal law is on occasion necessary, while at the same time, is an admission of the political failure to find a better way.

15.11 顏淵問爲邦。子曰："行夏之時，乘殷之輅，服周之冕，樂則韶舞。放鄭聲，遠佞人。鄭聲淫，佞人殆。"

Yan Hui asked about a viable state. The Master replied, "Introduce the calendar of the Xia dynasty, ride on the large yet plain chariot of the Yin, wear the ceremonial cap of the Zhou, and as for music, play the *shao* 韶 and *wu* 武. Abolish the 'music' from the state of Zheng and keep glib talkers at a distance, for the Zheng music is lewd and glib talkers are dangerous."

Comment: Perhaps the overriding message of this passage is the perception that good governance requires the transmission and embodiment of a continuing, compounding cultural legacy reaching back into a shared, incremental history. The cultural innovations of each succeeding dynasty are integral to an inclusive, hybridic, and evolving identity. This way of thinking is captured in Tang Junyi's cosmological postulate: "the one is many, many one" (*yiduobufenguan* 一多不分觀). There are many images in the culture of this distinctive value of a continuing intergenerational transmission: the *long* 龍 "dragon" composed of all animals as a symbol of imperial authority, the family and human-centered genealogical religiousness, the way of "family reverence" (*xiao* 孝) as the prime moral imperative, the continuing canonical core and its interlinear commentaries, and so on.

The contemporary philosopher Zhao Tingyang 趙汀陽 in many of his works has developed the notion of a *tianxia* 天下 or the "All-Under-Heaven" system as his way of explaining this cultural dynamic. He uses the metaphor of a centripetal whirlpool that over the centuries as a moving centripetal center draws into itself the vast diversity surrounding the Central Plain, and that continues to transform the many into a continuing hybridic one, a China that is one and many at the same time. The key cultural attractor that serves as the motive force behind the continuing civilization is the Chinese written character, and the continuing canonical record. With music being a major medium of discourse, Confucius underscores the complementary role of both the *shao* court music and the *wu* martial music in maintaining proper order. But discourse can be a source of moral diminution as well as growth, and not all aspects of the culture need be carried forward. In this respect, he sees the lewd music of Zheng and the machinations of glib talkers as being detrimental to the ethical, social, and political order.

16.13 陳亢問於伯魚曰："子亦有異聞乎？" 對曰："未也。嘗獨立，鯉趨而過庭。曰：'學詩乎？' 對曰：'未也。''不學詩，無以言。' 鯉退而學詩。他日又獨立，鯉趨而過庭。曰：'學禮乎？' 對曰：'未也。''不學禮，無以立。' 鯉退而學禮。聞斯二者。" 陳亢退而喜曰："問一得三，聞詩，聞禮，又聞君子之遠其子也。"

Chen Gang asked the son of Confucius, Boyu: "Have you been given any kind of special instruction?"

"No." he replied. "Once when my father was standing alone in the courtyard and as I hastened quickly by, he asked me, 'Have you studied the *Songs*?' I said, 'Not yet,' to which he replied, 'If you do not study the *Songs*, you will be at a loss as to what to say.' I deferentially took my leave and studied the *Songs*.

On another day when he was again standing alone in the courtyard, I hastened quickly by. He again asked me, 'Have you studied the *Rituals*?' I said, 'Not yet,' to which he replied, 'If you do not study the *Rituals*, you will be at a loss as to where to stand.' I deferentially took my leave and studied the *Rituals*. What I have learned from him then, are these two things."

Chen Gang, taking his leave, was delighted, and said, "I asked one question and got three answers. I learned the importance of the *Songs* and of the *Rituals*, but I also learned that exemplary persons (*junzi* 君子) do not treat their own sons as a special case."

Comment: From this passage we can see not only the centrality of these classics in the education of Confucius's students, but the practical way in which they would be used. Given that book culture is a much later Han dynasty development, the canonical texts referred to here would be part of an oral tradition and rote learning, with students being expected to know them by heart.[1] As the lives of the students would unfold, these texts could be drawn upon to provide them with a shared vocabulary of technical terms, metaphors, historical references, and allusions for organizing the many complexities of always novel experience. And owning the *Record of Rituals* in this way would again provide a shared structure of formal procedures through which to organize the activities of family and community as one moved through the various stages of a human life.

Another dimension of the importance of these texts would come from the way they would function as a shared language for diplomacy. Education within the Confucian academy was directed at preparing students who were coming to study with Confucius from all four quarters in preparation for social and political service. These classics provided a hugely disparate cultural geography a shared identity and a common axis that extended radially from a cultural center to the extremities. Facility with these texts would be the difference between the culturally refined and the less so, and between the able diplomat and the plodding functionary. Cf. 13.5.

Given the importance of "family reverence" (*xiao* 孝) as the prime moral imperative in Confucian philosophy, it might seem strange that members of Confucius's own family such as this son Boyu appear only infrequently in the text (5.1, 5.2, 17.10). Moreover, the instruction he gives his son is no different from that he would impart to any of his students. (17.9) Perhaps the last line in this passage provides some insight. Confucian education from earliest times down to today takes the institution of family as its underlying premise. Even today, teachers are called "teacher-father" (*shifu* 師父) or "teacher-mother" (*shimu* 師母), professional colleagues are referred to as "brothers" and "sisters," and classmates are "student-older-sister" (*xuejie* 學姐) and "student-younger-brother" (*xuedi* 學弟). Within this sense of family pervasive in the *Analects*, Boyu is only one among many of Confucius's children, and it would appear that Confucius felt stronger fatherly affection for some of his other students, Yan Hui in

---

[1] See Nylan, *Yang Xiong and the Pleasures of Reading and Classical Learning in China*.

particular.

The disciple Chen Gang (aka Ziqin) also appears in 1.10 and 19.25, in both cases asking about Confucius. The 19.25 passage is particularly curious, with Chen Gang referring to Confucius by his given name and suggesting Confucius could not possibly be superior in character to his disciple, Zigong.

17.10 子謂伯魚曰: "女爲《周南》、《召南》矣乎? 人而不爲《周南》、《召南》, 其猶正牆面而立也與?"

The Master said to his son, Boyu, "Have you mastered the 'South of Zhou' and 'South of Shao' sections of the *Book of Songs*? Striving to become a person without doing so is like trying to take your stand with your face to the wall."

Comment: Confucius once again underscores the importance of developing real facility with the canonical texts as integral to the education of his students, where his son Boyu is taken as simply one among them. An epistemology of comprehensiveness (*quan* 全) does in important measure the work of "truth" in these Confucian texts. Rather than presuming that there is one exclusive truth that will "true" a situation, the assumption is that the clearest way forward in any situation comes from having as many perspectives as possible. The best judgment can only be made on the basis of a panoramic view that provides access to a situation in all of its parts. This assumption is the epistemic version of the cosmological postulate: 一多不分觀 "many is one, one many." It is given this epistemic assumption that facing a wall becomes a metaphor for trying to establish oneself and to make one's contribution without the synoptic view provided by the proper kind of education. A knowledge of the *Songs* in particular is liberating in providing all of the accoutrements needed for effective communication. Cf. 17.9.

17.9 子曰: "小子! 何莫學夫詩? 詩, 可以興, 可以觀, 可以群, 可以怨。邇之事父, 遠之事君。多識於鳥獸草木之名。"

The Master said, "My young friends, why aren't any of you studying the *Songs*? Reciting the *Songs* can give you inspiration and strengthen your powers of observation, and can enhance your ability to get on with others and sharpen your critical skills. Near at hand it enables you to serve your father, and away at court it enables you to serve your lord. It instills in you the broad vocabulary necessary for making distinctions in the world around you: the birds and beasts, the grasses and trees."

Comment: Confucius gives the same instruction to all of his students that he gives to his son Boyu. He focuses on the way in which education through the *Songs* in particular provides students with the discursive capacities to function at an optimal level in their personal, social, and political experience. This passage has the usual radial structure, moving from personal development and the cultivation of immediate relations to service at the court. It is the *Songs* as the anonymous and commonly shared music of the people that, in having both powerful affective force and absolute veracity, serves the philosophical texts typically as the ultimate Q.E.D. endorsement for the arguments advanced.

Just as a trained botanist walking along a country road is able to experience nature's bounty in a way overlooked by the casual observer, so too students having developed a real facility with the vocabulary of the flora and fauna provided the *Songs* are able to bring these complex distinctions into their experience. But while such technical knowledge certainly brings complexity and resolution to the human experience, it is the embodiment of the feelings sedimented into the *Songs* that provides these students with the sense of belonging and the quality of responsiveness needed to get the most out of their journey through life. It is these verses that draw upon the powerful emotions of the people as they are expressed in the genuineness of their songs to serve as the highest celebration of the power of intense human feelings, feelings that in this Confucian tradition come to be seen as having a creative role in shaping the cosmic order.

Bringing Proper Order to the State (*zhiguo* 治國)

In the Confucian project of personal growth, the root must be set and firmly planted within the family itself. In reflecting on Confucian philosophy as a resource for an ecological political order, we must give full weight to the perceived isomorphism that obtains among the familial, political, and global orders as they are rooted in and emerge from a regimen of personal cultivation within the family. In *Expansive Learning* (*Daxue* 大學) as the first among the canonical *Four Books* that sets the Confucian project, we read:

古之欲明明德於天下者先治其國；欲治其國者先齊其家；欲齊其家者先修其身……自天子以至於庶人，壹是皆以修身爲本。

The ancients who sought to display their brilliant virtuosity to the whole world first effected proper order in their states; in seeking to effect proper order in their states, they first set their families right; in seeking to set their families right, they first cultivated their own persons. . . . From the emperor down to the common folk, everything is rooted in personal cultivation.

What then are the implications of this perceived isomorphism between family, state, and world for the proper functioning of governance at the local, state, and global orders? In the *Analects*, Confucius in speaking to the role of the ruler provides a classic statement of the distinctively Confucian conception of the political as what we might call a kind of Confucian "role politics:"

Analects 2.3: 子曰：「道之以政，齊之以刑，民免而無恥；道之以德，齊之以禮，有恥且格。」

The Master said: "Lead the people with administrative injunctions and keep them orderly with penal law, and they will avoid punishments but will not develop a sense of shame. Lead them with moral virtuosity (*de* 德) and keep them orderly through aspiring to propriety in their roles and relations (*li* 禮), and they will develop a sense of shame, and moreover, will order themselves."

Confucius draws a contrast here between the quality of rule achieved by invoking laws and policies on the one hand, and that attained through education and moral suasion on the other. In the first instance, the people can be made orderly through coercive measures, but do not in this process of external imposition develop the sense of shame that would reflect their own personal commitment to the shared values of the community. Such a model of governance is unilateral in separating the ruler from the ruled, and is made tenuous and at best interim by the fact that it is externally imposed without internal confirmation by the people. Although the practical Confucius would certainly allow that laws are necessary as second order injunctions, for him the most effective way for the ruler to promote order in the community is through moral education. Such education takes the form of the ruler serving the people as a role model by demonstrating the community's highest values in his own personal conduct, and purposively endorsing a sustained propriety in the family-based roles and relations of the people. When the people are thus inspired by the ruler both in conduct and exhortation to embody these family and communal values, their moral transformation brings with it a cultivated sense of shame the consequence of which is the people become self-ordering. And with this transformative moral education, the rulers need only reign over the people without having to impose their will upon them:

Analects 8.18: 子曰："巍巍乎！舜禹之有天下也，而不與焉。"
The Master said, "How majestic they were, Yao and Shun, who reigned over the world but did not rule it."

Social and political order originates with and is sustained by the people investing themselves heavily in their own family-based roles without any compulsion required from outside.

Analects 3.5: 子曰："夷狄之有君，不如諸夏之亡也。"
The Master said: "The Yi and Di barbarian tribes with rulers are not as viable as the various Chinese states without them."

Confucian "role politics" then is the symbiotic outcome of the ruler serving as a role model for the shared values of the community, and the people in their family and communal roles achieving a quality of propriety that sustains the social and political order.

The extended family system operative in China at the time of the compilation of the *Analects* was very different from the nuclear familial patterns of the contemporary West, especially as these patterns are expressed in the United States. Although trade and commerce had developed significantly, and China had entered the Iron Age in manufacture by the time of Confucius, it was basically an agrarian society with the family, as almost everywhere else, the basic economic unit of production, distribution, and consumption. Local communities were made up of one or more extended families or clans, and were largely self-sufficient. Larger and more centralized regulatory organizations, consisting of a monarch and retinue with significant ritual obligations combined with a bureaucracy based more on moral worth than wealth or lineage, was always a dream when not a reality. But for the early Confucians, the functions of these groups (uniformly called "the government" by sinologists which, while not incorrect, is nevertheless somewhat misleading) were circumscribed.[1] They were obliged to assist local communities of families and clans in achieving goals, significantly economic in nature, that they could not achieve on their own: building and maintaining roads, dikes and major irrigation systems; maintaining border defenses; developing postal and monetary systems; seeing that supplies of grain and seed were moved when necessary from bumper harvest to famine areas. These responsibilities were carried out in ways that preserved and enhanced the rich cultural heritage, requiring the governing organizatons to provide local schools and academies. Moreover, while the development of a detailed penal code occurred early on and bureaucratic institutions were established to enforce it, it would be a gross simplification to see the civilization as moving from rule by persons (and importantly, ritual propriety, *li* 禮) to rule by law. The power of the family metaphor in shaping perceptions of all social and political relations cannot be overstated. Indeed, it is this persistent family-based sociopolitical organization of Chinese society that has within this antique culture, late and soon, elevated the specific family values and obligations circumscribed by the term "family reverence" (*xiao* 孝) to serve as its governing moral imperative.

Much beyond these efforts the early Chinese state was not envisioned to go. While it did have manifold obligations, as just sketched, it was basically the family's task to sustain itself, with the able-bodied providing for the disabled, the elders educating the young, the healthy caring for the sick, the young providing security for the old, and the upright as models inspiring necessary reform among those who would stray from the straight and narrow. This division of labor between families and the central governing organizations in early China should not however, be seen as a divide

---

[1] In our translation of the *Analects,* the term *zheng* 政 is taken as verb, "governing effectively,"—in the sense of regulating—and not as the noun, "government." An essay by Tao Jiang suggests how Chinese "governments" were more akin to families than to governments in the modern Western sense. See Tao Jiang, "Intimate Authority: The Rule of Ritual in Classical Confucian Political Discourse," *Confucian Cultures of Authority*, ed. Peter D. Hershock and Roger T. Ames, Albany: State University of New York Press, 2006.

III. THE *ANALECTS* (*LUNYU* 論語): A BASIC CONFUCIAN VOCABULARY

between public and private spheres of life, for no such distinctions can be clearly drawn in Confucianism. The family encompassed virtually all of one's life. A person lacking kin altogether would be hard put to eke out even a bare subsistence, and it would in Confucian terms, be most difficult for such a person to flourish as a full human being.

I have argued elsewhere that the Confucian religious life is human and family-centered in "binding tightly" (L. *religare*) within family and community without any reference to a conception of an external monotheistic God.[①] There is an analogy here between Confucian religiousness and its vision of the political life that is likewise family focused, and then only by radial expansion, extended to the world beyond. The traditional Confucian way of life does not embrace the Aristotelian asymmetrical distinction between *oikos* and *polis*, between family/household and the realm of politics, with his *Politics* being understood as "the affairs of state" (*ta politika*). Instead, with a persistent isomorphism between family and state (*jiaguotonggou* 家國同構) throughout the early Confucian canons, we come to understand that the perceived primary source of both social and political order in this tradition is the institution of family as it is rooted in the prime moral imperatives of "family reverence" (*xiao* 孝) and its complement, "an achieved propriety in one's roles and relations" (*li* 禮). While Confucian texts certainly regard the abstract rule of law and the application of punishments as necessary institutions, at the same time they construe appeal to law as a clear admission of communal failure.

The *Analects* sets up a rather stark contrast between the efficacy of formal legal instruments and that of the tensile communal bonds woven out of robust family relations, with the ideal being that family and community through a cultivated sense of shame can become self-governing. Moral virtuosity in the person of the ruler is certainly perceived as an important factor in good governance, but this role model is most effective when such rulership takes the form of "reigning" rather than "ruling" with the people properly ordering themselves. At its most fundamental level, it is the proper functioning of roles in family and community and the commensurate sense of shame such roles produce within ritually choreographed relations that serve as the primary source of social and political order. A dynamic *li*

---

① Roger T. Ames, *Human Becomings: Theorizing Persons for Confucian Role Ethics*, Albany: State University of New York Press, 2021, pp. 255-258.

禮-structured family and community is a concrete and powerful guarantee of social solidarity, while abstract laws and policies can at best serve as only secondary injunctions.

III.11 Using Names Properly (*zhengming* 正名)

13.3 子路曰："衛君待子而爲政，子將奚先？" 子曰："必也正名乎！" 子路曰："有是哉，子之迂也！奚其正？" 子曰："野哉由也！君子於其所不知，蓋闕如也。名不正，則言不順；言不順，則事不成；事不成，則禮樂不興；禮樂不興，則刑罰不中；刑罰不中，則民無所錯手足。故君子名之必可言也，言之必可行也。君子於其言，無所苟而已矣。"

"Were the Lord of Wei to turn the administration of his state over to you, what would be your first priority?" asked Zilu.

"Without question it would be to ensure that names are used properly (*zhengming* 正名)," replied the Master.

"Really? That is so pedantic." responded Zilu. "What does it mean to use names properly anyway?"

"How can you be so obtuse!" replied Confucius. "Exemplary persons defer on matters they do not understand. When names are not used properly, language will not be used effectively; when language is not used effectively, matters will not be taken care of; when matters are not taken care of, propriety in roles and relations and in the playing of music will not be achieved; when propriety in roles and relations and in the playing of music is not achieved, the application of laws and punishments will not be on the mark; when the application of laws and punishments is not on the mark, the common people will not know what to do with themselves. Thus, when exemplary persons put a name to something, it can certainly be spoken, and when spoken it can certainly be acted upon. There is nothing careless in the attitude of exemplary persons toward what is said."

Comment: Confucius explains to his protégé Zilu what he means by the central Confucian precept, "using names properly" (*zhengming* 正名). In this exposition, Confucius uses "names" as "pragmatics" to do the work of an expanding range of different yet organically related modes of discourse on which the stability and prosperity of communal life depends, from language itself to the functioning of the institutions of law and governance. Most importantly, for Confucius the function of "naming," far from being primarily abstract, theoretical, and referential, has immediate, practical consequences for the quality achieved in the always changing life of the community.

I have benefited in thinking through the notion of *zhengming* 正名 from what I take to be the corroborative work of Jane Geaney who has also argued that this key philosophical terminology can only be understood if we locate it within the organismic and holistic process cosmology that gives these early texts their interpretive context. In looking at the dyadic pair, *mingshi* 名實, for example, she makes much of the oral/aural and visual distinction between them. She thus understands *shi* 實 conventionally translated as "substance" or "reality" as the "product of a process," that is, "the seen fruits of a continuing process." With *ming* 名, she makes a compelling case that it "refers first and foremost, to speech, and only incidentally to written characters as records of speech."[①]

Confucius is keenly aware of the performative and perlocutionary "ontology" of "relatings" or discourse—that is, the power that spoken names (*ming* 名) in the broadest sense have to shape the community and to command a desired world into being (*ming* 命). To thus "know" a world, far from being just a cognitive understanding, is to realize it in the sense of "making it real." Confucius is expounding upon precisely this point when he explains to his protégé Zilu what he means by the central Confucian precept, "using names properly" (*zhengming* 正名).

The expression *zhengming* 正名 has conventionally and perhaps unfortunately been translated as "the *rectification* of names." For Confucius, language is certainly and importantly retrospective in the sense that effective discourse requires the use of language according to received, stipulated definitions—for example, the deployment of proper titles and respect for the entitlements that accompany rank. Throughout the literature, Confucius has a strong commitment to such conventions, and to this extent, the idea of "rectification" certainly does part of the job. Simply put, established conventions provide stability and reinforce hard-won social, political, and cultural values. Thus, the past is importantly with us as guidance for novel experience. But because novel experience is always underdetermined, and must quite literally be taken on its own terms, the translation of this expression as "rectification of names" is inadequate at best, and

---

① Jane Geaney, *On the Epistemology of the Senses in Early Chinese Thought*, Honolulu: University of Hawai'i Press, 2002, pp. 18-19.

misleading at worst. To understand language as having only retrospective reference reduces it to a symbolic and representational means of mapping an already existing world—that is, knowing the world is finding the right name for its parts, and knowing what is what.

But language is much more. When spoken names are used properly, they are the engine that sustains, revitalizes, and amplifies appropriate relations. *Zhengming* 正名 as it is explained in this passage should certainly be understood as remembering and applying standards inherited from the past. But for Confucius, language is also importantly prospective and performative. There is the need for the community, grounded in the *gravitas* of its traditions, to continue to make productive adjustments and novel correlations within the evolving social and political structures. A thriving community must continuously reform, reconfigure, and reauthorize its institutions. The proper use of the spoken word is a continuing redefining of our terms of understanding, explanation, and performance through those semantic and phonetic associations that would enable us to make the most of our always changing world.

Confucius is trying to make several points in defining *zhengming* 正名 in this important passage that in degree confound our expectations. That is, with our commonsense being shaped so much by Aristotle, we are inclined to respect what are fundamental distinctions that inform our conception of discrete agency. We are inclined to separate "acting" (*prattein*) from "producing" (*poietin*), and an efficient cause or agent (*kinoun*) that initiates change from the material, formal and final causes that define the outcome of change. Confucius, does not begin from such ontological and teleological assumptions about discrete agency and agent-centered, productive activity. Rather, his starting point is the importance of the proper and productive use of language within the human community as it provides ambience for the ordinary affairs of the day.

The range of activities described in this *Analects* passage are irreducibly social and situational; persons, families, and communities become who they are discursively through what they say and do in their roles and relations—that is, through what Charles Taylor calls their "webs of interlocutions."[1] In this Confucian model of constitutive "relatings" then, we are

---

[1] Charles Taylor, *Sources of the Self: The Making of the Modern Identity*, Cambridge, MA: Harvard University Press, 1989, p. 36.

not individuals who associate in community, but rather because we associate effectively in community we become distinguished as unique individuals; we do not have minds and therefore speak with one another, but rather because we speak effectively with one another, we become like-minded with shared life-forms and values; we do not have hearts and therefore are empathetic with one another, but rather because we feel effective empathy with one another we become whole-hearted as a community.

13.15 定公問：" 一言而可以興邦，有諸？" 孔子對曰："言不可以若是其幾也。人之言曰：'爲君難，爲臣不易。' 如知爲君之難也，不幾乎一言而興邦乎？" 曰："一言而喪邦，有諸？" 孔子對曰："言不可以若是其幾也。人之言曰：'予無樂乎爲君，唯其言而莫予違也。' 如其善而莫之違也，不亦善乎？如不善而莫之違也，不幾乎一言而喪邦乎？"

Duke Ding inquired, "Is there any one maxim that can enable a state to prosper?"

"A maxim itself cannot have such an effect," said the Master, "but there is the saying, 'Ruling is difficult, and ministering is not easy either.' If the ruler really does understand the difficulty of ruling, is this not close to a maxim that would enable a state to prosper?"

"Is there any one maxim that can ruin a state?" he asked.

"A maxim itself cannot have such an effect," replied Confucius, "but there is the saying, 'I find little pleasure in ruling, save that no one will take exception to what I say.' If what one has to say is conducive to good consequences and no one takes exception, fine indeed. But if what one has to say is not conducive to good consequences and no one opposes him, is this not close to a maxim ruining a state?"

Comment: The default analogy for governance in the Confucian tradition is the institution of family. We see in the *Classic of Family Reverence* (*Xiaojing* 孝經) that "family reverence" (*xiao* 孝) as the prime moral imperative has application to the family, the polity, and the cosmos. Within the institutions of family and government organized around this doctrine of *xiao* 孝, the relations between parent and child and between ruler and minister respectively, have to be bilateral. The dynamic of *xiao* 孝 means the older generation has the responsibility to inherit the living cultural tradition and to transmit it to the next generation, and is thus entitled to their deference. And the younger generation having received and embodied the cultural legacy from the older generation rejoices in expressing this deference. But *xiao* 孝 also carries with it as a complement to this pattern of deference the solemn obligation on the part of the younger generation and of the ministers to remonstrate (*jian* 諫) with their elders and their ruler respectively when they deem it necessary. It is this collaterality between generations that guarantees proper governance at the levels of home and state.

The political version of this same *xiao* 孝 dynamic is at issue in this passage: "ruling is difficult, and ministering is not easy either." As the parent of the people, rulers must understand the heavy responsibilities that come with this role. When carried out conscientiously, just as with the flourishing family they will guarantee the flourishing of the state. But this is only part of the story. Ministers too have the obligation to speak up and remonstrate with the ruler when in their judgment the conduct of the ruler is not conducive to good outcomes. Again, the relationship is collateral, and the responsibility to each other works in both directions.

The first of these sayings might be an allusion to Emperor Yu in the *Book of Documents*, "The Counsels of the Great Yu" 書經大禹謨: 曰后克難厥后，臣克難厥難臣，政乃乂，黎民敏德 when he says: "If rulers are able to grasp the difficulties in what it means to rule, and ministers to grasp the difficulties in what it means to minister, government will be well-ordered and the people will aspire to virtuosity in their conduct." Cf. Legge, *Chinese Classics*, Vol. 3, p. 53.

12.11 齊景公問政於孔子。孔子對曰："君君，臣臣，父父，子子。"公曰："善哉！信如君不君，臣不臣，父不父，子不子，雖有粟，吾得而食諸？"

Duke Jing of Qi asked Confucius about governing effectively. Confucius replied, "The ruler must rule, the minister minister, the father father, and the son son."

"Excellent!" exclaimed the Duke. "Indeed, if the ruler does not rule, the minister not minister, the father not father, and the son not son, even if there were grain, would I get any of it to eat?"

Comment: This passage is frequently taken in tandem with 13.3 and 6.25 as being an expression of Confucius's doctrine of *zhengming* 正名: "using names properly." At a concrete level, the specific *dramatis personae* are important for establishing both the problem Confucius is addressing here, and the consequences that befall Duke Jing when he fails to take Confucius's advice. Confucius in 517 BCE visited the state of Qi and proffered this counsel about effective governing to the titular ruling duke (posthumously named Jing). Duke Jing's power was being usurped by his ministers at the same time that he was planning to override his eldest son's claim to the throne. In the end, the ministers taking advantage of the succession being unclear, assassinated their ruler and took possession of the state. The historical episode was in every way an example, of both ruler and minister, and of father and son, failing to live these roles properly. As a consequence, not only was the ruler unable to enjoy those provisions rightfully his, but he further lost both his state and his life.

At a more abstract level, there is also an important philosophical point that makes the conventional translation of *zhengming* 正名 as "rectification of names" misleading if not deficient. Within the process cosmology that serves as interpretive context for early Confucianism, the doctrine of "using names properly" (*zhengming* 正名) has to be understood holistically as having both retrospective and prospective reference. It requires not only living up to predetermined, stipulated expectations, but also deploying language effectively in a continuing present.

In addition to this prospective as well as retrospective doctrine of *zhengming* 正名, there are two other related correlative pairings that we find in the early Confucian and Legalist texts: that is, "naming and bringing to fruition" (*mingshi* 名實) and "naming and forming" (= accountability) (*xingming* 形名) respectively. In both cases, these expressions have to do with the demand for congruency between what is being proposed and what is being accomplished. It can be argued that in the Legalist case, *xingming* 形名 as a principle of bureaucratic control has to do with first defining policy or office clearly, and then insisting on absolute compliance, a tidy correspondence between claims and results.

But with *mingshi*, the issue is one of pragmatics (the vital relationship between an always changing context and an utterance). *Ming* 名 is conventionally translated as "name" and *shi* 實 is conventionally translated as "substance" or "reality," but the qualification is that both of these terms in Confucian cosmology must be understood gerundively, describing a continuing event rather than a discrete thing. *Ming* 名 and *shi* 實 are oral and visual respectively, and together reference the continuing, interdependent process of naming bearing tangible fruit. For example in the *Xunzi* 22.2 it states: 名無固實，約之以命實，約定俗成，謂之實名。名有固善，徑易而不拂，謂之善名。"Names are not fixed in their reference, but become so by mutual agreement. When there is mutual agreement and the reference becomes customary, it is said to be the referent. Names can be stable in their efficacy; when direct, easy to use, and not at odds with the phenomenon, they are said to be efficacious names." Within a process cosmology, names and their "fruit" are at once persistent and changing, with the issue being the felicitous use of language within the human community.

Compare 1.2 and 2.21 in which the argument is that effective familial relations are the root of both community and polity, and see 6.25 and 13.3 for the proper use of language.

6.25 子曰：" 觚不觚，觚哉！觚哉！"

The Master said, "A *gu* 觚 ritual vessel that is not being used as such—a *gu* 觚 indeed! A *gu* 觚 indeed!"

Comment: This passage is frequently invoked as an illustration of the Confucian doctrine of "using names properly" (*zhengming* 正名). The assumed interdependence of naming and context might prompt a useful distinction between a sometimes valuable *artifact*—that is, any object formed by human craft—and a precious *icon*—an object that has been a source of inspiration and devotion as it lives and functions within a particular cultural tradition.① John Dewey frames this same distinction with respect to art objects. When works of art "have lost their indigenous status, they have acquired a new one—that of being specimens of fine art and nothing else.... Objects that were in the past valid and significant because of their place in the life of a community now function in isolation from the conditions of their origin."②

I can make some sense of this laconic passage from the *Analects* by recounting my own personal experience with a *gu* 觚 ritual vessel. Indeed, I was so mesmerized by the shape and the elegance of a particular Shang dynasty bronze *gu* 觚 I first encountered at the Freer Gallery of Art in Washington DC that I acquired its image for the cover of our translation of *Focusing the Familiar: A Philosophical Interpretation and Translation of the* Zhongyong. In using the *gu* 觚 in this way, I suspect that I am a deserving target of Confucius's admonition for treating the *gu* 觚 as an object

---

① This distinction between an icon and an artifact is borrowed from an unpublished paper presented by David S. Blix, one of Wabash College's most celebrated teachers, at the American Academy of Religion conference in Atlanta in 2003.

② John Dewey, *Art as Experience*, New York: Penguin, 1934, p. 8.

and artifact rather than using it for its intended iconic purposes: "a *gu* 觚 indeed! A *gu* 觚 indeed!"

We might move beyond treating the *gu* 觚 ritual vessel as an artifact by relocating it within its indigenous culture and "reading" it through the lenses offered by our several academic disciplines. By viewing this object from these alternative perspectives, we might be able to "appreciate" the artifact in the sense of recovering its meaning and restoring its iconic value as it functioned within the life of its own culture. By viewing the *gu* 觚 historically, for example, we learn of how bronze ritual implements are almost synonymous with the Shang dynasty that achieved a high degree of metal mastery within a few centuries of its founding, and how the development of bronze production was catalytic in the emergence of the Chinese civilization itself. Such vessels served as markers of social, political, and indeed religious power that distinguished city-dwelling nobles from a rural peasantry. Again, by reading the *gu* 觚 ritual vessel economically, we are able to correlate the metal-winning efforts of this population living in the Yellow River basin with the magnitude of its surpluses and the nature of its expenditures. We are able to trace a transition from metal-working to large scale metal-production at fabrication centers that reflects exponential growth in the technological competence of the culture. The placement of the workshops and the quarters of bronze-working artisans in desirable urban locations tells us too of the growing prestige of their craft.

From a sociological vantage point, the *gu* 觚 ritual vessel tells the story of a hierarchical family and kinship structure dominated by a hugely literate aristocratic bureaucracy. This bureaucracy lent its counsel to a hereditary Shang house supported in this world largely by the labors of farmers and fishermen, a way of life watched over from the next world by a pantheon of former Shang kings. By reading the *gu* 觚 ritual vessel religiously, we learn of how this aristocratic population repaid the interest of the other world by expending its time and wealth on complex programs of ancestor reverence, and used its accumulated resources to develop an extraordinary civilization. Unlike other civilizations of the same period, most bronze metal was used for ritual vessels rather than for weapons. Such vessels were the accoutrements that attended regular sacrifices and libations in the various ancestral temples, and that ornamented mantic practices linking this world to the next. These ceremonies provided a conduit for communication between this living population and the ancestors who assisted them from beyond.

In thus "re-iconizing" the *gu* 觚 ritual vessel, we are perhaps better able to understand what Confucius means when he distinguishes between an iconic *gu* 觚, and a *gu* 觚 that is not a *gu* 觚—that is a *gu* 觚 as a merely aesthetic artifact.

7.18 子所雅言，詩、書、執禮，皆雅言也。
Occasions on which the Master would insist upon proper pronunciation were in reciting the *Songs* and the *Documents*, and in observing ritual propriety (*li* 禮). On all such occasions, the Master would use proper pronunciation.

Comment: Although advancing the argument that Confucian philosophy is fundamentally progressive, we must at the same time give full register to the conservative aspect of this Confucian project in which the traditional culture is transmitted from one generation to the next. In 7.1, Confucius insists he follows traditional ways and cherishes the ancients. The first responsibility of each generation is to embody the cultural legacy bequeathed to it, and in so doing, to keep the cultural corpus of the ancestors intact. One important element in this transmission is the proper pronunciation of the language in the classics and the emotive power of elocution. The diversity of the peoples and cultures that were drawn into the centripetal whirlpool that became China together with the ineluctable passage of time perpetuated a shared and persistent Chinese identity. At the same time, these same forces with the constant introduction of novel factors had a centrifugal effect on the cultural core, pulling it in all directions. The proper pronunciation of the classics set a standard Confucius felt important to preserve, while at the same time, this standard was open to the corrosive influences of both time and cultural differences. The pronunciation of the language used in reciting the classical canons was certainly necessary to preserve the emotive and aesthetic effects of these texts, but within an oral tradition it was much more. Elocution was integral to the internal rhyme scheme, cadence, tonality, and other mnemonic devices necessary to preserve it whole. Indeed, it was because the musicality of the language is so dependent upon personal transmission that it makes a text vulnerable to these ravages of time, with the early loss of the *Classic of Music* being a case in point.

1.3 子曰："巧言令色，鮮矣仁。"
The Master said, "It is a rare thing for glib speech and an insinuating

appearance to accompany consummate conduct (*ren* 仁).''

Comment: (Repeated in 17.17). Speech, ritualized propriety, the making of music, and meaningful gesticulation are all seen as discursive modes for effecting enjoyment. For Confucius, consummate persons are the "masters of ceremony" who through these various media of communication facilitate a social musicality. Thus, for Confucius, genuineness and sincerity in what is said and done are necessary conditions for growth in relations as the real substance of morality. Throughout the text, we see how exhortations to "make good on one's word" (*xin* 信) and to "do one's utmost" (*zhong* 忠) are modalities of relational transactions of the highest moral value because they are catalytic to such growth. Said the other way, duplicity in language and appearance is anathema to the integrity necessary for consummate conduct. In Confucian philosophy, glib speech and an insinuating appearance are not only unseemly ways of conducting oneself, they are fundamentally immoral.

5.5 或曰: "雍也仁而不佞。" 子曰: "焉用佞? 禦人以口給, 屢憎於人。不知其仁, 焉用佞?"

Someone said, "As for Zhonggong, he is a consummate person (*ren* 仁) but is not well-spoken."

The Master said, "What is the use of being well-spoken? A person who disputes with a glib tongue often earns the enmity of others. I cannot say whether or not Zhonggong is a consummate person, but of what use is being well-spoken?"

Comment: Even though Zhongyong is a young protégé much admired by Confucius, the Master is always reluctant to ascribe to anyone the distinction of being truly consummate. The term *ning* 佞 translated as both "well-spoken" and "glib" usually means the latter, but can have either one of these positive and negative connotations, depending upon context. In any case, the point being made by Confucius is that if the facility with language that makes one well-spoken is lacking in earnestness, it is duplicitous. As such, it is a long way from reflecting the sincerity and seriousness needed to become consummate as a person.

11.21 子曰: "論篤是與, 君子者乎? 色莊者乎?"

The Master said, "With those who are praised for being earnest in their words, the question is whether they really have the stuff of exemplary persons (*junzi* 君子), or are just pretending to be serious."

Comment: Again, Confucius is always concerned about the distinction between what appears to be, and what actually is. We must be discerning because language effectively deployed is at once the ground of moral growth, and the most frequent source of diminution. It is the performative power of language, even when duplicitous, that is Confucius's greatest concern. It is only those persons who are themselves consummate who are able to distinguish genuineness from dissemblance.

Throughout the text in different ways Confucius uses various modal distinctions as a basis for moral judgment: genuine versus feigning (9.12, 11.21, 13.18, 15.14, 17.13), sincere versus glib (1.3, 5.5, 5.25, 11.25, 14.32, 15.11, 16.4, 17.17, 17.18), enduring versus short-lived (4.2, 4.5, 4.6, 6.7, 12.1), optimally appropriate (*yi* 義) versus self-serving (*li* 利) (4.5, 4.9, 4.11, 4.12, 4.16, 14.23, 14.34), having ability versus seeking recognition (1.16, 4.14, 15.19, 14.30, 15.21). We can describe such judgments as objective in the sense of being determined by taking the full manifold of relevant factors into consideration rather than being biased or selective. Again, they are based upon the modality of actions: seriousness and commitment, sincerity, personal resolve, *how* more than *what*. These judgments can be said to be true, but in the aesthetic sense of being genuine like a true friend rather than as a matter of propositional logic. And they are thus usually too complex to resolve themselves into the binaries of right and wrong. In all of these cases, the capacity for such judgments must begin from one's own commitment to personal cultivation.

9.12 子疾病，子路使門人爲臣。病間，曰："久矣哉，由之行詐也！無臣而爲有臣。吾誰欺？欺天乎！且予與其死於臣之手也，無寧死於二三子之手乎！且予縱不得大葬，予死於道路乎！"

The Master being gravely ill, Zilu sent some of his disciples to serve as retainers. On improving slightly, Confucius said, "It has been a long time indeed that Zilu has been up to such pretenses. If I have no retainers and yet pretend to have them, who am I going to fool? Am I going to fool *tian* 天? Further, wouldn't I rather die in the arms of my disciples than in the arms of such retainers? And even though I do not get a grand state funeral, I am hardly dying by the roadside."

Comment: The Confucian doctrine of *zhengming* 正名 has conventionally been translated as "the *rectification* of names." For Confucius, language is certainly retrospective in the sense that effective discourse requires the use of language according to received, stipulated definitions—for example, the deployment of proper titles and respect for the entitlements that accompany rank. This is the point he is making here with respect to the rituals governing funerals. In the literature, Confucius has a strong commitment to such conventions as is in evidence here, and to this extent, the idea of "rectification" certainly has meaning. But to understand language as only retrospective reduces it to a symbolic and representational means of mapping an already existing world—that is, to know the world is simply to find the right name. Such a concept of "literal" language is inconsistent with the process cosmology and the "language games" that give these Confucian texts their interpretive context.

17.18 子曰：" 惡紫之奪朱也，惡鄭聲之亂雅樂也，惡利口之覆邦家者。"
The Master said, "I detest the fact that purple has stolen the place of red in noble dress; I detest the fact that the sounds of Zheng are corrupting our classical court music; I detest the fact that glib-tongued talkers bring down states and families."

Comment: Confucius lived at a time when the ritualized order of society rooted in the practices of the Shang dynasty and then promoted widely by the Zhou dynasty that followed it was in precipitous decline. One complicating factor in this degeneration was the continuing transition from an aristocratic to a meritocratic society. The redefinition of the term *junzi* 君子 from representing nobility of birth to becoming the designation for a moral exemplar and the growing prominence of the scholar-official class (*shi* 士) were both indications of this transition.

Although the doctrines of Confucius were instrumental in promoting meritocracy, true to his philosophical aestheticism he took it as his purpose to revive and reinstate the elegant, ritualized way of life he associated with the Duke of Zhou. In this passage, he singles out particular elements within the ritual practices that have been compromised. For example, while purple is a mixture of red and blue, red is a pure color. It seems that as early as the *Zuo Commentary to the Spring and Autumn Annals* Ai 17 there is a record of purple already taking the place of red as the color of noble dress. This passage is being alluded to in *Mencius* 7B37 in his commentary on the "village worthy." Cf. 15.11. Again, Confucius is keenly aware of the powerful influence of music on relational morality, and persistently rails against the lewd music of Zheng as having an impoverishing and disintegrative effect on the community.

17.13 子曰："鄉原，德之賊也。"

The Master said, "The 'village worthy' is virtuosity (*de* 德) under false pretenses."

Comment: These three passages 17.12, 17.13, and 17.14 are illustrative of a point frequently encountered in the *Analects*: genuineness is a necessary condition for moral conduct. Real growth can only occur when it is attended by a deep and abiding sincerity on the part of those in a shared relationship. *Mencius* 7B37 provides important commentary for this otherwise rather laconic remark:

曰："何如斯可謂之鄉原矣？"曰："'何以是嘐嘐也？言不顧行，行不顧言，則曰："古之人，古之人。"行何爲踽踽涼涼？生斯世也，爲斯世也，善斯可矣。'閹然媚於世也者，是鄉原也。"萬子曰："一鄉皆稱原人焉，無所往而不爲原人，孔子以爲德之賊，何哉？"曰："非之無舉也，刺之無刺也，同乎流俗，合乎汙世，居之似忠信，行之似廉潔，衆皆悅之，自以爲是，而不可與入堯舜之道，故曰'德之賊'也。孔子曰：'惡似而非者：惡莠，恐其亂苗也；惡佞，恐其亂義也；惡利口，恐其亂信也，惡鄭聲，恐其亂樂也；惡紫，恐其亂朱也；惡鄉原，恐其亂德也。'君子反經而已矣。經正，則庶民興；庶民興，斯無邪慝矣。"

"What kind of person is to be called a 'village worthy'?" asked Wan Zhang.

"The village worthy is one who would say: 'What is the point of having grand ambitions? With little relation between word and deed, the scholars keep saying "The Ancients this! And the Ancients that!" Why are they so reserved and unsociable? Having been born into this world, surely doing what the world expects you to do is a good thing'. In just this way they toady to the world."

"If the entire village praises him as an honorable man," said Wan Zhang, "and everywhere he goes he acts as an honorable man, why would the Master regard him as claiming virtuosity under false pretenses?"

"If you want to condemn the village worthy," said Mencius, "you have nothing on him. If you want to criticize him, there is nothing to criticize. He chimes in with the practices of the day and blends in with the ways of the world. Where he lives he seems to be conscientious and to live up to his word, and in what he does, he seems to have integrity. Everyone in the community likes him, and he even sees himself as doing what is right. And yet one cannot walk the way of a Yao or a Shun with such a person. This is why the Master says that he claims virtuosity under false pretenses.

"The Master said, 'As for my dislike and condemnation of what is specious: I dislike weeds lest they be confused with grain; I dislike flattery lest it be confused with what is proper for one to say; I dislike a glib tongue lest it be confused with integrity; I dislike the tunes of Zheng lest they be confused with music; I dislike purple lest it be confused with red; I dislike the village worthy lest he be confused with virtuosic conduct.'

"Exemplary persons must simply resort to the established norm. Where this norm is upheld, the common people will flourish, and where they flourish, there will be no perversity or ugliness."

Such a village worthy is overdetermined in the sense of form and appearance, making his conduct credible to those who would look to him as a model. It is his plausibility that Confucius finds so dangerous. He apes what is conventionally approved without the personal confirmation necessary to make it his own, and most people are unwittingly won over by him. Confucius is given the last word in this passage, summing up his concerns about the corrosive influence such a specious "model" can have on the quality of the culture.

There is a fundamental difference between doing something that is prompted by the anticipated approbation of others, and acting consistently and instinctively out of a cultivated moral virtuosity (*de* 德), a self-conscious moral virtuosity that in having been habituated, has become who you are. The village worthy exemplifies the distinction between form and substance found in the first chapter of *Five Modes of Virtuosic Conduct*: 仁形於內謂之德之行，不形於內謂之行 "Consummatory conduct in roles and relations (*ren* 仁) taking shape within is called moral virtuosity (*de* 德); where it does not take shape within, it is called merely doing what is deemed consummate." Again, we find this same distinction in *Mencius* 4B19: 舜……由仁義行，非行仁義也: "Shun ... acted upon his moral habit of being consummatory and optimally appropriate in his conduct rather than merely doing what was deemed consummatory and appropriate by others." There is an important difference between persons who are merely able to follow conventional values in acting in a way deemed proper by the community, and those who through an assiduous personal regimen are able to establish consummatory habits of conduct in their roles and relations, and whose conduct is then genuinely suffused by this moral virtuosity.

17.12 子曰："色厲而內荏，譬諸小人，其猶穿窬之盜也與？"
The Master said, "There are the faint of heart who put on a brave front. If we were to look among the petty people for an analogy for this kind of deceit, it is the house burglar who bores holes and scales walls."

Comment: For Confucius, genuineness is the standard for proper conduct. When we look among petty persons, the deception of the speciously brave coward can be compared to that of the thief who burgles under the cover of darkness. Both of them are just petty persons stealing something that is not their own.

17.14 子曰："道聽而塗說，德之棄也。"
The Master said, "Those who repeat whatever they hear in the streets and alleyways are at odds with virtuosic conduct (*de* 德)."

Comment: People who are the happy purveyors of gossip have no regard for the integrity defining of virtuosic conduct. Virtuosic conduct conduces to growth in relations, while spreading rumors poisons them.

19.8 子夏曰："小人之過也必文。"
Zixia said, "Petty persons are sure to gloss over where they have strayed."

Comment: A distinctive and defining feature of petty (or literally "small") persons is their imperviousness to moral growth. Not only are their relations with others barren, but far from learning from their own missteps, they cover them up. It is important here to read *guo* 過 that is conventionally translated as "faults, mistakes" as "straying" from the straight and narrow, or perhaps "missteps," in order to maintain the image of "walking the way" that is the pervasive metaphor in this text.

14.31 子曰："不逆詐，不億不信，抑亦先覺者，是賢乎！"
　　The Master said, "Without anticipating duplicity or suspecting bad faith, to still be the first to become aware of such conduct—is this not a mark of a superior person (*xian* 賢)?"

Comment: One of the points made repeatedly in the *Analects* is that the real danger of dissembling and hypocrisy lies in the fact that it is often so difficult to detect. The extended discussion of the "village worthy" is a case in point (17.13). One reason for this emphasis is certainly made evident in Confucius's distinction between conducting oneself out of a habituated virtuosity and merely doing those things conventionally deemed worthy. A second reason would be that persons who are truly consummate in their conduct expect as much from others, and giving others the benefit of the doubt, do not enter into relationships with the expectation that they will be deceived. At the same time, Confucius makes it clear that it is only persons themselves consummate in their conduct who are discerning and able to make informed moral judgments on the conduct of others (4.3). And again, while such exemplary persons might in fact be deceived, they cannot be duped (6.26), where to be deceived is for the properly trusting to be misled but to be duped is for the fool to become the victim of a swindle.

6.26 宰我問曰："仁者，雖告之曰：'井有仁焉。'其從之也？"子曰："何爲其然也？君子可逝也，不可陷也；可欺也，不可罔也。"
　　Zaiwo inquired, "If a consummate person (*ren* 仁) was told that there is another consummate person who has fallen in the well, would he go in after him?"
　　The Master replied, "How could this be? Exemplary persons (*junzi* 君子) can be sent to save the person, but not to jump in after him; they can be deceived, but not duped."

Comment: The terms "consummate persons" (*renzhe* 仁者) and "exemplary persons" (*junzi* 君子) are used interchangeably in this passage.
　　Zaiwo as portrayed in the *Analects* has the rare distinction of being Confucius's worst student. In 5.10, Confucius allows that Zaiwo's failure to match the word with deed has taught him to watch what people do rather than to take them at their word. There is an important difference between being deceived, which sometimes happens when one quite properly takes people at their word, and being duped, which would be foolish, and

amount to doing something that would diminish oneself as a person. For someone to jump into a well after another would be foolish not only because they are putting their own life at risk, but also because it is a wholly ineffective way of rescuing the person who had fallen in.

To be deceived can mean merely that the properly trusting are misled. But to be duped says something about the victim in the ruse, where it is the fool who becomes the mark in a swindle. This distinction is pursued in the *Mencius* 5A2. The first example is Shun taking a wife without informing his parents whom he knew would refuse his marriage. Shun's seeming violation of ritual propriety (*li* 禮) is trumped by his higher responsibility to his parents, that according to the precepts of "family reverence" (*xiao* 孝), is to provide them with an heir. Again, when Shun's parents and his brother Xiang attempt to kill him, he is not duped by them, and evades their attempts. Subsequently, he offers his brother Xiang a role in government. In so doing, Shun thereby fulfills the duty of fraternal respect (*ti* 悌). When asked whether Shun knew his family members were trying to take his life, Mencius says Shun was of course well aware of their machinations.

In response to these two episodes in the life of Shun, Mencius offers the following analogy:

昔者有饋生魚於鄭子產，子產使校人畜之池。校人烹之，反命曰："始舍之圉圉焉，少則洋洋焉，攸然而逝。"子產曰"得其所哉！得其所哉！"校人出，曰："孰謂子產智？予既烹而食之，曰：得其所哉？得其所哉。"故君子可欺以其方，難罔以非其道。

"Some time ago," said Mencius, "a gift of a live fish was made to Zichan of Zheng, and Zichan sent it to his groundskeeper to put in his pond. In fact, the groundskeeper cooked it up, and then reported back, 'When I first let the fish go, it seemed listless, but a little while later it came to life, and plunged into the depths.' Zichan replied, 'It found its element! It found its element!' The groundskeeper withdrew, and said, 'Who said this Zichan is a wise person? I have already cooked and eaten his fish, and he says 'It found its element! It found its element!' Indeed, the exemplary person can be deceived in how things are done, but he cannot be duped into abandoning the proper way (*dao* 道)."

Presumably Mencius's point is that Zichan's wisdom lies in the fact that, in spite of his trust in his groundskeeper being misplaced, his own conduct was impeccably consistent with the higher dictates of ritual propriety (*li* 禮) in receiving a gift and disposing of it properly. Just as Shun had been son to his parents and brother to his brother irrespective of their conduct, so Zichan had satisfied the ritual demands of receiving a gift irrespective of the conduct of his deceiving groundskeeper and was thus beyond reproach.

9.24 子曰："法語之言，能無從乎？改之爲貴。巽與之言，能無說乎？繹之爲貴。說而不繹，從而不改，吾末如之何也已矣。"

The Master said, "How could one but be inspired by what model sayings have to say. But the real value lies in being improved by them. How could one but take pleasure in kindly advice. But the real value lies in learning from it. What can be done with people who take pleasure in kindly advice but do not learn from it, or who comply with model sayings but are not improved by them."

Comment: A saying must be a doing. A major theme in the text is authentication in practice. The function of language is not simply to prompt the pleasure to be found in inspiring ideas. More importantly, its value lies in what is actually done as a result of what has been said. We often associate the mantra "the inseparability of knowing and doing" (*zhixingheyi* 知行合一) with the Ming dynasty philosopher, Wang Yangming, but this pragmatic assumption has deep roots in the classical canons. Indeed, the *Analects* itself as a repository of "model sayings" and "kindly advice" is an object lesson here. Its purpose is not simply to provide its readers with a vocabulary that will enable them to think cogently about moral issues. While it certainly is this too, more importantly is its goal to improve its readers as it is captured in the expression: "being transformed through education" (*jiaohua* 教化). The expectation is that given the inseparability of knowing and doing, a real understanding of the *Analects* will make its reader a better person.

17.19 子曰："予欲無言。"子貢曰："子如不言，則小子何述焉？"子曰："天何言哉？四時行焉，百物生焉，天何言哉？"

The Master said, "I think I will leave off speaking."

"If you do not speak," Zigong replied, "how will we your followers transmit the proper way?"

The Master responded, "What does *tian* 天 have to say? And yet the four seasons turn and the myriad things are born and grow in the process. And what does *tian* 天 have to say?"

Comment: Confucius is tough on the spoken word. For the practice-oriented Confucius, speaking always brings with it the danger of not being able to live up to one's words (*xin* 信). A major concern for him is the necessary congruence between word and deed that will keep speciousness and hypocrisy at bay. Since genuineness and sincerity are necessary conditions for growth in relations, Confucius makes much of the paronomastic play between being circumspect in what is said (*ren* 訒) and becoming consummate as a person (*ren* 仁) (12.3).

This passage in which Confucius alludes to the conduct of *tian* 天 also brings to mind *Focusing the Familiar* 30 in which Confucius himself is described hyperbolically in grand cosmic terms:

仲尼⋯⋯上律天時，下襲水土。辟如天地之無不持載，無不覆幬，辟如四時之錯行，如日月之代明。

Confucius . . . modeled himself above on the rhythm of the turning seasons, and below he was attuned to the patterns of water and earth. He is comparable to the heavens and the earth, sheltering and supporting everything that is. He is comparable to the progress of the four seasons, and the alternating brightness of the sun and moon.

Just as the ruler who governs with virtuosity is portrayed as the North Star with all of the stars circumambulating around it, so too throughout the literature sages are characterized in grand celestial terms, manifesting in their persons and conduct the brightness of the sun and the moon.

III.12 Exemplary Persons (*junzi* 君子) and Scholar-Officials (*shi* 士)

15.18 子曰："君子義以爲質，禮以行之，孫以出之，信以成之。君子哉！"

The Master said, "Having a sense of appropriate conduct (*yi* 義) as one's native quality (*zhi* 質), practicing it in achieving a ritual propriety in one's roles and relations (*li* 禮), expressing it with modesty, and consummating it in making good on one's word (*xin* 信): this then is the exemplary person (*junzi* 君子)."

Comment: This passage is important in providing a concrete example of how we should understand the expression, "native quality" (*zhi* 質). *Yi* 義 is the prosocial disposition we have within the vital roles and relations that constitute us to be deferential to and inclusive of the interests of others. As described here, *yi* 義 as a native quality is integral to achieving a life of ritual propriety by infusing our roles and relations with meaning. It is expressed through modesty and deference, and is consummated in living up to one's word.

What is revealed by this example is that *yi* 義 as a "sense" or "disposition" is not a given nature or potential that is then actualized and expressed in one's actions. Rather it is an incipient prosocial disposition activated and educated by the transactions of the life experience that then becomes integral to the continuing growth and consummation of a human narrative. We have to resist our tendency to first separate "native quality" from the narrative and then give it causal value. Native quality and narrative like root and tree are one thing, and grow together.

6.18 子曰：＂質勝文則野，文勝質則史。文質彬彬，然後君子。＂

The Master said, "When one's native quality (*zhi* 質) overwhelms the process of refinement (*wen* 文), the person is boorish; when refinement overwhelms the expression of one's native quality, the person has the officiousness of a scribe. It is only when one's native quality and refinement express a shared gentility that you have the exemplary person (*junzi* 君子)."

Comment: While the native quality of persons sets certain limits on the possibilities of growth, at the same time it does not impose a predetermined teleological design or end on them. Although persons are animals and thus might take on manual characteristics we might associate with a horse, there is still an important difference. The point though, is that like a work of art, exemplary persons emerge in their narratives in a contrapuntal relationship with their various environments—familial, social, political, cultural, natural—through which the most is made of their native quality as it is developed and is expressed in the transactional opportunities of their lives. The possibilities of both native quality and refinement are the consequence of the process of growth. The potential to become exemplary as a person, far from being some essential given, is a process that unfolds in the events of a life well-lived.

12.8 棘子成曰："君子質而已矣，何以文爲？" 子貢曰："惜乎！夫子之説，君子也。駟不及舌。文猶質也，質猶文也。虎豹之鞹，猶犬羊之鞹。"

Ji Zicheng inquired, "Exemplary persons (*junzi* 君子) are defined by their native quality and nothing else. What need have they of further refinement?"

Zigong replied, "It is a shame that the gentleman has spoken thus about the exemplary person—'a team of horses cannot retrieve his words.' Refinement is no different from one's native quality; one's native quality is no different from refinement. The hide of a tiger or leopard when shorn is no different from that of a dog or a sheep."

Comment: This passage rehearses two constant themes found throughout the text. First, there is a full recognition of the power of language to command a world into being. As such Ji Zicheng as a minister in the state of Wei has the social and political status that makes every word he utters a source of practical consequences.

The second theme requires us to resist our suppressed teleological assumptions that locate potential within something itself rather than within its narrative. In this Confucian cosmology, there is a collaterality in relations expressed in an unwillingness to separate root and tree, nature and nurture, potential and narrative, native quality and refinement. Just as the erstwhile "potential" of anyone emerges *pari passu* within their unfolding narrative at the intersection between person and world, so the native quality is integral to refinement. Native quality and refinement are aspectual and thus inseparable ways of looking at the same process of growth. That is, exemplary persons are to be found in their narratives. When it states that native quality is refinement, refinement native quality, the point is that exemplary persons are a consequence of how this quality evolves over time within the transactions that constitute their narratives.

Said another way, no one is born an exemplary person. Nature cannot be separated from nurture. Native quality is not some isolatable given that is then actualized in conduct. It is a disposition for becoming exemplary that is integral to and grows together with refinement, just as the root grows together with the tree. An important point is that the term translated here as "refinement" or "culture" (*wen* 文) is quite literally the complex patterns found on the pelts of animals such as the tiger and leopard. What makes a dog different from a tiger or leopard is the rather unremarkable, life narrative of a domesticated animal and that of two fiercely beautiful predators. Cf. 3.4, 3.8, 6.18. 9.14.

III. THE *ANALECTS* (*LUNYU* 論語): A BASIC CONFUCIAN VOCABULARY

7.33 子曰:"文,莫吾猶人也。躬行君子,則吾未之有得。"
　　The Master said, "In the niceties of cultural refinement (*wen* 文), I am perhaps like other people. But as far as personally succeeding in living the life of the exemplary person (*junzi* 君子), I have accomplished little."

Comment: In 7.25 we are told that "culture" is one of the four rubrics under which Confucius taught his students. But in 1.6 and elsewhere, we learn that Confucius subordinates the academic pursuits to the more practical project of cultivating one's personal conduct in family and community to the point of making it exemplary as captured in his neologism, "exemplary person" (*junzi* 君子). I describe *junzi* 君子 as a neologism because, even though in the literature it is a familiar social and political term indicating noble rank and status, Confucius not only redefines it as a moral term, but has made it one of his key terminologies and has given it enormous weight in his social and political philosophy. With characteristic modesty, Confucius demurs at claiming the kind of personal achievement that would elevate him to the high standards of social and political conduct he has invested in this term.

2.12 子曰:"君子不器。"
　　The Master said: "Exemplary persons are not functionaries."

Comment: "Exemplary" is a qualitative designation describing persons who through an ongoing commitment to personal growth demonstrate sociopolitical leadership, and who have thus become exemplary for their communities. Exemplary persons are not deemed such by virtue of a specific skill set or by demonstrated expertise, but by their contribution to the social and political life that qualifies them as a role model for those around them. There is the suppressed assumption that cultivated persons by virtue of their refinement and social influence are able to perform any task better than the technician. Exemplary persons with their wisdom understand the implications of instrumental technological knowledge for the overall quality of the human experience. Practically speaking, this presupposition has shaped traditional education for government service, defining it as a long process of personal refinement with training in any specialized skills being assigned an ancillary role.

　　A familiar contrast is made in the tradition from beginning to end, between the moral authority acquired through the quality of one's conduct and the leadership it enables on the one hand, and the kind of instrumental authority that comes with having the expertise to perform particular tasks on the other. Role models qualify as such not by virtue of what they can do, but by excellence in their achievements as persons and excellence in their actions that reflect it: *how* they do what they do. Such personal realization can only emerge and be expressed in the social and political activities defining of communal order, and for this reason, is heavily dependent upon effective communication. Correspondence between what is said and what is done is the basis of credibility, and the ground of social and political order.

The overlapping of consummate persons/conduct (*renzhe* 仁者) with exemplary persons/conduct (*junzi* 君子) as two dimensions of the project of becoming a sage (*shengren* 聖人) accounts for the fact that many characteristics of consummate persons are also the distinguishing features of exemplary persons. To the extent that both terms emphasize specific aspects in the general project of personal growth, the characteristics of a stern commitment to learning, personal cultivation, and ongoing refinement are held in common. Sagehood as a category like exemplary persons, is strongly associated with personal worth and the extended social and political sway that come with it, the difference lying in the epochal scope and scale of their influence.

5.4 子貢問曰: "賜也何如？" 子曰: "女器也。" 曰: "何器也？" 曰: "瑚璉也。"

>Zigong inquired, "And what do you think of me?"
>The Master replied, "You are a vessel."
>Zigong asked, "What kind of a vessel?"
>The Master replied, "You are the most precious and sacred kind of vessel."

Comment: In his asking this question, we might surmise that Zigong is fishing for a compliment. But what comes immediately to mind in Confucius's answer is 2.12: "Exemplary persons are not functionaries." *Qi* 器 as "functionaries" is the same term translated as "vessel" in this passage. Confucius's ambiguous and seemingly unkind description of Zigong prompts his further question. Confucius replies by stipulating the specific kind of vessel he is referencing as the *lian* 璉 and *hu* 瑚, sacrificial vessels for grain offerings used in the ancestral halls of the Xia and Shang dynasties respectively.

Zigong is of good birth and breeding, and was successful as both a statesman and a merchant. Eloquent and capable, he is still criticized by Confucius for the gap between his words and deeds that speaks of expedience in his conduct and for insufficient concern for the well-being of others. The ever-critical Confucius makes it clear to Zigong that in his judgment, he stands at a considerable distance from being exemplary as a person. Indeed, Zigong is being criticized by the Master as being a functionary, while at the same time being praised obliquely as being the very best kind of one.

14.42 子路問君子。子曰:"修己以敬。"曰:"如斯而已乎?"曰:"修己以安人。"曰:"如斯而已乎?"曰:"修己以安百姓。修己以安百姓,堯舜其猶病諸!"

Zilu asked about exemplary persons (*junzi* 君子). The Master replied, "Cultivating themselves they earn respect."

"Is that all there is to it?" asked Zilu.

"Cultivating themselves they bring accord to their peers."

"Is that all there is to it?" asked Zilu.

"Cultivating themselves they bring accord to the people broadly. Even a Yao or a Shun would find such a task daunting."

Comment: There is frequently an ambiguity in Confucius's use of the term "exemplary persons" (*junzi* 君子) that, while being newly invested by him with a strong moral sense, still carries the old political connotation of the formal role of ruler. For Confucius, the only road to becoming exemplary as a person is through demonstrated leadership in the social and political life of the people. This passage reminds us of 13.3 in which Zilu is rebuked by Confucius for his impulsive and facile response to Confucius when asked about the importance of the doctrine of *zhengming* 正名: "using names properly." Zilu's comment "is that all there is to it?" is an equally flippant response to what Confucius regards as the serious regimen of personal cultivation needed to carry out the social and political responsibilities for what it means to become an exemplary person. At issue here is nothing less than the quality in the conduct of persons that garners the respect of the people and thus enables them as rulers to promote real happiness, contentment, and security in their daily lives. Elevating the quality of the lives of the people in this way was something that the most sagacious of China's legendary rulers struggled to achieve.

12.4 司馬牛問君子。子曰："君子不憂不懼。"曰："不憂不懼，斯謂之君子已乎？"子曰："內省不疚，夫何憂何懼？"

Sima Niu inquired about exemplary persons (*junzi* 君子). The Master replied, "Exemplary persons are neither anxious nor apprehensive."

"Does just being free of anxiety and apprehension make one exemplary as a person?" he asked.

"On examining themselves there is nothing to be ashamed of, so why would they be worried or apprehensive?" replied Confucius.

Comment: It would seem that Confucius is responding sympathetically here to the plight of his student, Sima Niu. Sima Niu's oldest brother Huan Tui was the Minister of War in the state of Song who together with his other brothers fomented rebellion against their Song sovereign. Again, and closer to home, this same brother of Huan Tui on one occasion in a case of mistaken identity actually threatened the life of Confucius himself. During that episode, Confucius with his own life on the line expressed neither anxiety nor fear, but rather insisted that virtuosic conduct is the best response to Huan Tui's attempts at intimidation (7.23). While Sima Niu with such a family history might think he has every reason to be anxious and fearful, Confucius's counsel echoes his response to Huan Tui in insisting that if in your own conduct you are beyond reproach, what need is there for you to be concerned?

15.32 子曰："君子謀道不謀食。耕也，餒在其中矣；學也，祿在其中矣。君子憂道不憂貧。"

The Master said, "Exemplary persons (*junzi* 君子) make their plans around the proper way (*dao* 道) and not around sustenance. A life tilling the land can sometimes lead to hunger; a life of learning can sometimes lead to an official salary. But exemplary persons are anxious about the proper way, and not about poverty."

Comment: For Confucius, it is all about living the proper way. While farming that should be productive might fail to put food on the table, and while the life of the often-impoverished scholar might actually succeed in providing a good livelihood, neither hunger nor salary should enter into the equation. Exemplary persons are only anxious that their conduct might fail to contribute to the proper way and do not have a second thought for material well-being.

14.27 子曰：「君子恥其言而過其行。」
The Master said, "Exemplary persons (*junzi* 君子) would feel shame if their words were better than their deeds."

4.24 子曰：「君子欲訥於言而敏於行。」
The Master said, "Exemplary persons (*junzi* 君子) want to be slow to speak yet quick to act."

15.23 子曰：「君子不以言舉人，不以人廢言。」
The Master said, "Exemplary persons (*junzi* 君子) do not promote others because of what they say, nor do they reject what is said because of who says it."

2.13 子貢問君子。子曰：「先行其言而後從之。」
Zigong asked about exemplary persons (*junzi* 君子). The Master replied: "They first accomplish what they are going to say, and only then say it."

Comment: Given that Confucian morality is nothing other than growth in relations effected through what one says both verbally and through the various other modes of transactional discourse, a theme emphasized and repeated in the *Analects* is the need to find congruence between what one says and what one does. Said another way, persons define themselves as exemplary in their conduct by what they do rather than merely by what they say. This emphasis on success in practice is nothing but another way of saying that making good on one's word (*xin* 信) is a necessary condition for establishing the fiduciary community in which each member acknowledges their responsibility to act on behalf of the others. Passages 14.27, 4.24, 15.23 and 2.13 all make the same point with respect to word and deed, defining exemplary persons in this respect in the same terms as consummate persons (*ren* 仁).

15.20 子曰：「君子疾没世而名不稱焉。」
The Master said, "Exemplary persons (*junzi* 君子) despise the thought of ending their days without having established a name."

Comment: In Confucian philosophy, "person" is something that you do rather than what you are. In the same way "name" (*ming* 名) is something done as in "making a name for yourself." Names are thus gerundive: the process whereby one actually becomes the name one would like to be. "Confucius" is an accomplishment, a name (*ming* 名) that has borne fruit (*shi* 實) and has thus become real.

When we look at the complex naming practices in the Confucian tradition, proper names, sobriquets, style names, pen names, and so on, tend to be prospective and programmatic: what parents hope for their children, how scholars in their studies would like to be remembered, how one conjures up a self-image to which one can aspire. The challenge is to "make good on one's word" (*xin* 信), where the word itself is one's name.

Such a concern about making good on the substance of one's reputation has to be distinguished from the desire for celebrity and to reap benefits from merely being known. As with the relationship between what is said and what is done, the assumption is that there has to be an authentication in action that establishes a congruency between reputation and narrative.

16.8 孔子曰: "君子有三畏: 畏天命, 畏大人, 畏聖人之言。小人不知天命而不畏也, 狎大人, 侮聖人之言。"

Confucius said, "Exemplary persons (*junzi* 君子) hold three things in awe: the commands of *tian* (*tianming* 天命), great persons, and the words of the sages (*shengren* 聖人). Petty persons, knowing nothing of the commands of *tian* 天 do not hold it in awe, are contemptuous of great persons, and ridicule the words of the sages."

Comment: In the classical Confucian construction of religiousness, rather than an emphasis on supplication and obedience to some higher power, there is a concern that moral exemplars themselves become a source of meaningful change. That is to say, meaning, value, and purpose do not exist as a given standard in the image of a transcendent God-head, but are created and sustained in the interactions between human beings and *tian* 天. Hence there is the familiar mantra: "the continuity between and inseparability of the human and the cosmic orders" (*tianrenheyi* 天人合一). For Confucius, it is not only the *gravitas* of *tian* 天, but also the meaning-disclosing power of the best among human beings—the sages and other great persons—that should be the object of deference and awe. The commands of *tian* 天 certainly include circumstances over which human beings are able to exercise little control, but this ineluctable force also has a numinous aspect to be associated with the ancestors, the cultural heroes, and with the majesty of nature. Given the contrast between exemplary persons and "petty" or literally "small" persons, there is a warrant to read "great persons" as moral exemplars rather than as persons of high political station. On the other hand, in Confucian political philosophy the isomorphism between family and polity tends to soften considerably the familiar dialectical relationship of "us-and-them" assumed between people and political authority.

With respect to "petty persons," their social, political, and moral anemia arises from a failure on their part to recognize and to take advantage of the resources available to them to grow themselves as human beings. The cultural, natural, and religious propensities of *tian* 天 together with the wisdom of the cultural heroes and sages of the past constitute a shared repository of meaning available for each generation to draw upon for their sustenance. They use this repository in growing themselves as a flourishing community, and in the fullness of time, it is their responsibility to replenish the source with the best wisdom of the best people of their time and place.

16.10 孔子曰：" 君子有九思：視思明，聽思聰，色思溫，貌思恭，言思忠，事思敬，疑思問，忿思難，見得思義。"

Confucius said, "Exemplary persons (*junzi* 君子) always keep nine things in mind: in seeing they think about clarity, in hearing they think about acuity, in their countenance they think about cordiality, in their bearing and attitude they think about deference, in speaking they think about doing their utmost (*zhong* 忠), in conducting affairs they think about due respect, in entertaining doubts they think about the proper questions to ask, in their anger they think about regret, and in sight of gain they think about appropriate conduct (*yi* 義)."

Comment: The term repeated herein is *si* 思 translated as "think about." It is a generic term that covers the various modes of thinking: considering, pondering, calculating, reflecting on, ruminating, contemplating and so on. In the early literature *si* 思 is sometimes defined as *rong* 容 meaning "including," "forbearing," and "accommodating." With Confucius's constant valorization of flexibility, open-mindedness, deference, and inclusiveness, the assumption is that thoughtfulness in the sense of "paying attention to" leads to accommodation.

For example, if in seeing one has clarity both "in" mind and "of" mind, one is able to be discerning and to include much more within one's purview than one would otherwise. If in speaking there is a commitment to doing one's utmost to live up to one's word, one establishes the credibility necessary for growing relations in a flourishing community. If in sight of gain one is moved to accommodate the interests of all concerned, such inclusiveness leads to a greater quantum of equitable gain. In response to uncertainties, the most effective way of resolving such misgivings is to have the openness to seek out advice from those who would know better. Even in one's anger, to have the foresight to anticipate any negative consequences that might follow from acting upon it enables one to think again and perhaps to exercise forbearance.

17.24 子貢曰："君子亦有惡乎？"子曰："有惡：惡稱人之惡者，惡居下流而訕上者，惡勇而無禮者，惡果敢而窒者。"曰："賜也亦有惡乎？""惡徼以爲知者，惡不孫以爲勇者，惡訐以爲直者。"

Zigong said, "Do exemplary persons (*junzi* 君子) have things that they detest?"

"They do indeed," said the Master. "They detest those who happily pronounce on what is detestable in others; they detest those subordinates who would malign their superiors; they detest those who have courage yet do not temper it with proper manners; they detest those who, being determined to get what they want, are unrelenting. But Zigong, don't you too have things you detest?"

Zigong replied, "I detest those for whom earnestness passes for wisdom; I detest those for whom insolence passes for courage; I detest those for whom slander passes for being upright."

Comment: Confucius certainly makes much of how exemplary persons must strive to be open-minded, flexible, and accommodating, and embraces such a posture in his own person. At the same time, however, he is adamant that there are attitudes and modes of conduct that must not only be openly criticized, but must be roundly condemned. And the most credible persons to speak out against perversity are those who have in their own conduct risen high above it.

What the four contemptible dispositions enumerated here by Confucius seem to have in common is that each one of them—gossiping, impudence, rudeness, obstinacy—is an immediate source of social disintegration. When Zigong is asked what he would add to the list, his three choices are nuanced and intelligent. They all follow on Confucius's familiar abhorrence of dissemblance and duplicity, and Confucius's concern about something specious taking the place of what is genuine.

19.20 子貢曰："紂之不善，不如是之甚也。是以君子惡居下流，天下之惡皆歸焉。"

Zigong said, "The perversities of the Shang tyrant Zhou were nowhere near the extreme of what is now reported. That is why exemplary persons (*junzi* 君子) hate to dwell in the sewer—all of the world's filth finds its way there."

Comment: Passage 18.1 provides a brief synopsis of how different relatives of the last king of the Shang dynasty responded to the tyrant Zhou's perverse behavior, where each one of them did what they thought would serve the best interests of the Shang court:

微子去之，箕子爲之奴，比干諫而死。孔子曰："殷有三仁焉。"
The Viscount of Wei fled from him, the Viscount of Ji was enslaved by him, and Bi Gan in remonstrating with him was put to death. Confucius remarked: "The Shang dynasty had these three consummate persons."①

The Viscount of Wei was the elder brother of the tyrant Zhou who was born while their mother was still a concubine of Di Yi 帝乙, the former emperor. It was because their mother was installed as the official consort by the time of Zhou's birth that it was Zhou who inherited the throne. The story is recounted in the *Lushi chunqiu*. (*Mencius* 2A1 and 6A6 give a different account.)

The Viscount of Ji was Zhou's uncle. He sent Zhou into a rage with his remonstrances, and was subsequently enslaved. Bi Gan was also an uncle, and when he remonstrated with Zhou, Zhou responded by saying he had heard sages have seven openings in their hearts. He then proceeded to find out if Bi Gan was indeed a sage. Bi Gan in particular as this upright uncle of tyrant Zhou is much celebrated in the Confucian texts for his integrity

---

① The Dingzhou version of the text has "persons" (*ren* 人) rather than "consummate persons" (*ren* 仁).

and sacrifice.

Even so, Zigong is remarking here on a broader concern. In a tradition in which each dynasty writes the history of the one that has preceded it, there is a pattern of the new dynasty justifying the regicide that brought it to power by detailing the decadence of the former dynasty's last years and particularly by vilifying its last ruler as wantonly cruel and licentious. The fact that the regicides are often a family matter increases the need for rationalization. The example of the tyrant Zhou of the Shang who was overthrown by Kings Wen and Wu of the Zhou dynasty is the epitome of this practice. Zigong generalizes from this example, and his point here seems to be that exemplary persons as a matter of habit pass quickly over such exaggerations where and whenever they might appear, and are loathe to dwell on the gory details.

16.7 孔子曰:"君子有三戒:少之時,血氣未定,戒之在色;及其壯也,血氣方剛,戒之在鬭;及其老也,血氣既衰,戒之在得。"

Confucius said, "Exemplary persons (*junzi* 君子) have three kinds of conduct they guard against: in their youth when their vigor is still easily aroused, they guard against sexual promiscuity; in their prime when their vigor is at its height, they guard against conflict; in their old age when their vigor is on the decline, they guard against acquisitiveness."

Comment: Throughout the text, and particularly with the governing metaphor of "forging one's way" (*dao* 道), there is a keen awareness of the crucial role of physicality in human behavior herein captured in the expression "blood and vital energies" (*xueqi* 血氣) translated as "vigor." Embodied living means that the body is always a factor in dispositions for action. As a generalization that is perhaps as true today as ever, youth can easily be distracted by sexuality, mature persons by aggressiveness, and the aged by greed. The symbiotic relationship between body and mind (*xinshen* 心身) captured in the cognate relationship between "living body" (*ti* 體) and "embodied living" (*li* 禮) not only precludes the familiar dualistic deprecation of the physical, but makes the quality of person achieved through moral cultivation a holistic affair in which one's physicality becomes the external display of a moral inside. A corollary of this holistic understanding of the human experience would be to understand human dispositions not by emphasizing some and excluding others but by correlating the appropriateness of any particular inclination with the specific situation. Cf. 9.18, 15.13.

III. THE *ANALECTS* (*LUNYU* 論語): A BASIC CONFUCIAN VOCABULARY

14.6 子曰：" 君子而不仁者有矣夫，未有小人而仁者也。"

The Master said, "There have been occasions on which exemplary persons (*junzi* 君子) have failed to act in a consummate manner (*ren* 仁), but there has never been an instance of petty persons being able to act consummately."

Comment: We have to understand these Confucian moral categories such as exemplary or consummate persons as not only processual and open-ended, but also as being fallibilist. Such designations are summary attributions describing established habitudes rather than being final or categorical. It is for this same reason that petty persons in the absence of such habitudes can never act consummately.

The personal virtuosity expressed in either exemplary or consummate conduct is a matter of continuing disclosure rather than closure, is always situation-specific, is a matter of quality rather than right and wrong, and does not have any final formula or definition. With respect to consummate conduct (*ren* 仁), for example, in 6.7 Yan Hui is praised because 其心三月不違仁 "he could go for several months without departing from consummate thoughts and feelings" and we read explicitly that 死而後已 "the journey ends only with one's death." Cf. 4.6.

19.21 子貢曰：" 君子之過也，如日月之食焉：過也，人皆見之；更也，人皆仰之。"

Zigong said, "When exemplary persons (*junzi* 君子) go astray, it is like an eclipse of the sun and moon. When they stray, everyone sees it, and when they correct their course, everyone looks up to them."

Comment: With exemplary conduct being a sustained habitude rather than any kind of finality or closure, there is always the possibility that persons so described are vulnerable to qualitative lapses. With this persistent possibility that such persons might fail to live up to their highest aspirations, Confucius's real emphasis is not on an impossible perfection, but on acknowledging one's shortcomings and making a deliberate effort to reform them.

The social, political, and indeed religious influence of exemplary persons is such that celestial metaphors are frequently invoked to describe their conduct. As the moral beacons from which their communities set their bearings, the eyes of the world are upon them. Their sustained pattern of exemplary conduct as a model of emulation is certainly instructive, but any presumed perfection on their part might well make them less relevant to those below who are still struggling. Perhaps even more compelling than the achievements of these exemplars is their willingness to acknowledge their missteps and to make adjustments accordingly. Cf. *Mencius* 2B9 and *Analects* 1.8, 7.22.

12.16 子曰："君子成人之美，不成人之惡。小人反是。"

The Master said, "Exemplary persons (*junzi* 君子) help to bring out the best in others, not the worst. Petty persons do precisely the opposite."

Comment: How do exemplary persons influence others? Through their example. As we see in 6.30 能近取譬，可謂仁之方也已 "being able to correlate one's conduct with those near at hand can be said to be the method of becoming consummate as a person." Confucian ethics tends to rely more heavily upon analogy with concrete role models as its source of moral guidance than it does upon appeal to abstract rules or principles. The *Analects* and other Confucian canons introduce their readers to concrete historical figures and those situations that constitute a specific narrative as a point of reference for deliberating upon what are always novel challenges.

In 7.22 Confucius allows that 三人行必有我師焉 "in strolling in the company of just two other persons, I am bound to find a teacher." His point is that one learns from both the strengths and the weaknesses of others. Petty persons certainly can have the function of serving as negative role models, and Confucius makes much of this in his repeated contrast between them and exemplary persons. But at the same time, roles and relations within family and community are constitutive of personal identity, and as such, petty persons cannot be ignored. It would be enough that relations with such persons are barren, but in addition their disintegrating machinations are toxic and corrosive of the social fabric. For example, when innocent children learn to be deferential to their elders, there is a danger when these patterns of deference include petty persons and the misdirection that arises from their conduct.

8.6 曾子曰："可以托六尺之孤，可以寄百里之命，臨大節而不可奪也。君子人與？君子人也。"

Master Zeng asked rhetorically, "Are those to whom you can entrust an orphaned youth or can commission the command of a sovereign state, and those who in approaching great matters of life and death, remain unperturbed—are they exemplary persons (*junzi* 君子)? Such persons are exemplary indeed!"

Comment: Exemplary persons are not to be defined by any manifold of specific skills or actions, but by their credibility in all things large and small. The constant is their reliability and their conscientiousness in making good on their word. Throughout the *Analects*, the vocabulary of "credibility" has many variants, and is the preferred Confucian way of thinking about the notion of "truth" as fiduciary "trust."

6.27 子曰："君子博學於文，約之以禮，亦可以弗畔矣夫！"
　　The Master said, "Exemplary persons (*junzi* 君子) learn broadly of culture, discipline this learning through the practices of ritual propriety (*li* 禮), and moreover, in so doing, maintain their course without straying from it."

Comment: Repeated in 12.15. This passage sustains the familiar metaphor of forging forward on "the way." Exemplary persons through their regimen of personal cultivation come to reflect expansive learning and the embodiment of the cultural tradition on the one hand, and the disciplining, refining, and further elevating of this cultural legacy through full participation in ritual propriety on the other. In 1.12 we find the mantra: 禮之用，和爲貴 "an optimizing harmony (*he* 和) is the most valuable function of achieving propriety in our roles and relations (*li* 禮)." The notion that all learning as it literally "informs" and thus brings order to the human experience must be processed through the institutions and practices which conduce to a ritual propriety in family roles and relations is a persistant assumption in the text. Cf. 1.2, 2.3, 8.2, 12.1.

7.37 子曰："君子坦蕩蕩，小人長戚戚。"
　　The Master said, "Exemplary persons (*junzi* 君子) are calm and unperturbed; petty persons are always agitated and anxious."

Comment: Located within an ecological cosmology that gives primacy to vital relations, Confucian exemplars are defined by the quality of their cultivated relations rather than their status, and thus are always at ease in the world regardless of their station in life. Were petty persons simply "small" and self-isolating by their failure to cultivate relations, it would be better for all. But such persons are also embedded within families and communities, and their pursuit of personal advantage within these human nodes while being a source of agitation for themselves is also a distraction for all concerned. Cf. 12.16.

3.7 子曰："君子無所爭，必也射乎！揖讓而升，下而飲，其爭也君子。"

The Master said: "Exemplary persons (*junzi* 君子) are not competitive except when they must be in the archery ceremony. Greeting and making way for each other, the archers ascend the hall, and on returning they drink a salute. Even in contention they are exemplary persons."

Comment: Archery is one of the formal six arts (*liuyi* 六藝) that served as the general curriculum for Confucian personal cultivation. The locus of personal growth lies within their constitutive roles and relations rather than in any notion of discrete personhood. Hence, just as there is no ground for egoism, there is no room for altruism either. Personal growth is a matter of deference and mutual accommodation rather than the *agon* of contest. Even in the highly ritualized sport of archery that does entail a degree of competition, the quality of the exemplary person's performance lies in demonstrating an embodied sense of propriety rather than in any notion of victory. Virtuosity (*de* 德) is certainly a source of "gain" (*de* 得) as is suggested by this familiar paronomastic definition, but it is gain in the sense of growth won through patterns of deference rather than through the victory of contest.

13.26 子曰："君子泰而不驕，小人驕而不泰。"

The Master said, "Exemplary persons (*junzi* 君子) are imposing but are not arrogant; petty persons are the opposite."

Comment: We might take the meaning of *tai* 泰 from what was the pride of Confucius's state of Lu, the sacred and majestic mountain that has this same name. What then is the difference between being imposing, stately, majestic, and thus having *gravitas* on the one hand, and being "arrogant" on the other? The majesty of Mount Tai has deference conferred upon it by the people who live in its shadow, who stand in awe of its presence, and who associate their own identity with it. In 6.23 the notion of mountain is associated with consummate persons who stand large in the community as a beacon that other persons can use to set their moral bearings. In China, such mountains have a sacred aura as the site of royal sacrifices.

Arrogance, by way of contrast, comes from the Latin *arrogant*, "claiming for oneself," and is thus a bogus pride, undue exaggeration of one's own stature, a pretention to superiority. Rather than being conferred upon one by others, arrogance is offensive to other people because it is unwarranted and thus speciousness. This aesthetic contrast between what is genuine and what is duplicitous as a prominent criterion in making moral judgments is a familiar theme in Confucian philosophy. Cf. 20.2.

14.23 子曰："君子上達，小人下達。"
　　The Master said, "Exemplary persons (*junzi* 君子) aspire to what is lofty, while petty persons take the low road."

Comment: What is distinctive about Confucian morality is that what is "lofty" is irreducibly relational, and always requires a correlation between one's own particular circumstances and a vision of how one can elevate the situation by optimizing its creative possibilities for all concerned. Of course, successful precedents derived from prior correlations provide important guidance that can be accessed and thus become available for future analogizing. Reference to historical events and the model of cultural heroes thus has an important role in the best efforts of exemplary persons to take the high road and to find the best way forward.

The mountain appears frequently as a metaphor for the visibility and guidance provided by those who stand out in the community by virtue of their moral worth. Such an analogy contributes to the "walking the way" metaphor we find throughout the text. Cf. 13.26, 14.35.

12.5 司馬牛憂曰："人皆有兄弟，我獨亡。"子夏曰："商聞之矣：死生有命，富貴在天。君子敬而無失，與人恭而有禮。四海之內，皆兄弟也。君子何患乎無兄弟也？"
　　Sima Niu lamented, "Everyone has brothers except for me."
　　Zixia said to him, "I have heard it said:
　　'Life and death are a matter of one's lot;
　　Wealth and honor lie with *tian* 天.'
Since exemplary persons (*junzi* 君子) are respectful and impeccable in their conduct, are deferential to others and observe ritual propriety (*li* 禮) in their roles and relations, everyone within the four seas is their brother. Why would exemplary persons worry over having no brothers?"

Comment: This passage has frequently been cited to support the contention that *ming* 命 means fate or destiny. D.C. Lau calls it the best illustration of such an assumption.① But in fact this passage can be read in a way that offers something close to the opposite meaning. Zixia repeats a popular maxim that suggests there are circumstances beyond our human control. He takes one such circumstance that would seem to be positively unalterable: a person having no brothers. Zixia then explores a way of interpreting the "fate" of having no brothers that seems to allow that such a fate can in fact be changed.

To begin with, we know historically that Sima Niu did have brothers, one of them being the notorious Huan Tui. Huan Tui was the Minister of War in Song who, in a case of mistaken identity, made an attempt on the life of Confucius. In 7.23 in which this event is remembered, Confucius in response to this threat says: 天生德於予，桓魋其如予何？ "*Tian* 天 has nurtured this virtuosity here in me—what can the likes of Huan Tui do to me!" Sima Niu here as a student of Confucius seems to be disowning Huan Tui, altering the unalterable by refusing to interpret "brotherliness" in terms of his own facticity.

Zixia trumps Sima Niu by insisting on the reverse. That is, a factually brotherless person can alter the "propensity of circumstances" (*ming* 命) that has rendered him brotherless by redefining what it means to have brothers, thereby changing the meaning of the name (*ming* 名) "brother." Zixia asserts that the criterion determining brotherhood can be moral (fraternal) rather than biological (born of the same womb). This passage, far from justifying any kind of fatalism, demonstrates how redefinition can command an alternative world into being. It underscores the fluidity of circumstances and the inseparability of fact and value in how we choose to describe a situation.

19.1 子張曰："士見危致命，見得思義，祭思敬，喪思哀，其可已矣。"

Zizhang said, "Those scholar-officials (*shi* 士) who on seeing danger, are ready to put their lives on the line; who on seeing an opportunity for personal gain, think of what is optimally appropriate for all concerned (*yi* 義); who in performing sacrifices, think of proper respect; and who in participating in

---

① Confucius, *The Analects* (*Lunyu*), p. xxviii.

funeral ceremonies, think of real grief—such scholar-officials are deserving of our approbation."

Comment: Although Confucius is redefining the term *junzi* 君子 from "noble by birth" to "noble as exemplary persons," the only road to this personal achievement is still a matter of social and political service. This emerging class of scholar-officials (*shi* 士) seems to be educated apprentices in low-level government posts aspiring to become exemplary persons (*junzi* 君子) through their contributions to the social and political life of the community. It is the specific purpose of Confucius's own academy to produce such scholar-officials as a way of promoting proper governance. Confucius is seeking to transform the concept of the state as regulated by the imposition of external laws and policies into a community that through model leadership and consensus on appropriate family-centered values has become self-regulating. Zizhang provides the basic criteria on which these lower ranking aspirants in their prescribed activities might best be evaluated. Cf. 15.9.

4.9 子曰：" 士志於道，而恥惡衣惡食者，未足與議也。"
   The Master said, "Those scholar-officials (*shi* 士) who, having set their purposes on walking the proper way (*dao* 道), are at the same time ashamed of rude clothing and coarse food, are not worth engaging in discussion."

Comment: The *Analects* seems to use this term *shi* 士 in a specific way as a class of entry-level scholar-officials who are apprenticing for positions in the civil government. Just as with Plato in his Academy, Confucius's concern is to provide these young protégés with a moral education rather than merely administrative skills. As young scholar-officials, their purposes should be defined by the Confucian project captured in the expression, "walking the proper way" (*dao* 道), and not by the worldly comforts often afforded by government service. Confucius's goal in engaging this class of officials in discussion was to educate them rather than to train them. Their schooling certainly included the high standard of literacy and scholarship that would be required by their official duties, but more importantly, it was an education necessarily driven by their own personal resolve to apply themselves fully in a regimen of expansive learning, and in so doing, to aspire to become exemplary in their persons (*junzi* 君子). Cf. 1.14, 14.2.

8.7 曾子曰："士不可以不弘毅，任重而道遠。仁以爲己任，不亦重乎？死而後已，不亦遠乎？"

Master Zeng said, "Scholar-officials (*shi* 士) cannot but be strong and resolved, for their duties are heavy and their way (*dao* 道) is long. Where they take becoming consummate in their conduct (*ren* 仁) as their duty, is it not indeed a heavy one? And where their way ends only with their passing, is it not indeed a long one?"

Comment: "Scholar-officials" (*shi* 士) are interns in the project of becoming "exemplary persons" (*junzi* 君子), with most of Confucius's own students falling into this category. The metaphor of the challenging journey embarked upon by scholar-officials as they make their way through life is stated rather vividly. Perhaps the place to begin is with the contingent, participatory, and evolutionary nature of both "consummate conduct" (*ren* 仁) and "their way" (*dao* 道). Becoming consummately human is more than following in the footsteps of others. Human beings have an active and creative role in continuing, broadening, and extending this way, making *dao* 道 historically composite, incremental, and cumulative. The immediate relationship between *ren* 仁 as "person-making" and *dao* 道 as "world-making" does much to clarify the contingent and qualitative nature of both of them. It is because persons emerge from the dynamic interaction between always unique persons and always unique circumstances that both *ren* 仁 and *dao* 道 remain in degree obscure and indeterminate. Each generation has both the capacity and the obligation to build its connector to the next generation.

What makes the burden heavy and the way long is the responsibility of these always unique scholar-officials to actively forge their way both individually and together. On each page of the *Analects*, the text provides a concrete and continuing narrative of a cadre of such scholar-officials struggling to live up to the high standards laid down in the life of their hypercritical master, Confucius. It seems entirely appropriate that Master Zeng, one of the most distinguished among these scholar-officials, be the representative voice that both rues and celebrates the unremitting commitment needed to make their way along this most difficult road.

17.15 子曰："鄙夫！可與事君也與哉？其未得之也，患得之；既得之，患失之。苟患失之，無所不至矣。"

The Master said, "How can one possibly join together with reprobates in service to one's lord? Before such degenerates have been appointed to office, they are desperate they will not be. Once they are in office, they are then desperate they will lose their position. And in their desperation, they will stop at nothing to hang on to it."

Comment: Confucius states repeatedly that the scholar-officials he is preparing for public office must understand that the moral education they are receiving for civil service is an end in itself, and that it must not be instrumentalized. The important consideration is neither the appointment to office itself nor the status and rewards that come with such rank. Experience in civil service is a precondition for scholar-officials (*shi* 士) who would aspire to become exemplary persons (*junzi* 君子). They can only achieve real virtuosity in their conduct by making a singular contribution to the social and political order. Or said another way, in the absence of the opportunity provided by the responsibilities of public service, one does not have the forum to ascend to and habituate the highest levels of moral conduct integral to the definition of becoming exemplary as a person.

19.13 子夏曰：＂仕而優則學，學而優則仕。＂
Zixia said, "If while serving in public office one has a surplus of energy, it should be directed toward learning; if while studying one has a surplus of energy, it should be directed toward carrying out the duties of public office."

Comment: The character for "learning" or "study" (*xue* 學) in its earliest usage in fact means "teaching and learning" with these two occupations being mutually implicated, and with the teacher being first among the learners.[1] The early oracle bone form of *xue* 學 is a depiction of the national academy in which such teaching and learning take place.[2] This passage seems to be making a similar point. Confucius's vision of the relationship between civil service and moral education is that they are likewise mutually implicated. One does not pursue an education in order to gain office, nor

---

[1] See Roger T. Ames, "On Teaching and Learning (*Xueji* 學記): Setting the Root in Confucian Education," *Chinese Philosophy on Teaching and Learning*: Xueji (學記) *in the Twenty-First Century*, ed. Xu Di and Hunter McEwan, Albany: State University of New York Press, 2016.

[2] See Kwan Tze-wan's "Multi-function Character Database" 京津 4836.

does one enter office having completed one's education. On the contrary, Confucian learning understood as the cultivation of one's personal moral virtuosity is a life-long undertaking that includes both moral education and the intelligent, effective management of the responsibilities that come with social and political office.

13.20 子貢問曰: "何如斯可謂之士矣?" 子曰: "行己有恥, 使於四方, 不辱君命, 可謂士矣。" 曰: "敢問其次。" 曰: "宗族稱孝焉, 鄉黨稱弟焉。" 曰: "敢問其次。" 曰: "言必信, 行必果, 硜硜然小人哉! 抑亦可以爲次矣。" 曰: "今之從政者何如?" 子曰: "噫! 斗筲之人, 何足算也。"

Zigong inquired, "What must one be like to be called a scholar-official (*shi* 士)?"

The Master replied, "Persons who conduct themselves with a sense of shame and who, when sent to distant quarters, do not bring dishonor to the commission of their lord, deserve to be called scholar-officials."

"May I ask what kind of person would rank next?" asked Zigong.

"Persons whom their lineage would praise for their family reverence (*xiao* 孝) and whom their fellow villagers would praise as being deferential to their elders." he replied.

"And next?"

"Persons who always make good on their word (*xin* 信) and follow through in what they do, even though in their stubbornness they are just petty persons—they can still be considered next."

"What about those who are currently carrying out the offices of government?"

"Indeed! Such 'ladle and scoop' bean-counters hardly amount to much!"

Comment: From this passage, we learn the title of "scholar-official" (*shi* 士) is a recognized rank within the civil government with a standard that must be observed both at home and on diplomatic missions abroad. For Confucius, the first purpose of such moral education is to instill in scholar-officials the sense of shame that, without need of external compulsion, motivates them at home to live up to the expectations of their office and their community, and abroad to carry out their offices at a level that protects their lord from reproach.

Confucius's description of the next grade of official tells us much. First, Confucius locates us within the institutions of governance during his own time and throughout most of Chinese imperial history, where social and political order was largely maintained through family and clan regulation. We remember passage 2.21 in which Confucius insists living up to the values of family reverence (*xiao* 孝) and fraternal respect (*ti* 悌) is the ground and substance of all social and political order. We also learn the "scholar official" is a relatively low rank in civil government at the intersection between formal government service and the less formal local institutions and practices.

The description of the third grade is puzzling because so much emphasis in the text is invested in that modality of virtuosic conduct wherein living up to one's word (*xin* 信) and doing one's utmost (*zhong* 忠) are among the highest values. One way of reconciling this profile with the *Analects* as a whole would be to read it as a specific and rather severe reproach of Zigong himself, whose own personal weaknesses are captured herein. Confucius is the master of "tough love" in which he expresses his affection for his protégés in the sternest and most unsentimental terms. Even though Zigong is perhaps second only to Yan Hui as Confucius's most exceptional student, in the comparison with Yan Hui he is criticized for being distracted from the project of personal cultivation by his mercantile aspirations (11.19). Confucius instructs him on the need to put himself in the place of others (5.12, 15.24), and upbraids him for being unwarrantedly judgmental. Indeed, in 5.4 Zigong is damned by faint praise in being described by Confucius rather unkindly as being the best kind of a functionary.

The lowest grade of those who contribute to social and political order is saved for the petty bureaucrats who are presently serving in government and who Confucius is determined to replace with his own students as newly minted scholar-officials (*shi* 士). Since grain was a common unit for taxation, Confucius quite properly describes these minions as "ladle and scoop" bean counters.

12.20 子張問："士何如斯可謂之達矣？" 子曰："何哉，爾所謂達者？" 子張對曰："在邦必聞，在家必聞。" 子曰："是聞也，非達也。夫達也者，質直而好義，察言而觀色，慮以下人。在邦必達，在家必達。夫聞也者，色取仁而行違，居之不疑。在邦必聞，在家必聞。"

Zizhang inquired, "What do the scholar-officials (*shi* 士) have to do to be described as being 'outstanding'?"

"It depends upon what you mean by 'outstanding'?" replied the Master.

"I mean scholar-officials who are certain to be known, whether they are serving in public office or in the house of a ruling family." answered Zizhang.

"That is just being known." said the Master. "It is not being outstanding. Those scholar-officials who are outstanding are true to their native quality of seeking after what is most appropriate (*yi* 義) in their conduct. They examine what is said, are keen observers of demeanor, and are thoughtful in their deference to others. They are certain to be outstanding, whether serving in public office or in the house of a ruling family.

As for being merely known, such persons put on appearances to win a reputation for being consummate in their conduct (*ren* 仁) while their actions belie it. They have no misgivings about themselves being consummate, and are certain to be known by this pretense, whether serving in public office or in the house of a ruling family."

Comment: We first have to consider the interlocutor, Zizhang. He is criticized elsewhere by Confucius as lacking commitment in living up to his word and doing his utmost, and thus being more concerned about appearances than substance (2.18, 12.6, 12.10, 12.14, 15.6, 19.1, 19.3, 19.4). Hence, Confucius wants to make it clear to him specifically that there is an important distinction between a scholar-official who is simply known by others, and one who is truly distinguished. There is an allusion in this passage to 15.18 in which *yi* 義 as a native quality is integral to achieving a life of ritual propriety by infusing our roles and relations with meaning. Such meaning is expanded upon and expressed with modesty and deference, and is consummated in living up to one's word.

And again, being known by others raises the question of what they are known for. At the end of the day, scholar-officials who put on the appearance of being accomplished can be known not for actually having done anything, but for their self-deluding pretense to having done it.

Confucius profiles this new breed of civil servants as being morally outstanding by virtue of the quality they are able to effect in the relations they have with others, regardless of where they offer their service. I translate the term *da* 達 as "outstanding" in an effort to respect the "walking the way" (*dao* 道) metaphor that is pervasive in the text.

III.13 Harmony as an Optimizing Symbiosis (*he* 和)

1.12 有子曰: "禮之用，和爲貴。先王之道斯爲美，小大由之。有所不行，知和而和，不以禮節之，亦不可行也。"

An optimizing harmony (*he* 和) is the most valuable function of achieving propriety in our roles and relations (*li* 禮). In the ways of the Former Kings, the sustaining of this quality of harmony through achieving propriety in their roles and relations made them elegant, and was a guiding standard in all things large and small. But when things are not going well, to realize harmony just for its own sake without regulating the situation through an achieved propriety in roles and relations, will not work.

Comment: Master You is making an important distinction here between enforcing order and achieving harmony (*he* 和). That is, a putative "harmony" that is achieved by imposing external mechanisms and constraints as a means of enforcing order—the application of laws, policies, or rules—is dehumanizing to the extent that such "harmony" precludes personal confirmation and participation. Without an accord among persons being properly negotiated through our lived roles and relations, such actions can be meaningless or worse.

While this term *he* 和 is conventionally translated simply as "harmony," it is perhaps better understood as the aspiration to optimize the creative possibilities of any particular situation. In the case of Confucian ethics, for example, it is the concerted effort to make the most of one's roles as they are lived in family and community. Although we will find that in Confucian philosophy, "optimizing harmony" (*he* 和) is a generic idea with wide application in all human activities from the kitchen to the cosmos, what needs to be emphasized here is the assumption that when such aspirations have reference to human flourishing specifically, the harmony must necessarily be mediated through familial roles and relations for it to be robust, genuine, and enduring. It is the family that is the ultimate source and the indispensable ground of an achieved propriety (*li* 禮) in all of our roles and relations. Morality so understood describes the cultivation of a quality of conduct that is directed at making familial bonds stronger and thicker and more enduring.

13.23 子曰："君子和而不同，小人同而不和。"

The Master said, "Exemplary persons (*junzi* 君子) seek harmony not sameness; petty persons (*xiaoren* 小人), then, are the opposite."

Comment: In an attempt to understand what Confucius means by "harmony" (*he* 和), we might begin from how this term is defined in some of the classical texts. For example, the *Zuo Commentary to the Spring and Autumn Annals* Duke Zhao 20 reads:

齊侯至自田，晏子侍于遄臺，子猶馳而造焉。公曰："唯據與我和夫！"晏子對曰："據亦同也，焉得爲和？"公曰："和與同異乎？"對曰："異。和如羹焉，水、火、醯、醢、鹽、梅，以烹魚肉，燀之以薪，宰夫和之，齊之以味，濟其不及，以泄其過。君子食之，以平其心。君臣亦然。君所謂可而有否焉，臣獻其否以成其可；君所謂否而有可焉，臣獻其可以去其否。是以政平而不干，民無爭心。故《詩》曰：'亦有和羹，既戒既平。鬷假無言，時靡有爭。'先王之濟五味，和五聲也，以平其心，成其政也。聲亦如味：一氣，二體，三類，四物，五聲，六律，七音，八風，九歌，以相成也；清濁，大小，長短，疾徐，哀樂，剛柔，遲速，高下，出入，周疏，以相濟也。君子聽之，以平其心。心平德和。故《詩》曰：'德音不瑕。'今據不然。君所謂可，據亦曰可；君所謂否，據亦曰否。若以水濟水，誰能食之？若琴瑟之專壹，誰能聽之？同之不可也如是。"

The Marquis of Qi had returned from the hunt, and was being attended by Master Yan at the Chuan pavilion when Ju of Liangqiu galloped up to them. The Marquis remarked, "Only Ju is in harmony (*he* 和) with me!"

"All that Ju does is agree (*tong* 同) with you." said Master Yan. "Where is the harmony?"

"Is there a difference between harmony and agreement?" asked the Marquis.

"There is indeed." replied Master Yan. "Harmony is like making congee. We need water, fire, vinegar, sauce, salt, and plum preserves to cook the fish and meat, and we need to burn firewood as fuel in the cooking process. The cook blends these ingredients harmoniously to achieve the appropriate flavor. Where it is too bland, he adds flavoring, and where too thick, he dilutes it with water. When you partake of this congee, Sir, it lifts your spirits.

"The proper relationship between ruler and minister is also like this. Where the ruler gives his assent to something and yet there is something wrong with it, the minister must point out what is wrong to make things right. Where the ruler withholds his assent because there is something wrong and yet there is something right about it, the minister should point out where it is right in order to set aside what is wrong. In this way, governing will function smoothly without any setbacks and there will be no

quarreling over it in the minds of the people. Thus, the *Book of Songs* says:
> There is indeed the harmoniously blended congee;
> It is all prepared and properly seasoned.
> With nothing said the offering is there for the taking,
> And above and below are free of contestation.

"The Former Kings blended the five flavors and harmonized the five notes to lift their spirits and to bring success to their governance. Music functions similarly to flavoring. There is one field of sound; the two kinds of music: martial and civil; the three kinds of songs: airs of the states, odes, and hymns; the four quarters from which materials are gathered for making instruments; the five note pentatonic scale; the six pitch pipes; the seven sounds, the winds of the eight directions, and the nine ballads—all of which complement each other. There are distinctions between clear and turbid, small and great, short and long, quick and slow, plaintive and joyous, hard and soft, delayed and rapid, high and low, beginning and ending, and intimate and distant—all of which augment each other. You listen to these, Sir, and it lifts your spirits, which in turn enables you to govern with beneficence and harmony. Hence the *Book of Songs* says, 'There are no imperfections in the sounds of beneficence.'

"Now Ju is not acting in this way. Whatever you approve, Ju also approves; whatever you disapprove, Ju also disapproves. If you flavor water with water, who is going to eat it? If you keep playing the same note on your zither, who is going to listen to it? Such is the inadequacy of mere 'agreement.'"

Cf. Legge, *Chinese Classics*, Vol. 5 pp. 679, 684. See also 2.14 and 15.22.

"Harmony" as understood through these culinary, musical, and governing metaphors is an aesthetic that is only possible by fully respecting and accommodating the differences that obtain among the relevant constituents. Such an optimizing harmony requires the activating of difference to maximize the possibilities of the always unique ingredients in order that they enhance and thus make a difference for each other. We might describe this kind of harmony as an optimizing symbiosis.

2.14 子曰："君子周而不比，小人比而不周。"

The Master said: "Exemplary persons (*junzi* 君子) associating openly with others are not partisan; petty persons being partisan do not associate openly with others."

15.22 子曰："君子矜而不争，群而不黨。"

The Master said, "Exemplary persons (*junzi* 君子) are self-assured but not contentious; they associate with others, but do not form cliques."

Comment: These two passages 2.14 and 15.22 are a political application of the more general proposition of pursuing harmony by optimizing difference as it is expressed in 13.23. Just as an inclusive "optimizing appropriateness" (*yi* 義) challenges the boundaries set by "personal advantage" (*li* 利), such an inclusive harmony is the alternative to the exclusiveness of partisanship and cliquishness.

III.14 Making Friends (*you* 友)

19.3 子夏之門人問交於子張。子張曰："子夏云何？"對曰："子夏曰：'可者與之，其不可者拒之。'"子張曰："異乎吾所聞：君子尊賢而容衆，嘉善而矜不能。我之大賢與，於人何所不容？我之不賢與，人將拒我，如之何其拒人也？"

The disciples of Zixia asked Zizhang about establishing relations with others. Zizhang asked, "What has Zixia told you?"

They replied, "Associate with those who are worthy of your efforts; spurn those who are not."

Zizhang replied: "This is different from what I have learned. Exemplary persons exalt those of superior character and are accommodating of everyone, praise those who are truly efficacious, and are sympathetic with those who are less so. If in comparison with others, I am truly superior in character, who am I not able to accommodate? And if I am not superior in the comparison and people are thus going to spurn me, what basis do I have to spurn others?"

Comment: Zixia's account of making friends sounds arrogant and aloof while Zizhang's seems inclusive and accommodating. But the question is: Which of them is the better student, and which of them gives a better account of what they have learned from the Master? As to who is the better student, Confucius answers for us explicitly in 11.16 when he says 師也過，商也不及 "Zizhang oversteps the mark, and Zixia falls short of it," and thus

過猶不及 "one is as bad as the other." This is a good example of Confucius's hypercritical attitude toward his students.

When we look at the text carefully, however, we find a rather clear contrast between these two students that would recommend more serious consideration of Zixia's answer. Zixia is a man of letters, and is remembered by tradition as having had an important role in establishing the Confucian canon. He has a major place in the last five chapters of the *Analects* where he underscores the importance of learning. Confucius himself allows that he himself has gotten a great deal from his conversations with Zixia. Zixia defends himself against the charge of pedantry by insisting that personal relationships are what learning is all about. In the comparison, Zizhang, seems to be rash, caring more for appearances than for substance. Confucius is repeatedly critical of him for his failure to do his utmost and live up to his word. And Zizhang is criticized as well by some of his fellow students for being proud and distant (19.15, 19.16).

As we explore Confucius's understanding of the important role of friendship in the *Analects* as a whole, we find good reason to believe it is indeed Zixia rather than Zizhang who is true to Confucius's assumptions about what needs to be considered in making friends.

9.25 子曰："主忠信，毋友不如己者，過則勿憚改。"

The Master said: "Take doing your utmost and making good on your word as your mainstay. Do not have as a friend anyone who is not as good as you are. And where you have strayed, do not hesitate to mend your ways."

Comment: On this topic of friendship, commentators have often puzzled over what Confucius means when he cautions not once, but on two occasions (repeated in 1.8): "Do not have as a friend anyone who is not as good as you are." The logic that seems to follow from this advice is while the friends of an exemplary person will be precious few, the friends of a scoundrel will be legion. The simple point Confucius is making here, however, is that self-conscious personal growth is the outcome of relating effectively in our relationships. In "making friends," friends literally make each other. It is only through a regimen of personal cultivation in the most productive of such relationships that we have the opportunity to grow from some inchoate relational beginnings into distinguished and efficacious persons (*daren* 大人 or *shanren* 善人 or *chengren* 成人). It is for this reason the vocabulary of personal cultivation in Confucian philosophy is described in terms that frequently and specifically reference growth in magnitude from mere beginnings to those who, having been nourished through moral conduct, have added consequence. Such moral growth is purposeful; it starts here and goes there. As Confucius himself opines in 12.1, this project of cultivation to become consummate as a person 爲仁由己，而由人乎哉？ "is self-originating—how could it originate with others?"

But while this growth is self-originating and reflects purpose, such personal cultivation is by no means a solitary affair; it can only be pursued by nurturing the fecund relations that locate us within our everyday roles of family and community. This declaration to seek friendships only among the very best of persons is a clear acknowledgment that Confucius understands both personal growth and diminution as a function of associated living. And it prompts us to ask: Where in a "meaningful" friendship does meaning actually come from?

In a Platonic world wherein meaning has a transcendent reference, friendship is instrumentalized as a commitment to a common end. The conclusion of the reflection on friendship in the *Phaedrus*, for example, is that friends hold all things in common. And when what they hold in common is an *eros* directed toward the transcendent Good, they are *true* friends. Similarly, for the Christian, *philia* as the love among friends and family members, is subordinated to *agapē*, the love of a transcendent God channeled through His creatures as their love for one another.

For Plato's remarkable student Aristotle as well, commonality is the basis for friendship. While there are lower levels of incidental, contingent friendships that seek utility and pleasure, the few *true* friends by contrast are described as "another self" or "a second self." Such "friends in virtue" mirror one's own character as it is grounded in constant virtues and in the intellectual activity of *nous* which is identical in all people. Indeed, Aristotle appeals to the mirror metaphor to illustrate how the real friend in being similarly virtuous is a source of self-knowledge and corroboration.[①] He allows that "contemplative friendships" are higher than the practical kind and that such friendships are rare; they are only available to an elite circle

---

[①] Aristotle, *Complete Works*, 1213a20-26. See Yu Jiyuan, *The Ethics of Confucius and Aristotle: Mirrors of Virtue*, New York: Routledge, 2007, p. 4. See also 1209b12-19 and 1245a30-36.

of equally virtuous people.① There is a superiority of the theoretical life over the practical, and of the speculative vision over daily moral activities. Thus, for Aristotle, the eternal truth that can be grasped by *nous* must be given priority over friendship, even when it means turning away from one's own mentor—in his case, Plato. "While both are dear, piety requires us to honor truth above our friends."②

For Confucius, *contra* Plato and Aristotle, the ultimate source of meaning is not external but situational, and emerges through the self-conscious nurturing process of the friendship itself. And it is the ways in which friends are qualitatively superior to and different from each other that provide the opportunity for collaborative growth and advancement.

19.22 衛公孫朝問於子貢曰："仲尼焉學？"子貢曰："文武之道，未墜於地，在人。賢者識其大者，不賢者識其小者，莫不有文武之道焉。夫子焉不學？而亦何常師之有？"

Gongsun Chao of Wei asked Zigong, "With whom did Confucius study?"

Zigong replied: "The moral vision (*dao* 道) of Kings Wen and Wu has not collapsed utterly—it lives on in people. Those of superior character have grasped the greater part, while those of lesser quality have grasped a bit of it. Everyone has something of Wen and Wu's way in them. Who then did the Master not learn from? Again, how could there have been a single constant teacher for him?"

Comment: One of the most striking statements in this passage is the idea that *dao* 道—the proper way, the moral vision—lives on in people rather than in books or institutions. Again, this legacy has become so pervasive that it has in degree colored the entire population as a commonsense. While it is customary in this Confucian world for students to identify themselves with a particular teacher, such is not the case with Confucius who, true to his profile of being flexible and inclusive, has learned from everyone.

In many ways, the inclusiveness ascribed to Confucius himself is reflected in his own attitude towards diversity in education broadly. In the

---

① Aristotle, *Complete Works*, 1157b5-1158b11. See Yu Jiyuan, *Ethics of Confucius and Aristotle*, p. 214.

② Aristotle, *Complete Works*, 1096a11-16.

first passage of the *Analects* 1.1 we read:

有朋自遠方來，不亦樂乎？
To have fellow students coming from distant quarters—is this not a source of enjoyment?[①]

Peng 朋 in this passage means *menxia* 門下, students of the same master and stable, and would probably refer to the many followers of Confucius who came from foreign places. Friendship as fellowship is a classic illustration of the Confucian mantra 13.23: 君子和而不同 "Exemplary persons seek harmony not sameness." Importantly, it seems that the resources for productive friendships tend to be dispersed among people rather than belonging exclusively to particular paragons. Here we have such an example. When Zigong is asked who Confucius had as his teacher, his reply is inclusive in the sense that for Confucius everyone was, in greater or lesser degree, a source of personal growth. The message is that, since each person is different, Confucius has something—sometimes more, sometimes less—to learn from everyone.

7.22 子曰："三人行，必有我師焉。擇其善者而從之，其不善者而改之。"
The Master said: "In strolling together with just two other persons, I am bound to find a teacher in their company. Identifying their strengths, I follow them, and identifying their weaknesses, I reform myself accordingly."

Comment: The expression "strolling together with just two other persons" (*sanrenxing* 三人行) has come to mean we have something to learn from everyone. Confucius has a generous appreciation of both the positive and negative possibilities most relations with other people provide for us in our moral development. In the actions of others, we certainly see qualities to be admired and emulated, but we also see habits and behaviors that teach us what is best avoided.

13.28 子曰："切切、偲偲、怡怡如也，可謂士矣。朋友切切、偲偲，兄弟怡怡。"

---

① For the distinction between *peng* 朋 and *you* 友 see Hall and Ames, *Thinking from the Han*, pp. 257-269.

The Master said: "Persons who are critical and demanding yet amicable and accommodating can be called scholar-officials (*shi* 士). They need to be critical and demanding with their friends, and amicable and accommodating with their brothers."

Comment: The vital importance of the notion of friendship in Confucian role ethics cannot be overstated. In this Confucian tradition, to "make" friends is quite literally to participate in the "making" of each other to the extent that it is the friendship that becomes what is most concrete, while the discrete "individuals" who participate in the growth of the relationship become increasingly an abstraction from it. Within the web of Confucian relations, intimate friendships take on a transformative force that can only be adequately explained by understanding them as an extension and amplification of the family itself. As a dimension of a Confucian family-centered ethic, friendship serves as a definite, sometimes compensatory source of meaning and value. While immediate family relations are usually a matter of birth and blood, developed friendships are contingent, and entail diversity and deliberate choice. In seeking out and developing meaningful friendships beyond immediate family, these critical and self-conscious relations provide a latitude and a degree of intensity not usually characteristic of our relations with blood relatives. Confucius is keenly aware that freely chosen and expansive friendships bring with them resources for growth that in some important degree compensate for more homogeneous family relations, and in many ways, are our best opportunity for quantum personal growth.

The importance of friendship for Confucianism lies in its function as an open conduit that leads from the security and stability of one's own family out into the more uncertain and sometimes taxing social, political, and cultural realm. Confucius anticipates that friendships can in some ways be more challenging than intimate family relations. One can fairly take for granted the love and protection of one's immediate family, while successful life in the public sphere requires a higher degree of discrimination and a more critical sense of engagement. But then again, the dividends to be reaped from enduring friendships over a lifetime are truly substantial, introducing into personal productivity a deeper degree of difference. We might describe the role of friendship as a doorway through which erstwhile outsiders enter to join and to add a remarkable depth to the ranks of family relations. Cf. *Mencius* 4A19.

16.4 子曰:"益者三友,損者三友。友直,友諒,友多聞,益矣。友便辟,友善柔,友便佞,損矣。"

The Master said: "Having three kinds of friends will be a source of personal growth; having three other kinds of 'friends' will be a source of personal diminution. One stands to be improved by friends who are true, who make good on their word, and who are broadly informed; one stands to be injured by 'friends' who are ingratiating, who feign compliance, and who are glib talkers."

Comment: Not all erstwhile friendships are equally fertile. Indeed, our relations with others are not always benign. While our associations can certainly be an opportunity for growth, Confucius is aware that they can also be a source of personal attenuation. Confucius's point here is that there is a porous boundary on the institution of family that provides additional ground for a more deliberate and purposeful cultivation of friendships, and hence, one's own enhanced individuality as a person. Friends can differ from family in having the potential to provide a degree of growth and complexity that can often go beyond our more formal family bonds. These voluntarily chosen relations, as they develop, "come in the door" in the sense that in this Confucian world, close friends are frequently included as members of the extended family and are customarily referred to in family terms: brothers and sisters, uncles and aunties. Down to the present day, the classroom is very much a family affair, with it being presided over by "teacher-father" (*shifu* 師父) or "teacher-mother" (*shimu* 師母), and classmates being addressed as "student-older-sister" (*xuejie* 學姐) and "student-younger-brother" (*xuedi* 學弟).

16.5 孔子曰:"益者三樂,損者三樂。樂節禮樂,樂道人之善,樂多賢友,益矣。樂驕樂,樂佚遊,樂宴樂,損矣。"

Confucius said, "Finding enjoyment in three kinds of activities will be a source of personal growth; finding enjoyment in three other kinds of activities will be a source of personal diminution. One stands to be improved by the enjoyment found in attuning oneself to the rhythm of ritual propriety (*li* 禮) and music (*yue* 樂),[1] by the enjoyment found in speaking of what others

---

[1] The Dingzhou text just has "ritual propriety" (*li* 禮).

do well (*shan* 善), and by the enjoyment found in having a circle of many friends of superior character (*xian* 賢). One stands to be injured by finding 'enjoyment' in being arrogant, by finding 'enjoyment' in dissolute diversions, and by finding 'enjoyment' in the easy life."

Comment: "Enjoyment" (*le* 樂) is an important and under-remarked moral value in the *Analects*. Like "making music" (*yue* 樂) written with the same character, it is the "making of joy" and rejoicing felt in activities that conduce to moral growth. *Le* 樂 is the pleasure that comes with a sense of shared well-being, associating it immediately with the growth in relations defining of morality (1.15. 6.11. 6.23 7.16), education (1.1, 7.19), wisdom (3.23, 6.20, 6.23), and real friendship (1.1). In 16.4 with respect to friendship, those "friends" who are a source of personal diminution are spurious "friends." Again, any "enjoyment" that is to be found in arrogance, dissolute diversions, and the easy life is a spurious "enjoyment."

12.23 子貢問友。子曰："忠告而善道之，不可則止，無自辱焉。"
　　Zigong inquired about how to best treat one's friends. The Master replied, "Get the best results you can (*shan* 善) in doing your utmost (*zhong* 忠) to counsel them, and in leading them along the proper way (*dao* 道). But if in the end they are resistant then go no further—don't bring discredit on yourself in the process."

Comment: This passage is a good example of the pervasiveness of the "walking the way" metaphor. Confucius suggests that with those friends with whom we share the journey, we should pursue growth in our relationships as best we can. Such growth requires the best counsel we can offer, and serious attention to facilitating the best possible results for our friends along the way. If, however, certain friends resist our encouragement and our best advice and yet are still associated with us, they in their conduct can become a discredit to us. Friends can be a source of expansive growth or diminution.

　　In 4.26 this same logic is taken in the opposite direction where untoward conduct on our part can also preclude the opportunity for further growth in the relationship: 朋友數，斯疏矣 "if in counseling your friends you are unrelenting, they will have nothing to do with you."

III.15 Governing Properly (*zheng* 政)

2.21 或謂孔子曰："子奚不爲政？" 子曰："《書》云：'孝乎惟孝，友于兄弟，施於有政。'是亦爲政，奚其爲爲政？"

Someone asked Confucius, "Why are you not employed in government?"

The Master replied, "The *Book of Documents* says: 'It all lies simply in family reverence (*xiao* 孝). Being filial to your parents and finding fraternity with your brothers (*ti* 弟) is in fact carrying out the work of governing.' In doing these things I am participating in governing. Why must I be employed in government?"

Comment: Confucius is making an astute observation when he asserts that within this cultural tradition, the proper functioning of the institution of family is isomorphic with the socio-political order of the state. Yiqun Zhou marshals scholarly consensus behind her claim that premodern Chinese society was "for several thousand years largely a polity organized by kinship principles."[1] In weighing the extent to which social and political order was rooted in and dependent upon family relations, Zhou insists that in contrast with the Greeks, "the Chinese state was never conceived as a political community that equaled the sum of its citizens," and that "the relationship between the rulers and the ruled was considered analogous to the relationship between parents and children."[2] This contrast immediately recalls Fei Xiaotong's distinction between "the organizational mode of association" (*tuantigeju* 團體格局) as a sum of individuals and "the differential mode of association" (*chaxugeju* 差序格局) as a web of family relations.

On several occasions, Confucius makes the point that when the proper way (*dao* 道) does not prevail in the state, exemplary persons withdraw from involvement in governance. For example, 8.13 天下有道則見，無道則隱 "Be known when the way prevails in the world, but remain hidden away when it does not." Such withdrawal does not mean abandoning responsibility for the sociopolitical order. Rather, since such order is ultimately

---

[1] Yiqun Zhou, *Festival, Feasts, and Gender Relations in Ancient China and Greece*, New York: Cambridge University Press, 2010, p. 19.

[2] Yiqun Zhou, *Festival, Feasts, and Gender Relations in Ancient China and Greece*, pp. 17-18n51.

rooted in the flourishing family, it must be restored at this most fundamental level. Disorder at the higher level requires one to "go home" and cultivate the order at its root.

There is an important distinction between saying social and political order is "rooted in" the life of the family and that it is "derived from" this source. Given the isomorphism between family, state, and world, with the latter two being simulacra of the first, the relationship far from being causal, is contrapuntal and synergistic, with each enhancing the quality of the other.

2.3 子曰：道之以政，齊之以刑，民免而無恥；道之以德，齊之以禮，有恥且格。

The Master said: "If you lead the common people with policy and effect social order with punishments, they will avoid wrongdoing, but will not develop the appropriate sense of shame (*chi* 恥). If you lead the common people by modeling virtuosity in your conduct (*de* 德) and effect social and political order by encouraging propriety in roles and relations (*li* 禮), the people will not only develop a sense of shame, but will also order themselves."

Comment: These Confucian texts give primacy to the thick notion of "achieving propriety in one's lived roles and relations" (*li* 禮) as the source of sociopolitical order. As the primary criteria for moral judgment, such propriety must take the relevant, specific interests of all parties into account (*yi* 義). And while Confucians certainly regard abstractions such as the rule of law and the application of punishments as necessary social institutions, at the same time they construe any recourse to law as an unfortunate intervention that is a clear admission of communal failure. While the dynamics of *li* 禮 -structured family lineages provide a concrete normative pattern of relations for a thriving community, abstract precepts such as the application of laws or policies or its attendant threat of punishment, are at best only secondary, derivative injunctions. It is the moral virtuosity displayed in the role modeling of the rulers, the moral education that comes with the proper functioning of familial and social roles, and the commensurate sense of shame that develops within ritually choreographed family and community relations, that serve as a basis for a social and political consensus, and for critical assessment. Given the central role that *li* 禮 plays in proper governance and the fact that the ultimate goal is the "self-ordering" of the people, the question is whether we should understand the function of governance to be a more holistic "effecting of sociopolitical order" rather than a top-down "governing."

Just as we would argue against beginning from individual, deracinated persons as the subject of moral reflection, similarly we cannot begin from abstract principles as the presumptive determinants of what constitutes moral conduct. Just as particular persons embedded in their particular narratives are the proper subjects of evaluation, so also the standards of evaluation for such subjects are ultimately generalizations drawn from particular instances of human flourishing within our roles and relations, and are best applied with such an awareness.

The argument is that critical moral deliberation should begin from and return to the wholeness of experience. This being the case, any generic standard of adjudication can be no more than a generalization, and to give it a higher or exclusive value introduces the real danger of compromising the scope and imagination required for appropriate moral reflection. The specific narrative certainly has available to it generalizations that can serve as rules of thumb. But the ultimate source of these principles, virtues, and values is itself those compounding human narratives from which such generalizations are drawn. And further, any ostensive empirical generalization that might serve instrumentally as a putative "external" standard must again be adapted to the specific conditions of what are always unique situations. Cf. 20.2.

15.5 子曰: "無爲而治者，其舜也與? 夫何爲哉，恭己正南面而已矣。"

The Master said, "If anyone could be said to have effected proper order while remaining non-coercive in his actions (*wuwei* 無爲), surely it was the legendary sage-ruler Shun. What did he do? He simply assumed an air of reverence and faced due south."

Comment: This is the Confucian version of "noncoercive action" (*wuwei* 無爲) usually associated with the Daoist philosophical literature. In this conception of governance, patterns of deference make governing non-impositional, and make political "authority" morally authoritative rather than authoritarian. Compare *Analects* 2.3 in which the goal of proper governance is achieving a social and political consensus on what are ultimately familial values that then enables the people to become self-ordering through a shared sense of shame. Another factor in non-coercive action arises from the primary responsibility of rulers who, cognizant of the limits of any particular person, must find and promote the most worthy and talented ministers (13.2). For the idea that rulers in their role of exemplary models serve as beacons that orient the conduct of others, see also 6.23 and 17.3.

8.18 子曰: "巍巍乎! 舜禹之有天下也, 而不與焉。"
The Master said, "How majestic they were, Yao and Shun, who reigned over the world but did not rule it."

Comment: Sage-emperors Yao and Shun were in full possession of the world, and yet with the personal majesty of mountains, they remained aloof and did not impose themselves upon it. The highest level of moral governance enables the people through exemplary models and civic education to achieve a social and political consensus to become self-ordering (2.3). At the heart of Confucian political philosophy is its reliance upon the power of civility achieved through ritual propriety in the roles and relations of the people (*li* 禮) to sustain the social and political order without need for appeal to external regulation.

12.13 子曰: "聽訟, 吾猶人也, 必也使無訟乎!"
The Master said, "In hearing cases, I am the same as anyone. What we must strive for is to rid the courts of cases altogether."

Comment: Confucius's ideal society is one in which the application of laws is not necessary. Having said that, we must be careful not to misconstrue his attitude toward penal law. There can be no question that the Confucius depicted in the *Analects* advocated social and political order achieved through suasion and moral example. This preference for and emphasis on education, however, did not prevent the eminently practical Confucius from assigning penal law a role in his political philosophy as an unfortunate but necessary backstop to the omnipresent threat of disintegrating social order. Cf. 2.3, 13.3, 13.18, 12,12, 12.17, 12.18, 12.19, 20.2.

12.12 子曰: "片言可以折獄者, 其由也與?" 子路無宿諾。
The Master said, "If there is anyone who can decide a case listening to only one side, it is Zilu!" Zilu never procrastinates on a promise made.

Comment: Zilu is frequently criticized by Confucius as being insufficiently thoughtful and impetuous, a description of Zilu that is indeed reflected in this passage. While he might only hear one side of the case, the same honest Zilu always makes good on his promises, giving him the trust and confidence of the people. One interpretation of this passage might be that Confucius, far from disapproving of Zilu here, seems to be saying that even though Zilu's actions are often precipitous, his earnestness has earned him the goodwill of the people, and no one would want to take advantage of him. Thus, even when persons have the advantage of the court hearing only their side of a case without the opposing arguments, they would do so in a fair-minded way, enabling Zilu to decide the case without dispute.

16.2 孔子曰："天下有道，則禮樂征伐自天子出；天下無道，則禮樂征伐自諸侯出。自諸侯出，蓋十世希不失矣；自大夫出，五世希不失矣；陪臣執國命，三世希不失矣。天下有道，則政不在大夫。天下有道，則庶人不議。"

Confucius said, "When the proper way (*dao* 道) prevails in the world, ritual practices (*li* 禮), the music repertory (*yue* 樂), and punitive campaigns are initiated by the emperor. If the proper way does not prevail in the world, then such things are initiated by the various nobles. When they are initiated by the various nobles, it is unlikely the state will survive beyond ten generations. When they are initiated by the ministers, it is unlikely the state will survive beyond five generations. When the household stewards of the ministers seize command of the state, it is unlikely the state will survive beyond three generations. When the proper way prevails in the world, governing does not lie in the hands of the ministers; when the proper way prevails in the world, the common people do not debate affairs of state."

Comment: It would seem that in this passage and throughout the text, Confucius is condemning the current situation in the state of Lu where political power has devolved first to the powerful clans, and then to the household ministers of those same clans. For Confucius, proper political authority is a meritocracy that functions through patterns of deference. At the end of the day, there can only be one center. In 1.2, it states that:

其爲人也孝弟，而好犯上者，鮮矣；不好犯上，而好作亂者，未之有也。
... it is a rare thing for someone who has a sense of family reverence and fraternal responsibility (*xiaoti* 孝弟) to have a taste for defying authority. And it is unheard of for those who have no taste for defying authority to be keen on initiating rebellion.

III. THE *ANALECTS* (*LUNYU* 論語): A BASIC CONFUCIAN VOCABULARY

An entrenched sense of an "us-and-them" dialectic has deep roots in the Western philosophical narrative that can be traced back to the classical Greeks. This dialectical tradition including a loyal opposition and the questioning of authority that comes with speaking truth to power, has in certain contexts freighted the term "authority" with strongly negative authoritarian connotations.

By contrast, in the Confucian conception of the political, the immediate analogy is between family and polity, where the ruler serves as the parents of the people. The moral imperative that governs family, state, and cosmos is "family reverence" (*xiao* 孝). Randall Peerenboom gives us an interesting distinction between the Confucian ideal of "right thinking" and the liberal value of "right to think." A shared ideology that produces right thinking can in some cases be impositional and oppressive as a kind of indoctrination. In others it can also be a matter of freely won consensus.① In such a case, the substance of "right thinking" has to be tempered by the pluralistic and inclusive value of "harmony in difference" captured in the mantra: 13.23 君子和而不同 "exemplary persons seek harmony, not sameness." This general statement on the value of equity and diversity has a specifically political application expressed in several different ways. Cf. 2.14, 15.22.

20.2 子張問於孔子曰："何如斯可以從政矣？"子曰："尊五美，屏四惡，斯可以從政矣。"子張曰："何謂五美？"子曰："君子惠而不費，勞而不怨，欲而不貪，泰而不驕，威而不猛。"子張曰："何謂惠而不費？"子曰："因民之所利而利之，斯不亦惠而不費乎？擇可勞而勞之，又誰怨？欲仁而得仁，又焉貪？君子無衆寡，無小大，無敢慢，斯不亦泰而不驕乎？君子正其衣冠，尊其瞻視，儼然人望而畏之，斯不亦威而不猛乎？"子張曰："何謂四惡？"子曰："不教而殺謂之虐；不戒視成謂之暴；慢令致期謂之賊；猶之與人也，出納之吝，謂之有司。"

Zizhang inquired of Confucius, saying, "What kind of a person is it that can be given the reins of government?"

The Master replied, "A person who honors the five best practices and abstains from the four worst practices can be given the reins of government."

---

① Randall Peerenboom, "Confucian Harmony and Freedom of Thought: The Right to Think Versus Right Thinking," *Confucianism and Human Rights*, ed. Wm. Theodore de Bary, and Tu Wei-ming, New York: Columbia University Press, 1998, pp. 235-260.

"What are the five best practices?" asked Zizhang.

The Master replied, "Exemplary persons (*junzi* 君子) are generous and yet not extravagant, they demand hard work from the people and yet do not incur their ill-will, they have desires and yet are not greedy, they are commanding in appearance and yet not arrogant, and they have *gravitas* in their bearing and yet are not severe."

"What does it mean to be generous and yet not extravagant?" asked Zizhang.

The Master replied, "Provide the common people those things that will actually benefit them. Is this not being generous without being extravagant? Further, if you select those projects that the people can handle and get them to work at them, who will feel ill-will? In desiring to be consummate (*ren* 仁), be consummate; wherein could there be any greed? Exemplary persons, regardless of whether dealing with the many or the few, the great or the small, are always well-mannered. Is this not being commanding in appearance and yet not arrogant? Exemplary persons wear their caps and robes correctly, and are always polite in their gaze. With such an air of dignity, persons seeing them from far off hold them in awe. Is this not having *gravitas* in their bearing without being severe?"

"What then are the four worst practices?" asked Zizhang.

The Master replied, "To lead people to execution without having taught them properly is to treat them cruelly; to expect a job to be finished without having given proper notice is to be tyrannical; to enforce a timetable when slow in giving directions is to mistreat the people; to be reluctant in dispensing entitlements is to be officious."

Comment: What are the best practices in governing properly? The five enumerated here all have to do with the relationship between those who would govern and the governed: what it is proper to give to them and what it is proper to demand of them, what is proper to expect in one's transactions with them, and how to comport oneself in the treatment of the people that earns their respect. Zizhang only asks about the first of these best practices because "generosity" in its broadest sense covers them all. In the *Shuowen* lexicon, *hui* 惠 that I am translating here as "generous" is defined as *ren* 仁: being consummate in one's conduct. Even the necessary practice of corvée labor required of the people to sustain the public infrastructure that benefits everyone can be imposed on the people in a generous rather than onerous way. These best practices are irreducibly relational, inclusive, and accommodating of the interests of all concerned. The deference extended by the people to the imposing model of credible rulers is a sure sign they have been won over, and the confidence the people find in their rulers renders them self-ordering.

What are the worst practices? Not doing the job of ruling properly, and then making the people victims in the breach. In many ways, this passage is fair commentary on 2.3 that distinguishes between the top-down imposition of the regulative strategies of law and punishment on the one hand, and the pursuit of a social and political consensus on the other. Such a consensus can be achieved by providing a familial form of governance that wins over the people to its values and by the people thus cultivating a sense of shame that would dissolve any tension between personal and public interest. Cf. 7.38, 13.26, 17.8.

12.7 子貢問政。子曰："足食。足兵。民信之矣。"子貢曰："必不得已而去，於斯三者何先？"曰："去兵。"子貢曰："必不得已而去，於斯二者何先？"曰："去食。自古皆有死，民無信不立。"

Zigong asked about governing properly (*zheng* 政). The Master said to him: "Make sure there is sufficient food to eat, there are sufficient arms for defense, and the common people have confidence in their leaders."

"If you had to give up one of these three things," he said, "which should be given up first?"

"Give up the arms." he replied.

"If you had to give up one of the remaining two," he said, "which would it be?"

"Give up the food." he replied. "Death has been with us from ancient times, but if the common people do not have confidence (*xin* 信) in their leaders, the state cannot survive."

Comment: In responding to this question on proper governance, Confucius lists the three most obvious resources necessary for preserving the life of the state and its people: food for sustenance, arms for defense, and confidence for the state's sustainability. The term translated here as "confidence" is the central Confucian value of "living up to one's word" (*xin* 信) as viewed from the perspective of the people. When viewed from the perspective of the rulers, it properly references their perceived "credibility." Conventionally understood as the rulers being "trustworthy" and thus garnering the "trust" of the people, what is important and needs to be made clear is that good intentions are not enough to be *xin* 信; there has to be accountability in practice. Hence, both perspectives of confidence and credibility are covered in the more basic meaning of *xin* 信 as the ongoing achievement of "living up to one's word." Cf. 13.9.

12.14 子張問政。子曰："居之無倦，行之以忠。"
   Zizhang asked about governing properly (*zheng* 政), and the Master replied, "Be unflagging in the responsibilities of your office, and do your best in carrying them out."

Comment: A persistent theme in Confucian political philosophy is to encourage the best attitude for formulating policy rather than stipulating the specific policies themselves. Again, following upon such careful deliberation, be conscientious in carrying the findings into practice. Behind this theme is a recognition that since each situation will be unique, while the application of policies is best informed by past analogies, they must also be considered on their own specific terms. To be tireless in reflecting on the best policies to carry out certainly requires full consideration of those precedents that can provide guidance, but decisions made must be followed by resolve in achieving the best outcome under the specific circumstances. The correlation being made here is literally between "dwelling" (*ju* 居) in office, and "walking" (*xing* 行), that is, between deliberating over policy and putting it into practice: quite literally an exhortation to "walk the talk."

12.19 季康子問政於孔子曰："如殺無道，以就有道，何如？" 孔子對曰："子爲政，焉用殺？子欲善而民善矣。君子之德風，小人之德草。草上之風，必偃。"
   Ji Kangzi asked Confucius about governing effectively (*zheng* 政), saying, "What if I were to kill those who have abandoned the proper way in order to win over those who are in fact following it?"
   "If you govern effectively," Confucius replied, "what need is there for any killing? If you strive to be truly good (*shan* 善) in what you do, the common people will also be good. The virtuosity of exemplary persons is the wind, and that of petty persons is the grass. As the wind blows, the grass is sure to bend."

Comment: Confucius's point in this exchange is not to counsel Ji Kangzi on how he can have absolute sway over the people of Lu. To begin with, Ji

III. THE *ANALECTS* (*LUNYU* 論語): A BASIC CONFUCIAN VOCABULARY

Kangzi as prime minister and head of the Three Families, was seen by Confucius as a usurper of royal power, and we know that Confucius saw this interloper as someone who is not governing properly. For Confucius, governing effectively depends upon the extent to which rulers are exemplars of the values they would inculcate in their people. Again, the term *shan* 善 translated here as the ruler striving to be "truly good" in what he does, is not some qualitatively superior action or a character trait derived from some prior and higher virtue of "goodness" that inheres "in" a person, nor is it some general principle of "goodness" that informs and supervenes on an action as it is "done" by a person. "Good" in the sense of moral growth begins from relational activities within the continuing narrative, and only then can it serve as a general description of a person or action. *Shan* 善 is the gregarious activity of growing our relations and making them "meaningful" by "relating" to each other and communicating effectively: being truly good with, at, for, and in, what we do.

The moral sway that exemplary persons exert over others, far from being impositional or coercive, emerges out of the emulation of an authoritative model and out of the sense of shame born from identifying with the community in common cause. The wind is informing, not coercing, and the grass is receptive, not submissive. Under such sway, the application of law is unnecessary in achieving the desired social and political order. Proper governance emerges through the high expectations of the people who have been transformed by emulating an exemplary model.

This same *Analects* passage about the wind blowing and the grass bending is cited in *Mencius* 3A2 where Mencius offers his counsel to a crown prince on the death of the prince's father, the king. In this case as well, the message is that rulers must be exemplars to effect change in their people. But the important point being made begins from the recognition on the part of this particular crown prince that, because of a lack of seriousness in his own studies in the past, he is not held in high regard by his court or kinsmen. As a consequence of this failure, he as the newly anointed king will have difficulty securing their support in the affairs of state. The crown prince, following the advice given by Mencius to look to his own person, is able, by elevating his behavior and giving his people a model to emulate, to earn the respect of his court and to thus effect a change in their conduct. The crown prince is improved because of the expectations of his people, and his people are transformed by his exemplary conduct.

12.17 季康子問政於孔子。孔子對曰："政者，正也。子帥以正，孰敢不正？"

Ji Kangzi asked Confucius about governing properly (*zheng* 政), and Confucius replied to him, "Governing properly (*zheng* 政) is doing what is proper (*zheng* 正). If you, Sir, lead by doing what is proper, who would dare do otherwise?"

Comment: Confucius is using a paronomastic association to define proper governance. The root of the more specific term "governing properly" (*zheng* 政) is derived from the genus of "acting properly" (*zheng* 正). Hence, when the ruler acts properly in all things, governing properly is included among them. And given the didactic function of the ruler as a role model in this "role politics," when the ruler governs properly, the people respond to such governance with their own proper conduct.

12.18 季康子患盜，問於孔子。孔子對曰："苟子之不欲，雖賞之不竊。"

Ji Kangzi was troubled by the number of thieves, and asked Confucius for advice. Confucius replied to him, "Were you yourself not so greedy, the people would not steal if you paid them."

Comment: Confucius does not mince his words, laying the blame for the proliferation of thieves on the role model set by the prime minister Ji Kangzi himself. In this tradition, Mencius is often celebrated for speaking truth to power with his doctrine of justified regicide (see 1B8, 2B8). In 1B8 for example, Mencius is fearless in his response to King Xuan of Qi:

齊宣王問曰："湯放桀，武王伐紂，有諸？"孟子對曰："於傳有之。"曰："臣弒其君可乎？"曰："賊仁者謂之賊，賊義者謂之殘，殘賊之人謂之一夫。聞誅一夫紂矣，未聞弒君也。"

King Xuan of Qi inquired of Mencius, asking: "Was it the case that Tang deposed his sovereign Jie, and King Wu attacked his ruler Zhou?"

Mencius replied: "It is in the records."

King Xuan continued: "Is it permissible for a minister to kill his ruler?"

Mencius responded: "He who has done injury to those consummatory in their conduct (*ren* 仁) is called a thief, and he who has done injury to those appropriate in their conduct (*yi* 義) is called a mutilator. People of this ilk are called scoundrels. I have heard of the punishment of the scoundrel Zhou but I have heard nothing of regicide."

Xunzi like Mencius also advocates tyrannicide (13.9, 18.2).

As latter-day Confucians, the philosophers Mencius and Xunzi who both celebrate the person of Confucius seem to have come by their audacity honestly. Cf. 11.24.

13.1 子路問政。子曰﹕"先之，勞之。" 請益。曰﹕"無倦。"
Zilu inquired about governing properly (*zheng* 政).
The Master replied, "Set an example yourself and then demand hard work from the people."
"Please elaborate." he said.
"Be unflagging in your efforts." replied the Master.

Comment: Confucius offers the exuberant Zilu a rather cryptic response in this passage: literally, "before them, labor them." When asked for more, the Master adds "tirelessly." For Confucius, best practices in governance come from the kind of exemplary moral conduct on the part of the ruler that wins the people over. The objective is a social and political consensus that results in everyone working together. Confucius whose own sense of himself is someone who "continues his studies without respite and instructs others without growing weary" (7.2, 7.34) has no compunction in demanding assiduous effort from his protégés and in expecting real exertion from the people in carrying out their civic duties. Cf. 19.10, 20.2.

13.2 仲弓爲季氏宰，問政。子曰﹕"先有司，赦小過，舉賢才。" 曰﹕"焉知賢才而舉之？" 曰﹕"舉爾所知。爾所不知，人其舍諸？"
Zhonggong was serving as steward in the House of Ji, and asked about governing properly (*zheng* 政). The Master said to him, "Set an example yourself for those in office, pardon minor offences, and promote the most worthy (*xian* 賢) and able."
"How do you recognize the most worthy and able in order to promote them?" he asked.
The Master replied, "Promote those that you are sure about, and rely on others to do the same for those you are not."

Comment: Confucius states repeatedly that personal example must be given the highest priority in proper governance. One aspect of the exemplary model is generosity in dealing with colleagues expressed here as leniency in adjudicating small transgressions. The key responsibility in governing properly is to promote the very best, where "best" is defined both by moral worth and ability. In making these key appointments, there is an acknowledgment of the limits of any one person in doing so. Again, you lead the way with recognizing those you know to be most worthy and able, and give others the space to do the same.

1.5 子曰："道千乘之國：敬事而信，節用而愛人，使民以時。"

The Master said: "There is the proper way (*dao* 道) to lead a thousand-chariot state effectively. In carrying out your official duties respectfully, always make good on your word (*xin* 信). In being frugal in your expenditures, show true affection for your peers. And in putting the common people to work, do so only in the proper season."

Comment: The basis of good governance even for the largest state lies in optimizing one's relations with others. One must show respect, be frugal, and serve the interests of the common people by only requiring their corvée labor when it does not interfere with the pursuit of their own livelihood. Respect in one's relations with others is closely tied to making good on one's word, and it is true affection for others that prompts one to be sparing in the shared resources of the state.

2.20 季康子問："使民敬、忠以勸，如之何？" 子曰："臨之以莊則敬，孝慈則忠，舉善而教不能，則勸。"

Ji Kangzi asked: "How do you get the common people to be respectful, to do their utmost for you (*zhong* 忠), and to be eager in what they do?" The Master replied: "Oversee them with dignity and the people will be respectful; be filial to your elders (*xiao* 孝) and kind to your juniors, and the people will do their utmost for you; raise up those who are productive (*shan* 善) and teach those who are not, and the people will be eager."

Comment: For persons with political responsibility, there can be nothing more important than to cultivate a population who are properly respectful, who are keen to make good on their responsibilities, and who are earnest in carrying out their duties. Confucius's response is to encourage those in authority to earn the respect of the people by treating them with dignity, to earn their commitment to do their best for you by treating both elders and juniors as family members, and to get the most out of their talents by promoting those who are successful and instructing those who are not.

Such governing is not unilateral and impositional. Rather it requires elevating the people by cultivating civility in them through the *li* 禮 -informed roles and relations of family and community. Such a population in being won over to the shared values of the community, will thus become largely self-ordering. The objective is not to "govern" people, but to use a consensus on these shared values to effect a flourishing social and political order.

13.4 樊遲請學稼。子曰："吾不如老農。"請學爲圃。曰："吾不如老圃。"樊遲出。子曰："小人哉，樊須也！上好禮，則民莫敢不敬；上好義，則民莫敢不服；上好信，則民莫敢不用情。夫如是，則四方之民襁負其子而至矣，焉用稼？"

Fan Chi wanted to learn to farm. "A farmer would serve you better than me." said the Master. He wanted to learn to grow vegetables. "A market gardener would serve you better than me." said the Master.

When Fan Chi had left, the Master said, "This Fan Chi is certainly a petty person! If those above cherish the performance of ritual propriety (*li* 禮), none among the common people would dare be disrespectful; if those above cherish appropriate conduct (*yi* 義), none among the common people would dare be disobedient; if those above cherish making good on their word (*xin* 信), none among the common people would dare be duplicitous. This being the case, the common people from all quarters would flock here with their babies strapped to their backs. What need is there to talk of farming?"

Comment: Fan Chi throughout the text comes across as an avid enquirer, asking about consummate conduct (*ren* 仁) and wisdom (*zhi* 知) in 12.22 and 13.19. But he is not a quick study, repeatedly turning to his fellow students to get clear on what Confucius means by the instruction he has received. In this passage when Fan Chi asks Confucius how to grow a garden, Confucius gets impatient with him, calling him "a petty person" who clearly does not understand the difference in priority between growing yourself as a person in service to the community and state, and growing your vegetables for the table.

We have to be careful not to read this passage as Confucius disparaging or disrespecting the contribution of the farmer. To begin with, in the Confucian tradition historically, the status of the farmer who feeds the people is second only to the scholar who nourishes the people in a different way, both of them being sources of growth for the community. Again, the merchant and the soldier who contribute nothing and whose roles are thus perceived as parasitic on the community are held in relatively low esteem.

While there is a time and place to learn to farm, it is not part of the Confucian curriculum that seeks to provide students with what they need to be effective in public service. There is a coincidence between education and morality, and again between morality and effective governance in the sense that they are all achieved through fostering growth in relations. Those who have the responsibility for governing the people are perceived first and foremost as moral exemplars, and only secondarily as administrators.

13.16 葉公問政。子曰:"近者說,遠者來。"

The Governor of She asked about governing properly (*zheng* 政), and the Master replied, "When those close at hand are pleased, those at a distance will be drawn to you."

Comment: The Duke of She of the state of Chu appears in 7.18 asking Zilu about the person of Confucius. He returns in 13.18 where he tries to impress Confucius by recounting the anecdote about "True Goody" turning his errant "sheep-stealing" father over to the authorities. While the Duke is keen to claim a remarkable influence over his constituents in their submission to authority, Confucius offers him an alternative notion of moral governance. During the Spring and Autumn period and beyond, the Duke of She's state of Chu through its military rule grew from a small, marginal power to an expansionist kingdom. Confucius counters this history of top-down, impositional government with a familiar Confucian ideal of the people-centered, "middle-outward" pursuit of social and political consensus. The character for the "True King" (*wang* 王) is often defined paronomastically in the early literature as "repairing to" (*wang* 往), with the assumption that expansive growth for the state is a function of people seeking out and flocking to the moral ruler.

13.9 子適衛,冉有僕。子曰:"庶矣哉!" 冉有曰:"既庶矣。又何加焉?" 曰:"富之。" 曰:"既富矣,又何加焉?" 曰:"教之。"

Ranyou drove the Master's carriage on a trip to Wei. The Master remarked, "What a teeming population!"

Ranyou asked, "When the people are already so numerous, what more can be done for them?"

The Master said, "Make them prosperous."

"When the people are already prosperous," asked Ranyou, "what more can be done for them?"

"Teach them." replied the Master.

Comment: The practical Confucius takes economic well-being as a necessary condition for proper governance, giving it priority here even over education. The transformative education necessary for effective governance is predicated on the ruler's moral purchase as a role model, and the first criterion for such influence is his commitment to the welfare of the people. This same theme is carried through both in *Mencius* 1A5, 3A3, 3B3, 7A23 and *Xunzi* 9.4, and is echoed in contemporary China in the rights discourse that gives priority to second generation economic and welfare rights over first generation political rights. In other passages, Confucius takes moral education as having priority in turn over the population taking up arms and being sent to war on the assumption perhaps that belief in the rightness of one's cause is a necessary condition for victory (13.29, 13.30).

Is this passage contradicted by 12.7 in which Confucius gives priority to the confidence the people must have in the moral leadership of their rulers over both food and arms? We might ask if the rulers can have won the confidence of the people without first being perceived by the people as having committed themselves to their welfare? Again, an underlying assumption in Confucian political philosophy is that the people will "repair" (*wang* 往) to the True King (*wang* 王) where the people express their confidence in the rulership with their feet. Certainly, the teeming population in Wei is itself an indication of the quality of its moral leadership and its already having won over the confidence of the people (13.4). The discussion would seem to proceed on that assumption.

3.5 子曰："夷狄之有君，不如諸夏之亡也。"

The Master said: "The Yi and Di barbarian tribes with rulers are not as viable as the various Chinese states without them."

Comment: The Yi and Di are tribes that bordered the proto-Chinese states in the Central Plain to the east and north respectively. The Chinese language might reflect a certain contempt for such bordering tribes: after all, the Di 狄 tribes are classified under the "dog" (*quan* 犬) radical, the Man 蠻 tribes to the south are classified under the "beast/insect" (*chong* 虫)

radical, and the Mo 貊 tribes in the north are classified under the "reptile/legless insect" (*zhi* 豸) radical. An alternative more inclusive explanation would be that these tribes like other proto-Chinese peoples used animals as emblems, and that the *long* 龍, conventionally translated "dragon," is a totemic aggregation of such tribal symbolism.

If we factor in the Confucian assumption that the proper combination of moral leadership and suasion can produce a social and political consensus and thus inspire a self-ordering community, then the function of Confucian rulers is to reign rather than to rule (8.18). The best rulers simply assume a posture of reverence and face due south (15.5). The ideal of the Confucian state is to be free of litigation and punishments (12.13), and to be governed by a culture of shame achieved through the promotion of shared values (2.3). It is in this sense that in the flourishing Confucian state, social and political order is "middle-outward" rather than top-down or bottom-up.

13.17 子夏爲莒父宰，問政。子曰："無欲速，無見小利。欲速，則不達；見小利，則大事不成。"

Zixia was made the prefect of Jufu, and asked about governing properly (*zheng* 政).

The Master replied, "Don't try to rush things, and don't get distracted by small opportunities. If you try to rush things, you won't achieve your ends; if you get distracted by small opportunities, you won't succeed in the more important matters of government."

Comment: Confucius is offering his counsel to Zixia who is newly appointed to office in the state of Lu, recommending that he exercise patience and understand proper governance as a long-term proposition (see the *Comment* on 19.3, p. 315, for a profile of Zixia as one of Confucius's closest students). The pragmatic nature of Confucian political philosophy means that it is meliorative and incremental rather than being revolutionary. Hasty decisions and minor distractions can interfere with the important project of promoting the worthy and able, and in so doing, establishing the proper moral example among those who would govern as a catalyst for effecting a social and political consensus among the governed.

13.11 子曰："善人爲邦百年，亦可以勝殘去殺矣。誠哉是言也！"

The Master said, "It is said that 'If truly effective people governed the country for a hundred years, they would be able to overcome violence and dispense with killing altogether.' Such words could not be more true!"

13.12 子曰："如有王者，必世而後仁。"
The Master said, "Were a True King to arise, it would still take a generation before consummate conduct (*ren* 仁) would prevail."

Comment: 13.11 and 13.12 really serve as commentary on 13.17 in which Confucius makes the point that achieving proper governance requires time and patience. While using laws and punishment to enforce social and political order can be done immediately and is, in the short term, relatively efficient, creating a self-governing community grounded in cultivated civility is a long-term proposition. Order that is externally imposed upon the people is resented by them, and comes undone as soon as the external injunctions of law and punishment are removed. On the other hand, an emergent social order modeled on family and held together by shared values and the sense of shame that is entailed by this consensus is enduring.

14.41 子曰："上好禮，則民易使也。"
The Master said, "If those in high station cherish ritual propriety (*li* 禮), the common people will be easy to deal with."

Comment: The distinction being alluded to here is the difference between top-down rule by penal law and the promotion of a social cohesion that comes with educating the people in the shared values of ritualized propriety (*li* 禮). In the aspirations of Confucian political philosophy, much can be made of a further distinction between "authoritarian" and "authoritative" governance. The ruler serving as a role model who, in governing by example, effects self-governance among the people, is a strong theme. The classic statement of such values is 2.3. Cf. also 13.4.

Effecting Peace in the World (*pingtianxia* 平天下)

The *Analects* and the other canonical Confucian texts do not purport to lay out some generic formula by which everyone should live their lives. Rather, the personal model of Confucius remembered in these documents recalls the narrative of one special person: how he in his relations with others cultivated his humanity, and how he lived a fulfilling life, much to the admiration of those around him. Indeed, in reading the *Analects*, we encounter the relationally-constituted Confucius making his way through life by living his various and sometimes conflicted roles as best he can: his role as a strict and often judgmental teacher and mentor, as a scrupulous and incorruptible scholar-official, as a caring family member, as a concerned neighbor and member of the community, as an always critical and sometimes reluctant political consultant, as the grateful progeny of his progenitors, as an enthusiastic heir to a specific, living cultural legacy, and indeed, as a member of a chorus of joyful boys and men singing their way home after a happy day on the river Yi (11.26). In the teachings of Confucius that have been passed on from generation to generation with the purpose of remembering the events of his life, Confucius is portrayed as someone more inclined to appeal to the narratives of historical models than to invoke remote, abstract principles, to reference specific, concrete analogies than to apply putatively systematic theories, and to give voice to deeply felt exhortations than to issue imperatives. While Confucius seems keenly aware of the critical value of theorizing our practices in search of enhanced intelligence, he is also cognizant of the primacy of practice itself as both the source of the theorizing and the warrant for endorsing its results. The power and lasting value of his insights lie in the fact that many of these ideas are intuitively persuasive, and readily adaptable to the conditions of ensuing generations, including our own.

Confucius develops his insights around the most basic and enduring aspects of the ordinary human experience: that is, personal cultivation in family and communal roles, family reverence, deference to others, propriety achieved in our roles and relations, friendship, a cultivated sense of shame, moral education, a communicating community, a family-centered religiousness, the intergeneration transmission of culture, and so on. In so doing, he has guaranteed the continuing relevance of this compounding wisdom. In addition to being focused on such perennial issues, one further characteristic of Confucian philosophy that is certainly present in the words of Confucius himself and that has made his teachings so resilient, is the porousness and adaptability of his philosophy. His enduring contribution was simply to strive to take full ownership of the cultural legacy available during his time and place, to adapt this living wisdom from the past for the betterment of his own present historical moment, and then to recommend to future generations that they continue to do the same.

III. THE *ANALECTS* (*LUNYU* 論語): A BASIC CONFUCIAN VOCABULARY

Indeed, what makes this Confucian tradition more empirical than empiricism—that is, what makes Confucianism *radical* empiricism—is the fact that while grounded in the soil of an antique culture, it is also prospective and evolutionary in respecting the uniqueness of the omnipresent particular. Indeed, it alludes to the narrative of this one special person, Confucius, who lived such an exemplary life. Rather than advancing doctrines as universal principles or organizing experience around a taxonomy of natural kinds grounded in some notion of strict identity, Confucian philosophy proceeds from analogy with, and always provisional generalizations derived from, those *particular* historical instances of successful living. Confucius's signature neologism, "aspiring to consummate conduct in one's roles and relations" (*ren* 仁), for example, is not an appeal to some higher order, antecedent principle or generic virtue, but is rather a vision of the exemplary human life as it is aspired to through assiduous cultivation in one's personal relations. And in its realization, it can be of service to succeeding generations as a guiding source of value. Of course, any exemplary narrative is nested within and informed by a continuing confluence of the particular narratives of exemplary persons over time, including the life story of Confucius himself. And as a consummate exemplar who grows in meaning through the patterns of deference that define the social fabric of ensuing generations, Confucius serves as a role model within this living tradition to shape the way in which people come to live their own particular lives.

In trying to understand what constitutes religiousness in the Confucian tradition, we might begin from the fact that the very definition of "religion" in our best English language dictionaries usually takes some concept of a transcendent deity as its point of departure. The Oxford English Dictionary, for example, defines religion as "the belief in and worship of a superhuman controlling power, especially a personal God or gods." Such an understanding of religion propelled Western missionaries to search the Chinese canons for analogical equivalencies they could borrow to insinuate their own Abrahamic idea of God into the Chinese language. With this uncritical assumption that religion must begin from God, many if not most scholars concerned to define Confucian religiousness continue along this same path, beginning their foray into Chinese religiousness by appealing to some variation on the rather opaque Shang and Zhou dynasty notions of *shangdi* 上帝 and *tian* 天, where both of these terms in their own context seem to have some reference to ancestor reverence. In so doing, these exegetes beg the question of how to understand Confucian religiousness by having already transplanted a conception of "God" into a cosmology that is fundamentally "a-theistic," with gods best being represented by historical figures in the role of cultural heroes such as Confucius himself.

Taking Confucius as an example, having set his root in the life of his extended family, he introduces a notion of family-centered rather than God-centered religiousness that aspires to the optimal coordination of social, political, and indeed cosmic relations. He offers an alternative conception of religiousness expressed as a flourishing world that radiates outward from family life. In making this "a-theistic" argument, I am in good company. There is Marcel Granet's claim that "Chinese wisdom has no need for the idea of God,"① a characterization of Confucianism endorsed by many of our best sinologists Chinese and Western alike.② While such a description of a non-theistic "Chinese wisdom" might for some churchmen lower the bar and exclude this tradition from any important association with religion or religiousness, I would insist that Confucianism with its own alternative, family-centered understanding of religiousness requires an importantly different cluster of terms to give it robust expression. A key term needed to explain such a Confucian religiousness is the socio-religious idea of *li* 禮: "the pursuit of propriety in one's roles and relations." Again, I would argue that the persistently vague and thus protean term *tian* 天 denoting something very different from a transcendent and thus independent "Godhead," also has an important role to play in the way in which the family-centered Confucian religiousness comes to be articulated and expressed.

Although clearly having a formal, ceremonial reference, the preponderant significance of *li* 禮 in defining family and communal life lies in those personal, informal, and particular discursive activities that conduce to, and are indeed necessary for religious experience. *Li* 禮 as cognate with the character for "body or embodying," (*ti* 體) has a profoundly somatic dimension where body is often a more effective language than speech in the discourse necessary to strengthen the bonds among those participating in our various life forms. The *li* 禮 also have an affective aspect wherein feelings suffuse and fortify all of our relational activities, providing the communal fabric a tensile strength which resists the inevitable strains and

---

① Granet, *La pensée chinoise*, p. 478.
② See Ames, *Confucian Role Ethics*, Chapter 5 for this argument.

ruptures that attend associated living. *Li* 禮 is a process of personal articulation in the roles and relations one lives. It is what I have described as the growth and disclosure of an elegant disposition, an attitude, a posture, a signature style, and ultimately, a persistent identity. Refinement through the performance of *li* 禮 must be understood in light of the uniqueness of each participant engaged in the profoundly aesthetic project of cultivating themselves to become this exceptional and always inimitable person.

It is within the context of *li* 禮 as this achieved propriety in roles and relations that the ancestral/numinous/cultural/natural notion of *tian* 天 makes its contribution to our understanding of a Confucian family-centered religiousness. But *tian* 天, far from requiring what Friedrich Schleiermacher describes approvingly in *The Christian Faith* as "absolute dependence"—a self-abnegating deference to a self-sufficient, independent Deity—is instead an invitation for human collaboration with and contribution to the numinous aspect of our experience.① Indeed, the familiar mantra invoked to describe Confucian religiousness, *tianrenheyi* 天人合一, describes "the continuity between and inseparability of the cosmic and human order." It announces the continuity between the drama of human thinking and living, and the cultural and natural context within which this spectacle takes place. The *heyi* 合一 relation is a *yinyang* 陰陽 contrastive yet mutually entailing first-order relationship of two inseparable, "aspectual" features of experience that can only be understood in terms of each other. Just as with dyadic pairs such as "up and down" (*shangxia* 上下) and "the heavens and the earth" (*tiandi* 天地), the expression "the cosmic and the human" (*tianren* 天人) denotes a relationship that is one and two at the same time: two complementary aspects of the same phenomenon that cannot be fairly conceived of without reference to each other.

Importantly then, given the resolutely inseparable *heyi* 合一 relation between humans and their context, we must resist interpreting this expression as a "putting together" of what were two originally separate things, and instead read it in terms of their mutuality in difference. The concern is with the "depth of coalescence" (*du* 度) that can be cultivated and achieved in their first order relationality. And in this dyadic yet resolutely constitutive relationship, *tian* 天 together with human beings, is to be understood as mutually doing and undergoing, both shaping and being shaped by each

---

① Schleiermacher, *The Christian Faith,* p. 132.

other. It is thus that a correlative expression such as *tianren* 天人 is not simply descriptive, but is also prescriptive in encouraging the aspiration to an increasingly meaningful relationship.

It is only through deepening and achieving proper measure (*du* 度) in the correlative "human and cosmos" relationship (*tianren* 天人), and thus transforming this relation into one of sociality, and indeed of an evolving religiousness, that these exemplary persons can make their profound contribution to cosmic meaning. Such achieved harmony and clear resolution in our relationships is the very root from which the flourishing world order emerges, and as such, contributes to the life force that guides the cosmos with all of its bounty on its proper course. And on the human side, it is our unique sense of contribution, felt worth, and belonging within this dynamic cosmic life force that is the substance of real religious experience, and that gives life its profoundly religious significance.

The idea of *tianxia* 天下—conventionally translated as "all-under-Heaven"—is a familiar term in everyday Chinese parlance that simply means "the world." In the Chinese language *tianxia* 天下 can mean either "the world of China" or "the world" more broadly construed. In addition to this ordinary usage, *tianxia* 天下 is also a geopolitical term found throughout the ancient canonical literature that has a deeper philosophical and historical meaning. Over the past few decades, the significance of this technical term as a possible Chinese framework for thinking about a new and evolving planetary order and a new model of world governance—sometimes referred to as "All-under-the-Heaven System" (*tianxiatixi* 天下体系), primarily in the Chinese literature, has been a subject of much debate. Although the understandings of *tianxia* 天下 are many, within the Chinese process cosmology, they begin from an ecological understanding of international relations that acknowledges the mutuality and interdependence of all economic and political activity. *Tianxia* 天下 as "the world" assumes the primacy of vital relationality, thus relegating the nation state as a discrete, sovereign entity to the status of a second-order abstraction from the organic relations that constitute it. The Han dynasty Confucian philosopher, Wang Chong 王充 has a memorable passage that would insist the highest expression of Confucian religiousness by the most sagacious among us is to "family" the whole world:

聖人以天下爲家，不別遠近，不殊內外……聖人舉事求其宜適也……賢

聖家天下。(王充論衡 16.7-8)
Sages take the whole world (*tianxia* 天下) as their family without distinction between near or far, domestic or foreign... In their undertakings the sages seek what is optimally appropriate... The best and most sagacious would "family" the whole world.

III.16 Human Way-Making (*rendao* 人道)

5.13 子貢曰："夫子之文章，可得而聞也；夫子之言性與天道，不可得而聞也。"
Zigong said, "We can learn from the Master's cultural refinements, but will not hear him discourse on subjects such as human 'natural tendencies' (*xing* 性) and 'the way of *tian*' (*tiandao* 天道)."

Comment: In 9.4 it describes Confucius as a person not given to bold speculation or conjecture, and the rest of the *Analects* bears this out. The emphasis in the *Analects* is on *dao* 道 as "way-making" within the everyday human experience, and offers almost nothing that would carry us into the cosmological implications of this same term. We are told in 7.25 that Confucius is certainly glad to impart his insights into the received and evolving human culture. Confucius focuses on who we are, and what we have achieved as our cultural accomplishments, but seems reluctant to venture speculation upon what we humans and our world might become. Thus, given the ineluctable momentum within this process cosmology, we have to understand both human "natural tendencies" (*xing* 性) and "the way of *tian*" (*tiandao* 天道) as provisional and revisionist, and anticipate that they will continue to evolve in unexpected ways. Hence, Confucius is unwilling to speculate upon what the future might bode for human "becomings" and how the cosmos itself might continue to unfold. In the historical dialectic, when this conservative, almost exclusively human-centered emphasis in the earliest Confucian canons is challenged by the Daoists, Confucian texts such as *Focusing the Familiar* (*Zhongyong* 中庸) are prompted to respond by elevating the conversation and going cosmic in arguing human beings as meaning-makers have not only the capacity but also the responsibility to become co-creators with the cosmos.

15.29 子曰："人能弘道，非道弘人。"

The Master said: "It is persons who are able to broaden the way, not the way that broadens persons."

Comment: This key Confucian exhortation 人能弘道 "it is persons who are able to broaden the way" references a shared way of life inherited by each succeeding generation that then has the obligation to broaden and extend it. Each generation must build its own connector between generations for those who will follow it. In this Confucian tradition, the intergenerational transmission of civilization is the responsibility of two different but related conceptions of "family" (*jia* 家). There is the continuing civilization of the *daotong* 道統 or the "orthodox way" embodied in the elite social stratum of "the literati family lineage" or *rujia* 儒家. And then more broadly but importantly informed by the orthodox way of the literati lineage, there is the *xiaodao* 孝道 or "way of family reverence" that guides the lives of everyone within their extended family lineages or *jiazu* 家族, and that then radiates outward to become a civilizational "people" or *minzu* 民族.

9.17 子在川上，曰："逝者如斯夫！不舍晝夜。"
The Master was standing on the riverbank, and observed, "Isn't life's passing just like this, never ceasing day or night!"

Comment: Confucius waxes uncharacteristically speculative in describing the streaming of the human experience in the language of "passing" (*shi* 逝), a term used in the *Daodejing* 道德經 25 to describe the processual and reflexive nature of the cosmic *dao* 道:

> 吾不知其名，字之曰道，强爲之名曰大。大曰逝，逝曰遠，遠曰反。
> I do not yet know its name (*ming* 名). If I were to style it, I would call it "way-making" (*dao* 道), and if forced to give it a name, I would call it "magnificent" (*da* 大). Being magnificent, it is called passing (*shi* 逝), passing it is called distancing (*yuan* 遠), and distancing, it is called returning (*fan* 反).

In this *Daodejing*'s cosmogony (described again in 51), each event within this grand, fluid, and continuing process emerges to make its way forward both diachronically and synchronically. In this flow, it finds its consummation in achieving the uniqueness and complexity that, in making it truly distinctive, sets it at a distance from its contextualizing others. Having reached its apogee, it then subsequently folds back into the flow and thus returns to be transformed into something else.

Such a developed cosmogony made explicit in the *Daodejing* stands in stark contrast to a seemingly innocent observation Confucius makes as he stands at the intersection of the four streams that give his home near Qufu the county name *Sishui* 泗水. *Mencius* 4B18 provides a commentary on this passage, making Confucius's celebration of water an analogy for the deep "source" necessary to provide the life and vigor for personal growth. There is an interpretation of this passage perhaps more in keeping with the events of Confucius's own life. Confucius rues the ineluctable passage of time that, rather than rewarding him with the success he has craved and worked so hard for, has left him with a feeling of galloping frustration. Cf. 3.24. 5.7, 9.9, 9.14, 18.6.

6.17 子曰: "誰能出不由戶？何莫由斯道也？"
The Master said, "Since none can go out except through a gateway, how is it that none go out from this way (*dao* 道)?"

Comment: This passage is one more example of the pervasive "walking the way" metaphor. It provides us with a key to understanding the notion of "way" (*dao* 道) as it is associated with the two characters *you* 由: "to go out from" and the demonstrative pronoun, *si* 斯: "this." The analogy here is not that *dao* is some predetermined way that is to be walked, but rather that it serves as a "gateway" (*hu* 戶), providing both the direction whence to proceed, and access to the path forward. The way is not a given, but is specified as "this" way laid down by past generations that provides the bearings and the way forward for everyone in their own generation to forge and extend. It is because *dao* 道 is thus gerundive as something being "done" rather than simply something that "is" I have often translated it as "way-making." A passage in *Zhuangzi* 2 makes this same point about a way under construction in saying 道行之而成 "the way is made in the walking"—importantly, not in "the walking *of it*," but simply "in the walking."

3.24 儀封人請見。曰: "君子之至於斯也，吾未嘗不得見也。" 從者見之。出曰: "二三子，何患於喪乎？天下之無道也久矣，天將以夫子爲木鐸。"
A border official at the Yi crossing asked for an interview with the Master, saying: "I have always been accorded an interview with distinguished

persons who have made their way here."

Confucius's followers presented him. When the official emerged from the interview, he said: "Why worry over his loss of office, my friends? The world has long since lost its way (*dao* 道), and *tian* 天 is going to use your Master as its wooden bell-clapper to rouse it from its slumbers."

Comment: Confucius himself lived in a period in which the elegance provided by the ancient ritual practices had long been lost, and the quality of life available to succeeding generations had thus been compromised. As such, Confucius took it as his mission to clear what could be cleared from the path and forge a new connector for future travelers. Confucius's mission to locate the old road, cut it back, and set a trailhead on it for future generations is the grounding metaphor and a major theme in the *Analects*. Cf. 5.2, 5.7, 8.13, 11.24, 14.1, 14.36, 15.7, 18.7, and 19.19.

Yi is a town in the state of Wei that bordered Confucius's home state of Lu. This event might have occurred historically following an incident recorded in *Mencius* 6B6. Confucius departed the state of Lu precipitously following an occasion on which his counsel was ignored and he was slighted in a ritual sacrifice. In response to this mistreatment, Confucius first resigned his position as police commissioner before leaving. The implication of the official's prescient observation is that in the future, Confucius's mission will serve the Central Plain as a clarion call to restore the intergenerational transmission of the cultural legacy. This service will amplify his voice far beyond the influence he might have had in overseeing any particular political office.

The Dingzhou text does not have the phrase, "When the official emerged from the interview, he said." As such, it provides an alternative reading in which Confucius is still present. Although the border official's remarks are still directed at the followers of Confucius, they are on this redaction made within the context of the interview itself.

4.8 子曰:"朝聞道，夕死可矣。"

The Master said, "On the morning that I learn the proper way (*dao* 道) has prevailed in the world, I could die at dusk without regret."

Comment: The grammar of this cryptic passage lends itself to at least two possible readings. The translation here makes it a personal statement of Confucius's commitment to rejuvenating the cultural legacy, and is consistent with his sense of mission within the text as a whole. The second reading is: "If at dawn you learn of the way (*dao* 道), you can face death at dusk without regret." This second interpretation is defensible if we set aside the seemingly esoteric overtones, and read it in the same way as 7.30 仁遠乎哉？我欲仁，斯仁至矣 "How could consummate conduct (*ren* 仁) be at all remote? No sooner do I seek it than it has arrived." That is, *dao* 道 like *ren* 仁 is not a destination, but the roadway itself, and as soon as one has embarked upon this journey, one has in fact in an important sense already arrived. See also 9.19.

8.13 子曰："篤信好學，守死善道。危邦不入，亂邦不居。天下有道則見，無道則隱。邦有道，貧且賤焉，恥也；邦無道，富且貴焉，恥也。"

The Master said, "Make an earnest commitment to the love of learning (*haoxue* 好學) and be steadfast to the death in service to that way of living which produces the best results (*shandao* 善道). Do not enter a state in crisis, and do not tarry in one that is in revolt. Be known when the proper way prevails in the world, but remain hidden away when it does not. It is a disgrace to remain poor and without rank when the proper way prevails in the state; it is equally disgraceful to be wealthy and of noble rank when the proper way does not."

Comment: *Shandao* 善道 is "that way of living that produces the best results," where the modifier *shan* 善 often translated simply as "good" is not some qualitatively superior action or a character trait derived from some prior and higher virtue of "goodness" that inheres "in" a person. Nor is it some general principle of "goodness" that informs and supervenes on an action as it is "done" by a person. Indeed, as the shared and efficacious life-path one is walking together with others (*zhishanzhidao* 至善之道), *shan* 善 is most concretely imputed to the shared narrative rather than to the individual person. And it stands in contrast with the paths of those whose narratives are less so. Rather than referencing some antecedent, generic "virtue," it actually denotes first and foremost, a way of living and being in the world that is efficacious. "Good" in this sense of moral growth begins from discursive activities within the continuing narrative and only then can serve as a description of a person or action.

"Being steadfast to the death in service to that way of living that produces the best results" (*shandao* 善道) means that this personal commitment to a specific way of life can only be coordinated within the social and political life of the state when the proper way prevails there too. When the proper way prevails in the state, one's own efficacious way of living would include serving in office and enjoying the benefits that come with a shared flourishing. When the proper way does not prevail, however, one cannot allow oneself to be personally compromised by being in any way associated with the governance of a wayward state, and in particular, by profiting from it. Given that social and political order is rooted in personal cultivation within family and community, the only recourse one has in restoring order and thus continuing the proper way is to return home to the source.

For this contrast between states in which *dao* 道 prevails and those in which it doesn't, see also 3.24, 5.2, 5.7, 5.21, 8.13, 11.24, 14.3, 15.7, 16.2. 19.19.

6.24 子曰: "齊一變, 至於魯; 魯一變, 至於道。"
The Master said, "With one turn the state of Qi could become a Lu; with one turn the state of Lu could arrive at the proper way (*dao* 道)."

Comment: Confucius's own state of Lu was heir to the house of Zhou that in its early days had set the historical benchmark as the apogee of the cultural legacy. Repeatedly Confucius expresses his admiration for the Zhou. For example, 3.14: 周監於二代, 郁郁乎文哉! 吾從周 "The Zhou dynasty looked back to the Xia and Shang dynasties. Such a wealth of culture! I follow the Zhou." See also 7.5, 8.11, 8.20, 9.5, 15.11. It was because Confucius had such reverence for the cultural antecedents of Lu that, as seen by the frustration expressed here, he rues the fact that Lu is failing to live up to its own history.

Confucius's deep respect for Zhou has often been misunderstood as a kind of "Golden Age" cultural conservatism. A prominent representative of this interpretation is the esteemed political philosopher Hsiao Kung-chuan (Xiao Gongquan 蕭公權). Hsiao observes that "Confucius' political attitude was that of a compliant Chou [Zhou] subject, and that his political views were conservative."[1] Unquestionably Confucius evinces profound reverence for the institutions of the past, but this respect is by no means reducible to a simple reconstruction and replication of early Zhou institutions

---

[1] Hsiao Kung-chuan, *A History of Chinese Political Thought*, trans. Frederick W. Mote, Princeton: Princeton University Press, 1979, p. 98.

and culture. After all, in *Focusing the Familiar* 27, Confucius is reported to have said that 溫故而知新 "one must revise the old in order to realize the new:" Again, in *Focusing the Familiar* 28:

愚而好自用，賤而好自專，生乎今之世，反古之道。如此者，災及其身者也。

Being obtuse and yet being fond of depending on oneself, being base and yet insisting on being one's own advocate, being born into the present generation yet attempting to return to the ways of old—such a person will bring calamities down upon himself.

Confucius with his celebrated flexibility and sense of accommodation tempers his deep and abiding respect for antiquity (7.1) with the practical consideration that inherited institutions and their wisdom must be constantly reformed to accommodate the changing circumstances of an always evolving world. This prospective attitude to the past is captured succinctly in the expression from the *Changes*: "continuity in change" (*biantong* 變通). Cf. for example 2.11, 2.15, 13.5.

4.5 子曰："富與貴，是人之所欲也；不以其道得之，不處也。貧與賤，是人之所惡也；不以其道得之，不去也。君子去仁，惡乎成名？君子無終食之間違仁，造次必於是，顛沛必於是。"

The Master said, "Wealth and honor are what people seek after, but if they are the dividends of deviating from the proper way (*dao* 道), exemplary persons (*junzi* 君子) would have no part in them. Poverty and disgrace are what people abhor, but if they are the penalty for staying on the proper way, exemplary persons would not shun them. Wherein could exemplary persons who would abandon consummate conduct (*ren* 仁) make a name for themselves? Exemplary persons do not take leave of their consummate conduct even for the space of a meal. When they are harried, it is there; when in desperate circumstances, it is there."

Comments: The importance of "making a name" for exemplary persons is frequently referenced in the Confucian canons. For example, in the *Classic of Family Reverence*, we read:

立身行道，揚名於後世，以顯父母，孝之終也。

Distinguishing yourself and walking the proper way (*dao* 道) in the world; raising your name high for posterity and thereby bringing esteem to your father and mother—it is in these things that family reverence finds its consummation.

This aspiration to make a name should be read together with passages such as 1.1: 人不知而不慍，不亦君子乎？ "to go unacknowledged by others without harboring any frustration—is this not the mark of an exemplary person (*junzi* 君子)?" Exemplary persons are not on a quest for personal recognition, but are aware that a name is conferred on persons by others as an acknowledgment of their contribution to the community. Given that "name" (*ming* 名) refers primarily to the spoken word, it has the meaning of giving the best account of oneself that one can.

Another point being made in this passage is its emphasis on indefatigable devotion to a sustained modality of conduct—that is, the need for exemplary persons to be resolute and unrelenting in their commitment to consummate conduct, whatever circumstances might arise, and whatever they might require of them.

14.28 子曰："君子道者三，我無能焉：仁者不憂，知者不惑，勇者不懼。"子貢曰："夫子自道也。"

The Master said, "The path (*dao* 道) of the exemplary person (*junzi* 君子) has three conditions I have been unable to live up to in my own conduct: the consummate (*ren* 仁) are not anxious; the wise (*zhi* 知) are not in a quandary; the courageous (*yong* 勇) are not timid."

Zigong replied, "This is the path you yourself walk, Sir."

Comment: The idealized way of life referenced by the term "exemplary person" (*junzi* 君子) is a pattern of behavior in the world characterized by consummatory conduct, wisdom, and courage. An indication that one is indeed living such a life is the absence of any anxiety, perplexity, or timidity.

Important here is the coincidence between "persons" and their "narratives" (*dao* 道), where these are simply two aspectual ways of denoting the same thing. That is, lives lived and persons are one and the same thing. A person is a story rather than merely a discrete body. When we encounter a term such as *ren* 仁, for example, it is often unclear if the text is talking about persons (*renzhe* 仁者) or their conduct (*rendao* 仁道). The argument here is that gerundive persons as "human becomings" are what they do. This equivocation stands in contrast to any ontological assumption that persons come first and then such qualities of conduct reduce to the acquired character traits of those same persons. In the Confucian world, an understanding that would separate the noun from the verb in this way is to elide the rather important distinction between a leg and walking, between some discrete thing and an event that is happening in the world.

Confucius is lamenting here the fact that his own conduct falls short of this exemplary standard. Zigong, on the other hand as the disciple perhaps most responsible for the flattering profile of Confucius found in this text, identifies the person of Confucius with just such a way of life. Confucius's own demur far from diminishing him in fact complements his exemplary way with the additional quality of humility. Cf. 9.29.

5.16 子謂子產，"有君子之道四焉：其行己也恭，其事上也敬，其養民也惠，其使民也義。"

The Master remarked that Zichan accorded with the way (*dao* 道) of the exemplary person (*junzi* 君子) in four respects: he was gracious in his comportment, he was respectful in serving those above, he was generous in attending to the needs of the common people, and he was always appropriate (*yi* 義) in employing their services.

Comment: The term *junzi* 君子 translated here as "exemplary person" prior to Confucius had a specifically political meaning that denoted nobility of birth and office. It is demonstrably the case that with Confucius, this political category was appropriated and used to express the symbiotic relationship between political responsibility and moral growth. That is, the cultivation of one's person necessarily entails active participation in the family and in the social and political institutions of the community. Not only is this the locus of service to others, but it is also the forum in which the compassion and concern leading to one's own personal refinement is expressed. Said another way, one does not first become a *junzi* 君子 and then enter the arena of political life; rather, one can only *become* a *junzi* 君子 through responsiveness to the social and political obligations that emerge in communal living. Given the transition of *junzi* 君子 from a specifically political category to a moral one, and given their overlap in social and political responsibility, there is sometimes ambiguity in the text as to which of these two domains of meaning are being referenced.

In this passage, Zichan (another name for Gongsun Qiao d. 522 BCE), is a high minister of the small state of Zheng 鄭, and a contemporary of Confucius. Throughout the text we have generic statements characterizing the kind of moral life lived by exemplary persons, but such generalizations must be further qualified when they describe the conduct of concrete exemplars themselves. In this passage, the emphasis is specifically on the moral quality of Zichan in carrying out his political duties, focusing in particular on his own dignified demeanor and his respectful relationship with his superiors, and perhaps most importantly, on his generous treatment of the common people. Cf. 14.8, 14.9 and *Mencius* 5A2.

9.19 子曰: "譬如爲山，未成一簣，止，吾止也; 譬如平地，雖覆一簣，進，吾往也。"

The Master said, "As with piling up earth to erect a mountain, if with only one basketful short of completion I stop, I have stopped. As with filling in a ditch to level the ground, if having dumped in only one basketful I continue, I am progressing."

Comment: The Confucian project as it is sketched in the *Expansive Learning* takes personal cultivation as its root. In 12.1: 爲仁由己，而由人乎哉? "Becoming consummate in one's conduct is self-originating—how could it originate with others?" In this project, it is stated that it is an easy business to become consummate in one's conduct: 7.30 仁遠乎哉? 我欲仁，斯仁至矣 "How could consummate conduct (*ren* 仁) be at all remote? No sooner do I seek it than it has arrived." At the same time however, it is a project that while one is living, has no end: 8.7 仁以爲己任，不亦重乎? 死而後已，不亦遠乎? "Where they take becoming consummate in their conduct (*ren* 仁) as their charge, is it not a heavy one? And where their way ends only with their death, is it not indeed a long one?" The point Confucius is making here is that as long as his students have made the commitment to personal cultivation and do not relent, they are on their way.

The association between the metaphor of a mountain in all of its majesty and what it means to become consummate as a person is a familiar one. Mountains are prominent features of the landscape, especially in Confucius's home state of Lu, that provide a sense of place and direction. Reaching to the sky, they are not only stately but are indeed holy, lifting humankind up to touch the heavens. And given the Confucian epistemology of comprehensiveness in which the best view of anything is the most synoptic, mountains provide a 360-degree vantage point from which to view the events of the world. Recall 6.23 for example, where Confucius associates mountains with the most upright and outstanding of human beings: 仁者樂山 "those consummate in their conduct enjoy mountains."

8.9 子曰: "民可使由之，不可使知之。"
The Master said, "The common people can be encouraged to travel along the proper way, but they cannot be made to understand it."

Comment: Compare *Analects* 15.29 in which the way is something being built and extended by the cultural heroes of each generation. It is laid by some and traveled by many. The point being made here is that everyone can find a place on the way, even when they have not had much of a hand in constructing it.

Passages such as this one might offend against our egalitarian sensibilities, but it is important to remember Confucius's hierarchical standards are grounded in the assiduous effort needed to pursue a transformative moral education. In the opportunity for education, Confucius is demonstrably inclusive: 15.39 有教無類 "I teach (*jiao* 教) everyone, regardless of class distinctions or other such discriminations." His repeated contrast between exemplary and petty persons is not based upon blood or wealth or social status or race, criteria he explicitly rejects as being relevant to either education or moral growth. Rather, the first demand he makes of both himself and his students is on the unrelenting commitment to personal cultivation in the roles and relations that are defining of consummate human "becomings."

Cf. *Mencius* 3A4:

或勞心，或勞力；勞心者治人，勞力者治於人；治於人者食人，治人者食於人：天下之通義也。

Some labor with their minds and some with their backs. Those who labor with their minds rule over others while those who labor with their backs are ruled by others. Those who are ruled by others, feed them; those who rule others are fed by them. This is a precept accepted everywhere in the world.

18.6 長沮、桀溺耦而耕，孔子過之，使子路問津焉。長沮曰：" 夫執輿者爲誰？" 子路曰："爲孔丘。" 曰："是魯孔丘與？" 曰："是也。" 曰："是知津矣。" 問於桀溺，桀溺曰："子爲誰？" 曰："爲仲由。" 曰："是魯孔丘之徒與？" 對曰："然。" 曰："滔滔者天下皆是也，而誰以易之？且而與其從辟人之士也，豈若從辟世之士哉？" 耰而不輟。子路行以告。夫子憮然曰："鳥獸不可與同群，吾非斯人之徒與而誰與？天下有道，丘不與易也。"

Chang Ju and Jie Ni were yoked up ploughing the field. Confucius, passing their way, sent Zilu to ask them where to ford the river.

Chang Ju asked Zilu, "Who is that man holding the reins of your carriage?"

"He is Confucius," replied Zilu.

"The Confucius of Lu?"

"Indeed."

"Then he already knows where the ford is."

Zilu turned and asked Jie Ni the same question.

"Who are you?" asked Jie Ni.

"I am Zilu."

"You are that follower of Confucius of Lu?"

"The very one."

Jie Ni then said, "There is a deluge that has inundated the whole world. Who then is going to alleviate it? You follow after a scholar-official who would avoid people selectively. Wouldn't you be better off following those like us who avoid the world altogether?" As Jie Ni spoke he continued to turn the earth over the seeds.

Zilu departed and informed Confucius. Confucius, with some frustration, replied, "We cannot run with the birds and beasts. Am I not one among the people of this world? If not them, with whom should I associate? If the proper way (*dao* 道) prevailed in the world, I wouldn't need to alleviate the flood."

Comment: Chapter 18 in the *Analects* contains several passages that have Daoist-like recluses seeming to challenge Confucius's mission to reform the world. There are some linguistic resonances with *Zhuangzi's* "Autumn Floods" chapter. Taking fording the river as a metaphor for finding a way out of the deluge that has engulfed the world, Chang Ju's response to Zilu is that since your Master thinks he already has the answer, why ask me? Jie Ni suggests Confucius's partial method of giving a wide berth to a few bad rulers is not as good as the approach the recluses have taken in abandoning the world altogether.

On hearing the account of Zilu's conversation with these recluses, Confucius gives a decidedly Confucian defense, for good and for bad. From Confucius's perspective, these self-indulgent recluses have simply walked away from their obligation to other people and abandoned the world to chaos. For Confucius, we are all human beings, and as such, have both the capacity and the responsibility to set the world right. If all was as it should be, Confucius too would have the leisure to withdraw from the world and live the simple lives they have chosen.

While Confucius, given his espoused values, does make his case, the passage also reflects the limitations of these same anthropocentric metrics. The more expansive and inclusive Daoist answer might be that we need an anthropocosmic rather than merely a human-centered vision of the human experience: we need to see the world as the world in all of its parts. While the Confucian version of the pathetic fallacy places us at the center of the cosmos, an ecological civilization by contrast requires the acknowledgement of our association with and responsibility to all things, not just the human beings of this world. We can see that in response to this Daoist challenge, other classical Confucian texts such as *Focusing the Familiar* (*Zhongyong* 中庸) and the *Classic of Family Reverence* (*Xiaojing* 孝經) elevate human feelings to the level of having profound cosmic consequences.

18.7 子路從而後，遇丈人，以杖荷蓧。子路問曰："子見夫子乎？"丈人曰："四體不勤，五穀不分。孰爲夫子？"植其杖而芸。子路拱而立。止子路宿，殺雞爲黍而食之，見其二子焉。明日，子路行以告。子曰："隱者也。"使子路反見之。至則行矣。子路曰："不仕無義。長幼之節，不可廢也；君臣之義，如之何其廢之？欲潔其身，而亂大倫。君子之仕也，行其義也。道之不行，已知之矣。"

Zilu was accompanying the Master when he fell behind. He came across an old man using his staff as a carrying pole to tote his weed baskets.

"Have you seen my Master?" asked Zilu.

The old man replied, "You—'the kind of person whose limbs don't know the meaning of work, and who can't tell one kind of grain from another'— who could your Master be?" He then planted his staff in the ground and continued his weeding.

Zilu stood by him with his hands cupped respectfully in a salute. The old man invited Zilu to spend the night. He killed a chicken and prepared some special millet for the occasion, and presented his two sons to his guest. On the following day, Zilu took his leave, and reported the event to Confucius.

"He is a recluse." said the Master, and sent Zilu back to see him again. On Zilu's arrival, he discovered the old man had already left. Zilu remarked to his sons, "To refuse office is to fail to do what is most meaningful and appropriate (*yi* 義). If the differentiation between young and old cannot be abandoned, how could one think of abandoning what is appropriate between ruler and subject? In one's efforts to remain personally untarnished, one is ready to throw the most important relationships into turmoil. The opportunity of exemplary persons (*junzi* 君子) to serve in office is the occasion for them to bring into effect what they judge to be most meaningful and appropriate. That the proper way (*dao* 道) does not prevail—this is known already."

Comment: Unlike 18.6 in which Confucius does the talking, here it is Zilu. But the Confucian message is the same. The Confucian defense against this familiar Daoist injunction to withdraw from the world is to argue that just because the way does not prevail, we do not have license to abandon our responsibilities to each other in the roles and relations that define a human life.

It would seem that the "recluse" in this instance is more specifically a person who has refused to serve in government. Zilu observes that the old man in his relationship to Zilu himself has clearly not abandoned the proper distinction between young and old; in response to Zilu's gesture of respect, he invites him into his home to join with his family, and fetes him with the finest fare he has.

Zilu appeals to Confucianism's state and family isomorphism (*jiaguotonggou* 家國同構). He accuses the recluse of having his own self-serving reason of remaining unsoiled by government service. In being thus selfish, he is threatening the various distinctions in familial, social, and political roles that form the foundation of the sociopolitical order. Civil service for the Confucian is not only the opportunity for exemplary persons to make a difference; it is a profound obligation.

A seeming contradiction arises when we recall that Confucius repeatedly insists exemplary persons do not serve in government when the proper way does not prevail. But we do not want to read these passages as being simply expository and categorical. Zilu does make the Confucian point that exemplary persons do not turn their back on the world, and that in spite of the cost to themselves personally, they would still choose to advance their

III. THE *ANALECTS* (*LUNYU* 論語): A BASIC CONFUCIAN VOCABULARY

cause in striving to make the world a better place.

The fact that these polemical passages are included in the *Analects* can be read as reinforcing the openness and inclusiveness that has a high value for Confucius. They constitute a trope that has strong echoes in the Daoist literature. This passage in particular has an immediate resonance with an anecdote rehearsed in *Zhuangzi* 71/25/33 with a similar cast of players:

孔子之楚，舍於蟻丘之漿。其鄰有夫妻臣妾登極者，子路曰："是稷稷何爲者邪？"仲尼曰："是聖人僕也。是自埋於民，自藏於畔。其聲銷，其志無窮，其口雖言，其心未嘗言，方且與世違而心不屑與之俱。是陸沈者也，是其市南宜僚邪？"子路請往召之。孔子曰："已矣！彼知丘之著於己也，知丘之適楚也，以丘爲必使楚王之召己也，彼且以丘爲佞人也。夫若然者，其於佞人也羞聞其言，而況親見其身乎！而何以爲存？"子路往視之，其室虛矣。

When Confucius had arrived in the state of Chu, he took up lodgings at a roadhouse on Ant Knoll. The husband and wife in a neighboring house with all of their household servants had climbed up onto the roof to get a look at someone. Zilu asked Confucius: "All this fussing about—who is this person?"

"He is an assistant to the sages," replied Confucius. "He has buried himself among the common people, and has concealed himself in the fields. He is little known, but is boundless in his purposes. Even though he talks, he shows nothing of what he thinks and feels. It might well be that he is someone who lives contrary to our times and wants nothing to do with the likes of us. As one who has sunk to the bottom on dry land, could he be Yiliao from the south of the marketplace?"

Zilu asked Confucius if he could go and invite him over.

"Please don't." replied Confucius. "He knows I want to make a reputation for myself, and that on my visit to Chu I am sure to get the King of Chu to summon me. And he takes me to be a glib talker. Such being the case, if he would be ashamed to hear the words of a glib talker, how much more would he resist meeting me in person? And what makes you think he is still here?"

When Zilu went to see him, indeed his quarters were empty.

III.17 Confucius: One Special Person Extending the Proper Way (*dao* 道)

2.4 子曰:"吾十有五而志于學,三十而立,四十而不惑,五十而知天命,六十而耳順,七十而從心所欲,不踰矩。"

The Master said: "At fifteen, my heart-and-mind was set upon learning; at thirty I took my stance; at forty I was no longer doubtful; at fifty I realized the propensities of *tian* (*tianming* 天命); at sixty my ear was attuned; at seventy I could give my thoughts and feelings free rein without overstepping the boundaries."

Comment: The language used in this biographical passage is again consistent with the pervasive "walking the way" metaphor, describing Confucius's life as it unfolds step by step. Confucius's life is itself a concrete example of the Confucian project of personal cultivation that shapes both person and world. It depicts him striking out in a particular direction, taking up his place, knowing at each juncture which way to go, being fully cognizant of the terrain that surrounds him, making his way along a shared path by listening to everything being said,① and finally having cultivated a sense of moral direction, being able to go wherever he desires without fear of going astray. Importantly, *tianming* 天命 here is not to be read theistically as "the command of *tian* 天" that rings of divine command theory, but rather as the force of circumstances, the way of the world. Confucius places great emphasis upon the discursive nature of the human experience, and how effective communication at every stage has been essential to his personal growth.

11.26 子路、曾皙、冉有、公西華侍坐。子曰:"以吾一日長乎爾,毋吾以也。居則曰:'不吾知也!'如或知爾,則何以哉?"子路率爾而對曰:"千乘之國,攝乎大國之間,加之以師旅,因之以饑饉;由也爲之,比及三年,可使有勇,且知方也。"夫子哂之。"求!爾何如?"對曰:"方六七十,如五六十,求也爲之,比及三年,可使足民。如其禮樂,以俟君子。""赤!爾何如?"對曰:"非曰能之,願學焉。宗廟之事,如會同,端章甫,願爲小相

---

① There has been some speculation in the commentaries that "ear" in the expression 耳順 "my ear was attuned" might be a corruption, but the recently recovered Dingzhou version has this same character. Again, the aural metaphor abounds.

III. THE *ANALECTS* (*LUNYU* 論語): A BASIC CONFUCIAN VOCABULARY

焉。""點！爾何如？"鼓瑟希，鏗爾，舍瑟而作。對曰："異乎三子者之撰。"子曰："何傷乎？亦各言其志也。"曰："莫春者，春服既成。冠者五六人，童子六七人，浴乎沂，風乎舞雩，詠而歸。"夫子喟然嘆曰："吾與點也！"三子者出，曾晳後。曾晳曰："夫三子者之言何如？"子曰："亦各言其志也已矣。"曰："夫子何哂由也？"曰："爲國以禮，其言不讓，是故哂之。""唯求則非邦也與？""安見方六七十如五六十而非邦也者？""唯赤則非邦也與？""宗廟會同，非諸侯而何？赤也爲之小，孰能爲之大？"

Zilu, Zeng Xi, Ranyou, and Zihua were all sitting in attendance on Confucius. The Master said, "Just because I am a bit older than you do not hesitate on my account. You keep on saying, 'No one appreciates me!' but if someone were to do so, what would you do for them?"

"As for me," Zilu replied hastily, "give me a state of a thousand chariots to govern, set me in among powerful neighbors, harass me with foreign armies, and add to that, a widespread famine, and at the end of three years, I will have imbued courage in the people, and moreover, provided them with a sure direction."

The Master smiled at him, and then said, "Ranyou, what would you do?"

"Give me a small territory of sixty or seventy—or even fifty or sixty—*li* square, and at the end of three years, I will have made sure the common people have what they need. As for observing ritual propriety (*li* 禮) and the playing of music (*yue* 樂), these must wait upon an exemplary person (*junzi* 君子)."

And what would you do, Zihua?" asked the Master.

"Not to say that I have the ability to do so, but I am willing to learn. In the events of the Ancestral Temple and in the forging of diplomatic alliances, donning the appropriate ceremonial robes and cap, I would like to serve as a protocol officer."

"And what about you, Zeng Xi?" asked the Master. Zeng Xi ceased plucking his zither, and setting the instrument aside as it still sang, he sat up.

"I would choose to do something somewhat different from the others." he said.

"No harm in that," said the Master. "Each of you may speak your mind."

"At the end of spring, with the new clothes having been sewed, in the company of five or six young men and six or seven children, I would like for us to bathe ourselves in the river Yi, to revel in the cool breezes at the Altar for Rain, and then return home singing."

The Master heaved a deep sigh, and said, "I'm with Zeng Xi!"

Zilu, Ranyou, and Zihua all left, but Zeng Xi waited behind, and asked the Master, "What do you think of what my three fellow students have said?"

"Each of you has simply spoken his mind, that's all," replied the Master.

"Why did you, Sir, smile at Zilu?" said Zeng Xi.

"I smiled at him because he spoke of governing a state by means of ritual propriety, and yet in what he said there no accommodation at all," said the Master.

"Was it only Ranyou who did not speak of governing a state?" he asked.

"How can one speak of a territory of sixty or seventy—or even fifty or sixty—*li* square, and not be referring to a state?" replied the Master.

"Was it only Zihua, then, who did not speak of governing a state?" he asked.

"If the events of the Ancestral Temple and diplomatic alliances do not involve the various lords, then what are they? If he is only willing to serve as a minor protocol officer, who then is able to take up a major role?"

Comment: While Master Zeng was one of the Master's later disciples and one of the most prominent in the text, his father Zeng Xi 曾皙, also called Zeng Dian 曾點, was an earlier student. Zeng Xi appears only in this single passage of the *Analects*—one of the longest in the entire work. This portrait is most revealing of Master Zeng's father as a person, and tells us something of the other disciples as well. Importantly, it gives us an image of the always critical and yet still warmly human Confucius.

With this depiction of Zeng Xi, we get an insight into what Confucius really understands by ritual propriety (*li* 禮). Zilu's ambitious answer is that in governing a major state through ritual practices he can overcome all obstacles. Certainly, formal ritual practices together with full participation of the practitioners are defining of the life at high court and punctuate the turning of the seasons. But the importance of such an elegant way of life as an inspiration for the people cannot be overstated.

Confucius is keenly aware such practices have their roots in the daily lives of the people where family life itself is not only the primary source of social and political order, but of shared enjoyment as well. For Confucius, *li* 禮 is also a living, vibrant, and profoundly earthy tradition in which a religious reverence is to be found in song and dance and the ordinary pleasures of family and friends (3.4). The heart of ritual propriety is hearth and happiness with the deep concern that it must not ossify into rarified, often anemic, formalities.

It is significant that, given the inseparability of ritual propriety and the playing of music, Zeng Xi sets aside his reverberating zither to answer Confucius's question about what he would do if he were truly appreciated. And about Zeng Xi himself, we learn that in demonstrating his worth, he takes as his first priority the observance of just such ritual propriety. His answer and Confucius's response to it suggests that Zeng Xi, unlike the other three students, understands that any kind of political flourishing is going to depend upon setting a model of excellence for the people and encouraging them to find enjoyment through promoting ritual propriety in their roles and relations (2.3). Appropriate ritualized living like the proper use of language is a social discourse that is fundamental to effective governing (13.3). At the same time, Confucius himself in appreciating Zeng Xi's response is making it clear that the path to governing effectively must at times also include simple pleasures and playfulness. While governing is certainly a serious business, if it becomes too much so at the expense of life's enjoyments, a zealousness to rule "properly" can lead to precisely the opposite result.

7.1 子曰："述而不作，信而好古，竊比於我老彭。"
The Master said, "Following the proper way, I do not forge new paths. With confidence I cherish the ancients. In these respects, I am comparable to Old Peng."

Comment: Confucius here is giving an account of how he thinks about his own personal role in the transmission of the literati learning. When Confucius allows that in "following the proper way, I do not forge new paths," he is clearly disassociating himself from the term *zuo* 作 that is conventionally understood as "initiating" or "innovating." Respecting the significance of the "walking the way" metaphor here, I have translated it as "forging." Allowing that *zuo* 作 throughout the canonical texts is often coupled with the term "sages" (*shengren* 聖人), one interpretation of Confucius's demurring from this association might be his sincere deference to the cultural innovations of the sages, while at the same time being yet another expression of his familiar modesty.

But there are commentators across the centuries who have read this passage literally and have thus portrayed Confucius as a cultural fundamentalist. As early as the *Mozi*, for example, Confucius is taken at his word as being wholly a transmitter, and is criticized roundly for offering the world a lifeless conservatism:

> 又曰:"君子循而不作。"應之曰:"古者羿作弓,杼作甲,奚仲作車,巧垂作舟,然則今之鮑函車匠皆君子也,而羿、杼、奚仲、巧垂皆小人邪?且其所循人必或作之,然則其所循皆小人道也?"
>
> Again, the Confucians say: "Exemplary persons follow and do not innovate." But we would respond by saying: "In ancient times, Yi introduced the bow, Yu introduced armor, Xizhong introduced the carriage, and the tradesman Qiu introduced the boat. Such being the case, are today's tanners, smiths, carriage-makers, and carpenters as their followers all exemplary persons, and are Yi, Yu, Xizhong, and the tradesman Qiu as innovators simply petty persons? Further, since whatever the Confucians are following had to be introduced by someone, doesn't this mean that what they are in fact following are the ways of petty persons?"[①]

The logic of this Mohist criticism is impeccable if we take Confucius's self-description to be expository rather than as an expression of his profound deference to the cultural tradition, and again as a token of his personal modesty. And just such a Mohist criticism of Confucian traditionalism is alive and well in the commentarial tradition as it has continued down to the present day. The contemporary political philosopher, Hsiao Kung-chuan [Xiao Gongquan] 蕭公權, for example, describes this ostensive Confucian conservatism at length as the project of "emulating the past" (*fagu* 法古).[②] More recently, Edward Slingerland, in interpreting this same passage from the *Analects*, aligns himself with a retrospective understanding of a Confucianism that would harken back to the Golden Age of the Zhou dynasty. Slingerland observes:

> It is more likely that transmission is all that Confucius countenanced for people in his age, since the sagely Zhou kings established the ideal set of institutions that perfectly accord with human needs.[③]

Contra this fundamentalist and purist reading of Confucius—a position

---

[①] *Mozi* 63/39/19. See also 81/46/50.
[②] Hsiao Kung-chuan, *A History of Chinese Political Thought* Volume 1, trans. F. W. Mote, Princeton: Princeton University Press, 1979, pp. 79-142.
[③] Edward Slingerland (trans.), *Analects: With Selections from Traditional Commentaries*, Indianapolis: Hackett Publishing, 2003, p. 64.

that I must disagree with profoundly—I want to suggest that this passage speaks rather to Confucius's understanding of the nature and the dynamics of intergenerational transmission. And in this process of genealogical transmission, the vital patterns of deference captured in the notion of "family reverence" (*xiao* 孝) serve as a key factor.

Borrowing the language of the *Book of Changes* (*Yijing* 易經), I would argue that Confucius as he is remembered historically is in fact a particularly good example of the cosmological assumptions that grounds this canonical text. He, consistent with the language of the *Changes*, assumes that the unfolding of the natural and cultural narratives can best be expressed in terms of "continuity in change" (*biantong* 變通) and of "ceaseless procreation" (*shengshengbuyi* 生生不已). To describe Confucius in these terms is not to deny that, with his constant appeal to the core canons of the tradition, he is anything but a most effective transmitter of a persistent worldview and of an abiding commonsense. Indeed, his personal *gravitas* is derived importantly from the authority Confucius garners by the traditional assumption it was he who compiled, or at least edited, the canonical *Five Classics*. At the same time, however, with Confucius's own unique contribution to the development of a specific and profoundly novel vocabulary, he is also an exemplar of philosophical innovation within a living tradition. Indeed, we can appreciate his modesty in resisting the suggestion he has been an innovator and is thus a sage, and we can again allow that he was without question an effective transmitter. But we still have substantial evidence to comfortably assert that Confucius was also an innovator of the first order who established a vocabulary for personal cultivation and took the tradition in significantly new directions.

7.28 子曰:"蓋有不知而作之者，我無是也。多聞擇其善者而從之，多見而識之，知之次也。"
    The Master said, "There are presumably those who would forge new paths without the knowledge that would warrant it, but I am not of this kind. I learn much, select out of it what works well, and then follow it. I observe much, and remember it. But this is not the highest level of wisdom."

Comment: Innovation must be rooted in a comprehensive understanding of what has come before. While Confucius was certainly a dedicated intermediary within a living tradition, he was also singularly responsible for introducing, redefining, and elaborating upon a set of key terms as the authorized philosophical vocabulary for an evolving Confucianism: *ren* 仁 (aspiring to consummate conduct in one's roles and relations), *junzi* 君子 (exemplary persons), *yi* 義 (an optimizing appropriateness), and *li* 禮 (achieving propriety in one's roles and relations). Again, it is Confucius who promoted personal cultivation as the defining characteristic of the Confucian project, and who grounds Confucian role ethics and the vision of the consummate life in "family reverence" (*xiao* 孝). This being the case, it is not surprising that when Zhu Xi 朱熹 selects the *Four Books* as the core texts of the Confucian tradition, he canonizes the *Analects* and the *Mencius* as the second and third texts respectively, giving as his explicit reason for including them that they provide the fundamental vocabulary for this Confucian project. In addition, these two texts make available to the tradition, narrative examples of such cultivation in the role models of Confucius and Mencius themselves.

10.24-26 寢不尸，居不容。見齊衰者，雖狎，必變。見冕者與瞽者，雖褻，必以貌。凶服者式之。式負版者。有盛饌，必變色而作。迅雷風烈，必變。升車，必正立執綏。車中，不內顧，不疾言，不親指。色斯舉矣，翔而後集。曰："山梁雌雉，時哉！時哉！" 子路共之，三嗅而作。

In sleeping, he did not assume the posture of a corpse, and when at home alone, he did not kneel in the formal posture he would assume were he entertaining guests.

On encountering someone in mourning dress, even those with whom he was on intimate terms, he would always assume a solemn visage. On coming across someone wearing a ceremonial cap or someone who is blind, even though they were persons of frequent acquaintance, he would invariably pay his respects.

On meeting up with a person in mourner's attire, he would lean forward on the crossbeam of his carriage. He would do the same on encountering an official with state census records on his back.

On being presented with a sumptuous table, he would always assume a solemn demeanor and rise to his feet.

On experiencing a sudden clap of thunder or fierce winds, he would change his countenance.

In mounting his carriage, he would always stand upright and grasp the cord. While riding in the carriage, he would not turn his head to look inward, speak hastily, or point at things.

III. THE *ANALECTS* (*LUNYU* 論語): A BASIC CONFUCIAN VOCABULARY

Comment: This detailed portrait of Confucius rehearses a succession of snapshots that are revealing of the quality of Confucius's responsiveness to particular circumstances and of his unrelenting attention to proper countenance. It discloses a pattern of proper conduct on the part of this particular human being in the particular circumstances of his life.

One way to distinguish an inclusive and holistic Confucian role ethics from more formalized and thus reductionistic principle-based ethical theories is to give an account of how in this Confucian moral vision, the particular, the informal, and the contextualizing aspects of experience, far from being discounted or marginalized, in fact take on central importance. Such are the resources that can be drawn upon to maximize the productive outcome of always particular human activities. Certainly the formal aspect in all of its guises has an indispensable role in structuring our practices and in the further refinement of conduct. But it is because the moral vision of Confucian role ethics is concerned with coordinating the contribution of each aspect of experience in achieving the totality of the effect that the normative language to which it appeals, and the sense of order to which it aspires, is in the Whiteheadian sense, fundamentally aesthetic.[①] The ethical aesthetic—the need for elegance and moral artistry in ethics—means that in this holistic understanding of human conduct all aspects of the life experience have more or less relevance, and thus have some value for determining a worthwhile outcome.

The outcome or effect itself is most often characterized in these texts in the aesthetic language of authenticity or duplicity rather than by appeal to the rationalizing language of right and wrong, or good and evil. There is a perceived, inseparable relationship between elegance and morality, and conversely, between baseness and immorality. On being asked about family reverence (*xiao* 孝), for example, Confucius would insist that this moral imperative cannot be satisfied by some set of formally prescribed, reduplicative activities that would resolve to a binary right or wrong. Rather *xiao* 孝 is dependent upon the specific attitude expressed in the countenance and the actions as they are being carried out (2.8). This ethics of proper responsiveness is elaborated upon in great detail in these middle books of the *Analects* wherein the life habits of Confucius are displayed as a model for the ages.

[①] A.N. Whitehead, *Modes of Thought*, New York: Macmillan, 1938, pp. 60-63.

10.8 食不厭精，膾不厭細。食饐而餲，魚餒而肉敗，不食。色惡，不食。臭惡，不食。失飪，不食。不時，不食。割不正，不食。不得其醬，不食。肉雖多，不使勝食氣。惟酒無量，不及亂。沽酒市脯不食。不撤薑食。不多食。祭於公，不宿肉。祭肉不出三日。出三日，不食之矣。食不語，寢不言。雖疏食菜羹，瓜祭，必齊如也。

In his staple cereals, Confucius did not object to them being milled, and in his dishes, he did not object to the food being cut up fine.

If the cereal was damp and mildewed, and tasted unusual, and if the fish or meat had spoiled, he would not eat them. If the food was off color or smelled strange, he would not eat it. If the food was not properly cooked or the dining hour had not arrived, he would not eat. He would not eat food that was improperly prepared, or that was lacking the appropriate condiments and sauces.

Even when meat was abundant, he would not eat it in disproportionate amount to the staple foods.

Only in his wine did he not limit himself, although he never got inebriated.

He would not consume store-bought wine or dried meats from the marketplace.

When he had eaten his fill, he would not take more, even if the ginger had not yet been cleared.

Comment: In our reading of the *Analects*, there is a tendency to give short shrift to the middle books 9-11 as a series of intimate portraits depicting the historical person, Confucius. But in fact, in overlooking these personal details and life habits, we are in danger of missing the real substance of Confucius's moral vision. We must not lose sight of the fact that Confucian role ethics ultimately and invariably has to do with specific persons in their specific situations. The middle chapters of the *Analects* provide a series of concrete images in the life of Confucius—how he ate, and drank, and sat, and dressed, and how he engaged different people under different circumstances. These passages provide the images and the anecdotes that brought this exemplary teacher to life for his immediate protégés, and for the numerous generations of students that have followed after them down to our present day.

Confucius was certainly a flesh-and-blood historical person who lived, taught, and died some twenty-five centuries ago. He consolidated in his own time a formidable legacy of wisdom that has been passed down and

III. THE *ANALECTS* (*LUNYU* 論語): A BASIC CONFUCIAN VOCABULARY

applied through the ages to shape the character of an entire culture and beyond. In and of itself, the profoundly personal model of Confucius remembered by his protégés through those intimate snapshots of his life collected in the middle chapters of the *Analects* and other canonical texts, has its own value and meaning.

10.12 席不正，不坐。
Confucius would not sit unless the mats were properly placed.

Comment: The placement of the mats would reflect the status and purposes of the others present relative to Confucius's own rank and obligations. This protocol of proper seating arrangements according to perceived status in all kinds of gatherings is still very much a part of the *li* 禮 in China today. *Zheng* 正 as "proper" is not merely "rectification" or "correct conduct" as in an appeal to some external standard, but also "proper conduct" as it can best be determined inclusively by those specific persons within any particular situation. The Latin *proprius*, "making something one's own," gives us a series of reflexive cognate expressions that are useful in translating key Confucian philosophical terms such as "ritual propriety" (*li* 禮) and "appropriateness" (*yi* 義) to capture this sense of participation and personalization.

10.13 鄉人飲酒，杖者出，斯出矣。鄉人儺，朝服而立於阼階。
When drinking wine at a village function, Confucius would wait for those with walking sticks to depart before taking his leave.

Comment: These passages from the middle chapters reveal the extent to which ordinary life was punctuated by public events that would invariably include eating and drinking, and how attentive Confucius himself was to the dictates of ritual propriety and social etiquette. Of course, the allusion to walking sticks is a reference to showing deference to the most aged in the company as an expression of "family reverence" (*xiao* 孝).

7.34 子曰："若聖與仁，則吾豈敢？抑爲之不厭，誨人不倦，則可謂云爾已矣。"公西華曰："正唯弟子不能學也。"
The Master said, "How would I dare to consider myself a sage (*sheng* 聖) or a consummate person (*ren* 仁)? What can be said about me is simply that I continue my studies without respite and instruct others without growing

weary."

Gongxi Hua remarked, "It is precisely this quality of commitment we students are unable to learn from you."

Comment: On the one hand, Confucius displays his usual modesty in demurring ascriptions to him of the Confucian ideals of sage and consummate person. But on the other hand, he does express in clear terms what is really important to him in his own conception of himself. He has no need to make grand claims about his own accomplishments; such compliments if deserved at all are properly conferred on a person by others. But here and in many other places as well, Confucius does insist on his unrelenting resolve in the project of personal cultivation effected through the inseparable and complementary occupations of teaching and learning. And his student Gongxi Hua is astute in allowing it is this quality of resolve that is what is so distinctive about Confucius as a mentor and role model, and that such dedication cannot be taught. Cf. 7.1 and *Mencius* 2A2 for similar descriptions.

15.3 子曰："賜也，女以予爲多學而識之者與？" 對曰："然，非與？" 曰："非也，予一以貫之。"

The Master said, "Zigong, do you take me to be someone who has learned a great deal and who can remember it all?"

He replied, "I do indeed. Is it not so?"

"No, it is not," said the Master, "I just pull everything together on one continuous thread."

Comment: It is significant that Confucius's interlocutor in this passage is the well-bred and eloquent Zigong who is credited with providing a most becoming portrait of Confucius. The usual self-effacing modesty of Confucius is in evidence here, with him setting aside the assumption that he is a scholar of great erudition. At the same time, he repeats the expression of "pulling everything together on one thread" from 4.15 where in conversation with Master Zeng he claims there is a coherent logic to his teachings. In that passage, after Confucius departs Master Zeng is asked by the other students what Confucius means by "one thread," Master Zeng says 夫子之道，忠恕而已矣 "the way of the Master is simply doing one's utmost (*zhong* 忠) and putting oneself in the other's place (*shu* 恕), nothing more." D.C. Lau describes these two activities as two aspects of the same method of becoming consummate in one's conduct (*ren* 仁). Confucius is perhaps saying all of his teachings are captured in this one neologism *ren* 仁 that is introduced in the *Analects* and repeated more than a hundred times. This same method is restated in 6.30 as 夫仁者，己欲立而立人 "exemplary persons establish others in seeking to get established themselves." The Confucian wisdom here is that if my neighbor does better, I do better. Good teachers can only be as much if they have good students, and having a great student will make them a great teacher. Persons can only grow themselves as moral exemplars through a sustained process of deferring to the needs and aspirations of other people, and in the process, creating a field of meaningful relations. Importantly, it is the quality of the people in their "field of selves" that is a key resource for their own flourishing.

7.13 子之所慎：齊，戰，疾。
There were three things the Master approached with special care: fasting, warfare, and illness.

Comment: Confucius is here respecting his own definition of wisdom 知之爲知之，不知爲不知，是知也 as "know what you know and know what you do not know" (2.17). That is, all three of these topics require special care from Confucius because they take him to the boundaries of his professed competence. Confucius's commitment to a culture of ritual propriety requires that he pay careful attention to the formalities of fasting both physically and intellectually in preparation for sacrifices. In 10.7, we are given some of the details of such preparations. His expertise with respect to such sacrifices is limited to an understanding of their function in galvanizing order within the human community. At the same time, he demurs explicitly on any claim to having privileged access to the world of the spirits. Elsewhere we learn that Confucius had nothing to say about strange happenings, the use of force, disorder, or the spirits (7.21).

The complex topic of warfare that would seriously affect the domestic and the geopolitical order as they are grounded in the structures and institutions of ritual propriety also requires the most serious attention. On an occasion when Duke Ling of Wei sought Confucius's counsel on the deployment of troops, Confucius allows that he has never made a study of military matters. And sorely offended by having been asked such a question, on the following day Confucius promptly departs (15.1).

With respect to illness, we see in the many passages detailing the life habits of Confucius he takes great care in not consuming spoiled food or drink. See for example, 10.9 where he will not eat sacrificial meat that is more than three days old, and 10.8 in which he seems particularly concerned with the quality of both his food and wine. Again in 10.16 when gifted with medicine by the head of the Ji family, Confucius's accepts it as a courtesy, 丘未達，不敢嘗 "but not knowing its effects, I dare not take it."

9.4 子絕四：毋意，毋必，毋固，毋我。

There were four things the Master abstained from entirely: He would not conjecture, he would not claim or demand certainty, he was not inflexible, and he was not self-absorbed.

Comment: In a process cosmology that eschews any strong sense of teleology or idealism, the focus is on making the most of the "very now" rather than anticipating the actualization of some delayed end. As a personal regimen, these abstentions locate conduct relationally in what is most immediate in the human experience, and are focused on shaping the kind of habitual disposition that is most effective in responding concretely to what are always changing circumstances. While we might allow that these four abstentions are of a piece, each being implicated in the others, we might also ask: What can we infer about Confucius's self-conscious moral agency from each of these abstentions when they are analyzed individually?

In the first abstention, Confucius is described as refraining from conjecture, speculation, or surmise (*wuyi* 毋意). And this is indeed the portrait of Confucius we find in the *Analects*. Confucius is *not* a person of principle. That is, we do not find him acting upon broad, theoretical assumptions determined by principles ostensibly existing prior to and informing any particular situation. Instead, he is a person whose agency seems diffused within, and responsive to, the here-and-now events of a particular human narrative, with the continuing theorizing of practice being motivated by producing more intelligent outcomes. Most of the language that expresses his moral vision is modal rather than referencing specific actions, exhorting his students to a particular attitude in action rather than compliance with any specific rules of conduct. We should act with self-conscious resolve (*cheng* 誠) in our actions, and be conscientious (*zhong* 忠) in what we do, and we should be assiduous in our studies (*haoxue* 好學) and credible (*xin* 信) in our relations with others. Such an emphasis on modality rather than content reflects the fact that most of our actions are a function of

III. THE *ANALECTS* (*LUNYU* 論語): A BASIC CONFUCIAN VOCABULARY

persisting existential commitments in our various roles and relations rather than being determined seriatim by a staccato series of fragmented choices. And again, the very complexity of life itself requires that optimal moral actions will necessarily be a matter of responding efficaciously to specific circumstances, precluding the possibility of the best response being determined in advance.

From the textual tradition that remembers the life of Confucius, we witness a person who is not given to habits of thinking and acting that depend upon the seeming clarity and facility provided by remote, theoretical abstractions. Rather, he would rely pragmatically upon more immediately accessible, demonstrable information. He seems focused upon weighing up and acting upon the untidy, concrete possibilities readily available in the complex roles and events of our lives. The structure and rhythm of his narrative emerge from his best efforts to pursue and sustain propriety within what are for him sanctified roles and relations (*li* 禮).

The second abstention in this description of Confucius is his reluctance to claim or demand certainty. Such reticence to invoke the fixed and final as imperatives or universal laws is based upon his fundamental respect for change and novelty. It reflects an awareness of the open-ended complexities of lives lived within a cosmology of "ceaseless procreation in the continuing 'now,'" a profound sense of on-going and ineluctable transformation captured in the mantra associated with the *Book of Changes*: *shengshengbuyi* 生生不已. And this process of generative procreation is made normative in a complementary passage in the same text: 天地之大德曰生 "The greatest capacity of the cosmos is life itself." This passage asserts that we are born into, grow together with, and live on within, our contextualizing and always evolving natural, social, and cultural relations. And it is our self-conscious growth itself within this ecological context that is the substance of cosmic morality. The sense of agency within this process first and foremost emerges out of a purposeful and deliberate devotion to the vital, always collaborative roles we live in our continuing personal narratives. This defining feature of focus-field agency requires of us not only our unrelenting attention to continuing growth in these roles, but also sufficient moral imagination to be aware of and responsive to our always shifting circumstances. Irreducibly complex persons are vital and inherently active, and in their continuing deference to, and collaboration with others, they must necessarily remain provisional, revisionist, and accommodating in all they do. While aspiring to consummatory conduct, there is for them, neither finality nor closure.

Confucius's third, closely related commitment is to a flexibility in his actions that follows from this same abjuring of certainty. Such flexibility is required from reflexive persons who, being keenly aware of the transactional and associated nature of the human experience, acknowledge their own imbricated identities as variable and yet resolute foci within the contextualizing fields of environing others. Such focus-field agents have to be understood as irreducibly transactional, consciously shaping and being shaped in their vital patterns of relations. At the end of the day, such agency can only be negotiated through established habits of commitment and deference. While such agency is necessarily passive in the archaic sense of invariably "suffering" the actions of others, it must at the same time find the right balance in also being self-conscious, animated, purposeful, and projective. Simply put, morally responsible lives can only be lived through a flexible responsiveness in the activities that come to define our identities.

And the final abstention for Confucius is refraining from being self-absorbed. Critically self-aware agency that is irreducibly social cannot afford to be egoistic or self-obsessed. Such focus-field agents as they become increasingly enculturated through the semiotic processes and symbolic competencies that shape them in their associations, develop their own inflected and reflexive sense of themselves out of their *intra*-subjective relations with others. Such hylozoistic agents—at once psychic and profoundly physical—certainly live their many roles through their discursive, vital, and carnal bodies. But as they strive to achieve personal coherence in the changing configuration of their equally organic physical and social relations, such bodies have a porous membrane that is continually internalizing, incorporating and embodying their experience as integral to their evolving identities. Such focus-field agents must exercise their cultivated capacity to be responsive to their environments, while at the same time exhibiting that quality of a relationally-defined autonomy that comes with the absence of coercion in the activities they share with others. Such a relational autonomy is the direct consequence of collaborative lives lived within these environments in which the values and purposes of a web of collaborators become coincident with one's own.

14.38 子路宿於石門。晨門曰:"奚自?"子路曰:"自孔氏。"曰:"是知其不可而爲之者與?"

III. THE *ANALECTS* (*LUNYU* 論語): A BASIC CONFUCIAN VOCABULARY

Zilu spent the night at Stone Gate. The morning gatekeeper asked him, "Where have you come from?"

"From the residence of Confucius." replied Zilu.

"Isn't he the person who keeps trying although he knows it is all in vain?" asked the gatekeeper.

Comment: There are many passages in the *Analects* in which we are told by Confucius himself and by others who know of him that the times are not amenable to his teachings, and that he is thus doomed to a life of simmering frustration. Although Confucius enjoyed great popularity as a teacher and many of his students found their way into political office, his enduring disillusionment was that he personally achieved only marginal influence in the practical politics of the day. As a *philosophe* rather than a theoretical philosopher, he wanted to be actively involved in the improvement of the human condition through the production of the social and political intelligence needed to make a difference. Although there were many occasions on which important political figures sought his services and advice during his years in his home state of Lu, he held only minor offices at court. When finally Confucius was appointed as police commissioner late in his career, his advice was not heeded, and the court of Lu did not treat him with appropriate courtesy. Early in his career Confucius had made several brief trips to neighboring states, but late in his life having been mistreated in the performance of court sacrifices at home, he determined to take his message on the road and spent more than a decade as an itinerant counselor. This passage might be the record of an event in this late adventure.

13.10 子曰: "苟有用我者。期月而已可也，三年有成。"

The Master said, "If someone were to make use of me in the offices of governing, in the course of one year I could make a difference, and in three years I would really have something to show for it."

Comment: This wishful reflection might well come from the period of a disappointed Confucius traversing the states of the Central Plain in vain as an itinerant counselor. These were troubled times, and there was a great adventure and much danger in offering his wisdom to the competing political and military leaders of his day. In his fifties he traveled widely, and on several occasions remembered in the *Analects* found himself in mortal danger (9.5).

14.35 子曰："莫我知也夫！"子貢曰："何爲其莫知子也？"子曰："不怨天，不尤人。下學而上達。知我者，其天乎！"

The Master sighed, saying, "No one appreciates me!"

Zigong replied, "Why doesn't anyone appreciate you, Sir?"

The Master said, "I don't hold any ill-will against *tian* 天 nor blame other people. I study what is near at hand and aspire to what is lofty. It is only *tian* 天 who appreciates me!"①

Comment: Confucius on his extensive travels was no more successful in securing preferment abroad than he was at his home in the state of Lu. He eventually returned to Lu and lived out his last years as a counselor of the lower rank and, according to later accounts, continued his compilation of the classics. We can only surmise that Confucius left this life a few years later in 479 BCE as a disappointed if not exasperated teacher who was never able to find the high political office he desperately sought in his best efforts to really make a difference in the world.

14.39 子擊磬於衛。有荷蕢而過孔氏之門者，曰："有心哉！擊磬乎！"既而曰："鄙哉！硜硜乎！莫己知也，斯己而已矣。深則厲，淺則揭。"子曰："果哉！末之難矣。"

The Master while in the state of Wei was playing on the stone chimes. Someone toting his baskets and passing by the gate of Confucius's residence, exclaimed, "How heavy-hearted is this playing of the stones!" With the piece coming to an end, the person continued, "How crude is this stubborn

---

① Compare *Daodejing* 70 in which this same phenomenon of the wisest among people being overlooked is given expression within the Daoist context:

吾言甚易知，甚易行。天下莫能知，莫能行。……知我者希，則我者貴。是以聖人被褐懷玉。

What I have to say is very easy to understand

And is very easy to carry out,

Yet there is no one in the world who is able to understand it

And no one who is able to put it into practice....

But even if those who understand me are rare,

I am to be highly prized.

Thus it is that sages dress in burlap

Yet conceal jade in their bosom.

qing-qing-ing! If there is no one who appreciates you, just give it up!
  'If the water is deep, you take the plunge,
  If it is shallow, you lift your skirts.'"
  The Master remarked, "That would certainly make an end of it! And it would be so easy too!"

Comment: This passage might recall the event recorded in 3.24 and *Mencius* 6B6 in which Confucius precipitously and with indignation resigned from the office as police commissioner in the state of Lu, and set out to tour the other political centers on the Central Plain in search of employment. The person who hears Confucius performing his music is a singularly interesting character who as a peasant farmer can cite the *Book of Songs* from memory. Even though the stone chimes is an instrument played in the court orchestra that would reflect the rank and breeding of Confucius as the player, the farmer has no compunction in pronouncing judgment on Confucius's performance. The appearance of such scholar-recluses reprimanding the persistent and tenacious Confucius is a familiar trope (3.24, 14.32, 14.38, 18.5, 18.6, 18.7). The *Songs* 34 is being interpreted here to say intelligence requires us to adapt to the times rather than being obstinate in pursuing a hopeless mission. And Confucius's response is what we might expect: While it is easy enough to give up, I will never relent (9.19).

17.5 公山弗擾以費畔，召，子欲往。子路不說，曰：" 末之也已，何必公山氏之之也。" 子曰：" 夫召我者而豈徒哉？ 如有用我者，吾其爲東周乎？ "
  Gongshan Furao was plotting rebellion using the Bi stronghold, and summoned Confucius to join him. Confucius wanted to go.
  Zilu was upset, and said to Confucius, "Even if we have nowhere else to turn, why on earth must we go to this man Gongshan?"
  The Master replied, "How could this person who is summoning me be doing so for no reason? If there were someone who would use me, I would give him a 'Zhou of the east.'"

Comment: Here as elsewhere we find a frustrated Confucius so eager for political office that it clouds his judgment. The intrepid Zilu is not going to allow Confucius to do the wrong thing. It is significant that Confucius consistently takes the early Zhou dynasty as his inspiration in his reverie on exercising proper governance.
  There are different versions of this event. For example, this story as

reported in the *Zuo Commentary to the Spring and Autumn Annals* has Gongshan Furao revolting against Lu, but the report does not include his calling Confucius to join him. In other accounts, at the time of this revolt, Confucius is Minister of Justice, and sends forces to defeat Gongshan. Bi was a magistrate in service to the Ji family who had usurped the ducal power in Lu, and had joined forces with Yang Huo, a steward to the Ji family who was the leader of the insurrection. When Confucius's life was threatened in the state of Chen, it was apparently because of a physical similarity he bore to this rebellious minister Yang Huo (7.23, 12.5).

17.7 佛肸召，子欲往。子路曰："昔者由也聞諸夫子曰：'親於其身爲不善者，君子不入也。' 佛肸以中牟畔，子之往也，如之何！" 子曰："然。有是言也。不曰堅乎，磨而不磷；不曰白乎，涅而不緇。吾豈匏瓜也哉？焉能繫而不食？"

Bixi summoned Confucius, and Confucius wanted to go to him. Zilu said, "In past I have heard you say, Master, 'Exemplary persons (*junzi* 君子) will have nothing to do with someone who personally behaves badly.' Bixi is plotting rebellion having taken the Zhongmou stronghold. How could you justify going to assist him?"

"You are right." said the Master. "It is as you say. But is it not also said, 'In the case of what is hardest, grinding will not wear it thin.' Is it not said, 'In the case of what is whitest, dying will not turn it black.' Am I just some kind of gourd? How can I allow myself to be strung up on the wall and not be eaten?"

Comment: 17.5 and 17.7 allude to historical occasions on which Confucius is so frustrated from having been excluded from political office that he is tempted to throw his lot in with some characters of questionable reputation who are undertaking projects of questionable political legitimacy. There is some dramatic effect in the fact that Confucius not only thinks better of the invitations, but is repeatedly restrained from joining these conspiracies by his most impulsive and martial student, Zilu. The only way we can justify Confucius's positive response to these solicitations is that the ducal powers of Lu had long been usurped by powerful families and ministers, and he was keen to see the power restored to the rightful ruler.

Confucius certainly relents, but he still argues that with an upright person such as himself—the hardest and the whitest—even if he were to join in the revolt, he could not be tarnished by those whose motivations are not as pure. And he further laments that his destiny seems to be like that of a useless gourd hanging on the wall rather than something that can be put into productive service.

The gourd metaphor comes alive when we remember the exchange between Hui Shi and Zhuangzi in *Zhuangzi* 1. It is because gourds are seen to be of little use that Zhuangzi can criticize his good friend for not having the ingenuity and imagination to find a way to make use of them.

15.1 衛靈公問陳於孔子。孔子對曰："俎豆之事，則嘗聞之矣；軍旅之事，未之學也。"明日遂行。

Duke Ling of Wei asked Confucius about military formations. Confucius replied, "I have heard something about the arrangement of ritual vessels, but I have never studied military matters." On the following day, he left the state.

Comment: In a world beset with military intrigue that is a prelude to the carnage of the Warring States period, Confucius makes it clear that unlike so many of the other itinerant philosophers, his counsel has to do with proper governance rather than winning wars.

The *Zuo Commentary to the Spring and Autumn Annals* Ai 11 has a related passage:

孔文子之將攻大叔也，訪於仲尼。仲尼曰："胡簋之事，則嘗學之矣；甲兵之事，未之聞也。" 退，命駕而行，曰："鳥則擇木，木豈能擇鳥？" 文子遽止之，曰："圉豈敢度其私，訪衛國之難也？" 將止。魯人以幣召之，乃歸。

Kong Wenzi was about to attack Taishu, and went to Confucius for advice. Confucius said to him, "I have studied the use of ritual vessels, but I have never learned anything about arms." He withdrew, and ordered his carriage harnessed for his departure, saying, "The bird chooses the tree on which to roost; since when can the tree choose the bird?" Wenzi hurriedly detained him, saying, "I was not asking your advice for my own sake, but to prevent the troubles that are befalling our state of Wei." Confucius was going to stay, but when an envoy from Lu came with a ceremonial monetary gift to summon him, he returned home.

See *Analects* 5.15 for another reference to this same Kong Wenzi. Duke Ling asks Confucius explicitly about "battle formations" (*chen*

陳). There is a paronomastic relationship between the term being used here *chen* 陳 that actually means "displaying, laying out" and the cognate term *zhen* 陣 meaning battle formation. That is, "battle formation" (*zhen* 陣) is defined as "displaying" (*chen* 陳), suggesting the most important function of carrying a sword and scabbard, or parading in battle formation, is making an overt display of prowess that will effectively deter an enemy. In the *Sun Bin Art of Warfare* where this notion of fixed battle formation becomes a major theme, *chen* 陳 is used throughout as a loan character for *zhen* 陣. Here Confucius is playing on this association to correlate the deployment of troops with the laying out and displaying of ritual vessels.

17.1 陽貨欲見孔子，孔子不見，歸孔子豚。孔子時其亡也，而往拜之，遇諸塗。謂孔子曰："來！予與爾言。"曰："懷其寶而迷其邦，可謂仁乎？"曰："不可。""好從事而亟失時，可謂知乎？"曰："不可。""日月逝矣，歲不我與。"孔子曰："諾。吾將仕矣。"

Yang Huo wanted Confucius to come and see him, and when Confucius would not oblige, Yang Huo sent him a suckling pig as a gift. Confucius, waiting for a time when Yang Huo would not be home, went to acknowledge the gift. Confucius however happened to meet up with Yang Huo on the road.

Yang Huo called out to Confucius, "Come over here! I have something I would like to speak to you about." Continuing, Yang Huo said, "Can you call someone consummate in his conduct (*ren* 仁) who hoards his treasure of talent while his country loses its way? I should say not. Can you call someone wise (*zhi* 知) who has always wanted to serve in office but who repeatedly misses the opportunity to do so? I should say not. The days and months are passing; the years will not wait for us."

Confucius replied, "Alright, alright. I will serve in office then."

Comment: Yang Huo was the chief steward of the Ji household. Just as the Ji household had usurped the ducal power of the state of Lu, Yang Huo was plotting to usurp it once again by wresting it from the hands of the Ji family. Given Confucius's stature in the state and his reputation for being incorruptible, Yang Huo was keen to win his allegiance. Confucius of course was in the double bind of wanting to support neither the usurping Ji family nor Yang Huo's equally indefensible machinations.

Yang Huo's ploy in presenting Confucius with this gift was that ritual obligation required Confucius to call upon him to thank him. Confucius looks to counter Yang Huo's move with a similar ruse, but he is undone by running into Yang Huo on the road. Yang Huo's analogy that correlates Confucius's talents with a piece of hoarded treasure remembers Zigong's analogy of an exquisite piece of jade that has been stored away for safekeeping in 9.13:

子貢曰:"有美玉於斯, 韞匵而藏諸? 求善賈而沽諸?" 子曰: "沽之哉! 沽之哉! 我待賈者也。"

Zigong said, "We have an exquisite piece of jade here—should we box it up and put it away for safe keeping, or should we try to get a good price for it and sell it off?"

The Master replied, "Sell it! By all means, sell it! I am just waiting for the right price!"

And Yang Huo's definition of wisdom as public service reminds us of a similar definition given by Confucius in 12.22. A fuller and yet different report on this Yang Huo encounter occurs in *Mencius* 3B7. For the historical details, see the account in the *Zuo Commentary to the Spring and Autumn Annals* (cf. Legge, *Chinese Classics*, Vol. 5, pp. 765ff).

9.9 子曰: "鳳鳥不至, 河不出圖, 吾已矣夫! "

The Master said, "The auspicious phoenix does not appear; the Yellow River does not yield up its magical chart. All is lost with me!"

Comment: In his waning years, Confucius who had devoted his life to the mission of lifting the world out of precipitous decline through the inspiration provided by the Zhou ritual order, expresses his frustration. The phoenix was a bird associated with the rule of Shun portending the arrival of this sage-king. And the magical chart was a drawing by Fu Xi inspired by a dragon that had emerged from the Yellow River. The phoenix and the magical chart were thus auspicious symbols that had appeared with the arrival of civilization itself. For the now aged Confucius, the possibility of a cultural renaissance was a quickly fading dream.

14.29 子貢方人。子曰: "賜也賢乎哉? 夫我則不暇。"

Zigong was given to judging other people. The Master said, "It is because Zigong is of such superior character himself that he has time for this. I myself have none."

Comment: While the *Analects* certainly celebrates the person of Confucius, it is a long way from hagiography. The modesty and humility of Confucius is one of his most endearing characteristics, but there are also several examples in the text of a critical Confucius's droll sense of humor. While Confucius is self-deprecating, he makes no secret of the high standards he demands of himself, and of his protégés as well. With the one exception of Yan Hui, Confucius seems loath to offer any kind of compliments to his students. There are anonymous passages in the text where the students are listed as *dexing* 德行 "excelling in their conduct" and *yanyu* 言語 "excelling in eloquence" (11.3 echoed in *Mencius* 2A2) but other places also where they are characterized most unkindly (11.18): 柴也愚，參也魯，師也辟，由也喭 Zigao is obtuse; Zeng is thick; Zhuansun is biased; Zilu is rough and rude. Confucius as a teacher is a hard taskmaster who is often hypercritical of his students. See 5.4, 5.10, 5.11, 11.3, 11.16, 11.17, 11.19, 11.22, 11.26, 16.1, 17.21.

17.4 子之武城，聞弦歌之聲。夫子莞爾而笑，曰:"割雞焉用牛刀?"子游對曰:"昔者偃也聞諸夫子曰:'君子學道則愛人，小人學道則易使也。'"子曰:"二三子! 偃之言是也。前言戲之耳。"

The Master, on approaching the town of Wucheng, heard the sounds of stringed instruments and singing. He smiled, saying, "Why would someone want to use an ox cleaver to kill a chicken?"

Ziyou responded, "In past I have heard you say, Master: 'Exemplary persons (*junzi* 君子) who study the proper way (*dao* 道) truly love others while petty persons who do so are much easier to employ.'"

The Master replied, "My young friends, what Ziyou has said is right. What I was saying was just in fun."

Comment: From 6.14 we learn that Ziyou is the magistrate of this town of Wucheng, a small military fortification in Lu. If Confucius's student Zixia errs on the side of book learning and Zilu is too impetuous, Ziyou seems to have emphasized the formal side of the Confucian teachings—the rites and rituals—at the expense of warmth and good humor. A good example is 19.12 where Ziyou is critical of those students of Zixia who are engaged in the trivial occupations of housekeeping when he thinks they should be getting on to the serious business of the rituals and music.

Confucius's criticism seems to be one of proportion: that is, Ziyou is bringing a string quartet to a picnic. Confucius would allow that just as Zixia's students should begin at the beginning by learning competence in everyday housekeeping affairs before embarking on the higher goal of becoming proficient in rites and music, Ziyou too should make sure his people have what they need in their daily lives before introducing them to high culture. Confucius seems to be saying that Ziyou is educating the ordinary townspeople under his charge in the niceties of rituals and music way beyond their needs, and is then making a show of it.

Ziyou's seemingly wounded response is to justify his conduct by citing something Confucius himself has said in past. Ziyou's point is that in his best efforts to be exemplary in his conduct he has tried to express his proper love for the people by educating them in the important and difficult matters of mastering ritual and music rather than by taking some easy way out. In the end, Confucius seems contrite in offering his apologies for having hurt Ziyou's feelings.

17.20 孺悲欲見孔子，孔子辭以疾。將命者出戶，取瑟而歌。使之聞之。

Ru Bei sought a meeting with Confucius, but Confucius declined to entertain him, feigning illness. Just as the envoy carrying Ru Bei's message was about to depart, Confucius got out his lute and sang a song, making sure that the messenger heard him.

Comment: This somewhat humorous anecdote reflects a Confucius who, understanding the very personal nature of music, uses his own performance of it to send a curt message to Ru Bei. All we know of Ru Bei is that he appears in the *Record of Rituals* (*Liji* 禮記) 21.41/113/12 where he is sent to Confucius from the court by Duke Ai to learn about mourning rituals. What we might surmise from this passage is that Ru Bei although having some status in the court, is still presumptuous in calling on Confucius. If Ru Bei wants to seek an audience with Confucius, he should follow the proper protocols. Confucius, his teacher in such etiquette, chooses this novel way of chastening him.

17.16 子曰："古者民有三疾，今也或是之亡也。古之狂也肆，今之狂也蕩；古之矜也廉，今之矜也忿戾；古之愚也直，今之愚也詐而已矣。"

The Master said, "In the old days, the common people had three faults that people of today have managed to do away with. Of old, rash people were merely reckless, but nowadays they have managed to overcome all restraint. Of old, proud people were merely smug, but nowadays they are quarrelsome and easily provoked. Of old, obtuse people were only frank and direct, but nowadays they have become nothing less than scammers."

Comment: More humor. Confucius is being facetious in his criticism of the ordinary people of his time, saying obliquely that society in general has gone from bad to worse. One of Confucius's main frustrations was his failure to be appointed to political office where he might have had some influence in elevating the quality of the lives of the people. This concern was animated by his feeling that society in his own time in the absence of a strong ritual structure had become thoroughly decadent. Not only was the contemporary population inferior to that of ancient times in their moral standing, but even what could be identified as the faults of those earlier people had become more acute in their present iteration.

III.18 A Family-Centered Religiousness (*tian* 天)

11.12 季路問事鬼神。子曰："未能事人，焉能事鬼？" 敢問死。曰："未知生，焉知死？"

Zilu asked how to serve the spirits and the gods. The Master replied, "Not yet being able to serve other people, how could you be able to serve the spirits?"

He said, "May I ask about death?" The Master replied, "Not yet understanding life, how could you understand death?"

Comment: For some interpreters, Confucius's reticence to hold forth on the spiritual world is a clear indication of his commitment to a kind of secular humanism. This humanistic reading is reinforced by a second passage 6.22 in the *Analects* when Fan Chi asks Confucius about "wisdom." Confucius does not attempt to formulate the kind of generic, formal definition of virtues such as "justice" and "courage" that are familiar to us from the Platonic dialogues. Rather he exhorts Fan Chi as this person Fan Chi to address his own problem of getting his priorities right:

務民之義，敬鬼神而遠之，可謂知矣。
To devote yourself to what is most appropriate (*yi* 義) for the people, and

to show respect for the ghosts and spirits while keeping them at a distance can be called wisdom.

Given the speculative assumptions that have such a central place in our own Abrahamic beliefs, this counsel to pursue a practical efficacy in one's relations with others while keeping ghosts and spirits at a distance has persuaded many commentators that Confucius has a lack of interest in, if not an aversion to, the demands of a cultivated religiousness.

We need to remember the close association the character for "optimal appropriateness" (*yi* 義) had historically with the practice of sacrifice. It alludes to a communal decorum necessary to perform such ceremonies properly (see the *Lexicon* entry). The important connection between the two phrases in this passage is their focus on family and community-centered religious practices that certainly respect but at the same time marginalize the spiritual world.

In interpreting such passages, while some would ascribe to Confucius a disenchanted humanism, we might also look for another reading more consistent with his own family-centered religious assumptions. We might conclude, for example, that for Confucius, real religiousness rather than lying in the reverence for and supplication to remote supernatural entities, is to be found in cultivating bonds much nearer to home. Such an alternative religiousness is manifested as a shared, family-centered spirituality to be achieved in aspiring to live inspired lives within our families and communities as they are informed by ancestral reverence. We have seen that for Confucius, growth is centered in a commitment to personal cultivation within intimate family and community relations, a process that then extends outward radially and reflexively to the cosmic totality. There is an interpenetrating center and periphery, where the most self-consciously intense feelings have the greatest extended reach and influence, and where this inclusiveness is refracted back to strengthen one's own personal resolution.

More concretely, we might infer that for Confucius, there is a direct and inseparable link between the self-conscious deference, veneration, and gratitude expressed within the moral life at home, and the quiet, reassuring spirituality we associate with the expression of reverence for the ancestors and with natural piety. Or said more simply, such Confucian religiousness is nothing other than the sense of cosmic belonging that is inspired by our achieved sense of felt worth within our most immediate and intimate relations.

In his reflections on the meaning of death in classical China broadly, David Keightley allows that death was perceived as "unproblematic." Of course, his claim is not that the end of life was approached by people free of any fear and trepidation. He means rather that death was not considered unnatural, perverse, or horrible. Chinese "natural" death is contrasted with the enormity and unnaturalness of death in the Judeo-Christian tradition, where such mortality is conceived as divine animus meted out for human disobedience. While there is an uneasiness manifested in Chinese folk religion visions of the "Yellow Springs" (*huangquan* 黄泉, *diyu* 地獄) as a name for the netherworld, there is a marked absence of the morbidity, gloom, and tragedy we would associate with the Greek, Roman, and medieval European conceptions of death.[①]

7.21 子不語怪，力，亂，神。

The Master had nothing to say about strange happenings, the use of force, disorder, or the spirits.

Comment: In 9.4 Confucius is described as being disinclined to make conjectures (*wuyi* 毋意). In particular, he seems to be reluctant to speculate about the world of the strange and supernatural, and seems to find his own kind of religiousness closer to home. What he does speak about at great length is a kind of spirituality if not sacredness that emerges within community lived through ritualized roles and practices. If the etymology of religion (L. *religare*) does actually mean "to bind tightly," then *li* 禮 would seem to be the key term for understanding such family-centered religiousness, serving as the social grammar and producing those meaningful bonds that reinforce the strength of the communal fabric. *Li* 禮 begins from a ritualized devotion to the family and lineage, and then extends to sacralize our roles and relations in community more broadly. When we pursue

---

[①] David Keightley, "Early Civilization in China: Reflections on How it Became Chinese," *Heritage of China: Contemporary Perspectives on Chinese Civilization*, ed. Paul S. Ropp, Berkeley: University of California Press, 1990. See also Roger T. Ames, "War, Death and Ancient Chinese Cosmology: Thinking Through the Thickness of Culture," *Mortality in Traditional Chinese Thought*, ed. Amy Olberding and Philip J. Ivanhoe, Albany: State University of New York Press, 2011.

optimal appropriateness (*yi* 義) in our transactions with others, we are again remembering the history of this term and the decorum in communal sacrifices it denotes.

On such an understanding of religiousness, the traditional Chinese Spring Festival alive and well today should be understood as a profoundly religious event. We witness in this largest regularized migration of any population in human history, a phenomenon wherein the predominantly immigrant urban centers disgorge their populations. Almost every person in the country using any manner of transportation available returns to their native place for an extended period of serious familial and indeed moral "re-creation." This recreation is engaged in by a population who, through a lifetime of moral education, have had reverence for family, elders, teachers, and communities inculcated into them. They take their "native place" (*laojia* 老家) as a prime defining factor in their personal identity, and "family reverence" (*xiao* 孝) as their prime moral imperative. Acting upon this family reverence, people everywhere return to their roots to renew their most intimate relations, thereby regenerating the tensile strength within family relations that will allow them to return to the cities several weeks later, and to carry on for another year.

7.35 子疾病，子路請禱。子曰："有諸？"子路對曰："有之。誄曰：'禱爾于上下神祇。'"子曰："丘之禱久矣。"

The Master was gravely ill, and Zilu asked if he could pray on his behalf. The Master said, "Is this done?"

Zilu replied, "Yes, indeed. The invocation says that 'we pray for you to the gods of the heavens above and the earth below.'"

The Master said, "Then I have already been praying for myself for a long time now."

Comment: The ardent Zilu, worried at the gravity of Confucius's illness, wants to recommend the ailing Confucius to the gods with his solemn prayers. Confucius's response is simple: Everything he has done throughout his entire life has been his very best effort to recommend himself to whatever powers there might be. We come away from such passages with the understanding that Confucius's sense of religiousness has more to do with his having lived a morally meaningful life within family and community than with gods, giving him a feeling of worth and belonging. He has done his best. Supplication to the unknown and anticipation of some afterlife have little meaning for Confucius, even during his last moments.

11.23 子畏於匡，顏淵後。子曰："吾以女爲死矣。" 曰："子在，回何敢死？"

When the Master was surrounded in Kuang, Yan Hui had fallen behind. The Master said to him, "I had given you up for dead."

"While you are still living," Yan Hui replied, "how could I dare to die?"

Comment: Yan Hui with this comment reveals that Confucius is a father figure for him, and true to the spirit of family reverence (*xiao* 孝), he could not countenance departing this world while Confucius still needs his services. Again, ironically the inclusion of this passage in the text has the dramatic effect of remembering that Yan Hui in fact died young. For the record of this incident of being surrounded in Kuang, see 9.5. Cf. also 17.1.

11.9 顏淵死。子曰："噫！天喪予！天喪予！"

When Yan Hui died, the Master cried, "Oh my! *Tian* 天 is the ruin of me! *Tian* 天 is the ruin of me!"

Comment: Confucius is profoundly vague himself when he refers to terms such as *tian* 天 that are already in themselves vague references. Here the term seems to be merely an exclamation of his powerlessness over the ineluctable force of circumstances rather than communicating any specific religious significance. *Tian* 天 especially in its association with the term "the propensity of things" (*ming* 命) seems to be a reference to those things in a life over which we have the least control. In any case, on such matters we always run the risk of saying more on Confucius's behalf than he himself might have wished to say.

11.10 顏淵死，子哭之慟。從者曰："子慟矣。" 曰："有慟乎？非夫人之爲慟而誰爲！"

When Yan Hui died, the Master grieved for him with sheer abandon. His followers cautioned, "Sir, you grieve with such abandon." "I grieve with abandon?" the Master replied. "If I don't grieve with abandon for Yan Hui, then for whom?"

Comment: When Yan Hui died, his father who was also a student of Confucius was aware of Confucius's deep affection for this extraordinary student, and asked Confucius to dispose of his carriage in order to provide

Yan Hui with an outer coffin (11.8). Again, the other students of Confucius knowing of this special relationship between the Master and Yan Hui likewise wanted to have a lavish burial for him (11.11). In both instances, Confucius refuses the requests because he is persuaded that Yan Hui is shown the greatest degree of respect not with undue extravagance, but by following proper ritual protocols that would preclude such excesses. Even though Confucius would insist on following these formal conventions, he is at the same time inconsolable in his expression of grief. In such ritual matters, the ultimate measure is sincerity. Confucius's treatment of Yan Hui's death is a portrait of him being true to his word when he says in 3.4: 禮，與其奢也，寧儉；喪，與其易也，寧戚。 "In aspiring to ritual propriety, it is better to be modest than extravagant; in mourning, it is better to express real grief than to worry over formal details."

10.11 雖疏食菜羹，瓜祭，必齊如也。
Even with a simple meal of coarse grains and vegetable gruel, Confucius invariably made an offering, and did so with solemnity.

Comment: Such a description of Confucius sharing his food with his ancestors underscores the centrality of a sense of ritual propriety pervasive in the most ordinary events of his daily life. This family-centered religiousness is a holistic form of religiousness, a "way of life" rather than just one discrete element within the cultural sensorium. There are the "big moment" sacrifices (which are certainly important) but perhaps even more significant is the keen and persistent awareness of one's place in the intergenerational transmission of a cultural and genealogical tradition expressed through a deferential attitude in everything one does.

8.21 子曰："禹，吾無間然矣。菲飲食，而致孝乎鬼神；惡衣服，而致美乎黻冕；卑宮室，而盡力乎溝洫。禹，吾無間然矣。"
The Master said, "With the sage-king Yu, I can find no flaw. He was simple in his food and drink and yet was generous in his offerings to the gods and to the spirits of his ancestors. He wore coarse clothing and yet was lavish in his ceremonial robes and cap. He lived amidst the humblest circumstances and yet devoted all of his strength to the construction of drainage canals and irrigation ditches. With Yu, I can find no flaw."

Comment: Yu was the founding emperor of the Xia dynasty. And although there is no written record that dates from this time some four millennia ago, the detail with which his reign is remembered speaks to the power of tradition and its oral transmission. During the reigns of Emperors Yao and Shun, the Central Plain of China was constantly being inundated with floods, impeding the growth of this early civilization. Yu inherited the task of taming the floods from his father, and making a careful study of the hydrography of the world, he developed a system for water control including irrigation canals and dredging protocols that brought the waters to heel, and made the subsequent prosperity of the Yellow River basin and beyond a possibility. He is remembered in this passage and elsewhere as a selfless emperor who both lived and looked like an indentured laborer when he was working on the water projects, and who took on the pomp and regalia of the court only as required in performing the ancestral rites to fulfil the weighty responsibility of his station.

9.5 子畏於匡。曰："文王既沒，文不在茲乎？天之將喪斯文也，後死者不得與於斯文也；天之未喪斯文也，匡人其如予何？"

When the Master was surrounded in the town of Kuang, he said, "With King Wen long dead, does not our cultural heritage (*wen* 文) reside here in us? If *tian* 天 were going to destroy this legacy, we latecomers would not have had access to it. If *tian* 天 is not going to destroy this culture, what can the people of Kuang do to me!"

Comment: Confucius had left the state of Wei and was on route to Chen when he passed through the town of Kuang. The people of Kuang had recently suffered injury at the hands of Yang Huo, the rebellious chief steward of the Ji family. The Ji family had usurped the ducal powers in the state of Lu, and Yang Huo was plotting with other officials to challenge the family itself on its hold on power. Confucius being from Lu and resembling Yang Huo in his appearance, was mistaken for him. For this historical incident, see also *Analects* 11.23, 17.1, and *Mencius* 3B7.

The self-understanding of Confucius in broad strokes is that he self-consciously sees himself as continuing an antique tradition reaching back into the second millennium BCE. As he says in 3.14: 周監於二代，郁郁乎文哉！吾從周 "The Zhou dynasty looked back to the Xia and Shang dynasties. Such a wealth of culture! I follow the Zhou." This Zhou culture transmitted through the many generations who have come before has been bequeathed to the people of his own day.

III. THE *ANALECTS* (*LUNYU* 論語): A BASIC CONFUCIAN VOCABULARY

In this passage, Confucius is playing on the name of one of the founders of the Zhou dynasty, King Wen (or King "Culture") and the Zhou "cultural" legacy. Throughout the *Analects*, Confucius is portrayed as embracing as his sacred mission the responsibility to rejuvenate and perpetuate the highly ritualized culture inherited from the early Zhou dynasty some 500 years earlier. One distinctive element in this cultural tradition was the ancestral/religious/cultural/natural idea of *tian* 天, conventionally translated into English as "Heaven."

As it reports specifically in *Focusing the Familiar* 17, *tian*'s 天 bounty has been and continues to be shared with the human world in direct proportion to the achieved virtuosity of those in positions of social and political authority. Appealing to the paronomastic relationship between the homophonic terms "virtuosity" (*de* 德) and "getting, gaining" (*de* 得), we can say that there is a contrapuntal relationship between human virtuosity and the largesse humankind receives from *tian* 天.

The philosophical and religious notion of *tian* 天 is profoundly recondite in the Chinese classics, with language such as "distant" (*yuan* 遠) and "dark" (*xuan* 玄) being invoked to describe it. The fact that the Chinese tradition itself has not realized any real precision in the vocabulary of a distinctively Chinese family-centered religiousness has facilitated a sustained misreading of its general import by many Western interpreters. Indeed "religion" as it is understood among contemporary scholars broadly is a conception of Western "religion" that either collapses the Confucianism into its ranks as in the 1893 World Parliament of Religions, or ignores the Confucian alternative form of religiousness altogether.

It is clear that human beings in this relationship derive much benefit from the ancestral/religious/cultural/natural resources denoted by *tian* 天. *Tian* 天 certainly provides human beings with the various environing contexts needed for human flourishing, and serves as an object of cosmic numinosity to revere and to emulate. But given the doctrine of first-order constitutive, internal, and organic relations we discern in this Confucian worldview, we must allow that just as humans are importantly shaped by *tian* 天, *tian* 天 is also in turn shaped in some way and in some degree by human beings. The quality of human flourishing is to be measured by the extent to which *tian* 天 itself is made both different and more because of the human contribution to cosmic order. It is the collaborative, mutually generative relationship between *tian* 天 and the highest order of human beings, the sages, that provides such a stark contrast with the Abrahamic traditions. Indeed, the need to cultivate a "depth of coalescence" (*du* 度) in this *tianren* 天人 relationship can be brought to bear on how we might want to think about "the continuity between and inseparability of the human and the cosmic orders" (*tianrenheyi* 天人合一) and the human transformation of *tian* 天.

19.23 叔孫武叔語大夫於朝，曰："子貢賢於仲尼。"子服景伯以告子貢。子貢曰："譬之宮墻，賜之墻也及肩，窺見室家之好。夫子之墻數仞，不得其門而入，不見宗廟之美，百官之富。得其門者或寡矣。夫子之云，不亦宜乎！"

Shusun Wushu said to the other ministers at court, "Zigong is a better man than Confucius."

Zifu Jingbo reported this to Zigong.

Zigong replied, "Let us take a perimeter wall as our analogy. My wall is shoulder high, so one can catch a glimpse of the charm of the buildings inside. The Master's wall, on the other hand, is massive, rising some twenty or thirty feet in the air. Without gaining entry through the gate, one cannot see the magnificence of the ancestral temple or the lavishness of the estate inside. Since those who gain entry are few indeed, is it at all surprising that the minister speaks as he does?"

Comment: 19.23, 19.24, and 19.25 are of a piece. A stark contrast is struck between the self-understanding of a modest and always humble Confucius painfully aware of his own limitations, and the celebration by his students of a Confucius who as a sage takes on cosmic proportions. As we witness throughout the canonical Confucian texts, they repeatedly correlate these always unique sages with *tian* 天 by characterizing them metaphorically in grand, celestial terms. The vague notion of *tian* 天 is thus brought into focus and made determinate by taking on the visage of a particular human face. There is much textual evidence that sagacity is the ultimate "depth of coalescence" (*du* 度) in the first-order *tianren* 天人 relationship. That is, the best among human beings are nothing less than a co-creative and transformative moral force in the cosmos. In these classical Confucian canons, human sagacity is understood not only as having the capacity to introduce epochal transformations in the human experience, but also as having a transformative influence on the quality of *tian* 天 and an amplificatory effect on the moral meaning of the cosmos broadly.

19.24 叔孫武叔毀仲尼。子貢曰："無以爲也，仲尼不可毀也。他人之賢者，丘陵也，猶可踰也；仲尼，日月也，無得而踰焉。人雖欲自絶，其何傷於日月乎？多見其不知量也！"

    Shusun Wushu spoke disparagingly of Confucius. Zigong responded, "Do not do this! Confucius cannot be disparaged. The superior character of other people is like a mound or a hill that can still be scaled, but Confucius is the sun and moon that no one can climb beyond. When people cut themselves off from the sun and moon, what damage does this do to the sun and moon? It would only demonstrate that such people do not know their own limits."

Comment: Repeatedly throughout the canons the person of Confucius takes on cosmic measure. If Confucius can elevate the worth of human "becomings" by insisting in 15.29 that they "are able to broaden the way," (*rennenghongdao* 人能弘道), we can extend this celebration of humanity by joining Zhu Xi in proclaiming that "the sages can continue and carry out the workings of *tian*" (*shengrennengjitianliji* 聖人能繼天立極).[1]

19.25 陳子禽謂子貢曰："子爲恭也，仲尼豈賢於子乎？" 子貢曰："君子一言以爲知，一言以爲不知，言不可不慎也。夫子之不可及也，猶天之不可階而升也。夫子之得邦家者，所謂立之斯立，道之斯行，綏之斯來，動之斯和。其生也榮，其死也哀，如之何其可及也。"

    Chen Ziqin said to Zigong, "You are only being deferential—how could Confucius be superior in character to you?"

    Zigong replied, "Exemplary persons (*junzi* 君子) must be ever so careful about what they say. On the strength of a word others can deem them either wise (*zhi* 知) or foolish. The Master cannot be matched just as a ladder cannot be used to climb the sky. Were Confucius to have become a head of state or of a clan, it would have illustrated the saying:

    He gave them a place and they took a stand,
    He led them forward and they followed,
    He brought peace and they flocked to him,
    He aroused them and they achieved harmony.
    In life he was glorious,
    And in death he was mourned.

---

[1] See Zhu Xi's 朱熹 preface to his commentary on the *Zhongyong* 中庸章句 in his commentary on the *Four Books* 四書章句集注.

How could anyone be his match?"

Comment: The relationship between *tian* 天 and the human world is fecund and generative, with the challenge for these "two" aspectual worlds to work together collaboratively to broaden and extend the cosmic order in building the connector for their own time and place. With its hypothetical, this passage rehearses the persistent theme of a willing Confucius who, to the profound detriment of his own time, was never given an opportunity to demonstrate how his ideas and his moral influence could change the world. Such change would have to wait upon the transmission of his teaching to later ages.

8.19 子曰:"大哉,堯之爲君也! 巍巍乎! 唯天爲大,唯堯則之。蕩蕩乎! 民無能名焉。巍巍乎! 其有成功也;煥乎,其有文章!"
    The Master said, "How great indeed was Yao as ruler! How majestic! Only *tian* 天 is truly awesome, and only Yao modeled himself upon it. How vast and boundless—the common people could not find words adequate to praise him. How majestic was he in his accomplishments, and how brilliant was he in his cultural achievements."

Comment: Since our conventional words of praise cannot do justice to the magnitude of Yao and his accomplishments, he is described hyperbolically with language usually used to celebrate the grandeur of nature: majestic like the mountains, vast like the oceans, truly awesome like the heavens above. Given that Confucian morality is fundamentally growth in relations, the virtuosity of supreme personalities can only be described in terms of the scale of growth they inspire. And again, the religious aspect of such cultural heroes elevates them by invoking the celestial language of the sun, moon, and stars, and the turning of the seasons. Yao's accomplishments pile up like the sacred mountains and his cultural achievements shine everywhere. Such a description of Yao evokes the familiar mantra used to describe Confucian religiousness as "the continuity between and inseparability of the human and the cosmic orders" (*tianrenheyi* 天人合一).

IV. THE *MENCIUS* (*MENGZI* 孟子): EXTENDING THE VOCABULARY

Mengzi 孟子 or "Master Meng" (4th century BCE) is latinized as "Mencius," and his given name is Meng Ke 孟軻. He was born in the state of Zou (now in modern Shandong province) just a short distance from the birthplace of Confucius. Confucius lived at the end of the Spring and Autumn period (770-476 BCE) and Mencius in the early years of the Warring States period (475-221 BCE). A major change in the century between the death of Confucius and the birth of Mencius was the exponential escalation in internecine violence as the contending states on the central plains vied for empire. Confucius before Mencius had spent a decade during the latter part of his life traveling from state to state as an itinerant counselor, trying to persuade rulers of the wisdom and political effectiveness of his teachings. Mencius followed the Master in this respect, and spent much of his career traveling with a retinue from state to state recommending a form of governance infused with Confucian values as the best way to succeed in the competition for political supremacy. An important turn comes with Mencius's emphasis on the application of Confucian values to the immediate and vital project of proper government. The focus of "consummate conduct" (*ren* 仁), for example, is extended to become "consummate governance" (*renzheng* 仁政). Again, Mencius expands upon Confucius's contrast between an inclusive optimizing "appropriateness" (*yi* 義) and the pursuit of exclusive "personal profit" (*li* 利), but he extends the context from the personal to the political. For this same reason, the doctrine of "the mandate of *tian*" (*tianming* 天命) also becomes a major theme with *tian* 天 making its will known through its people to overthrow an ineffective ruler.

We might fairly describe Mencius's political philosophy as the extension of a Confucian "role ethics" to a "role politics." The argument for Confucian role ethics begins from the focus-field, relationally-constituted understanding of persons and the associative nature of the human narrative in all of its parts. Nothing and no one does anything by themselves. As soon as we ask and then stipulate what kind of association is involved, the morally neutral notion of "association" becomes the normative project of living a particular familial, social, or political role as mother, neighbor, or ruler. A politics of roles begins from appealing to the narratives of historical and legendary sage-rulers—role models—as a way of defining the role of the political ideal: the True King. As in the teachings of Confucius, the suasive force of the moral ruler is a major factor in the "education by example" provided for the people. Although the various historical sages are all particular and thus unique, the one constant, generic characteristic they share is the responsibility they assume for providing for the welfare of the common people. In addition to appealing to these historical role models, Mencius also repeats his detailed formula for the rule of the True King that includes land reform, division of labor, ecological intelligence in the use of natural resources, and perhaps the most important factor, the people's moral education. Where Confucius is the First Teacher to his students, Mencius might be seen as the First Counselor to those who would rule.

It is fundamental to understanding the *Mencius* as a text that it be read dialectically as taking a philosophical stand against the Mohists who became a major intellectual challenge for the Confucian philosophers over these centuries. The Mohists make morality largely a matter of compliance with external doctrines, elevate the notion of *tian* 天 to serve as an "objective" standard that redefines its relationship with humankind, advocate for austerity in the expenditure of what are limited resources, and promote a kind of populism that challenges Confucian literati elitism.

There are also important differences of emphasis between Mencius and Confucius himself in the project of cultivating moral competence. The *Analects* 1.2, for example makes family feeling the starting point of consummate conduct:

君子務本，本立而道生。孝弟也者，其爲仁之本與？
Exemplary persons (*junzi* 君子) concentrate their efforts on the root, for the root having been properly set, the vision of the moral life (*dao* 道) will grow therefrom. As for family reverence and fraternal responsibility, it is, I suspect, the root of consummate conduct (*ren* 仁).

Confucius places a great deal of emphasis on the love of learning and the personal growth that is achieved through the cultivation of one's own moral character. In the *Analects*, the deepening and even enchanting of the ordinary human experience is made possible through enculturation and living the ritualized life. We are witness to snapshots of the actual narrative of Confucius himself as an object lesson in what it means to become a distinguished and revered role model for the ages.

IV. THE *MENCIUS* (*MENGZI* 孟子): EXTENDING THE VOCABULARY

In the *Mencius* on the other hand, the project of personal cultivation is still a central theme, but the example provided by Confucius himself is in degree superseded by a more abstract and theoretical justification for this regimen of cultivation: the realization of the "natural propensities" (*xing* 性) through making the most of embodied "heartminding" (*xin* 心) within the context of immediate family and community relationships. Broadly speaking, in the interpretive literature, Mencius has come to be widely understood as arguing that human nature is good. That is, it is assumed by many commentators that Mencius is forwarding an *a priori* conception of an abstract, innate, essential human nature, a given, inborn potential for goodness that is then actualized in the life experience.① As this interpretive

---

① In *A Daoist Theory of Chinese Thought*, Hong Kong: Oxford University Press, 1992, Chad Hansen, concerned that "most of Graham's appreciative herd of Mencius worshipers still think that the problems of moral reform dictate Mencius' status-quo solution" (p. 194) argues that Mencius' "innatist" interpretation of *xing* 性 precludes the possibility of moral reform all together. Hansen insists that "The content—the detailed structure of the nature of the moral plant—is not the result of external factors.... Morality is internal in this sense" (p. 174), and hence "There is an absolutely correct thing to do in each situation" (p. 178) because "Nature programs *xin* [heart-and-mind] to generate that action" (p. 177). Hansen summarizes Mencius' innatist position in the following terms:

> We could understand Mencius as arguing that humans have an entire innate moral grammar. That moral grammar enables them to process any morally neutral external structure and produce the morally right line of behavior. But moral rightness has no metaphysical basis other than its situational production by the heart. That would preserve Mencius' claim that morality is metaphysically internal rather than external. (p. 187)

P.J. Ivanhoe, *Ethics in the Confucian Tradition,* Atlanta: Scholars Press, 1990, acknowledges the merit of Angus Graham's novel insistence that "*the proper course of development* defines human nature" (p. 34), but insists that morality is not "existential" in any sense of being dependent upon human choices, but rather is simply "the manifestation of human nature" (p. 33). "Human nature has a specific *content* . . . These different parts are arranged in a very special structure and the shape of this structure emerges as an individual matures" (p. 47).

Benjamin Schwartz, *The World of Thought in Ancient China*, Cambridge, MA: Harvard University Press, 1985, pp. 175, 179 defines the term *xing* 性 as "an innate tendency toward growth or development in a given, predetermined direction" and as "a 'heavenly endowed' or 'heavenly ordained' tendency, directionality, or potentiality of growth in the individual."

Donald Munro, *Concept of Man in Contemporary China, (Continued on next page)*

literature stands, Mencius offers a clear explanation of what we can become as "human *beings*."

Indeed, we need to ask the important question here: Where are we today in our received reading of the *Mencius*? The contemporary philosopher Tang Junyi 唐君毅 has developed a robust interpretation of "native human propensities" (*xing* 性) that rejects such essentialistic claims. And there are Angus Graham's important insights into an alternative, narrative understanding of "native human propensities" (*xing* 性) that explicitly challenges the appropriateness of translating this character as "human nature." But the intervention of such scholars seems to have made little difference in how the *Mencius* continues to be read and understood. Taking Graham as an example, he abandons his own earlier essentialist reading and has provided a relatively full account of a more capacious interpretation of *xing* 性 in his *Disputers of the Tao* and elsewhere.[①] In highlighting the importance of recovering this interpretive context, Graham has been continuing the important work of scholars such as Marcel Granet, Tang Junyi, Fei Xiaotong, and Joseph Needham who have come before him. But his arguments and insights continue to be largely ignored or misunderstood.

Bringing Graham's revisionist reading of Mencius on "native human propensities" (*xing* 性) and our own elaborations on the relationally constituted person into summary form, we might begin by observing that "heartminding" (*xin* 心) is a moral sensorium that, motivated by the prosocial "four inclinations" (*siduan* 四端), references the native physical, social, and cultural conditions of human "becomings" at their incipience as vital matrices of shared family and communal bonds (*renyilizhi* 仁義禮智). For Mencius who locates persons within family and community, these vital bonds incline them toward positive moral growth (*shan* 善) in those discursive roles and relations. These native conditions are not only a generic

---

(Continued from previous page) Ann Arbor: University of Michigan Press, 1979, pp. 19-20, 57 in commenting on the opening passage of the *Zhongyong*:
This means that a person's nature being so decreed, cannot be altered through human action; it is a "given" that exists from birth. The Neo-Confucians also affirmed the fixed character of man's essential nature... The Chinese immediately associate the panhuman with the innate and the innate with the unchangeable.

① This is my argument in "Reconstructing A.C. Graham's Reading of *Mencius* on *xing* 性: A Coda to 'The Background of the Mencian Theory of Human Nature' (1967)," *Having a Word with Angus Graham: At Twenty-five Years into his Immortality*, ed. Carine Defoort and Roger T. Ames, Albany: State University of New York Press, 2018.

description of the pattern of relations of persons as they are born into, live, and grow within the continuing narrative of a mature culture, they are also normative as providing a resource for moral growth in the specific roles we live. Although it is possible through inattention and a lack of effort to lose this capacity for prosocial growth in our relations, such a native predilection inclines us otherwise; if in fact we commit ourselves to living according to the promptings of these native moral propensities that animate the inchoate pattern of our relations, we grow and acquire increasing moral influence within our families and communities.

Again, Mencius's notion of "heartminding" (*xin* 心) defies the familiar dichotomies of cognition and affect, body and mind, agent and action, inner and outer, subject and object, nature and nurture, and so on. Thus, if we want to do justice to the complexity of *xin* 心, rather than translating it simply as "heartmind" that challenges only the first among these many dualisms, we might have to render it as "vital, resolute, and focused bodyheartminding within our field of experience." As such, it denotes a particular focal identity within an extended field of relations, and is thus holographic, with "the myriad things of the world all implicated here in me." The living *xin* 心 is a fundamentally relational and vital narrative, and is only made formal and discrete as a second order abstraction.

"Native human propensities" (*xing* 性) on the other hand is the human propensity to cultivate this native pattern of relations (*xin* 心) and, when we "make the most" of these initial relations (*jinqixin* 盡其心), we are able to realize who we are in our roles within family and community. The cultivation of our *qi* 氣 within the context of our discursive relations (*zhiyan* 知言) is what funds such personal growth and conduces to virtuosity in conduct. By cultivating both the intensity (*zhigang* 至剛) and the resolution (*cheng* 誠) of this *qi* 氣, the *qi* 氣 becomes intentional and deliberate (*zhi* 志). Such *qi* 氣 expressed as purposeful actions is animated by our commitment to achieving optimal appropriateness (*yi* 義) in what we do. And it is the habituation of this optimal appropriateness in our conduct that serves as the most productive disposition we can achieve in our best efforts to make our own surging "flood-like" contribution to the reach and influence (*zhida* 至大) of the proper way (*dao* 道).

In order to distinguish the Mencian *xing* 性 from an essentialist understanding of human nature, we might need to clarify the notion of "potential" and underscore the inseparability of person and context in this Confucian conception of relationally constituted, focus-field persons. The "potential" for becoming human is not something innate or inborn "within" persons exclusive of their family relations. In the first place, there is no such person. Since persons are constituted by their relations, the "potential" of persons in fact emerges *pari passu* from out of the specific, contingent transactions that, in the fullness of time, eventuate in these particular persons located within these particular families achieving their symbiotic identities. Thus, the best sense we can make of "potential" here is that, rather than being something ready-made and then actualized, it evolves collaboratively with the ever-changing circumstances; rather than being generic or universal, it is always unique to the career of relational persons; and rather than existing as an inherent and defining endowment, it can only be known post hoc after the unfolding of the particular narrative.

The argument, then, is that the preponderance of the content of what comes to be our "human propensities" (*renxing* 人性) is acquired rather than given as it is consolidated and expressed in the habitude of "consummatory conduct in roles and relations" (*ren* 仁), "acting optimally appropriate in meaningful relations" (*yi* 義), "realizing propriety in these roles and relations" (*li* 禮), and "acting with intelligence and wisdom" (*zhi* 智). "Natural propensities" (*xing* 性) are no more an essential and inborn given than is "consummatory conduct" (*ren* 仁). Both are a source and a product: that is, *ren* 仁 is the assiduous extension of tentative native conditions in a robust narrative that is informed by habituated patterns of consummate conduct. "Acting with intelligence and wisdom" is not simply applying wisdom to inform a situation, but is rather a condition or quality of acting that arises through an achieved efficacy in one's actions.

In the absence of those biological, psychological, and metaphysical assumptions that lie behind the notion of the discrete individual, it is the continuing cultivation of unity and resolve in the deliberate purposes of physically and socially diffused and yet resolute persons that become the signature of our always unique and increasingly coherent personal identities. There is thus an important and repeated distinction that the *Mencius* and other texts make between simply making retail choices to act according to established conventions on the one hand, and achieving the resolution and focus that consolidates these norms as the structure, unity, and agency of our role-bearing personal identities on the other. And an achieved propriety in the roles and relations of our narrative identities (*li* 禮) is reflected in the symbiotic growth and luster of our lived bodies (*ti* 體). Indeed, just as virtuosity in the roles that we live comes to distinguish us with a sense of worth and felt belonging within our families and communities, so the bodily aspect of this virtuosity is manifested in the warm and glowing complexion of our human physicality.

It is only in giving Mencius's notion of "native human propensities" (*xing* 性) such a narrative reading that we can get past Xunzi's caricature of him as naturalizing morality: that is, as having asserted that simply acting according to what we are born with is good. And we can thus appreciate the extent to which the insights of Mencius are indeed an extension of the intrepid Confucius, demanding as Mencius does assiduous effort in and full commitment to the project of becoming consummately human. Mencius, true to Confucius and to the Zisizi lineage, rejects technical or contrived morality in favor of the spontaneous expression of natural concrete feelings that emerge in familial and communal living. "Spontaneous" in this context, far from suggesting randomness or impetuosity, is being able to get the most out of the possibilities of a situation by having cultivated an appropriate and thus productive disposition. It is the spontaneity of the master carpenter, the calligrapher, the inspired potter; it is the spontaneity of Confucius who in *Analects* 2.4 reports on the consummatory nature of his own cultivation: 六十而耳順，七十而從心所欲，不踰矩 "at sixty my ear was attuned; at seventy I could give my heart-and-mind free rein without overstepping the boundaries."

Mencius's political philosophy is an extension of his moral, social, and political psychology. He develops his central doctrine of "extending kindness and concern" (*tui'en* 推恩) that begins with family feelings and is then projected outward into community, polity, and cosmos. In order for a ruler to take good care of the people, he needs to extend his empathetic family feelings radially outward in an inclusive and accommodating way. Mencius not only exhorts the ruler to take care of the material well-being of his people, but also to give them a share in the pleasures that he by virtue of his station has come to enjoy.

Such a Confucian morality is nothing other than the growth in relationships that is achieved in acting upon one's empathy for others. In this doctrine of "extending kindness and concern" (*tui'en* 推恩), we have a reinforcement of the argument in Mencius's social psychology that the prosocial "four inclinations" (*siduan* 四端) are the starting point of moral growth, situating the inchoate infant within a nexus of family and community relations as its locus. Mencius's doctrine of extension has immediate resonance with Confucius's method for becoming consummate in one's conduct: that is, of "putting oneself in the place of others and then doing one's best" (*zhongshu* 忠恕).

IV.1 An Interpretive Context for Reading the *Mencius*

3A5　墨者夷之因徐辟而求見孟子。孟子曰："吾固願見，今吾尚病，病愈，我且往見，夷子不來！"他日，又求見孟子。孟子曰："吾今則可以見矣。不直，則道不見；我且直之。吾聞夷子墨者，墨之治喪也，以薄爲其道也；夷子思以易天下，豈以爲非是而不貴也；然而夷子葬其親厚，則是以所賤事親也。"徐子以告夷子。夷子曰："儒者之道古之人若保赤子，此言何謂也？之則以爲愛無差等，施由親始。"

The Mohist Yi Zhi sought an interview with Mencius through the good offices of Xu Pi. Mencius replied: "I certainly would like to meet him, but I am not feeling well these days. When I recover, I will go and see him; no need for him to come to me."

On another day, Yi Zhi again came to seek an audience with Mencius, and Mencius said: "I can certainly meet with him today. If he is not advancing in a straight line, he will not see his proper way forward. I want to set him right. I have heard that Yi Zhi is a Mohist. In carrying out their funerals, Mohists take frugality as their standard. Since Yi Zhi thinks to convert the world to this line of thinking, he must believe that any other way simply will not do. And yet in providing a funeral for his parents, Yi Zhi was most lavish. In acting thusly, he must have been doing them a grave disservice."

Master Xu told Yi Zhi what Mencius had said, and Yi Zhi replied: "According to the Confucian way, it says the ancients in treating others acted as though they were 'caring for a newly born baby'." What does this expression mean? It means that they loved the people without distinction, even though they would allow that such love should first be extended to one's own parents."

Comment: A familiar point of contention between the followers of Confucius and those of Mozi was the scale of funeral expenses, where the Confucians see lavish funerals as a way of honoring their seniors, and Mohists see it as a waste of resources better spent on providing everyone with a minimum standard of living. Mencius assumes the Mohist Yi Zhi who is seeking an audience with him must hold this same view about frugality in funerals, and that a conversation with him would be a good occasion for

Mencius to set him right. For Mencius, such a minimalist doctrine is not only a mistaken view, but indeed is an unnatural one. Mencius points out to Master Xu a contradiction in Yi Zhi's own conduct. When his own parents died, in spite of his Mohist beliefs, he naturally gave them a proper funeral, putting Yi Zhi in the awkward position as a Mohist of mistreating his parents by so honoring them.

But Yi Zhi has an answer. He cites an expression from the Confucian classic, the *Book of History*, in which it implies that the ancients treated everyone the same: that is, as if "caring for a newly born baby." For Yi Zhi, this is the same thing as the Mohist doctrine of inclusive care (*jian'ai* 兼愛), although he would allow the first expression of such an inclusive love is properly due to one's own parent.

徐子以告孟子。孟子曰："夫夷子信以爲人之親其兄之子爲若親其鄰之赤子乎？彼有取爾也。赤子匍匐將入井，非赤子之罪也。且天之生物也，使之一本，而夷子二本故也。蓋上世嘗有不葬其親者，其親死，則舉而委之於壑。他日過之，狐狸食之，蠅蚋姑嘬之。其顙有泚，睨而不視。夫泚也，非爲人泚，中心達於面目，蓋歸反虆梩而掩之。掩之誠是也，則孝子仁人之掩其親，亦必有道矣。"徐子以告夷子。夷子憮然爲間曰："命之矣。"

Master Xu reported these words to Mencius, who replied: "Does Yi Zhi believe people really have the same affection for a neighbor's newly born baby that they have for their own nephews? What can we take from his example? Only that we deem the baby in crawling towards the mouth of the well to be innocent. Nature in giving birth to things gives them one root, but Yi Zhi wants to give them two. Now in high antiquity there were certainly cases where people did not bury their parents. When their parents died, they simply carried the bodies out and threw them into a ditch. But then subsequently when passing by, they saw foxes and other animals feeding on them, and flies and other insects consuming them. Perspiration broke out on their brow, and they averted their eyes. This perspiration, far from being for the sake of other people, was the physical expression of their innermost feelings. They then went home and came back with shovels and baskets, and covered the bodies. If burying was really the right thing to do for them, then when we see children who are filial and persons who are consummate in their conduct burying their parents, this must also be the proper way of doing things."

When Master Xu told Yi Zhi what Mencius had said, Yi Zhi replied: "I see his point."

Comment: On being informed of Master Xu's conversation with Yi Zhi, Mencius again appeals to the natural feelings of human beings who love those closer to them than those far away, underscoring the natural logic of the Confucian doctrine of graduated love rather than the inclusive, undifferentiated care for all advocated by the Mohists. In examining Yi Zhi's example of how caring for a baby is a natural instinct that extends to all (alluding perhaps to the famous "child and the well" example in 2A6), Mencius has two answers. First, human beings respond instinctively to a dangerous situation involving a baby not out of love, but because the baby is innocent and helpless. Again, nature in giving life to human beings provides them with one continuous love that begins in family and extends outward in a pattern of differentiation. But Yi Zhi chooses to make two out of one by claiming first we are naturally undifferentiating in our care, but at the same time, we should express this concern first with respect to our parents.

Then Mencius conjures up a story about how human beings out of their innermost feelings have come to recognize the naturalness of loving their parents, and have institutionalized such love through the practices of the funeral and burial. For the Mohists, the argument is that morality is an externally imposed standard; for Mencius and the other classical Confucians, the natural inclinations that activate such a morality come from within. The notions of family reverence (*xiao* 孝) and consummate conduct (*ren* 仁) are simply terms that capture what it is natural for human beings to do.

When Mencius's argument is conveyed to Yi Zhi, he allows that he has been instructed by it.

3B9 公都子曰：" 外人皆稱夫子好辯，敢問何也？" 孟子曰："予豈好辯哉？予不得已也。天下之生久矣，一治一亂。當堯之時，水逆行，氾濫於中國。蛇龍居之，民無所定。下者爲巢，上者爲營窟。《書》曰：'洚水警余。' 洚水者，洪水也。使禹治之，禹掘地而注之海，驅蛇龍而放之菹。水由地中行，江、淮、河、漢是也。險阻既遠，鳥獸之害人者消，然後人得平土而居之。堯、舜既没，聖人之道衰。暴君代作，壞宮室以爲汙池，民無所安息；棄田以爲園囿，使民不得衣食。邪説暴行又作，園囿、汙池、沛澤多而禽獸至。及紂之身，天下又大亂。周公相武王，誅紂伐奄，三年討其君，驅飛廉於海隅而戮之。滅國者五十，驅虎、豹、犀、象而遠之。天下大悦。《書》曰：'丕顯哉，文王謨！丕承哉，武王烈！佑啓我後人，咸以正無缺。' 世衰道微，邪説暴行有作，臣弒其君者有之，子弒其父者有之。孔子懼，作《春秋》。《春秋》，天子之事也。是故孔子曰：'知我者其惟春秋乎！罪我者其惟春秋乎！'"

Master Gongdu said: "Outsiders all describe you as someone who loves to debate. Why is this?"

"How could I be someone who loves to debate?" replied Mencius. "I just have no other option. The world has been around for a long time, and sometimes there is order and sometimes chaos. At the time of Emperor Yao, the waters all reversed their natural courses causing flooding that inundated the central states. Serpents and dragons took up residence among the common people, depriving them of a normal life. Those people who dwelt in the lower reaches made nests while those in the higher areas occupied cave dwellings.

"In the *Book of Documents* it is recorded: 'The floodwaters were a warning to us all.' The floodwaters here refer to the Great Flood, and it was Yu who was sent to bring them under control. Yu dug out channels and led the water to the sea. He drove the serpents and dragons into the wetlands. It was this water as it made its way through the channels that became the Yangtze, the Huai, the Yellow, and the Han rivers. It was only when the various dangers that preempted a settled life receded and the animals of the field who were harmful to humans were eliminated that people could clear the land and take up their lodgings.

"With the passing of Yao and Shun, the ways of the sages fell into decline and one despot after another arose. They razed the buildings and houses to make their ponds, leaving the common people with nowhere to take shelter. They cleared the farmlands to make their parks, robbing the people of their staples. Heretical teachings and violence once again arose, and with a proliferation of parks, ponds, and wetlands, the wild animals of the field returned. By the time the despot Zhou arrived on the scene, the world had sunk into utter chaos. The Duke of Zhou served under King Wu in punishing the despot Zhou, and in attacking Yan, he spent three years in leading a punitive expedition against its ruler. Driving Fei Lian to the water's edge he there dispatched him. There was great rejoicing in the world as he laid waste to some fifty states and drove away the wild tigers, leopards, rhinos, and elephants. The *Book of Documents* says:

How resplendent were the strategies of King Wen,
How resilient were the many accomplishments of King Wu.
You have bequeathed blessing upon us as your descendants
So that all might live properly and without fault.

"But once again the age fell into decline and the proper way into darkness. Heretical teachings and violence once more reared their heads to the extent that there were cases of ministers killing their lords and sons killing their fathers. Confucius was so concerned he compiled the *Spring and Autumn Annals*. It was because the *Spring and Autumn Annals* was the business of the emperor alone Confucius said: 'It is because of this one document, the *Spring and Autumn Annals*, some will come to understand me and yet others to denounce me.'"

Comment: Mencius rehearses the vicissitudes of a broad swath of Chinese history, from Yu's bringing order to the world by bringing the Great Flood under control through to the era of King Wen, Wu, and the Duke of Zhou. It was through the combined efforts of these model rulers that they were able to reestablish proper order after the decline that ended with the rule of the Shang dynasty's last emperor, the despot Zhou. But again, proper order has not endured. Confucius in his own time of social and political decline had to compile the *Spring and Autumn Annals* as a text into which he could encode his judgments on the few successes and many failures that had marked governance during this period. In so doing, he interjected his veiled opinions into a text that belonged to the emperor, predicting for this reason that while some would be glad to have his insights, others would roundly condemn his *lese majeste*. Mencius anticipates the way in which this particular canonical text, the *Spring and Autumn Annals*, inspired a continuing tradition of "classical learning" (*jingxue* 經學) in which many commentaries were written to lift and clarify Confucius's salutary judgments out of this laconic text.

Leibniz and Jesuit Figurists made much of the correlation they found between Yu's Great Flood and the stories of Noah and the Great Deluge found in Genesis. In fact, these records provide a rather clear contrast between the Great Yu who with his ingenuity and perseverance was able to redirect and bring the waters under control as a prelude to the development of human civilization, and Noah who distinguished himself by his piety and obedience to an angry God. The biblical flood as a reversal of creation and a new beginning was an act of divine animus directed against a world that was lacking in the righteousness necessary to serve as the foundation for human civilization.

"聖王不作，諸侯放恣，處士橫議，楊朱、墨翟之言盈天下。天下之言，不歸楊，則歸墨。楊氏爲我，是無君也；墨氏兼愛，是無父也。無父無君，是禽獸也。公明儀曰：'庖有肥肉，廄有肥馬，民有飢色，野有餓莩，此率獸而食人也。'楊墨之道不息,孔子之道不著,是邪說誣民,充塞仁義也。仁義充塞,則率獸食人,人將相食。吾爲此懼,閑先聖之道,距楊墨,放淫辭,邪說者不得作。作於其心,害於其事;作於其事,害於其政。聖人復起,不易吾言矣。昔者禹抑洪水而天下平,周公兼夷狄驅猛獸而百姓寧,孔子成《春秋》而亂臣賊子懼。《詩》云:'戎狄是膺,荆舒是懲,則莫我敢承。'無父無君,是周公所膺也。我亦欲正人心,息邪說,距詖行,放淫辭,以承三聖者;豈好辯哉?予不得已也。能言距楊墨者,聖人之徒也。"

"No sage-kings have since arisen, and the vassal lords have thrown off all restraint. Unemployed scholar-officials make free with their opinions, and the doctrines of Yang Zhu and Mo Di fill the world. If the doctrines that prevail in the world are not those of Yang Zhu, then they come from Mo Di. Yang Zhu's doctrine of everyone for themselves amounts to the repudiation of one's sovereign lord, while Mo Di's doctrine of inclusive concern (*jian'ai* 兼愛) is a repudiation of the special affection persons should have for their own father. To repudiate one's father and one's sovereign lord is to join the wild beasts of the field. Gongming Yi has said: 'Your kitchens are full of prime cuts of meat and your stables have well-fed horses, and yet the common people have the pallor of hunger and in the countryside they are dying of starvation. This is leading animals to the table to consume human beings.'

"If the ways of Yang and Mo go unchecked and the proper way of Confucius is not proclaimed, heretical teachings will deceive the common people and the moral values of consummate conduct (*ren* 仁) and optimal appropriateness (*yi* 義) will be stifled once and for all. When such values are stifled, it leads animals to devour humans, and ultimately to humans devouring each other. This then is my concern. I want to protect the proper way of the former sages, drive out the teachings of Yang and Mo, and get rid of their wanton ideas so that such heretical theories do not arise. What arises in the heartmind will do injury to what one does. What arises in what one does will do injury to the business of governance. Were the sages to appear among us again today, they would not say anything different.

"In ancient times, Yu controlled the floods and the world was at peace. The Duke of Zhou then quelled the northern and southern barbarians and drove away the wild animals, bringing security to the people. Confucius compiled the *Spring and Autumn Annals*, bringing fear to corrupt ministers and unfilial sons. In the *Book of Songs* 300, it says:

Suppressing the Rong and Ti barbarians
And marching against Jing and Shu,
There are none left who would dare to give us contest.

It was those who would repudiate their fathers and sovereign lords that the Duke of Zhou struck down. I too want to carry on the work of these three sages in putting an end to heretical teachings, in arresting improper conduct, and in getting rid of wanton ideas, and in doing this, to establish what is proper in the hearts of the people. What option do I have but to debate? I have no choice. Those who with their words can drive out the teachings of Yang and Mo are the true followers of these sages."

Comment: Mencius's characterization of the followers of Yang Zhu and Mo Di is an intentionally skewed account of their doctrines, but it is a caricature that has become particularly influential with the ascent in the Song and Ming dynasties of a Mencian orthodoxy that made Mencius the heir to Confucius himself. Although Mozi advocated the precept of inclusive care (*jian'ai* 兼愛), for example, he still allowed that there must be special regard for one's own family members, most importantly, for one's parents. And Yang Zhu's erstwhile egoist position described here as "everyone for themselves" is again a purposeful distortion. It is likely that Yang Zhu in fact declared he would give away nothing of his own person to possess the world, reassuring news indeed for his sovereign lord.

7B26 孟子曰："逃墨必歸於楊，逃楊必歸於儒。歸，斯受之而已矣。今之與楊、墨辯者，如追放豚，既入其苙，又從而招之。"

Mencius said: "Those who abandon the Mohist doctrines are sure to turn to those of the Yang school, and those who abandon the Yang doctrines are sure to turn to the Confucian school. When they turn to us, we should just receive and accept them. But now it is as if those who would debate with the Yangists and Mohists are chasing after a stray pig. Not only do they want to put the pig back in the sty, but they want to hogtie it as well."

Comment: Such passages make it clear that historically there was a dialectical relationship among these lineages—the Mohists, the Yangists, and the Confucians. In retrospect, it is best perhaps to interpret them contextually as engaging and responding to each other. And it is the Mohists in particular who cultivate the linguistic skills needed to be experts in debate. For Mencius, the doctrines of the three traditions are such that there is a natural progression for people to be won over from Mohism and Yangism to the Confucian position. But even when the former Mohists and Yangists have been properly converted, Mencius rues the fact that arguments against them seem to rage on. In these debates, the advocates of Confucian doctrines not only want to show that the Mohists and Yangists are the devil, but moreover, that the devil is an ass.

7A26 孟子曰: "楊子取爲我，拔一毛而利天下，不爲也。墨子兼愛，摩頂放踵利天下，爲之。子莫執中。執中爲近之。執中無權，猶執一也。所惡執一者，爲其賊道也，舉一而廢百也。"

Mencius said: "Master Yang would have everything for himself. If in pulling out one hair it could benefit the entire world, he would have none of it. For Master Mo it was all about inclusive and indiscriminate love. If by shaving himself from head to heel he could benefit the world, he would do it in an instant.①

"Zimo takes the middle way between them. Holding onto the middle is closer to getting it right. But if he thus holds the middle without proper calibration, it is the same as holding on to one extreme. What is to be condemned for holding on to one of these extremes is that it cheats the proper way. It is to hold up one thing to the neglect of a hundred others."

Comment: Mencius sets up Master Yang and Master Mo as the extremes of egoism and altruism respectively. And then he places Zimo as someone who tries to steer the middle course between them, but who in taking them as the two choices without calculating all of the other possibilities is still affirming one or the other. The choice is between selecting one position as it is determined by these two extremes, or the proper way (*dao* 道) that can only be known by considering all of the possibilities.

The epistemic critique we find in many of the canonical Confucian texts does not rely heavily upon the language of right and wrong or true and false that follow from either-or thinking. Instead, criticism often takes the form of insisting someone has only limited knowledge—having access to only one perspective on a situation while being insufficiently aware of the many others.

---

① Carine Defoort uses this "body hair" trope in her argument against the standard readings of Mozi and Yang Zhu that have emerged historically from this Mencian caricature. See her essay, "Unfounded and Unfollowed: Mencius's Portrayal of Yang Zhu and Mo Di" in *Having a Word with Angus Graham: At Twenty-Five Years into His Immortality*, ed. Carine Defoort and Roger T. Ames. Albany: State University of New York, 2018.

The best way of looking at anything in the human experience is the most comprehensive view that includes as many perspectives as possible. This then is an argument for a Confucian epistemology of comprehensiveness (*quan* 全). At the end of the day, the best we are entitled to is not truth or certainty, but only an intelligent and edifying conversation that will provide us with as many perspectives as possible and thus the most panoramic view of things.

In the process cosmology that was made explicit in the *Book of Changes*, the epistemic vocabulary seems to reflect a "mapping" of a way forward in which any severe distinction between subject and object, and between the theoretical and the practical, is moot. "Knowing" (*zhi* 知) allows for a productive "forging ahead" within a particular situation, and thus promises practical efficacy rather than truth: that is, "finding our way forward" (*zhidao* 知道), "unraveling the patterns within the context" (*lijie* 理解), "seeing with full clarity" (*liaojie* 瞭解), "seeing from a height far into the distance" (*liaowang* 瞭望), "getting through with facility" (*tongda* 通達), "being well acquainted with everything" (*baishitong* 百事通) and so on.

This sense of mapping carries over into the modern Chinese language in which the expression for "I know" is quite literally "I am walking the way, I am realizing the way" (*wozhidao* 我知道), thus suggesting both the grasping of a specific bearing on where we are going and knowing how best to get there. To know is to be cognizant of prevailing conditions, to have the imagination to see their possibilities, and through virtuosic relationality (*ren* 仁) within one's own community, to have achieved the deference of others necessary to rally support behind and enthusiasm for a chosen future. Importantly, in the transitive "I know the way" (*wozhidao* 我知道), "the way" (*dao* 道) is not the "object" of knowledge as such, but has a real subjective and performative dimension. *Dao* 道 is a qualitative way of conducting one's life in the world that entails both subject and object, and the attributes of the subject as well as the modality of the activities taking place. *Dao* 道 defies Aristotle's philosophy of grammar, having as much to do with the conditions of the subject as with the object, and having as much to do with the quality of understanding as it does with the conditions of the world as understood. Knowing tells us as much about the *ren* 仁 quality of the person who "knows" as it does about something known, as much about a particular disposition to act as it does about the modality of acting itself. And then given the irreducibly social nature of persons themselves, knowing becomes a sociology of knowing rather than the activity of a single knower.

6B4 宋牼將之楚，孟子遇於石丘。曰："先生將何之？"曰："吾聞秦楚構兵，我將見楚王說而罷之。楚王不悅，我將見秦王說而罷之，二王我將有所遇焉。"曰："軻也請無問其詳，願聞其指。說之將何如？"曰："我將言其不利也。"曰："先生之志則大矣，先生之號則不可。先生以利說秦楚之王，秦楚之王悅於利，以罷三軍之師，是三軍之士樂罷而悅於利也。爲人臣者懷利以事其君，爲人子者懷利以事其父，爲人弟者懷利以事其兄。是君臣、父子、兄弟終去仁義，懷利以相接，然而不亡者，未之有也。先生以仁義說秦楚之王，秦楚之王悅於仁義，而罷三軍之師，是三軍之士樂罷而悅於仁義也。爲人臣者懷仁義以事其君，爲人子者懷仁義以事其父，爲人弟者懷仁義以事其兄，是君臣、父子、兄弟去利，懷仁義以相接也。然而不王者，未之有也。何必曰利？"

Song Keng was on his way to the state of Chu when Mencius encountered him at Shiqiu. Mencius asked him, "Where are you going, Sir?"

"I have heard the states of Qin and Chu have gone to war." replied Song Keng. "I am going to seek an audience with the King of Chu to persuade him to put a stop to it. If the King of Chu is not happy with this, I will seek out the King of Qin and try to persuade him instead. I am sure to get somewhere with one of them."

"Without going into all of the details, what will be the substance of your argument? How will you persuade them?"

"I am going to make the case there is no profit (*li* 利) in warfare."

"I greatly admire your intentions in this, Sir, but I think your mantra is wrong-headed. If you make profit the motive, and are able to persuade the two kings to cease their hostilities because of their love for profit, then the soldiers in their armies too will want to quit the field for the sake of profit. When profit is the motive for ministers serving their ruler, sons serving their fathers, and younger brothers serving their elders, this will mean that such relations are based solely on the love of profit to the exclusion of any concern for morality: that is, concern for what is most consummate and appropriate (*renyi* 仁義) in what they do. To follow such a course of action is to court disaster.

"If on the other hand you make moral conduct the motive, and are able to persuade the two kings to cease their hostilities because of their love of doing what is consummate and appropriate, then the soldiers in their armies too will want to quit the field for the sake of doing what is consummate and appropriate. When doing what is consummate and appropriate is the motive for ministers serving their ruler, sons serving their fathers, younger brothers serving their elders, this will mean that such relations are based solely upon the love of doing what is consummate and appropriate to the exclusion of any concern for profit. To follow such a course of action is to become a True King."

Comment: Beginning in the *Analects* (4.16, 14.12, 16.10, 19.1), a central Confucian doctrine is the contrast between conduct motivated by the opportunity for exclusive personal profit (*li* 利) and that undertaken in pursuit of an inclusive optimal appropriateness (*yi* 義). Such a contrast introduces an alternative conception of "objectivity" into the ethical discourse. The Confucian sense of an objective standard is not a principle that precedes and can be applied as an objective norm to any particular situation exclusive of subjective concerns. Rather, Confucian objectivity emerges from an optimizing appropriateness that takes all relevant interests into account in any particular situation. Such objectivity as the moral objective will always be situation specific with historical instances of "objectivity" serving as instrumental analogies rather than as determinative principles.

A complication arises from the fact that "profit" in the sense of "benefit" is not in itself necessarily exclusive. In *Analects* 20.2 for example: 因民之所利而利之，斯不亦惠而不費乎？ "Provide the common people those things that will actually benefit (*li* 利) them. Is this not being generous without being extravagant?" In the tension between the Confucians and the Mohists, it is this second sense of profit as inclusive "benefit" that is appealed to as a standard for the Mohists. Perhaps the most important difference between these two philosophies lies in the contrast between a self-consciously always situation-specific and reflexive "appropriateness" (*yi* 義) for the Confucians as opposed to an erstwhile external, "objective" rightness for the Mohists. For the Mohists, this sense of rightness must be consistent with the "purposes of 'Heaven'" (*tianzhi* 天志) as constituting and making available to human beings an externally grounded, objective criterion for morality.

Even so, the "external" standard of the Mohist is a publicly determined and implemented objective norm, and while certainly conservative and impositional, it still remains as one possible extreme within the assumed framework of a correlative relationship between *tian* 天 and the human world. That is, the "purposes of *tian* 天" are negotiated and then function within the parameters of "the continuity between and inseparability of the human and the cosmic orders" (*tianrenheyi* 天人合一). As such, as a putatively objective standard, it is of a fundamentally different quality of "objectivity" than that derived from the dualistic, two-world order we would associate with the conventional Abrahamic notion of the perfection, and thus the aseity or self-sufficiency, of an independent, transcendent God. To capture these different understandings of the term *yi* 義, we might appeal to the distinction that obtains among 1) a Confucian prospective standard of what is "optimally appropriate" within each unique situation, 2) a Mohist conception of a negotiated yet abstract "rightness," and 3) an Abrahamic conception of "righteousness" as a divine command theory where one comports oneself according to the wholly independent will of a transcendent, self-sufficient God.

IV.2 Continuing on the Way of Confucius

4A27 孟子曰: "仁之實, 事親是也; 義之實, 從兄是也; 智之實, 知斯二者弗去是也; 禮之實, 節文斯二者是也; 樂之實, 樂斯二者, 樂則生矣; 生則惡可已也, 惡可已, 則不知足之蹈之手之舞之。"

Mencius said: "The substance of consummate conduct (*ren* 仁) lies in serving one's parents and the substance of being optimally appropriate (*yi* 義) lies in deference to one's elder brothers. The substance of living wisely (*zhi* 智) lies in holding resolutely to and never abandoning these two precepts; the substance of ritual propriety (*li* 禮) lies in the adjustment and refinement achieved in these two precepts; the substance of music (*yue* 樂) lies in finding enjoyment in these two precepts. Where there is enjoyment there is life, and where there is life, how can it be arrested? And when it cannot be arrested, unconsciously the feet tap and the hands dance."

Comment: Mencius here elaborates upon the key philosophical cluster of terms around which the *Analects* has shaped its Confucian project. The two foundational precepts of consummate conduct (*ren* 仁) and optimal appropriateness (*yi* 義) find their fruition in the flourishing of vital family roles and relations. The other concepts that are grounded in and augment these values are the wisdom that is achieved in living these roles optimally, the refinement that comes with cultivating them, and the musicality that accompanies the performance of them as the ultimate source of human enjoyment. Where there is such enjoyment, life itself is manifested most obviously in the way in which this virtuosity is expressed in the spontaneous movements of the human body. The ultimate appeal to life itself echoes the zoetological assumptions made explicit in the *Changes* that serves as the interpretive context for the *Mencius*.

4A19 孟子曰："事，孰爲大？事親爲大；守，孰爲大？守身爲大。不失其身而能事其親者，吾聞之矣；失其身而能事其親者，吾未之聞也。孰不爲事？事親，事之本也；孰不爲守？守身，守之本也。曾子養曾皙，必有酒肉；將徹，必請所與；問有餘，必曰：'有。'曾皙死，曾元養曾子，必有酒肉；將徹，不請所與；問有餘，曰：'亡矣。'將以復進也。此所謂養口體者也。若曾子，則可謂養志也。事親若曾子者，可也。"

Mencius said: "To whom do we owe the greatest degree of service? It is to our parents. To what should we have the greatest degree of vigilance? With respect to our persons. I have heard of those who are vigilant with respect to their persons being able to serve their parents, but never of those who are not being able to do so. There are many services we must render, but serving our parents is the root of them all. There are many things requiring vigilance, but vigilance with respect to our persons is the root of them all.

"Master Zeng in taking care of his father Zeng Xi always provided him with meat to eat and wine to drink. When he was about to clear the table, Master Zeng would always ask to whom the food left over should be given. On being asked if there was food left, he always answered in the affirmative. When his father had died and Zeng Yuan was taking care of Master Zeng, he too would provide his father with meat to eat and wine to drink. But when he was about to clear the table, he would never ask to whom the leftover food should be given. And when asked if there was food left over, the answer was always in the negative, with the intention of serving his father the same food again. This is what is called taking care of the mouth and stomach while Master Zeng was caring for his father's wishes. In serving our parents, we should follow Master Zeng."

Comment: Master Zeng is the paragon of family reverence (*xiao* 孝), and in the Confucian culture, family reverence is the prime moral imperative. It is the basis of the family lifeworld and the intergenerational embodiment necessary for the transmission of the living culture. Hence, the most important duty we have is taking care of our parents, and the ultimate standard by which persons are to be measured lies in how devoted they are in carrying out this responsibility.

The specifics of Master Zeng's conduct as described here are not a template for family reverence; it is the serious attitude that underlies his behavior together with the modality of conduct that is its proper measure. Mencius is again following Confucius here. In *Analects* 2.7, Confucius insists merely providing sustenance is no more than what we do for our animals, and in *Analects* 2.8, he makes it clear it is the bounce in the step rather than what we actually provide or do, that is the appropriate standard for family reverence. Taking care of the parent's needs is necessary, but fathoming their wishes and thus caring for them is a much higher consideration.

4A5 孟子曰："人有恒言，皆曰'天下國家'。天下之本在國，國之本在家，家之本在身。"

Mencius said: "There is a popular adage spoken among the people who all say: 'The world, the state, the family.' The world is rooted in the state, the state in the family, and the family in one's own person."

Comment: Confucius and Mencius both insist the ultimate source of meaning is personal cultivation. The *Analects* 12.1 states: 爲仁由己，而由人乎哉？ "Becoming consummate in one's conduct is self-originating—how could it originate with others?" And again, the *Expansive Learning* 1 states: 自天子以至於庶人，壹是皆以修身爲本 "from the emperor down to the common folk, everything is rooted in personal cultivation." At the same time, Mencius rehearses the symbiotic relationship the *Expansive Learning* 1 finds in the mantra 修身齊家治國平天下 "cultivating one's person, setting the family right, effecting order in the state, and bringing peace to the world."

4A26 孟子曰："不孝有三，無後爲大。舜不告而娶，爲無後也，君子以爲猶告也。"

Mencius said: "There are three ways of failing to observe family reverence (*xiao* 孝), and to be without progeny is the most serious among them. It is because Shun's taking of a wife without first asking his parent's permission was in an effort to guarantee his issue that exemplary persons interpret his case as though Shun had in fact gotten their approval."

Comment: Continuing one's family lineage in a tradition so heavily invested in family life and that takes "family reverence" (*xiao* 孝) as the prime moral imperative is certainly a serious concern. The sense of continuity that comes with the assumption that progenitors live on in their progeny provides a source of continuing felt-worth for each generation, a sense of belonging, and the mainstay of a family-centered religiousness.

But what is important here is that for a family to be without progeny is not only to fail to continue one's own blood lineage, it is also a failure to produce the human conduits through which the transmission of the living cultural tradition itself takes place. It is certainly a grave offence against a person's own parents and grandparents for whom the continuity of sacrificial offerings will be ruptured. But even graver is the transgression against the collective ancestors who were the founders and transmitters of the antique civilization itself. Given that Confucian morality simply put is continuing growth in relationships, to be without the progeny needed to attend to the living civilization bequeathed to one by one's ancestors in this broadest sense can be interpreted as nothing less than an acute moral lapse.

It should be clear that what we are referencing here is not simply the transmission of a physical lineage. The living body (*ti* 體) and our embodied living (*li* 禮) is the conveyance of the cultural corpus of knowledge through which a living civilization itself is preserved and extended: linguistic facility and proficiency, religious doctrines and mythologies, the aesthetics of refined living, the modeling of mores and values, instruction and apprenticeship in cognitive technologies, and so on. Our bodies are certainly our physicality, but they are also the medium through which the entire body of culture has been inherited, interpreted, elaborated upon, and reauthorized down through the ages.

Thus, according to the opening chapter of the *Classic of Family Reverence* (*Xiaojing* 孝經), keeping the cultural "body" intact is the process of embodying the tradition fully, drawing upon it creatively as a resource for distinguishing oneself in the world, and contributing dividends to its resources by establishing a name for oneself and one's family that will be remembered by posterity. In this way, the evolving corpus of the cultural tradition—the civilization itself—is continued in each person and embodied in each succeeding generation.

Ralph Waldo Emerson in his essay, "American Civilization," provides us with a rather simple physical image to make a rather profound statement about the intergenerational march of a continuing civilization:

Civilization depends on morality. Everything good in man leans on what is higher. This rule holds in small as in great. Thus, all our strength and success in the work of our hands depend on our borrowing the aid of the elements.[1]

Emerson uses the image of a carpenter hewing wood to remark on the utter futility of individuals striking out and "going it alone" in this world:

> You have seen a carpenter on a ladder with a broad-axe chopping upward chips and slivers from a beam. How awkward! at what disadvantage he works!

For Emerson, such aberrant individuality stands in stark contrast to the felicity of squaring civilization behind our shoulders and living lives that are propelled by the moral and cultural *gravitas* of a shared and continuing cultural tradition:

> But see him on the ground, dressing his timber under him. Now, not his feeble muscles, but the force of gravity brings down the axe; that is to say, the planet itself splits his stick.

Emerson's image of lives empowered by the weight and momentum of a common civilization recalls the Confucian exhortation in 15.29 that 人能弘道 "it is persons who are able to broaden the way"—a way we walk together and for which each generation has the stern obligation to construct the connector that will extend it to the next generation.

5A2 萬章問曰："《詩》云：'娶妻如之何？必告父母。'信斯言也，宜莫如舜。舜之不告而娶，何也？"孟子曰："告則不得娶。男女居室，人之大倫也。如告，則廢人之大倫，以懟父母，是以不告也。"萬章曰："舜之不告而娶，則吾既得聞命矣；帝之妻舜而不告，何也？"曰："帝亦知告焉則不得妻也。"
    Wan Zhang said: "In the *Book of Songs* 101 it says:
    How does a person go about taking a wife?
    He must inform his parents.

---

[1] Emerson, "American Civilization," *Atlantic Monthly* 9 (1862), pp. 502-511.

No one is as proper as Shun, and yet how was it that Shun took his wives without informing his parents?"

"If Shun had informed his parents he would not have been permitted to marry them." replied Mencius. "For a man and woman to cohabit is one of the most important among human relations. Shun did not inform his parents because for him to have to forsake this most important of all relations would have incurred Shun's resentment towards them."

"It is now clear to me why Shun took his wives without informing his parents," said Wan Zhang, "but how was it that the Emperor Yao in giving his two daughters in marriage to Shun did not inform the parents?"

"The Emperor also knew that were he to inform the parents, they would not have permitted the marriage." said Mencius.

Comment: One way of reading this passage is that in the moral hierarchy, family reverence (*xiao* 孝) takes precedence over the observation of specific proprieties (*li* 禮). Shun's first and highest responsibility to his parents is to provide them with an heir and this can only be accomplished through marriage. Knowing that his parents will not permit his pending marriage, Shun overrides his obligation to inform them of his intentions in order to serve his higher obligation to them. Emperor Yao in not informing Shun's parents apparently followed this same reasoning.

萬章曰：" 父母使舜完廩，捐階，瞽瞍焚廩。使浚井，出，從而揜之。象曰：'謨蓋都君咸我績。牛羊父母，倉廩父母，干戈朕，琴朕，弤朕，二嫂使治朕棲。' 象往入舜宮，舜在床琴。象曰：'鬱陶思君爾。' 忸怩。舜曰：'惟茲臣庶，汝其于予治。' 不識舜不知象之將殺己與？" 曰："奚而不知也？象憂亦憂，象喜亦喜。" 曰："然則舜偽喜者與？"

Wan Zhang remarked: "Shun's father and mother having sent Shun to repair a granary, removed the ladder. Then his father the Blind Man put the granary to the torch. They sent him to sink a well, and following after him, sealed it up. Shun's younger half-brother Xiang said: 'All of the credit for covering over this 'great politician' belongs to me. His animals and granaries go to father and mother, but I will take his spear and shield, his lute, his bow, and my two sisters-in-law can be sent to attend to my couch.'

"Xiang then went to Shun's palace, and on entering found Shun sitting on his bed playing the lute. Xiang said to him: 'It is only because I was so anxious about you that I have come,' and his face flushed red. Shun replied: 'It is because my subjects are so numerous that I need you to help me in governing them.' I am not really sure if Shun knew that Xiang had been trying to kill him."

"How could he not know? When Xiang was concerned, he too was concerned, and when Xiang was pleased he too was pleased."

"In that case, was Shun just pretending to be pleased?"

Comment: Half-brother Xiang thinking that his plot to murder Shun had succeeded, decides on how to partition the spoils. But going to Shun's residence to secure his gains, he finds Shun is at leisure, alive and well. Embarrassed, Xiang tries to explain himself, but Shun instead of accusing him of his misdeeds asks for his assistance in the task of governing. Wan Zhang having recounted this story, wonders aloud if Shun was aware that his own family was trying to take his life.

曰："否。昔者有饋生魚於鄭子產，子產使校人畜之池。校人烹之，反命曰：'始舍之圉圉焉，少則洋洋焉，攸然而逝。'子產曰：'得其所哉！得其所哉！'校人出，曰：'孰謂子產智？予既烹而食之，曰：得其所哉？得其所哉。'故君子可欺以其方，難罔以非其道。彼以愛兄之道來，故誠信而喜之，奚偽焉？"

"No." said Mencius. "Some time ago a gift of a live fish was made to Zichan of Zheng, and Zichan sent it to his groundskeeper to release it in his pond. In fact, the groundskeeper cooked it up, and then reported back, 'When I first let the fish go, it seemed listless, but a little while later it came to life, and plunged into the depths.' Zichan replied, 'It found its element! It found its element!' The groundskeeper withdrew, and said, 'Who said this Zichan is a wise person? I have already cooked and eaten his fish, and he says 'It found its element! It found its element!' Indeed, the exemplary person (*junzi* 君子) can be deceived in how things are done, but they cannot be duped into abandoning the proper way (*dao* 道). It was because Xiang came to him as his loving brother that Shun really believed him and was pleased. How could he be just pretending?"

Comment: How does Mencius's analogy of Zichan and the groundskeeper relate to the attempts made by Shun's family on his life? Zichan does not have control over the actions of other people and as any trusting person, might be taken in by them. But the implication here is that, just as in the case of Shun, the wise Zichan is fully aware of what is going on. The important thing is that Zichan does have control over his own actions, and in this respect, is impeccable in his proper response to having received a gift. Similarly, Shun responds to the machinations of his parents and brother by rising above their depravity. Indeed, he is compelled by such conduct to double his efforts in continuing to be a filial son (*xiao* 孝) and a good older brother (*ti* 悌). In the distinction between being deceived and being duped, in the first instance a person is properly trusting and then let down by being deceived by someone else who is thus the wrongdoer. But in the second case, a person in being duped is made a mark because of their own weakness of character.

5A1　萬章問曰："舜往于田，號泣于旻天，何爲其號泣也？" 孟子曰："怨慕也。" 萬章曰："父母愛之，喜而不忘；父母惡之，勞而不怨。然則舜怨乎？" 曰："長息問於公明高曰：'舜往于田，則吾既得聞命矣；號泣于旻天，于父母，則吾不知也。' 公明高曰：'是非爾所知也。' 夫公明高以孝子之心，爲不若是恝，我竭力耕田，共爲子職而已矣，父母之不我愛，於我何哉？"

Wan Zhang inquired of Mencius: "When Shun took to the fields, he wailed and sobbed to the high heavens. Why did he do this?"

"He was torn between his despondency (*yuan* 怨) and his yearning." said Mencius.

Wan Zhang replied: "It is said: 'When father and mother love you, being pleased by it, you must not indulge yourself. When father and mother despise you, even though you make every effort on their behalf, you must not feel resentment (*yuan* 怨) towards them.'[①] Do you mean to say that Shun was in fact resentful?"

"Chang Xi asked Gongming Gao, saying: 'From you I have come to see clearly why Shun took to the fields, but why he wailed and sobbed to the high heavens and to his father and mother, this I still don't understand.' 'This is something quite beyond you.' replied Gongming Gao. Gongming Gao certainly did not believe that a truly filial son could console himself and become indifferent in such matters by saying I exhaust myself in tilling the fields and do everything that a proper son should do, so if my parents do not return my love, what is it to me."

Comment: The term *yuan* 怨 usually means resentment or enmity where, like in fearing something, it is directed at a particular object or situation. And in the doctrine of family reverence with respect to parents, such

---

[①] D.C. Lau points out this quotation appears in the *Record of Rituals* (*Liji* 禮記) 31.9/140/20 attributed to Master Zeng, the paragon on family reverence (*xiao* 孝). See D.C. Lau (trans.), *Mencius*, London: Penguin, 1970, p. 138.

IV. THE *MENCIUS* (*MENGZI* 孟子): EXTENDING THE VOCABULARY

resentment is much discouraged. *Analects* 4.18 says quite typically:

事父母幾諫。見志不從，又敬不違，勞而不怨。
In serving your father and mother, remonstrate with them gently. On seeing that they do not heed your suggestions, remain respectful and do not act contrary. Although concerned, voice no resentment (*yuan* 怨).

But *yuan* 怨 like anxiety can also mean an intransitive sadness, despondency, despair that has no particular object. This second meaning of *yuan* 怨 is the better description of Shun's feelings, where such despondency is coupled with his yearning for the situation to be different. Gongming Gao's point is that in spite of the fact that Shun does everything he can to overcome the situation, this does not relieve Shun of his despair.

"帝使其子九男二女，百官牛羊倉廩備，以事舜於畎畝之中。天下之士多就之者，帝將胥天下而遷之焉。爲不順於父母，如窮人無所歸。天下之士悅之，人之所欲也，而不足以解憂；好色，人之所欲，妻帝之二女，而不足以解憂；富，人之所欲，富有天下，而不足以解憂；貴，人之所欲，貴爲天子，而不足以解憂。人悅之、好色、富貴，無足以解憂者，惟順於父母，可以解憂。人少，則慕父母；知好色，則慕少艾；有妻子，則慕妻子；仕則慕君，不得於君則熱中。大孝終身慕父母。五十而慕者，予於大舜見之矣。"
"Emperor Yao sent his nine sons, two daughters, and all of his officials provisioned with herds of cattle and sheep, and with an abundant store of grain, to serve Shun in his plowing of the fields. All of the scholar-officials of the world flocked to Shun's side, and the Emperor was about to abdicate his throne to him. But because he could not find accord with his father and mother, he was like a dejected person with nowhere to turn.
"Everyone wants the scholar-officials of the world all to admire them, but even this was not enough to relieve Shun's anxiety. Everyone loves beauty, but being given the Emperor's two daughters in marriage was not enough to relieve his anxiety. Everyone desires wealth, but having all of the wealth of the world was not enough to relieve his anxiety. Everyone desires to be honored, but being honored as the Emperor was not enough to relieve his anxiety. The reason that these advantages—admiration, beauty, wealth, honor—were insufficient to relieve his anxiety was because the only resolution would be finding true accord with his father and mother.
"When young, a person yearns after his mother and father; when he

becomes aroused by beauty he yearns after the young and fair; when he has a wife and family he yearns after them; when he is appointed to office he yearns after his lord, and failing to gain his lord's approval, he becomes frustrated. But in all of this, the truly filial son to the end of his days yearns after his father and mother. I see in the great Shun a person who at fifty years old was still yearning."

Comment: Although Shun as the heir to Yao received everything a person could possibly want—admiration of his fellows, beautiful wives, wealth and honor as well—none of these attainments could quell his natural yearning for the love of his parents. Shun is a clear example of the power of "family reverence" (*xiao* 孝) as a moral imperative. Perhaps Shun is celebrated in the literature for his filial devotion because, in spite of his steadfast longing for the affection of his perverse and unnatural parents, his love went unrequited for so long. In *Focusing the Familiar* 17, for example, he is singled out by Confucius as a great model of family reverence (*daxiao* 大孝):

舜其大孝也與！德爲聖人，尊爲天子，富有四海之內。宗廟饗之，子孫保之。

Now Shun—there was a person of great filiality (*xiao* 孝). His virtuosity (*de* 德) was that of a sage (*shengren* 聖人), he was venerated as the Son tian 天, and his wealth extended to everything in the world. In the ancestral hall he received sacrifices, and generation after generation of progeny have preserved his name.

4A28 孟子曰："天下大悅而將歸己。視天下悅而歸己，猶草芥也。惟舜爲然。不得乎親，不可以爲人；不順乎親，不可以爲子。舜盡事親之道而瞽瞍厎豫，瞽瞍厎豫而天下化，瞽瞍厎豫而天下之爲父子者定，此之謂大孝。"

Mencius said: "The greatest happiness felt by the entire world was turning to Shun. But Shun looked upon this fact as if it were so much straw. For Shun, to fail to have the affection of his parents was to fail to be a person; to fail to have an accord with his parents was to fail to be a son. Shun did everything possible in the service of his parents, and only in the very end was his father the Blind Man pleased. That the Blind Man in the end was finally pleased transformed the world, and set for it a model of what it means to be father and son. This is what is meant by the greatest example of family reverence."

IV. THE *MENCIUS* (*MENGZI* 孟子): EXTENDING THE VOCABULARY

Comment: This passage would seem to be the denouement of the saga of Shun's lifelong attempt to overcome the antipathy of his parents and to win their affection. While there is certainly an unsettled question that remains with respect to the Blind Man's role as a father, it is Shun's resolve and his unrelenting perseverance that has given the tradition one of its most lasting examples of family reverence. That this outcome sets a template for father-son relations is a stretch.

7A45 孟子曰: "君子之於物也，愛之而弗仁；於民也，仁之而弗親。親親而仁民，仁民而愛物。"

Mencius said: "Exemplary persons (*junzi* 君子) having a love for all things in general, still do not seek a consummatory relationship with them. Seeking a consummatory relationship with the common people, they still do not extend family affection to them. Exemplary persons expressing family affection to their kinsmen seek a consummatory relationship with the common people; seeking a consummatory relationship with the common people they have a love for all things in general."

Comment: One familiar value in Confucian philosophy is the notion of graduated love that extends radially outward from family members to the community, and then to the world at large. We learn to love by being loved; we develop self-esteem by being appreciated by others. This value reflects the central role that family has as the entry point for developing moral competence, and as the basis for not only sociopolitical order, but cosmic order itself. Cosmologically the starting point is "life" (*sheng* 生), and the family is the site of procreation. The term *ai* 愛 is usually translated as "love," but as D.C. Lau points out in his translation of this same passage, it also has by extension the meaning of being "sparing," "frugal," "judicious."[1]

How can this term *ai* 愛 mean love and frugality at the same time? In the sense of "love," it is used broadly in the canons to mean everything from the bond between husband and wife to loving the common people. It is often glossed as "consummate conduct" (*ren* 仁) and "kindness, generosity, favoring" (*hui* 惠).

---

[1] *Mencius*, trans. D.C. Lau, London: Penguin Books, 1970, p. 192.

Genuine love is certainly expressed through favors and generosity, but also entails deference and respect. True love means taking someone or something on their own terms without overwriting them with expectations or conditions that are not of their own making. The logic is that when we are partial to something, we want to keep it whole. Hence, we are sparing of it and circumspect in our dealings with it, being keen to allow it to be fully who or what it is. In this circle of love, family affection is at the center, with the responsibility of consummate conduct in the treatment of the common people being next, followed again by an attitude of love expressed as being partial and thus judicious in dealing with things in general.

7A40 孟子曰："君子之所以教者五：有如時雨化之者，有成德者，有達財者，有答問者，有私淑艾者。此五者，君子之所以教也。"

Mencius said: "There are five aspirations exemplary persons (*junzi* 君子) have in their teaching: transforming their students like the timely rains, enabling students to achieve virtuosity in what they do, facilitating students in realizing their talents, providing students with a forum for discussion, and offering other students who have to make their own way a worthy exemplar. These five objectives then are what exemplary persons pursue in their teaching.

Comment: Like the life and growth enabled by the spring rains, the role of exemplary teachers is to provide their students with an education that is fundamentally transformative. The talents and communication skills of students need to be nurtured, but even more important is the cultivation of a true virtuosity in their conduct. An important function of exemplary teachers is the role model they are able to provide for those students who do not have the benefit of their personal instruction, and who thus must make their own way. The limits of the best of teachers are not their own classroom. Throughout these Confucian canons, we find a coincidence between education and morality, where students in becoming educated are also becoming moral human beings.

4A18 公孫丑曰："君子之不教子，何也？" 孟子曰："勢不行也。教者必以正；以正不行，繼之以怒。繼之以怒，則反夷矣。'夫子教我以正，夫子未出於正也。' 則是父子相夷也。父子相夷，則惡矣。古者易子而教之，父子之間不責善。責善則離，離則不祥莫大焉。"

Gongsun Chou asked Mencius, "Why is it that exemplary persons (*junzi* 君子) do not teach their own children?"

Mencius replied: "Because the conditions are not conducive to it. Teachers must necessarily do what is proper, but when their instruction is not acted upon they become frustrated. Such frustration leads to grievances between teacher and student. 'You teach me by showing me the proper thing to do, but then you act otherwise.' Thus, father and child become aggrieved of each other, and when this happens you have a bad situation. The ancients would teach each other's children, where father and child would not be put in the situation of demanding goodness from each other. Where there is such a demand, it causes estrangement, and there is no greater misfortune than estrangement between father and child."

Comment: In Confucianism, there is an isomorphism between family and classroom captured in the conventional language of "teacher-father" (*shifu* 師父), "teacher-mother" (*shimu* 師母), "student-older-sister" (*xuejie* 學姐), and "student-younger-brother" (*xuedi* 學弟). Even so, Mencius provides practical advice that respects the difference between the role of teacher and that of parent. While the relationship between teacher and student requires a formal propriety (*zheng* 正), the relationship between parent and child is characterized by a natural affection more fragile than such propriety. We know that "family reverence" (*xiao* 孝) is the prime moral imperative in Confucian ethics and politics, and that integral to this doctrine is the obligation of the younger generation to remonstrate (*jian* 諫) with their elders. Such remonstrance however, needs to be clearly distinguished from accusations and blame. In *Analects* 4.18 it is made clear that such remonstrance on the part of the younger generation must be "gentle" (*ji* 幾), and must be attended by respect and acquiescence because family relations demand as much, and at the very least, the younger person is not necessarily right.

In *Mencius* 4B30 there is the case of a young man Kuang Zhang who becomes estranged from his father over a moral issue. The argument as in this passage is that where friends should properly demand goodness from each other, for father and child to do so might be a source of serious injury to their mutual affection. Again, in *Analects* 13.28 it states that one must be critical and demanding of one's friends, but amicable with one's family members. The subtle but important differences that obtain among these three roles—parent and child, teacher and student, and friend and friend—require that it is best to be pre-emptive, and avoid situations in which conflict might arise. We choose our friends, and because they are our most important resource for personal growth, in our relations we must be critical and demand much from them. At the other end of the spectrum, while family members are crucial in providing the entry point for the development of moral competence, we are offered little choice in the relationships, and must be generous in our accommodation of them. There is little to theorize in "because he is my brother."

The teacher-student relationship resides between family and friend, and while it is highly selective on the part of both teacher and student as in the case of teacher Confucius and student Yan Hui, this special relationship has the potential to become a sacred bond that optimizes the possibilities of both familial intimacy and the open-ended opportunities for shared growth that the best of friends provide.

3B7 公孫丑問曰:"不見諸侯何義?" 孟子曰:"古者不爲臣不見。段干木踰垣而辟之,泄柳閉門而不內,是皆已甚。迫,斯可以見矣。陽貨欲見孔子而惡無禮,大夫有賜於士,不得受於其家,則往拜其門。陽貨瞰孔子之亡也,而饋孔子蒸豚;孔子亦瞰其亡也,而往拜之。當是時,陽貨先,豈得不見?曾子曰:'脅肩諂笑,病于夏畦。'子路曰:'未同而言,觀其色赧赧然,非由之所知也。'由是觀之,則君子之所養可知已矣。"

Gongsun Chou asked Mencius, "What is the meaning of the fact that you do not seek out interviews with the various feudal lords?"

Mencius replied, "In ancient times, if one was not in service as a minister to a state, one did not seek an interview with its lord. Duangan Mu climbed over a wall to avoid such an interview; Xie Liu bolted his door and would not open it. But perhaps this is taking things too far. If pressed by one of the feudal lords, one may agree to an interview with him.

"Yang Huo wanted Confucius to come and see him, but did not want others to think he had no sense of ritual propriety (*li* 禮). When a minister gives a gift to a scholar-official (*shi* 士) but the scholar-official is not at home to personally receive it, it is incumbent upon the scholar-official to go to the minister's home to pay his respects and express his gratitude. Yang Huo waited until Confucius was out, and then presented a steamed suckling pig at his home. But then Confucius waited until Yang Huo was out, and went to pay his respects at the minister's residence. One might ask: On this occasion, since Yang Huo had in fact first paid his respects to Confucius, how could Confucius have refused to go and see him?

"Master Zeng said, 'It is harder to cringe and smile obsequiously than it is to tend the garden in the heat of summer.' 'To have to speak with someone you do not want to, and further, to have to humble oneself in his presence—I would find such conduct unthinkable' said Zilu. From such reports we can know what exemplary persons (*junzi* 君子) would want to cultivate in themselves."

Comment: Yang Huo's ploy here is to create a situation in which Confucius would have no choice but to come and seek an interview with him. The point is that while exemplary persons must necessarily conduct themselves in a way that is consistent with ritual proprieties and social expectations, they must also avoid situations in which protocol requires them to defer to people they do not respect. Master Zeng and Zilu are both cited to reinforce the profound discomfort an honorable person feels when obliged to defer to a reprobate simply because they are of higher status. In his response to Yang Huo's machinations, Confucius demonstrates both imagination and a good sense of humor.

This passage would seem to be a commentary on the same but abbreviated story found in *Analects* 17.1. See the *Comments* on this *Analects* passage (p. 380) for the profile of Yang Huo, and for a very different outcome.

6B16 孟子曰: "教亦多術矣，予不屑之教誨也者，是亦教誨之而已矣。"

Mencius said: "Pedagogy has many different techniques, and my not deigning to instruct someone is in itself a form of teaching."

Comment: Mencius like Confucius is an eager teacher, but again like Confucius his single highest expectation of his students lies in the quality of their commitment and assiduous application. Confucius in *Analects* 7.8 famously says: 舉一隅不以三隅反，則不復也 "If on instructing students on one corner they do not come back to me with the other three, I will not repeat myself," and again in 15.8 不可與言而與之言，失言 "to speak with people who are not worth the effort is to waste your words." Confucius as a serious teacher in commenting on his students offers little that is complimentary and much that is critical. Importantly, the standard being set demands resolve and hard work on the part of students rather than irrelevant considerations such as social class and bloodline. Simply put, as teachers neither Confucius nor Mencius would suffer fools.

7A33 王子墊問曰："士何事？"孟子曰："尚志。"曰："何謂尚志？"曰："仁義而已矣。殺一無罪，非仁也，非其有而取之，非義也。居惡在？仁是也；路惡在？義是也。居仁由義，大人之事備矣。"

Prince Dian asked Mencius, "What is the business of scholar-officials (*shi* 士)?"

"To be lofty in their purposes." replied Mencius.

"What does it mean for them to be lofty in their purposes?" asked Prince Dian.

"Being consummate (*ren* 仁) and optimally appropriate (*yi* 義) in their conduct, nothing more." said Mencius. "It is contrary to being consummate in one's conduct to take one innocent life; it is contrary to having a sense of optimal appropriateness to take something that does not belong to you. Where do scholar-officials dwell? In consummate conduct? What road do they travel? One of optimal appropriateness. Dwelling in consummate conduct and setting off on the road of optimal appropriateness is everything needed in the business of being a great person."

Comment: Prince Dian is the son of the King of Qi, and thus a member of the aristocracy. The scholar-officials (*shi* 士) are a literate class first emerging at the time of Confucius who have been educated (as well as trained) in preparation for a role in government. As suggested here, the substance of their education is to produce students who not only have the skill-set necessary to carry out the work of governance, but more importantly, who are lofty in their purposes and disposed to moral conduct in everything they do. Mencius has followed Confucius as a teacher of moral education in preparing his students for civil service, and also follows him here and throughout the text in the trope of the "walking the proper way" metaphor.

7B16 孟子曰："仁也者，人也。合而言之，道也。"

Mencius said: "Aspiring to consummate conduct in your roles and relations (*ren* 仁) is becoming a person (*ren* 人); and when these two words—consummate conduct and your person—can be spoken together, you are walking the proper way (*dao* 道)."

Comment: "Walking the proper way" (*dao* 道) refers to excelling in one's own particular narrative as it is nested in the narratives of family, community, and the mature culture. From this passage and other examples we could cite, we must allow that *ren* 仁 seems to be situation-and-

IV. THE *MENCIUS* (*MENGZI* 孟子): EXTENDING THE VOCABULARY

person-specific. At the same time, however, given the fact that each situation is holographic and thus focal within a narrative field, *ren* 仁 also has a holistic, narrative quality to it. As such, *ren* 仁 must be understood as having all of the personal differences and habits of conduct of the particular person implicated within it. *Ren* 仁 can only be achieved in any particular situation when we take into account the virtuosity of whole persons (*ren* 人) living the full range of their different roles. *Focusing the Familiar* says as much:

> Aspiring to consummate conduct in your roles and relations (*ren* 仁) is becoming a person (*ren* 人); and loving your family members is what is of greatest consequence.①

Indeed, I would argue that this holistic, normative, role-based, and narrative meaning of *ren* 仁 allows us to claim that *ren* 仁 itself is one clear way that the notion of role ethics is being referenced in classical Confucianism. To be clear on this, *ren* 仁 denotes the aspiration to an achieved virtuosity in the unique roles and relations that constitute our specific, continuing narratives. And further, generalizations made off of these particular roles like erstwhile "principles," function as guidelines that assume their evolving definition as they are shaped by and emerge out of the collective confluence of our concrete behaviors. Being a father is both an always particular role and a useful generalization. As such, roles as they are lived produce such generalizations for succeeding generations about how past exemplars in their actions might serve literally as "role models" to guide our present conduct and be of service in the critical evaluation of it.

2A7 孟子曰："矢人豈不仁於函人哉？矢人唯恐不傷人，函人唯恐傷人。巫匠亦然，故術不可不愼也。孔子曰：'里仁爲美。擇不處仁，焉得智？' 夫仁，天之尊爵也，人之安宅也。莫之禦而不仁，是不智也。不仁、不智、無禮、無義，人役也。人役而恥爲役，由弓人而恥爲弓，矢人而恥爲矢也。如恥之，莫如爲仁。仁者如射，射者正己而後發。發而不中，不怨勝己者，反求諸己而已矣。"

Mencius said, "Could it be that the arrow-maker is less consummate in his conduct (*ren* 仁) than the shield-maker? After all, the worry of the

---

① *Zhongyong* 20: 仁者人也，親親爲大。

arrow-maker is that his arrows will fail to hurt people while the worry of the shield-maker is that his shields will fail to protect them. The medical practitioner and the coffin-maker is another case in point. It is for this reason one must take great care in choosing one's occupation.

"Confucius said, 'In taking up one's residence, it is the presence of consummate persons that is the greatest attraction. How can anyone be called wise who, in having the choice, does not dwell among consummate persons?'

"Now being consummate is that nobility in conduct most revered by *tian* 天, and the most comfortable dwelling place for the human being. Since there is nothing standing in the way, to fail to be consummate in our persons is a lack of wisdom. To be neither consummate in conduct nor wise guarantees the absence of ritual propriety (*li* 禮) and a sense of appropriateness (*yi* 義), making one a mere servant to others. To thus be a servant and to be ashamed of serving others is like the bow-maker being ashamed of making his bows, or the arrow-maker being ashamed of making his arrows. If you are truly ashamed of being a servant, nothing is better than becoming consummate in your conduct. A consummate person can be likened to an archer. The archer releases his arrow only after having taken his proper stance. When he misses the mark, he does not resent those who have bested him, but simply turns inward to find his error."

Comment: This passage seems to be a commentary on *Analects* 4.1, wherein Confucius makes the point that wisdom requires us to seek out and dwell among good people because our association with such people conduces to growth in the quality of our own lives. At the same time, just like the craftsmen, we are responsible for artistry in crafting our own lives and for the quality of the product we are able to produce. The ultimate responsibility for being consummate in one's conduct begins with ourselves. In *Analects* 12.1 it states: 爲仁由己，而由人乎哉？ "Becoming consummate in one's conduct is self-originating—how could it originate with others?"

Consummate conduct is both divinely sanctioned and the most comfortable abode in which we can reside. To fail to cultivate the prosocial conduct in our roles and relations prompted by our natural moral inclinations makes us less than, and subordinate to, those who would do so, and should properly be a source of shame. If the makers of offensive weapons such as bows and arrows should be ashamed of their occupations because the ultimate goal of what they make is injury to other people, those who have been subordinated to others through their own failure to cultivate their persons should be ashamed because they too have nothing good to offer others. The way out of such servitude is the consummate quality of conduct that begins from one's own commitment, and that then provides an opportunity for the personal growth of not only oneself but of others too. Just as with archers who miss their mark, the adjustments needed in the artistry of becoming consummately human must begin from within.

5B8 孟子謂萬章曰: "一鄉之善士斯友一鄉之善士，一國之善士斯友一國之善士，天下之善士斯友天下之善士。以友天下之善士爲未足，又尚論古之人。頌其詩，讀其書，不知其人，可乎? 是以論其世也。是尚友也。"

Mencius spoke to Wan Zhang saying: "The best kind of scholar-officials (*shanshi* 善士) in the village will seek out friends among their counterparts in that village; the best kind of scholar-officials in the state will seek out friends among their counterparts in the state; the best kind of scholar-officials in the world will seek out friends among their counterparts in the world. Discovering that seeking out friendships with the best scholar-officials in the world is still not enough, these same scholar-officials will go back in history to talk with the ancients. In reciting their poetry and studying their writings, how could these scholar-officials not come to know these ancients intimately? In thus discussing the world in which the ancients lived their lives, how could these ancients but become their 'friends in history?'"

Comment: We have here a definition of friendship that in many respects repeats that found in the *Analects* where Confucius insists persons should only befriend those who are better than themselves. There is a recognition in this method of making friends that the quality of those we befriend is the most immediate and fertile resource for growing ourselves as persons. What is novel in Mencius's definition of friendship is the inclusion of "friends in history" who are available to us through a careful study of their lives and teachings. Throughout the Confucian canons there is the assumption that the cultural progenitors live on in their writings and their music, and astute students can therefore find them and speak with them directly in their best efforts to embody the living tradition.

4A12 孟子曰: "居下位而不獲於上，民不可得而治也。獲於上有道，不信於友，弗獲於上矣。信於友有道，事親弗悦，弗信於友矣。悦親有道，反身不誠，不悦於親矣。誠身有道，不明乎善，不誠其身矣。是故誠者，天之道也；思誠者，人之道也。至誠而不動者，未之有也；不誠，未有能動者也。"

Mencius said: "If persons in a lower station do not enjoy the confidence of those above, they will not be able to govern the common people effectively. But there is a way for them to win over the confidence of those above. If they are not trusted by friends, they will not win over the higher authorities. But there is a way of winning the trust of friends. If in serving their parents, they are not able to make them happy, they will not have the trust of friends. But there is a way of making their parents happy. If in turning personally inward they cannot find resolve (*cheng* 誠), they cannot make their parents happy. But there is a way of finding resolve in one's person. If they are unclear on what constitutes efficacious conduct, they will not be able to find resolve in their persons.

"It is thus that resolve is the way-making of *tian* 天, while reflecting on things with resolution is the way-making of human beings. There has never been a person of the highest resolve who has not been able to move others while there has never been anyone without this personal resolve who has been able to move anyone at all."

Comment: This passage is reminiscent of the *Expansive Learning* in which there is a radial extension from person to family to community to proper governance and ultimately, to cosmic order. It uses language that alludes directly to *Mencius* 7A4 of turning inward and finding personal resolve in my coalescence with the myriad things all implicated here in me. True to the emphasis in the *Mencius* on proper governance, it establishes an immediate symbiosis between personal cultivation, governing effectively, and a flourishing cosmos. In this passage, the feeling of resolve (*cheng* 誠) in personal growth is elevated as a natural force that correlates a person's inner intensity with cosmic reach and influence, and establishes humankind as a co-creator with the heavens and the earth: the "three forces" (*sancai* 三才). Elevating resolve to become a force that shapes the emerging natural order locates human life and growth as integral to what is fundamentally a moral cosmos. This cosmic association of *cheng* 誠 with creativity and resolve is developed further in *Focusing the Familiar* 16:

夫微之顯，誠之不可掩如此夫。
Such is the way that the inchoate is made manifest and that resolve cannot be repressed.

And it occurs again in *Focusing the Familiar* 20:

誠者，天之道也；誠之者，人之道也。誠者不勉而中，不思而得，從容中道，聖人也。誠之者，擇善而固執之者也。

Resolve is the way-making of *tian* 天; applying resolve is the way-making of becoming consummately human. Resolve is achieving equilibrium and coalescence without coercion; it is succeeding without reflection. Freely and easily traveling at the center of way-making—this is the sage. Resolve is selecting what is efficacious and holding on to it firmly.

The ultimate statement of this cosmic notion of resolve (*cheng* 誠) is found in *Focusing Familiar* 25 in which 性之德也，合外內之道也 "the virtuosity achieved in one's natural propensities" is correlated with "the way-making that integrates what is more internal and what is more external." In cultivating ourselves by growth in our relations, we bring resolution and meaning to the cosmos.

IV.3 The Vocabulary of Mencius's Moral Sensorium

living, birthing, growing (*sheng* 生), *qi* (氣), inner/outer (*neiwai* 內外), thinking and feeling, heartmind, "bodyheartminding" (*xin* 心), speaking (*yan* 言), intending (*zhi* 志), thinking, feeling, and reflecting (*si* 思), desiring (*yu* 欲), the four inclinations (*siduan* 四端), loving (*ai* 愛), embodying (*ti* 體), growing the native human propensities (*xing* 性), sagacity (*shengren* 聖人), resolve/resolution (*cheng* 誠), putting oneself in the other's place, empathy (*shu* 恕), courage (*yong* 勇)

2A2 公孫丑問曰："夫子加齊之卿相，得行道焉，雖由此霸王，不異矣。如此，則動心否乎？"孟子曰："否，我四十不動心。"曰："若是，則夫子過孟賁遠矣。"曰："是不難，告子先我不動心。"曰："不動心有道乎？"曰："有。北宮黝之養勇也；不膚撓，不目逃，思以一豪挫於人，若撻之於市朝；不受於褐寬博，亦不受於萬乘之君；視刺萬乘之君，若刺褐夫；無嚴諸侯，惡聲至，必反之。孟施舍之所養勇也，曰：'視不勝猶勝也；量敵而後進，慮勝而後會，是畏三軍者也。舍豈能為必勝哉？能無懼而已矣。'孟施舍似曾子，北宮黝似子夏。夫二子之勇，未知其孰賢，然而孟施舍守約也。昔者曾子謂子襄曰：'子好勇乎？吾嘗聞大勇於夫子矣：自反而不縮，雖褐寬博，吾不惴焉；自反而縮，雖千萬人，吾往矣。'孟施舍之守氣，又不如曾子之守約也。"

Gongsun Chou asked Mencius, "If you, Sir, were to become the prime minister of the state of Qi and were to succeed in promoting the proper way therein, it would not be at all surprising to find that the King of Qi would become the leader of the various nobles or even a True King. If you were to bring this about, would such a dramatic change give you any feelings of anxiety (*dongxin* 動心)?"

"No," replied Mencius: "It wouldn't. From turning forty on, I have not suffered from any anxiety."

"If this is so, Sir, you are far more courageous (*yong* 勇) than the legendary Meng Ben."

"It is really no great accomplishment. Master Gao overcame his anxieties long before I did."

"Is there some way to cultivate this control over one's anxieties?"

"Indeed, there is." said Mencius. "The way Beigong You used to steel his courage was to never yield an inch or avert his glare, thinking the least slight was tantamount to taking a pummeling by the crowd in the marketplace. He was no more inclined to suffer insult from the lord of a great state than he was from a bumpkin in rags. Running his sword through the lord of the great state or the bumpkin was all the same to him. Fearless in the presence of the powerful, no slur was forgiven.

"Meng Shishe described his way of steeling his courage in the following terms. 'Victory or defeat is all the same to me. He who advances only after taking the enemy's measure and who engages only after deliberating on his chances of victory is to stand in awe of the enemy's armies. If I can't be invincible, I can certainly be fearless.'

"Meng Shishe was like Confucius's protégé Master Zeng, and Beigong You was like Zixia. I couldn't say which of these two had the superior courage, but Meng Shishe had really grasped its meaning.

"There was an occasion on which Master Zeng said to Zixiang, 'Do you hold courage in high regard? I heard the Master speak about the greatest kind of courage. If on reflection I am in the wrong, then even a bumpkin in rags would be a source of intimidation. But if I am doing what is right, then though the enemy be legion, I can march ahead steady on.' Master Zeng's grasp of the true meaning of courage goes way beyond Meng Shishe's mere fortitude (*qi* 氣)."

Comment: Why would Mencius or anyone else feel anxious (*dongxin* 動心)

if, because of his own sagely counsel, the ruler of Qi becomes a True King? In the Western commentaries, *dongxin* 動心 is variously translated as "moved," "stirred," "agitated," and "perturbed." Zhu Xi glosses it as "fear" (*kongju* 恐懼) and "perplexity" (*yihuo* 疑惑). Many of the commentators suggest that Mencius in mentioning the age of forty is an allusion to the *Analects* 2.4 in which Confucius rehearsing his own growth states that "at forty I was no longer doubtful" (*sishierbuhuo* 四十而不惑). "Anxiety" is concern respecting some uncertain future event that agitates and disturbs the mind, and keeps it in a state of painful unease.

What is the difference between fear and anxiety? And what is the perceived relationship between anxiety and *yong* 勇: "bravery, valor, courage?" The word "courage" in English comes from the Latin *cor* meaning "heart." Aristotle defines courage as acting courageously in a qualified way: at the right time, in the right manner, with the right motivation, for the right reason. Courageous acts are conducted with an eye on the correct purpose:

> The courageous man withstands and fears those things which it is necessary [to fear and withstand] and on account of the right reason, and how and when it is necessary [to fear or withstand] them, and likewise in the case of being bold (1116b17-19).

In Plato's *Phaedo*, Socrates argues that everyone except the philosopher is courageous out of fear that the alternative will be worse than the consequences of the courageous action—for example, the fear of being seen as a coward by your comrades-in-arms. True courage for Plato is to act on behalf of wisdom.

Interestingly, the ancient form of this character "courage" on the bronzes is sometimes written as *yong* 恿 ("urging, inciting") 㦺 with the heart radical, a character that is attested as late as the bamboo strips: 㦺. The later stylized form of the character 勇 uses the signific *li* 力 meaning "strength, force, power" that was originally a pictograph of a primitive farming tool used for turning the soil, thus emphasizing the physical rather than the mental and emotional aspect of courage.

Mencius gives four different examples of bravery or courage: Meng Ben, Beigong You, Meng Shishe, and Master Zeng. How do we distinguish among them? What is the motivation in each case? Meng Ben is the paragon of animal courage as being fierce and invincible. Beigong You is motivated by a sense of honor where he will brook no insult. Meng Shishe seems to make a death resolve similar to the Japanese *bushi* 武士 that precipitates an immediate response to any situation without any deliberation or calculation regarding the chances of victory or defeat. Jim Behuniak makes the point that these examples of courage reflect the pervasive question of whether morality is a function of "inner" intentions or "outer" conditions:

> Beigong Yu represents a form of courage conditioned by external circumstance; his concern is with disgrace in the face of others. Mengshi She represents courage fueled by unbending internal conviction; external circumstances will have no bearing on this conduct. Each form of courage disconnects the transactional circuit of human engagement by introducing either an internal factor, resoluteness, or an external factor, conditioning. The inflexible posture of each form of courage results from the reduction of human conduct into one or the other category.... The form of courage Mencius endorses, however, restores continuity between the internal and the external (*nei/wei* 內外), something that Mencian notions consistently do.[①]

Mencius takes Meng Shishe to be a higher form of courage than Beigong You because he is animated by inner purpose as opposed to simply external conditions. But it is Master Zeng who has the holistic understanding of courage as the coordination of an appropriate inner moral responsiveness to most effectively and productively manage all outer conditions. Master Zeng is one of Confucius's most prominent disciples conventionally associated with "family reverence" (*xiao* 孝), where the ultimate standard for *xiao* 孝 is optimal appropriateness (*yi* 義) for all concerned, a necessary condition for true courage. It is Master Zeng who makes the immediate connection between true courage and morality.

曰：" 敢問夫子之不動心與告子之不動心，可得聞與？" "告子曰：' 不得於言，勿求於心；不得於心，勿求於氣。' 不得於心，勿求於氣，可；不得於言，

---

① James Behuniak, Jr., *Mencius on Becoming Human*, Albany: State University of New York Press, 2005, p. 36.

IV. THE MENCIUS (MENGZI 孟子): EXTENDING THE VOCABULARY

勿求於心，不可。夫志，氣之帥也；氣，體之充也。夫志至焉，氣次焉；故曰：'持其志，無暴其氣。'" "既曰：'志至焉，氣次焉。' 又曰：'持其志，無暴其氣' 者何也？" 曰："志壹則動氣，氣壹則動志也，今夫蹶者趨者，是氣也，而反動其心。"

Gongsun Chou said, "Would it be possible for you to speak to the issue of how you, Sir, and Master Gao both came to terms with your anxieties?"

"According to Master Gao, 'If I don't get something from what is being said (*yan* 言), I don't bother seeking it out by thinking it through (*xin* 心). And thus, not getting it from thinking it through, I don't seek it out by turning to *qi* 氣.' I think that Master Gao is quite right in saying that if he doesn't get it from thinking it through, he ought not to bother seeking it out by turning to *qi* 氣, but I do not agree that if he doesn't get it from what is being said, he should not bother seeking it out by thinking it through. It is our intentions (*zhi* 志) that guide our *qi* 氣, and it is this *qi* 氣 that fills our bodies. And it is because our *qi* 氣 follows wherever our intentions take us that it is said: 'Be firm in your intentions and do not distress your *qi* 氣'."

"Since you have already said that 'our *qi* 氣 follows wherever our intentions take us,' what is your point in adding 'be firm in your intentions and do not distress your *qi* 氣'?"

Mencius replied, "If one is set in one's intentions, it will affect one's *qi* 氣, and if there is intensity in one's *qi* 氣, it will affect one's intentions. We can say that running and jumping certainly just makes us breathe faster (*qi* 氣), but it also quickens the heartbeat."

Comment: Speaking (*yan* 言), thinking something through (*xin* 心), and *qi* 氣 are three different levels of discursive interaction. The question is: are they separate and distinct, or aspectual and mutually entailing? There is the example of *Analects* 6.23 仁者樂山，知者樂水 "The wise enjoy water; those consummate in their conduct enjoy mountains." Persons who are wise and consummate in their conduct are being distinguished as such, and yet wisdom and consummatory conduct are symbiotic like the relationship between the mountain and the rain, and they are thus aspects of one and the same person. Again each of these three modes of discourse needs to be understood by appeal to the language of "forming" and "functioning" (*tiyong* 體用). Since the interlocutors in any discursive interaction are at once shaping and being shaped, structure and function are both in play. And each of the three discourses is to be evaluated on the basis of the appropriateness and meaningfulness (*yi* 義) of the outcome.

If you cannot grasp the best path forward from what is being said in the ideas of the philosophical doctrines available to you (*yan* 言), look for the best way in the intentions (*zhi* 志) that emerge in the process of thinking these ideas through. Mencius's revision of Master Gao's statement is first that the intentions which develop from thinking something through must inform the original doctrines themselves. Secondly, the course the *qi* 氣 will follow will in turn be set by the intentions that emerge in thinking things through. And thirdly, even though the *qi* 氣 will follow these intentions, the process of thinking things through and the movement of *qi* 氣 are still symbiotic and have an effect on each other. In his physical analogy, Mencius is saying that even though running and jumping occasion faster breathing (*qi* 氣), such activity also produces the quickening palpitations in the heartmind (*xin* 心) that are analogous to one's intentions (*zhi* 志). Any activity and stimulation in our *qi* 氣 can have consequences that affect the intentions arising from our thinking things through, and hence they can affect each other.

In 7A24, Mencius associates the exercise of intentionality with flowing water:

流水之為物也，不盈科不行；君子之志於道也，不成章不達。
It is the nature of flowing water that it does not advance until every low-lying hollow has been filled. For exemplary persons whose intentions (*zhi* 志) are set on the proper way, they do not move forward on this path without having some real achievements to show.

The intentions of exemplary persons are set on the proper way, but are also flexible in responding to the conditions that are found along it.

In speech-act theory, locutionary acts by definition have meaning such as providing information, asking questions, describing something, or even announcing a verdict. Speech-acts have a locutionary sense or meaning, an illocutionary force in doing something, and a perlocutionary result. This is but to say that illocutionary acts as a "doing" are performative in some cases, such as "I do," "ready, aim, fire," and "we find the defendant guilty." A perlocutionary act on the other hand is an action or state of mind that is the consequence of something said when persuading, convincing, scaring, enlightening, inspiring or otherwise affecting the listener.

Can these same characterizations of linguistic discourse be carried over into the *xin* 心 "thinking-and-feeling" and into the *qi* 氣 "forming and functioning" discourses? What is interesting in the Confucian cosmology is that these same kinds of linguistic distinctions also apply to Confucian epistemology in which "knowing" is necessarily a "doing." We could invent a new language for "epistenary" (as opposed to locutionary) acts where knowing is "il-epistenary" in having force in realizing something, and "per-epistenary" force in having affective consequences. If we reflect on *xin* 心 as "thinking and feeling," these functions like language are a source of meaning. They happen in the world as interwoven with the events of our lives. They have intentional force and do things in precipitating and guiding our actions, thus having real consequences for the quality of communal life. If we reflect on *yangqi* 養氣 as a discourse, it follows this same pattern.

"敢問夫子惡乎長？" 曰："我知言，我善養吾浩然之氣。" "敢問何謂浩然之氣？" 曰："難言也。其爲氣也，至大至剛，以直養而無害，則塞于天地之間。其爲氣也，配義與道；無是，餒也。是集義所生者，非義襲而取之也。行有不慊於心，則餒矣。"

"May I ask after your success in this respect, Sir?"

Mencius replied: "I realize what is being said (*zhiyan* 知言), and I am good at nourishing my flood-like *qi* 氣 (*haoranzhiqi* 浩然之氣)."

"May I ask what you mean by 'flood-like *qi* 氣'?"

Mencius replied: "It is difficult to put into words. It is activating our *qi* 氣 to have its most extensive reach and its most intensive resolution. If we nurture it faithfully and without respite, it will fill up all between the heavens and the earth. As the achieved quality of our *qi* 氣, it is of a piece with sustaining optimal appropriateness in our conduct (*yi* 義) and with moving resolutely forward in our way-making (*dao* 道). Without this quality of *qi* 氣, we will starve. Flood-like *qi* 氣 is what is born of the cumulative habit of optimally appropriate conduct, and is not something that can be had through merely random acts of appropriateness. If one does anything that would cause disappointment in our thinking and feeling, it starves."

Comment: The expression "realizing what is being said" (*zhiyan* 知言) might well be an allusion to a passage in the *Analects* 20.3 wherein Confucius insists that: 不知言，無以知人也 "persons who do not realize what is being said (*buzhiyan* 不知言) have no way of understanding other people." It is important to appreciate the performative implications of the term *zhi* 知—conventionally translated as "knowing." Rather than delimiting this capacity as simply "knowing" something cognitively, I have rendered it here as "realizing" in the performative sense of "making something real." As it is captured in the phrase "the inseparability of knowing and doing" (*zhixingheyi* 知行合一) made popular by Wang Yangming, in the Confucian tradition from earliest times, "knowing" entails something done. Hence, "knowing" is a continuing practical process rather than an achieved state of mind. This being the case, the notion of "understanding other people" has to be taken in the sense of making some kind of difference in the lives of others, if not in fact having some transformative effect upon them. One immediate implication of this non-dualistic way of thinking is the absence and irrelevance of the familiar knowledge/wisdom dichotomy. There is thus also a challenge to the usual way of thinking about a mirroring alignment between an exclusive objectivity and truth, where an alternative inclusive sense of objectivity means that "knowing" must be the most panoramic view on and comprehensive engagement with any particular situation.

This claim about "realizing what is being said" (*zhiyan* 知言) parallels the phrase "nourishing my flood-like *qi* 氣" in suggesting we must understand human relations semiotically as a "relating to" within the irreducibly social "thinking and feeling." "Relating to" is making meaning. In grasping the discursive nature of relatedness, we can then understand that the quality of those relations which constitute our own particular identities is nothing other than the quality of our sustained conversations with others over time. The quality of the persons we are to become is a direct consequence of our ability to communicate effectively and meaningfully within our families and communities.

And the parallel with the second accomplishment here is clear. Mencius's nurturing his "flood-like *qi* 氣" like the semiotic and symbolic exchanges needed in understanding others is also a modality of discourse, a resonant relationship with one's environing context. By "cultivating and nourishing" (*yang* 養) both the intensity (*zhigang* 至剛) and the resolution (*cheng* 誠) of this *qi* 氣, the *qi* 氣 becomes intentional and deliberate (*zhi* 志). The cultivation and configuration of our *qi* 氣 within the context of our discursive relations (*zhiyan* 知言) is what funds such personal growth in our relations and conduces to virtuosity in our conduct. Such *qi* 氣 expressed as purposeful actions is animated by our commitment to achieving optimal appropriateness (*yi* 義) in what we do. Mencius's claim is that when his *qi* 氣 is properly nurtured and achieves its most "intensive resolution" (*zhigang* 至剛) within his own person, it provides him with the greatest "extensive magnitude" (*zhida* 至大) in the influence he then comes to have on the world.

And this same radial and symbiotic "intensive focus" and "extensive field" dynamic is then repeated a second time in the language of *dao* 道 and *yi* 義: that is, Mencius is able to acquire reach and influence (*dao* 道) through habituating a quality of meaningful resolution in the relations that constitute his own person (*yi* 義). For Mencius, to nourish his *qi* 氣 most successfully is to achieve the greatest degree of meaning and thus resolution within his most extensive field of *qi* 氣. In just this manner, sustained virtuosity in the quality of his conduct (*daode* 道德) is attained as he acquires the greatest degree of potency and effectiveness (*de* 德) in relation to the most far-ranging elements of his various environments (*dao* 道). It is in this sense that the nurturing of one's *qi* 氣 has flood-like, even cosmic consequences.

Again, we might use the familiar language of *jingshen* 精神 that as a binomial is conventionally translated as "spirit, vigor, vitality, drive" to capture this same dynamic between the intensity of focus and the enhanced extension of one's field. *Jing* 精, conventionally translated as "essence," is not some ontological essence to be contrasted with accidents or attributes, but is the concentrated source of personal vitality, both physical and intellectual that is inherited from parents and acquired from various forms of nourishment. *Jing* 精 is the sap of life, a tangible, life-giving energy, the potency of semen. And *shen* 神, conventionally translated as "spirit," is not the spiritual as opposed to the corporeal, but is this same *jing* 精 vitality as it comes to flow, course through, pervade, and be manifested through the functional activities of the mind and the body as a whole as they extend radially to transform the world. *Shen* is the mystery of how we become "great souled" in our expansive and inspired living. As the "Great Commentary" on the *Book of Changes* A5 reports: 陰陽不測之謂神 "what cannot be fathomed by appeal to *yin* 陰 and *yang* 陽 is what we call the truly mysterious (*shen* 神)."

Confucianism advocates for a sense of growth that is centered in a commitment to personal cultivation within intimate family and community relations, and that then extends outward symbiotically both radially and reflexively to the cosmic totality. There is an interpenetrating center and periphery, where what is most extensive is reflected back to fortify what is most intensive, and what is most intensive has the greatest extensive reach and influence. Important in this passage is Mencius's assertion that human beings, through a regimen of personal cultivation in our various levels of discourse, can exercise an influence over the configuration of our *qi* 氣 cosmos.

Indeed, Mencius is suggesting that we can have a "flood-like," cascading impact on the moral quality of the world to the extent that it "fills all between heaven and earth." Confucius did. Buddha did. Socrates and Jesus did. Alternatively, if we fail to cultivate our resolutely discursive identities—if we do not nourish our *qi* 氣 and thus fail to configure it in a way that is continuous with our morality—we disappoint and thus ultimately "starve" (*nei* 餒) our thinking and feeling. The underlying zoetology of "birthing, living, growing" (*sheng* 生) as it is expressed in the "art of living" is made explicit in this metaphor of being starved, where it is the nature of life that in order for it to be sustained and grow, it must be nourished.

"我故曰：告子未嘗知義，以其外之也。必有事焉，而勿正，心勿忘，勿助長也。無若宋人然：宋人有閔其苗之不長而揠之者，芒芒然歸，謂其人曰：'今日病矣！予助苗長矣！' 其子趨而往視之，苗則槁矣。天下之不助苗長者寡矣。以爲無益而舍之者，不耘苗者也；助之長者，揠苗者也，非徒無益，而又害之。"

"This is why I have said that Master Gao has never understood appropriateness (*yi* 義) because he externalizes it. Instead, in cultivating this moral *qi* 氣, you must work at it diligently without pause, but must not be dogged. You must be mindful, but must not force its growth.

"You do not want to be like that farmer in the state of Song. There was a farmer of Song who was worried that his grain was not growing properly, and went around the field tugging on the seedlings to help them grow. Weary from his labors, he returned home and reported to the others: 'Today I am really bushed! I was helping the grain seedlings to grow.' His son ran out to take a look at the crop, and sure enough the seedlings were all withered and brown.

"If the truth be known, there are not many people in this world who can refrain from tugging on their seedlings. There are those who abandon the crop because they think they do not make any difference, and so do not even weed the field. And then there are those who tug on the seedlings to help them grow. Far from helping the grain grow, such people in fact do it serious harm."

Comment: Master Gao has failed to understand *yi* 義 as a standard of judgment. He makes it a matter of externally derived and imposed regulation rather than seeing it as aspiring to an inclusive and optimal appropriateness in one's conduct. For Master Gao, *yi* 義 is a matter of *yan* 言 with what is said being formulated as "doctrine." Mencius in suggesting that Master Gao "externalizes" *yi* 義 associates Gao with the Mohists, the doctrines of whom Mencius decries as having an unwarranted yet powerful role in the philosophical discourse of this period.

In this Mencian ethic, there is a tacit awareness of what Bernard Williams also concluded during his own long and distinguished career as an ethicist. Williams in his search for "thick," "world-guided," and "action-guiding" ethical concepts is famous for having reservations about the capacity of any moral theory to tell us what is right, what is wrong, and what we ought to do. In the preface to *Moral Luck*, Williams announces:

> There cannot be any very interesting, tidy or self-contained theory of what morality is, nor, despite the vigorous activities of some present practitioners, can there be an ethical theory, in the sense of a philosophical structure which, together with some degree of empirical fact, will yield a decision procedure for moral reasoning.[①]

Williams is saying here that no ethical theory, no ready-made set of rules, no moral system, can in any particular situation tell us what is the right course of action. The best response to our moral quandaries must emerge out of intelligent reflection on the specific conditions of experience, where much of human flourishing is dependent upon dexterity in the exercise and application of our moral imagination. In our search for doing what is most appropriate, the abstract and theoretical are certainly important, but can at best have only an instrumental function in providing direction and some general guidance for such immediate deliberations.

Mencius's alternative to Master Gao is not to "internalize" *yi* 義, but rather to make its cultivation a collaboration between persons and their world—what *Focusing the Familiar* 25 refers to as 合內外之道 "the way-making that integrates what is more internal and what is more external."

---

① Bernard Williams, *Moral Luck: Philosophical Papers* 1973-1980, New York: Cambridge University Press, 1981, pp. ix-x.

It is this same "internal-external" dynamic we find in *Mencius* 7A4:

萬物皆備於我矣。反身而誠，樂莫大焉。強恕而行，求仁莫近焉。
Is there any enjoyment greater than, with the myriad things of the world all implicated here in me, to turn personally inward and to thus find resolution with these things? Is there any way of seeking to become consummate in my person more immediate than making every effort to act empathetically by deferring to the interests of others?

One must be assiduous in the project of cultivating the moral *qi* 氣. But in so doing, one must in this collaboration be accommodating with the contextualizing others in order to realize what is optimally appropriate for everyone and everything concerned. Mencius uses his horticultural analogy to make the point that, while carefully attending to what crops need is essential, to violate the underlying premises of how crops themselves grow naturally and to thus become a "seedling tugger" (*zhumiaozhangzhe* 助苗長者) is not only counterproductive, but disastrous. The "seedling tugger," like Master Gao, is depending upon some external mechanism to activate growth when it must be activated by the intentions in the thinking and feeling of the heartmind itself.

Of course, the immediate association with the "seedlings" here is Mencius's "four inclinations" (*siduan* 四端), an expression that is often translated as the "four sprouts" or "four shoots." Again, growth of these four inclinations is dependent upon our natural, prosocial disposition towards efficacious conduct (*shan* 善). This native disposition can be compromised and even lost utterly either by failing to cultivate it or through the imposition of externally derived doctrines on our natural human proclivities.

"何謂知言？" 曰："詖辭知其所蔽，淫辭知其所陷，邪辭知其所離，遁辭知其所窮。生於其心，害於其政；發於其政，害於其事。聖人復起，必從吾言矣。" "宰我、子貢善爲説辭；冉牛、閔子、顏淵善言德行。孔子兼之，曰：'我於辭命，則不能也。' 然則夫子既聖矣乎？"

"What does it mean to realize what is being said (*zhiyan* 知言)?" asked Gongsun Chou.

"In language that is one-sided, I understand where the speaker's bias lies; in language that is excessive, I know where the speaker has gotten bogged down; in language that is deviant, I know where the speaker has gone astray;

in language that is evasive, I know why the speaker is at the end of his tether. Where these four kinds of language arise in our thinking and feeling, they are sure to impair government policy, and where they emerge in government policy, they are sure to impair its implementation. Were a sage to arise in the world again, he would certainly concur with what I am saying here."

Gongsun Chou said, "Zaiwo and Zigong excelled in the eloquence of their speech; Ran Niu, Minzi, and Yan Hui excelled in explaining virtuosic conduct. Although Confucius excelled in both, he said of himself that 'I can never find the right words.' Since you understand both, Sir, does this mean you are already a sage?"

Comment: As with the cultivation of *qi* 氣 above, the ultimate criteria in the productive use of language is aspiring to the quality of communication that conduces to achieving what is most meaningful and optimally appropriate (*yi* 義) in relating to each other. Mencius makes the connection between four kinds of disintegrative language—speech that is biased, excessive, deviant, and evasive—and the four kinds of speakers who would use such inappropriate language. He is making the same point as the *Analects*: to "realize what is being said" is to be able to discriminate and "to know other people."

A second connection Mencius makes here is between the use of inappropriate language and ineffective governance. One important transition we find between the vocabulary of the *Analects* and the emphasis found in the *Mencius* is the extension of a Confucian vocabulary of personal cultivation to the challenges of proper governance. This reorientation reflects the exponential rise in internecine violence among the states on the Central Plain. Mencius's insight here is immediately reminiscent of the doctrine of "using language properly" (*zhengming* 正名) announced in *Analects* 13.3:

名不正，則言不順；言不順，則事不成；事不成，則禮樂不興；禮樂不興，則刑罰不中；刑罰不中，則民無所錯手足。故君子名之必可言也，言之必可行也。君子於其言，無所苟而已矣。

When names are not used properly, language will not be used effectively; when language is not used effectively, matters will not be taken care of; when matters are not taken care of, propriety in roles and relations and in the playing of music will not be achieved; when propriety in roles and relations and in the playing of music is not achieved, the application of laws and punishments will not be on the mark; when the application of laws and punishments is not on the mark, the people will not know what to do with themselves. Thus, when exemplary persons put a name to something, it can certainly be spoken, and when spoken it can certainly be acted upon. There is nothing careless in the attitude of exemplary persons toward what is said.

The logic of the text then turns from concern about effective governance, dependent as it is upon the effective use of language, to the role of the sage as the virtuosic communicator. Sageliness is defined here first as eloquence in speaking, and then as being good at explaining virtuosic conduct. But it seems that such an abstract theoretical definition of effective communication is not sufficient in a holistic tradition requiring a thicker explanation inclusive of concrete practice. What is of note here is that Mencius's own student Gongsun Chou goes beyond the theoretical account of sagely virtuosity in his appeal to the lives of historical role models who define concretely what is meant by a moral life. He begins his examples from several of the most distinguished students of Confucius, then on to Confucius, and finally to his own teacher, Mencius.

曰:"惡!是何言也?昔者子貢問於孔子曰:'夫子聖矣乎?'孔子曰:'聖則吾不能,我學不厭而教不倦也。'子貢曰:'學不厭,智也;教不倦,仁也。仁且智,夫子既聖矣乎。'夫聖,孔子不居,是何言也?" "昔者竊聞之:子夏、子游、子張皆有聖人之一體,冉牛、閔子、顏淵則具體而微,敢問所安。"曰:"姑舍是。"曰:"伯夷、伊尹何如?"曰:"不同道。非其君不事,非其民不使;治則進,亂則退,伯夷也。何事非君,何使非民;治亦進,亂亦進,伊尹也。可以仕則仕,可以止則止,可以久則久,可以速則速,孔子也。皆古聖人也,吾未能有行焉;乃所願,則學孔子也。"

"My goodness!" replied Mencius, "What on earth are you talking about? Once Zigong asked Confucius, 'Are you a sage Master?' and Confucius responded, 'A sage I am not. I just continue to study without respite and instruct others without growing weary.' Zigong said, 'To study without respite is wisdom (*zhi* 智) and to instruct others without respite is consummate conduct (*ren* 仁). If you, Master, are consummate in your conduct and also wise, you are already a sage.' Now if being called a sage is something that even Confucius would not countenance, how can you say this of me?"

Gongsun Chou said, "I once heard it said that Zixia, Ziyou, and Zizhang all had something of Confucius's sagacity, while Ran Niu, Minzi, and Yan Hui were smaller versions of him. Which kind of person, Sir, would you choose to be?"

"Let's not bother with them for the moment," replied Mencius.

"What about Bo Yi and Yi Yin then?"

"They did not follow the same path as Confucius," replied Mencius. "To serve only the lord of his choice, to preside over only those of the common people he wanted to, to take office only when the world was orderly, and to abandon it when disorder arose—this was Bo Yi. To serve any lord, to preside over any of the common people, and to take office regardless of the conditions that prevailed in the world—this was Yi Yin. To serve in office when he should serve in office, to step down when he should step down, to continue when he should continue, and to leave when he should leave—this was Confucius. All are our sages of old, and have attained to something I could never reach, but even so, what I really aspire after is to learn the way of Confucius."

Comment: Rather than debating the abstract criteria necessary for defining the sage, the conversation turns to a comparison of historical exemplars who are popularly associated with sageliness. One condition of being considered a sage seems to be the personal modesty necessary to reject such a characterization by one's juniors, a condition evidenced by both Confucius and Mencius. In responding to Gongsun Chou's second ascription of sageliness to the most distinguished disciples of Confucius, although Mencius does ask for temporary respite, he is not rejecting this line of inquiry in which historical examples are evoked in trying to find a definition for what it means to be a sage. Hence, Gongsun Chou introduces some other examples of reputed sages of more ancient vintage, Bo Yi and Yi Yin.

For Mencius, these two earlier Zhou dynasty sages in providing a contrast with Confucius illustrate how Mencius thinks about the highest exemplar. Mencius allows that they are all "our sages of old," and as such, have much to recommend them. But at the same time, both Bo Yi and Yi Yin are partial and incomplete. The best answer and the best example is the one that is most "comprehensive," and that illuminates most fully any particular issue in all of its complexity. It is interesting that the term *quan* 全 we translate as "comprehensive" is defined in the early lexicons qualitatively and aesthetically as well as quantitatively. The *Shuowen* for example defines *quan* 全 as *wan* 完 meaning "complete," where complete has both the meaning of "full" or "total" (*bei* 備) as well as "completely beautiful" (*wanmei* 完美). It also defines *quan* 全 as pure and flawless jade: "pure jade is said to be *quan*"(*chunyuyuequan* 純玉曰全).

Here Confucius rather than just being the right example is qualitatively the better one. The epistemic critique we find in many of the classical Confucian texts does not rely heavily upon the binary language of right and wrong, or true and false that would follow from a reality-appearance and essence-attribute kind of ontological dualism. Rather, they often take the form of insisting someone knows only one aspect of a situation while being insufficiently aware of the others.

For example, the *Xunzi* has a whole chapter entitled "Dispelling Obsessions" (*jiebi* 解蔽) that opens with the charge: 凡人之患，蔽於一曲而闇於大理 "The affliction most people have is they are obsessed with one corner and cannot see the big picture." Xunzi then goes on to criticize his contemporaries Mozi, Shen Dao, Shen Buhai, and Hui Shi, accusing each of them in their doctrines of grasping only one corner of the whole. Indeed, Xunzi takes Zhuangzi as an example, saying of him that 莊子蔽於天而不知人 "being so obsessed with 'nature' (*tian* 天), he does not know human beings."

"伯夷、伊尹於孔子，若是班乎？" 曰："否。自有生民以來，未有孔子也。"
"然則有同與？" 曰："有。得百里之地而君之，皆能以朝諸侯，有天下；行一不義，殺一不辜，而得天下，皆不爲也。是則同。" 曰："敢問其所以異。" 曰："宰我、子貢、有若，智足以知聖人，汙不至阿其所好。宰我曰：'以予觀於夫子，賢於堯、舜遠矣。'子貢曰：'見其禮而知其政，聞其樂而知其德，由百世之後，等百世之王，莫之能違也。自生民以來，未有夫子也。'有若曰：'豈惟民哉？麒麟之於走獸，鳳凰之於飛鳥，泰山之於丘垤，河海之於行潦，類也。聖人之於民，亦類也。出於其類，拔乎其萃，自生民以來，未有盛於孔子也。'"

"Were Bo Yi and Yi Yin on a par with Confucius then?" asked Gongsun Chou.

"Not at all. In the entire history of the human race, there has never been another Confucius."

"This being so, did the three of them have anything in common?"

"Indeed." replied Mencius. "Were any of them to be made ruler over a tiny territory of a hundred square *li*, they could have won the allegiance of the various nobles and unified the world. On the other hand, were they offered the world in exchange for one inappropriate deed or the execution of one innocent person, none of them would have taken it. In this respect, they were similar."

"May I ask in what ways they differed?"

IV. THE *MENCIUS* (*MENGZI* 孟子): EXTENDING THE VOCABULARY

"Zaiwo, Zigong, and You Ruo were wise enough to understand what it means to be a sage, and would never have let their personal feelings color their judgment. Even so, Zaiwo said, 'In my opinion, Confucius goes way beyond Yao or Shun.' Zigong said, 'From examining the ritual practices of a state, Confucius could discern government policy, and from listening to its music he could gauge the character of its ruler. In the evaluation of the rulers for a hundred generations to come, none of them will be able to get away with contravening his teachings. In the entire history of the human race, there has never been another Confucius.'

"You Ruo said, 'Is it just among human beings that we vary so greatly? In what way is the unicorn different in kind from the brute of the field, the phoenix different from other winged creatures, Mount Tai different from other protuberances of earth, and the oceans and seas different from puddles of water? The sage too is same in kind as the common people. As it is said:

Although coming out from amongst their kind
He towers high above the crowd.

In the entire history of the human race, there has never been anyone greater than Confucius.'"

Comment: Even though Confucius stands apart, the three sages under discussion are similar in that, given the opportunity, they would all have brought proper governance to the world. Further, in doing so, none of them would stray from "optimal appropriateness" (*yi* 義) as their ultimate standard of judgment. Here again we see Mencius's preoccupation with governance.

The text begins by insisting that the most distinguished students of the Master were given to a quality of objectivity in their judgments that would preclude any hyperbolic celebration of their teacher. The passage then concludes with a panegyric to Confucius. They describe Confucius in hagiographic if not even religious terms that bring to mind the familiar mantra invoked to describe Confucian religiousness: "the continuity between and inseparability of the human and the cosmic orders" (*tianrenheyi* 天人合一). We find Confucius throughout this early literature described in celestial terms in being compared to the sun and the moon, and in naturalistic terms with his actions being elevated to the scale of the turning of the seasons and having the majesty of earth's mountains and rivers.[1] Confucius

---

[1] See for example, *Analects* 19.23, 24, and 25 and *Zhongyong* 30.

is repeatedly included in a pantheon of ancient sages, but is always the one who is singled out as being qualitatively far above everyone else. Cf. 5B1.

We also have some insight here into what Mencius and later Xunzi might mean by the claim that "the sage is same in kind as the common people." We have to be conscious of the teleological assumptions we bring to such claims. John Dewey cautions us in our search for good explanations regarding things against the inveterate habit of referring "the peculiarities" of any particular specimen back to something that stands behind it and guarantees it as a particular instance of some formal genus or natural kind:

> We dispose all too easily of the efforts of the schoolmen to interpret nature and mind in terms of real essences, hidden forms and occult faculties, forgetful of the seriousness and dignity of the ideas that lay behind. We dispose of them by laughing at the famous gentleman who accounted for the fact that opium put people to sleep on the ground it had a dormitive faculty. But the doctrine, held in our own day, that knowledge of the plant that yields the poppy consists in referring the peculiarities of an individual to a type, to a universal form, a doctrine so firmly established that any other method of knowing was conceived to be unphilosophical and unscientific, is a survival of precisely the same logic.①

What then do Mencius and Xunzi actually mean when they make the claim that all persons can become sages? Mencius in his moral psychology challenges us to reflect upon how we begin life as initially shallow, relatively passive and yet complex patterns of relations within family and community. He calls our native disposition at birth the "four inclinations" (*siduan* 四端). These four inclinations are not only productive of a cultivated human efficacy (*shan* 善), but also provide the ground for the Mencian claim that everyone, given these initial conditions, can aspire to behave sagaciously in their conduct. By pursuing focus and resolution in living these embodied roles and relations, we gradually evolve discursively into what are always unique and hopefully somewhat coherent personal identities. Indeed, for Mencius, those who, by virtue of assiduous effort emerge as the

---

① John Dewey, *The Middle Works of John Dewey* (1899-1924), ed. Jo Ann Boydston, Carbondale: Southern Illinois University Press, Vol. 4, pp. 6-7.

most distinctive and distinguished among us, become exemplary within our extended fields of selves, and become objects of deference within our communities.

For Mencius then, and Xunzi too, human beings are not "potentially" sages by virtue of some self-same, innate trait defining of all members of our species who then, by virtue of this trait, reduplicatively become sages. Rather the collaboration between our initial inclinations and the possibilities that emerge from our transactions with our world can produce sagacious conduct. There is an important difference between saying everyone has some inherent potential for becoming a sage, and everyone who behaves like a sage is a sage. The potential for becoming a sage only emerges *pari passu* in the transactional events that constitute the substance of a human life. That is, when the best among us behaves habitually and consistently with sagacity in their conduct, they are then sages. Said simply, sages are what sages do. And Mencius 6B2 makes this point explicitly in saying it is sagacious conduct that makes someone a sage:

> 曹交問曰："人皆可以爲堯舜，有諸？" 曰："……堯舜之道，孝弟而已矣。子服堯之服，誦堯之言，行堯之行，是堯而已矣。"
>
> Cao Jiao inquired: "Is it the case that we all have the capability of becoming Yaos and Shuns?"
>
> Mencius replied: " . . . The way-making of Yao and Shun was nothing but family reverence and deference to elders. If you wear Yao's clothes, speak his words, and do what he does, then you *are* a Yao."

7A4 孟子曰："萬物皆備於我矣。反身而誠，樂莫大焉。強恕而行，求仁莫近焉。"

Mencius said, "Is there any enjoyment greater than, with the myriad things of the world all implicated here in me, to turn personally inward and find resolution with all things? Is there any way of seeking to become consummate in my person more immediate than making every effort to act empathetically in deferring to the interests of others?"

Comment: Aristotle's ontological answer to "What is a man?" found at the very beginning of the *Categories* defines the subject "man" in terms of essence or substance—what is the "being" of the human being? The questions of "Where? When? His active state?" and so on, follow after this primary question, providing the various contingencies that in sum give a full predication of the subject. Notably, the "Why?" and "How?" are absent because these questions for Aristotle need not be asked. *Eidos* as the formal cause and *telos* as the final cause are already implicated in the ontological answer to "What is a man?" This ontological subject in Aristotle's "biopsychology" treatise, *De Anima*, is associated with a soul as the "source of movement" (the generative cause), "the end" (the teleological cause), and "the essence of the whole living body" (the ontological nature).① The form that the subject takes distinguishes it from formless matter (*hyle*), and actualizes matter from the state of potentiality (*dynamis*) to the state of actuality (*entelechia* or *energia*) of its final cause (*telos*).

This kind of Greek ontological thinking has little relevance for the Confucian process cosmology. What I have termed zoetology or "the art of living" is the Confucian alternative to ontology, and since life is growth, the primary Mencian questions are "Whence?" and "Whither?" This passage provides a clear statement of the focus-field conception of persons assumed in the early Confucian literature. That is, human "becomings" (and they must be plural) emerge through growth in context that can be called their *ziran* 自然, or "self-so-ing." The *zi* 自 can be foregrounded as "self" as the achieved, inimitable uniqueness of each particular persons, as the existentially projective purposes of this self, and as the unbounded matrix of relations that coalesce to constitute the *ran* 然 or presencing of this particular person. Growth in such relations is always productive of novel possibilities.

This gestalt shift from ontology to zoetology also requires that we think of "me" and "world" in eventful, processual terms rather than as bounded "things:" We have to resist separating form from function, and must rather think in terms of an unbounded but focal symbiotic process of forming and functioning, with new opportunities for forming always emerging within enhanced functioning. When Mencius says that "the myriad things of the world" are "all implicated here in me," he is thus declaring that the cosmic totality is implicated in each vital impulse of the embodied narratives of always unique persons. We are living cells within a social organism, a social organism within a natural ecology, and a centered ecology within an

---

① Aristotle, *The Complete Works of Aristotle: The Revised Oxford Translation*, ed. Jonathan Barnes, Princeton: Princeton University Press, 1984, Part 2, Ch. 4, 415b9-12, p. 661.

unbounded and unsummed cluster of ecologies.

If we are not externally related in standing "outside" of each other, what then is the nature of the relationships of persons, one to another? The focus-field understanding of relationally-constituted persons is one answer to this question, beginning as it does from the doctrine of internal, constitutive relations. This focus-field model requires a gestalt shift in our understanding of persons in which their particular identities and the unsummed totality—their foregrounded, always unique foci and their overlapping fields—are two holographic and thus mutually entailing ways of perceiving the same phenomenon. By way of analogy, just as each unique note as it is played within the context of a symphony has implicated within it the entire performance and must thus be evaluated accordingly, so each focal event—that is the identity expressed through each moment in a person's life—has implicated within it this person's entire, unbounded, narrative field. The Confucian project is optimizing the possibilities as they become available in the correlative interactions between existential subject and its contextualizing world that over time compound to constitute its narrative identity. Increased resolution in the focal identity of Confucius results in an expanding field of influence. Across the centuries, the meaning of the person Confucius and the values he represents have become increasingly focused and intelligible, and the field of influence of his ideas has spread from the state of Lu across East Asia and to the world.

There is a symbiosis in consolidating the pattern of relations within one's own focal identity, and the expanding field of relevance of this identity outward as it affects the world beyond. As expressed here, there is a symbiosis between "going inward" (*fanshen* 反身) to bring these same relations into meaningful resolution (*cheng* 誠), and exerting every effort to defer to and find the optimally appropriate fit in the expanding circle of empathetic relations (*qiangshu* 強恕) as these relations converge to constitute a personal identity. The shift here is between who I am becoming and what my world is becoming, between foregrounding the resolution of the insistent particularity of my life's narrative (*de* 德), and the construal of the unbounded totality from my own particular perspective (*dao* 道). What is important here is that *fanshen* 反身 and *qiangshu* 強恕 are not simply a process of discovery, but are in both instances a complex project of creative personal growth and extension.

Focusing the Familiar 25 describes this focus-field symbiosis:

成己，仁也；成物，知也。性之德也，合内外之道也。

Completing oneself is achieving virtuosity in one's roles and relations (*ren* 仁); completing all things is advancing wisdom in the world (*zhi* 知). Such is the virtuosity achieved through one's natural propensities and the way-making that integrates what is more internal and what is more external.

This Confucian focus-field model of person stands in contrast to the familiar realist separation of self and world, of inner and outer domains, where we are private, discrete subjects who share a mind-independent, objective world. This inner-outer dualism presupposes a doctrine of second order, external relations that obtain among independent things. And such a dualism brings with it the familiar intellectualist exercise called "*intro*-spection," a journey that turns inward away from the objective world to examine the representations of that world as they constitute our own private "states of mind." That is, introspection is usually understood as a turning away from our normal outward orientation toward the objective world in order to perform a reflective examination of our own internal mental states and our subjective feelings that mirror that world.

Inspired by this Mencian understanding of "thinking and feeling," however, we might want to challenge this assumption about turning "inward" by inventing an alternative term—"*intra*-spection"—as being a more appropriate descriptor. Michael Sandel opts for the search for an "*intra*subjective" rather than "intersubjective" conception of self, with the understanding that "*intra*-" means "on the inside, within," and references internal and constitutive relations as they function within a given entity itself.[①] "*Intra*-" has organic, ecological implications—an inside without an outside. Thus, *intra*-specting means examining the relations not between erstwhile separate internal and external domains, but rather scrutinizing those organic relations that obtain among the things that together constitute a group or entity—in this case, the ecological pattern of relations as they converge to constitute one's own focal identity, and the identity of the family, the community, and so on. We foreground the unique cell as it is constituted by its relations in the organism, or we foreground the organism as it is construed from the perspective of this particular cell. The neologism

---

[①] Michael Sandel, *Liberalism and the Limits of Justice*, Cambridge: Cambridge University Press, 1982, pp. 62-63.

"*intra*-spection" signals the fact that the vital process of "*looking into* our own thinking and feeling" is at the same time a *looking outward* into the quality of the coalescence we, in our experience of "thinking and feeling" have achieved within the ecology of our contextualizing world.

Such a "subjective" process parallels the more "objective" orientation in which we extend our reach and influence by deferring to our environing others in order to cultivate optimally productive relations with them. Indeed, since "the myriad things are all implicated here in me," in "making the most of our thinking and feeling" (*jinqixin* 盡其心) both in symbiotically bringing increased resolution to our own identities (*zhigang* 至剛) and thus extending our influence in the world (*zhida* 至大), we are literally bringing the entire cosmos into more meaningful moral focus from our own unique perspectives (*daode* 道德).

7A1 孟子曰："盡其心者，知其性也。知其性，則知天矣。存其心，養其性，所以事天也。夭壽不貳，修身以俟之，所以立命也。"

Mencius said: "Those who make the most of their 'bodyheartminding' (*xin* 心) realize their natural propensities (*xing* 性). And those who realize their natural propensities then realize *tian* 天. It is by consolidating their thinking and feeling and nourishing their natural propensities that they do service to *tian* 天. No matter whether short or long-lived, cultivating our own persons is how we wait for whatever will ensue. It is how we make a commitment and get on with our lives."

Comment: This passage advocates for making the most of our "bodyheartminding" (or "embodied thinking and feeling") and the symbiotic, expansive phases that occur in the process of doing so. Such an effort enables us to grow our initial conditions in family and community fully, and in so doing, to make our own distinctive contribution to the realization of our natural and cosmic context.

It is important to appreciate the performative implications of the term *zhi* 知—conventionally translated as "knowing." Rather than delimiting this capacity as simply "knowing" something cognitively, I have rendered it here as "realizing" in the performative sense of "making something real". This interpretation is further reinforced by avoiding the frequent eliding of the distinction between *xin* 心 and *xing* 性 (itself 心 + 生) where both are interpreted as merely denoting our initial native conditions. We must acknowledge the parallel in this passage between the activity of "making the most of their *xin* 心" (*jinqixin* 盡其心) and the vital process of "growing" the *xin* 心 itself indicated by the "growth" (*sheng* 生) element within the character *xing* 性 itself. That is, to "realize their natural propensities" (*zhixing* 知性) is to "grow their *xin* 心" (*shengqixin* 生其心) and thus make the most of it (*jinqixin* 盡其心).

Xin 心 and *xing* 性 as 1) native conditions and as 2) the ultimate product of cultivation respectively, have a clearly different reference at the beginning of the process of personal growth. At this early stage, the distinction between them must not be elided. *Xin* 心 as the "four inclinations" (*siduan* 四端) that describe our native conditions is to be distinguished from our "natural propensities" (*xing* 性) as the process of the growth itself. But as the process unfolds, *xin* 心 and *xing* 性 gradually converge as terms denoting the same result—that is, the consummate *xin* 心 is the emerging product of the spontaneous process of growth, while *xing* 性 is that spontaneous process of growth that has "made the most of" and produced this consummate *xin* 心.

Xin 心 can be parsed at first as the initial, native conditions—what Mencius calls the "four inclinations" (*siduan* 四端)—available for growth. Then in "making the most" of this resolute and deliberate *xin* 心 through assiduous cultivation, the consummate *xin* 心 as the product of this cultivation, becomes the same referent as *xing* 性. When the process of growth has run its course, there is no equivocation in the shared identity of *xin* 心 and *xing* 性. It is at this juncture then, that 仁，人心也 "consummatory conduct is *xin* 心" (6A11).

This passage provides further insight into "the continuity between and inseparability of the human and the cosmic orders" (*tianrenheyi* 天人合一). As we see in this passage, "those who make the most of their 'body-heartminding' (*xin* 心) realize their natural propensities (*xing* 性)." And again, "those who realize their natural propensities then realize *tian* 天" or the world around them that gives them context. What is clear here is that such achieved moral virtuosity is neither some characteristic pattern of behavior established by complying with external, antecedent principles, nor is it a personal identity that emerges from the reduplication of an erstwhile internal, innate human nature. Rather, this virtuosity is the product of a collaboration between persons and their worlds. Again, the conduct inspired by these "four inclinations" is not only generative in producing efficacy (*shan* 善) in our familial and communal relations, but also provides the ground for the Mencian claim that everyone, in the narratives that can be shaped out of activating these initial conditions, can aspire to behave sagaciously in their conduct. The ultimate measure in thus behaving with sagacity is the quality of the collaborative relationship between persons and *tian* 天 in a moral cosmos. Just as persons in their projects of personal cultivation profit from the natural and cultural context provided by *tian* 天, so *tian* 天 too is extended and deepened through the galvanizing and elevating activities of our sages.

In 7B24 a clear distinction is established between *ming* 命 as "capacities" and *xing* 性 as "propensities." The notion of *ming* 命 is relational, referencing the interface between the limits of our human capacities and those elements in the human experience such as the length of a life itself over which we have the least control. By contrast human propensities (*xing* 性) is the term Mencius chooses to denote those outcomes in the human experience that carry the strongest human signature: that is, our ability to purposely and deliberately nurture our familial, communal, and ultimately cosmic roles. Even the seemingly ineluctable circumstances in the career of a human being—our life span being either short or long-lived as the example given in this passage—are still in some degree negotiable. Far from denoting a predetermined, irrevocable fate or destiny, *ming* 命 is simply the limits against which the process of personal cultivation must advance. There being no guarantee of long life or good fortune, our best attitude is to optimize our possibilities, and through unrelenting effort at personal cultivation in our roles and relations, to do the best we can with what we have.

7B25 浩生不害問曰：「樂正子何人也？」孟子曰：「善人也，信人也。」「何謂善？何謂信？」曰：「可欲之謂善，有諸己之謂信，充實之謂美，充實而有光輝之謂大，大而化之之謂聖，聖而不可知之之謂神。樂正子，二之中、四之下也。」

Haosheng Buhai asked Mencius: "What kind of person is Master Yuezheng?"

Mencius replied: "He is a good (*shan* 善) person with real integrity (*xin* 信)."

"What do you mean by a 'good' person and having 'integrity'?" asked Haosheng Buhai.

Mencius replied: "What I mean by good is what is worth desiring, and what I mean by having integrity is embodying such desires in oneself. To bring these desires to full fruition in oneself is what I mean by becoming commendable, and to bring them to full fruition and shine forth is what I mean by becoming illustrious. Becoming thus illustrious and transforming the world accordingly is what I mean by sagacity, and being unfathomably sagacious in what is done is what I mean by deific (*shen* 神). Master Yuezheng has realized the first two of these qualities in his conduct, but has achieved something less than the last four."

Comment: In thus defining "good" (*shan* 善) itself as "what is worth desiring," Mencius is making the point that what animates our natural inclinations to pursue moral growth is our desire to become consummate in our conduct (*ren* 仁). Angus Graham comments that this inexorable progression of moral growth is motivated by the agreeable feelings we derive from it: "The process once launched accelerates, like fire catching, because we discover the pleasure of it."[①]

There is an important grammatical difference between the denotative "is what is meant by" (*zhiwei* 之謂) and the conative "is termed" (*weizhi* 謂之). The former expression defines its antecedent explicitly, while the latter connotes or references some "aspect" of a greater whole. Here Mencius is giving his denotative definitions of these several important terms.

In this passage, Mencius is reinforcing the distinction between "capacities" (*ming* 命) and "propensities" (*xing* 性) he has made in 7B24. The desiring that animates the kind of moral conduct most distinctively human and over which we have the greatest degree of control provides the project for the "human becoming." It is a trajectory that begins in discursive relations and culminates in the highest kind of deific sagacity that Mencius would associate with Confucius himself. While Mencius is glad to praise Master Yuezheng here, he also makes it clear that what he has achieved is only the first two phases in the steep ascent necessary to become most consummately human.

What is defining of the sage here is bringing to full fruition a quality of conduct wherein the human and the numinous coalesce as one (*tianrenheyi* 天人合一). This achievement makes the sages the counterpart of *tian* (*peitian* 配天) and as such, they transform the world. As we witness throughout the canonical Confucian texts, the vague notion of *tian* 天 takes on the visage of a particular human face as they repeatedly characterize

---

① A.C. Graham, *Disputers of the Tao*, p. 126.

these always unique sages metaphorically in grand, celestial terms: "King Wen shines in the heavens"[1] and "Confucius is the sun and the moon."[2] The quality of conduct and the depth of coalescence (*du* 度) required to be deemed truly sagacious is couched in language that references nothing less than the elevation of the human experience to a level that invites hyperbole. In spite of its seemingly impossible demands and unreachable heights, Mencius posits this transformation as a real possibility. For him, there are documented historical precedents in the lives of both the ancient sages and the very recent exemplar, Confucius himself. Perhaps it is Mencius's conviction it is the recent life of Confucius as the greatest sage in human history that makes the achievement of sagacity a much more concrete possibility. The designation of sage, far from being the actualization of some given human potential, is the recognition of an aesthetic achievement reserved for a few unique persons remembered in history. Through the introduction of their singular, otherwise inconceivable innovations such as the written word and the compilation of the philosophical canons, they have elevated what it means to be human into something celestial and deific, and have thus become full collaborators with *tian* 天.

But sagacity is not merely measured by their innovations. The sages become sages only through their capacity to use such new technologies to transform the ordinary lives of the people into extraordinary lives. These towering paragons raise their voices on behalf of humanity as a whole to sing the joyful music of the cosmos. It ought not to be surprising that sages (*shengren* 聖人), standing in stark contrast to the stagnation occasioned by "small persons," are defined by their discursive virtuosity. The earliest form of the character for the term sage, *sheng* 聖, as it is found on the oracle bones is composed of the combination of the graphs for "ear" (*er* 耳) and "mouth" (*kou* 口) 𦔮, suggesting that at least one characteristic held in common by the always unique members of this highest order of humanity, in all of their hearing and saying, is their shared virtuosity as communicators.[3] Sages are able to hear what is to be heard, and when they speak,

---

[1] *Wuxingpian* 15: 聖者，禮樂之所由生，五行之所和也。和則樂，樂則有德，有德則邦家興。文王之見也如此。文王在上也，於昭於天。此之謂也。

[2] *Analects* 19.24: 叔孫武叔毀仲尼。子貢曰："無以爲也，仲尼不可毀也。他人之賢者，丘陵也，猶可逾也；仲尼，日月也，無得而逾焉。人雖欲自絶，其何傷於日月乎？多見其不知量也！"See also *Analects* 19.21 and 25.

[3] Kwan, "Database," 甲骨文合集 CHANT 0693.

they change the world.

By "deific" here is what might be described as a process of euhemerization. Euhemerus was a 4th C. BCE Greek thinker who advanced the theory that the complex Greek mythologies and their persona are the allegorical and imaginative interpretations of what were originally historical people and events. In an analogical way, "Gods" in this Chinese one-world, genealogical cosmology are "gods" with a lower case "g" rather than "Gods" as a separate order of being. That is, they are largely "dead people"—ancestors and cultural heroes now dead—who are remembered, elevated, and revered as meaning-makers responsible for the enculturalization of the human experience (*wenhua* 文化). The perceived coincidence between objectivity and truth has persuaded traditions informed by Greek philosophy that historicity is the rational account that sanitizes "the story" of what has gone before. That is, *logos* as rational explanation is used to discipline *historia* by cleansing it of a fictive and fanciful *mythos*. The role of *mythos* in Confucian assumptions about history seems to have had a more positive value. Confucius while a historical, flesh and blood teacher, was from the Han dynasty designated an institutionalized, cultural "god" to be revered with all of the temples and formal observances appertaining thereto.

7A21 孟子曰："廣土衆民，君子欲之，所樂不存焉；中天下而立，定四海之民，君子樂之，所性不存焉。君子所性，雖大行不加焉，雖窮居不損焉，分定故也。君子所性，仁義禮智根於心，其生色也睟然，見於面，盎於背，施於四體，四體不言而喻。"

Mencius said, "To have a vast territory with a teeming population is something desired by exemplary persons (*junzi* 君子), but what they find enjoyment in does not lie in acquiring such things. To stand at the center of the world and bring stability to all of the common people would for them be a source of enjoyment, but what is habituated as their human propensities (*xing* 性) does not lie in achieving such things. Because the lot in life of exemplary persons is already settled and secure, what is habituated as their propensities (*xing* 性) is neither enhanced by their having great influence in the world, nor diminished by their being mired in difficult circumstances.

"What exemplary persons habituate as their human propensities—that is, their inclinations to act consummately in their roles and relations (*ren* 仁), to act with optimal appropriateness (*yi* 義), to achieve propriety (*li* 禮), and to act wisely in these same roles and relations (*zhi* 智)—are all rooted in their heartmind (*xin* 心). And the physical complexion that develops in this endeavor first glows radiantly on their faces, is further reflected in their carriage, and then extends throughout their extremities. Without their bodies having to say anything at all, everyone is keenly aware of this personal growth."

Comment: Although exemplary persons certainly desire and would find pleasure in noble undertakings such as ruling a flourishing state and bringing peace and stability to the whole world, attaining this kind of political standing does not affect who they aspire to become as persons. That is, their commitment to, and the substance of, their personal cultivation is not a function of such contingencies.

What first attracts our notice in this passage is the verbal use of "human propensities" (*xing* 性)—not just the propensities themselves, but what we are able to produce in the cultivating of them (*suoxing* 所性). It is something that we "do" and "become" rather than just "have."

Commenting on the assumed inseparability of physical and moral growth reflected in this passage, Angus Graham observes:

> Moral inclinations belong to nature in the same way as the physical growth of the body. They germinate spontaneously without having to be learned or worked for, they can be nourished, injured, starved, they develop if properly tended but their growth cannot be forced.[①]

We need to be careful in how we parse the human journey from animality to sagehood referenced in 4B19: 人之所以異於禽獸者幾希 . . . "What distinguishes people from the brutes is ever so slight . . ." The familiar and oft repeated analogy in the *Mencius* between the "four inclinations" and the "body with its four limbs" is important in at least two respects. First, the growth in our personal relations and of our bodies is profoundly but not exclusively physical (rather than metaphysical), and is prompted by the agreeable feelings we have as we participate in the ongoing conversation enabled by our irreducibly social thinking and feeling. Like the body, our moral habits find nourishment and growth when they are exercised regularly.

And secondly, the virtuosity that emerges in the radial growth of our

---

① Graham, *Disputers of the Tao*, p. 125.

relations inspired as it is by the promptings of the inchoate heartmind produces a qualitatively transformed moral physicality that elevates the embodied human experience into something refined and elegant—what Richard Shusterman has termed a "somaesthetic."[1] Stated simply, the distinction between human animality and sagacity is not one grounded in the differences between our physical and intellectual qualities. Virtuosic conduct is necessarily embodied, and as it is habituated, it is expressed through a quality of action that is at once physically and intellectually compelling. Indeed, the sensuous and intellectual as complementary aspects of our persons are perceived as no more than two different ways of viewing and evaluating the same phenomenon.

4B19 孟子曰:"人之所以異於禽獸者幾希,庶民去之,君子存之。舜明於庶物,察於人倫,由仁義行,非行仁義也。"

Mencius said: "What distinguishes people from the brutes is ever so slight, and while the common run of people might lose their grasp on this difference, exemplary persons (*juzi* 君子) preserve and develop it. Shun was wise to the way of all things and had real insight into human roles and relationships. He acted upon his moral habit of being consummatory and optimally appropriate in his conduct rather than merely doing what was deemed consummatory and appropriate by others."

Comment: For Mencius, the gregarious impulse that prompts growth in relations and guides us in the direction of efficacious moral conduct (*shan* 善) is at first only incipient growth, and thus, as we have seen, is certainly at risk of being either ignored or even worse, lost. Xunzi caricatures Mencius as offering a naturalistic interpretation of *xing* 性—"what you are born with makes you good." But *contra* Xunzi, for Mencius becoming "great persons" requires much more than simply avoiding the loss of our initial inclination to relate to others in a meaningful way.[2] In spite of

---

[1] See for a representative example, Shusterman, *Body Consciousness*.

[2] *Xunzi* 23: 孟子曰:"人之學者,其性善。"曰:是不然。是不及知人之性,而不察乎人之性偽之分者也。凡性者,天之就也,不可學,不可事。禮義者,聖人之所生也,人之所學而能,所事而成者也。不可學,不可事,而在人者,謂之性。Mencius says that "since human beings can be educated, their *xing* is good." I would argue that this is not so. Mencius in his lack of understanding of the human *xing* 性, is unable to discern the distinction between *xing* 性 itself and deliberate *(Continued on next page)*

Mencius's own emphatic rejection of the tautological naturalism ascribed to him by Xunzi (that is, humans are good because they are good), it is this impoverished teleological interpretation of Mencius (*xing* 性 is an unlearned given that makes us good) that has not only persisted in the literature after Xunzi, but in fact largely prevails among commentators even today. The mantra *renxingshan* 人性善 understood as "human nature is good" is an interpretation that is pervasive in the contemporary commentary on Mencius, both Western and Chinese alike.

Michael Sandel, in his search for a robust, *intra*-subjective alternative to a deracinated individualism, pointedly observes that for most Western commentators at least:

> To speak of human nature is often to suggest a classical teleological conception, associated with the notion of a universal human essence, invariant in all times and places.[1]

Indeed, the uncritical assumption for many if not most commentators is that for Mencius, *xing* 性 references a universal, inborn, fixed, self-sufficient endowment defining of all human beings that programs us naturally as human beings to be moral in what we do.

But in the *Mencius*, there is in fact an inordinate emphasis on the role of unremitting personal cultivation in growing and consolidating the virtuosic habits that are expressed in and are defining of an always unique, exemplary life. This process at one end begins from our initial animality with the minimalist human advantage of the incipient "four inclinations," and extends at the other end to the possibility of attaining the habitude of full-blown, epoch-changing, human sages as our loftiest prospect.

Mencius makes a frequently found distinction between just doing something that is prompted by the approbation of others, and by way of

---

(Continued from previous page) activity (*wei* 偽). Speaking generally, *xing* 性 is what is given by nature; it can neither be learned nor acquired. Moral dispositions such as aspiring to propriety in our roles and relations (*li* 禮) and acting on moral precepts (*yi* 義) are the products of the sages, and hence are something that can be learned and applied, acquired and mastered. What cannot be learned and cannot be acquired but is simply inherent in persons is what is called *xing* 性.

[1] Sandel, *Liberalism*, p.50.

contrast, acting consistently out of a cultivated, evolving moral habitude. We need to register the vital distinction that is being made here between persons who are merely able to follow conventional values in acting in a way deemed virtuosic by the community, and a sage like Shun. Shun through an assiduous personal regimen is able to actually become consummatory in his roles and relations, and to act from this cultivated habitude of virtuosity.

In the Aristotelian ontological conception of person, one cannot rescind one's humanity. But in Mencius, since becoming human is an achievement, there is the possibility of loss and failure. The Mencian idea that humans can lose their claim on their humanity and revert to their animality is also found in 4B28. Even though once lost, the possibility of becoming human might still be recovered, there is still a warrant in the interim to look on some humans as less than human. The propensities for growth on Ox Mountain might still be restored, but in the meantime, people are prone to see and treat Ox Mountain as little more than a barren hill. There are perhaps negative implications of such an assumption for issues such as the dignity of the human being, the presumed sanctity of human life, and the defense of human rights on the one hand, and positive ones such as the possibility of overcoming our human exceptionalism and speciesism on the other.

2A6 孟子曰："人皆有不忍人之心。先王有不忍人之心，斯有不忍人之政矣。以不忍人之心，行不忍人之政，治天下可運之掌上。"

Mencius said, "Everyone has a heartmind (*xin* 心) that cannot endure the suffering of others. And it was because the Former Kings had such a heartmind they established compassionate governance. When, inspired by this compassionate heartmind, they were able to put compassionate governance into practice, bringing proper order to the world was as easy as turning something over in the palm of their hand."

Comment: Given the political challenges that distinguished the world of Mencius, there is this familiar pattern in the *Mencius* of correlating his moral psychology with the promotion of proper governance.

"所以謂人皆有不忍人之心者，今人乍見孺子將入於井，皆有怵惕惻隱之心，非所以內交於孺子之父母也，非所以要譽於鄉黨朋友也，非惡其聲而然也。由是觀之，無惻隱之心，非人也；無羞惡之心，非人也；無辭讓之心，非人也；無是非之心，非人也。惻隱之心，仁之端也；羞惡之心，義之端也；辭讓之心，禮之端也；是非之心，智之端也。人之有是四端也，猶其有四體也。有是四端而自謂不能者，自賊者也；謂其君不能者，賊其君者也。凡有四端於我者，知皆擴而充之矣，若火之始然，泉之始達。苟能充之，足以保四海；苟不充之，不足以事父母。"

"What I mean in saying that everyone has a heartmind that cannot endure the suffering of others is that were anybody suddenly to see an infant about to topple into a well, their heartmind would be moved by alarm and compassion. And this fact would have nothing to do with cultivating a relationship with the parents of the infant, or making a name for themselves among friends and villagers, or having an aversion to the wailing of an infant.

"From this one example, we can infer that anyone who lacks such a sense of empathy is not human, anyone who lacks a sense of shame is not human, anyone who lacks a sense of respect is not human, and anyone who lacks a sense of discrimination is not human. Our heartmind in feeling pity at perceived suffering disposes it toward consummate conduct in our roles and relations (*ren* 仁); our heartmind in feeling shame at perceived crudeness disposes it toward appropriate conduct in our roles and relations (*yi* 義); our heartmind in its feelings of modesty and deference disposes it toward propriety in our roles and relations (*li* 禮); our heartmind in feeling a sense of discrimination disposes it toward wisdom in our roles and relations (*zhi* 智).

"Persons have these four inclinations (*siduan* 四端) just as they have their four limbs. Those people who would say that although they have these four inclinations, they are unable to act upon them are damaging themselves. And those who would say that their ruler is unable to act upon them are damaging their ruler.

"Now acknowledging that these four inclinations are defining of us, the process of realizing the development and fruition of them is like a fire beginning to blaze, or a spring of water beginning to gush forth. Persons who are able to bring them fully to fruition can vouchsafe everyone within the four seas; persons unable to do so cannot even be of service to their own parents."

Comment: In this passage, Mencius introduces us to what he calls our incipient "four inclinations" (*siduan* 四端)—that is, the constitutive conditions he is able to generalize about the human experience and that he identifies with the inchoate heartmind (*xin* 心). It is these four inclinations that stir us to moral conduct. Commenting on this passage, Angus Graham observes that the analogy between cultivating our four inclinations and nourishing our bodies is an apposite one:

> It is essential to Mencius' case that although moral education is indispensable it is, like the feeding of the body, the nourishing of a spontaneous process.... A man becomes bad, not because the incipient impulses are missing from his constitution, but because he neglects and starves them.[①]

Graham underscores the analogy here between physical and moral growth. In both cases such growth occurs because of the natural conditions of the organism and the effort that must be invested in their development. And the terms "constitution" and "incipient impulses" used here to describe these natural conditions are important because Mencius is referencing the native inclinations we have within our relations as human beings.

The *Mencius* uses the metaphors of a run-away fire and surging water to emphasize the precipitous nature of this moral growth. Graham comments that this inexorable progression of moral growth is motivated by the agreeable feelings we derive from it:

> The process once launched accelerates, like fire catching, because we discover the pleasure of it.[②]

The attribution to Mencius of a notion of an essential "human nature" is certainly a counterintuitive assertion within the context of a holistic *qi* 氣 cosmology that begins from the primacy of process and vital relationality. In this cosmology, the assumption is that change is pervasive, and as such, that everything is disposed to transformation. *Xin* 心 by referencing the initial conditions and propensities of human "becomings" captured in the aspectual language of *renyilizhi* 仁義禮智, acknowledges that in loving families and communicating communities, infants are born into roles informed by "consummatory conduct" (*ren* 仁), "appropriateness and meaning" (*yi* 義), "an achieved sense of propriety" (*li* 禮), and "intelligence and wisdom" (*zhi* 智). Radically situated within these fecund associations, such infants through participating in the various discursive activities of life are inclined

---

[①] Graham, *Disputers of the Tao*, pp. 126, 129.
[②] Graham, *Disputers of the Tao*, p. 126.

to efficacious growth (*shan* 善). This nonanalytic *renyilizhi* 仁義禮智 language of "the four inclinations" is "aspectual" in that each term provides a particular perspective on the same relationally-constituted, vital phenomenon, and anticipates how this inchoate, socially embedded infant, located within a grammar of familial and cultural conditions, will be inclined to grow and mature as a source of communal and ultimately cosmic meaning.

We might take the roles of the infant as informed by intelligence and wisdom (*zhi* 智) as an example. Such an attribution is not a claim that infants have some internal and innate repository of knowledge that they then apply to the situations of their lives. Rather, wisdom is a quality of conduct that arises gradually within the social activities of which infants are a part, informed as these activities are by the values of their families, their communities, and the mature culture into which they are born. Reading "conduct" etymologically as *con-* ("together, "with") and *duct* ("leading"), such wisdom is a profoundly participatory activity manifested in the ongoing transactions infants have with their environing others, and the interactions their environing others have with them. Indeed, without ready access to a mature wisdom, the lives of infants would likely be perilous and quite short.

Again, *xin* 心 as "four inclinations" is no more an essential and inborn "given" than is the tendency infants have toward "consummate conduct in their roles and relations" (*ren* 仁). Such consummate conduct is initially no more than an incipient relational disposition, an inclination, a tendency, but with assiduous effort within this matrix of relations, it gradually evolves to become an acquired virtuosity in the roles and relations that unfold within the personal narratives of family and community. All of these "four inclinations" are fairly described as native conditions that, in the fullness of time and with the continuing growth of what are initially only tentative dispositions, gradually thicken to become those qualitatively achieved habits of conduct in the roles and relations that constitute our personal narratives and identities.

4B12 孟子曰："大人者，不失其赤子之心者也。"

Mencius said, "Truly great persons do not surrender the heartmind (*xin* 心) of the newly born infant."

Comment: We must resist an expository reading of this passage that might essentialize and reify heartmind, cleaving it off from the narrative as some essential "original mind" that is either overwhelmed by the distractions that come with life in the world, or is reduplicated in the growth of the infant into a mature person. It is better to understand Mencius here as simply making a point. And the point being made is that activating the native inclinations of the relationally-constituted infant is a necessary condition upon which the project of ultimately becoming exemplary in our persons depends. The symbiosis between root and tree is instructive, where growth is a holistic process with each growing the other in their shared narrative. Mencius's description of incipient "inclinations" not only introduces the radically embedded newborn babe as the locus of the growth of these "inclinations," but further defines the "constitution" of this infant in terms of these same organic relations. That is, the newborn babe emerges *in medias res* as an inchoate narrative nested within the larger pattern of the more mature narratives of family and community. The growth of an infant born into the concrete matrix of the family and communal relations of a mature culture can be captured both descriptively and prescriptively by an appeal to the intense socializing impulses of these constitutive bonds.

While infants have these inclinations within the conditions that attend their emergence in the world, such positive tendencies if not cultivated can be lost to them (*shi* 失). Such an assertion stands in contrast to an ontological conception of human nature that, being defining of what a person is, cannot be surrendered.

6A8 孟子曰: "牛山之木嘗美矣，以其郊於大國也，斧斤伐之，可以爲美乎？是其日夜之所息，雨露之所潤，非無萌蘖之生焉，牛羊又從而牧之，是以若彼濯濯也。人見其濯濯也，以爲未嘗有材焉，此豈山之性也哉？雖存乎人者，豈無仁義之心哉？"

Mencius said, "The trees on Ox Mountain were flourishing, but because the mountain is located in the suburbs of a great population center and the axes and hatchets would chop away at them, how could the trees continue to thrive? Of course, night and day they do have some respite, and the rains and dew do give them moisture, so there was certainly no lack of new growth. But then again with the cattle and sheep being pastured there to graze, the mountain has become as barren as it is. People seeing its barrenness come to think it never had any wooded areas on it. Wherein is this the natural condition of the mountain? And by analogy, how can whatever resides within the breasts of human beings be other than a heartmind (*xin* 心) with its propensity for acting consummately (*ren* 仁) and with optimal appropriateness (*yi*

義)?"

Comment: The analogy here is between the mountain that naturally has flourishing stands of trees and the natural propensity of human beings to have flourishing heartminds. When the mountain is encroached upon and conditions evolve so that the mountain is stripped bare of its foliage, people gradually come to think this is how it has always been. How can this barrenness be the natural condition of the mountain, and how can human beings have heartminds without the propensities for acting consummately and finding optimal appropriateness in their roles and relations? Important here is that just as the nature of the mountain is defined in terms of the relationship between its native conditions and the activities of the world around it, so the natural propensities of human beings are a function of the relationship between their native tendencies and the sources of nourishment provided by their environment. Neither mountain nor heartmind is complete in itself, and the growth in both cases begins from and is sustained by environmental rather than metaphysical factors.

"其所以放其良心者，亦猶斧斤之於木也，旦旦而伐之，可以爲美乎？其日夜之所息，平旦之氣，其好惡與人相近也者幾希，則其旦晝之所爲，有梏亡之矣。梏之反覆，則其夜氣不足以存；夜氣不足以存，則其違禽獸不遠矣。人見其禽獸也，而以爲未嘗有才焉者，是豈人之情也哉？故苟得其養，無物不長；苟失其養，無物不消。孔子曰：'操則存，舍則亡；出入無時，莫知其鄉。'惟心之謂與？"

"The way in which people let go of their native heartmind and its prosocial propensities (*liangxin* 良心) is just like the axes and hatchets chopping down the trees. If day in and day out, the axes chop away, how can the trees thrive? Now if in spite of the fact that night and day people are restored by their breathing in the sweet air, still their likes and dislikes become increasingly idiosyncratic, it is because what they are doing during the daytime is allowing the gains made in their energy to dissipate. If this dissipation continues, the sweet air of the night will have no restorative force, and when this happens, such persons become little better than brutes. Other people witnessing their brutishness, come to think of such persons as never having had any native resources. But how could this be their actual human condition (*qing* 情)?

"Thus, if taken care of properly, there is nothing that will not grow, but if it is deprived of such care, there is nothing that will not wither away.

Confucius said, 'Hold onto it and it will survive; give it up and it will perish. Coming and going at random, no one knows which way it is headed.' Wasn't he talking about the heartmind (*xin* 心) here?"

Comment: Note that heartmind is defined in this passage by reference to consummate conduct (*ren* 仁) and optimal appropriateness in one's roles and relations (*yi* 義), activities that are irreducibly social. This is immediately relevant to how we are to understand the expression "their native heartmind and its prosocial propensities" (*liangxin* 良心) in what follows. The *Shuowen* lexicon defines *liang* 良 in 良心良能 as "good at" (*shan* 善). Zhu Xi and Wang Fuzhi gloss this term in the same way. *Liang* 良 is used on the oracle bones and bronzes descriptively as a fine steed 良馬 and a stout warrior 良士. *Liang* 良 originally references a corridor (*lang* 廊) in a residence that makes living better by providing air flow. Hence, some contemporary commentators gloss *liang* 良 as *shen* 甚 meaning "superlative." On the oracle bones, *liang* 良 describes the aroma of food rising from the cooking pot. Just as *shan* 善 emerges in an irreducibly social context as a function of the discursive and gregarious nature of the human being, *liang* 良 references another modality of discourse: the giving, getting, and sharing of food. While certainly allowing Mencius has a thick concept of initial conditions, at the same time we should resist decontextualizing and metaphysicalizing the "native heartmind" (*liangxin* 良心) as some *a priori*, innate faculty defining of discrete individuals. *Xin* 心 is social and communal, not individual, and the expression *liangxin* 良心 is another way of describing the initial relational conditions that promote productive associations, the natural propensity for prosocial conduct of the "four inclinations" (*siduan* 四端).

Confucius underscores the claim that being human is something we do rather than what we are, and morality in this tradition is nothing other than activity that conduces to growth in relations. Importantly, in what is quoted from Confucius here is characterizing the heartmind in terms of its transactions and direction rather than its substance.

7A15 孟子曰:"人之所不學而能者,其良能也;所不慮而知者,其良知也。孩提之童無不知愛其親者,及其長也,無不知敬其兄也。親親,仁也;敬長,義也;無他,達之天下也。"

Mencius said: "What people are able to do without learning anything are their 'native capacities' (*liangneng* 良能); what they are able to realize without deliberation is their 'native wisdom' (*liangzhi* 良知). There are no toddlers who are unaware that they love their parents, and as they grow up, there are none who are unaware of the respect they have for their elders. Affection for parents is an expression of consummate conduct (*ren* 仁); respecting elders is an expression of a sense of optimal appropriateness (*yi* 義). For no other reason than this, such values have to be encouraged throughout the world."

Comments: Important for this passage is to begin from the examples given, and to thus resist isolating, essentializing, or metaphysicalizing these native capacities. Mencius makes the point that morality is a collaboration between persons and world rather than something derived from some external source. The love of children for their parents and the respect the younger generation expresses toward their elders are irreducibly relational values located within and informing familial roles and relations. There can be no children without parents, nor any elders without their juniors. No one can be *ren* 仁 or *yi* 義 by themselves.

Again, with this Mencian exhortation to promote and disseminate such native values throughout the world, his emphasis is on the growth in such values from their incipient form as native inclinations within relations to thick patterns of habitualized moral conduct. If we were going to formulate a minimalist morality that would be inclusive and thus have relevance to all cultures, it would have to begin with family feeling as bedrock and in need of no further theorizing or persuasion. The Er Cheng 二程 commentary on this passage states the relationship between the native heartmind (*liangxin* 良心) with its native capacities (*liangneng* 良能) and native wisdom (*liangzhi* 良知), is one of "forming and functioning" (*tiyong* 體用), where activating one's abilities and acting wisely not only give shape to but also grow the heartmind. On the relationship between the native capacities and native wisdom, the Cheng brothers describe it in terms of "the inseparability of knowing and doing" (*zhixingheyi* 知行合一)—specifically, the resources needed for intelligent practice.

7B21 孟子謂高子曰:"山徑之蹊，間介然用之而成路；爲間不用，則茅塞之矣。今茅塞子之心矣。"

Mencius said to Master Gao, "If the narrowest of mountain paths is used regularly, it will quickly become a trail, but if for the briefest time it goes unused, it will become overgrown. At the moment, Sir, your heartmind (*xin* 心) is overgrown."

Comment: The metaphor repeated here is the growth of foliage, but this passage takes it in the opposite direction from the denuding of Ox Mountain. The heartmind can either suffer from conditions that arrests its growth so that its natural inclinations wither away, or it can be impeded by overgrowth that stymies its capacity to perform its proper function effectively. In both cases, the emphasis is on the function of the heartmind and its proper measure of growth.

Implied by the metaphor, the specific criticism being made of Master Gao is he is not exercising his heartmind properly. He, as with the Mohists, is committed to the notion that morality is a matter of external arrangement where conduct is regulated from some outside source. In 2A2 we see that when Master Gao is not able to derive his norms from what is being said in some external, doctrinal source (*yan* 言), he doesn't bother seeking them out in thinking the ideas through (*xin* 心). With such an attitude, Master Gao is failing to appreciate the important symbiotic relationship between the internal and the external where it is collaboration between the natural inclinations of the heartmind and its irreducibly social context that is the source of moral growth.

6A12 孟子曰: "今有無名之指屈而不信，非疾痛害事也，如有能信之者，則不遠秦楚之路，爲指之不若人也。指不若人，則知惡之；心不若人，則不知惡，此之謂不知類也。"

Mencius said, "Now take a person whose ring finger is bent so that it cannot be properly extended. Even though the finger does not hurt or interfere with his work, if he knew of someone who could straighten it for him, he would not think Qin or Chu too distant a place to travel. This is because his finger is not as good as those of other people. If such a person is ashamed of the fact his finger is not as good as other people but feels nothing when his heartmind (*xin* 心) is not up to par, this is called being unaware that these two disfigurements are the same in kind."

Comments: It is significant that when Mencius is looking for appropriate metaphors to express his moral psychology, he usually appeals to natural growth in either foliage or the human body. Indeed, he begins from correlating the natural growth of the heartmind to that of the physical body, where such moral growth is immediately visible both in the quality of personal conduct and in the radiance of their countenance.

The last line here could be interpreted as "isn't there something wrong with this person's priorities?" which would seem to make good sense. But such a reading might inadvertently insinuate a blanket qualitative distinction between the physical and the mental. What Mencius is in fact saying is that both disfigurements are of a kind in being unnatural and a condition we should make every effort to remedy, with the limited function of the finger being less pressing perhaps than that of the heartmind.

7B35 孟子曰: "養心莫善於寡欲。其爲人也寡欲，雖有不存焉者，寡矣; 其爲人也多欲，雖有存焉者，寡矣。"

Mencius said, "There is no better way to nourish one's heartmind (*xin* 心) than to reduce one's desires. For those who in their persons make their desires few, even though there is something lost in doing so, it is minimal. But for those who in their persons have many active desires, even though they have conserved something in having them, it again will not be much."

Comment: While personal agitation in a Platonic world takes the form of tensions among the rational, volitional, and appetitive forces raging within a tripartite human soul, for Mencius such disquiet arises from conflicted external distractions. The native disposition of the heartmind as it is defined by the four inclinations (*siduan* 四端) locates the human experience within our morally charged, familial and social roles. Given the irreducibly relational nature and function of the heartmind, its nourishment comes from growth in the quality of coalescence it achieves in these same natural relations.

Desire is not a bad thing. Indeed, in 7B25 Mencius defines "good" itself (*shan* 善) explicitly as "what is worth desiring" (*keyu* 可欲). In 7A21 we also note that exemplary persons quite properly desire social and political responsibility and find real enjoyment in the opportunity to bring peace and security to the world. At the same time, such achievements are only contingencies, and not integral to the cultivation of the natural propensities for prosocial growth. While desires and the pleasures they afford are in themselves and in proper measure, natural to the heartmind, when experienced in excess, such disintegrating tensions can interfere with the singular purpose (*zhi* 志) and resolution (*cheng* 誠) that the heartmind needs to be optimally effective in cultivating one's own person, and in fostering a flourishing environment.

6A7 孟子曰："富歲，子弟多賴；凶歲，子弟多暴，非天之降才爾殊也，其所以陷溺其心者然也。今夫麰麥，播種而耰之，其地同，樹之時又同，浡然而生，至於日至之時，皆孰矣。雖有不同，則地有肥磽，雨露之養、人事之不齊也。故凡同類者，舉相似也，何獨至於人而疑之？聖人，與我同類者。故龍子曰：'不知足而爲屨，我知其不爲蕢也。' 屨之相似，天下之足同也。"

Mencius said, "In years of plenty the young men tend to be lethargic, while in lean years they tend to be aggressive. It is not that their endowed capacities are any different, but it occurs because the different environments have taken their toll on their heartminds. Take barley for instance. If in sowing it and turning the soil, the ground is the same and the time of planting is the same, the stalks of barley will grow and by the time of the summer solstice, the crop will all ripen. If there is any change in the yield, it is due to differences in the quality of the soil, the quantity of moisture received, or the amount of human attention invested.

"Thus, since things of the same kind are generally alike in their development, why should we question this pattern when it comes to the human being? The sage and I are of the same kind. Thus, it is that Master Long said: 'Even though the shoemaker is not sure of the size of someone's foot in making a grass sandal, I am sure he is not going to weave a basket.' Grass sandals are similar because feet are about the same."

"口之於味，有同耆也；易牙先得我口之所耆者也。如使口之於味也，其性與人殊，若犬馬之與我不同類也，則天下何耆皆從易牙之於味也？至於味，天下期於易牙，是天下之口相似也。惟耳亦然。至於聲，天下期於師曠，是天下之耳相似也。惟目亦然。至於子都，天下莫不知其姣也。不知子都之姣者，無目者也。"

"When it comes to taste, our palates are partial to the same things. Yi Ya was just the first among us to really grasp what our palates like. If in fact our palates varied in their natural inclinations in the same way horses and dogs are different in kind from human beings, then how is it that everyone's palate follows Yi Ya in what they like? When it comes to taste, the fact that everyone is partial to Yi Ya's cooking is fair evidence that everyone's palate is similar.

"The same thing is true with the ear. When it comes to music, that everyone is partial to Shi Kuang is fair evidence everyone's ear is similar. And the same is true with the eye. When it comes to Zidu, anyone who would dispute his good looks would have to be blind."

IV. THE *MENCIUS* (*MENGZI* 孟子): EXTENDING THE VOCABULARY

"故曰：口之於味也，有同耆焉；耳之於聲也，有同聽焉；目之於色也，有同美焉。至於心，獨無所同然乎？心之所同然者何也？謂理也、義也。聖人先得我心之所同然耳。故理義之悅我心，猶芻豢之悅我口。"

"Thus it is said: In taste our palates are partial to the same flavors, in music our ears to the same sounds, and in beauty our eyes to the same forms. How could it be with respect to the heartmind (*xin* 心) alone we have nothing in common? What then do heartminds have in common? I would say it is a sense of coherence (*li* 理) and of appropriateness (*yi* 義). The sages were just the first among us to really grasp what our heartminds have in common. Thus, it is a sense of coherence and appropriateness that are pleasing to my heartmind in the same way meat from livestock is pleasing to my palate."

Comment: Mencius is making the point that things of a particular kind (*lei* 類), whether it be young men, barley, or sages, are all similar in their native conditions, and that their differences are a function of the circumstances they encounter in the process of growth and maturation. How are we to understand this claim?

An essentialist Aristotelian reading would locate the most important potential of things in their given "natures"—their formal and final causes—making their maturation the actualization of these causes. A narrative reading on the other hand, would allow that the native inclinations of things are indeed similar, but that the potential for what they will become emerges in the cultivation that attends this growth and the symbiotic transactions they have with the content of their various environments over their particular careers. Given the available conditions, there is a holistic symbiosis in which the root grows the tree and the tree nourishes the root.

Mencius certainly rejects any claim that things are determined solely by their environments, but this is not to argue that through the actualization of some internally sufficient cause they are self-determining and self-sufficient. Instead, the argument is that things emerge in the coordination of organisms with their environments, whether it be seeds becoming barley or young men becoming sages. His emphasis is upon the proper and adequate nourishment needed, be it plants incorporating the nutrients of rain and soil into themselves in the process of deliberate cultivation, or human beings nourishing the growth of their initial moral inclinations through the habituation of patterns of conduct that then evolve into full and exemplary narratives. A persistent theme in Mencius is how such growth surges exponentially once the root is properly set.

It is interesting here that Mencius goes beyond the "four inclinations" in what he takes to be the commonalities obtaining among different heart-minds, identifying a sense of coherence (*li* 理) and of appropriateness (*yi* 義) as something we all share. What these two terms have in common is first they are both one and many at the same time. The uniqueness and meaning in the growth of the one are informed by the many that offers it context. The *li* 理 of any particular thing is unique to it, locates it by analogy within a particular kind, and defines it by virtue of its relations within the totality. That is, *li* 理 is 1) the coherence of the relations that come together to constitute a uniquely particular thing, 2) the kind of thing it is as it is determined through analogy with other things, and 3) the coherence of a world construed from its perspective in the most general terms. The many changing events of a life are brought together as a coherent moral narrative by the insistent perspective that persists as one's identity within that narrative. Analogously, *yi* 義 is a pattern of relations optimally appropriate for me, by extension for us, and ultimately for everyone in the most general terms.

A second commonality between *li* 理 and *yi* 義 is that they are not simply descriptive, but also normative—they are an achieved coherence and optimization rather than just a report on what is. And a third commonality that follows from the first two is that, in defining what is optimally coherent and optimally appropriate, both terms reference the quantum of meaning achieved in the pattern of relations. Both intelligence and morality are nothing more than the correlating of different things and events for optimum efficacy, and the increased growth and resolution produced in that process.

6A15 公都子問曰："鈞是人也，或爲大人，或爲小人，何也？" 孟子曰："從其大體爲大人，從其小體爲小人。" 曰："鈞是人也，或從其大體，或從其小體，何也？" 曰："耳目之官不思，而蔽於物。物交物，則引之而已矣。心之官則思，思則得之，不思則不得也。此天之所與我者。先立乎其大者，則其小者不能奪也。此爲大人而已矣。"

Master Gongdu asked Mencius: "Since all are equally human, how is it some persons become exemplary while others are wholly deficient?"

"Those who follow their higher capacities (*dati* 大體) become superior; those who follow their lower ones (*xiaoti* 小體) become inferior." replied Mencius.

"Since all are equally human, how is it some would follow their higher capacities while others would follow their lower ones?" he asked.

"Our physical senses such as looking and listening are not reflective, and thus can be deceived by external things. When one thing is thus engaged by another, they do no more than distract each other. The office of the heart-mind on the other hand is thinking and feeling. But it can only accomplish something if it actually thinks and feels. We have been given this as our native ability. If we begin by attending to these higher capacities, the inferior ones will not be able to wrest control from them. This is all there is to becoming a superior person."

Comment: That some people become so much better than others speaks to the vital role that disciplined, habituated conduct has in growing what after all are only one's initial conditions. Mencius reiterates the point that the initial conditions can only become productive if they are actively engaged, and that it is this deliberate conduct itself that makes all the difference, indeed a quantum difference, in the quality of one's person.

It is significant that the eyes, ears, and heartmind itself are described herein as "offices" or "functions" (*guan* 官), not reifying them, but instead treating them as activities. There is the omnipresent inseparability of forming and functioning (*tiyong* 體用) in the erstwhile nature of "things" that must be respected. This gerundive priority, making these offices verbal nouns, is a warrant for translating them as a situated "looking," "listening," and "thinking and feeling" respectively. Indeed and importantly, it is the reflective capacity of the heartmind with its thinking and feeling that informs the other offices within the sensual sensorium, thereby transforming mere "looking" into "seeing" and mere "listening" into "hearing."

The office of these higher capacities of "thinking and feeling" enables us to "accomplish something" in the sense of "getting" (*de* 得), where "getting" is cognate with its homophone *de* 德 meaning "virtuosity." This is but to say that the expression of intelligence and moral competence in our actions are a function of "getting" in the sense of cultivating those relationships that locate us within a particular context, thereby growing them and thus making them our own. By contrast, what defines "petty persons" (*xiaoren* 小人) and makes them "wholly deficient" is the absence of such growth. Lacking interest in their relations, they are stunted in their growth and remain aberrant individuals.

4B28 孟子曰:"君子所以異於人者,以其存心也。君子以仁存心,以禮存心。

仁者愛人，有禮者敬人。愛人者，人恒愛之；敬人者，人恒敬之。"

    Mencius said, "What makes exemplary persons (*junzi* 君子) different from the common lot lies in preserving their heartmind (*xin* 心). They do so through their consummatory conduct (*ren* 仁) and through aspiring to propriety in their roles and relations (*li* 禮). To be consummatory in one's conduct is to love others; to achieve propriety in one's roles and relations is to respect others. Those who love others are always loved by others, and those who respect others are always respected by others."

    Comment: Our initial inclinations toward efficacious moral conduct are incipient and thus tenuous, and must be acted upon in order to be sustained and grown into a habituated pattern of conduct. These inclinations take the form of doing our best to make the most of our relations with others (*ren* 仁) and of achieving the proper patterns of deference in the roles that we live within family and community (*li* 禮). The Chinese term translated as "love" here is *ai* 愛, and means love in the sense of affection, but also thus grudging something in the sense of wanting to maintain it whole and in its entirety. In 1A7, King Hui of Liang says 我非愛其財而易之以羊也。宜乎百姓之謂我愛也。"It is not that begrudging (*ai* 愛) the expense I changed the ox for a sheep. But I am not surprised the people would say of me I am miserly (*ai* 愛)." The economy of consummatory conduct is a kind of love where, in the effort to optimize the possibilities of any relationship, one must begin from taking others on their own terms and allowing them their integrity. Such is the meaning of truly cherishing others. The propriety that can be achieved in our roles and relations is a function of the deference and respect people show to each other; we learn to love by being loved, and learn to respect by being respected. In loving and respecting others, we activate the same feelings in them.

"有人於此，其待我以橫逆，則君子必自反也：我必不仁也，必無禮也，此物奚宜至哉？其自反而仁矣，自反而有禮矣，其橫逆由是也，君子必自反也，我必不忠。自反而忠矣，其橫逆由是也，君子曰：'此亦妄人也已矣。如此，則與禽獸奚擇哉？於禽獸又何難焉？'"

    "If someone were to treat exemplary persons with appalling disrespect, they would surely search themselves, saying: 'I must have failed to act consummately or I must have failed to achieve propriety in my roles and relations. How else could such a situation arise?'

    "If on searching themselves, they discover they have behaved consummately and with propriety, and the appalling treatment continues, they would surely reflect: 'I must have failed to do my best for this person.'

"But if on searching themselves they discover they have done their best for this person, and the appalling treatment continues, such exemplary persons would say, 'Such a person must be quite mad and not know what he is doing. This being the case, he is no different from an animal, and how can I blame an animal?'"

Comment: The response of exemplary persons to appalling conduct on the part of others is to look for its source in failings in their own conduct. Have they failed in their application of empathetic "dramatic rehearsal" (*shu* 恕) in determining what is the best course of action with respect to another, and then have they failed to act with conscientiousness upon their determination of what is best (*zhong* 忠)? As is repeated in the *Analects*, in ascertaining what to do in one's relations with others, the first step is 己所不欲，勿施於人 "do not impose on others what you do not want imposed on you." At the end of the day, the central concern of exemplary persons is maintaining their own standards. As such, their first instinct is to examine their own conduct in terms of what they have done themselves and the consequences their actions have had for others. They are not given to the kind of reflex blame and resentment that would only diminish themselves. When the status as a human being is determined by morality and culture rather than other ontological considerations, there is still a warrant as in 4B19 for regarding other people as no more than animals. Such a perception is certainly positive in being a challenge to human exceptionalism, but it can also have obvious negative implications and consequences.

"是故君子有終身之憂，無一朝之患也。乃若所憂則有之：舜，人也，我，亦人也。舜爲法於天下，可傳於後世，我由未免爲鄉人也，是則可憂也。憂之如何？如舜而已矣。若夫君子所患則亡矣。非仁無爲也，非禮無行也。如有一朝之患，則君子不患矣。"

"Thus, while exemplary persons are always concerned as a matter of temperament, they are not given to unexpected bouts of anxiety. In being concerned, it is of this kind. Shun was a person, as am I. Shun became a model for the world that could be handed down to later generations, and yet I am nothing but an ordinary person. This then is something worth worrying about. What can I do about this concern? There is nothing to do short of becoming a Shun myself.

"When it comes to anxieties, exemplary persons simply do not have them. They do not act in any way that is less than consummate, and do not do anything that is not consistent with ritual propriety. Even when unexpected problems arise, exemplary persons are not anxious about them."

Comment: Exemplary persons respond to the rudeness of others through a pattern of introspection and concern about their own conduct that conduces to personal growth, and at the same time, remain free of the kind of blame and resentment that would make them less. Similarly, the kind of concern that is commensurate with being exemplary as a person is to aspire to becoming a sage by cultivating the habitude of a sage in one's own conduct. Since their actions are consistently consummate and always in accord with ritual propriety, exemplary persons cannot be vexed by other matters, nor can unfortunate episodes that might arise detract from their comportment. Exemplary persons have one concern alone: that is, the quality of their own conduct.

7A27 孟子曰：" 飢者甘食，渴者甘飲，是未得飲食之正也，飢渴害之也。豈惟口腹有飢渴之害？人心亦皆有害。人能無以飢渴之害爲心害，則不及人不爲憂矣。"

Mencius said, "A famished person will find anything to eat delicious; a thirsty person will find anything to drink quite divine. Neither of them will be good at discerning the quality of the fare because their hunger and thirst intrude upon their judgment. How can it be that just the workings of the palate can suffer from deprivation? The heartmind (*xin* 心) is open to the same kind of threat. If people can avoid the same starving of their heartmind that cripples the palate, they will have no concern in their comparison with others."

Comment: Mencius is consistent in his analogy between the necessity of nourishing the body properly and attending to the kind of nourishment required to grow the moral habitude as it takes shape as the heartmind. Just as the palate can be cultivated and provide proper guidance with respect to food, so the heartmind can be cultivated to ensure that persons in their moral habits are able to rise above the rest. This Confucian zoetology (*shengshenglun* 生生論) that begins from life and growth prompts a cluster of familiar metaphors that are focused on nourishing the life experience in all of its aspects.

6A11 孟子曰："仁，人心也；義，人路也。舍其路而弗由，放其心而不知求，哀哉！人有雞犬放，則知求之；有放心而不知求。學問之道無他，求其放心而已矣。"

Mencius said, "Consummatory conduct (*ren* 仁) is the human heartmind (*xin* 心), and acting appropriately (*yi* 義) is its way forward. It is a pity indeed when persons abandoning their proper way forward, fail to follow it, and when allowing their heartmind to get away, are oblivious to the need to chase after it. When their dogs and chickens get away, they go after them, but when their heartmind gets away, they can't be bothered. The proper way to learning is nothing more than going after the heartmind that got away."

Comment: In this passage, Mencius appeals to the familiar Confucian metaphor of "walking the way." He places real emphasis on the opportunity the initial natural inclinations (*siduan* 四端) of the heartmind provides human beings for moral growth and refinement as these inclinations are represented by consummate conduct (*ren* 仁) and acting appropriately (*yi* 義). He exhorts us to not let this incipient disposition get away from us given that our entire future regimen of personal cultivation is dependent upon securing it. Mencius repeatedly expresses his concern about the possibility of losing hold on our moral inclinations at the incipient stage, but when we compare this text with the *Analects*, we might wonder why there is not a stronger emphasis on the institution of family as the entry point for developing moral competence.

7B24 孟子曰："口之於味也，目之於色也，耳之於聲也，鼻之於臭也，四肢之於安佚也，性也，有命焉，君子不謂性也。仁之於父子也，義之於君臣也，禮之於賓主也，知之於賢者也，聖人之於天道也，命也，有性焉，君子不謂命也。"

Mencius said, "The mouth's penchant for taste, the eye's for color, the ear's for sound, the nose's for smell, and the body's for comfort—these are all human propensities (*xing* 性), and yet because our capacities (*ming* 命) also have a role in these sensations, exemplary persons are not given to referring to these aptitudes as human propensities (*xing* 性). A penchant for consummate conduct (*ren* 仁) in the roles of father and son, for appropriateness (*yi* 義) in the roles of ruler and subject, for ritual propriety (*li* 禮) in the roles of guest and host, for wisdom (*zhi* 知) in the roles that make persons superior and that sages have within the way-making of *tian* (*tiandao* 天道), are capacities we have (*ming* 命), yet because our human propensities (*xing* 性) also have their place, exemplary persons are not given to referring to such moral habits as mere capacities."

Comment: We as persons are born into a manifold of family and community relations, and by virtue of these thick initial conditions, have feelings of pity at suffering, feelings of modesty and deference, a sense of propriety and a sense of approval and disapproval. Indeed, we have the beginnings of a full moral sensorium. This sensorium as a general description of the conditions that obtain at birth is rooted in our thinking and feeling (*xin* 心). It is in acting upon these native inclinations that, in a collaboration between persons and world, they can be cultivated to constitute our particular narratives as distinctively human lives. Mencius reserves the term "human propensities" (*xing* 性) to reference the growth within those transactions that make persons distinctively human. In so doing, he places a heavy emphasis on the critical role of context:

> 居移氣，養移體，大哉居乎！夫非盡人之子與？
> Context alters one's vital energies just as what one eats alters one's body. Huge indeed is the function of context. Would we not otherwise just be anybody's son?①

It is in this sense then we might claim that relatively speaking, persons are less importantly similar and more importantly distinctive cultural achievements. And again, in more general terms, what it means to become distinctively human as a species is a generalization made from the collective history of our achievements within our particular narratives. It is for this reason Mencius claims that: 天下之言性也，則故而已矣 "the various doctrines on human propensities (*xing* 性) that have been discussed in the world are all a matter of invoking historical precedents, and nothing more."②

It is important to note that Mencius chooses to reserve the use of the term *xing* 性 for what is most exclusively and distinctively human. *Ming* 命 as "capacities" is used here as elsewhere in the *Mencius* to designate those conditions in the life experience over which we have less rather than more

---

① *Mencius* 7A36.
② *Mencius* 4B26.

influence and control: that is, the various instincts and physiological functions that enable us to sustain life and that in sum, are life itself. *Xing* 性 as "human propensities" by contrast refers to those outcomes in our roles as human beings that carry the strongest human signature: our ability to purposely and deliberately cultivate our familial, communal, and ultimately cosmic roles, and in so doing, to elevate the human experience into an elegant and exemplary narrative. In rehearsing these roles, Mencius begins radially and expansively from the most basic familial roles to the transformative role the lives of the sages have had as epochal meaning-makers that expand the cosmic order itself.

Again, we should note both *ming* 命 and *xing* 性 are animated by our desires. In 7B25, Mencius defines "good" (*shan* 善) explicitly as "what is worth desiring" (*keyu* 可欲). Since such "good" is fundamentally the outcome of discursive relations within family and community, it is the quantum of such growth that Mencius would associate with *xing* 性 as the substance of morality.

In the distinction drawn here between our "human propensities" (*xing* 性) and our "capacities" (*ming* 命), there is a clear emphasis on the moral and cultural dimensions of life that are most uniquely human. And the more biologically and physiologically defined aspects of the human experience, while also open to cultivation, are shared by animals more broadly, and are thus treated as less remarkable. It is important, however, that the distinction Mencius chooses to make between our *xing* 性 and our *ming* 命 here not be reduced to some simple dichotomy between the mental and the physical, the intellectual and the sensual, the psychical and the somatic. Indeed, the intellectual and physical aspects of our persons are inseparable in our best efforts to elevate the human experience, and both reflect such growth. What makes us distinctively human is our propensity for moral growth as it is expressed through the virtuosity of our embodied actions. For Mencius, not only is our physicality an integral aspect of such human activity, but just as with our cognitive and affective competencies, the cultivated transformation of the physical is reflective of the unremitting effort invested in becoming consummately human.

Another important insight we can derive from this passage is the role of what Confucius has called "using names properly" (*zhengming* 正名). Mencius is referencing the power that human beings have in the illocutionary and normative force of naming. Language when used effectively as it is interwoven with our life forms has the power to realize a particular world in the sense of making that world real. By insisting upon this distinction between "propensities" and "capacities," Mencius is elevating one modality of personal cultivation over another, celebrating our ability to reach beyond the cultivation of those vital capacities that enable us to continue living, and to transform this same quantum of life creatively into an exemplary moral narrative.

6A6 公都子曰："告子曰：'性無善無不善也。' 或曰：'性可以爲善，可以爲不善；是故文、武興，則民好善；幽、厲興，則民好暴。' 或曰：'有性善，有性不善；是故以堯爲君而有象；以瞽瞍爲父而有舜；以紂爲兄之子，且以爲君，而有微子啟、王子比干。' 今曰'性善'，然則彼皆非歟？"

Master Gongdu said, "According to Master Gao, our natural human propensities (*xing* 性) are neutral, inclined neither toward good (*shan* 善) nor bad conduct. But others would say that such propensities have the capability for either good or bad conduct. It is for this reason that when Kings Wen and Wu flourished, the common people were given to doing good, but when Kings You and Li arose the people resorted to violence. And then there are yet others who would say that the natural human propensities of some people are inclined to good conduct, while those of others are inclined to do bad things. It is for this reason there were wicked people such as the Xiang even with Yao as their ruler. There was a filial son such as Shun even with the despicable Blind Man Gusou as his father, and loyal subjects such as Viscount Qi of Wei and Prince Bi Gan even with the despot Zhou as both relative and ruler. Now when you say the natural human propensities are inclined to do good, does this mean all of these other views are wrong?"

Comment: Master Gongdu gives Mencius three alternatives to Mencius's claim that human propensities tend toward goodness: (1) human propensities are neutral and thus must be disciplined by externally imposed doctrines, (2) these propensities are fickle, and can be influenced one way or the other by the sway of the external environment, and (3) for some people such propensities tend toward good and for others, bad, regardless of the external conditions. The first two of these alternatives assume the conduct of persons is governed by forces external to them; the third view is that conduct is dependent on internal conditions alone regardless of external influence. It is Mencius's claim about such propensities tending toward goodness that is in fact holistic, including both internal and external conditions.

孟子曰："乃若其情，則可以爲善矣，乃所謂善也。若夫爲不善，非才之罪也。惻隱之心，人皆有之；羞惡之心，人皆有之；恭敬之心，人皆有之；是非之心，人皆有之。惻隱之心，仁也；羞惡之心，義也；恭敬之心，禮也；是非之心，智也。仁義禮智，非由外鑠我也，我固有之也，弗思耳矣。故曰：'求則得之，舍則失之。'或相倍蓰而無筭者，不能盡其才者也。"

"If we are talking about what people actually are (*qing* 情)," replied Mencius, "then they have the capability to become good. This is what I mean by 'good.' If in fact they do bad things, it is not the fault of their native resources. In the thinking and feeling (*xin* 心) of everyone there is a sense of empathy, of shame, of respect, and of discrimination. It is the sense of empathy that enables them to conduct themselves consummately (*ren* 仁) in their roles and relations; it is the sense of shame that enables them to conduct themselves with optimal appropriateness (*yi* 義); it is the sense of respect that enables them to conduct themselves with ritual propriety (*li* 禮); it is the sense of discrimination that enables them to conduct themselves wisely (*zhi* 智). The propensity to act consummately, to act appropriately, to act with ritual propriety, and to act wisely is not something fused onto me from some external source; it is what I have had all along, but have simply failed to reflect upon.

"Thus it is said, 'Look for it and you will find it, set it aside and you will lose it.' There are certainly some people who are twice, five, countless times better than others, but this is only because some people are not able to make the most of their native resources."

Comment: There are two importantly different ways of reading this passage. One way is that Mencius is making a claim about what it means to be a human "being" reminiscent of Aristotle's ontological definition of the man in the marketplace. Aristotle's *Categories* is the first text of the *Organon* in the standard *Corpus Aristotelicum*. And Aristotle's initial project in the *Categories* is to identify the set of questions that must be asked to give a full account of what can be predicated of a subject, with his own concrete example of this subject being "the man in the marketplace." In the several different versions of these categories found throughout his corpus, "What is a man?" is not only his first question but is also his primary one. Its primacy lies in the fact that, in Aristotle's answer to this question, he introduces an ontological disparity by first identifying the necessary essence or substance of the subject (Gk. *ousia*, L. *substantia*)—What "is" a man?

followed then by questions that distinguish this person's various secondary and contingent attributes: "What is 'in' a man?" Aristotle explains this ontological distinction between substance and attribute in the following terms:

> To give a rough idea, examples of substance are man, horse; of quantity: four-foot, five-foot; of qualification: white, grammatical; of a relative: double, half, larger; of where: in the Lyceum, in the market-place; of when: yesterday, last-year; of being-in-a-position: is-lying, is-sitting; of having: has-shoes-on, has-armour-on; of doing: cutting, burning; of being-affected: being-cut, being-burned.[1]

For Aristotle, the "What?" question has primacy because it provides us with the essential subject: that is, what identifies the underlying self-sufficient substance of what the man *is*. The various other questions prompted by the remaining secondary conditions—quantity, quality, relation, place, time, position, state, action, and affection—seek to provide us with the full complement of attributes that are "in" a subject or can be said "of" a subject as contingent and conditional predicates, none of which can exist without supervening on this subject. In Aristotle's own language:

> All the other things are either said of the primary substances as subjects or in them as subjects. . . . So if the primary substances did not exist it would be impossible for any of the other things to exist.[2]

It is interesting and important to note that Aristotle's set of questions do not include "Why?" or "How?" because his substance ontology has causal and teleological entailments that already provide the answers to them—that is, why the man exists and what he will become when he actualizes his formal and final causes. Importantly, the potential of the man's formal essence and his final *telos* as a man, makes such explanatory questions such as Whence? and Whither? moot.

Angus Graham reflects on the extent to which this substance ontology

---

[1] Aristotle, *The Complete Works of Aristotle: The Revised Oxford Translation*, ed. Jonathan Barnes, Princeton: Princeton University Press, 1984, 1b25-2a4.
[2] Aristotle, *The Complete Works*, 2a35-2b7.

individuates and decontextualizes the man by locating his potentialities as residing essentially within him:

> Aristotle's thinking is noun-centered; he starts with the substance identified as man, and before introducing any verb but "to be" can already ask "When was he in the marketplace?" and "Where was he yesterday?" but not "Whence?" or "Whither?"[①]

Aristotle's ontology introduces the notion of simple location and of discrete individuality, and favors the noun form grammatically—the "man" in the marketplace—as the ground for the attributes that can then be ascribed to him.

One of the corollaries of an Aristotelian substance ontology that gives privilege to such an isolated, individual subject is the experience of the world as being populated by discrete things or objects that "object" to us in standing off independent of us. And a second corollary of this ontology is the doctrine of external relations it assumes: that is, it construes these various independent objects each with its own essential integrity as first-order, discrete things—what they really are—and then any relations that might conjoin them as only second-order, contingent relations they subsequently contract.

The second way of reading Mencius's claim here is that he is making a descriptive rather than a metaphysical assertion, and is giving an account of human "becomings" rather than a human "being." Graham cautions us about ascribing ontological assumptions to Chinese cosmology, using as his specific example the tendency commentators have had to treat this Mencian idea of "human propensities" (*xing* 性) as referencing some "transcendent origin, which in Mencian doctrine would also be a transcendent end."[②] Graham, rejecting the relevance for Mencius of an essentializing Greek idealism (*eidos*) and the radical teleology (*telos*) that follows from it, would locate his notion of *xing* 性 within the generic features of an early Chinese process or "event" ontology in which putative "things" and their contexts are interdependent and thus inseparable. It is just such a worldview that I and my collaborators following scholars such as Marcel Granet,

---

① Graham, *Studies in Chinese Philosophy*, p. 391.
② Rosemont, *Chinese Texts and Philosophical Contexts*, p. 287.

Tang Junyi, Fei Xiaotong, Joseph Needham, and Graham himself have argued for at length as the most appropriate interpretive context for understanding these classical Confucian texts.①

I would argue that the basic misreading of this passage arises from a dualistic, realist interpretation of the distinction between inside and outside as being exclusive and essential rather than as being transactional, experiential, and mutually entailing. The point is that these "four inclinations" locate relationally-constituted persons within a stream of experience that must acknowledge their subjective dispositions as well as their objective behavior. Moral conduct is a collaboration between persons and their worlds rather than being a pattern of behavior derived solely from the outside as environmental influences, or for that matter, solely from the inside as the actualization of a given human nature.

Mencius clarifies what he means in saying our human propensities are inclined toward good conduct. In 7B25 he defined "good" (shan 善) as "what is worth desiring" (keyu 可欲). And in this passage, given what humans actually are, "good" is something they "have the capability to do" (keyiwei 可以爲) in the sense of it being possible for them to do it rather than it being a necessary condition, something they must do. This suggests that shan 善 as efficacy is a quality of activity that can be achieved within one's context if so desired rather than denoting some innate quality of character one owns and must act upon irrespective of one's circumstances.

The Confucian notion of "good" (shan 善), rather than referencing some antecedent, generic "virtue," begins from what we actually are (qing 情), and means first and foremost, "moral growth" achieved through effective communication in our roles and relations. Of course, the identities of persons are certainly grounded in their thick native beginnings within the environing relationships of family and community which, as a received and thus retrospective inheritance integral to who they are, needs to be both nurtured and protected from loss or injury. And the conduct of such persons is certainly guided by the normative generalizations that a cultural

---

① See for example David L. Hall and Roger T. Ames, *Thinking from the Han*, pp. 23-78, and Roger T. Ames and Henry Rosemont, Jr., *The Analects of Confucius: A Philosophical Translation*, pp. 20-45. See also Roger T. Ames. *Confucian Role Ethics: A Vocabulary,* Honolulu and Hong Kong: University of Hawai'i Press and Chinese University Press joint publication, 2011, especially Chapter 2, "An Interpretive Context for Understanding Confucianism."

tradition has best remembered in its customs and institutions. But such identities and the realization of the highest aspirations of persons only emerge prospectively in the process of these initial relationships achieving thick resolution as they are cultivated, grown, and consummated over their lifetimes. Their potential far from being an antecedent given, in fact emerges most significantly in the always transactional events that in sum constitute lives lived in the world.

For Mencius, *xin* 心 here references the initial native conditions captured in the "four inclinations" (*siduan* 四端) formula of the inchoate *xin* 心 comprised of *renyilizhi* 仁義禮智. That is, *xin* 心 is our native inclination toward consummate conduct (*ren* 仁), appropriate behavior (*yi* 義), an achieved propriety (*li* 禮), and wisdom (*zhi* 智) as these tendencies are expressed in our roles and relations. The "four inclinations" are the multivalent aspects of *xin* 心 referencing our preliminary and at first inchoate pattern of roles and relations in the ambient family, community, and culture that constitute our focal identity at birth, and that are then thickened as our narratives unfold. It is an appreciation of this irreducibly relational and intentional understanding of *xin* 心 together with the vital, generative import of *xing* 性 that saves us from what I take to be a common and thus familiar misinterpretation of Mencius as advocating a fixed, universal, and essentialist doctrine of human nature.

What it means to become human, far from referencing an antecedent given that takes us back to our origins or forward to some pre-determined end, is in fact a provisional and emergent process within the context of an evolving cosmic order. Again, the "potential" for becoming human is not simply some causal "beginning" or teleological "end." It is not some inborn, essential potential exclusive of context and family relations, or some potential that is actualized as the ineluctable process of growth toward some predetermined ideal. To begin with, in this Chinese natural cosmology, there are no such deracinated, individual persons who live outside of context and family relations. Persons do not live their lives inside their skins; they exist in their associations, and only in their associations. And since persons in their nested, narratives-within-narratives are constituted by these evolving, eventful relations, the "potential" of persons and their achieved identities in fact emerge *pari passu* from out of the specific, contingent transactions of their lives.

What is at stake here is the deliberate Mencian answer to perhaps our most basic and important philosophical question: What does it mean to become fully human? How do we explain the birth, life, and growth of the human "being"? Do we appeal to reduplicative causal accounts (the infant is a ready-made adult), by teleological accounts (the infant is simply preliminary to the existing ideal)? Or do we posit the notion of human "becomings" that appeals to a contextual, narrative account available to us through a phenomenology of reflective and purposeful personal action? How do we define what it means to be a human "being?" Do we offer speculative assumptions about innate, isolatable causes that locate persons outside of the roles and relations in which they live their lives? Or alternatively, do we explain them as having "become" human by taking full account of the initial, native conditions and context within in which persons are inextricably embedded, and then go on to assay the full accretion of consequent action as their life stories unfold?

This passage concludes with the observation that the process of personal cultivation that enables one to become consummately human is largely dependent upon assiduous application. This then is the equalizer among persons. It is the sustained effort to make the most of our native conditions rather than any difference in kind that distinguishes cultivated persons from the crowd. These native conditions here are *cai* 才, a term that like the *siduan* 四端 as sprouts or seedlings, references breaking through the ground as first growth. Worthy of note is the fact that for Mencius, although persons are the same in kind, the ultimate differential between ordinary people and those human "becomings" who take full advantage of the possibilities inherent in the disposition and evolving conditions of the human experience is exponential growth. *Xing* 性, far from being an internal, regulative design that produces legions of identical, reduplicated human beings, is a dynamic and complex process of growth that produces a full range of persons who by virtue of their resolve are exponentially different in their quality as persons.

"《詩》曰: '天生蒸民, 有物有則。民之秉夷, 好是懿德。' 孔子曰: '爲此詩者, 其知道乎! 故有物必有則; 民之秉夷也, 故好是懿德。'"

"The *Book of Songs* 260 says:
Tian produces the throngs of common people;
And everything thus produced has its standards.
Were the common people to hold fast to their norms
They would be given to merit and virtuosity (*de* 德).
And Confucius commented: 'Whoever composed this song knew of what he

spoke. Indeed, everything that is produced certainly has its standards. It is because the common people hold fast to their norms they come to cherish the beauty of virtuosity in their conduct.'"

Comment: Citing the *Book of Songs* is a familiar practice in the philosophical canons that serves as a Q.E.D. clincher for the argument presented. The term *ze* 則 translated here as "standards" appears on the bronzes as 剘 and references the practice of inscribing laws and regulations on the bronze vessels as a way of making these edicts public and thus broadly known.① We have to resist a dualistic reading of the relationship between *tian* 天 and human beings from which we would be prompted to infer the standards for things are set by some external source. Human beings emerge within a *tian* 天 ecology with each of them being implicated in the other. Given this correlative relationship, the standards emerge as the most appropriate way of maintaining what is a symbiotic relationship.

In contrast to the three alternative understandings of our natural human propensities (*xing* 性) described at the beginning of this passage that would locate norms either as exclusive external standards or as an exclusive internal nature, this song concludes by asserting the standards for human actions emerge from conduct that is a collaboration between native human conditions and social environment in which these tendencies are cultivated and brought to maturation. It is by holding fast to such standards that human beings are able to thrive and to experience the beauty of achieving real virtuosity in their conduct.

6A1 告子曰: "性猶杞柳也，義猶桮棬也；以人性爲仁義，猶以杞柳爲桮棬。" 孟子曰: "子能順杞柳之性而以爲桮棬乎？將戕賊杞柳而後以爲桮棬也？如將戕賊杞柳而以爲桮棬，則亦將戕賊人以爲仁義與？率天下之人而禍仁義者，必子之言夫！"

"Our natural propensities (*xing* 性) are like the willow tree," said Master Gao, "and our sense of appropriateness (*yi* 義) is like cups and bowls. Cultivating these natural propensities into a moral habitude of consummate conduct (*ren* 仁) and appropriateness is like making the willow tree into our cups and bowls."

"Are we able to accord with the natural propensities of the willow tree in

---

① Kwan, "Database," 西周晚期 CHANT 10176.

making it into our cups and bowls?" asked Mencius. "Or is it only once we have violated the natural propensities of the willow tree that we are able to make them? If we must violate the natural propensities of the willow tree before we can make the cups and bowls, then must we also violate the natural propensities of human beings before we can encourage a moral habitude of consummate conduct and appropriateness? These doctrines of yours are certain to lead the people of the world to believe that cultivating such a moral habitude would be a disaster!"

Comment: The two metaphors Mencius uses consistently for the cultivation of a moral habitude from our natural propensities are the natural growth of the human body, and of foliage. Aristotle's ontological conception of persons would locate the generative, formal, and final causes of such growth within persons themselves. Master Gao's position by contrast would assert such moral growth is dependent on the imposition of external doctrinal constraints that can be imposed on them to shape them in the proper way. Mencius, as an alternative to these two internal and external conceptions of moral growth, proposes a radical contextualism in which both the inchoate natural inclinations that activate our natural propensities for moral growth and the environing conditions through which this growth is nourished and extended, are integral to the process itself. For Mencius, Master Gao's doctrine of an externally imposed, contrived morality is a grave distortion of the natural process.

Given his consistent appeal to horticultural metaphors, the danger here in reading Mencius as an alternative to Master Gao, is to ascribe to Mencius the strong Greek commitments to "species" (*eidos*) and "design" (*telos*) in a way that would associate his position with Aristotle. Mencius, far from assuming our natural propensities are going to produce rolling fields of identical human "beings," exhorts each of us to aspire to a sageliness as the ultimate expression of our own assiduous, always particular, regimen of personal cultivation.

James Behuniak addresses Mencius's use of the botanical metaphor explicitly:

Before we think of the botanical metaphor in terms of an end-driven teleology and equate *xing* 性 with a uniform, predetermined "nature" on that basis, let us briefly attempt to locate this metaphor in its own context. . . . When Mencius describes growth, the stress is on the irrepressible process of emergence, a process located within nourishing conditions. The seed is the beginning of an emergent process. . . . This is a process shaped within environing conditions; it is not teleological in any strict, end-driven sense. In the Chinese tradition, the seed is not described as containing its own end; rather the process would appear to determine its end, since not all seeds come to fruition. . . . Generally in this tradition, the mention of botanical growth in a literary context does not evoke generic traits that are simply "actualized" in the process of growth.①

Behuniak goes on to make the point that throughout the classical canons, botanical growth is usually associated with a certain environment, often using the expression that a particular locale "has" (*you* 有) its regional foliage as particular to its climate and conditions. In an analogous way, he argues the locale that "has" human beings is the family and that the features that condition human growth are familial relations.

> Like everything else that grows in early China, humans are rooted and nourished *somewhere*. So, if it can be said that the southern mountains "have" mulberry trees, it is suggested here that families "have" humans.②

And it is precisely those specific features of family and communal living that are captured in the specific conditions of the "four inclinations" (*siduan* 四端).

To be clear, the "four inclinations" describe the initial matrix of family, social, and political relations that "have" the infant, and serve as the locus for personal moral growth. In this sense, Mencius is consistent with the sentiments expressed in the *Analects* 1.2 which states:

> 其爲人也孝弟，而好犯上者鮮矣……孝弟也者，其爲仁之本與。
> It is rare indeed for someone who has a sense of family reverence and fraternal deference to have a taste for defying authority. . . . As for family reverence and fraternal deference, these are, I suspect, the root of becoming consummate in one's roles and relations.

---

① Behuniak, *Mencius on Becoming Human*, pp. xiii-xiv.
② Behuniak, *Mencius on Becoming Human*, p. xvi.

The same connection between the familial and the political is made in *Mencius* 1A1:

> 未有仁而遺其親者也，未有義而後其君者也。
> There have never been persons consummate in their conduct (*ren* 仁) who have left their parents behind and there have never been persons with a sense of appropriateness (*yi* 義) who have placed their rulers last.

This Mencian emphasis upon the irreducibility of person and context is pervasive. For example, in 4A11:

> 孟子曰："道在邇而求諸遠，事在易而求諸難：人人親其親、長其長，而天下平。"
> Mencius said: "The proper way is right before us and yet it is sought after at some great distance; things are easy and yet they are sought after in what is difficult. Were everyone to love their parents and defer to their elders, peace would prevail in the world."

In *Mencius* 3A5, the argument against what Mencius interprets as the Mohist position of dissolving family affection by extending the same concern to all people (*jian'ai* 兼愛) is his insistence that human beings only have one root in their immediate, concrete family relations:

> 夫夷子信以爲人之親其兄之子爲若親其鄰之赤子乎？⋯⋯且天之生物也使之一本，而夷子二本故也。
> Does Master Yi really believe persons will have the same affection for their neighbor's baby as they do for their own nephew? . . . When nature (*tian* 天) gives birth to things it just gives them one root but Master Yi wants them to have two.

Nature in giving humankind life provides them with one continuous love that begins in family and extends outward. But Yi Zhi chooses to make two out of one by claiming that we are naturally inclusive in our care for others, but at the same time, we must direct this concern first to our parents.

There is a major philosophical point to be made here. Angus Graham reports that "the absence of terminations to mark abstract nouns interferes with forming an abstract concept."[1] What does he mean? Definition is an act of predication. The difference between substance ontology and a Confucian process cosmology is that while "things" when defined essentially presumably can be fully predicated and thus "defined" within fixed limits, a process cosmology with continuing, interpenetrating events resists such boundaries. From the *Analects*, for example, we learn that, because the notion of "consummate conduct" (*ren* 仁) is irreducibly relational and processual, far from being a generic virtue with a fixed definition, is person- and situation-specific. Generalizations are then made from specific instances. The same is true with other erstwhile "virtues," *de* 德 and "the good," *shan* 善 among them. We read in the *Book of Documents*: 德无常师，主善为师。善无常主，协於克一 "Virtuosity is without anything to take as its constant norm; it takes what is good as its norm. Again, what is good is without anything to take as its constant norm; it brings together what can be done on an individual basis."

As such, Graham understands *shan* 善 and other such modalities "not as a quality but as a way of behaving."[2] It is on this basis that Confucian ethics appeals to modalities of behavior rather than concrete precepts defining of right and wrong: that is, to acting with resolution (*cheng* 誠), with integrity (*xin* 信), with virtuosity (*de* 德), with felicity (*shan* 善), and so on. Specific actions in any particular situation are determined analogically out of past experience, and are always contextual, presupposing a local set of conditions and considerations. By the same logic, the processual nature of this cosmology means that in the absence of absolute limits, generalizations, horizons, and probabilities must do the work of the universals and laws that provide structure for classical Greek philosophy.

6A2 告子曰："性猶湍水也，決諸東方則東流，決諸西方則西流。人性之無分於善不善也，猶水之無分於東西也。"孟子曰："水信無分於東西，無分於上下乎？人性之善也，猶水之就下也。人無有不善，水無有不下。今夫水，搏而躍之，可使過顙；激而行之，可使在山。是豈水之性哉？其勢則然也。人之可使爲不善，其性亦猶是也。"

"Our natural propensities (*xing* 性) are like surging water." said Master

---

[1] A.C. Graham, *Disputers of the Tao: Philosophical Argument in Ancient China*, La Salle, IL: Open Court, 1989, p. 426. See also pp. 398-399, 423-427.

[2] Graham, *Disputers of the Tao*, p. 424. See the discussion in Behuniak, *Mencius on Becoming Human*, pp. 61-62.

Gao. "If we open a path for water to the east, it will flow eastward; if we open a path for it to the west, it will flow westward. Our inability to separate our natural propensities into those that would do good and those that would do otherwise is like our inability to separate water into that which would flow east and that which would flow west."

"Water certainly has no inclination to flow eastward as opposed to westward," replied Mencius, "but does the same hold true in its flowing upwards or downwards? The natural propensity of human beings toward doing good is like water's propensity to flow downward. There is no one who is not inclined to do good just as there is no water that is not inclined to flow downwards.

"With water, by slapping it and making it jump, we can splash it above our heads, and by blocking it off and making it flow backwards we can create a reservoir on the top of a mountain, but what has this got to do with the natural propensity of the water? Such things only occur because we have manufactured the situation. That persons can be made to act badly is because as in the case of the reservoir of water their natural propensities have been overridden."

Comment: D.C. Lau has translated this same passage as:

> It is certainly the case ... that water does not show any preference for either east or west, but does it show the same indifference to high and low? Human nature is good just as water seeks low ground. There is no man who is not good; there is no water that does not flow downwards.

The problem with Lau's translation in saying "human nature *is* good, just as water *seeks* low ground," is that it does not respect the symmetry of the sentence. Given the parallel structure, the text is saying that human propensities (*xing* 性) are an inclination in personal growth whereby one *seeks to* become *shan* 善, not that *xing* 性 in itself "is" already *shan* 善. A more careful reading of this passage is the claim that good conduct is *an inclination* of our natural propensities (*xing* 性) rather than a predetermined condition, and we must cultivate this inclination in what we do.①

---

① This more careful reading was suggested to me in correspondence with Vytis Silius at Vilnius University.

To begin, there are two important points to be made here. First, the appeal to surging water is a familiar metaphor in the text, and is a fair indication of how much weight Mencius chooses to place on the irrepressible surge of growth that occurs when this natural inclination is followed. Secondly, *shan* 善 as it is defined in 7B25 is "what is worth desiring" (*keyu* 可欲). What animates our moral growth is our desire to become consummate in our persons.

For the infant, the four inclinations that anticipate moral growth are the thick, irreducibly biological, familial, social, and cultural conditions defining of its situation. These discursive bonds are thus by nature resolutely relational and inclusive, and a source of rapid moral articulation (*shan* 善) as they become increasingly robust. As suggested by the character itself that references communication, *shan* is "good" in the sense of moral growth within the continuing narrative. Relations are fundamentally a relating to, a giving an account, a conversation. It is only from this continuing discursive process that "good" can be abstracted as a summary description of persons or their actions. Said simply, newborns as concrete facts are constituted by the relations that define them, and as they follow the discursive promptings within the matrix of these relations, they grow their various roles into emerging personal identities. Infants in these relations are animated and projective, they are alive and active, and develop their inflected and reflexive sense of themselves within the expansive *intra*subjective roles and relations that come to constitute them.

Importantly, it is the radial, constitutive, and transactional nature of relations themselves and their propensity to produce meaning that locate newborns within an inchoate habitude, and thus dispose them to positive moral growth. An infant conceived of as a discrete and separate "individual" is nothing more than a retrospective abstraction from this same manifold of relations. The erstwhile "goodness" (*shan* 善) of infants, far from being some innate and isolatable endowment, is the product of the vital disposition they have toward prosocial growth. *Shan* 善 refers to the felicitous growth within the semiotic processes and symbolic competencies as they are occuring that come to shape them as human "becomings."

6A3 告子曰："生之謂性。" 孟子曰："生之謂性也，猶白之謂白與？" 曰："然。""白羽之白也，猶白雪之白；白雪之白猶白玉之白與？" 曰："然。""然則犬之性猶牛之性，牛之性猶人之性與？"

Master Gao insisted: "It is what you are born with (*sheng* 生) that is meant by 'natural propensities' (*xing* 性)."

"Is saying that 'it is what you are born with that is meant by natural propensities' the same thing as saying 'white' is what is meant by 'white'?" responded Mencius.①

"Indeed, it is." replied Master Gao.

"Then is the whiteness of white feathers the same as the whiteness of snow, and the whiteness of snow the same as the whiteness of jade?"

"Yes, it is." replied Master Gao.

"Would it follow then, that the natural propensities of a dog are the same as the natural propensities of an ox, and the natural propensities of an ox are the same as the natural propensities of a human being?"

Comment: Master Gao's naturalization of *xing* 性 here is the same position Xunzi ascribes to Mencius and uses to challenge his understanding of natural propensities. Xunzi himself follows Confucius in arguing for the assiduous effort needed to achieve moral competency, and wants to distinguish himself from Mencius by suggesting that Mencius thinks otherwise. In this effort, Xunzi seems to be offering a self-serving caricature of Mencius's position on natural propensities (*xing* 性):

孟子曰："人之學者，其性善。"曰：是不然。是不及知人之性，而不察乎人之性偽之分者也。凡性者，天之就也，不可學，不可事。

Mencius says "since human beings can be educated, their natural propensities (*xing* 性) are good." I would argue this is not so. Mencius in his lack of understanding of our natural propensities (*xing* 性), is unable to discern the distinction between natural propensities themselves and deliberate activity (*wei* 偽). Speaking generally, natural propensities are what is given by nature; they can neither be learned nor acquired.

Xunzi in criticizing Mencius begins by assuming his own understanding of *xing* 性 as being an unlearned "given" is incontrovertibly what *xing*

---

① As D.C. Lau points out, because *sheng* 生 and *xing* 性 are used interchangeably in these early texts and were close in pronunciation, Mencius is able to impute a tautology to Master Gao: "A is A." This tautology allows Mencius to draw the *reductio* analogy that just as "white is white," the *xing* 性 of one thing is the same as another. See D.C. Lau (trans.), *Mencius*, Hong Kong: Chinese University Press, 1984, p. 225.

性 actually means. Such being the case, according to Xunzi's logic, when Mencius says our *xing* 性 inclines us in our conduct to do good, Mencius is at the same time asserting being good is unlearned and does not require deliberate effort. Such an assertion would mean being good is as easy as falling off a log. It is simply being human. Of course, this naturalistic interpretation of *xing* 性 that Xunzi is imputing to Mencius—what you are born with makes you good—is explicitly rejected here by Mencius as a *reductio ad absurdum*.

6A4 告子曰: "食色, 性也。仁, 内也, 非外也; 義, 外也, 非内也。"孟子曰: "何以謂仁内義外也?" 曰: "彼長而我長之, 非有長於我也; 猶彼白而我白之, 從其白於外也, 故謂之外也。" 曰: "異於白馬之白也, 無以異於白人之白也; 不識長馬之長也, 無以異於長人之長歟? 且謂長者義乎? 長之者義乎?" 曰: "吾弟則愛之, 秦人之弟則不愛也, 是以我爲悦者也, 故謂之内。長楚人之長, 亦長吾之長, 是以長爲悦者也, 故謂之外也。" 曰: "耆秦人之炙, 無以異於耆吾炙, 夫物則亦有然者也, 然則耆炙亦有外歟?"

"The need for food and sex is a matter of our natural propensities (*xing* 性)." said Master Gao. "Being consummate in our roles and relations (*ren* 仁) comes from within rather than from without, while our sense of what is appropriate in these roles and relations (*yi* 義) comes from without, not from within."

"What do you mean when you say being consummate in our roles and relations comes from within while our sense of what is appropriate in them comes from without?" asked Mencius.

"When I defer to that old person over there as an elder, this sense of deference is not something I already have. It is just as when something is white and I acknowledge it to be white. The external thing is white and I am simply acknowledging it to be so. This is what I mean by 'comes from without.'"

"But a sense of appropriateness is different from whiteness." said Mencius. "There is no difference in acknowledging a white horse to be white and a white-haired man to be the same, but is this to say there is no difference between the way in which we treat an old horse and an elderly person? And again, does the sense of appropriateness lie in the person's being elderly, or in the person's being treated as an elder?"

Master Gao said: "It is because he is my younger brother I love him, but if he is the brother of some stranger from Qin, I do not. This means the criterion for finding pleasure lies in my relationship to him, and thus I say it 'comes from within.' But deferring to an elder from the state of Chu is just the same as deferring to an elder in my own family. This means the criterion for my finding pleasure lies with their elderliness, and thus I say it 'comes from without.'"

"My enjoying roasted meat received from a person from Qin is no different from enjoying it prepared by myself." said Mencius. "If my enjoying anything at all is just the same, how can it follow my enjoying roasted meat is something that comes from without?"

Comment: Mencius as a Confucian would have no quarrel with Master Gao's first claim: the need for food and sex is a matter of our natural propensities. In fact, by returning to the example of food in the last section, Mencius seeks to refute Master Gao's argument that some aspects of morality—the sense of what is appropriate—is a matter of external imposition.

Yang Bojun 楊伯峻 in his commentary on this passage points out:

> The "Admonishments" chapter of the *Guanzi* 管子戒篇 states: 仁從中出，義由外作。"Consummate conduct emerges from within; appropriateness is a matter of external imposition." Master Gao holds the same position here. The "Canons and Commentary B" chapter of the *Mozi* Book 10 says: 仁，愛也；義，利也。愛利，此也，所愛所利，彼也。愛利不相爲內外，所愛利亦不相爲內外。其爲仁，內也，義，外也，舉愛與所利也，是狂舉也。
> "*Ren* 仁 is love; *yi* 義 is utility. Love and utility are 'this;' being loved and giving utility are 'that.' Love and utility are not a matter of internal and external (meaning they are both internal). And being loved and giving utility are not a matter of external and internal (meaning they are both external). Taking *ren* 仁 as internal and *yi* 義 as external is to match love with what gives utility, and is absurd." It is a much clearer logical refutation of Master Gao's thesis than Mencius's criticism.①

But there is another section of the *Mozi* 墨子尚同上 that is also relevant:

---

① Yang Bojun 楊伯峻, 孟子譯注, Beijing: Zhonghua Shuzhu, 1960, pp. 256-257. Cf. Ian Johnston, *The Mozi: A Complete Translation*, Hong Kong and New York: Chinese University Press and Columbia University Press joint publication, 2010, p. 272.

IV. THE *MENCIUS* (*MENGZI* 孟子): EXTENDING THE VOCABULARY

子墨子言曰：古者民始生，未有刑政之時，蓋其語，人異義。是以一人則一義，二人則二義，十人則十義。其人茲眾，其所謂義者亦茲眾。是以人是其義，以非人之義，故交相非也。

Mozi said: "Of old when the common people first appeared it was a time without law or governance. There was a saying: People have a different sense of what is right (*yi* 義). If there is one person, there is one right, if two then two, and if ten then ten. The more people, the more things were said to be right. It was a situation in which people would affirm their own standard and reject that of others, and thus one of mutual rejection."

The chaos of having so many opinions was the Mohist logic behind establishing public offices and standards, where norms are thus taken to be a matter of external decree.[①]

Mencius is keen here to advance his argument that the relationships implicated in the "four inclinations" (*siduan* 四端) which include both "consummate conduct" (*ren* 仁) and "a sense of appropriateness" (*yi* 義) whether expressed in deference to elders or love for others, all have an internal as well as an external aspect. In the first example, Mencius rejects Master Gao's suggestion that deference to elders is external with the argument that deference is initiated by the young person who is defering rather than from anything done on the elder's part. Mencius would abjure the "Euthyphro problem" where Socrates insists that principles of adjudication must be prior to and separate from the objects of our judgment. For Socrates, something must be determined to be intrinsically and thus externally good—good in itself—rather than being deemed good as a summary judgment on its always relational narrative.

Socrates famously asks Euthyphro whether something is holy because it is loved by the gods, or is loved by gods because it is holy. And Socrates then answers his own question by insisting on the latter. Continuing in this same dialogue, Socrates makes a further point in support of his answer through a rather convoluted grammatical argument that concludes by claiming that anything loved as holy must itself be both logically and temporally prior to its being loved. That is, the thing must have some essential characteristic itself that then induces the accident or attribute of its being loved. Simply put, you have to have an "it" before it can be loved.

[①] Ian Johnston, *The Mozi*, p. 51.

Of course, the success of such an argument is dependent upon a logic grounded in a substance ontology that allows for a clear distinction between essences and their attributes, between something and its contextualizing relations. We might recall Aristotle's ontological and thus isolating "What?" question that would answer what can be said "of" the man in the marketplace. This answer stands in contrast to the subsequent ancillary questions that identify what can be attributed to, and thus be "in" the subject once substantially understood.

But this same argument falters in an event ontology where the essence and attribute dualism has no purchase, and where what is putatively "essential" is simply a generalization made off of a pattern of evolving relationships within a narrative. That is, something being holy, far from being a quality intrinsic to the thing itself, is a function of what an event means for those persons within its continuing context. An old church in Wales made quite holy by the faithful in its own time can become someone's rather ordinary house when its congregation has dispersed and faded away. As such, it is only a provisional convenience if not a grammatical nicety for us to describe the church as being holy rather than as "holy-ing" under a specific set of conditions. Something being holy is both temporal and situational. It is a function of having over time become valorized as holy, and continues as such as long as it is loved by the gods and anyone else who would invest their reverence in it. Further, in this alternative eventful logic and *contra* Socrates, the actual content of something that is "holy-ing" or continually "becoming" holy changes over time rather than being some essential and unchanging property that defines it. All this is but to say that what something is, what it does, and what it means for other things, are no more than aspects of its continuing narrative. Things are what they are because of their place and function within the wholeness of experience.

Consummate and optimally appropriate persons are the product of comporting themselves in their roles and relations in consummate and optimally appropriate ways. And what it means for them to be designated consummate and appropriate is a summary generalization made about such conduct. In all cases, the enjoyment one derives from acting morally, whether it is deferring to elders of one's own family or elders in general, or loving brothers or brothers in general, although having an external aspect in being directed toward other persons, also has an internal aspect as being expressive of one's own natural inclinations. The point that is ubiquitous in Mencius is morality cannot be reduced simply to external circumstances or imposition.

4B18 徐子曰: "仲尼亟稱於水, 曰: '水哉, 水哉! ' 何取於水也。" 孟子曰: "原泉混混, 不舍晝夜, 盈科而後進, 放乎四海。有本者如是, 是之取爾。苟爲無本, 七八月之間雨集, 溝澮皆盈; 其涸也, 可立而待也。故聲聞過情, 君子恥之。"

Master Xu said: "There were several occasions on which Confucius heaped praise on water, saying: "My that water! My that water!" What was it that Confucius found so admirable about it?"

Mencius replied: "Water that has a deep source cascades forward unceasing day and night, filling all of the low-lying hollows as it advances to find its way to the sea. Things that have a deep source are like this, and it is what Confucius found admirable about it. If it did not have a deep source, it would be like standing water that collects from the summer rains, filling the drains and gutters only to dry up in no time at all. It is thus that exemplary persons would be ashamed to have a reputation that goes beyond their deeds."

Comment: Mencius uses the metaphor of surging water repeatedly to describe the irrepressible vigor of the natural human propensities as these inclinations drive the production of moral growth. In this passage, however, the focus is upon the source that sustains the water and that nourishes such growth. Just as standing water with no source is gone in a moment with no lasting effects, so the reputation of exemplary persons will not endure if it in substance is no more than a few good deeds. This passage brings to mind 4B19 in which the sage Shun is described as:

由仁義行, 非行仁義也。
... acting upon his moral habit of being consummatory and optimally appropriate in his conduct rather than merely doing what was deemed consummatory and appropriate by others.

And again 2A2:

浩然之氣……是集義所生者, 非義襲而取之也。
Flood-like *qi* 氣 ... is what is born of the cumulative habit of optimally appropriate conduct, and is not something that can be had through merely

random acts of appropriateness.

It is only those actions with a deep source, grounded in and expressive of a living and aggregating moral habitude, that are the real substance of moral action.

Important here is the concept of "source" as it would be understood within this process cosmology. As with notions such as "potential," "root," "nature," and "cause," the "source" is not conceived on the model of God creating the world—as an independent, bounded and self-contained reservoir that as an initial beginning feeds an independent stream. Source is not something separate from its issue that then needs conceptually to be put back together. Rather, it is the whole creative narrative that is real. As with the relationship between *dao* 道 and the myriad things (*wanwu* 萬物), "source" and "recipient," "creator" and "creature," are aspectual terms—two alternative ways of entertaining the same phenomenon. The "source" of the sages then, is nothing more than their stories: their accumulating and thus habituated narratives of sagacious conduct.

6B2 曹交問曰："人皆可以爲堯舜，有諸？" 孟子曰："然。" "交聞文王十尺，湯九尺，今交九尺四寸以長，食粟而已，如何則可？" 曰："奚有於是？亦爲之而已矣。有人於此，力不能勝一匹雛，則爲無力人矣；今日舉百鈞，則爲有力人矣。然則舉烏獲之任，是亦爲烏獲而已矣。夫人豈以不勝爲患哉？弗爲耳。徐行後長者謂之弟，疾行先長者謂之不弟。夫徐行者，豈人所不能哉？所不爲也。堯舜之道，孝弟而已矣。子服堯之服，誦堯之言，行堯之行，是堯而已矣。子服桀之服，誦桀之言，行桀之行，是桀而已矣。" 曰："交得見於鄒君，可以假館，願留而受業於門。" 曰："夫道若大路然，豈難知哉？人病不求耳。子歸而求之，有餘師。"

Cao Jiao inquired: "Is it the case that we all have the capability of becoming Yaos and Shuns?"

"Indeed." Mencius replied.

"I have heard that King Wen was ten units tall, and Tang was nine. Now how can I measure up to them when I stand at nine units four, and have only rice to eat?"

Mencius replied: "What difference does that make—just do it. If there is someone who is unable to lift a small chicken, he is indeed a weakling. But say instead this same person were able to lift a hundredweight. He is indeed a strong man. This is but to say anyone who can lift the same weight as the strongman Wu Huo is a Wu Huo. How can the concern lie in not being equal to the task rather than just not doing it?

"For a young person to walk slowly behind his elders is proper deference, while walking quickly and jostling ahead of them is a lack of the same. How could walking slowly be something this person cannot do? It is just he doesn't do it. The way-making of Yao and Shun was nothing but family reverence and deference to elders. If you wear Yao's clothes, speak his words, and do what he does, you *are* a Yao. Again, if you wear the clothes of the tyrant Jie, speak his words, and do what he does, then you *are* a Jie."

Cao Jiao said: "I am going to go and call on the lord of Zou to ask him for lodging because I want to stay and be your student."

Mencius replied: "The proper way is like a broad thoroughfare—how can it be hard to find? It is just that people are remiss in seeking it out. If you go back and look for the proper way, there will be teachers enough for you."

Comment: There are two possible interpretations here that hang on the distinction between "are" or "do." Do we understand "potential" ontologically ("the science of being in itself") as an essential capacity that makes a person a person, or "zoetologically" ("the art of living") as the possibilities that emerge *pari passu* in one's narrative as a transactional collaboration between person and world? On the first interpretation, everyone by virtue of some innate capacity has the potential to lift a hundredweight, to be the strongman Wu Huo, and to be a sage like Yao. Or alternatively, if they fail to exercise this same innate capacity, they are weaklings and become a tyrant Jie.

The second possible interpretation is that anyone who in making the most of their transactional narratives does any of these exceptional things, in the fullness of time becomes what they do. The stress is on the process of personal cultivation and the various possibilities that increase with personal growth. *Mencius* 2A6 describes this unbridled growth made possible by our initial inclinations:

凡有四端於我者，知皆擴而充之矣，若火之始然，泉之始達。

Now acknowledging these four inclinations are defining of us, the process of realizing the development and fruition of them is like a fire beginning to blaze, or a spring of water beginning to gush forth.

And there is Shun's example of such growth in 7A16:

若決江河，沛然莫之能禦也。
. . . like a breach in the dikes of the Yangtze or Yellow rivers that nothing could contain.

The examples Mencius offers are telling. Does Mencius think everyone has some *initial* physical capacity to lift a hundredweight and thus be a Wu Huo? Wrong question. There are people who have been able to apply themselves in the world and in so doing, optimize the possibilities that arise out of living such an exceptional narrative. Were any one of us able to do what strongman Wu Huo does, they too would be a Wu Huo. The point Mencius is making here is that you are what you do, where what you do in every moment is changing who you are and the possibilities of who you will become.

Mencius repeatedly analogizes moral cultivation with physical nourishment and growth. Just as everyone seeks to nourish and strengthen their body, we are all able in the activities of our roles and relations able to behave in a moral way. Everyone in "simply acting with family reverence and deference to elders" (*xiaoti'eryiyi* 孝弟而已矣) is acting sagaciously. Yao and Shun did nothing more in their becoming sages. But there are sages and there are sages. The difference lies in making the assiduous, unrelenting effort of a Yao or Shun to become superlative exemplars of what can be done.

It is perhaps not incidental that Mencius uses the example of walking in the company of one's elders. The metaphor of "walking the way" and extending the road is pervasive throughout these Confucian canons: that is, growing the relationships that shape us on the shared journey of our narratives. Walking this proper way as a vision of the moral life should be patently clear to everyone, and does not depend upon any particular teacher to show them the way. All we need to do is do it.

As in other passages, it would seem that losing the momentum provided by our native inclinations toward establishing a pattern of moral conduct is not irreversible as long as there is life. Like the case of Ox Mountain, we can make an effort to revive the original conditions that allow for growth. If we "go back and look for the proper way," it is not hard to find.

7A16 孟子曰："舜之居深山之中，與木石居，與鹿豕遊，其所以異於深山之野人者幾希；及其聞一善言，見一善行，若決江河，沛然莫之能禦也。"

Mencius said: "When Shun was deep in the mountains living among the rocks and trees and wandering about with the deer and wild boar, the difference between him and the wild men of the mountains was ever so slight. But on hearing just one fine word and seeing just one fine deed it was like a breach in the dikes of the Yangtze or Yellow rivers that nothing could contain."

Comment: This passage uses the metaphor of surging water to clarify the distinction between what are similar beginnings and the exponentially expansive effects of personal cultivation. Where the sage Shun in his low beginnings is no different from the most unrefined of persons, once his project of personal cultivation is initiated in his associations with others, it is irrepressible, surging forward to transform the world.

IV.4 Role Politics and Consummate Governing (*renzheng* 仁政)

1A7 齊宣王問曰:"齊桓、晉文之事可得聞乎?"孟子對曰:"仲尼之徒無道桓文之事者,是以後世無傳焉,臣未之聞也。無以,則王乎?"曰:"德何如則可以王矣?"曰:"保民而王,莫之能禦也。"曰:"若寡人者,可以保民乎哉?"曰:"可。"曰:"何由知吾可也?"曰:"臣聞之胡齕曰:王坐於堂上,有牽牛而過堂下者,王見之,曰:'牛何之?'對曰:'將以釁鍾。'王曰:'舍之!吾不忍其觳觫,若無罪而就死地。'對曰:'然則廢釁鍾與?'曰:'何可廢也?以羊易之!'不識有諸?"曰:"有之。"曰:"是心足以王矣。百姓皆以王為愛也,臣固知王之不忍也。"王曰:"然;誠有百姓者。齊國雖褊小,吾何愛一牛?即不忍其觳觫,若無罪而就死地,故以羊易之也。"曰:"王無異於百姓之以王為愛也。以小易大,彼惡知之?王若隱其無罪而就死地,則牛羊何擇焉?"王笑曰:"是誠何心哉?我非愛其財而易之以羊也。宜乎百姓之謂我愛也。"曰:"無傷也,是乃仁術也,見牛未見羊也。君子之於禽獸也,見其生,不忍見其死;聞其聲,不忍食其肉。是以君子遠庖厨也。"王說,曰:"《詩》云:'他人有心,予忖度之。'夫子之謂也。夫我乃行之,反而求之,不得吾心。夫子言之,於我心有戚戚焉。此心之所以合於王者,何也?"

King Xuan of Qi asked of Mencius: "Can you tell me about the affairs of King Huan of Qi and Duke Wen of Jin?"

Mencius replied: "Since none of the followers of Confucius spoke about the affairs of King Huan and Duke Wen, there has been nothing passed down to later times, and thus I have heard nothing of them. But if you have no objection, I could speak on becoming a True King."

"What kind of virtuosity defines the conduct of the True King?"

"If you take good care of the common people, nothing can prevent you from becoming a True King."

"Can someone like me really take good care of the common people?"

"Certainly."

"How do you know this?"

"I heard this anecdote from Hu He. He said your Majesty was sitting at the head of the hall when some persons passed by the lower part of the hall leading an ox. Your Majesty having seen them, asked: 'What are you doing with the ox?' 'We are going to use its blood to consecrate a newly cast bell.' they replied. Your Majesty said: 'Release the ox. I cannot bear to watch it trembling with fear like an innocent person being led to the execution ground.' The persons responded: 'In that case, do we give up the consecration of the bell?' 'How could we do that?' your Majesty replied. 'Use a sheep in its place.' I don't know if this event really happened." said Mencius.

"It did indeed." said the King.

"Within the heartfelt feeling you expressed here is the makings of a True King. The people all thought you begrudged the ox, but I know for sure that you could not bear its suffering."

"You are right," said the King. "But is it true that the people thought this? Even though the territory of Qi is small, how could I begrudge one ox? I could not bear the trembling of the ox like an innocent person being led to the execution ground, and thus I replaced it with a sheep."

"Your Majesty must not think it strange that the people in seeing you exchange the larger animal for the smaller one thought of you as being miserly. How could they know your real reason? After all, if you were pained by an innocent animal going to its death, what is the difference between the ox and the sheep?"

The King laughed and said: "What was I really feeling? It certainly wasn't that I begrudged the expense, but then I did exchange the ox for a sheep. It only makes sense that the people would think me miserly."

"They meant no harm." said Mencius. "Yours was an act of consummate conduct (ren 仁). You had seen the ox but not the sheep. This is the way exemplary persons respond to animals. Once having seen the animals alive they cannot bear to see them die, and having heard their cries, they cannot bear to eat their meat. It is for this reason that exemplary persons give the kitchen a wide berth."

The King was delighted and said, "The *Book of Songs* 198 does have the following passage:
The feelings do belong to other persons,
But it is I who has been able to take the measure of their motives.
It is referring to you, Mencius. I certainly did this thing, but in reflecting on it and trying to fathom why I did it, I did not know my own mind. But when you put it into words, just such feelings welled up in me. How is it then that these feelings are consonant with being a True King?"

Comment: Mencius in a straightforward way makes "taking good care of the people" the substance of becoming a True King. He goes on to analyze King Xuan's motives in exchanging a sheep for an ox in the blood consecration of a bell that the King himself does not understand. This particular example ought to alert us to the continuing centrality of sacrifice in the social, political, and religious life of this period. While the people are inclined to see the King as being motivated by economic reasons, Mencius focuses on the uncalculated responsive feelings the King has for the innocent animal. Such empathetic feelings are a necessary condition for "taking good care of the people" and thus becoming a True King.

曰：「有復於王者曰：『吾力足以舉百鈞，而不足以舉一羽；明足以察秋毫之末，而不見輿薪。』則王許之乎？」曰：「否。」「今恩足以及禽獸，而功不至於百姓者，獨何與？然則一羽之不舉，爲不用力焉；輿薪之不見，爲不用明焉；百姓之不見保，爲不用恩焉。故王之不王，不爲也，非不能也。」曰：「不爲者與不能者之形何以異？」曰：「挾太山以超北海，語人曰：『我不能。』是誠不能也。爲長者折枝，語人曰：『我不能。』是不爲也，非不能也。故王之不王，非挾太山以超北海之類也；王之不王，是折枝之類也。」

Mencius said: "If in my reply to your Majesty I were to say 'I am strong enough to lift three-quarters of a ton, but not enough to lift a feather; my sight is keen enough to see the tip of an autumn hair, but not enough to see a cartload of firewood,' would you accept my claim?"

"I would not." said the King.

"How then can it be that your kindly concern is enough to reach the animals, but the merits of your governance do not get through to the people? In fact the single feather not being lifted is because no effort was made to do so; the cartload of wood being unseen is because no effort was made to look at it. And the people not being properly cared for is because you haven't shown them any kindly concern. Thus, your not being a True King is simply a matter of what you have failed to do; it is not because you are unable to do it."

The King asked: "What would be a good example of the difference between not doing and not being able to do?"

"If you say to others that I am unable to tuck Mount Tai under my arm and leap over the North Sea, this is really a case of being unable to do something. But if you say to others that I am unable to massage the joints of an elder for him, this is a matter of not doing it rather than being unable to do it. Hence, your not being a True King is not a case of tucking Mount Tai under your arm and leaping over the North Sea, but one of not massaging the joints of an elder."

Comment: Mencius's distinction between being unable to do something and simply not doing it really has broad application, and is key to understanding his claim that everyone can become a sage. King Xuan with his empathy toward animals is able to extend this kindness to his relationship with the people and provide them with proper care. Similarly, human beings given their prosocial propensities are able to cultivate these inclinations in what they do into a habituated pattern of conduct, and thus become sages. Becoming a True King or a sage is not some essential potential belonging to all human beings as a natural endowment to then be realized. Nor is the project of becoming a True King heroic in the sense of someone being able to do something extraordinary that others cannot do. Rather such accomplishments are simply the outcome of having the personal resolve to do what is ordinary in an extraordinary way.

"老吾老，以及人之老；幼吾幼，以及人之幼。天下可運於掌。《詩》云，'刑于寡妻，至于兄弟，以御于家邦。'言舉斯心加諸彼而已。故推恩足以保四海，不推恩無以保妻子。古之人所以大過人者，無他焉，善推其所爲而已矣。今恩足以及禽獸，而功不至於百姓者，獨何與？權，然後知輕重；度，然後知長短。物皆然，心爲甚。王請度之！"

"Treat your own aged relatives as they should be treated and extend this same treatment to the aged of others; treat your own young as they should be treated and extend this same treatment to the young of others. If you do this, you can turn the world over in the palm of your hand. As it says in the *Book of Songs* 240:

He served as a model for his own consort
And extended this influence to all of his brothers,

And thus he brought order to his family and the state.
These words simply say that King Wen took these feelings and projected them onto others. It is thus that extending your kindly concern is sufficient to take good care of all within the four seas, while not doing so leaves you unable to care for even your own wife and children. The one way in which the ancients were able to surpass all others was simply in their extraordinary capacity to extend what they did. How then can it be that your kindly concern is enough to reach the animals, but the merits of your governance do not get through to the people? By weighing things up we come to know their weight, and by taking their measure we come to know their extension. This calculation applies to everything, how much more with our feelings. I would ask your Majesty to take the measure of your feelings."

Comment: Mencius lays out his central doctrine of "extending kindly concern" (*tui'en* 推恩) that begins with family feelings and is then projected outward into community, polity, and cosmos. King Huan has the appropriate feelings, but in order to take good care of the people he needs to extend these same feelings radially in an inclusive and accommodating way. Morality is not only irreducibly relational, but is also something done within those relations. It is nothing other than the growth in relationships achieved in acting upon one's empathy for others. With the use of "heartminding" (*xin* 心) here, we have reinforcement of the argument that the prosocial "four inclinations" (*siduan* 四端) in Mencius's moral social psychology are the starting point of moral growth, situating the inchoate infant within a matrix of family and community relations. Mencius's doctrine of extension is a variation on and has the same centrality in his role ethics as Confucius's method for becoming consummate in one's conduct: that is, of "putting oneself in the place of others and then doing one's best" (*zhongshu* 忠恕). Mencius in using the expression "taking the measure" (*du* 度) reflects the fact morality is a deepening of the relations within the social ecology as they already exist rather than the outcome of bringing two separate things into relation.

"抑王興甲兵，危士臣，構怨於諸侯，然後快於心與？"王曰："否。吾何快於是？將以求吾所大欲也。"曰："王之所大欲可得聞與？"王笑而不言。曰："爲肥甘不足於口與？輕煖不足於體與？抑爲采色不足視於目與？聲音不足聽於耳與？便嬖不足使令於前與？王之諸臣皆足以供之，而王豈爲是哉？"曰："否。吾不爲是也。"曰："然則王之所大欲可知已，欲辟土地，朝秦楚，苢中國而撫四夷也。以若所爲求若所欲，猶緣木而求魚也。"王曰："若是其甚與？"曰："殆有甚焉。緣木求魚，雖不得魚，無後災。以若所爲求若所欲，盡心力而爲之，後必有災。"曰："可得聞與？"曰："鄒人與楚人戰，則王以爲孰勝？"曰："楚人勝。"曰："然則小固不可以敵大，寡固不可以敵衆，弱固不可以敵强。海内之地方千里者九，齊集有其一。以一服八，何以異於鄒敵楚哉？蓋亦反其本矣。"

"Or perhaps your Majesty can only find pleasure in raising armed troops, imperiling your officers and ministers, and inciting the enmity of the other vassal lords?"

"Not at all. How could I find pleasure in such things? I only want to satisfy my one great desire."

"Would your Majesty share with me the object of this great desire?"

The King smiled, but remained silent.

"Could it be the taste of the food on your table does not satisfy your palate? Or the seasonality of your garments does not satisfy your body? Or the colorful embellishments around you do not satisfy your eyes? Or the singing and music played for you does not satisfy your ears? Or the attendants and favorites who surround you do not satisfy your wants? Given that your various ministers can provide you with all of these things, it cannot be them."

"No, my great desire is not in satisfying any of these things."

"That being the case, then I can surmise what your one great desire must be. You want to open up new territory, to make vassals of the states of Qin and Chu, rule over the central kingdoms, and win over all of the barbarian tribes on the borderlands. But to do what you are doing to realize this desire is like climbing a tree to catch a fish."

"That bad?" said the King.

"Yes," said Mencius, "but even worse. Though you are not going to catch any fish by looking for them up in the trees, at least there will be no calamity that will follow in its wake. But to do what you are doing to realize what you desire, and further to put your whole heart into it, is a sure recipe for disaster."

"How so?" asked the King.

"If the people of Zou went to war with those of Chu, who does your Majesty think would be the victor?"

"The people of Chu would win."

"This is true because the small is no match for the large, the few no match for the many, the weak no match for the strong. There are nine expanses of territory within the Four Seas with each of them occupying a thousand *li* square, and the combined lands of Qi make up only one of these. How is one trying to subdue eight any different from Zou trying to vanquish Chu? We need to get back to the fundamentals."

Comment: In order to counsel King Xuan effectively, Mencius needs to find out his real ambitions. King Xuan denies he has any desire to make war or requires any material gratifications that go beyond those available in his own court, but he does allow he has one great desire. Although the King remains silent on this desire, Mencius is able to infer from what has been said that it is to become sovereign over the entire world. By the fourth century BCE as the Warring States period was coming to a close, it had become clear to all contenders for empire that this tournament was a winner-take-all, zero-sum game. Philosophers such as Mencius with entourage in tow toured the various courts to share their wisdom on how to accomplish this single enterprise. We can discern fundamentals in the way of things; after all, fish are not to be sought in the treetops. Mencius uses a war analogy to make his case to the King that in the way of things, small trying to defeat large is never a good logic for success. But laying aside force of arms and the coercion it entails, there is an alternative strategy basic to effecting political order that can be relied upon.

"今王發政施仁，使天下仕者皆欲立於王之朝，耕者皆欲耕於王之野，商賈皆欲藏於王之市，行旅皆欲出於王之塗，天下之欲疾其君者，皆欲赴愬於王。其若是，孰能禦之？" 王曰："吾惛，不能進於是矣。願夫子輔吾志，明以教我。我雖不敏，請嘗試之。" 曰："無恆產而有恆心者，惟士爲能。若民，則無恆產，因無恆心。苟無恆心，放辟邪侈，無不爲已。及陷於罪，然後從而刑之，是罔民也。焉有仁人在位罔民而可爲也？是故明君制民之產，必使仰足以事父母，俯足以畜妻子，樂歲終身飽，凶年免於死亡；然後驅而之善，故民之從之也輕。今也制民之產，仰不足以事父母，俯不足以畜妻子；樂歲終身苦，凶年不免於死亡。此惟救死而恐不贍，奚暇治禮義哉？王欲行之，則盍反其本矣：五畝之宅，樹之以桑，五十者可以衣帛矣。雞豚狗彘之畜，無失其時，七十者可以食肉矣。百畝之田，勿奪其時，八口之家可以無飢矣。謹庠序之教，申之以孝悌之義，頒白者不負戴於道路矣。老者衣帛食肉，黎民不飢不寒，然而不王者，未之有也。"

"Now were your Majesty to become consummate in the governance you dispense (*renzheng* 仁政), it would make all of those in the world who serve in an official capacity want to have a place in your Majesty's court, all of those who till the land to want to till in your Majesty's fields, all of the merchants practicing their trade to want to warehouse their goods in your Majesty's marketplaces, all of the travelers making their way in the world to want to do their traveling on your Majesty's roadways, and all of those who feel aggrieved of their rulers to present their petitions to your Majesty. This being the case, who could possibly hold them back?"

"I am muddle-headed," said the King, "and not able to see a path forward. I hope you will help me find my way by instructing me clearly. Even though I am a slow learner, I will try to do my best to practice what you say."

"It is only scholar-officials (*shi* 士) who, in the absence of constancy in their material well-being, are still able to maintain constancy in their thoughts and feelings. As for the common people, a lack of constancy in their thoughts and feelings can be traced directly to the absence of constancy in their material well-being. With a lack of constancy in their thoughts and feelings, they will be given over to every kind of license and depravity, stopping at nothing. To inflict punishments when they have thus sunk into crime is to entrap the people. How could it be that there is a consummate person in authority when entrapping the people is allowed?

"It is for this reason enlightened rulers will regulate the material well-being of the common people to guarantee that looking up there is sufficient for them to serve their parents and looking down there is sufficient to support their wives and children, that from good years there will be enough to live happily with a full stomach, and in bad years they will escape the ravages of starvation. In just this way, such rulers usher the people towards a happy life, and thus make it easy for them to follow.

"As for today, in the provisioning of the people, looking up there is not enough to serve their parents, and looking down there is not enough for their wives and children. Good years only promise them a hard life, and in bad years there is no escape from starvation. If mere survival is beyond their grasp, what leisure do they have to cultivate propriety (*li* 禮) and appropriateness (*yi* 義) in their roles and relations?

"If your Majesty really wants to dispense consummate governance, you need to stop and go back to the basics. If mulberry trees are planted within the five-*mu* compounds, those who have reached fifty years can wear garments made of silk. If in the raising of chickens, pigs, dogs, and swine the animals are allowed their breeding time, those who have reached seventy years can have meat to eat. If those with a plot of a hundred *mu* are not robbed of their seasons, a family with eight mouths to feed will not go hungry. If care is taken in the education provided by the village schools to teach the moral imperatives of family reverence and deference to elders (*xiaoti* 孝悌), you won't see old grey heads on the roadways carrying heavy loads on their backs. When the aged have silk to wear and meat to eat, and the common people are neither cold nor hungry, this then is the very definition of the True King."

Comment: If the King provides his people with consummate governance, he creates a centripetal vortex that, without coercion and of their own accord, will draw all of the people of the world in all of their different occupations, toward his rule. The fundamental obligation the ruler has to the common people is to guarantee their welfare. While perhaps scholar-officials who by definition have received a Confucian moral education can be relied upon regardless of material well-being, the common people without being provided an adequate livelihood are vulnerable to every depravity. For the ruler to fail in his basic responsibility to take care of the people and then to punish them for what is a predictable outcome is perverse. Mencius then in his exhortation to the King to "go back to the basics" lays out his familiar formula for the welfare of the people that includes land reform, division of labor, ecological intelligence in the use of natural resources, and perhaps the most important factor, their moral education.

5B1 孟子曰: "伯夷, 目不視惡色, 耳不聽惡聲。非其君不事, 非其民不使。治則進, 亂則退。橫政之所出, 橫民之所止, 不忍居也。思與鄉人處, 如以朝衣朝冠坐於塗炭也。當紂之時, 居北海之濱, 以待天下之清也。故聞伯夷之風者, 頑夫廉, 懦夫有立志。"

Mencius said: "As for Bo Yi, he would not look at anything unseemly or listen to anything indecent. He would not give service to anyone save the ideal ruler, and would not take command of anyone save the ideal people. When order prevailed, he would step up to serve; when chaos set in, he would withdraw. He could not endure dwelling in a place where perverse governance was dispensed and where perverse people found a home. He thought of taking up company with some rude villager to be no different from sitting down in the mud and ashes in his full court attire. Living at the time of Zhou, the last evil ruler of the Shang dynasty, he took up residence on the shores of the North Sea to wait for the waters to clear. Thus it was that on hearing of the comportment of Bo Yi, the insatiably greedy would become honest and clean, and the weak and cowardly would find their resolve."

Comment: Given the political malaise that prevailed at the end of the Warring States period, Mencius is preoccupied with the task of establishing consummate governance (*renzheng* 仁政) in the world as the only antidote. Rather than positing a set of principles or drafting a constitution that would capture his vision of proper governing, Mencius alludes to a set of historical figures who in their conduct can serve as political role models. He takes Bo Yi as a sage of old who was scrupulous in his conduct, always remaining beyond and above any reproach. Bo Yi would only deem to participate in the world when he could remain unsullied by the baseness and perversity of those around him. Being incorruptible, he serves the tradition as a beacon that can attract the avaricious and the cowardly toward his light, and that can inspire them to change their ways.

"伊尹曰：'何事非君？何使非民？'治亦進，亂亦進。曰：'天之生斯民也，使先知覺後知，使先覺覺後覺。予，天民之先覺者也。予將以此道覺此民也。'思天下之民匹夫匹婦有不與被堯舜之澤者，如己推而內之溝中，其自任以天下之重也。"

"Yi Yin said: 'Who is the ruler I would not serve; who are the common people I would not command? I will give service regardless of whether order prevails or chaos sets in.' Again he said: '*Tian* 天 in giving birth to the common people expects those who are first aware of things to awaken those who follow. Since I am the first to be enlightened among the common people, I am going to rouse them with this proper way.' His thinking was this. On seeing ordinary men and women who had not yet enjoyed the favor of living according to the way of Yao and Shun, it was as if he had pushed them off this proper path into the gutter. Such was Yi Yin's sense of responsibility."

Comment: Yi Yin, unlike Bo Yi, threw himself into the world without concern for any deleterious effects it might have on him personally. He was a sage who serves the tradition as a paragon of responsibility, seeing himself as having a duty to maintain the ways of Yao and Shun regardless of the conditions that prevail in the world. For him, there was no thought of being contaminated by other people, but only of his solemn duty to use his own understanding of the proper way to guide those who are less fortunate. Yi Yin thus serves the tradition as a role model in the obligation each person has to both transmit and to share with others the values passed on from generation to generation.

"柳下惠不羞汙君，不辭小官。進不隱賢，必以其道。遺佚而不怨，阨窮而不憫。與鄉人處，由由然不忍去也。'爾爲爾，我爲我，雖袒裼裸裎於我側，爾焉能浼我哉？' 故聞柳下惠之風者，鄙夫寬，薄夫敦。"

"Liu Xiahui found no shame in serving a corrupt ruler nor would he refuse a lowly appointment. In attending court, he did not conceal his talents, and would invariably follow the proper way. He showed no resentment when passed over, nor did he feel aggrieved when in desperate circumstances. On sitting down with some local villager, he was so thrilled he could not break away. 'You are you, and I am me,' he said. 'Even if you stood beside me as naked as a newt, how could such behavior bring any discredit to me?' Thus it was on hearing of the comportment of Liu Xiahui, small-minded persons would become accommodating, and unkind persons generous."

Comment: Liu Xiahui was the selfless and altruistic sage, contributing his considerable talents in his service to the government and to the people without any thought of his own personal advantage or advancement. His unbounded kindness and devotion to others revealed a generosity of spirit that could transform smallness in all of its forms into something welcoming and generous.

"孔子之去齊，接淅而行；去魯，曰：'遲遲吾行也，去父母國之道也。'可以速而速，可以久而久，可以處而處，可以仕而仕，孔子也。"

"When Confucius departed the state of Qi, he set off without letting the washed rice dry, but when he took leave of the state of Lu, he said 'Let's just go slowly—this is the way one should leave the state of one's parents.' If he should rush off, he would rush off; if he should tarry, he would tarry; if he should retire, he would retire; if he should take office, he would take office—this then was Confucius."

Comment: Confucius is described here as the capacious sage—the sage that can respond appropriately to each and every situation. Felicity in what can be accomplished is always a matter of a comprehensive understanding of the circumstances, and flexibility in finding the best way forward. As with *Sunzi: The Art of Warfare*, each battlefield is particular and waits upon the formulation of a unique response. While each of the other sages described in this passage reflects an admirable pattern of conduct, to the extent that they are one thing rather than another, they are limited. The claim here is that the conduct of Confucius is all of them and more, much more.

孟子曰："伯夷，聖之清者也；伊尹，聖之任者也；柳下惠，聖之和者也；孔子，聖之時者也。孔子之謂集大成。集大成也者，金聲而玉振之也。金聲也者，始條理也；玉振之也者，終條理也。始條理者，智之事也；終條理者，聖之事也。智，譬則巧也；聖，譬則力也。由射於百步之外也，其至，爾力也；其中，非爾力也。"

Master Meng said: "Among the sages, Bo Yi was the unsullied sage, Yi Yin the highly responsible sage, Liu Xiahui the amiable and obliging sage, and Confucius the timely sage. It is Confucius who can be called the one who gathered up all of the great accomplishments. One who gathers up all of the great accomplishments is like a musical performance opening with bells and then following up with the jade tubes to bring it to a close. To open by striking the bells is a beginning that sets and modulates the tone; to close with jade tubes is an ending that continues and modulates the proper tone. To begin by setting the proper tone is the stuff of wisdom (*zhi* 智); to finish up by maintaining the proper tone is the stuff of sageliness (*sheng* 聖). Wisdom can be compared to skill; sageliness to strength. It is like shooting an arrow from beyond a hundred paces. For the arrow to reach the target is a matter of strength, but for the arrow to hit the mark—this is more than mere strength."

Comment: Mencius appeals to role models rather than abstract principles. The middle chapters of the *Analects* provide a series of snapshots in the life of Confucius—how he ate, and drank, and sat, and dressed, and how he engaged different people under different circumstances. And although these images are sometimes regarded as being of more biographical than philosophical interest, in a tradition in which aspirational role models do much of the work of regulative principles, these passages are in fact hugely important philosophically for our understanding of role ethics and role politics. These passages provide the images and the anecdotes that brought this exemplary teacher to life for his immediate protégés, and for the numerous generations of students that have followed after them down to our present day. It is within these core chapters that the person of Confucius is described as having four things he could not personally countenance—four abstentions that reveal much about Confucius's self-understanding and his own values:

There were four things the Master abstained from entirely: He would not conjecture, he would not claim or demand certainty, he was not inflexible, and he was not self-absorbed.①

In the Confucian process cosmology that eschews any strong sense of teleology or idealism, the focus is on the musicality achieved in making the most of the very now. As a personal regimen, these abstentions locate conduct relationally in what is most immediate in the human experience, and focus on shaping a habitual disposition most effective in responding concretely to what are always changing circumstances.

The positive implication of these four abstentions taken in sum is that, for Confucius, living an ethical life is much more than subscribing to a moral catechism or complying with some predetermined set of imperatives. From these strictures, we can infer an overarching, hermeneutical disposition in his own desired habits of action. We can tell that he has a commitment to pragmatic engagement rather than abstract speculation, an attitude of openness and accommodation rather than a need for finality, a willingness to be flexible rather than any intransigence or obstinacy, and a sensitivity and deference to the needs of others rather than an inordinate concern for his own personal advantage. This habituated disposition then is what motivates the virtuosic if not indeed sagacious conduct we associate with the person of Confucius who has served as *the* ultimate role model for an entire cultural tradition.

Mencius's musical metaphor is meant to capture the scale and the quality of Confucius's contribution as "the one who gathers together all of the great accomplishments" (*jidachengyezhe* 集大成也者): that is, Confucius is the historical figure who has most fully embodied the living tradition in his own person as it travels on from generation to generation. The musical metaphor speaks to the consummatory nature of the eventful human experience, with its beginnings and endings, only to begin again. In the performance of a piece of music as in the cadence of life itself, there has to be deliberate modulation from beginning to end through the whole piece, with a proper beginning and an appropriate and receptive ending. Such an achieved musicality is the highest expression of the human experience. Again, with the archery metaphor, the sagacity Confucius shares with these

---

① *Analects* 9.4: 子絕四：毋意，毋必，毋固，毋我。

other role models gives him the strength to get the arrow to the target, but beyond simply the strength, it is some additional, particular kind of responsive wisdom that enables him to always hit the mark.

3A4 有爲神農之言者許行，自楚之滕，踵門而告文公曰："遠方之人聞君行仁政，願受一廛而爲氓。"文公與之處。其徒數十人，皆衣褐，捆屨，織席以爲食。陳良之徒陳相與其弟辛負耒耜而自宋之滕，曰："聞君行聖人之政，是亦聖人也，願爲聖人氓。"陳相見許行而大悅，盡棄其學而學焉。陳相見孟子，道許行之言曰："滕君則誠賢君也；雖然，未聞道也。賢者與民並耕而食，饔飧而治。今也滕有倉廩府庫，則是厲民而以自養也，惡得賢？"孟子曰："許子必種粟而後食乎？"曰："然。""許子必織布然後衣乎？"曰："否。許子衣褐。""許子冠乎？"曰："冠。"曰："奚冠？"曰："冠素。"曰："自織之與？"曰："否。以粟易之。"曰："許子奚爲不自織？"曰："害於耕。"曰："許子以釜甑爨，以鐵耕乎？"曰："然。""自爲之與？"曰："否。以粟易之。""以粟易械器者，不爲厲陶冶；陶冶亦以械器易粟者，豈爲厲農夫哉？且許子何不爲陶冶，舍皆取諸其宮中而用之？何爲紛紛然與百工交易？何許子之不憚煩？"曰："百工之事固不可耕且爲也。"

There was a person named Xu Xing who taught the doctrines of Shen Nong. Coming to Teng from the state of Chu, he went to the gates of Duke Wen, and said to him: "I am a person who has come from a distant land, having heard you are putting into practice consummate governance (*renzheng* 仁政). I would like to be given a plot of land to work and to become one of your people." The Duke gave him a place to live.

Xu Xing had a following of a few dozen people who wore plain hemp and made their living by weaving sandals and mats.

Chen Xiang and his brother Chen Xin, both followers of Chen Liang, carrying their ploughs and shares on their backs, came to Teng from the state of Song. They said to the Duke: "We have heard you are putting into practice the governance of the sages, in which case you are a sage. We would like to be the people of a sage."

Chen Xiang met up with Xu Xing and was delighted at his teachings. Abandoning what he had learned before, he committed himself to study with Xu Xing. On meeting Mencius, Chen Xiang shared with him the words of Xu Xing: "The Lord of Teng is certainly a worthy ruler. Even so, he has yet to have learned the proper way (*dao* 道). Worthy rulers earn their keep by tilling the land with their people. They carry out their administration while all the time cooking their own meals. Now the ruler of Teng in having his granaries and treasure houses oppresses his people in order to take care of himself. How can this be considered worthy?"

"Does Master Xu eat only the grain he has planted and grown himself?" asked Mencius.

"Indeed." replied Chen Xiang.

"Does Master Xu wear only the cloth he has woven for himself?"

"No. He wears plain hemp."

"Does Master Xu wear a cap?"

"He does."

"What kind of a cap?"

"A cap made from raw silk."

"Did he weave it for himself?"

"No. He exchanged grain for it."

"Why doesn't he weave it for himself?"

"It would take him away from his tilling the fields."

"Does Master Xu use an iron pan and an earthenware steamer for cooking his food, and does he use an iron ploughshare in tilling the fields?"

"Yes, he does."

"Does he make these implements for himself?"

"No, he exchanged grain for them."

"Exchanging grain for his pots and farming tools is not oppressing the potter and blacksmith. And the potter and blacksmith exchanging their wares for grain are hardly oppressing the farmers. Here is an idea. Why doesn't Master Xu become a potter and a blacksmith himself, and make everything he has need of in his own home? Why bustle about bartering with all of the different tradesmen? Why not save himself all this trouble?"

Chen Xiang replied: "There is no way someone can carry out the occupations of the various tradesmen while at the same time tilling the fields."

Comment: This passage explores different models of governance, and reveals several assumptions that Mencius has about best practices. The story begins from the familiar trope that a burgeoning population is the sign of consummate governance captured in the paronomastic definition of "king" (wang 王) as "repairing to" (wang 往): that is, the people from all over the world will repair to the True King. The image is that, having heard of the good governance by Duke Wen in the state of Teng, large groups of people carrying their worldly possessions on their backs make their way from distant quarters to join his population. The groups describe Duke Wen as practicing "consummate governance" (renzheng 仁政), and as practicing "sagely governance" (*shengrenzhizheng* 聖人之政), with the second group announcing that if Duke Wen is practicing sagely governance, he is *ipso facto* a sage. An important Mencian assumption here is if you act like a sage, you are a sage.

The leaders of both groups of people are teachers of popular doctrines. Xu Xing teaches the ideas of Shen Nong, the founding father of agriculture, and Chen Xiang the teachings of a contemporary, Chen Liang. In the course of things, Chen Xiang and his people come under the sway of Shen Nong's teachings, and on the basis of them, come to question the worthiness of Duke Wen's governance. According to the teachings of Shen Nong, a truly worthy ruler works the fields and administers the government at the same time, and to do less is to be a burden to the people.

Mencius is brought into the conversation, and questions the assumption that different persons carrying out different functions in the society is a source of oppression. He makes the argument for the impossibility of any one person covering all of the occupations necessary to live an ordinary life, and for an appropriate division of labor and a bartering system among tradesmen and farmers that will provide everyone with what they need.

"然則治天下獨可耕且爲與？有大人之事，有小人之事。且一人之身，而百工之所爲備，如必自爲而後用之，是率天下而路也。故曰：或勞心，或勞力；勞心者治人，勞力者治於人；治於人者食人，治人者食於人，天下之通義也。當堯之時，天下猶未平，洪水橫流，氾濫於天下，草木暢茂，禽獸繁殖，五穀不登，禽獸偪人，獸蹄鳥迹之道交於中國。堯獨憂之，舉舜而敷治焉。舜使益掌火，益烈山澤而焚之，禽獸逃匿。禹疏九河，瀹濟漯而注諸海，決汝漢，排淮泗而注之江，然後中國可得而食也。當是時也，禹八年於外，三過其門而不入，雖欲耕，得乎？"

"Could it be the case that ruling the world is the exception—the one occupation that can be carried out while at the same time tilling the fields? There are important people and those who are less so. Moreover, in the case of any one person, given what they get from the various tradespersons, if they had to make all such things themselves before they could use them, the world would descend into chaos with everyone out on the street. Hence the saying: 'Some labor with their minds and some with their backs. Those who labor with their minds rule over others while those who labor with their backs are ruled by others. Those who are ruled by others, feed them; those who rule others are fed by them.' This is a precept accepted everywhere in the world.

"During the era of Emperor Yao, the world had yet to find its peace. Flood waters flowed across the lands, inundating the whole world. The land was overgrown, the beasts of the field multiplied, and the domesticated grains did not grow to be harvested. The wild animals pressed in upon human settlements, and the tracks of the wild birds and beasts even crisscrossed the central kingdoms. Yao alone had to take on this worry. He raised up Shun and gave him the authority to bring proper order to the world. Shun appointed Yi to handle clearing the land by fire. Yi took his torch to the mountains and wetlands, and burned out the overgrowth, sending the wild animals into hiding. Yu dredged the nine rivers, cleared out the Ji and Luo rivers and drained them into the sea, deepened the Ru and Han rivers, built up the dikes for the Huai and Si rivers and drained them into the Yangtze. Only then could the people of the central kingdoms produce the food they needed. During this time, Yu spent eight years away from home, and when passing by his gate three times, he never entered. Even if he wanted to till the fields, could he have done so?"

Comment: The division of labor is a necessary condition for everyone to have their own occupation and to make their contribution to the community. The main argument here is first that among these occupations, ruling the world is a sufficiently taxing and selfless undertaking that even if these rulers wanted to till the fields, they would not have the time to do so. Secondly those who are capable of this important occupation of governing are made important because of their ability to succeed in overseeing those projects that serve the interests of everyone. In the past, in the absence of the intervention of sagely rulers, life for everyone was harsh and unhappy. When the ancient sage rulers tamed the environment and quelled the floods, they made it possible for the people to seek their livelihood.

The language here is certainly elitist, and reflects the hierarchical nature of aristocratic society both in ancient times and in Mencius's own day. But the elitism is not based on hereditary rule or social class defined by wealth or bloodline. Mencius's argument is for a meritocracy in which all of the occupations necessary to provide society with what it needs are filled by those persons who are able to best carry them out on behalf of the society as a whole. Mencius must work hard at the argument here because those who till the land and grow the crops in the Confucian scheme of things are accorded high social status.

"后稷教民稼穡，樹藝五穀；五穀熟而民人育。人之有道也，飽食、煖衣、逸居而無教，則近於禽獸。聖人有憂之，使契爲司徒，教以人倫，父子有親，君臣有義，夫婦有別，長幼有敘，朋友有信。放勳曰：'勞之來之，匡之直之，輔之翼之，使自得之，又從而振德之。'聖人之憂民如此，而暇耕乎？"

"Houji taught the people how to sow and reap their crops, and how to plant and grow the various grains. When these grains ripened, the people flourished. But human beings also have their proper way (*dao* 道). Even when they have full stomachs, warm clothing, and comfortable housing, without education they are little more than animals. The sagely Yao was much concerned about this situation, and sent Xie as Minister of Education to teach the people by appealing to propriety in human roles and relations: that is, there is affection to be had in the roles of father and son, the pursuit of optimal appropriateness (*yi* 義) to be had in the roles of lord and minister, proper distinctions to be made in the roles of husband and wife, a productive hierarchy to be observed in the role of elders and juniors, and fidelity to be achieved in the role of friend and friend. Emperor Yao said to Xie:

Draw them to you in their labors,
Steer them onto the straight and narrow,
Minster to them and give them your aid,
And make them happy in being who they are.
Being solicitous of them, raise them up to virtuosic conduct.

With the sage-king's concern for his people being such, did he really have the leisure to till the fields?"

Comment: Houji (literally, "millet lord") was minister to Shun and a legendary cultural hero associated with the introduction of millet as the staple grain before the introduction of wheat. During the reign of Yao with the assistance of Shun, the land was cleared, and Yu drained the waters to make the cultivation of crops possible. When the material needs of the people had been taken care of—a necessary condition for further civilization—Yao sent his Minister of Education with explicit instructions on how to elevate the people out of their animality into moral human beings. The intimate relationship between specific ethical values and social roles is historicized here, taking this relation-based vocabulary of role ethics back to the earliest stages in the evolution of human civilization. In this passage we can see how "life and growth" (*sheng* 生) as the underlying cosmic value brings a symbiotic coherence to growth in the cultivation of their crops, growth in the education of the people, and growth in their moral sensibilities.

The argument is that the proper occupation of the sage-King is the unrelenting attention to the well-being of his people that leaves him little leisure for anything else. He has little enough time for either working in the fields or indulging himself in the dividends made possible by his civilizing leadership.

"堯以不得舜爲己憂，舜以不得禹皋陶爲己憂。夫以百畝之不易爲己憂者，農夫也。分人以財謂之惠，教人以善謂之忠，爲天下得人者謂之仁。是故以天下與人易，爲天下得人難。孔子曰：'大哉堯之爲君！惟天爲大，惟堯則之，蕩蕩乎民無能名焉！君哉舜也！巍巍乎有天下而不與焉！' 堯舜之治天下，豈無所用其心哉？亦不用於耕耳。"

"Yao's greatest concern was not being able to find a Shun, and Shun's greatest worry was not being able to find a Yu or a Gao Yao. Now someone whose only worry is with the difficulties of tilling a hundred *mu* plot of land is just a farmer. Sharing one's wealth with others is generosity; instructing others in how to do good things is called doing one's best (*zhong* 忠); finding the best person on the world's behalf is called being consummate in one's conduct (*ren* 仁). It is thus that giving the world to someone is easy enough to do, but finding the right person to give it to is difficult indeed.

"Confucius said: 'How great indeed was Yao as ruler! How majestic! Only *tian* 天 is truly awesome, and only Yao modeled himself upon it. How vast and boundless—the common people could not find words adequate to praise him. How majestic was he in his accomplishments, and how brilliant was he in his cultural achievements. How majestic they were, Yao and Shun, who reigned over the world but did not rule it.'[①] How could it be that Yao and Shun had any choice but to use their intelligence in ruling the world? It was only that they didn't use it in tilling the fields."

Comment: The greatest challenge for those who provide sagely leadership is to exercise their intelligence in perpetuating their sagely rule. This requires them to find the right people who can assist them while they are in office, and to then succeed them at the proper time. Emperor Yao passed over his own son in abdicating his throne to Shun, and Shun again abdicated to the Great Yu who founded the Xia dynasty. Gao Yao was the Minister of Justice who first served Emperor Shun and then Yu. What is

---

[①] *Analects* 8.18, 19.

significant in the transition of this sagely lineage is that its succession was based on merit and performance rather than blood, and that the transfer of power was abdication at the right time rather than on the emperor's death. Teaching others to do good things themselves is more worthy than the generosity of sharing one's wealth with others. But both teaching and sharing as examples of exemplary conduct pale in comparison to the perspicacity of a sage-king finding the best person to succeed him. The epochal impact that continuity in sagely rulership has is vast in its proportions. The language Confucius uses to describe Yao and Shun is hyperbolic, elevating them to truly cosmic status by bringing them into comparison with the awesomeness of *tian* 天 and with the majesty of nature. How, asks Mencius, can such grand virtuosity be compared to merely tilling a plot of land?

"吾聞用夏變夷者，未聞變於夷者也。陳良，楚產也，悅周公、仲尼之道，北學於中國。北方之學者，未能或之先也。彼所謂豪傑之士也。子之兄弟事之數十年，師死而遂倍之！昔者孔子沒，三年之外，門人治任將歸，入揖於子貢，相嚮而哭，皆失聲，然後歸。子貢反，築室於場，獨居三年，然後歸。他日，子夏、子張、子游以有若似聖人，欲以所事孔子事之，彊曾子。曾子曰：『不可；江漢以濯之，秋陽以暴之，皜皜乎不可尚已。』今也南蠻鴃舌之人，非先王之道，子倍子之師而學之，亦異於曾子矣。吾聞出於幽谷遷于喬木者，未聞下喬木而入于幽谷者。《魯頌》曰：『戎狄是膺，荊舒是懲。』周公方且膺之，子是之學，亦為不善變矣。"

"I have heard of using the ways of the proto-Chinese Xia people to convert the barbarians, but I have never heard of such people being converted to barbarian ways. Chen Liang was a son of Chu who, enamored of the teachings of the Duke of Zhou and Confucius, traveled north to study in the central kingdoms. Even the northern scholars were unable to best him in anything. He is what is called an esteemed scholar-official (*shi* 士) of the highest order. You and your brothers served him for decades, but then on his death, you just up and turned away from him.

"In the past when Confucius died, after the three-year mourning period had lapsed, his protégés packed up and prepared to return home. On going in to take their leave of Zigong, they stared at each other and wept until they had all lost their voices, and only then departed for home. But Zigong came back, and building a hut in the cemetery, remained there for another three years before eventually returning home. On another occasion, Zixia, Zizhang, and Ziyou thinking Master You resembled the Sage, all wanted to serve him in the same way they had served Confucius. They tried to make

IV. THE *MENCIUS* (*MENGZI* 孟子): EXTENDING THE VOCABULARY

Master Zeng join them, but Master Zeng said: 'Washed by the waters of the Yangtze and Han rivers and bleached by the autumn sun, the purity of his whiteness was incomparable.'

"Now in your case you are really different from Master Zeng. You have turned your back on your Master and been converted to the chirping-tongue teachings of the southern barbarians who themselves denounce the ways of the Former Kings. I have heard of those who would ascend out of the darkest valley to perch atop the highest tree, but I have never heard of anyone wanting to abandon such lofty heights to descend into the depths. The Hymn of Lu states: 'He struck down the Rong and Di barbarians of the west and north, and punished the Jing and Shu tribes.' While the Duke of Zhou wanted to strike down such people, you want to learn their ways. This is certainly a turn for the worse."

Comment: Having leveled his criticisms first at the teachings of Xu Xing who would insist that worthy rulers join their people in the fields, Mencius then turns to castigate the messenger Chen Xiang himself for having abandoned the solid teachings of Chen Liang and taken up with Xu Xing and the heresies of the south. Chen Liang was a southerner who had converted to the ways of the north, and had so excelled that he became an exemplary scholar unparalleled among his northern colleagues. Xu Xing on the other hand is what Mencius regards as a southern barbarian whose teachings condemn the traditions of the north.

Mencius draws an analogy between Chen Xiang's crime in switching teachers with the disciples of Confucius who after the death of their Master tried to get Master Zeng to join them in transferring their loyalties and services to one among them, Master You. Master Zeng refuses them, remaining loyal to both the person and the teachings of Confucius even after his death, declaring this special teacher was without equal. Mencius further cites the hymns of the northern state of Lu from the classic, the *Book of Songs* 300, that celebrate how their royal ancestors had struck down and disciplined the southern barbarians, and had thus preserved and passed on their own civilized traditions to posterity.

What has clearly piqued Mencius's wrath and provoked his assault on Chen Xiang is that the narrative of Chen Xiang himself is the opposite of his former teacher, Chen Liang. While Chen Liang came from the south and was won over to civilized northern ways, Chen Xiang has come from the civilized northern state of Song and has allowed himself to be converted to the ways of the southern barbarians.

"從許子之道，則市賈不貳，國中無僞；雖使五尺之童適市，莫之或欺。布帛長短同，則賈相若；麻縷絲絮輕重同，則賈相若；五穀多寡同，則賈相若；屨大小同，則賈相若。"曰："夫物之不齊，物之情也；或相倍蓰，或相什百，或相千萬。子比而同之，是亂天下也。巨屨小屨同賈，人豈爲之哉？從許子之道，相率而爲僞者也，惡能治國家？"

Chen Xiang said: "If we follow the way of Xu Xing, prices in the marketplace will be uniform, and there will be no duplicity in the state. Even if a small boy is sent to the market, no one will cheat him. The price will be constant when the lengths of cloth or silk are the same, when the weight of hemp, flax, and raw silk are the same, when the quantity of the various grains are the same, and when shoes regardless of size are the same."

Mencius replied: "That things are not equal is the way things actually are. Some are worth twice or five times as much, sometimes ten or a hundred times as much, and sometimes a thousand or ten thousand times as much. To make everything uniform will only bring chaos to the world. If large shoes and small shoes go for the same price, who is going to make the large ones? To follow the ways of Xu Xing is to lead us into deceiving each other. How would one be able to govern a state in this way?"

Comment: Chen Xiang counters Mencius's rebuke by invoking Xu Xing and his argument that standardization itself in eliminating duplicity is sufficient to bring order to the community. But Mencius will not have it. For him, the idea that things can be decontextualized and thus equalized violates a fundamental insight into the human experience. All things in different contexts have a different value, and to assert otherwise is to recommend chaos. If we are looking for the source of duplicity, it is nothing other than the advocacy of those policies that offend against the very nature of things.

3A2 滕定公薨，世子謂然友曰："昔者孟子嘗與我言於宋，於心終不忘。今也不幸至於大故，吾欲使子問於孟子，然後行事。"然友之鄒問於孟子。孟子曰："不亦善乎！親喪，固所自盡也。曾子曰：'生，事之以禮，死，葬之以禮，祭之以禮，可謂孝矣。'諸侯之禮，吾未之學也；雖然，吾嘗聞之矣。三年之喪，齋疏之服，飦粥之食，自天子達於庶人，三代共之。"然友反命，定爲三年之喪。父兄百官皆不欲也，曰："吾宗國魯先君莫之行，吾先君亦莫之行也，至於子之身而反之，不可。且《志》曰：'喪祭從先祖。'曰：'吾有所受之也。'"

Duke Ding of Teng passed away. The Crown Prince said to Ranyou: "I have never forgotten the advice I got from Mencius years ago when I spoke with him in the state of Song. At this moment having encountered this most unfortunate turn I would ask you to go and consult with Mencius on how I should proceed."

Ranyou went to Zou and inquired of Mencius who then responded: "Very good indeed. In the death of one's parents, one ought to give of oneself utterly. Master Zeng said: 'While living, serve them according to the observances of ritual propriety (*li* 禮); when dead, bury them and sacrifice to them according to the observances of ritual propriety—such can be called filial conduct (*xiao* 孝).' I have not made a study of the ritual practices of the vassal lords, but even so, I have learned something about them. There is a three-year mourning period, the funeral garment of hemmed unwoven hemp, and thin gruel for sustenance. During the three dynasties, everyone from Emperor to the ordinary people followed this regimen."

Ranyou returned and reported on his commission, and the Crown Prince mandated a three-year mourning period. His older relatives and the various officials were much opposed, observing that "None of the earlier rulers of the ancestral state of Lu practiced such things, and nor have any of our own former rulers done so. It is not proper for you alone to act contrary to established practices. Moreover, the *Records* state explicitly 'In funerals and sacrifices follow the practices of the ancestors.' 'We have a tradition to respect.' they insisted."

Comment: The Crown Prince of Teng who after his father's passing is to succeed him to the throne thus consults with Mencius on how he should proceed. An important consideration here in this aristocratic culture is the central importance of ritual practices and sacrifices. Far from being mere formalities, they are themselves integral to the identity of the people themselves as the embodying progeny of a living tradition, and thus to the effecting of social and political order in the present moment. We might recall the intimate relationship between the language of sacrifice and achieving of optimally appropriate and meaningful community captured in the notion of *yi* 義. This Mencius passage echoes *Analects* 19.17:

曾子曰:"吾聞諸夫子:人未有自致者也,必也親喪乎!"

Master Zeng said, "I have heard the Master say: Even those who have yet to give of themselves utterly are sure to do so in the mourning of their parents."

Mencius ascribes to Master Zeng, the paragon of filial conduct in the tradition, a saying that in *Analects* 2.5 is spoken by Confucius himself. It underscores the importance of ritual observances in treating parents properly while living and again when they have passed. Mencius rehearses the strict three-year funeral practices that have defined the lives of all social classes and have been passed on throughout the remembered history. From the time of Confucius onward, the mission of the Confucian lineage of scholar-officials has been to renovate and to restore the ritual structure of a now decadent Zhou dynasty. When the Crown Prince follows Mencius's advice and mandates the strict ancient practices, his family and the court in opposing such measures appeal to their own understanding of the ancestral tradition based on recent practices.

謂然友曰："吾他日未嘗學問，好馳馬試劍。今也父兄百官不我足也，恐其不能盡於大事，子爲我問孟子！"然友復之鄒問孟子。孟子曰："然；不可以他求者也。孔子曰：'君薨，聽於冢宰，歠粥，面深墨，即位而哭，百官有司莫敢不哀，先之也。'上有好者，下必有甚焉者矣。君子之德，風也；小人之德，草也。草上之風，必偃。是在世子。"然友反命。世子曰："然；是誠在我。"五月居廬，未有命戒。百官族人可，謂曰知。及至葬，四方來觀之，顏色之戚，哭泣之哀，吊者大悅。

The Crown Prince said to Ranyou, "In the past I have not given myself to my studies, being fonder of horses and swordsmanship. I am afraid my older relatives and our ministers do not hold me in high regard, and will not do their utmost for me in the affairs of state. Please go and consult with Mencius for me."

Ranyou again went to Zou to ask Mencius for his advice.

"I understand," said Mencius, "but the Crown Prince cannot get the answer from others on this matter. Confucius said, 'When the ruler dies, the crown prince would have all of the various officials place themselves under the command of the prime minister. He would eat only thin gruel, his face would turn ink-black, and taking his proper place, he would weep. None of the various ministers and officers of the court would dare but grieve because the crown prince has set this example.' When a superior shows a passion for something, those below are sure to be even more zealous. 'The virtuosity of exemplary persons is the wind, while that of petty persons is the grass. As the wind blows, the grass is sure to bend.' This matter lies with the Crown Prince alone."

Ranyou returned and reported his conversation to the Crown Prince.

"Of course, he is right," said the Crown Prince. "This matter really does lie with me and me alone."

For five months, the Crown Prince stayed in the mourning shed, and issued no orders or proscriptions. All of his ministers and clansmen praised him, and said of him he understood the observance of ritual propriety. When the time came for the burial ceremony, people came from all over to observe it. The agony shown in his countenance and the anguish felt through his tears moved all of the mourners deeply.

Comment: This passage echoes *Analects* 14.40:

子張曰："《書》云：'高宗諒陰，三年不言。'何謂也？"子曰："何必高宗，古之人皆然。君薨，百官總己以聽於冢宰，三年。"

Zizhang said, "The *Book of Documents* says: 'When the Shang dynasty king Gaozong dwelt in the mourning shed, he did not speak for three years.' What is the meaning of this passage?"

The Master said, "It was not only Gaozong—all of the ancients did the same. When the ruler died, all of the various ministers would come together and place themselves under the command of the prime minister for a period of three years."

In *Analects* 12.19 again we read: 君子之德風，小人之德草。草上之風，必偃 "The virtuosity of exemplary persons is the wind, while that of petty persons is the grass. As the wind blows, the grass is sure to bend." The metaphor of the wind and grass is repeated in this passage where Mencius is offering his counsel to a crown prince on the death of his father. He advises the prince to follow the dictates of Confucius in restoring the three-year standard in mourning practices for his court. Again, the message herein is certainly that rulers must be exemplars to effect change in their people. But the important point being made begins from the recognition on the part of this particular Crown Prince that, because of a lack of seriousness in his studies in the past, he is not held in high regard by his court and kinsmen. As a consequence of this failure, he as the newly anointed king will have difficulty securing their support in the affairs of state. The Crown Prince, following the advice given by Mencius to look to his own person is able, by elevating his behavior and giving his people a model to emulate, to earn the respect of his court and to thus effect a change in their conduct. As Mencius says in 4A12, 至誠而不動者，未之有也 "There has never been a person of the highest resolve who has not been able to move others." The Crown Prince is improved because of the expectations of his people, and his people are transformed by his exemplary conduct. This passage is a good example of the continuity between role ethics and role politics as the primary source of sociopolitical order.

1A3 梁惠王曰："寡人之於國也，盡心焉耳矣。河內凶，則移其民於河東，移其粟於河內。河東凶亦然。察鄰國之政，無如寡人之用心者。鄰國之民不加少，寡人之民不加多，何也？" 孟子對曰："王好戰，請以戰喻。填然鼓之，兵刃既接，棄甲曳兵而走。或百步而後止，或五十步而後止。以五十步笑百步，則何如？" 曰："不可，直不百步耳，是亦走也。" 曰："王如知此，則無望民之多於鄰國也。"

King Hui of Liang said: "I have done everything in my power for my state. When there was a bad harvest in the middle region, I moved many of the people over to the east side of the river, and transported grain to the affected middle region. When the eastern region had a bad harvest, I did the opposite. In examining the administration of my neighboring states, I don't see anyone acting with the same degree of concern. And yet the populations of the neighboring states do not decrease and neither does mine get larger. Why is this?"

"You are fond of war." said Mencius. "Allow me to use a war analogy. To the pounding of the drums the armies have crossed swords and are engaged. On one side the soldiers abandon their armor. Some soldiers, dragging their weapons behind them, don't stop until they have run a hundred paces, while others stop after having run only fifty paces. What would you think if one of the soldiers who ran only fifty paces ridiculed those who ran a hundred?"

"Unacceptable." said the King. "In spite of the fact the soldier did not run a hundred paces, he still ran."

"If you understand this," said Mencius, "then why would you expect that your people would be more numerous than your neighbors?"

Comment: One sure sign of consummate governance is an increasing population. In the *Shuowen* lexicon, the True King (*wang* 王) is defined paronomastically as "repairing to" (*wang* 往) with the implication people flock to exemplary leaders. King Hui gives Mencius a report on how he has sought to provide for his people, and then wonders why his population has not increased. Mencius criticizes King Hui obliquely for his fondness of war by using a military analogy. Just as deserters fleeing the battle are not getting the job of war done, King Hui's governance when compared with his neighboring states is a matter of one ruler being as bad as the next. None of them are getting the job done.

"不違農時，穀不可勝食也；數罟不入洿池，魚鱉不可勝食也；斧斤以時入山林，材木不可勝用也。穀與魚鱉不可勝食，材木不可勝用，是使民養生喪死無憾也。養生喪死無憾，王道之始也。五畝之宅，樹之以桑，五十者可以衣帛矣；雞豚狗彘之畜，無失其時，七十者可以食肉矣；百畝之田，勿奪其時，數口之家可以無飢矣；謹庠序之教，申之以孝悌之義，頒白者不負戴於道路矣。七十者衣帛食肉，黎民不飢不寒，然而不王者，未之有也。狗彘食人食而不知檢，塗有餓莩而不知發；人死，則曰：'非我也，歲也。'是何異於刺人而殺之，曰：'非我也，兵也。'王無罪歲，斯天下之民至焉。"

"If you do not offend against the agricultural calendar, there will be more grain than can be eaten; if you do not allow closed-mesh nets to be used in the ponds and wetlands, there will be more fish and turtles than can be eaten; if the axes and hatchets are allowed into the forests only at the right time, there will be more lumber than can be used. When the grain, fish, and turtles are more than can be eaten and the lumber more than can be used, the common people will be able to nourish the living and bury their dead with no enmity towards anyone. Providing such adequate resources is the first step on the way to becoming a True King.

"If mulberry trees are planted within the five-*mu* compounds, those of fifty years can wear garments made of silk. If in the raising of chickens, pigs, dogs, and swine, all of the animals are allowed their breeding time, those of seventy years can have meat to eat. If those with a plot of a hundred *mu* are not robbed of their seasons, a family with many mouths to feed will not go hungry. If care is taken in the education provided by the village schools to teach the moral imperatives of family reverence (*xiao* 孝) and deference to elders (*ti* 悌), you won't see old grey heads on the roadways carrying heavy loads on their backs. When those of seventy years have silk to wear and meat to eat, and the common people are neither cold nor hungry, this then is the very definition of a True King.

"Dogs and swine are eating the food of the people without being restrained, and people in not getting any grain from the granaries are dying of starvation on the roadways. When people die and you say: 'It is not me, it is the harvest.' How is this different from running a person through with a knife and saying 'It was not me who killed him, it was the knife'? If your Majesty would just stop blaming the harvest, the people of the world would come to you."

Comment: Mencius's concept of the True King might be an abstraction, but the detailed system he advances for consummate governance is concrete. He offers a set of land reforms that include a standardized size of the living compound and farming plot. By regulating the peoples' use of resources according to the almanac, they will produce more than enough in their various occupations of making silk, cutting timber, raising domestic animals, and tilling the fields. Corvée labor and animal breeding have to be done at the right time. Mencius provides instructions on how through ecologically-sensitive management the forests and streams will provide an abundance of resources. Importantly, there is also an educational component to consummate governance where the curriculum in the government-run village schools needs to inculcate into the people those values that come with the moral imperatives of family reverence and respecting their elders.

7B1 孟子曰:"不仁哉梁惠王也！仁者以其所愛及其所不愛，不仁者以其所不愛及其所愛。"公孫丑問曰:"何謂也？"梁惠王以土地之故，糜爛其民而戰之，大敗，將復之，恐不能勝，故驅其所愛子弟以殉之，是之謂以其所不愛及其所愛也。

Mencius said: "King Hui of Liang was indeed immoral. Those who are consummate in their conduct (*ren* 仁) stretch what they love to reach what they don't love; those who are immoral stretch what they don't love to reach what they do love."

Gongsun Chou asked: "What do you mean?"

"What it means to stretch what you don't love to reach what you do love is this: King Hui of Liang in order to expand his territory sent his people off to war to be reduced to pulp. On suffering a resounding defeat, he tried again, and afraid he might not win, he urged on his son whom he loved dearly to sacrifice his own life along with his people."

Comment: What King Hui coveted was only increased territory gained through conquest. What he failed to love was his people, and this failure cost him his own son who got caught up in his machinations. Consummate conduct that begins with growth in family roles and relations is the substance of morality. To behave in the opposite manner results in a diminution in relations, and is immoral. Given the isomorphism assumed between state and family in Confucian political philosophy, morality in the role of a ruler is expressed through his love and concern for his people. Mencius's persistent criticism of King Hui of Liang is his concern for personal profit (*li* 利) that is pursued at the expense of being consummate in his conduct and doing what is moral (*ren* 仁). A moral ruler as the parents of the people is one who extends the love for his own children to his love for the people. But King Hui being quite impervious to such love is quite willing to declare war on other states and not only sacrifice his people in the attempt to serve his interests, but even his own son.

7A24 孟子曰: "孔子登東山而小魯，登泰山而小天下，故觀於海者難爲水，遊於聖人之門者難爲言。觀水有術，必觀其瀾。日月有明，容光必照焉。流水之爲物也，不盈科不行；君子之志於道也，不成章不達。"

Mencius said: "Confucius in climbing Eastern Mountain made the state of Lu small; in climbing Taishan he made the world small. Similarly, it is difficult for someone who has contemplated the ocean to take the rivers and lakes seriously and it is difficult for one who has wandered in the courtyard of a sage to take the doctrines of others seriously. The technique in contemplating water is that you must watch its billowing waves; the brightness of the sun and moon are sure to light up every swell and ripple. It is the nature of flowing water that it does not advance until every low-lying hollow has been filled. For exemplary persons whose intentions are set on the proper way, they do not move forward on this way without having some real achievements to show."

Comment: Mencius has a repertoire of familiar metaphors. In the canonical texts we see Confucius ascend as a sage to be compared to the sun and the moon and to the turning of the seasons. From his lofty heights, all is made small and manageable. To be witness to the vast oceans and to have heard the words of sages makes other vistas shrink by comparison. Confucius's fascination with and praise of water is described in 4B18, a passage that bears comparison with this one. Just as Confucius's view from Taishan reduces the complexity of the world to something that can be turned in the palm of his hand, the brightness of the heavenly bodies enables him to penetrate and see through every ripple in the movement of water. Just as the flowing water advances by filling in every crack and cranny, the resolve of exemplary persons fills in every imperfection to create their own inimitable pattern of achievements as they advance on the proper way. An epistemology based on a panoramic and comprehensive view of things, and the "advancing on the proper way" metaphor are both familiar Confucian themes.

4A14 孟子曰:"求也爲季氏宰,無能改於其德,而賦粟倍他日。孔子曰:'求非我徒也,小子鳴鼓而攻之可也。'由此觀之,君不行仁政而富之,皆棄於孔子者也。況於爲之強戰? 爭地以戰,殺人盈野; 爭城以戰,殺人盈城。此所謂率土地而食人肉,罪不容於死。故善戰者服上刑,連諸侯者次之,辟草萊、任土地者次之。"

Mencius said, "Ranyou was the chief steward of the Ji clan, and though he had no success in reforming the quality of their conduct, he was able to double their tax revenues. Confucius said, 'This man Ranyou is no disciple of mine. If you my young friends, want to sound the charge and take him down, be my guest.' From this example, we know Confucius rejected any students who would enrich a lord that was not dispensing consummate governance (*renzheng* 仁政)—how much more so those ministers who would wage war on their lord's behalf. When such rulers contend for land by waging war, the carnage fills the fields; when they contend for fortified cities by waging war, the carnage fills the walled enclaves. This is what is called teaching the land to devour human flesh. Death is too good for such people. Thus, those who are effective at waging war should suffer the harshest punishment, those who forge alliances among the vassal lords should suffer the next harshest, and those who open up the frontiers for homesteading should be next in line."

Comment: Confucius had high hopes for the young Ranyou and his acumen for administrative affairs (*Analects* 5.8 and 6.8). Ranyou himself on several occasions expresses a desire to learn more about governance (13.9, 11.26). At the same time, Ranyou does not seem to be a serious or able student in the refinements of ritual practices and music that are at the heart of effecting sociopolitical order. It was probably because of this deficiency that Confucius sees Ranyou as lacking initiative in promoting consummate governance, a familiar failing remarked upon here and elsewhere (11.22, 3.6, 6.8, 16.1).

IV. THE *MENCIUS* (*MENGZI* 孟子): EXTENDING THE VOCABULARY

Mencius is citing an event that is also described in *Analects* 11.17:

季氏富於周公，而求也爲之聚斂而附益之。子曰："非吾徒也。小子鳴鼓而攻之，可也。"

Even though the House of Ji is wealthier than the Duke of Zhou, Ranyou in gathering revenues for them added even more to their coffers. The Master said, "This man is no disciple of mine. If you my young friends want to sound the charge and bring him down, be my guest."

The *Zuo Commentary* on the *Spring and Autumn Annals* (Duke Ai 11: Cf. Legge, *Chinese Classics*, Vol. 5, p. 826) discusses this same incident:

季孫欲以田賦，使冉有訪諸仲尼，仲尼曰，丘，不識也，三發，卒曰，子爲國老，待子而行，若之何子之不言也。仲尼不對，而私於冉有曰，君子之行也。度於禮，施取其厚，事舉其中，斂從其薄，如是則以丘亦足矣，若不度於禮，而貪冒無厭，則雖以田賦，將又不足，且子季孫若欲行而法，則周公之典在，若欲苟而行，又何訪焉，弗聽。

    The head of the House of Ji, Ji Sun wanted to use the land tax system to increase their revenues, and sent Ranyou to solicit Confucius's advice. Confucius said to him, "I know nothing of these matters."

    Several times inquiries were made of Confucius, and finally the head of the Ji clan said to him, "You are a senior adviser to the state, and I am waiting for you to carry out its business. What is the meaning of your silence?"

    Confucius did not reply, but privately said to Ranyou, "The exemplary ruler in his conduct observes ritual propriety. In what he gives he is generous, in carrying out his affairs he does what is fitting, and in what he exacts in taxation he tries to be moderate. This being the case, according to the Qiu ordinance the taxes being levied are quite enough. If Ji Sun and his clan do not act in accordance with ritual propriety, but instead are insatiable in their greed, even if they exact a land tax, it will not be enough. If they want to act lawfully, there are the statutes of the Duke of Zhou; if they want to act otherwise, why are they seeking advice from me?" Confucius's counsel was not heeded in this matter.

Ranyou continues to follow the directives of the House of Ji and implemented the tax system. In the *Record of Rituals* (*Liji* 禮記) 43.2/166/21 it says clearly,

百乘之家，不畜聚斂之臣。與其有聚斂之臣，寧有盜臣。
A family of a hundred chariots is not entitled to a revenue collector. Rather than employing one, wouldn't they be better off hiring a robber?

Although it might seem the last category listed of those rulers who would open up the frontiers for homesteading would redound to the benefit of the people, in fact, their own motivation in doing so really lies in benefiting themselves. The main reason for poverty among the people was not inadequate farmland, but excessive taxation and protracted wars.

4A20 孟子曰："人不足與適也，政不足間也。惟大人爲能格君心之非。君仁莫不仁，君義莫不義，君正莫不正。一正君而國定矣。"
Mencius said: "Those persons in charge are not worth our reprimand and their governance is not worth our censure. It is only the great person who is able to right what is wrong in the heart and mind of the ruler. Where the ruler is consummate in his conduct (*ren* 仁), none will be otherwise; where the ruler is appropriate in his conduct (*yi* 義), none will be otherwise; where the ruler is proper in his conduct (*zheng* 正), none will be otherwise. Once the ruler is proper in his conduct, the state will be secure."

Comment: Mencius gives a clear statement of what he takes to be the transformative influence of the ruler as a role model for the state. The highest responsibility of those who would give the ruler counsel is not to be critical of the day-to-day workings of government on personnel or policy, but rather to effect a dramatic change in the moral competence of the ruler himself. The able counselor must be a teacher, and the subject taught must be empathy for the people. The moral competence of the ruler is gauged primarily through the concern he feels for the welfare of the common people. In many ways this is a summary statement of both the approach Mencius himself took to influencing governance, and the philosophy of governance we find throughout the *Mencius*. As we find in the case of King Hui of Liang, Mencius embracing such a charge is difficult and dangerous, and is seldom successful.

1B5 齊宣王問曰："人皆謂我毀明堂。毀諸？已乎？"孟子對曰："夫明堂者，王者之堂也。王欲行王政，則勿毀之矣。"王曰："王政可得聞與？"對曰："昔者文王之治岐也，耕者九一，仕者世祿，關市譏而不征，澤梁無禁，罪人不孥。老而無妻曰鰥。老而無夫曰寡。老而無子曰獨。幼而無父曰孤。此四者，天下之窮民而無告者。文王發政施仁，必先斯四者。《詩》云：'哿矣富人，哀此煢獨。'"

King Xuan of Qi asked Mencius: "Everyone says I should demolish the Hall of Light. Should I tear it down or not?"

"The Hall of Light is the hall of the True King." replied Mencius. "If you are going to use it to practice the governance of a True King, then by all means leave it standing."

"How about enlightening me on this governance of the True King?" asked the King.

"In ancient times, King Wen administered a territory called Qi." replied Mencius. "The tax on land tilled by farmers was one part of nine, officials were entitled to a hereditary stipend, the passes and marketplaces had regular inspections but no levy was imposed, there were no prohibitions placed on the wetlands, and the guilt of individuals did not extend to their wives and children. An aged man without a wife is called a widower; an aged woman without a husband is called a widow; the aged without children are called childless; the young without a father are called orphans. These four categories of people are the world's most destitute with no one to speak on their behalf. King Wen in dispensing his consummate governance (*renzheng* 仁政) gave priority to all four of them. As it says in the *Book of Songs* 192: 'It is all happiness for the wealthy, but only grief for the solitary and dejected.'"

Comment: The Hall of Light as an ancient institution was a sacred structure of symmetrical design visited by the emperor in carrying out various sacrifices linked to the calendar. It is often used as a metonym for the governance of the True King. Such is its immediate association here with King Wen of the Zhou dynasty. For him, the governance of the True King is a social and political system in which everyone and everything has its proper place. On the government side there is a proper structure for collecting taxes and for regulating public spaces. Resources are properly shared, and punishments are meted out fairly. Of particular note, there is a welfare system in which the beneficence of the True King is most in evidence. He gives the highest priority to the proper care of the most vulnerable members of the community. Consummate governance is the effecting of sociopolitical order as a holistic, systemic affair that is both inclusive and participatory, with each member of the society being included without remainder. The isomorphism of family and state in which the concept of the political includes the proper ordering of the family extends the political responsibility of the True King to familial roles and relations.

王曰:"善哉言乎!"曰:"王如善之,則何爲不行?"王曰:"寡人有疾,寡人好貨。"對曰:"昔者公劉好貨,《詩》云:'乃積乃倉,乃裹餱糧,于橐于囊。思戢用光。弓矢斯張,干戈戚揚,爰方啟行。'故居者有積倉,行者有裹糧也,然後可以爰方啟行。王如好貨,與百姓同之,於王何有?"王曰:"寡人有疾,寡人好色。"對曰:"昔者大王好色,愛厥妃。《詩》云:'古公亶甫,來朝走馬,率西水滸,至于岐下。爰及姜女,聿來胥宇。'當是時也,內無怨女,外無曠夫。王如好色,與百姓同之,於王何有?"

"Well-spoken," said the King.

"If you deem these words to be well-spoken then why not put them into practice?" said Mencius.

"I have an infirmity in my fondness for wealth." said the King.

"In ancient times Gong Liu was fond of wealth," replied Mencius. "The *Book of Songs* 250 says:

He piled it up and filled his granaries,
He loaded bags and sacks with various provisions
On the idea that such stores brought glory to his state.
Laying out the bows and arrows
And making a display of the spears, halberds, and battle-axes,
Only then did he commence the march.

Thus, it was only when those who remained at home had full granaries and those setting off were fully provisioned that Gong Liu undertook the march. If you share your fondness for wealth with your people, how can it prevent you from becoming a True King?"

"I have an infirmity in my fondness for women." said the King.

"In ancient times, King Tai had a fondness for women, loving his consort and his concubines. The *Book of Songs* 237 says:

The ancient prince King Tai
Set off at daybreak with his galloping steeds
And following the bank of the river to the west
He arrived at the foot of Mount Qi.
Together with the Lady Jiang
He stayed there and took up his abode.

At that time, there were no girls in the homes pining for a husband and no young men in the community going to waste. If you share your fondness for women with your people, how can it prevent you from becoming a True King?"

Comment: Mencius is not deterred by King Xuan's confession that he has an inordinate interest in wealth and women. The single most important criterion for consummate governance is its inclusiveness. Whatever wealth and pleasure is available to the court becomes an asset rather than a liability when these same resources are shared and enjoyed by everyone.

1B4 齊宣王見孟子於雪宮。王曰："賢者亦有此樂乎？"孟子對曰："有。人不得，則非其上矣。不得而非其上者，非也；爲民上而不與民同樂者，亦非也。樂民之樂者，民亦樂其樂；憂民之憂者，民亦憂其憂。樂以天下，憂以天下，然而不王者，未之有也。"

King Xuan of Qi invited Mencius for an audience in his Snow Palace. The King said: "Do the worthy and wise rejoice in such things?"

"They do," replied Mencius. "But if there are people who do not get to partake of such things, they are sure to find fault with those in power. Their thus finding fault with those in power because they themselves lack a share in the rejoicing is certainly inappropriate, but holding authority over the people and yet not sharing the joy with them is equally wrong. When the ruler rejoices in the joy of the people, the people will also rejoice in his joy; when the ruler worries over the people's concerns, the people will also worry over his concerns. The ruler whose joy is shared by the world and whose concerns are those of the world is the definition of the True King."

Comment: From Mencius's perspective, the ruler is heavily burdened by the many concerns that necessarily accompany his responsibility to serve the people, and thus there is nothing wrong with him finding respite in the luxuries that attend his station. But a persistent theme in Mencius's political philosophy is the isomorphism between family and state that extends to the shared enjoyment of ruler and his people, and to the shared concern of ruler and his people. When all of the ruler's feelings of both enjoyment and concern are shared with his people—that is, where there is true empathy between ruler and ruled—the ruler has defined himself as the True King.

"昔者齊景公問於晏子曰：'吾欲觀於轉附、朝儛，遵海而南，放於琅邪。吾何修而可以比於先王觀也？'晏子對曰：'善哉問也！天子適諸侯曰巡狩，巡狩者巡所守也；諸侯朝於天子曰述職，述職者述所職也。無非事者。春省耕而補不足，秋省斂而助不給。夏諺曰："吾王不遊，吾何以休？吾王不豫，吾何以助？一遊一豫，爲諸侯度。"今也不然：師行而糧食，飢者弗食，勞者弗息。睊睊胥讒，民乃作慝。方命虐民，飲食若流。流連荒亡，爲諸侯憂。從流下而忘反謂之流，從流上而忘反謂之連，從獸無厭謂之荒，樂酒無厭謂之亡。先王無流連之樂，荒亡之行。惟君所行也。'景公說，大戒於國，出舍於郊。於是始興發補不足。召大師曰：'爲我作君臣相說之樂！'蓋徵招角招是也。其詩曰：'畜君何尤？'畜君者，好君也。"

"In the past Duke Jing of Qi asked Master Yan: 'I want to make a royal progress to Zhuanfu and then Chaowu, and to follow the seaside south to Langya. How can I carry out this tour of inspection in such a way that it bears comparison with those of the Former Kings?'

"'What a wonderful question.' replied Master Yan. 'When the emperor would travel to visit the vassal lords it was called a tour of inspection. The purpose of the tour was to make an inspection of the lands under their charge. When the vassal lords would travel to the court of the emperor it was called a report on their duties of office. The purpose of this report was to provide an account of how they are carrying out their official responsibilities. Both practices are undertaken with good reason. In the spring, the tour is to inspect the tilling of the fields and to help out when the seed for sowing is insufficient. In the autumn it is to inspect the harvest and to help out when the crops are insufficient. There is an adage passed on from the Xia dynasty that says:

> If our King does not make his royal progress
> How can we find our respite?
> If our King does not make his tour,
> How can we gain his assistance?
> In his progress and in his tour
> He sets the measure for the vassal lords.

Today things are different.

> The troops march in and consume all of the provisions,
> Leaving the hungry without food
> And the weary without rest.
> The common people, with eyes askance and with much complaining,
> Are driven into depravity.
> The vassal lords offend against their mandate
> By being cruel to the people.
> Food and drink stream like water.

IV. THE *MENCIUS* (*MENGZI* 孟子): EXTENDING THE VOCABULARY

The vassal lords drift and tarry, are wild and lost,
Such conduct making them a grave concern.
What is meant by "drifting" is going downstream with no thought of return. What is meant by "tarrying" is moving upstream with no thought of return. What is meant by "wild" is never tiring of pursuing the chase. What is meant by "lost" is never getting tired of the pleasures of inebriation. The Former Kings found no pleasure in such behaviors. Only you my lord can set your own proper course.'

"Duke Jing was much pleased. He drew up a grand proclamation in the capital and then left his palace to go out to its outskirts and dwell in a lowly shed. He began to open up his granaries to assist those who were in need. Summoning his Grand Musician, he said: 'Compose some music for me that expresses the happiness the ruler and his subjects are enjoying together.' This was the origin of the *Zhishao* and *Jueshao* pieces in which the song says: 'What could the ruler we love do wrong?' A lord who is loved is cherished by his people."

Comment: King Xuan of Qi is himself one of the modern-day vassal lords. Duke Jing of Qi (r. 546-488) is cited by Mencius as one of the King's enlightened precursors who wanted to model his conduct as ruler on the Former Kings. Mencius recounts the advice given to the Duke by Master Yan, one of his ministers, explaining that the official activities of both the emperor and the vassal lords have their purposes. The royal tour of inspection made by the emperor has the dual function of making sure the needs of the common people in the planting of their crops and their harvesting of them are taken care of properly. The second function is the conduct of the emperor serves as a role model for the vassal lords themselves. On the other hand, the purpose of the vassal lords attending the emperor's court is their accountability: they must provide a report on how they have lived up to the responsibilities of their offices. In citing a saying that traces back to the hoary history of the Xia dynasty, the minister Yan is remarking that the spirit of interdependence between emperor and vassal lords which informs this pattern of governance has an important role in the continuing cultural legacy.

Minister Yan again recounts how in their own times, the vassal lords have failed to emulate the model of the Former Kings, exploiting the common people and driving them to despair. In their wantonness and cruelty, these vassal lords have become a source of grave concern. In their decadent conduct they have no direction, and are given over to the pleasures of the table and the hunt. Master Yan concludes by exhorting Duke Jing to set his own course. Duke Jing is not only persuaded by Master Yan's advice, but immediately acts upon it by making a grand announcement of his plans. As a ceremonial gesture he removes himself to a small hovel distant from his royal comforts, and begins a pattern of generous conduct in which his royal resources are made available to those in need. To remember this occasion, he commissions music to be composed that celebrates the shared rejoicing of the ruler and his subjects.

4A2 孟子曰: "規矩, 方員之至也; 聖人, 人倫之至也。欲爲君盡君道, 欲爲臣盡臣道, 二者皆法堯舜而已矣。不以舜之所以事堯事君, 不敬其君者也; 不以堯之所以治民治民, 賊其民者也。孔子曰: '道二: 仁與不仁而已矣。' 暴其民甚, 則身弒國亡; 不甚, 則身危國削。名之曰'幽厲', 雖孝子慈孫, 百世不能改也。《詩》云: '殷鑒不遠, 在夏后之世', 此之謂也。"

Mencius said: "The compass and the set square are the templates for the round and the square; the sages are the templates in human relations. For those who would be rulers by doing everything expected of a ruler, and for those who would be ministers by doing everything expected of a minister, they need only to emulate Yao and Shun respectively, nothing more. To do other than serve a ruler as Shun served Yao is to disrespect the ruler; to do other than govern the common people as Yao governed them is to do injury to the people. Confucius said: 'There are two ways and two ways only: being consummate in your conduct (ren 仁) and being otherwise.' When a ruler inflicts real violence on his people, he will be assassinated and his state will perish. Where such negligence is in a lesser degree, his person will be endangered and the territory of his state will be pared away. Such rulers will become known as 'the Benighted' and 'the Cruel,' and even if they have the most dutiful and affectionate sons and grandsons, their progeny will be unable to change this stigma for a hundred generations. The *Book of Songs* 255 captures what I mean in saying: 'The object lesson for the Shang rulers was not at all remote; it was made flesh and blood in the last ruler of the Xia.'"

Comment: Mencius is heavily invested in the suasive power of role models; certainly positive models but negative ones as well. Yao and Shun provide positive models for both ruler and minister, and the proper relationship that should obtain between them. At the other extreme, appealing to the authority of Confucius himself, Mencius is not shy about stating clearly what happens to rulers who inflict violence on their people. In reflecting on sagely governance or political collapse, the single criterion on which a ruler is to be evaluated is the welfare of the common people. Again, appealing to the authority of the *Book of Songs*, Mencius rehearses a passage that remembers how the last ruler of the Xia dynasty, Jie, was cruel and violent and thus brought about the dynasty's ruin. The tyrant Jie serves as a constant and immediate negative model for the rulers of the Shang dynasty who succeeded the Xia on how not to govern.

4A4 孟子曰:"愛人不親反其仁,治人不治反其智,禮人不答反其敬。行有不得者,皆反求諸己,其身正而天下歸之。《詩》云:'永言配命,自求多福。'"

Mencius said: "If your love for others is unrequited, reflect on the quality of your own conduct; if in your governing of others you fail, reflect on the quantum of wisdom you are dispensing; if the propriety you show to others is not answered in kind, reflect on the respect you have shown them. When your conduct does not succeed in its purposes, always look for the reasons within yourself. When you are proper in your own person (*zheng* 正), the entire world will repair to you. As it says in the *Book of Songs* 235: 'May he forever live up to the responsibilities of his charge, and thus seek for himself an abundance of good fortune.'"

Comment: In his exhortation to rulers to serve as role models for their people, Mencius underscores the importance of cultivating the habit of critical self-reflection. Without blame or recriminations, one's failings should be an occasion to look into the quality of one's own person and redouble one's efforts to live up to the responsibilities of one's office. When rulers are successful in conducting themselves properly, their populations will multiply and they will prosper.

7A22 孟子曰:"伯夷辟紂,居北海之濱,聞文王作興,曰:'盍歸乎來!吾聞西伯善養老者。'太公辟紂,居東海之濱,聞文王作興,曰:'盍歸乎來!吾聞西伯善養老者。'天下有善養老,則仁人以爲己歸矣。五畝之宅,樹墻下以桑,匹婦蠶之,則老者足以衣帛矣。五母雞,二母彘,無失其時,老者足以無失肉矣。百畝之田,匹夫耕之,八口之家足以無飢矣。所謂西伯善養老者,制其田里,教之樹畜,導其妻子,使養其老。五十非帛不煖,七十非肉不飽。不煖不飽,謂之凍餒。文王之民,無凍餒之老者,此之謂也。"

Mencius said: "Bo Yi fled the wicked ruler Zhou, and took up residence on the shores of the Northern Sea. On hearing of the innovations brought about by King Wen, he was moved and remarked 'Why should I not return? I have heard King Wen excels at taking care of the aged.' Taigong fled the wicked ruler Zhou, and took up residence on the shores of the Eastern Sea. On hearing of the innovations brought about by King Wen, he was moved and remarked 'Why should I not return? I have heard that King Wen excels at taking care of the aged.' When someone in the world excels at taking care of the aged, consummate persons (ren 仁) will take such a person to be their sanctuary.

"When mulberry trees are planted beneath the walls of a five-*mu* compound from which the woman of the house can make her silk, then the aged are bound to have garments made of silk to wear. When their five mother hens and two sows do not miss their breeding season, the aged are bound to have some meat to eat. When the man of the house has a hundred *mu* of field to till, a home with eight mouths to feed is bound to escape hunger.

"What it means to say King Wen excels at caring for the aged is that he instituted land reform, taught the people how to plant their fields and raise their animals, and gave guidance to the womenfolk on how to take care of the aged. Those at fifty years who do not get silk to wear are not warm enough and those at seventy years who do not taste meat cannot eat their fill. To be neither warm enough nor have a full stomach is called being destitute. This means then that among the common people of King Wen, none of the aged were left destitute."

Comment: This passage alludes to the familiar story of the brothers Bo Yi and Shu Qi who protested against the Zhou vassal state overthrowing its Shang dynasty overlords and becoming the succeeding dynasty. In this account, Jiang Taigong who was a counselor to King Wu takes the place of Shu Qi. Jiang Taigong had protected the brothers Bo Yi and Shu Qi when they accosted the chariot of King Wu in protest against King Wu's assassinating his lord, and thus made a show of their loyalty to the Shang dynasty. The important message in this passage is that King Wen's "caring for the aged" is not simply a report on his charity and kindness. Rather it is a reflection on the complex land reform and agricultural system King Wen established to guarantee the welfare of all of his people, including the most vulnerable among them. In 1A3 and 1A7 Mencius recommends the specifics of King Wen's agricultural system to King Hui of Liang, but without attributing it to King Wen. See also 4A13.

IV. THE *MENCIUS* (*MENGZI* 孟子): EXTENDING THE VOCABULARY

7A23 孟子曰："易其田疇，薄其稅斂，民可使富也。食之以時，用之以禮，財不可勝用也。民非水火不生活，昏暮叩人之門戶，求水火，無弗與者，至足矣。聖人治天下，使有菽粟如水火。菽粟如水火，而民焉有不仁者乎？"

Mencius said: "Ease the work of the common people in planting their field crops and lighten your taxes and levies to allow them to thrive. If foods are consumed according to their season and other commodities are used according to social protocols, there will be plenty of everything to go around. The common people cannot live without access to fire and water, and yet when there is a knock on the door in the evening and someone is asking after fire and water, the fact is they are never refused. This is because we have such things in abundance. In their governing of the world, the sages tried their best to make the various provisions as abundant as fire and water. When this is so, how can there be anyone among the common people who is less than consummate in their conduct (*ren* 仁)?"

Comment: For Mencius, a major factor in effecting sociopolitical order is for those who are responsible for the administration of the state to organize the production and consumption of resources in such a way that the material well-being of the people is assured. When the necessities of life are had in abundance, a public morality will also thrive. Said the other way, poverty itself is a social problem that invariably brings desperation and crime in its wake. The assumption is that if those in authority are successful in alleviating poverty, most criminality will recede of its own accord.

2A3 孟子曰："以力假仁者霸，霸必有大國，以德行仁者王，王不待大。湯以七十里，文王以百里。以力服人者，非心服也，力不贍也；以德服人者，中心悅而誠服也，如七十子之服孔子也。《詩》云：'自西自東，自南自北，無思不服。'此之謂也。"

Mencius said: "The ruler who complements force with feigning consummate conduct (*ren* 仁) is a hegemon, and as such this ruler needs a big and powerful state. The ruler who with virtuosity puts into practice consummate conduct is a True King and has no need to rely upon size. Tang did as much with just 70 *li* square and King Wen with 100 *li* square. Subjugating the people with force is not winning over their hearts but only putting down any resistance. When you win them over with moral virtuosity, there is happiness in their hearts and sincerity in their compliance. Such was the case with Confucius and his seventy protégés. In the *Book of Songs* 244 it says: 'From every direction—east and west, north and south—none thought but to follow.'"

Comment: Mencius contrasts the relationship between the hegemon and his people with that of the True King. While the hegemon must rely upon strength and size, the True King gains the loyalty of the people through exemplary conduct and moral suasion. The hegemon is authoritarian in his rule, imposing order on the people and quelling any resistance. The True King by contrast is authoritative, winning over the people who happily defer to his moral leadership. Invoking the model of Confucius with his extended family of protégés brings to mind a perceived isomorphism in the effects of family, education, morality, and proper governance as they all contribute to a flourishing sociopolitical order.

7A30 孟子曰：" 堯舜，性之也；湯武，身之也；五霸，假之也。久假而不歸，惡知其非有也。"

Mencius said: "While Yao and Shun habituated morality and Tang and Wu embodied it, the Five Hegemons only feigned it. But if these hegemons feign such morality without remiss over an extended period of time, who is to say it does not become their own?"

Comment: The term "native human propensities" (*xing* 性) is used as a verb here, making the point that for Mencius, it is something done rather than something merely "had." It is a situated, narrative process of growing these prosocial relational propensities rather than actualizing some given potential. The importance of the body and embodiment in Mencius and Confucian philosophy broadly cannot be overstated. Far from being incidental to moral growth, embodiment is perceived as the tangible outside of an inside that gives clear testimony to moral transformation. In this perceived hierarchy Yao and Shun are the paradigmatic sage kings and Tang and Wu are something less. We can see for Mencius that moral governance far from being essentialized, is habituated and transformative to the extent that hegemons who would act like True Kings over an extended period of time, become True Kings. To say "everyone can become a sage" is not a claim about some universal innate potential, but only to say that since sagacity is nothing more or less than what one does, so do it. The pathway from hegemon to True King is no different.

1B12 鄒與魯鬨。穆公問曰："吾有司死者三十三人，而民莫之死也。誅之，則不可勝誅；不誅，則疾視其長上之死而不救，如之何則可也？" 孟子對曰：
"凶年饑歲，君之民老弱轉乎溝壑，壯者散而之四方者，幾千人矣；而君之倉廩實，府庫充，有司莫以告，是上慢而殘下也。曾子曰：'戒之戒之！出乎爾者，反乎爾者也。' 夫民今而後得反之也。君無尤焉。君行仁政，斯民親其上，死其長矣。"

Following a skirmish between Zou and Lu, Duke Mu asked Mencius: "In this incident in which thirty-three of my officials have been killed, none of the common people would risk their lives in their defense. My dilemma is there are too many of these people to punish, and yet if I let them go unpunished, I allow them to glare at their leaders and render them no aid as these officials go off to their deaths. What do you think I should do?"

Mencius replied: "The lean years of famine have affected several thousands of your people. The old and the frail have found their way into the ditches and gutters while the able-bodied have scattered in all directions. At the same time, while your granaries are full and your storehouses are bursting, not one of your officials has said anything to you. Such is the callousness of those in authority and the injury they have inflicted on the people below. Master Zeng has said: 'Be warned. Be warned. What goes around comes around.' It is only now that the people have been able to pay them back. You my lord should not be blaming the people. When the ruler practices consummate governance (*renzheng* 仁政), the common people will love those in authority and will die for their leaders."

Comment: The answer to Duke Mu's dilemma is the people should not be punished at all. The relationship between the rulers and the ruled is reciprocal. A prime directive of consummate governance is to provide for the material welfare of the common people. And when this responsibility is fulfilled, the people will support their rulers. But a callous administration that fails to take care of the people will find that such callousness will be returned in kind. As you sow, so shall you reap. Mencius is uncharacteristically politic in allowing that since Duke Mu of Zou was not properly informed by his officials on the suffering of his people, the blame lies with the officials rather than the Duke himself.

1A4 梁惠王曰："寡人願安承教。" 孟子對曰："殺人以梃與刃，有以異乎？"
曰："無以異也。" 曰："庖有肥肉，廄有肥馬，民有飢色，野有餓莩，此率獸而食人也。獸相食，且人惡之。爲民父母，行政不免於率獸而食人。惡在其爲民父母也？仲尼曰：'始作俑者，其無後乎！' 爲其象人而用之也。如之何其使斯民飢而死也？"

King Hui of Liang said to Mencius: "I am earnest in wanting to have your instruction."

"Is there any difference between killing someone with a bludgeon or a knife?" replied Mencius.

"I don't see any difference." said the King.

Mencius said: "Your kitchens are full of prime cuts of meat and your stables have well-fed horses, yet the common people have the pallor of hunger, and in the countryside, they are dying of starvation. This is leading animals to the table to consume human beings. Human beings detest the sight of animals eating each other. And yet if you as the father and mother of the people are practicing policies that are responsible for leading animals to consume the people, wherein are you their parents? Confucius has said: 'Those people who invented burial surrogates should properly be without posterity.' Yet how can using human figures in such a way be as bad as starving actual people to death?"

Comment: Mencius is both candid and courageous in his condemnation of King Hui's governance. For Mencius, there is nothing wrong with rulers enjoying the luxuries of their station when these same rulers have guaranteed a sufficient livelihood for the common people. The problem is one of economic inequity: the ruler has more than he needs, and the people have nothing. Given the isomorphism between family and state, the ruler is properly parent to the people. To have well-tended animals while the people are starving to death is an offense against family reverence (*xiao* 孝) wherein the elder generation is responsible for the well-being of their progeny. During the highly cultured Shang dynasty and well into the Zhou, human blood sacrifice was common in funerary and many other institutionalized practices, where the sheer number of victims executed testifies to the importance of this religious and political spectacle. Over the centuries, the sacrifice of living human victims gradually gave way to burying surrogates in the tombs. While burying human figures is certainly better than burying the actual thing, Confucius still finds the very concept objectionable. If animals killing each other makes us uncomfortable, how much more so should the idea of animals being provisioned in the place of human beings?

IV.5 Maintaining *Tian's* Mandate (*tianming* 天命)

1B8 齊宣王問曰：" 湯放桀，武王伐紂，有諸？" 孟子對曰："於傳有之。" 曰："臣弒其君可乎？" 曰："賊仁者謂之賊，賊義者謂之殘，殘賊之人謂之一夫。聞誅一夫紂矣，未聞弒君也。"

King Xuan of Qi inquired of Mencius: "Did it really happen that Tang, the founder of the Shang dynasty banished Jie, the last ruler of the Xia, and that King Wu, founder of the Zhou dynasty, attacked Zhou, the last ruler of the Shang?"

Mencius replied: "The historical records tell us as much."

"Is it permissible then for a minister to commit regicide?"

Mencius said: "A person who would mutilate those who are consummate in their conduct (*ren* 仁) is called a mutilator; a person who would mutilate those who are appropriate in their conduct (*yi* 義) is called a maimer, and those who would thus mutilate and maim are called scoundrels. I have heard that the scoundrel Zhou has been punished, but I have heard nothing of regicide."

Comment: King Xuan cites the historical record in which founders of new dynasties have overthrown their rulers. As king, he puts Mencius on the spot in asking if regicide is legitimate. A familiar trope in the historical records is the last ruler of each dynasty is cruel and debauched, thereby lending legitimacy to those who effect his removal. Of course, it is the succeeding dynasty that writes the history of the one that has come before.

This political option is institutionalized early in the Zhou tradition as the "mandate of *tian*" (*tianming* 天命): the divinely sanctioned removal of an unworthy ruler. And the ultimate criterion for exercising this option is the mandate of *tian* 天 as it is expressed through the will of the people. If the ruler has failed to live up to the fundamental responsibility of promoting the welfare of the people, he has not satisfied the conditions of rulership, and thus according to the Confucian doctrine of "using names properly" (*zhengming* 正名), he is not a ruler. While *tian* 天 "commands" a particular person to be ruler, it is the virtuosic conduct of the ruler as acknowledged by the people that must "command" the respect of *tian* 天 for the mandate to be continued.

The bilateral nature of all relations is a fundamental precept in this relational cosmology; all relationships run in both directions. In the relationship between the authority of the proper way (*dao* 道) and the human being, for example, *dao* 道 is certainly a guiding force in the human experience to the extent that in *Focusing the Familiar* 1 we read: 不可須臾離也 "we cannot quit it for an instant." At the same time, however, in *Analects* 15.29: 人能弘道，非道弘人 "It is persons who are able to broaden the way, not the way that broadens persons." Similarly in the doctrine of "family reverence" (*xiao* 孝), respect for the authority of the older generation is complemented by the stern obligation of the younger generation to remonstrate (*jian* 諫) when their elders are perceived to be straying from the proper path. With the isomorphism between the family and state, this obligation translates immediately into the need for the loyal minister to remonstrate with the ruler when he is perceived to have taken the wrong turn.

The many stories that remember the last ruler of the Shang dynasty, the tyrant Zhou 紂, recount his debauchery and cruelty to all of those around him, particularly with respect to punishments that maim and mutilate. Making it even worse, many of his victims were elder members of his extended family. It is for this reason he was given the posthumous name Zhou: a horse crupper that in securing the saddle at the back, is most likely to be fouled by the horse. It is on the basis of this political doctrine of *tianming* 天命 that Mencius insists no ruler had been deposed; only a scoundrel has been properly punished.

5B9 齊宣王問卿。孟子曰："王何卿之問也？"王曰："卿不同乎？"曰："不同。有貴戚之卿，有異姓之卿。"王曰："請問貴戚之卿。"曰："君有大過則諫，反覆之而不聽，則易位。"王勃然變乎色。曰："王勿異也。王問臣，臣不敢不以正對。"王色定，然後請問異姓之卿。曰："君有過則諫，反覆之而不聽，則去。"

King Xuan of Qi asked Mencius about the role of high ministers. "What kind of high ministers are you asking about?" replied Mencius.

"Aren't they all the same?" asked the King.

"By no means." replied Mencius. "There are the hereditary ministers related by blood to the ruler, and then there are those ministers who have a different surname."

"Can I ask about the hereditary ministers who are blood relatives to the ruler?"

"When the ruler is guilty of major wrongdoings, they must remonstrate with him, but when this is done repeatedly to no avail, they must depose

him."
The King became agitated, and his color changed visibly.
"Your Majesty must not be offended." said Mencius. "When the King seeks counsel from his ministers, the ministers are obliged to provide an honest response."
Having regained his composure, the King then asked about those high ministers who are unrelated.
"When the ruler is guilty of major wrongdoings," said Mencius, "they must remonstrate with him, but when this is done repeatedly to no avail, they must quit their office."

Comment: Important here is the foundational role of family in all matters, including the responsibility for consummate governance. With the ruler, the authority of family members as high ministers comes from their being closest to if not in fact integral to the exercise of power. A particular ruler rules in the name of the ruling house. With the privileges that appertain to this high status comes their shared responsibility for the welfare of the governed.

In formulating his doctrine of "family reverence" (*xiao* 孝), Confucius in *Analects* 4.18 says:

事父母幾諫。見志不從，又敬不違，勞而不怨。
In serving your father and mother, remonstrate with them gently. On seeing that they do not heed your suggestions, remain respectful and do not act contrary. Although concerned, voice no resentment.

Confucius is setting what he takes to be the proper boundaries on remonstrance. Just because the younger generation is uncomfortable with the conduct of their parents, such a judgment is not their warrant to find blame. The difference between remonstrance and finding blame is that the former is inclusive while the latter is exclusive: that is, the difference between "we can do better" as opposed to "you are doing something wrong." In any case, the younger generation must continue to function and do their best within the family circle. But at the end of the day, even within the irrevocable bonds of family, the ultimate criterion for the conduct expressive of family reverence is *yi* 義: "doing what is optimally appropriate for all concerned in the particular circumstances."

Perhaps a key in this passage for the ruler being deposed by his hereditary ministers is the stipulated condition that he be guilty of "major wrongdoings" where counsel is no longer an option. In the *Analects* 13.18 account of "True Goody" who turns his father in to the authorities for stealing a sheep, Confucius's response is "being true" means that a son "covers" for his father. Even though the son covering for his father seems nepotistic, he is still obligated to do whatever is necessary by way of both behavioral reform and compensation to make the situation "right" (*yi* 義).

5A5 萬章曰: "堯以天下與舜, 有諸?" 孟子曰: "否。天子不能以天下與人。""然則舜有天下也, 孰與之?"曰: "天與之。""天與之者, 諄諄然命之乎?"曰: "否。天不言, 以行與事示之而已矣。"曰: "以行與事示之者如之何?"曰: "天子能薦人於天, 不能使天與之天下; 諸侯能薦人於天子, 不能使天子與之諸侯; 大夫能薦人於諸侯, 不能使諸侯與之大夫。昔者堯薦舜於天而天受之, 暴之於民而民受之, 故曰: 天不言, 以行與事示之而已矣。"

"Was it the case that Yao gave the world to Shun?" asked Wan Zhang.

"No." said Mencius, "An emperor cannot give the world to someone else."

"Who gave Shun the world then?" he continued.

"*Tian* 天 gave it to him." replied Mencius.

"In saying that *tian* 天 gave it to him, does this mean that *tian* 天 repeatedly and earnestly exhorted Shun to take this on?" asked Wan Zhang.

"No." said Mencius. "*Tian* 天 does not speak. It simply made this transition known through its various acts and deeds."

"How does this happen?" Wan Zhang asked.

"The emperor can recommend someone to *tian* 天, but cannot make *tian* 天 give this person the world; the various nobles can recommend someone to the emperor, but they cannot make the emperor enfeoff him as a noble; the various ministers can recommend someone to the nobles, but they cannot make the nobles give him office. In ancient times, Yao recommended Shun to *tian* 天 and *tian* 天 accepted the recommendation. Again, Yao commended Shun to the common people, and they accepted his commendation. It is thus I say that *tian* 天 does not speak but simply made its acceptance known through its various acts and deeds."

曰: "敢問薦之於天而天受之, 暴之於民而民受之, 如何?"曰: "使之主祭而百神享之, 是天受之; 使之主事而事治, 百姓安之, 是民受之也。天與之, 人與之, 故曰: 天子不能以天下與人。舜相堯二十有八載, 非人之所能爲也,天也。堯崩，三年之喪畢，舜避堯之子於南河之南。天下諸侯朝覲者，不之堯之子而之舜；訟獄者，不之堯之子而之舜；謳歌者，不謳歌堯之子而謳歌舜，故曰天也。夫然後之中國，踐天子位焉。而居堯之宮，逼堯之子，是篡也，非天與也。《太誓》曰：'天視自我民視，天聽自我民聽'，此之謂也。"

"How then did *tian* 天 accept Shun on Yao's recommendation, and how did the common people accept Shun on Yao's commending Shun to them?" asked Wan Zhang.

Mencius answered: "When Shun was made master of the sacrifices, the various gods and spirits welcomed the offerings. It was thus *tian* 天 accepted him. When Shun was put in charge of the affairs of state and the affairs were well-managed, he had credibility with the common people. It was thus the common people accepted him. Since it was *tian* 天 and the people who gave the world to Shun, I said that the emperor cannot give it to someone else. Shun assisted Yao in governing for some twenty-eight years. This is not something people can do; it is the workings of *tian* 天.

"When Yao died and the three years of mourning came to an end, Shun, giving wide berth to Yao's son, relocated to the southern reaches of Nanhe. But when the various nobles sought audience with the emperor, they did not go to Yao's son but to Shun instead. When a legal case was to be settled, they did not go to Yao's son but again to Shun. And when the minstrels and poets composed their songs, their verses were not in praise of Yao's son, but rather of Shun. It is thus I said that it was the workings of *tian* 天. It was only thereafter that Shun returned to the central states and assumed the throne. If Shun had himself taken over the palace and ousted Yao's son, it would have been a matter of usurpation, and not something given to him by *tian* 天. This is what it means when in the 'Great Oath' of the *Book of Documents* it says: '*Tian* 天 sees as the common people see; *tian* 天 hears as the common people hear.'"

Comment: A pillar of Confucian political philosophy in the transmission of authority is the transfer of the mandate of *tian* (*tianming* 天命) as the claim to legitimacy. What is important in this account is the role of meritocracy. After Shun had served Emperor Yao in a ministerial capacity for decades, Yao passes over his own son in recommending Shun be installed as emperor. But in the hierarchy, the will of the ruler can only be expressed as a matter of recommendation rather than appointment. Shun had proven himself in carrying out the important religious rituals of state and in promoting the welfare of the people. His appointment comes through signs that originate with *tian* 天, the most important of which is the acceptance by the common people as it is made manifest in their actions.

After Yao's passing and the proper mourning observances, Shun withdrew from the court to allow for Yao's son to succeed his father. But the vassal lords in seeking audience on government matters and the common people in writing the popular record for posterity in their actions made the transition to Shun plain. The mandate (*ming* 命) is not a unilateral action taken on the part of some higher power, but a multilateral and inclusive process expressed through the ineluctable force of circumstances itself.

V. THE *FOCUSING THE FAMILIAR* (*ZHONGYONG* 中庸): THE HIGHEST EXPRESSION OF THE CONFUCIAN PROJECT

Focusing the Familiar (*Zhongyong* 中庸) is traditionally attributed to Kong Ji 孔伋 (483-402 BCE), a grandson of Confucius born to Confucius's son Boyu 伯魚 who himself appears in the *Analects*. Kong Ji is best known by his "style" name, Zisizi 子思子 or "Master" Zisi. This attribution is made in the biography of Confucius in the *Records of the Grand Historian* (*Shiji* 史記) and in some other early sources. In 1973, in the archaeological find at Mawangdui 馬王堆, Changsha, documents buried in c. 168 BCE were discovered that have been attributed to the school of Zisi, if not Zisi himself. Again, in the more recent find at Guodian 郭店 in Hubei province in 1993, new texts recovered in the tomb of "the Tutor to the Eastern Palace," probably the teacher of the crown prince of Chu, have also been attributed to the Zisi lineage. We should not, however, put too much credence in the idea that *Focusing the Familiar* or any of the other texts associated with Zisizi's name were necessarily from his own hand. Typically, texts were one element in a continuing lineage that perpetuated the teachings of earlier generations. Over time, a corpus of curricular materials would accumulate, receiving their authority through attribution to a defining figure in the transmission. Several contemporary scholars including Li Xueqin 李學勤 and Pang Pu 龐樸 have suggested, quite plausibly, that there was a composite collection of writings under the name of Zisi (perhaps similar in structure to the Daoist classic, the *Zhuangzi*) that evolved during the century between Confucius's death and Mencius's birth, and that a good portion of the materials recovered at the Mawangdui and Guodian sites and

V. THE *FOCUSING THE FAMILIAR* (*ZHONGYONG* 中庸): THE HIGHEST EXPRESSION OF THE CONFUCIAN PROJECT

other archeological sources are remnants of it.

Along with other documents associated with the name Zisizi, *Focusing the Familiar* was first canonized and incorporated into the *Record of Rituals* (*Liji* 禮記), a compendium of rites that emerged initially in several forms in the early Han dynasty. But *Focusing the Familiar* also had a life of its own, appearing as an independent text in the court bibliographies across the centuries with many accrued commentaries. Although regarded through the tradition as a document of enormous wisdom, *Focusing the Familiar* achieved another level of prominence when it was canonized a second time as one of the *Four Books* compiled and annotated by the Southern Song dynasty philosopher, Zhu Xi 朱熹 (1130-1200) who saw this text as the highest statement of the Confucian vision of the moral life. Zhu Xi divided *Focusing the Familiar* into numbered sections, and wrote a searching and detailed commentary on it. The *Four Books* with Zhu Xi's commentary became the standard primer for the imperial examination system, and from the Song dynasty to the beginning of the twentieth century, this canon and its evolving commentaries provided a shared vocabulary among Chinese intellectuals.

In *Focusing the Familiar*, the "aspectual" notions of "achieved propriety in one's roles and relations" (*li* 禮), "embodied living within one's roles and relations" (*ti* 體), and the aspiration to "an optimizing harmony" (*he* 和) provide a framework for the highest statement of the Confucian project. The Confucian ethic of roles as an alternative to rule-based ethics begins from its acknowledgement of the native human capacity to collaborate creatively with our environments in pursuit of a consummatory, aesthetic end. As the *locus classicus* among the Confucian canons in celebrating human beings as having both the capacity and the responsibility to be full co-creators with the heavens and the earth, *Focusing the Familiar* opens with the oft-cited passage:

天命之謂性，率性之謂道，修道之謂教。
What *tian* 天 commands is called our native human propensities; acting upon these propensities is called way-making; advancing this way is called education.

One possible reading of *Focusing the Familiar* that comes immediately to mind when the text is located within its own historical context would be to interpret it dialectically as a Confucian argument against the Mohist camp, a philosophical lineage that constituted a pervasive and powerful polemical force during this pre-Qin period. A Mohist interpretation of this opening line of the text would have construed the relationship between *tian* 天 and the human being in a decidedly conservative, more "theistic" direction by suggesting that "Heaven" (*tian* 天) largely imposes its natural and moral order on the human world from without (*wai* 外).① Chris Fraser provides a summary description of this Mohist understanding of the intentions or "purposes of 'Heaven'" (*tianzhi* 天志) as constituting and making available to human beings an externally grounded, objective standard:

> The Mohists justify their consequentialist ethics by appeal to the intention of Heaven (*Tian*), which they believe provides an objective criterion of morality.... The crux of the Mohists' appeal to Heaven is that as the highest, wisest moral agent, Heaven conducts itself in a way (a *dao*) that unfailingly sets an example of correct ethical norms. Its intentions are consistently or reliably humane and right. To obtain an objective criterion of moral right and wrong, then, we can observe Heaven's conduct and notice the norms it is committed to and enforces.②

To be clear, I would argue (and I think Fraser would agree) that the "external" standard of the Mohist is a publicly determined and implemented objective norm, and while certainly conservative and impositional, it still remains as one possible extreme within the assumed framework of a correlative relationship between *tian* 天 and the human world. That is, the "purposes of *tian*" are negotiated and function within the parameters of "the continuity between and inseparability of the human and the cosmic orders" (*tianrenheyi* 天人合一). As such, it should not be construed as a meta-ethical divine command theory in the way this doctrine is usually

---

① This Mohist claim that moral order is ultimately derived from an external source is the basis of a frequently encountered debate in the Confucian texts, with the *Mencius* being perhaps the clearest case in point. See for example, the *Mencius* 6A chapter.

② Chris Fraser, "Mohism", *The Stanford Encyclopedia of Philosophy* (Fall 2012 Edition), Edward N. Zalta (ed.), URL = http://plato.stanford.edu/archives/fall2012/entries/mohism/. See also Chris Fraser, *The Philosophy of the Mozi: The First Consequentialists*. New York: Columbia University Press, 2016, esp. pp. 117-121.

V. THE *FOCUSING THE FAMILIAR* (*ZHONGYONG* 中庸): THE HIGHEST EXPRESSION OF THE CONFUCIAN PROJECT

understood. As a putatively objective standard, the Mohist view entails a fundamentally different kind of "objectivity" than that derived from the dualistic, two-world order we would associate with the conventional Abrahamic notion of the perfection, and thus the aseity or self-sufficiency, of an independent, transcendent God.

Still, this clear degree of difference did not prevent James Legge as a Christian proselytizer from finding an analog for his Christian theism in translating the first line of this text:

> What Heaven has conferred is called THE NATURE; an accordance with this nature is called THE PATH *of duty*; the regulation of this path is called INSTRUCTION.

While Legge thought his own theistically inspired reading of this opening passage gave the text a good beginning, he rued the hubris that would elevate human sages to be on a par with *tian* 天 that he found in the rest of the document. The extent to which the remainder of *Focusing the Familiar* not only strays from but flatly contradicts what Legge really wanted the first line to say was a grave disappointment to this honest translator, leading him to append a stinging indictment of this canonical text to serve as fair warning to its readers that it is a blasphemy of the first order:

> It begins sufficiently well, but the author has hardly enunciated his preliminary apophthegms, when he conducts into an obscurity where we can hardly grope our way, and when we emerge from that, it is to be bewildered by his gorgeous but unsubstantial pictures of sagely perfection. He has eminently contributed to nourish the pride of his countrymen. He has exalted their sages above all that is called God or is worshipped, and taught the masses of the people that with them they have need of nothing from without. In the meantime it is antagonistic to Christianity. By-and-by, when Christianity has prevailed in China, men will refer to it as a striking proof how their fathers by their wisdom knew neither God nor themselves. (Legge, *Chinese Classics*, Vol. 1, p. 55)

Indeed, as Legge grudgingly allows, the remainder of *Focusing the Familiar* is a sustained argument for a Confucian interpretation of this first line that will accommodate neither a soft Mohist nor a much stronger

Christian theism. This alternative Confucian interpretation provides a robust answer to what is perhaps our most basic philosophical questions: How do we become consummately human in our persons through the cultivation of those expansive local and ultimately cosmic relations that locate us within our cultural, social, and natural worlds? And how do we in so doing, ensure that "the heavens and the earth maintain their proper places and all things flourish in the world?" *Focusing the Familiar* can be read as an inspired account of the commonplace characterization of Confucian religiousness as "the continuity between and inseparability of the human and the cosmic orders" (*tianrenheyi* 天人合一) in which the human being must step up to assume the status of co-creator with the heavens and the earth. Importantly, this prescription is not to be understood as the bringing together and conjoining of two separate domains. Rather, and similar to the mutually implicated dyadic pairs, *yinyang* 陰陽 and *daode* 道德, this mantra describes the deliberate growth of those first-order constitutive relations already defining of the human and cosmic orders as continuous and inseparable aspects within the human experience.

The Confucians in arguing here against the Mohist assertion that cosmic order is divinely imposed upon the human world, are not simply advancing the claim that human beings have an active role to play in the production of cosmic order. Indeed, the Confucians go on to insist that, in this aspiration to live inspired lives, human beings contribute in an intense and inimitable way to the refulgent spirituality of the cosmos. Moreover, this spirituality far from being unilateral or singular in purpose as is implied by the Mohist notion of "the purposes of 'Heaven'" (*tianzhi* 天志), is multivalent, pluralistic, and inclusive. The myriad things obey no single unifying principle, but achieve their harmony and their diversity through resourcing the interpenetrating differences that obtain among them to make a difference for each of them. Stated more simply, according to this text, the Confucian vision of the moral life is enhanced and all things in the world flourish when powerful human feelings achieve coalescence in their relations with their environing others, and are orchestrated together with them into a productive, optimal harmony.

Confucian role ethics is a radial way of thinking about the moral life, with human feelings grounded as they are at a focal familial center to then be extended outward by cosmic way-makers in their best effort to "family" the world in which we live. Our warrant for translating the title of the text, "*Zhongyong*" 中庸, as "*Focusing the Familiar*," is the fact that "familiar"

V. THE *FOCUSING THE FAMILIAR* (*ZHONGYONG* 中庸): THE HIGHEST EXPRESSION OF THE CONFUCIAN PROJECT

and "family" share the same etymological root: L. *familiaris* "domestic, private, belonging to a family, of a household." Just as the focusing of a camera lens brings its subject into clearer focus, so the focusing of our most intimate relations bring them into clearer and more meaningful resolution. This seminal text appeals directly to this superlative sense of "harmony" in its own iteration of the holistic and aspirational Confucian project of optimizing familial, political, and cosmic relations.

Focusing the Familiar serves as an object lesson in a Confucian cosmology that requires of human co-creators the production of added significance, and in so doing, the expansion of the cosmic order. It exhorts its readers to exercise their capacity of *ars contextualis*—"the art of contextualizing"—to strive with imagination to take full advantage of both the indeterminate energy that honeycombs the determinate world, and the profound differences that always unique human beings have in their relations with those things present-to-hand in their various environments.

While the opening statement of *Focusing the Familiar* is conceivably the words of Zisizi himself, the chapters that follow from it co-opt the authority of Confucius to support its interpretation of the Confucian project and the cosmic force of human feelings. The first chapters expound on the term *zhongyong* 中庸, a vague binomial that prior to *Focusing the Familiar* had appeared only once in the *Analects* 6.29 from the mouth of the Master himself:

子曰:"中庸之爲德也,其至矣乎!民鮮久矣。"
The Master said, "It takes the highest degree of virtuosity to bring focus to what is familiar in the ordinary affairs of the day. That such virtuosity is rare among the people is an old story."

Some of these early *Focusing the Familiar* chapters are an attempt to define the term *zhongyong* explicitly (2, 3, 7, 8, 9, 11); a few other passages attempt to illuminate what is meant by the character *zhong* 中 by itself as "focus" or "coalescence" (6, 10). What is clear is that the chapters in this first portion of the text attempt to link the notion of *zhongyong* 中庸 with full human participation in the "way-making" (*dao* 道) of the cosmos.

The text continues with the ordinary lives of people in their families and communities as these lives have been informed and inspired by the model provided by exemplary persons who have come before (10, 11, 12, 13,

15). The felt lives of the ordinary people being thus transformed, serve as a motive force as they come to be implicated in the epochal lives of the sages. That is, the sages become sages only through their capacity to transform the lives of the ordinary people into extraordinary lives. These towering paragons then raise their voices on behalf of humanity as a whole, to sing the joyful music of the cosmos.

The middle chapters of the text recount how the sages and cultural heroes have taken the everyday human experience within family and ancestral lineages, and by promoting the pursuit of a ritualized propriety in family and community relations (*li* 禮), have aestheticized this experience and done their best to make what is ordinary, extraordinary. In so doing, they have in important degree elevated and enchanted the lives of the people. There is an important point made repeatedly: *Tian*'s 天 bounty has been and continues to be shared with the human world in direct proportion to the achieved virtuosity of those in positions of social and political authority. Appealing to the paronomastic relationship between the homophonic terms "virtuosity" (*de* 德) and "getting or gaining" (*de* 得), we can say that there is a contrapuntal relationship between human virtuosity and the largesse of *tian* 天. A pervasive dynamic in these Confucian canons, simply put, is that in the lives of exemplary persons, there is an immediate correlation between their achieved resolution rooted within their own narratives, and the expansive reach and influence they have in the world around them. In thus recounting the history of the collaborative origins of human culture, the text marshals the hoary sages and cultural heroes to join Confucius in endorsing *Focusing the Familiar*'s decidedly Confucian interpretation of the transformative cosmic force of human feelings.

Chapter 25 of *Focusing the Familiar* provides a straightforward and substantial statement of several cosmological assumptions that further expand upon the theme expressed in the opening chapter. It is the indeterminate aspect of our experience coupled with human resolution to make a difference that provides the space for humans to participate as responsible players in the creative cosmic advance. The chapter itself is an elaboration on a passage found in the *Mencius* 4A12 that has elevated the term *cheng* 誠, conventionally translated as "sincerity" or "honesty" but rendered here as "resolve," to cosmic status as a source of transformation:

是故誠者，天之道也，思誠者，人之道也。

V. THE *FOCUSING THE FAMILIAR* (*ZHONGYONG* 中庸): THE HIGHEST EXPRESSION OF THE CONFUCIAN PROJECT

Resolve is the way-making of *tian* 天, while reflecting with resolution on things is the way-making of human beings.

The *Mencius* is ascribing to resolution as it is achieved in our intense human feelings, the potential to become a powerful force in shaping cosmic order. In this appropriation and elaboration of the uniquely Mencian reading of human resolution (*cheng* 誠) as a cosmic force, the text has added Mencius to Confucius and the early sages as one more sponsor of its Confucian interpretation of the cosmic reach and influence of human feelings.

Focusing the Familiar, with Confucius, the sages and cultural heroes, and Mencius all endorsing its interpretation of the Confucian project, it has only to bring in the compelling voice of the *Book of Songs* to complete its score. It is the *Book of Songs* as the anonymous and commonly shared songs of the people, that in having powerful affective force and absolute veracity, serves typically as the ultimate Q.E.D. endorsement within many if not most of the Confucian canonical texts. As we move through the final concluding chapters of *Focusing the Familiar*, the bottomlessness and the boundlessness of the heavens and the earth that provide the natural context for the human experience are described in hyperbolic language (26). An important cosmological point made explicitly here is that each particular event that emerges as integral to cosmic order, is unique and without replication, making the process of procreation unlimited in its bounty:

天地之道，可壹言而盡也。其爲物不貳，則其生物不測。
The way of heaven and earth can be captured in one phrase: since events are never duplicated, their proliferation is unfathomable.

In this crescendo, with quickening pace and animation, the text goes on to describe the human complement to these natural processes of procreativity made by sages and exemplary persons who spread the proper way throughout the world (27). It is through the exemplary rulership of the True King (28) that the role of the human actor is extended both culturally and politically to the furthest reaches of the cosmos. These more generic descriptions then give way to the specific and concrete example of Confucius himself (30) who is portrayed in grand, celestial language that makes his life a counterpart to the cosmic process of procreation itself in which the human and the natural operations converge as one.

Making the point that this cosmic process continues unabated, the penultimate chapters 31 and 32 describe in majestic and exuberant language the singular transformative impact of "those of utmost sagacity in the world" (*tianxiazhisheng* 天下至聖) and "those of utmost creative resolve in the world" (*tianxiazhicheng* 天下至誠) respectively. Finally, the last chapter (33) registers perhaps most dramatically the now galloping momentum of the generative procreative process. The text breaks out into the celebratory, full-throated verses of the *Book of Songs* and moves rapidly toward its denouement in a veritable "Ode to Joy." It is these verses that draw upon the powerful feelings of the people and the genuineness of their songs to serve as the last and most powerful endorsement for the Confucian reading of this text: that is, the celebration of the power of intense human feelings in the collaborative processes of cosmic procreativity.

V.1 Chapter 1: The Confucian Project: "The Continuity Between and Inseparability of the Human and the Cosmic Orders" (*tianrenheyi* 天人合一)

天命之謂性，率性之謂道，修道之謂教。道也者，不可須臾離也，可離非道也。是故君子戒慎乎其所不睹，恐懼乎其所不聞。莫見乎隱，莫顯乎微。故君子慎其獨也。

What *tian* 天 commands is called our native human propensities (*xing* 性); acting upon these propensities is called way-making (*dao* 道); advancing this way is called education (*jiao* 教). As for this way-making, we cannot quit it even for an instant. Could we quit it, it would not be proper way-making. It is for this reason that exemplary persons are so concerned about what is not seen, and so anxious about what is not heard. There is nothing more present than what is imminent, and nothing more manifest than what is inchoate. Thus, exemplary persons are ever concerned to consolidate their virtuosic habits as an inner disposition for action.

Comment: In translating this opening line as "What *tian* 天 commands is called our native human propensities...," I am following the interpretation of the term "native human propensities" (*xing* 性) that Tang Junyi endorses in his extensive commentary generally, and on this passage specifically. Tang insists that:

V. THE *FOCUSING THE FAMILIAR* (*ZHONGYONG* 中庸): THE HIGHEST EXPRESSION OF THE CONFUCIAN PROJECT

所謂天命之爲性，非天以一指定命運規定人物之行動運化，而正是賦人物以多多少少不受自己過去之習慣所機械支配，亦不受外界之來感之力之機械支配，而隨境有一創造的生起而表現自由之性。

What is meant in this opening passage by such a claim is not that *tian* 天 according to some fixed fate determines the conduct and progress of human beings. On the contrary, *tian* 天 endows humans with our native human propensities (*xing* 性) that, being more or less free of the mechanical control of established habits and of external intervening forces, undergo a creative advance within their contextualizing situation that is expressive of this spontaneity.[1]

Each of the two paragraphs that follow from this opening statement offers an interpretation of this first line that can be read as a succinct and explicit statement of the Confucian project. This first chapter sets the problem for the entire document and provides a summary answer not just once but twice. *Focusing the Familiar* is, from beginning to end, a celebration of the continuing contributions of those human beings who embrace and take responsibility for their co-creative role in the cosmos captured in the mantra, "the continuity between and inseparability of the human and the cosmic orders" (*tianrenheyi* 天人合一). Expanding upon this central theme, these two introductory paragraphs provide us with several cosmological corollaries that follow from the primacy invested in vital relationality.

In the recently recovered documents associated with the name Zisizi, there are five philosophical terms that have been identified as key to his doctrines: *tian* 天 (conventionally translated as "Heaven"), "commanding" (*ming* 命), "native human propensities" (*xing* 性), "bodyheartminding" (*xin* 心), and "feelings, actuality" (*qing* 情). The prominence of "feelings" (*qing* 情) in particular has occasioned a rereading of the corpus of texts in this formative period. In just the opening line of this chapter, we have encountered three of these five terms: *tian* 天, *ming* 命 ("commanding"), and *xing* 性 ("native human propensities"), providing a good reason for the traditional association of the authorship of the text with this grandson of Confucius. An argument can be made that even though the two additional Zisizi terms—"feelings" (*qing* 情) and "bodyheartminding" (*xin* 心)—do not appear in this first chapter explicitly, they are implicit in what is being

---

[1] Tang Junyi, *Complete Works*, Vol. 4, p. 100.

said about the intimate role of human feelings in cosmic flourishing. The semantic content if not the two remaining Zisizi terms themselves are referenced obliquely, making up the full complement of five key terms with these surrogates. And then later in the text, the increasing centrality of *cheng* 誠—"sincerity, honesty, integrity, resolve"—elevated to cosmic proportions as a kind of "co-creativity" reinforces the claim that human "feelings" have a prominent role in shaping the cosmos.

In the first paragraph of this opening chapter, human beings are taken to be integral to the creative cosmic process. As we cultivate and enculturate ourselves, we have a recursive relationship within the context of this generative advancing of cosmic order, shaping and being shaped at the same time. And we cannot extricate ourselves from this responsibility. Importantly, it is the imminent, inchoate, and thus underdetermined penumbra of the emerging cosmic order that provides cultivated persons with the opening and the opportunity to function as co-creators, and to collaborate fully with the heavens and the earth in achieving a flourishing world. Moreover, through the reflexive internalization and consolidation of this virtuosic conduct in their own persons in this focus-field dynamic, they come to have this entire flourishing cosmos implicated in their personal project of becoming fully who they are.

Indeed, exemplary persons have the capacity through an achieved inner resolve and the personal cultivation that follows from it, to produce increased significance in all of the relations that constitute them and their world. This process is illustrative of the Confucian assumption that creativity is always a situated, collaborative undertaking as *creatio in situ*. Given that Confucian morality is nothing more or less than deliberate growth in relations, these exemplars are thus able to achieve cosmic stature as a continuing source of moral meaning in their increasingly intimate relationship with their world. Any reticence with respect to the remoteness, vastness, and externality of the cosmos gives way to an awareness of an increasingly mutual and indeed "social" coalescence with this world funded by feelings of deference, belonging, and trust. It is this same sense of the inseparability of the human and the natural worlds that is inspiring the contemporary movement in the social sciences and humanities to herald an Anthropocene epoch by challenging the nature/social dualism and, in remembering the etymology of "social" as "company" and "alliance," embracing nature as a social category.[1]

Contemporary scholar Liang Tao on the basis of recently recovered archaeological texts has argued convincingly that the meaning of the last phrase in this passage—故君子慎其獨也—is best understood as the need for those who would be exemplary "to internalize and consolidate the five modes of virtuosic conduct as a habitual disposition for acting with moral virtuosity."[2]

喜怒哀樂之未發,謂之中;發而皆中節,謂之和;中也者,天下之大本也;和也者,天下之達道也。致中和,天地位焉,萬物育焉。

The moment at which joy and anger, grief and pleasure, have yet to arise we can call a nascent equilibrium; once these feelings have arisen, that they find coalescence we can call an optimizing harmony. This notion of equilibrium is the great root of the world; an optimizing harmony then is the advancing of way-making in the world. When equilibrium is sustained and an optimizing harmony is fully realized, the heavens and the earth maintain their proper places and all things flourish in the world.

Comment: This second passage then, begins from a description of the initial conditions of humankind—those latent, native but as yet unexpressed feelings—that provide us with the relational resources for engaging the world and for enchanting the cosmos. And it is because we are able to cultivate ourselves as responsive, feeling creatures that we can develop the capacity to become a truly transformative force suffusing the ceaseless process of procreation. The notion of "feelings" here has to be read as a human responsiveness that has the potential to function in a deepened, capacious, and inclusive way. As David Wong and others have argued, we do not find the Greek separation of emotions and reason in these classical Confucian texts, or any assumed tension between these capacities that might

---

[1] See Gisli Palsson et al., "Reconceptualizing the 'Anthropos' in the Anthropocene: Integrating the Social Sciences and Humanities in Global Environmental Change Research," *Environmental Science & Policy* 28 (2013), pp. 3-13.

[2] See Liang Tao 梁涛, "Zhu Xi dui 'Shendu' de Wudu jiqi zai Jingxue Quanshi zhong de Yiyi" 朱熹對"慎獨"的誤讀及其在經學詮釋中的意義, *Zhexue Yanjiu* 哲學研究 (2004), 第 3 期, pp. 48-54.

follow from such a disjunction.① Our feelings in this broad, cosmic sense seek their own satisfaction by pursuing a productive continuity within the contours of the concrete world, a world we actually come to embody in recognizing and acting upon the inseparability of person and context.

But such feelings become a powerful resource only when they are properly cultivated to achieve both coalescence (*zhongjie* 中節) and a superlative harmony (*he* 和) in these expansive relations, and in so doing, to give rise to the personal resolution needed to produce a flourishing world. It is only through the deepening of the proper measure (*du* 度) in the correlative "human and cosmos" relationship (*tianren* 天人), and thus transforming this relationship into one of sociality, and indeed of an evolving religiousness, that these exemplary persons can make their profound contribution to cosmic meaning. Such an achieved harmony and clear resolution in our relationships is the very root from which the flourishing world order emerges, and as such, contributes to the life force that guides the cosmos with all of its bounty, on its proper course. On the human side, it is our unique sense of felt worth and belonging within this dynamic cosmic life force that is the substance of real religious experience, and that gives *Focusing the Familiar* as a text its profound religious significance.

We might note that the first paragraph begins with "what *tian* 天 commands is called our native human propensities," introducing what if interpreted in a theistic way might be taken as a "given" endowment. The second paragraph on the other hand begins from human feelings where when these feelings are optimized, all things in the cosmos flourish. This reflects a tension between a theistic reading of this first line and chapter 25 that interprets "human propensities" not as something given in the human experience, but as the result of an optimizing resolve that makes this conduct consummate and that in turn inspires wisdom in the world:

性之德也，合外内之道也，故時措之宜也。
Such is the virtuosity achieved in one's natural propensities and the way-making that integrates what is more internal and what is more

---

① David B. Wong, "Is There a Distinction Between Reason and Emotion in Mencius?", *Philosophy East and West* 41, No. 1 (1991), p. 31. Myeong-seok Kim disputes Wong's claim in her subsequent essay, "Is There No Distinction between Reason and Emotion in *Mengzi*?", *Philosophy East and West* 64, No. 1 (2014).

external. Thus, when and wherever one applies this virtuosity, it is fitting.

V.2 Chapters 2, 3, 5, 8: Explaining the Term *zhongyong* 中庸

2. 仲尼曰:"君子中庸,小人反中庸。君子之中庸也,君子而時中;小人之中庸也,小人而無忌憚也。"

Confucius said: "Exemplary persons bring focus to the familiar affairs of the day; petty persons bring confusion to them. Exemplary persons are able to bring focus to the familiar affairs of the day because, being themselves exemplary, they constantly abide in equilibrium. Petty persons bring confusion to these affairs because, being petty persons, they lack the requisite scruples and concern."

3. 子曰:"中庸其至矣乎! 民鮮能久矣!"

The Master said: "Focusing the familiar affairs of the day is a task of the highest order. That it is rare among the common people is an old story."

5. 子曰:"道其不行矣夫。"

The Master said: "This proper way, alas, is not being traveled at all!"

8. 子曰:"回之爲人也,擇乎中庸,得一善,則拳拳服膺而弗失之矣。"

The Master said: "Yan Hui chose the path of focusing the familiar affairs of the day, and on gaining something worthwhile from doing so, would clasp it tightly to his breast and not lose it—such was the likes of Yan Hui."

Comment: These opening passages of *Focusing the Familiar* are lethargic and pessimistic, setting up a contrast with the text as it gathers momentum in the middle chapters with increasing optimism about the human condition, and then gallops at the end toward its bold crescendo in celebrating the boundless possibilities of human beings as co-creators of cosmic order.

We have translated the obscure term *zhongyong* 中庸 as "focusing the familiar affairs of the day" in the sense of deepening and bringing into clearer resolution the pattern of relationships that constitute our ordinary human experience. With "familiar" and "family" having the same root, it means cultivating and bringing into meaningful resolve one's relationships in family, community, polity, and cosmos. Another translation we have used elsewhere is "hitting the mark in the everyday." Stated simply, *zhongyong* 中庸 celebrates the creative human capacity for growing and bringing our concrete, everyday relationships into clearer focus as a source of increased significance, that is, cognitive, affective, moral, aesthetic, and religious meaning.

Prior to the *Focusing the Familiar*, the term *zhongyong* 中庸 that is used as its title occurs only once in the philosophical literature in *Analects* 6.29 where it comes from the mouth of Confucius himself:

子曰:"中庸之爲德也,其至矣乎! 民鮮久矣!"
The Master said: "The virtuosity that comes with bringing focus to the familiar affairs of the day is of the highest order. That it is rare among the common people is an old story."

In its effort to appropriate the prestige of Confucius for its own interpretation of the Confucian project, *Focusing the Familiar* repeats the *Analects* passage almost verbatim and then adds to it several other passages that serve as further explanation. This term *zhongyong* 中庸 has been interpreted and translated many different ways, and even on occasion differently by the same author: "The Doctrine of the Mean," "according to the Constant Mean," "the state of equilibrium and harmony" (Legge), "the Mean-in-Action" (E.R. Hughes), "Central Harmony" (Ku Hung-ming 辜鴻銘), "the Unwobbling Pivot" (Ezra Pound), "the Mean" (D.C. Lau 劉殿爵), "Centrality and Commonality" (Tu Wei-ming 杜維明), "Using the Centre" and "Central and Constant" (Johnston and Wang), "applying the mean" (Slingerland), "the Middle Way" (Leys).

The now conventional translation as "The Doctrine of the Mean" of course recalls Aristotle's account of virtues as a rational determination of a mean located between the two extremes of defect and excess. For example, courage is a mean between cowardice (defect) and foolhardiness (excess). This culturally reductive interpretation of *zhongyong* 中庸 can lead to a misconstrual of what the text itself purports to say.

A process cosmology with its focus and field dynamic will hardly yield itself to "a mean and extremes" vocabulary. Aristotle's rational calculation of the relationship between distinctive emotions (courage, generosity, and so on) and "actions" (acting courageously, generously) in the construction

V. THE *FOCUSING THE FAMILIAR* (*ZHONGYONG* 中庸): THE HIGHEST EXPRESSION OF THE CONFUCIAN PROJECT

of a virtuous character contrasts dramatically with *Focusing the Familiar*'s treatment of a more vectorial and dispositional sense of feelings as they come to be focused (*zhong* 中) and thus productive of an optimal and sustained harmony (*he* 和) in the routine events of our lives.

Aristotle provides a strategy that enables individual agents to make choices disciplined by acquired character and rational deliberation, appealing to metaphors such as navigation and medicine. *Focusing the Familiar* by contrast tends to be more holistic. It advocates optimizing the creative possibilities of the ever-changing circumstances within which the human experience takes place. The shifting equilibrium that underlies this optimizing process is both embedded within and consistently promotes communal life forms (*li* 禮). Practice is resolutely communal, and rather than being governed by individual choices, is animated by those interpersonal dispositions created by coordinating roles and relationships effectively. It is not impersonal reason, but holistic, *li* 禮 -informed affective habits that direct experience. Unstinting attention to proper roles and relations produces not only appropriate dispositions, but ultimately a profound human-centered religiousness that comes to elevate a flourishing community. In such circumstances, the terms of extremes and mean must be translated into the language of field and focus. The habit of being resolved in the familiar affairs of the day and thus bringing resolution to one's field of experience, is accomplished through dispositional adjustments in communal *li* 禮 -living rather than through individual deliberation and choice.

In our best efforts to understand *zhongyong*, we could also appeal to a distinction between first problematic analogical or correlative thinking and second problematic causal or rational thinking. First problematic thinking is neither strictly cosmogonical nor cosmological in the sense of presupposing an initial beginning or a single-ordered world respectively. This mode of thinking accepts the priority of change or process over rest and permanence, presumes no ultimate agency responsible for the general order of things, and seeks to account for states of affairs by appeal to correlative procedures rather than to agencies or rationalizing principles.

The presuppositions of second problematic or rational, causal thinking are the understanding of "cosmos" as a single-ordered world that is the consequence of some principle or agency of construal (the demiurge, *nous*, the Unmoved Mover, the Will of God, and so on) in its overcoming of an initial chaos. There is a priority given to stasis over change and motion often expressed as a priority of being over becoming. And there is the tacit or explicit claim that the states of affairs comprising the world are grounded in, and ultimately determined by, these agencies of construal.

A form of first problematic thinking is dominant in classical Confucian culture, while perhaps recessive in the received Greek tradition. And second problematic thinking is the cultural dominant in classical Greek philosophy, while being recessive in classical China.

V.3 Chapter 12: The Proper Way of Exemplary Persons (*junzi* 君子)

君子之道費而隱。夫婦之愚，可以與知焉，及其至也，雖聖人亦有所不知焉；夫婦之不肖，可以能行焉，及其至也，雖聖人亦有所不能焉。天地之大也，人猶有所憾，故君子語大，天下莫能載焉；語小，天下莫能破焉。《詩》云："鳶飛戾天，魚躍于淵。"言其上下察也。君子之道，造端乎夫婦，及其至也，察乎天地。

The proper way (*dao* 道) of exemplary persons (*junzi* 君子) is both broad and hidden. The dullest of ordinary men and women can know something of it, and yet even the sages (*shengren* 聖人) in trying to penetrate to its furthest limits do not know it all. The most unworthy of common men and women are able to travel a distance along it, yet even the sages in trying to penetrate to its furthest limits are not able to travel it all.

As grand as the world is, people still have their dissatisfactions. Thus, were exemplary persons to discourse on the profundity of their way, there is nothing in the world that could take its weight; were they to discourse on its subtlety, there is nothing in the world that could further refine it. The *Book of Songs* 239 says:

The hawks soar to the limits of the heavens;
The fishes plunge to the furthest depths.

This passage gives expression to its height and its depth. The proper way of exemplary persons has at its beginning the simple lives of ordinary men and women, and at its furthest limits it sheds its light upon the entire world.

Comment: In the radical empiricism of Confucian philosophy, everything starts here and goes there. There is a centered and unbounded radiality that commences from what is close at hand and extends to the furthest limits. Such is the definition of the proper way of exemplary persons. Near

V. THE *FOCUSING THE FAMILIAR* (*ZHONGYONG* 中庸): THE HIGHEST EXPRESSION OF THE CONFUCIAN PROJECT

at hand, it is accessible to the most common of the people, and even the most unworthy can walk on it awhile. In its nuance, it carries us plunging into what is as yet only incipient in what we are experiencing, and in the acuity it provides, it lifts us soaring upward to the most panoramic view of things to see how they all fit together. Still, at its extremes, it extends beyond the reach of the most sagacious of people.

V.4 Chapter 15: Family as the Trailhead of the Proper Way (*dao* 道)

君子之道，辟如行遠必自邇，辟如登高必自卑。《詩》曰："妻子好合，如鼓瑟琴；兄弟既翕，和樂且耽。宜爾室家，樂爾妻帑。"子曰："父母其順矣乎！"

The proper way of exemplary persons is analogous to traveling a long way, where you must set off from what is near at hand. It is analogous to climbing to the lofty heights, where you must begin from the lowliest ground. The *Book of Songs* 164 says:

> The loving relationship with wife and children
> Is like the strumming of the zither and the lute;
> In the harmonious relationship between older and younger brothers
> There is an abundance of enjoyment and pleasure.
> Be appropriate in your house and home
> And bring joy to your wife and progeny.

The Master said: "And how happy your father and mother will be."

Comment: The journey is always from near to far, and the climb is from low to high. The notion of *zhongyong* 中庸 as "focusing the familiar" is rooted in family reverence (*xiao* 孝) as the prime moral imperative, and begins from a flourishing family life. At the same time, the steep climb and the heights to be reached, far from taking us away from this beginning, is the musicality achieved in elevating and enchanting what is ordinary, and relishing the delight to be found in the deepening of the everyday. Progress along the way of exemplary persons is made through the assiduous effort in the project of personal growth needed to qualitatively transform what is at once most basic and yet most profound in the human experience. There is no destination on this shared journey, and rejoicing in the events to be experienced along the way is always better than the inn.

V.5 Chapter 17: The Cosmic and the Human as a Contrapuntal Dynamic

子曰:"舜其大孝也與! 德爲聖人, 尊爲天子, 富有四海之内。宗廟饗之, 子孫保之。故大德必得其位, 必得其禄, 必得其名, 必得其壽。故天之生物, 必因其材而篤焉。故栽者培之, 傾者覆之。《詩》曰:'嘉樂君子, 憲憲令德! 宜民宜人, 受禄于天。保佑命之, 自天申之!'故大德者必受命。"

The Master said: "Now Shun—there was a person of great filiality (*daxiao* 大孝)! His virtuosity (*de* 德) was that of a sage (*shengren* 聖人), he was venerated as the Son of *tian* 天, and his wealth extended to his rule over everything in the world. In the ancestral hall he received sacrifices, and generation after generation of progeny have preserved his name. Thus, those of the greatest virtuosity (*dade* 大德) are certain to gain status, emoluments, reputation, and longevity. For the generosity of *tian* 天 in giving birth to and nurturing things is certain to be in response to the quality of the things themselves. It is thus those trees that are planted properly are provided nourishment while those that are not will topple. The *Book of Songs* 249 says:

So good and happy is the ruler:
Such an abundant display of illustrious virtuosity.
He treats the common people appropriately,
He treats his kinsmen appropriately,
He receives his emoluments from *tian* 天;
Tian 天 protects him in office and bestows on him its charge (*ming* 命).
It is from *tian* 天 that all of his bounty is redoubled.

Those of the greatest virtuosity are thus certain to receive *tian's* 天 charge."

Comment: The always collaborative life and growth of the cosmos is captured here in the phrase "the generosity of *tian* 天 in giving birth to and nurturing things is certain to be in response to the quality of the things themselves." It is telling that the contrapuntal dynamic between the largesse of *tian* 天 and human virtuosity (*de* 德) is explained under the rubric of "family reverence" (*xiao* 孝).

The second term that describes the deepening of the relationship between human beings and the cosmos is "virtuosity" (*de* 德), where the locus of the cultivation and the expression of such personal virtuosity is in the first instance the family, and then by extension, the community, the polity, and the cosmos. The radiality of this "virtuosity" is expressed explicitly in the verse selected from the *Book of Songs* where it extends outward with the ruler's "family" of common people and kinsmen at the center.

On the human side, it is Shun, son of the cruel Blind Man, who is celebrated as having through sheer perseverance finally won his father's favor. Shun accomplished what is celebrated as the greatest historical example of family reverence that, in *Mencius* 4A28 as here, is called "the great filiality" (*daxiao* 大孝). More generally, there is a perceived isomorphism between state and family with the ruler being father and mother to the people, and an isomorphism between state and cosmos with the emperor being the Son of *tian* (*tianzi* 天子). Shun was both ruler and Son of *tian* 天. Throughout the Confucian canons, the same normative terms are used to both describe and prescribe order in the human and in the cosmic realms: not only "the proper way, way-making" (*dao* 道), "coherence" (*li* 理), "inscription, ornamentation, culture" (*wen* 文), "life, living, procreation" (*sheng* 生), "ease" (*yi* 易), and "simplicity" (*jian* 簡), but also seemingly specifically human values such as "family reverence" (*xiao* 孝), "virtuosity" (*de* 德), "resolve, sincerity" (*cheng* 誠), and even "consummate conduct" (*ren* 仁) are elevated as cosmic forces. The cosmos has a moral order that can be expressed through this shared vocabulary having application to both the natural and the human worlds.

V.6 Chapter 19: Effecting Order Through Family Reverence (*xiao* 孝)

子曰："武王、周公，其達孝矣乎！夫孝者：善繼人之志，善述人之事者也。春、秋修其祖廟，陳其宗器，設其裳衣，薦其時食。宗廟之禮，所以序昭穆也；序爵，所以辨貴賤也；序事，所以辨賢也；旅酬下爲上，所以逮賤也；燕毛，所以序齒也。踐其位，行其禮，奏其樂，敬其所尊，愛其所親，事死如事生，事亡如事存，孝之至也。郊社之禮，所以事上帝也；宗廟之禮，所以祀乎其先也。明乎郊社之禮、禘嘗之義，治國其如示諸掌乎！"

The Master said: "King Wu and the Duke of Zhou—there indeed stood two exemplars of family reverence (*xiao* 孝)! Family reverence means being good at continuing the purposes of one's predecessors and at maintaining their ways. In the proper season, they made repairs to the ancestral temple, laid out the sacrificial vessels of their ancestors, exhibited the robes used in funerary observances, and sacrificed with the newly harvested crops.

"They made use of ritual practices (*li* 禮) in the ancestral temple as their way of arranging the tablets of the departed generations appropriately on the left and right sides; they deferred to the titles of office as their way of recognizing degrees of nobility; they used the sequence of the services as their way of distinguishing those most worthy; they used the drinking pledges in which those below toast their superiors as their way of reaching down to include the lowliest, and they took into consideration the color of the hair as their way of seating participants according to their seniority.

"Taking up the places of their forebearers, carrying out their ritual observances (*li* 禮), playing their music (*yue* 樂), showing respect (*jing* 敬) to those whom they esteemed, extending their affections to those of whom they were fond, serving their dead as though they were living, and serving those who are long departed as though they were still here—this then is family reverence at its highest.

"The sacrificial observances to *tian* 天 at the winter solstice in the southern suburbs of the capital and to the earth (*di* 地) at the summer solstice in the northern suburbs are ways of serving the high ancestors. Ritual observances performed in the ancestral temple are the way of making sacrifices to one's forebearers. For one who has a clear understanding of the sacrificial observances to *tian* 天 and the earth, and the various ceremonies such as the Grand *di* 禘 sacrifice and the autumnal *chang* 嘗 sacrifice performed in the ancestral temple, the governing of the world is as easy as turning something over in the palm of one's hand."

Comment: The Confucian sense of the intergenerational transmission of social, political, and indeed cosmic order is grounded in the institution of family reverence (*xiao* 孝). Family reverence begins from maintaining the ancestral temple and its accoutrements, and performing the sacrifices at the proper times. It is the organizing principle that locates everyone according to their titles and achievements, living and dead alike, in their proper place, and is the basis of the protocols that galvanize the family-centered hierarchical structures. With family as the governing cultural metaphor and a narrative understanding of human "becomings," social and political hierarchies as they punctuate the human experience are perceived as the natural order of things. With each generation in the fullness of time achieving its identity by inheriting and embodying the cultural tradition, and then extending it for their own time and place, the ancestors and their values live on.

In this ritualized way of organizing the human experience, it is not the hierarchical structure of these relations themselves that is problematic. It is only when such hierarchical relations are compromised by coercion that there is a pernicious diminution in their value and effectiveness. When the ritually-informed social order functions optimally, a relational rather than an individual autonomy is achieved in this self-ordering process.

V.7 Chapter 21: The Foundational and the Creative Aspects of Education

自誠明，謂之性；自明誠，謂之教。誠則明矣，明則誠矣。

Understanding born of creative resolve (*cheng* 誠) is what we call the expression of our natural human propensities (*xing* 性); creative resolve born of understanding is what we call learning (*jiao* 教). Where resolve then understanding; where understanding then resolve.

Comment: The word "education" has two principal roots that are relevant here—L. *educare* and *educere*. The first root *educare* means "cultivating, rearing, bringing up," while the second *educere* means "educing, evoking, leading forth, drawing out." The customary, habitual, and ritualistic aspect of education as *educare* leans toward transmission from teacher to student, and requires discipline in the fundamentals. *Educere* suggests the more creative, personal, and expansive understanding of education, where teacher and student learn together. This evocative sense of *educere* references novel and imaginative elaborations in one's own best efforts at personal cultivation, and is productive of new knowledge.

By identifying education with first embodying and then advancing the proper way, the Confucian texts are invested in both the foundational and the creative aspects of education. The first line of the text that might well come from Zisizi himself states:

天命之謂性，率性之謂道，修道之謂教。

What *tian* 天 commands is called our natural propensities (*xing* 性); drawing out these natural propensities is called the proper way (*dao* 道); improving upon this way is called education (*jiao* 教).

The more conservative *educare* has a fundamental if not the primary role to play in passing on the details of the rich cultural heritage from one generation to the next. Hence, to say that the function of education is not primarily that of transmission and training but of innovation would be misleading. It is in fact an achieved symbiotic balance between the *educare* and *educere* aspects of education that is emphasized in this chapter.

Grasping the gist of this laconic passage requires some sensitivity to the nuance and complexity of the central terms and of their relationship with each other. Creative resolve (*cheng* 誠) as the spontaneous expression of our natural propensities is a responsiveness to the world that leads to a secure *understanding* of it. In this context, "understanding" means primarily deferring to, appropriating, and accommodating the "*what*" of learning (*educare*). But the process continues. As creative resolve emerges again, it is prompted by imaginative projection that takes us beyond our existing *understanding* of the world to initiate new "learning" (*jiao* 教), an "improving upon the proper way" and extending it further. Such learning requires imagination: the thinking and feeling that will carry us outside of the box and go beyond it. Importantly, the proper way is vital and constantly being extended through the continuing human production of meaning. Resolve (*cheng* 誠) in the first instance is productive of understanding (*educare*), where such secure understanding in turn animates the creative capacity of resolve to extend the proper way (*educere*). It is in this sense that there is a wholeness and inclusiveness to resolve, such that Chapter 25 declares 誠者物之終始，不誠無物 "Resolve is the beginning and the end of things, and without this resolve, there would be nothing."

V.8 Chapter 25: Resolve (*cheng* 誠) as a Collaborative and Reflexive Creativity

誠者自成也，而道自道也。誠者物之終始，不誠無物。是故君子誠之為貴。誠者非自成己而已也，所以成物也。成己，仁也；成物，知也。性之德也，合外內之道也，故時措之宜也。

Resolve (*cheng* 誠) is self-consummating and its way-making is self-directing. Resolve is the beginning and the end of things, and without this resolve, there would be nothing. It is thus that, for exemplary persons, it is resolve that is prized. But resolve is not simply the self-consummating of one's own person; it is what consummates everything. Completing oneself is achieving virtuosity in one's roles and relations (*ren* 仁); completing all things is

V. THE *FOCUSING THE FAMILIAR* (*ZHONGYONG* 中庸): THE HIGHEST EXPRESSION OF THE CONFUCIAN PROJECT

advancing wisdom in the world (*zhi* 知). Such is the virtuosity achieved in one's natural propensities and the way-making that integrates what is more internal and what is more external. Thus, when and wherever one applies this virtuosity, it is fitting.

Comment: An important feature of cosmology generally is that, far from being some remote speculation on the turning of the heavens, it is typically a projection onto the world initially derived from the ordinary activities of the everyday human experience: love and strife, law and chaos, friend and foe, male and female, and so on. In the cosmology implicit in early Confucian philosophizing, the pursuit of cosmic harmony begins with personal cultivation in family and community relations at home, and then ripples out to suffuse the polity and the furthest horizons of the cosmos, both of which are construed as a direct extension of personal feelings and familial relations.

We should note that *cheng* 誠 is a familiar human sentiment usually translated as "sincerity," "honesty," or "integrity." This chapter in *Focusing the Familiar* is itself a commentary on a passage found in the *Mencius* 4A12 that has elevated *cheng* 誠, translated here as "resolve," as a technical term to cosmic status to stipulate it as a source of creativity and transformation:

> 是故誠者，天之道也，思誠者，人之道也。
> Resolve is the way-making of *tian* 天, while reflecting with resolution on things is the way-making of the human being.

This cosmic association of *cheng* 誠 with creativity and resolve has been anticipated in *Focusing the Familiar* 16:

> 夫微之顯，誠之不可掩如此夫。
> Such is the way that the inchoate is made manifest and that resolve cannot be repressed.

Cheng 誠 occurs again as a technical term with this same cosmological connotation in *Focusing the Familiar* 20:

> 誠者，天之道也；誠之者，人之道也。誠者，不勉而中，不思而得，從

容中道，聖人也。誠之者，擇善而固執之者也。

Resolve is the way-making of *tian* 天; applying resolve is the way-making of becoming human. Resolve is achieving coalescence without coercion; it is getting what you are after without reflection. Traveling freely and easily at the center of way-making—this is the sage. Resolve is selecting what is efficacious and holding on to it firmly.

Here in Chapter 25, we witness a familiar image of an increasingly inner intensity and resolve being extended outward to have vast cosmic reach and consequence. In the *Mencius* and in these middle passages of *Focusing the Familiar*, *cheng* 誠 as resolve is elevated and projected onto the cosmos to describe the process of procreation itself, making the resolve of intense human feelings not only integral to its operations, but a source of the world's boundless capacity for growth. It is because of the cosmic power of this sentiment that resolve (*cheng* 誠) is revered by all exemplary people who understand most profoundly that the process of personal consummation (*ren* 仁) is at once collaborative and reflexive, both a source of family and community solidarity, and of a critical self-awareness. Such personal growth is coterminous with the growth of the joyful wisdom that inspires a flourishing world (*zhi* 知).

Here also we have the explicit statement that, *contra* the Mohists, subjectivity and objectivity (*neiwai* 內外) in the achieved virtuosic relationships which constitute our insistent identities (*de* 德) are a matter of aspect rather than exclusivity, a matter of degree rather than kind. What is subjective and objective are inseparable aspects of our way-making (*dao* 道). They enable us, in the process of coalescing with the content of our environments, to achieve what is optimally fitting in these relations (*yi* 宜) on the objective side, while more subjectively, to find and dispose ourselves in the most appropriate way (*yi* 義). Earlier in *Focusing the Familiar* 20, "what is optimally appropriate" (*yi* 義) as the source of moral growth has been defined paronomastically as "what is most fitting" (*yi* 宜) in any particular situation. This association provides a warrant for reading this character *yi* 宜 here as what is optimally appropriate as a source of moral as well as phenomenal significance. Moral appropriateness is the source of meaningful relations, bringing them internally into focus and resolve, and making them externally available as a source of cosmic flourishing. In this development of the uniquely Mencian reading of human resolution as a cosmic force, the text has added Mencius to Confucius and the early sages as one more sponsor of its Confucian interpretation of the cosmic reach and influence of human feelings.

As a footnote, the first lines can be read in two different ways. One reading is that the phrase 誠者自成也 "resolve is self-consummating" is merely rhetorical, and is then flatly contradicted by what follows when it states: 誠者非自成己而已也 "but resolve is not simply the self-consummating of one's own person."

Alternatively, the "self-" (*zi* 自) in the expression "self-consummating" (*zicheng* 自成) in this opening line is being used in the inclusive, symbiotic sense in which "self" and "other" are in tandem "self-completing." In the parallel structure of this opening line, *cheng* 誠 is paired with the holistic notion of *dao* 道 described as 而道自道也 "its way-making is self-directing." Since *dao* 道 clearly precludes any exclusive "other," I would think that the inclusive reading of "self-" (*zi* 自) in this first line makes better sense of the passage. Such a reading is reinforced by the holistic characterization of *cheng* 誠 that follows: 誠者物之終始，不誠無物 "Resolve is the beginning and the end of things, and without this resolve, there would be nothing." Such being the case, when it states: 誠者非自成己而已也 "but resolve is not simply the self-consummating of one's own person," the text is further clarifying the point that self and world evolve symbiotically.

V.9 Chapter 30: Confucius as a Force of Nature

仲尼祖述堯、舜，憲章文、武；上律天時，下襲水土。辟如天地之無不持載，無不覆幬，辟如四時之錯行，如日月之代明。萬物并育而不相害，道并行而不相悖，小德川流，大德敦化，此天地之所以爲大也。

Confucius revered Yao and Shun as his ancestors and carried on their ways; he emulated and made illustrious the ways of King Wen and Wu. He modeled himself above on the rhythm of the turning seasons, and below he was attuned to the patterns of water and earth. He is comparable to the heavens and the earth, sheltering and supporting everything that is. He is comparable to the progress of the four seasons, and the alternating brightness of the sun and the moon.

All things flourish together and do not cause injury to one another; their various ways are traveled together and are not conflicted. Their lesser virtuosities are seen as flowing streams; their greater virtuosities are seen as grand transformations. This is why the heavens and the earth are so grand.

Comment: Confucius is described here retrospectively as the embodiment of a continuing genealogical stream that flows from the remote ancestors down to his own time and beyond. The entire living cultural tradition is present in the person of Confucius, and is then extended over the centuries as Confucius continues to define the Chinese cultural identity. The ancestors themselves and their culture live on. In earlier chapters we have seen how the vocabulary of the human moral order such as "family reverence" (*xiao* 孝) and "virtuosity" (*de* 德) and "sincerity, resolve" (*cheng* 誠) is coincident with the natural order. In this chapter, Confucius is characterized as not only bringing the entire cultural tradition into holographic focus, but also as the embodiment of a cosmic morality inherent in the natural order itself: the harmonious turning of the seasons, the collaborative alternations of sun and moon.

There are many important implications that come along with this perceived convergence of the human and natural orders in the person of the sage. First of all, the remote and obscure concept of *tian* 天 that has both cosmic and human reference takes on a warm and immediate human visage in the person of Confucius. Confucian sages being epochal in their meaning and influence, ascend in the heavens to celestial proportions that all can see. There is a profound human-centered religious import in this pattern of sages becoming elevated as moral beacons for the ages. Again, the contrapuntal relationship between the human and natural worlds makes them mirrors of each other. Just as human beings in their project of personal cultivation are much benefited from the abundant resources of the natural and cultural context into which they are born, the natural order becomes a social category as it is complemented and enriched by the contributions of human sages. And the celebration of the beauty of the natural order in the poesy of the human being makes humankind into a natural category. The contemporary philosopher Li Zehou 李澤厚 insists the proper understanding of the mutuality of the human and cosmic orders can be captured in the symbiotic and synergistic language of "the naturalization of the human" (*rendeziranhua* 人的自然化) and "the humanization of the natural world" (*ziranderenhua* 自然的人化).

The second paragraph observes how it is the impulse of all things in the cosmos to collaborate in a shared flourishing and how their narratives take them along a common road. The ecological vitality that animates the complex transactions among things produces procreative growth and a process of generative transformation. Acknowledging the paronomastic implications of "virtuosity" (*de* 德) and "gaining, getting" (*de* 得), we can read the concluding sentence as reporting minor coalescences among things creates a steady flow while major coalescences among them brings with it the grand transformations. The greatness of the world lies in its bottomless fecundity.

V.10 Chapter 31: Optimal Sagacity (*zhisheng* 至聖)

唯天下至聖，爲能聰明睿知，足以有臨也；寬裕溫柔，足以有容也；發強剛毅，足以有執也；齊莊中正，足以有敬也；文理密察，足以有別也。溥博淵泉，而時出之。溥博如天，淵泉如淵。見而民莫不敬，言而民莫不信，行而民莫不說。是以聲名洋溢乎中國，施及蠻貊；舟車所至，人力所通，天之所覆，地之所載，日月所照，霜露所隊；凡有血氣者，莫不尊親，故曰配天。

Only those of the world with the utmost sagacity:
    have sufficient perspicacity and agility of mind to oversee the world;
    have sufficient tolerance and flexibility to win them the forbearance of others;
    have sufficient energy and fortitude to maintain their grip on things;
    have sufficient poise and impeccability to command respect;
    have sufficient refinement and discernment to be discriminating.
So broad, vast, and profoundly deep, in a timely way they express this virtuosity. So broad and vast like the heavens themselves; so profoundly deep like a bottomless abyss:
    they appear and all defer to them,
    they speak and all have confidence in what they say,
    they act and all find pleasure in what they do.
It is for this reason that their fame spreads out over the Central States, extending to the Man and Mo barbarians on the frontiers:
    everywhere that boats and carriages ply,
    everywhere that the human presence penetrates,
    everywhere that is sheltered by the heavens and borne up by the earth,
    everywhere that is illuminated by the sun and moon,
    everywhere that the frosts and dew settle—
all creatures that have breath and blood revere and love them.
Thus it is said they are the complement of *tian* 天.

Comment: We might correlate this chapter with the one that comes just before it. While Chapter 30 characterizes the person of Confucius as a force of nature, here in Chapter 31 Confucius as the person of "utmost sagacity" in similarly hyperbolic language is described as a comparable force within the precincts of the human world as well. Alternatively, we might read this chapter as turning from Confucius specifically to offer a more generic description of human sagacity itself.

There is much textual evidence to understand sagacity as the ultimate degree of coalescence (*du* 度) in the first-order, coterminous, and constitutive human-cosmic (*tianren* 天人) relationship. As we witness throughout the canonical Confucian literature, the texts repeatedly correlate these always unique sages with *tian* 天 by characterizing them metaphorically in grand, celestial terms, projecting onto the vague notion of *tian* 天 the details of a particular human face and its exemplary narrative. In these classical Confucian canons, human sagacity is understood not only as having the capacity to introduce epochal transformations in the human experience, but also as having a transformative influence on the quality of *tian* 天 and an amplificatory effect on the moral meaning of the cosmos broadly. This highest order of human "becomings" with their production of human culture are inseparable from the flourishing of nature's sublimities. That is, human beings are nothing less than a co-creative and transformative moral force in the cosmos. Confucius elevates the worth of human "becomings" by insisting that they "are able to broaden the way" (*rennenghongdao* 人能弘道). Similarly, the collaboration between sages and the cosmos can be understood as the inspiration behind Zhu Xi's proclamation that "the sages can continue and carry out the workings of *tian* 天" (*shengrennengjitianliji* 聖人能繼天立極).①

Through the patterns of deference described herein, the lives of the people are implicated in the narratives of the sages themselves. We are familiar with the liberal notion of individual autonomy, but in this holographic Confucian world the lives of the sages bring with them a kind of a relational autonomy. The sages through their achieved virtuosity establish a way of being in the world that, without coercion, draws the human and

---

① See *Analects* 15.29 and Zhu Xi's 朱熹 preface to his commentary on the *Zhongyong* 中庸章句 in his commentary on the *Four Books* 四書章句集注.

natural energy of an epoch into their narratives, and their exceptional model becomes a guiding vector for the cosmic flourishing of their time and place.

V.11 Chapter 32: Optimal Resolve (*zhicheng* 至誠)

唯天下至誠，爲能經綸天下之大經，立天下之大本，知天地之化育。夫焉有所倚？肫肫其仁！淵淵其淵！浩浩其天！苟不固聰明聖知達天德者，其孰能知之？

Only those of the world with utmost resolution are able to separate out and braid together the many threads on the great loom of the world. Only they set the great root of the world and realize the transforming and nourishing processes of the heavens and the earth. How could there be anything on which they depend?

So earnest, they are consummate (*ren* 仁);
So profound, they are a bottomless abyss (*yuan* 淵);
So pervasive, they are *tian* (*tian* 天).

And only those whose own capacities of discernment and sagely wisdom extend to the powers of *tian* 天 could possibly realize this.

Comment: The text does make a distinction between those of the world with utmost sagacity (*zhisheng* 至聖) and those with utmost resolution (*zhicheng* 至誠), but the fact that they both become coincident with *tian* 天 suggests these are indeed two aspectual ways of describing the same phenomenon. Zhu Xi in his commentary on this chapter says 然至誠之道，非至聖不能知；至聖之德，非至誠不能爲，則亦非二物矣 "Since only those of utmost sagacity are able to understand the way of utmost resolution, and only those of utmost resolution are able to carry out the virtuosity of the sage, we are not referencing two separate things here." This assumption is borne out when the language that gives an account of the transformative power of resolution overlaps in specific detail with the one reporting on the influence of sagacity. It is those who with utmost sagacity and utmost resolution who are able to become co-creators with "the transforming and nourishing processes of the heavens and the earth."

V.12 Chapter 33: The *Book of Songs* (*Shijing* 詩經) as a Confucian "Ode to Joy"

《詩》曰:"衣錦尚絅",惡其文之著也。故君子之道,闇然而日章;小人之道,的然而日亡。君子之道,淡而不厭,簡而文,溫而理,知遠之近,知風之自,知微之顯,可與入德矣。

The *Book of Songs* 88 says:
Over her brocade skirts
She wears a plain robe.

This means she did not like to make a display of her elegance.

Thus it is that the ways of exemplary persons while hidden away every day become more conspicuous; the ways of petty persons while in clear sight every day fade further away. The ways of exemplary persons are plain but not dull, they are simple yet refined, they are congenial yet coherent. It is only those who know the nearness of the distant, the origins of what has become customary, and the brilliance of what is subtle that can enter the gates of virtuosity.

《詩》云:"潛雖伏矣,亦孔之昭!"故君子內省不疚,無惡於志。君子所不可及者,其唯人之所不見乎!

The *Book of Songs* 192 says:
Although the fish have dived down to hide themselves on the bottom
Still the light makes them easy to see.

It is thus that exemplary persons on introspection find no fault and have nothing improper in their intentions. It is only what exemplary persons themselves cannot get to that others cannot see.

《詩》云:"相在爾室,尚不愧于屋漏。"故君子不動而敬,不言而信。

The *Book of Songs* 256 says:
Watch yourself as you dwell in your own residence,
Be without shame even in the most secluded corner.

It is thus that exemplary persons are respected without lifting a finger, and are credible without having spoken a word.

《詩》曰:"奏假無言,時靡有爭。"是故君子不賞而民勸,不怒而民威於鈇鉞。

The *Book of Songs* 302 says:

V. THE *FOCUSING THE FAMILIAR* (*ZHONGYONG* 中庸): THE HIGHEST EXPRESSION OF THE CONFUCIAN PROJECT

Entering and attending to the sacrifice in silence
At such a time there is no contention.

It is thus that exemplary persons without having to reward the common people are still able to get their best, and without any display of anger are held in awe more than any cleaver or axe.

《詩》曰:"不顯惟德! 百辟其刑之。"是故君子篤恭而天下平。

The *Book of Songs* 269 says:
Without making a show of his virtuosity
The various vassals model themselves on his example.

It is thus that exemplary persons being earnest and reverential, the world is at peace.

《詩》曰:"予懷明德,不大聲以色。"子曰:"聲色之於以化民,末也。"

The *Book of Songs* 241 says:
Harboring the highest virtuosity in your breast
You have no need of loud words or intimidating looks.

The Master said: "Loud words and intimidating looks are worthless in the transforming of the common people."

《詩》曰:"德輶如毛",毛猶有倫;"上天之載,無聲無臭",至矣!

The *Book of Songs* 260 says:
The influence of his virtuosity is as light as a feather.

But even a feather is too heavy in the comparison.

The *Book of Songs* 235 says:
The natural world around us goes about its work without the need of sound or scent.

How magnificent!

Comment: In this final chapter, *Focusing the Familiar* breaks into a veritable "Ode to Joy" in the sense that it is a celebration of the capacity of exemplary persons as co-creators with the heavens and the earth to make meaning and inspire the world. Just as in the *Analects*, the *Mencius*, and the *Xunzi*, *Focusing the Familiar* appeals to the *Book of Songs* more than any other source as an authority for its claims. One element in this authority arises from the association the *Book of Songs* has with Confucius himself and with Confucian education. The *Records of the Grand Historian* (*Shiji* 史記) credits Confucius with having collected some three thousand songs from the archives of the feudal courts, and then selecting out over three hundred of them in compiling the *Book of Songs*. Further, the tradition attributes its preface to one of Confucius's most prominent followers, Zixia. It is clear that Confucius regarded this text as an essential element in his curriculum, and his esteem for it helped to establish it as one of the *Five Classics*. From the Han dynasty on, the expression "the *Songs* and the *Documents*" (*ShiShu* 詩書) was used to characterize a Confucian education.

Viewing the role of the *Book of Songs* in Confucius's curriculum, it may be said to serve several purposes. First, it contains a wealth of important historical information about the cultural tradition, and lends stability to contemporary society by providing a sense of its roots and its genealogical narrative. It is a repository of cultural values that can be learned by succeeding generations. But more than simply a conduit of historical information to be learned, it is a source of creative reflection. It stimulates students to pursue personal cultivation, to exercise their imagination, to ascend to levels of heightened awareness, and to develop a deepened sense of sociability.

The *Songs* are not expository as a linear, sequential explanation of ethical imperatives that can be replicated in reproducing the moral person. Rather, it is an authoritative record of personal, social, and political experiences that, given creative adaptation, can serve as a source of inspiration for addressing issues in the present moment. As a work of art, it encourages refinement and aesthetic sensitivity. It is a source of a vocabulary that can improve oral and written skills and provide a richer medium for organizing and articulating the human experience. Important in the whirlpool of the Spring and Autumn political affairs, the *Songs* provided a shared currency for couching sensitive issues in an indirect manner. A close familiarity with the images and metaphors of the *Songs* was an essential skill for any diplomat or would-be statesman. Confucius himself summarizes the didactic function of the text in *Analects* 17.9:

子曰："小子！何莫學夫詩？詩，可以興，可以觀，可以群，可以怨。邇之事父，遠之事君。多識於鳥獸草木之名。"

The Master said, "My young friends, why aren't any of you studying the *Songs*? Reciting the *Songs* can give you inspiration and strengthen your powers of observation, and can enhance your ability to get on with others

V. THE *FOCUSING THE FAMILIAR* (*ZHONGYONG* 中庸): THE HIGHEST EXPRESSION OF THE CONFUCIAN PROJECT

and sharpen your critical skills. Near at hand it enables you to serve your father, and away at court it enables you to serve your lord. It instills in you the broad vocabulary necessary for making distinctions in the world around you: the birds and beasts, the grasses and trees."

In reciting and mastering the *Songs* and in searching for ever-widening latitude in interpreting them, students of the text locate themselves between a received tradition and always novel circumstances.

The contents of the *Book of Songs* dating from c. 1100-500 BCE is highly composite. It includes folk songs that reveal the concerns and values of early Zhou China, romantic odes about life among the nobility at court, political laments, festive ballads, ceremonial hymns, celebrations and dirges. While the *Songs* is one of our most valuable windows on the world of the early Zhou dynasty, it is a window with a rather opaque pane of glass. There are many difficulties with the language of the text. As poetry it tends toward elliptical, symbolic, and evocative expression that is at best highly elusive. Again, the frequent use of archaic and provincial language renders the *Songs* extremely difficult to interpret. For readers without the competence of its historical context, many of the allusions to customs and the subtleties of cultural institutions are now meaningless.

But Confucius activates this productive vagueness. The ambiguity of the text and the remoteness of the original authorial intentions, far from being an obstacle, serve to extend its range of interpretive possibilities in adapting it to the present human condition. The conservative Han dynasty commentators, for example, long removed from the world of the *Songs* and in an effort to reinforce the values of their own time, were quite happy to read the coupling in ribald fertility celebrations of the autumn harvest as metaphors for proper social interaction and solidarity.

The *Book of Songs* is used by philosophers to punctuate a particular philosophical point with the expectation that it adds to their argument in several ways. Philosophers in tailoring passages to serve their purposes provide clarification for the text in exchange for claiming its prestige in reinforcing their argument. And the *Songs* is persuasive by virtue of its being held in high esteem by the audience of the philosophical text. Again, the source of the unauthored song is the daily life of the people, and thus as the sound from the ground has absolute sway. The spontaneity and genuineness of the songs come from the fact that they are most often offering either blame or praise—an irrepressible protest against oppression or a public outpouring of approbation for some good deed. When a philosophical text bursts into song, it is taking full advantage of the reader's assumption that these songs do not lie. Thus, invoking a song not only clarifies the argument, but celebrates its veracity. The song also dramatizes the argument and charges it emotionally by bringing the more general and abstract assertions of the philosophical text down to earth, locating them in seemingly specific historical situations. Thus, a well-placed song not only lends veridical force to the philosopher's claims, but invests the claims with passion, and carries them to a crescendo.

VI. THE *CLASSIC OF FAMILY REVERENCE* (*XIAOJING* 孝經): THE PRIME CONFUCIAN MORAL IMPERATIVE

The date of composition of the *Classic of Family Reverence* is uncertain. Because Master Zeng appears prominently in the text, we know it could not in any case have been written much before he died in 436 BCE. It is first cited in another text (*Lüshichunqiu* 呂氏春秋) that is known on independent grounds to have been composed no later than 239 BCE. Thus, we can feel confident the *Classic of Family Reverence* was composed sometime during the Warring States period at the height of the labor convulsions that anticipated the birth of imperial China.

The lack of a specific date for the composition of the text carries over to the question of authorship. We do not know who wrote or edited the document. One tradition attributes the work to Confucius himself; another allows that the words were his but Master Zeng wrote them down. Still a third account, developed later, attributes the composition of the work to the disciples of Master Zeng—to students at two removes from Master Zeng and three from the Master himself. The fact Master Zeng is referred to honorifically as "Master" in itself recommends this third tradition as more probable. In any event, little said in the *Classic of Family Reverence* is out of keeping with what we know of Confucius and Master Zeng from the *Analects*, and it is consistent with their conversations as they appear in the *Record of Rituals* (*Liji* 禮記). We can thus surmise the text in its present form very probably dates from the early Han period if not earlier, and thus has been read and studied by some eighty generations of Chinese students and scholars.

VI. THE *CLASSIC OF FAMILY REVERENCE* (*XIAOJING* 孝經): THE PRIME CONFUCIAN MORAL IMPERATIVE

One indication of the importance of this text is the stature of the participants in the serious debates that surrounded it during its transmission, and the ferocity with which these scholars and officials advanced their arguments. In 719 the Tang Emperor Xuanzong 唐玄宗 commanded his Confucian officials to provide him with a definitive text of the *Classic of Family Reverence*. In response, one of his ministers, Liu Zhiji 劉知幾, wrote a document entitled *Twelve Items of Evidence* that advocated a return to the ancient script redaction of the text associated with the Han dynasty commentator, Kong Anguo 孔安國. This same document rejected the modern script version associated with the Zheng Xuan 鄭玄 commentarial tradition that had been edited by Liu Xiang 劉向 and had served as the basis for the popularly received text, claiming it was a later forgery. Another minister of Emperor Xuanzong, Sima Zhen 司馬貞, challenged Liu Zhiji's assertions, providing his own evidence that in fact it was the ancient script version endorsed by Liu that was a spurious text concocted by later Confucians, and that both the Kong and Zheng commentarial traditions had to be consulted. Emperor Xuanzong, in an attempt to restore order, ultimately insisted that indeed both versions had to be preserved, revising his own 712 commentary in 743. He then had the text and his imperial commentary literally carved in stone in order to perpetuate its influence in the world, and had it placed before the entrance to the Chang'an academy as his endorsement of its canonical stature. From then on, his imperial commentary superseded the Kong and Zheng commentaries as providing the standard text.

Again in the Northern Song dynasty, the great statesman Wang Anshi 王安石 wrote his "Explanations of the *Classic of Family Reverence*" based on the modern script text, only to inspire the equally prominent Sima Guang 司馬光 to find a copy of the ancient script version in the national archives to compile his counterpoint, "An Exposition of the Ancient Script *Classic of Family Reverence*." And thereafter the Southern Song philosopher Zhu Xi 朱熹 wrote his famous "Amended Text of the *Classic of Family Reverence*" 孝經刊誤, arguing that only a third of what was purported to be the *Classic of Family Reverence* was in fact the original text. Subsequently, the imperial commentary of Emperor Xuanzong and the amended text of Zhu Xi competed for authority within the academy, eclipsing any influence of the original Kong and Zheng commentaries.

From its origins in the prehistoric past, an ever-evolving Chinese culture has been unique among the world's civilizations, both in terms of its unbroken continuity, and in the rich and varied institutional, material, and conceptual artifacts its peoples have produced. At the same time, this richness and variety guarantees many of these artifacts will have at least partial counterparts in other civilizations, thus making it difficult to isolate, in brief compass, what it is about Chinese culture that does indeed make it unique. Nevertheless, upon entering into China's past, certain major themes emerge as they are repeatedly expressed in different facets of Chinese life. One of these themes is the centrality of the family that has thoroughly permeated the socio-political, economic, metaphysical, moral, and religious dimensions of Chinese history since at least the early Neolithic period. A fair argument can be made that all relationships within a Chinese world—social, political, and indeed cosmic relations—are conceived of as familial. In the classroom the teacher is "teacher-father or teacher-mother (*shifu* 師父 or *shimu* 師母)" and students are "older-sister student and younger-brother student (*xuejie* 學姐 and *xuedi* 學弟)." From earliest times the Emperor was known as the "Son of 'Heaven' (*tianzi* 天子)" and as "father and mother of the heavens and the earth (*futianmudi* 父天母地)." Later his country-level civil servants who represented the dragon throne were colloquially designated as the "father-mother officials (*fumuguan* 父母官)." And in the cosmos, even the heavens and the earth (*tiandi* 天地 or *qiankun* 乾坤) stand in a familial relationship to one another.

To be sure, family structures and associated values are found in virtually every culture past and present. Kinship relations have been a central focus of anthropological field studies since the discipline began, and family values have been prominent in the development of Western civilization since the days of the Hebrew scriptures. Eight of the Ten Commandments are negatively phrased; the obligation to honor our parents is one of the two that is not. In China, family values were discernible as fundamental throughout the culture. Physical evidence of ancestral sacrifices has been found in archaeological remains from as early as the fifth millennium BCE. It should therefore come as no surprise that "family reverence" (*xiao* 孝) was one of the most basic and defining values of the Chinese people, especially the early Confucians. Indeed, one may even go so far as to say that for them, filial reverence was a *necessary* condition for developing any of the other human qualities they deemed integral to a consummate life. In the Confucian tradition, human morality and the personal realization it inspires is grounded in the cultivation of family feeling as it is reflected in the isomorphism between family and political order. In the *Analects of Confucius* 1.2, we read:

VI. THE *CLASSIC OF FAMILY REVERENCE* (*XIAOJING* 孝經): THE PRIME CONFUCIAN MORAL IMPERATIVE

有子曰："其爲人也孝弟，而好犯上者，鮮矣；不好犯上，而好作亂者，未之有也。君子務本，本立而道生。孝弟也者，其爲仁之本與！"

Master You said: "It is a rare thing for someone who has a sense of family reverence and fraternal responsibility (*xiaoti* 孝弟) to have a taste for defying authority. And it is unheard of for those who have no taste for defying authority to be keen on initiating rebellion. Exemplary persons (*junzi* 君子) concentrate their efforts on the root, for the root having been properly set, the vision of the moral life (*dao* 道) will grow therefrom. As for family reverence and fraternal deference, these are, I suspect, the root of becoming consummate in one's conduct (*ren* 仁)."

While nowhere does the *Classic of Family Reverence* advocate the abolition of the aristocracy, it does make it clear that true aristocrats are such because of the nobility of their exemplary qualities, not their bloodlines. Ten of the eighteen chapters of this text, in a pattern typical of the early Confucian canons, conclude with a quote from the *Book of Songs* (*Shijing* 詩經). Although regularly cited in support of some weighty aesthetic, ethical, political, and religious points that Confucius and other early philosophers wished to make, the original 305 verses that comprise the *Songs* are just that: songs to be intoned or chanted aloud. Collectively they paint a picture of life in early historical China. Indeed, it is because the *Book of Songs* is an anonymous reflection on life in early China capturing the honest feelings of the people broadly, that it has had enormous affective force in closing an argument or endorsing some interpretive observations. The veracity of the *Book of Songs* is quite simply beyond dispute, making it a favorite device among philosophers for terminating discussion by clinching their point.

In sum then, the reader of the *Classic of Family Reverence* needs to keep in mind the routine life of the people during the period in which this document was compiled, and to appreciate how these practices lived on in the tradition to shape the values and the character of Chinese culture. The text's call to preserve the past and respect tradition may be construed not merely as the lament of reactionary and authoritarian intellectuals, but also as containing the keen insight that much of who and what we are is always linked to the past. It is a complex and even fluid past in the sense that it is constantly being reinterpreted by those in the present moment in service to the arcs of change that will bring about a desired future.

VI.1 Chapter 1: Setting the Theme and Illuminating Its Meaning (開宗明義章)

仲尼居，曾子侍。子曰：＂先王有至德要道，以順天下，民用和睦，上下無怨。汝知之乎？＂曾子避席曰：＂參不敏，何足以知之？＂子曰：＂夫孝，德之本也，教之所由生也。復坐，吾語汝。身體髮膚，受之父母，不敢毀傷，孝之始也。立身行道，揚名於後世，以顯父母，孝之終也。夫孝，始於事親，中於事君，終於立身。《大雅》云：＇無念爾祖，聿修厥德。＇＂

Confucius was at leisure at home, and Master Zeng was attending him. The Master said: "Do you understand how the Former Kings were able to use the model of their consummate virtuosity (*de* 德) and their vital way (*dao* 道) to bring the world into accord? And how the people on this account were able to attain harmony (*he* 和) and to live with each other as good neighbors, and benefactors and beneficiaries did not resent each other?"

Master Zeng rose from his mat to respond, and said: "I am not clever enough to understand such things."

"It is familial reverence (*xiao* 孝)," said the Master, "that is the root of moral virtuosity (*de* 德), and whence education (*jiao* 教) itself is born. Please sit down again, and I will explain it to you.

"Your physical person with its hair and skin are received from your parents. Vigilance in not allowing anything to do injury to your person is where family reverence begins; distinguishing yourself and walking the proper way (*dao* 道) in the world; raising your name high for posterity and thereby bringing esteem to your father and mother—it is in these things family reverence finds its consummation. This family reverence then begins in service to your parents, continues in service to your lord, and culminates in distinguishing yourself in the world.

"In the 'Greater Odes' section of the *Book of Songs* 235 it says:
How can you not remember your ancestor, King Wen?
You must cultivate yourself and extend his virtuosity."

Comment: In classical Confucianism, Confucius' protégée Master Zeng 曾子 is the paradigmatic figure most closely associated with the fullest expression of "family reverence" (*xiao* 孝). In the *Classic of Family Reverence*, Confucius begins by elevating *xiao* 孝 to be Confucianism's highest moral imperative, declaring that this "way of family reverence" is the very substance of morality and education: "It is family reverence (*xiao* 孝)

VI. THE *CLASSIC OF FAMILY REVERENCE* (*XIAOJING* 孝經): THE PRIME CONFUCIAN MORAL IMPERATIVE

that is the root of moral virtuosity, and whence education (*jiao* 教) itself is born." The opening chapter of this text goes on to provide us with the familiar radial progression we find consistently in the Confucian literature from a determinate center to an unbounded extreme. It begins from respect for one's own person as what is closest at hand, extends such concern to the care for one's family and kin, and then culminates in dedicating one's service to one's ruler and to posterity. In this passage, King Wen— that is, King "Culture" (*wen* 文)—is singled out as the source from which the current generation draws its inspiration and to whom, with the cultural dividends it can accrue, will make appropriate return.

The charge in this passage to keep the body intact certainly refers to a person's own carnal physicality, but it also lends itself to an importantly broader, cultural reading. That is, each succeeding generation has the responsibility of keeping the corpus of culture it comes to embody whole and alive. Indeed, we might offer the following as an alternative reading of the concluding citation from the *Book of Songs*: "How can you fail to embody the culture of your ancestors? You must cultivate yourself and extend its reach and influence."

Confucian role ethics in substance is perpetuated through family lineages that have complex political, economic, and religious functions. There are two cognate characters integral to the dynamics of "family reverence" (*xiao* 孝) in the intergenerational transmission of the continuities of the family lineage: *ti* 體 ("embodying," "body," "forming and shaping," "category," "class") and *li* 禮 ("ritual," "achieving propriety in one's roles and relations"). Without the formal and determinate dimension provided by the living body (*ti* 體), and without the social grammar afforded by meaningful roles and relations (*li* 禮), there is real question of whether cultural refinement would be possible. Put simply, determinate forms in their many different variations—body, ritual, language, the institutions of family and ancestral reverence, and so on—are a necessary condition for cultural refinement. It is the collaboration of form and vitality—the "living body" (*ti* 體) and its "embodied living" (*li* 禮)—that extends the tradition. Embodiment provides the narrative site for the conveyance and the continuing refinement of the culture, and allows a living civilization in all of its parts to be perpetuated: its language, its mores and values, its religious rituals, its aesthetics of cooking, song, and dance, and so on.

VI.2 Chapter 2: The Emperor as Son of *Tian* (天子章)

子曰: "愛親者，不敢惡於人；敬親者，不敢慢於人。愛敬盡於事親，而德教加於百姓，刑於四海。蓋天子之孝也。《甫刑》云: '一人有慶，兆民賴之。'"

The Master said: "The emperor who loves (*ai* 愛) his own parents would not presume to dislike the parents of others, and who respects (*jing* 敬) his own parents would not presume to be rude to the parents of others. With love and respect being fully expressed in this service to his parents, such conduct will educate and morally transform (*dejiao* 德教) the people, serving them as a model in all corners of the world. Such then is the family reverence of the emperor. The *Book of Documents* says: "Where this one person behaves so well in serving his parents, the entire population will look up to his example."

Comment: A fundamental precept in Confucian political philosophy is the suasive force of the ruler as moral exemplar captured here with the term *dejiao* 德教: morally transformative education. This assumption is grounded in the perceived coincidence between morality and education, both of which are a function of growth in relations. The chapters 3-6 that follow extend the influence of family reverence as an organizing structure from the person of the emperor himself, down to his hereditary vassal lords, to the ministers and high officials, and then on to the lower officials, culminating by bringing in the common people. Family reverence is expressed in the proper use of resources, in respect for traditional customs and dress, in having circumspection in the use of language, in the appropriateness of conduct, and in the continuation of ancestral sacrifices, with the aspiration being to bring the world into proper accord (*shun* 順). The isomorphism between family and state is immediately in evidence when the love and devotion within the family and the respect for parents has its political application as loyalty to one's lord (*zhong* 忠). We will see in Chapter 15 that this same *zhong* 忠 as "doing one's best" at home and "loyalty" to one's lord is qualified by the stern obligation the younger generation and loyal ministers have to remonstrate (*jian* 諫) with those above when the conduct of elders and one's lord is perceived as morally suspect.

VI. THE *CLASSIC OF FAMILY REVERENCE* (*XIAOJING* 孝經): THE PRIME CONFUCIAN MORAL IMPERATIVE

VI.3 Chapter 6: The Common People (庶人章)

用天之道，分地之利，謹身節用，以養父母，此庶人之孝也。故自天子至於庶人，孝無終始，而患不及者，未之有也。

By making the most of the seasonal cycle (*dao* 道) and discriminating among the earth's resources to best advantage, and by being circumspect in their conduct and frugal in what they consume, they take proper care of their parents. Such then is the family reverence of the common people.

Thus it is for the emperor down to the common people, the way of family reverence is inclusive and comprehensive, and there should be no one concerned they are inadequate to their task.

Comment: The function of family reverence (*xiao* 孝) in bringing accord to the world is extended to the use of natural resources in the lives of the common people. This sequence of chapters from 2-6 is reminiscent of *Expansive Learning* 1 in which it states: 自天子以至於庶人，壹是皆以修身爲本 "from the emperor down to the common folk, everything is rooted in personal cultivation." This Confucian project of personal cultivation is expressed in many different ways in the roles and occupations that define the human community, but the one commonality is family reverence is the prime moral imperative and the substance of education for everyone.

VI.4 Chapter 7: The Three Powers and Resources (三才章)

曾子曰："甚哉，孝之大也！"子曰："夫孝，天之經也，地之義也，民之行也。天地之經，而民是則之。則天之明，因地之利，以順天下。是以其教不肅而成，其政不嚴而治。先王見教之可以化民也，是故先之以博愛，而民莫遺其親，陳之德義，而民興行。先之以敬讓，而民不爭；導之以禮樂，而民和睦；示之以好惡，而民知禁。《詩》云：'赫赫師尹，民具爾瞻。'"

Master Zeng said, "Incredible—the profundity of family reverence!"

The Master continued, "Indeed, family reverence is the constancy of the heavenly cycles, the appropriate responsiveness (*yi* 義) of the earth, and proper conduct on the part of the people. It is the constant workings of the heavens and the earth that the people model themselves upon. Taking the illumination (*ming* 明) of the heavens as their model and making the most of the earth's resources, they bring the world into proper accord. This is the reason education can be effective without being severe, and governance can maintain proper order without being harsh.

"The Former Kings saw their teachings (*jiao* 教) were able to transform the people. Thus, setting their own example of magnanimity (*bo'ai* 博愛) before the people, none of them would neglect their parents; demonstrating moral virtuosity and appropriateness (*yi* 義) in their own actions, the people were inspired to conduct themselves accordingly; setting their own example of respect (*jing* 敬) and reverence before the people, they did not contend among themselves; guiding the people with ritual propriety (*li* 禮) and music (*yue* 樂), the people found harmony (*he* 和) and accord with each other; showing the people what they deemed acceptable and unacceptable, the people understood what was proscribed. The *Book of Songs* 191 says, 'Illustrious Grand Tutor Yin, the people all look up to you.'"

Comment: As announced in *Focusing the Familiar* 22, 唯天下至誠……可以與天地參矣 "Only those in the world of utmost resolve . . . can take their place in a triad with the heavens and the earth." The intense human feeling of "resolve" (*cheng* 誠) with its power to make meaning is elevated to cosmic status. In the *Classic of Family Reverence* the prime moral imperative "family reverence" (*xiao* 孝) is also invested with such cosmic force. And the argument here is that in this Confucian cosmology, human culture as the product of a collaboration with the cosmos, far from being artificial as an exception to nature, is as natural as birdsong, the barking of dogs, the turning seasons, and the falling rains. It is this perceived Confucian "nature-culture" that is captured in the mantra, "the continuity between and inseparability of the human and the cosmic orders" (*tianrenheyi* 天人合一). What is most natural arises from aligning the operations of human arts and technologies with the values the human world shares with the heavens and the earth.

In this chapter, the grand analogy is just as the ruler in his moral virtuosity integrates his conduct with the moral order of nature, so the common people in their conduct are transformed by the exemplary role model set by the ruler. Important here is a first order, symbiotic relationship that obtains among the three powers wherein each is inspired and animated by the others. Rather than mere imitation or replication, there is a productive synergy among them.

VI.5 Chapter 8: Effecting Sociopolitical Order Through Family Reverence (孝治章)

子曰："昔者明王之以孝治天下也，不敢遺小國之臣，而況於公、侯、伯、子、男乎？故得萬國之歡心，以事其先王。治國者，不敢侮於鰥寡，而況於士民乎？故得百姓之歡心，以事其先君。治家者，不敢失於臣妾，而況於妻子乎？故得人之歡心，以事其親。夫然，故生則親安之，祭則鬼享之。是以天下和平，災害不生，禍亂不作。故明王之以孝治天下也如此。《詩》云：'有覺德行，四國順之。'"

The Master said: "Of old when the enlightened kings (*mingwang* 明王) used family reverence (*xiao* 孝) to effect proper order in the world, they would not presume to neglect the ministers of the smallest state, how much less so the dukes, earls, and other members of the high nobility. Thus, all of the different vassals participated wholeheartedly in their service to these Former Kings. Those who would effect proper order in the vassal states would not presume to ignore the most dispossessed, how much less so the lower officials and common people. Thus, the people all participated wholeheartedly in their service to these former lords. Those who would effect proper order in their families would not presume to overlook their servants and concubines, how much less so their wives and children. Thus, all of the people participated wholeheartedly in their service to their parents. In such a world, the parents while living enjoyed the comforts parents deserve, and as spirits after death took pleasure in the sacrificial offerings made to them.

"Hence the world was harmonious (*he* 和) and free of strife, natural disasters did not occur, and man-made calamities were averted. In this way the enlightened kings used family reverence to effect order in the world. The *Book of Songs* 256 says: 'So admirable is the moral virtuosity of his conduct that all of the states from the four quarters accord with him.'"

Comment: Family reverence (*xiao* 孝) is the basis for effecting order in the state from top to bottom. In Confucian philosophy, rather than appealing to an "us" and "them" rhetoric, there is a perceived symbiotic relationship between proper social and political order. From the king down to the common people, everyone including the deceased ancestors are included in the social organism, and have their proper role within it. We must be cognizant of the important function the solemnity of ancestral sacrifice has in reinforcing a sense of structure, continuity, and belonging. And we must also note that natural disasters as well as man-made calamities are omens interpreted in this tradition as announcing a failure in governance, reflecting the aspectual and mutually entailing nature of the "three powers" relationship (*sancai* 三才).

VI.6 Chapter 9: Sagely Governance (聖治章)

曾子曰：" 敢問聖人之德，無以加於孝乎？" 子曰：" 天地之性，人爲貴。人之行，莫大於孝。孝莫大於嚴父。嚴父莫大於配天，則周公其人也。昔者，周公郊祀後稷以配天，宗祀文王於明堂，以配上帝。是以四海之内，各以其職來祭。夫聖人之德，又何以加於孝乎？故親生之膝下，以養父母日嚴。聖人因嚴以教敬，因親以教愛。聖人之教，不肅而成，其政不嚴而治，其所因者本也。父子之道，天性也，君臣之義也。父母生之，續莫大焉。君親臨之，厚莫重焉。故不愛其親而愛他人者，謂之悖德；不敬其親而敬他人者，謂之悖禮。以順則逆，民無則焉。不在於善，而皆在於凶德，雖得之，君子不貴也。君子則不然，言思可道，行思可樂，德義可尊，作事可法，容止可觀，進退可度，以臨其民。是以其民畏而愛之，則而象之。故能成其德教，而行其政令。《詩》云：'淑人君子，其儀不忒。' "

Master Zeng said: "May I presume to ask if there is anything in the moral virtuosity (*de* 德) of the sages (*shengren* 聖人) more profound than family reverence?"

The Master replied: "Of all of the creatures in the world, the human being is the most noble. In human conduct there is nothing more important than family reverence; in family reverence there is nothing more important than venerating one's father; in venerating one's father there is nothing more important than placing him on a par with *tian* 天. And the Duke of Zhou was able to do this.

"Of old the Duke of Zhou performed the *jiao* 郊 sacrifice on the outskirts of the capital to the first ancestor of the House of Zhou, Hou Ji, to place him on a par with the numinous *tian* 天. And in the Hall of Light he performed the ancestral sacrifice to his father, King Wen, to place him on a par with the numinous *shangdi* 上帝. It was for this reason the all of the nobility within the four seas came each according to his office to assist in the sacrifices. How then could there be something in the moral virtuosity of the sages more profound than family reverence?

"Affectionate feeling for parents begins at their knee, and as children take proper care of their fathers and mothers, this veneration increases with the

VI. THE *CLASSIC OF FAMILY REVERENCE* (*XIAOJING* 孝經): THE PRIME CONFUCIAN MORAL IMPERATIVE

passing of each day. The sages build upon this veneration in their teachings about respect, and build upon this affection in their teachings about love. In these teachings proffered by the sages they are able to be effective without being severe. That in their governing they achieve proper order without being harsh is because what they are building upon lies at the very root.

"The proper way (*dao* 道) between father and son is their natural propensities (*xing* 性) that by extension become the appropriate relationship (*yi* 義) between ruler and minister. There is no bond more important than father and mother giving life to their progeny, and there is no generosity more profound than the care and concern this progeny receives from their ruler and parents.

"It is for this reason that to love others while not loving one's parents is depravity (*beide* 悖德), and that to respect others while not respecting one's parents is a sacrilege (*beili* 悖禮). To base the norms to be followed upon such perversity would leave the people without any standards. No decency is to be found in this—only decadence (*xiongde* 凶德). Even though such persons might enjoy a measure of success, exemplary persons (*junzi* 君子) would find nothing to admire.

"Exemplary persons are nothing like this. They are concerned that what they say be credible, and that what they do be a source of rejoicing (*le* 樂). Their moral virtuosity (*de* 德) and their sense of appropriateness (*yi* 義) is to be esteemed and they are to be emulated in what they do. In their bearing and deportment they are to be looked up to, and in their undertakings they are to be taken as a standard. It is in this way that they care for their people. This is why the people, holding them in awe, love them, and taking them as their models, emulate them. Thus, they are able to succeed in dispensing their moral education (*dejiao* 德教) and in carrying out effective policies.

"The *Book of Songs* 152 says: 'This good man, our lord, in his comportment he is beyond reproach.'"

Comment: The conduct of the Duke of Zhou is a paradigm for family reverence that includes proper deference to the founding ancestor of the House of Zhou and his father as well, elevating them both to be on a par with the intense numinous forces of *tian* 天 and *shangdi* 上帝. What does this mean?

The wisdom of the sages invested in shaping their institutions around the value of family reverence (*xiao* 孝) lies in the fact that they are constructing the social and political edifice on firm ground. As the text states:

其所因者本也 "what they are building upon lies at the very root." In a Confucian world, because persons are born into family relations that are considered constitutive of their persons, their "natural propensities" (*xing* 性) are a combination of initial conditions and acting upon their prosocial inclinations. Their cultivated cognitive, moral, aesthetic, and religious sensibilities emerge out of their shared narratives within the locus of family. That is, persons rather than being perceived as discrete entities defined by common traits are to be understood from their inchoate beginnings as embedded in and nurtured by unique, transactional patterns of relations. The notion of ritual practices (*li* 禮) locates what we refer to as "moral" conduct within the transactions of thick and richly textured patterns of vital relations.

Family affection is thus natural in the human experience. Beginning immediately at birth, such feelings only grow stronger with the passage of time. While coming from within, such feelings are shaped and given definition in the various roles and relations that make up family, communal, and political living. Deference to one's parents is the natural response of children to the life they are given, and to the love and generosity the parents extend to them. Such deference becomes respect, and in the fullness of time, respect becomes reverence. Thus it is that the ultimate commitment of children to their parents lies in the solemn sacrifices they perform to their ancestors and to the vague but intense spiritual world associated with the notions of *tian* 天 and *shangdi* 上帝. Confucius in *Analects* 3.12 in saying: 吾不與祭，如不祭 "If I myself do not participate in the sacrifice, it is as though I have not sacrificed at all" is speaking specifically to the practice of sacrifice, but in fact he is expressing a commitment to a reverential way of life in all of its parts.

Persons become exemplary not through performing heroic deeds, but by providing the common people with a model for living a life informed by family reverence as their guiding moral imperative. It is the lives of these exemplary persons that come to define the moral vocabulary of the people, and serve as role models in a transformative moral education. It is thus that the people are able to channel their natural feelings in ways that give optimal service to the flourishing community and its family-centered religiousness.

VI.7 Chapter 12: Expanding upon the Essential Way (廣要道章)

子曰：" 教民親愛，莫善於孝。教民禮順，莫善於悌。移風易俗，莫善於樂。安上治民，莫善於禮。禮者，敬而已矣。故敬其父，則子悅；敬其兄，則弟悅；敬其君，則臣悅；敬一人，而千萬人悅。所敬者寡，而悅者衆，此之謂要道也。"

The Master said: "There is nothing more effective than family reverence (*xiao* 孝) for teaching (*jiao* 教) the common people about love and family affection; there is nothing more effective than deference toward elders (*ti* 悌) for teaching the people about ritual propriety (*li* 禮) and accord; there is nothing more effective than music (*yue* 樂) for elevating the customs and cultural habits of the people; and there is nothing more effective for securing the place of the lord and bringing proper order to the people than ritual practices.

"The practices of ritual propriety are simply a matter of respect (*jing* 敬). Thus, the son finds pleasure in respecting his father; the younger brother finds pleasure in respecting his elder brother; the minister finds pleasure in respecting his lord; and all of the people find pleasure in respecting the emperor. Those who are respected are few, but those who find pleasure in showing this respect are legion. This is what is called the essential way (*dao* 道)."

Comment: Even though the moral imperative of family reverence (*xiao* 孝) is in many respects straightforward and intuitively simple, the moral implications are manifold and deep. The generic concept of family reverence is dirempted into a cluster of terms made specific by the feelings expressed in different roles and relations within the family, community, and polity. In its broadest compass, *xiao* 孝 is the motive force behind the intergenerational transmission of the cultural legacy in all of its parts. To ground a vision of the consummate human life in family reverence is to assert each succeeding generation is the teacher of the generation that is to follow it. It is important to keep this idea of generational continuities and changes via lineages in mind when reading these canonical texts. The engine that provides both the intensity in this transmission and its continuing momentum is the symbiotic relationship between respect and pleasure. Feelings of respect are directed by the older generation toward the living tradition it is inheriting from those who have come before. And as this cultural legacy comes to define them and to infuse their lives with meaning, a sense of profound pleasure and gratitude rises up within them. Again, when this older generation turns to view the younger generation following behind them, they sense this same deference as it is expressed towards them as their heirs come to embody both the transmitted legacy and the additional cultural connector the older generation has constructed in their own time. This sense of embodiment means ancestors and family elders quite literally live on in their progeny, and the body of living culture remains intact. The acknowledgment of "if not for them, no me" makes the ancestors and elders an object of reverence and a source of joy.

VI.8 Chapter 13: Expanding on the Utmost Moral Virtuosity (廣至德章)

子曰：" 君子之教以孝也，非家至而日見之也。教以孝，所以敬天下之爲人父者也。教以悌，所以敬天下之爲人兄者也。教以臣，所以敬天下之爲人君者也。《詩》云：'愷悌君子，民之父母。' 非至德，其孰能順民如此其大者乎！"

The Master said: "Exemplary rulers (*junzi* 君子) in their teachings (*jiao* 教) on family reverence do not travel daily from one family to the next to meet with each of them individually. That they are teaching family reverence is their way of showing respect (*jing* 敬) for every father in the world; that they are teaching fraternal deference (*ti* 悌) is their way of showing respect for every older brother in the world; that they are teaching ministerial deference is their way of showing respect for every lord in the world.

"The *Book of Songs* 251 says: 'The kind and congenial lord—he is the father and mother of the people.' If he were not someone of consummate moral virtuosity, how could he be the person to bring such remarkable accord to the people?"

Comment: The term *junzi* 君子 that can be rendered either "lord" or "exemplary person" is somewhat ambiguous in this passage, where it is unclear if it is referencing the political position of the lord or those persons of exemplary character. The citation from the *Book of Songs* at the end suggests the former, but it also allows us to combine the two. Exemplary rulers do not need to go from door to door to school the people. They teach by way of the values they choose to teach and how they model these same values in their own lives. The advocacy of exemplary persons for the doctrine of family reverence (*xiao* 孝) and the values of fraternal (*ti* 悌) and ministerial deference that follow from it sets the prime moral imperative for the cultural tradition and each generation that carries it forward. And living according to these precepts themselves and thus becoming role models for the people, they expand the reach and influence of this imperative.

VI.9 Chapter 15: On Remonstrance (諫諍章)

曾子曰:"若夫慈愛、恭敬、安親、揚名,則聞命矣。敢問子從父之令,可謂孝乎?"子曰:"是何言與,是何言與!昔者天子有爭臣七人,雖無道,不失其天下;諸侯有爭臣五人,雖無道,不失其國;大夫有爭臣三人,雖無道,不失其家;士有爭友,則身不離於令名;父有爭子,則身不陷於不義。故當不義,則子不可以不爭於父,臣不可以不爭於君;故當不義,則爭之。從父之令,又焉得爲孝乎!"

Master Zeng said: "Parental love (*ai* 愛), reverence and respect (*jing* 敬), seeing to the well-being of one's parents, and raising one's name (*ming* 名) high for posterity—on these topics I have received your instructions. I would presume to ask whether children can be deemed filial (*xiao* 孝) simply by obeying every command of their father."

"What on earth are you saying? What on earth are you saying?" replied the Master. "Of old, an emperor had seven ministers who would remonstrate with him, so even if he had no vision of the proper way (*dao* 道), he still did not lose the world. The high nobles had five ministers who would remonstrate with them, so even if they had no vision of the proper way, they still did not lose their states. The high officials had three ministers who would remonstrate with them, so even if they had no vision of the proper way, they still did not lose their clans. If the lower officials had just one friend who would remonstrate with them, they were still able to preserve their good name (*ming* 名). If a father has a son who will remonstrate with him, he will not behave reprehensibly (*buyi* 不義).

"Thus, if confronted by reprehensible behavior on his father's part, a son has no choice but to remonstrate with his father, and if confronted by reprehensible behavior on his ruler's part, a minister has no choice but to remonstrate with his ruler. Hence, remonstrance is the only response to immorality. How could simply obeying the commands of one's father be deemed filial?"

Comment: In this text, the familiar Confucian vocabulary—"consummate person or conduct" (*ren* 仁), "optimal appropriateness" (*yi* 義), "ritual propriety" (*li* 禮), and "wisdom" (*zhi* 智)—is somewhat muted by a sustained focus upon family reverence (*xiao* 孝) as the root from which the entire tradition grows. In this holistic way of understanding morality, these other terms that define the Confucian tradition derive their relevance and meaning from being rooted within the context of the flourishing family. Simply put, when family reverence is functioning effectively within the home, all is well within the community, the polity, and indeed, the cosmos. Family reverence is the root, and as *Analects* 1.2 states explicitly, 本立而道生 "the root having been properly set, the vision of the moral life (*dao* 道) will grow therefrom." Although it is not certain the *Classic of Family Reverence* records the actual words of Confucius, based upon the received corpus, the centrality of the notion of family reverence in classical Confucian philosophy cannot be disputed. It is intimately and organically linked to the cluster of other concepts central to this philosophical and religious tradition.

We must resist any simplistic equation between family reverence (*xiao* 孝) and blind obedience. *Xiao* 孝 that is inclusive of the deference children owe their elders must be distinguished clearly from the unilateral *paterfamilias* we associate with Roman law as the juridical *patria potestas* or power and privilege of the father who owns the lives of his children. Indeed, in the Confucian tradition, there are times when being truly filial within the family, as being a truly loyal minister within the court, requires courageous remonstrance (*jian* 諫) rather than automatic compliance. And indeed, in this doctrine of family reverence, such remonstrance is not perceived as merely a possibility or an option one might choose, but as a stern if not sacred obligation. One unremarked aspect of the "two-ness" of consummate person/conduct (*ren* 仁) that parallels this key role of remonstrance, is the cultivation of a critical self-awareness and sense of shame that can serve as a perspective from which to critique one's own roles as well as those of others.

Clearly obedience and loyalty, while necessary qualities of exemplary persons (*junzi* 君子), are not sufficient; what is also needed is the commitment at all times to do what is optimally appropriate (*yi* 義) within the larger familial, moral, and spiritual context. We can see and appreciate, perhaps, how both obedience and loyalty, on the one hand, and remonstrance on the other, are to be valued as the complementary dimensions of family reverence, contributing as they do to becoming *ren* 仁 persons on the basis of *li* 禮 behavior within family and community. And we can equally see how the political importance of obedience to authority and yet of courageously challenging this authority when necessary, might conduce to good governance.

Indeed, *Xunzi* 29 takes on this same theme, and devotes an entire chapter to various stories that provide concrete examples of how blind obedience to the older generation, far from promoting family reverence, offends against this very same value by producing different but consistently dire consequences.

VI.10 Chapter 18: Mourning for Parents (喪親章)

子曰：" 孝子之喪親也，哭不偯，禮無容，言不文，服美不安，聞樂不樂，食旨不甘，此哀戚之情也。三日而食，教民無以死傷生。毀不滅性，此聖人之政也。喪不過三年，示民有終也。爲之棺槨衣衾而舉之，陳其簠簋而哀戚之；擗踴哭泣，哀以送之；卜其宅兆，而安措之；爲之宗廟，以鬼享之；春秋祭祀，以時思之。生事愛敬，死事哀戚，生民之本盡矣，死生之義備矣，孝子之事親終矣。"

The Master said: "When filial children are in mourning for a parent, they weep without prolonged wailing, they participate in the funeral ceremony (*li* 禮) with little attention to their personal appearance, and they speak plainly without trying to be eloquent. They are uncomfortable in elegant clothing, are unable to find any enjoyment (*le* 樂) in listening to music (*yue* 樂), and have no appetite for fine food. This is because of their feelings of distress.

"After three days, they break their fast in order to teach (*jiao* 教) others not to harm the living on account of the dead, and not to threaten life through a lack of restraint. This is the policy laid down by the sages. The course of mourning must not exceed three years to make it clear to the people they must find closure.

"The inner and outer coffins are prepared, the burial shroud is readied, the corpse is dressed and covered, and is then lifted into the coffin. The funerary vessels are set out with grief and sorrow. Beating their breasts and stamping their feet, weeping and wailing, the mourners escort the coffin to the gravesite. Divination is used to determine the proper location, and the body is interred in peace. The ancestral temple is prepared to make offerings to the spirit of the deceased, and the spring and autumn sacrifices are performed to provide occasion to cherish the memory of the departed.

"When their parents are alive they are served with love (*ai* 愛) and respect (*jing* 敬), and when deceased they are served with grief and sorrow. This is the basic duty being discharged by the living, the fulfilling of the appropriate obligations (*yi* 義) between the living and the dead, and the consummation of the service filial children owe their parents."

Comment: A continuous thread integral to the doctrine of family reverence is the love and respect to be paid parents when alive, and the proper grief and sorrow due them on the occasion of their death. These feelings of distress continue during the prescribed mourning period, and are vented in the pattern of sacrifices that celebrate their memory. These natural feelings have been institutionalized by the sages in great detail as a way of revering the dead in service to the continuing life of the family and the tradition itself. In all of this reverence for family, there is an emphasis upon a personal authenticity over external formalities. There is also insight into the fact that grief can lead to excesses which will compromise the living, doing them real harm. Just as there is a healthy death, there is a healthy sense of grieving where the living themselves must remain whole in order to remember properly those who have departed.

VII. THE *FIVE MODES OF VIRTUOSIC CONDUCT* (*WUXINGPIAN* 五行篇): THE INTERIM BETWEEN CONFUCIUS AND MENCIUS

Five Modes of Virtuosic Conduct (*Wuxingpian* 五行篇) is an ancient but only recently recovered document. Two versions of this text belonging to what the scholar Guo Moruo in the 1940s came to call the Zisizi-Mengzi lineage (SiMengxuepai 思孟學派) have been recovered in two separate archaeological sites. The first find was at Mawangdui 馬王堆, Changsha, Hunan in 1973 on a silk text dating to 168 BCE, and then the second was at Guodian 郭店, Jingmen 荊門, Hubei in 1993 on bamboo strips dating from c. 300 BCE. The fact that redactions of this same text have been found at such a physical and temporal distance from each other speaks to the perceived importance of the document within its own historical context. This seminal document is in the same lineage as *Focusing the Familiar* that, as we have seen above, argues that human beings through personal cultivation have both the capacity and the responsibility to serve as

VII. THE *FIVE MODES OF VIRTUOSIC CONDUCT* (*WUXINGPIAN* 五行篇): THE INTERIM BETWEEN CONFUCIUS AND MENCIUS

co-creators with the heavens and the earth. Again, in this same lineage are the *Mencius* and the *Expansive Learning* that share themes, terminology, and images with *Five Modes of Virtuosic Conduct*. This corpus of texts is revealing of how early Confucianism in taking persons and their worlds as being symbiotic in their growth, emphasized the important contribution human beings make to cosmic flourishing.

The version of *Five Modes of Virtuosic Conduct* found at Guodian with the two characters *wuxing* 五行 as a title on the first bamboo strip corroborated the speculations by contemporary scholar Pang Pu 龐樸 that the untitled version in the earlier Mawangdui find was in fact this ancient text. Several scholars including Li Xueqin 李學勤 and Pang Pu have quite plausibly suggested that there was a composite collection of writings under the name of Zisizi (perhaps similar to the inner and out chapters structure of the Daoist classic, the *Zhuangzi*) that evolved during the period between Confucius and Mencius. They speculate that an important portion of the materials recovered at Guodian, Mawangdui, and other archaeological sources might be remnants of this earlier compilation. In the court bibliography of the *History of the Former Han* 漢書藝文誌, we have a text listed under Zisizi's name in 23 chapters that only disappeared from the record a millennium later with the Song dynasty history. This suggestion of a composite Zisizi text is reinforced by a compilation by Southern Song dynasty scholar Wang Zhuo 汪晫 entitled *The Complete Works of Master Zisi* 子思子全書. Its nine chapters like the *Zhuangzi* are divided into Inner and Outer sections. While this Song dynasty reconstruction contains much of what has been ascribed to Master Zisi, it does take liberties with the actual materials and also includes quotations from texts considered spurious.[①]

Given the current state of the research on the Si-Meng lineage, we can speculate that at least portions of *Five Modes of Virtuosic Conduct* are to be located in the fourth century BCE prior to the other texts in this tradition: the *Mencius*, *Expansive Learning*, and *Focusing the Familiar*. Perhaps in reflecting on the significance of *Five Modes of Virtuosic Conduct*, we might begin retrospectively by recalling that Zhu Xi recommended a close reading of the *Analects* because it provides the vocabulary for the Confucian project. Not only does *Five Modes of Virtuosic Conduct* continue to appeal to and promote the same technical philosophical vocabulary

---

① https://www.kanripo.org/text/KR3a0054/001#1a.

authorized by the *Analects*, but it seeks to further develop and establish correlations among these various terms of art. There is a commitment in this text to elaborate upon the key philosophical concepts not only individually, but in terms of how they interpenetrate with and are derivative of each other. For example, while we might observe that the two terms *ren* 仁 (consummate conduct) and *zhi* 知 (wisdom) appear in tandem in many passages in the *Analects*, *Five Modes of Virtuosic Conduct* attempts to shed light on the philosophical implications of this correlation by arguing for the significance of their interdependence, and then goes on to introduce a similar correlation between consummate conduct (*ren* 仁) and sagacity (*sheng* 聖) (VII.4-7). In the *Analects*, there is a perceived intimate relationship between wisdom (*zhi* 知) and way-making (*dao* 道) on the one hand, and the language of human enjoyment and flourishing on the other: *yue* 悦 (1.1, 6.12, 13.25) and *le* 樂 (1.1, 1.15, 6.11, 6.20, 6.23). This same theme is again made explicit in *Five Modes of Virtuosic Conduct*: *yue* 悦 (VII.11-14, 19) and *le* 樂 (VII.17). Further, the seldom remarked upon contrast in the *Analects* between exemplary persons (*junzi* 君子) who have achieved moral virtuosity and scholar-officials (*shi* 士) who emulate the *junzi* 君子 in aspiring to such conduct is made explicit and further clarified in this newly recovered text:

五行皆形於內而時行之，謂之君子。士有志於君子道，謂之志士。
Those for whom all of the five modes of virtuosic conduct have taken shape within and who act upon them in a timely way are called exemplary persons (*junzi* 君子). Those scholar-officials (*shi* 士) whose intentions are set on the way of exemplary persons are called scholar-officials with a purpose (VII.3).

Beyond this terminological continuity with the *Analects*, prospectively we find shared metaphors and specific allusions to *Five Modes of Virtuosic Conduct* in the later *Mencius*. The rather direct linguistic and conceptual resonances between *Five Modes of Virtuosic Conduct* and the *Mencius* suggest that whoever produced the *Mencius* was aware of a version of this earlier text, and drew upon it in several different ways. For example, *Mencius* seems to offer a commentarial elaboration on the metaphor in the *Five Modes of Virtuosic Conduct* VII.10: 金聲而玉振之，有德者也 "To open with bells and then rally others with jade tubes is to have moral virtuosity

VII. THE *FIVE MODES OF VIRTUOSIC CONDUCT* (*WUXINGPIAN* 五行篇): THE INTERIM BETWEEN CONFUCIUS AND MENCIUS

(*de* 德)." In *Mencius* 5B1 we read:

集大成也者，金聲而玉振之也。金聲也者，始條理也；玉振之也者，終條理也。始條理者，智之事也；終條理者，聖之事也。
One who gathers up all of the great accomplishments is like a musical performance opening with bells and then following up with the jade tubes to bring it to a close. To open with striking the bells is a beginning that sets and modulates the tone; to close with jade tubes is an ending that continues and modulates the proper tone. To begin by setting the proper tone is the stuff of wisdom (*zhi* 智); to finish up by maintaining the proper tone is the stuff of sageliness (*sheng* 聖).

Such commentary is reminiscent of how the *Mencius* 3A2 elaborates on *Analects* 12.19 on the theme of 君子之德風，小人之德草 "The excellence of the exemplary person is the wind, while that of the petty person is the grass" and of how *Mencius* 7B37 expands upon the rather laconic reference to the "village worthy" (*xiangyuan* 鄉原) in *Analects* 17.13.

More substantially then, there is much in *Five Modes of Virtuosic Conduct* that anticipates the elaborate moral social psychology developed in the *Mencius*, beginning of course with the explicit sequencing of the "four inclinations" (*siduan* 四端) as the first four of the five modes of virtuosic conduct, *renyilizhi* 仁義禮智. In *Mencius* 7A21, Mencius observes:

君子所性，仁義禮智根於心。
What exemplary persons habituate as their human propensities—that is, their inclinations to act consummately in their roles and relations (*ren* 仁), to act with optimal appropriateness (*yi* 義), to achieve propriety (*li* 禮), and to act wisely in these same roles and relations (*zhi* 智)—are all rooted in their heartmind (*xin* 心).

And then Mencius in 7A1 describes this same process of habituation in a similar way:

盡其心者，知其性也。
Those who make the most of their "bodyheartminding" (*xin* 心) realize their natural propensities (*xing* 性).

An achieved harmony among these four modalities is described in both texts specifically in the language of efficacious conduct (*shan* 善) VII.1-2, VII.18. In its opening chapter, *Five Modes of Virtuosic Conduct* argues for a personal habituation of these modalities of conduct that begins from mere inclination and then through living a morally virtuosic narrative eventuates in the symbiotic process of drawing them together in establishing one's personal identity. A second expression shared by *Five Modes of Virtuosic Conduct* and the *Mencius* that captures this sense of "habituated conduct" is *zhongxin* 中心 as in "habituated concern" (*zhongxinzhiyou* 中心之憂). *Mencius* 6A15 in describing the central role of the heartmind (*xin* 心) within the human physical and mental sensorium seems to be an elaboration of the *Five Modes of Virtuosic Conduct* VII.25:

耳目鼻口手足六者，心之所役也。
The ears, eyes, nose, mouth, hands, and feet are the six attendants of the heartmind.

Beyond the *Mencius*, *Expansive Learning* and *Focusing the Familiar* are texts traditionally associated with the name of Confucius's grandson, Zisizi and are probably of later provenance, being compiled sometime after the appearance of the *Mencius*. Stylistically, both of these texts have passages that echo the "if x then y, if y then z" inferential sequencing we find throughout *Five Modes of Virtuosic Conduct*. The most immediate and perhaps most important link shared by all three of these texts is the expression *shenqidu* 慎其獨 that captures the Mencian notion of a coherent and integrated personal identity emerging from the habituation of the various modes of virtuosic conduct. In the commentary to the Mawangdui version of *Five Modes of Virtuosic Conduct* this process is explained as:

獨然後一，一也者，夫五爲□（一）心也，然後得之。
Having consolidated these modalities, they become one. And this 'one' then refers to the five modalities that, having been consolidated as the [one] heartmind, is then taken as one's personal identity.

Expansive Learning and *Focusing the Familiar* both understand this expression *shenqidu* to refer to the process of exemplary persons consolidating their virtuosic habits as a resolute disposition for action in the sense

VII. THE *FIVE MODES OF VIRTUOSIC CONDUCT* (*WUXINGPIAN* 五行篇): THE INTERIM BETWEEN CONFUCIUS AND MENCIUS

of the several modalities becoming one. In the language of the *Expansive Learning* 2, "becoming resolved in purpose" (*chengqiyi* 誠其意) is given as a precondition for *shenqidu*.

The importance of *Five Modes of Virtuosic Conduct* in the Si-Meng lineage is immediately evident in a critical reference to Zisizi and Mencius in the "Contra Twelve Masters" 非十二子 chapter of the *Xunzi*. Following the initial recovery of the version of *Five Modes of Virtuosic Conduct* at Mawangdui, Xunzi's death in 238 BCE had served as a *terminus ad quem* for its compilation. Scholars led by Pang Pu saw *Five Modes of Virtuosic Conduct* as either contemporaneous with or later than the *Mencius*. But with the more recent Guodian find from c. 300 BCE, the date for the end of the process of compilation has now been set much earlier.

The scathing indictment of *Five Modes of Virtuosic Conduct* in the *Xunzi* reads as follows:

略法先王而不知其統, 然而猶材劇志大, 聞見雜博。案往舊造説, 謂之五行, 甚僻違而無類, 幽隱而無説, 閉約而無解。案飾其辭, 而祇敬之, 曰：此真先君子之言也。子思唱之, 孟軻和之。世俗之溝猶瞀儒, 嚾嚾然不知其所非也, 遂受而傳之, 以爲仲尼子弓爲茲厚於後世：是則子思孟軻之罪也。

There are those who, only superficially subscribing to the way of the Former Kings, do not understand its real substance. Even so, their talents were abundant and their purposes grand, and what they had seen and heard was both varied and vast. Basing their ideas on ancient lore, they have concocted their new doctrine and call it *Five Modes of Virtuosic Conduct* (*Wuxing* 五行). In fact, this doctrine is perverse and bizarre. It is a lot of obscure and impenetrable nonsense. They dress it up in eloquent language, and with great reverence say: "These are truly the words of the exemplary persons of old." Zisizi sang this song, and Mencius chimed in with it. The deluded and foolish Confucians of our present day are thrilled with this doctrine and are wholly oblivious to where it goes wrong. They inherit it and have passed it on, thinking that on the basis of it, Confucius and Zigong will be celebrated by later generations. This then is the crime of Zisizi and Mencius.

Herein Xunzi is associating the names of Zisizi and Mencius with the doctrine of "five modes of virtuosic conduct" (*wuxing* 五行), a prescription for moral behavior initially distinct from, but perhaps later developed into the "five phases" (*wuxing* 五行) cosmological theories attributed to Zou Yan 鄒衍 (also written 騶衍) (305-240 BCE) that go by the same name. The fact that we have an earlier moral doctrine and a later seemingly unrelated cosmological theory both called *wuxing* 五行, has generated at least two explanations for Xunzi's rather severe condemnation of this doctrine.

One possible interpretation of the indictment is that the ever-practical Xunzi takes exception to scholars introducing a connection between the moral doctrine of Zisizi and Mencius and the increasingly popular "five phases" speculations about cosmic operations that Xunzi believes ought not to be a concern for the human world. Consistent with Confucius's abstention from pronouncing on speculative questions (*Analects* 9.4), Xunzi is adamant that human beings should invest their efforts in personal and communal cultivation, and not waste their time conjecturing about things they cannot and should not hope to understand. It has been claimed by some scholars such as John Knoblock that this passage in the *Xunzi* is ambiguous in that it is not immediately clear from the language whether Xunzi is criticizing Zisizi and Mencius themselves or rather the inappropriate coopting and contaminating of their "five modes of virtuosic conduct" doctrine by those latter-day Confucians who are given to speculating on cosmic mysteries. On this interpretation, it is most probable Xunzi's complaint is directed at the misappropriation of the term *wuxing* 五行 as a cosmological theory by his contemporaries and is aimed at the complicity of his fellow Confucians in promoting this distortion.

In Knoblock's attempt to resolve this ambiguity, he points out that even Xunzi himself applies the expression "five modes of virtuosic conduct" (*wuxing* 五行) to appropriate human deportment elsewhere in his writings in a positive sense, albeit with a content clearly different from the specific five moral virtuosities announced by Zisizi and Mencius.

There is a second, alternative explanation of Xunzi's complaint against the *wuxing* 五行 doctrine associated with Zisizi and Mencius that might be more plausible. To begin with, we have no corroborating evidence that the *wuxing* 五行 cosmological theory that emerges in the Han dynasty was current as early as Xunzi. Given Xunzi's antipathy to such speculations and his eagerness to speak out against what he perceives to be heterodox philosophical ideas, the absence of any clear reference to this development would suggest that the target of Xunzi's ire is probably the moral doctrine associated with Zisizi and Mencius.

VII. THE *FIVE MODES OF VIRTUOSIC CONDUCT* (*WUXINGPIAN* 五行篇): THE INTERIM BETWEEN CONFUCIUS AND MENCIUS

In other contexts, Xunzi is anything but shy about voicing loud and sustained objections to the ideas of Mencius, especially Mencius's attempt to define the "natural human tendencies" (*xing* 性) as the prosocial "four inclinations" (*siduan* 四端). Again, given Xunzi's practical turn, the elevation of the fifth of the five modes of virtuosic conduct, human sagacity (*sheng* 聖), to serve as a profoundly creative cosmic force would undoubtedly be received by Xunzi as "a lot of obscure and impenetrable nonsense."

And finally, this passage from the *Xunzi* condemning Zisizi and Mencius is anything but ambiguous. It describes the *wuxing* 五行 doctrine as a gross distortion of the technical vocabulary established by the *Analects*. While I would read the *Xunzi* itself as a rather conservative commentary on many of the themes found in the *Analects*, both *Five Modes of Virtuosic Conduct* and the *Mencius* take these doctrines associated with Confucius and in terms of both tone and content, expand upon them with real philosophical imagination. Xunzi who sees himself as the proper heir to Confucius, denounces the hyperbolic language in which these distortions are presented, deplores the popularity it has garnered among his contemporary Confucians, and blames Zisizi and Mencius by name and in unequivocal terms, for their crime of promoting what he takes to be a heretical Confucianism. Xunzi's rejection of the *wuxing* 五行 doctrine would appear to be an opening volley in what then becomes a contest between two importantly distinct interpretations of Confucian philosophy: the Xunzi lineage that had considerable prominence in the early Han dynasty, and the Si-Meng lineage that later and in the fullness of time was to supersede it.

The Mawangdui version of *Five Modes of Virtuosic Conduct* is divided into two sections, the classic itself (*jing* 經) and an explanatory gloss (*shuo* 説). In recent scholarship, the contemporary scholar Chen Lai 陳來 has followed Pang Pu in reflecting on the Xunzi indictment cited above. In explanation of the phrase 子思唱之, 孟軻和之 "Zisizi sang this song, and Mencius chimed in with it," Chen Lai has argued in great textual detail that we have good grounds to speculate that the "classic" section itself is from the hand of Zisizi (or at least his lineage), and that the explanatory gloss (*shuo* 説) with so many allusions to a decidedly Mencian Confucianism was appended by Mencius himself (or his lineage). With considerable scholarly support, this would date the classic itself to somewhere around 400 BCE and the commentary sometime before Mencius's death around 300 BCE.

The Guodian version has only the "classic" section, but Chen Lai takes the first half of it to be the classic with the latter passages being an amplificatory commentary on the first section. This format of classic and commentary is familiar from the *Expansive Learning* (*Daxue* 大學) where I have divided this text into the "classic" as part 1 and then the "commentary" on the classic as parts 2 and 3. Other texts such as the *Guanzi* 管子 and *Mozi* 墨子 also have this kind of structure. Another example of such a Si-Meng collaboration might be *Focusing the Familiar* traditionally ascribed to Zisizi. We have suggested that at least the opening chapter using a specifically Zisizi vocabulary might be traced back to Zisizi himself, while the remaining portion of the text might be commentary from the Mencian lineage that mounts a sustained argument for a decidedly Confucian rather than Mohist reading of "the continuity between and inseparability of the cosmic and human orders" (*tianrenheyi* 天人合一).

Although the Mawangdui and Guodian versions of the *Five Modes of Virtuosic Conduct* are more or less the same, this "less" entails some important differences. Chen Lai has summarized existing scholarship that has identified three important points on which the two versions differ.[①] First, in the opening passage in VII.1, the ordering of the five modes is different, with the Guodian version having "consummate conduct" (*ren* 仁), "appropriateness" (*yi* 義), "ritual propriety" (*li* 禮), "wisdom" (*zhi* 智), and "sagacity" (*sheng* 聖), while the Mawangdui version has the order *ren* 仁, *zhi* 智, *li* 禮, *yi* 義, *sheng* 聖. This alternative sequence in the Mawangdui version is important because it separates "wisdom" (*zhi* 智) and "sagacity" (*sheng* 聖) that are coupled as a major theme in the Guodian version. Indeed, this coupling is the second important difference.

In VII.17, the Guodian version makes the claim that:

聖智，禮樂之所由生也，五行之所和也。

Sagacity and wisdom are whence ritual propriety and music arise, and are what bring harmony to the five modes of virtuosic conduct.

By contrast, the Mawangdui version elevates "consummate conduct" (*ren* 仁) and "appropriateness" (*yi* 義) to this high status:

仁義，禮樂所由生也，五行之所和也。

---

① Chen Lai 陳來, 竹帛《五行》與簡帛研究, Beijing: SDX Joint Publishing Company, 2009, p. 143.

VII. THE *FIVE MODES OF VIRTUOSIC CONDUCT* (*WUXINGPIAN* 五行篇): THE INTERIM BETWEEN CONFUCIUS AND MENCIUS

Consummate conduct and appropriateness are whence ritual propriety and music arise, and what bring harmony to the five modes of virtuosic conduct.

While in the Guodian version, sagacity (*sheng* 聖) and wisdom (*zhi* 智) are the source of the other modes of virtuosic conduct, in the Mawangdui the other modes are derivative of consummate conduct (*ren* 仁) and appropriateness (*yi* 義).

The third difference between the two versions is consistent with the prior two. In VII.13, the Guodian version has:

仁, 義禮所由生也, 四行之所和也。
Consummate conduct is whence appropriateness and ritual propriety arise, and is what brings harmony to the four modes of proper conduct.

By contrast, the Mawangdui version has:

仁義, 禮智之所由生也, 四行之所和也。
Consummate conduct and appropriateness are whence propriety and wisdom arise, and are what bring harmony to the four modes of virtuosic conduct.

Here again, in the Mawangdui text consummate conduct and appropriateness are given pride of place, and wisdom is made derivative of them.

In summary, while the Guodian version links sagacity (*sheng* 聖) and wisdom (*zhi* 智) together and gives them the highest status, they are challenged in the later Mawangdui version by the coupling of consummate conduct (*ren* 仁) and appropriateness (*yi* 義), giving them prominence. The substantial differences between the two redactions then can be construed as a contrast between intellectual insight in the Guodian text, and moral virtuosity in Mawangdui. This means that although we recognize the important continuities between Zisizi and Mencius in referring to a Si-Meng lineage (*SiMengxuepai* 思孟學派), we also have to acknowledge that significant doctrinal differences emerged over its ongoing evolution. Through an analysis of the classical corpus, Chen Lai goes on to survey the Warring States philosophical literature and to demonstrate that the coupling of sagacity and wisdom together with keenness of hearing and visual acuity (*congmingshengzhi* 聰明聖智) that we find in the Guodian version of the *Five Modes of Virtuosic Conduct* became a pervasive and influential theme in the pre-Qin Confucian, Legalist, Militarist, and Mohist writings, whether it was celebrating this intellectual perspicacity as the highest level of sagely wisdom, or decrying it as we find in the Daoist texts.[①]

While allowing that the correlation between sagacity and wisdom did become an important theme in *Five Modes of Virtuosic Conduct*, the coupling of consummate conduct (*ren* 仁) and appropriateness (*yi* 義) also has an important role. They do come first in the sequence of the five modes as they are listed in VII.1. Again, in VII.5-7, consummate conduct (*ren* 仁) comes first in the linking of consummate conduct (*ren*), wisdom (*zhi* 智), and sagacity (*sheng* 聖). And in VII.18, consummate conduct (*ren*) is 四行之所和 "what brings harmony to the four modes of virtuosic conduct" and 義禮所由生 "whence appropriateness and ritual propriety arise."

Chen Lai's historical contextualizing and careful analysis is helpful in appreciating the importance and the complexity of this Zisizi text within the early philosophical dialectic. Perhaps one way of resolving the issue of what particular terms are emphasized and given higher status is to understand them ecologically as "aspectual" rather than as "analytically" separable categories, and thus as different perspectives on the same phenomenon. The aspiration to a kind of "efficacy" (*shan* 善) and "optimizing symbiosis" (*he* 和) among these various aspects is inclusive while at the same time having its own internal logic, with some of the categories taking priority over others in different situations. This pattern of thinking is captured in the notion of "the inseparability and mutual entailment of one and many" (*yiduobufenguan* 一多不分觀) wherein the many are always implicated in the one.

To take the example of the importance of the heartmind (*xin* 心) in governing the physical sensorium given in VII.25, the heartmind holds sway over the functions of the other different elements of the body's sensorium, and coordinates their various activities into a single, efficacious unity. This theme of an efficacy achieved through the activation and coordination of the differences that are implicated in all virtuosic conduct has physical as well as moral and political application. While the heartmind governs the senses, far from being an independent, external imposition on

---

① Chen Lai 陳來, 竹帛《五行》與簡帛研究, pp. 143-149.

VII. THE *FIVE MODES OF VIRTUOSIC CONDUCT* (*WUXINGPIAN* 五行篇): THE INTERIM BETWEEN CONFUCIUS AND MENCIUS

these senses, its function emerges within the pattern of relations defining the physical and cognitive ecology as a guiding impetus and intentionality that makes the most of its possibilities.

In parsing the text, I have followed the standard 28 sections, taking the earlier Guodian bamboo strip text as the master document and informing it with the Mawangdui silk version and its commentary.

VII.1: Habituating Moral Virtuosity

五行。仁形於内謂之德之行，不形於内謂之行。義形於内謂之德之行，不形於内謂之行。禮形於内謂之德之行，不形於内謂之行。智形內謂之德之行，不形於内謂之行。聖形於内謂之德之行，不形於内謂之行。①

Five Modes of Virtuosic Conduct: Consummatory conduct in roles and relations (*ren* 仁) taking shape within is called moral virtuosity (*de* 德); where it does not take shape within, it is called merely doing what is deemed consummate. Appropriate conduct (*yi* 義) taking shape within is called moral virtuosity; where it does not take shape within, it is called merely doing what is deemed appropriate. An achieved ritual propriety in roles and relations (*li* 禮) taking shape within is called moral virtuosity; where it does not take shape within, it is called merely doing what is deemed proper. Wisdom (*zhi* 智) taking shape within is called moral virtuosity; where it does not take shape within, it is called merely doing what is deemed wise. Sagacity (*sheng* 聖) taking shape within is called moral virtuosity; where it does not take shape within, it is called merely doing what is deemed sagacious.

Comment: The opening chapter of *Five Modes of Virtuosic Conduct* explains how a person's conduct becomes habituated as characteristic, identity-forming patterns of moral virtuosity. This continuing process of cultivation first produces efficacy (*shan* 善) in human relations and then culminates in a world-changing moral virtuosity (*de* 德) shared by both persons and their world. This passage makes the same distinction we find in the *Mencius* between 1) doing something prompted by the anticipated approbation of others, and 2) acting consistently and instinctively out of a cultivated moral virtuosity (*de* 德), a self-conscious virtuosity that in

---

① The order on the Mawangdui version is different: *ren* 仁, *zhi* 智, *yi* 義, *li* 禮, and *sheng* 聖.

having been habituated, has become who you are. There are persons who are merely able to follow conventional values in acting in a way deemed proper by the community, and then there are those who through an assiduous personal regimen, having established consummatory habits of conduct in their roles and relations, are then able to act out of this moral virtuosity. Chen Lai makes the point that the expression "taking shape within" (*xingyunei* 形於內) does not mean the internalization of something that comes from the outside, but rather references the locus and point of origination for such activity: "For this reason, it is only when 'taking shape within' is in fact consummate conduct (*ren* 仁) that comes from within and takes shape without that it is a moral virtuosity expressed out of one's own moral propensities."[①] What requires clarification is the origin of such moral virtuosity. Chen Lai observes that the text is ambiguous on this point. It neither states clearly whether moral virtuosity (*dexing* 德性) is the endowment of *tian* 天 and as such a natural condition, or whether it is the result of the personal cultivation of exemplary persons and is thus something nurtured.[②] I would argue that the alternative to something derived or imposed from without in these Confucian texts is a process of habituation that is a collaboration between initial human propensities and the world. As it states in *Mencius* 7A30 where *xing* 性 (conventionally translated as "human nature") is used as a verb:

孟子曰:"堯舜,性之也;湯武,身之也;五霸,假之也。久假而不歸,惡知其非有也。"

Mencius said: "While Yao and Shun habituated morality and Tang and Wu embodied it, the Five Hegemons only feigned it. But if these hegemons feign such morality without remiss over an extended period of time, who is to say it does not become their own?"

How then does this cultivated moral virtuosity "take shape within" to become habituated conduct? In interpreting this passage, we might appeal to the familiar Confucian expression *shenqidu* 慎其獨 to shed light on the way in which such conduct becomes consolidated "within." We encountered

---

① See Chen Lai 陳來, 竹帛《五行》與簡帛研究, pp. 120-121: 因此, 形于內謂之德之行, 實際是説仁自內發動而形于外, 才是德之行, 才是由德性發出的德行。
② Chen Lai 陳來, 竹帛《五行》與簡帛研究, p. 124.

VII. THE *FIVE MODES OF VIRTUOSIC CONDUCT* (*WUXINGPIAN* 五行篇): THE INTERIM BETWEEN CONFUCIUS AND MENCIUS

the expression *shenqidu* 慎其獨 in the analysis of the first chapter of *Focusing the Familiar* where I have interpreted it as the process of exemplary persons consolidating their virtuosic habits as a resolute disposition for action. The interlinear commentary included in the Mawangdui version of this *Five Modes of Virtuosic Conduct* document offers its explanation of this same expression *shenqidu* 慎其獨. This commentary is explicit in referencing *xin* 心 or "heartminding" as the personal identity produced when these five patterns are set as the root of virtuosic conduct. The commentary reads and is explained as:

慎其獨也者，言舍夫五而慎其心之謂也。獨然後一，一也者，夫五爲□（一）心也，然後得之。

The expression '*shenqidu*' 慎其獨 means getting rid of the distinction among the five modes of conduct and bringing focus to one's heartmind. Having consolidated these modalities, they become one. And this 'one' then refers to the five modalities that, having been consolidated as the [one] heartmind, is then taken as one's personal identity.

This expression *shenqidu* 慎其獨 is similar in import to VII.25 in which the heartmind holds sway over its six physical attendants that could otherwise be a source of external distraction by coordinating a unifying symbiosis among them. The meaning of this expression *shenqidu* 慎其獨 found in *Expansive Learning* (*Daxue* 大學) has much the same meaning as when it occurs here in *Five Modes of Virtuosic Conduct*. It is defined as "becoming resolute in one's thoughts and feelings" (*chengqiyi* 誠其意): that is, cultivating and consolidating a habitual disposition of conduct to be expressed consistently as one's moral virtuosity.

VII.2: Humans Can Broaden the Way and Sages Can Continue and Carry Out the Workings of *Tian* 人能弘道, 聖人能繼天立極 ①

德之行五，和謂之德，四行，和謂之善。善，人道也。德，天道也。君子無

---

① See Zhu Xi's 朱熹 preface to his commentary on the *Zhongyong* 中庸章句 in his commentary on the *Four Books* 四書章句集注.

中心之憂則無中心之智，無中心之智則無中心之悦，無中心之悦則不安，不安則不樂，不樂則無德。[君子無中心之憂則無中心之聖，無中心之聖則無中心之悦，無中心之悦則不安。不安則不樂，不樂則無德。] ①

When harmony (*he* 和) is achieved among these five modes of virtuosic conduct, it is called moral virtuosity (*de* 德), while achieving harmony among only the first four of them is called efficacy (*shan* 善). Efficacy is human way-making (*rendao* 人道), while moral virtuosity is the way-making of *tian* (*tiandao* 天道).

If exemplary persons (*junzi* 君子) have no habituated concern, they will be lacking in habituated wisdom (*zhi* 智); if they are lacking in habituated wisdom, they will be lacking in habituated delight; if they are lacking in habituated delight, they will not be at ease; if they are not at ease, they will not find enjoyment; and if they do not find enjoyment, they will be lacking in moral virtuosity.

[If exemplary persons (*junzi* 君子) are lacking in habituated concern, they will be lacking in habituated sagacity (*sheng* 聖); if they are lacking in habituated sagacity, they will be lacking in habituated delight; if they are lacking in habituated delight, they will not be at ease; if they are not at ease, they will not find enjoyment (*le* 樂); and if they do not find enjoyment, they will be lacking in moral virtuosity.]②

Comment: Having previously made the important distinction between mere conduct and a habituated moral virtuosity, this passage of *Five Modes of Virtuosic Conduct* then offers the reader a distinction between efficacy (*shan* 善) as the way-making of the human being, and moral virtuosity (*de* 德) as the way-making of *tian* 天, a distinction repeated below in VII.9. This distinction between human way-making and the way-making of *tian* 天 that assigns "moral virtuosity" (*de* 德) to *tian* 天 is made curious by the fact that the text has up to this point used the same term "moral virtuosity" (*de* 德) to describe the quality of *human* conduct achieved when it has been habituated by human beings as their accustomed way of behaving. In this text then, the same term moral virtuosity (*de* 德) is used to

---

① In the Guodian version, this passage ends without the second "sageliness" sequence that has been added here on the basis of the Mawangdui text.
② The correlation of "wisdom" (*zhi* 智) and "sagacity" (*sheng* 聖) is a defining theme of this text.

VII. THE *FIVE MODES OF VIRTUOSIC CONDUCT* (*WUXINGPIAN* 五行篇): THE INTERIM BETWEEN CONFUCIUS AND MENCIUS

describe both the way-making of *tian* 天, and the way-making of consummate human beings.

To appreciate what is meant here by the distinction between "human way-making" and "the way-making of *tian* 天" we need first to suspend our uncritical yet default Abrahamic theological assumptions and thus resist any temptation to think this dichotomy is referencing two exclusive domains. The *tian*-human (*tianren* 天人) collaboration in way-making captured in the mantra "the continuity between and inseparability of the human and the cosmic orders" (*tianrenheyi* 天人合一) is an emergent, increasingly inspired way of being in the world that always has both a human and a cosmic aspect. Here the text states a harmonious integration of the first four modes of virtuosic conduct as moral virtuosity (*de* 德) produces human efficacy (*shan* 善). But when the fifth mode of virtuosic conduct is added to this harmony—that is, the sagacity of human beings (*sheng* 聖)— it produces a moral virtuosity (*de* 德) to be associated with *tian* 天.

In this text then, moral virtuosity (*de* 德), far from being described exclusively as the way-making of *tian* 天, is in fact expressed as a collaboration between *tian* 天 and the way-making of the highest order of humanity, the sages. The relationship itself is first order, while *tian* 天 and humankind are a second order horizon within this relationship. Given that the sages are the paramount exemplars of what is humanly possible, this moral virtuosity is manifested in the world as the consummate expression of the operations of both sagacious human beings and the contextualizing *tian* 天 as, in their collaborative activities, they find a real depth of coalescence and meaning (*du* 度). Not only is such sagacity to be understood as the human being achieving the reach and the influence of *tian* 天, but moreover *tian* 天 itself is deepened and extended by this accumulating human sagacity. Just as human sagacity is naturalized to become integral to cosmic order, *tian* 天 and the natural order are socialized to become integral to the human experience. This shared virtuosic conduct not only underscores the primacy of the *tianren* 天人 relationship over the secondary distinction between *tian* 天 and *ren* 人, but also makes the important point that human beings in their role as sages can continue and extend the work of *tian* 天.

This insight into the mutuality of the way-making of human beings and *tian* 天 expressed through sagacious conduct is further strengthened when we reflect on the four inclinations (*siduan* 四端) of "heartminding" (*xin* 心) that for Mencius are defining of the native human conditions. These are the relationships that locate the human being within family and community, and that are thus available for personal cultivation. Of course, as we have seen in this *Five Modes of Virtuosic Conduct* chapter, these first four modes of virtuosic conduct *renyilizhi* 仁義禮智 are identical with the "four inclinations" (*siduan* 四端) of the Mencian heartmind (*xin* 心). As we also find in *Mencius* 7A1: 盡其心者知其性也。知其性則知天矣 "Those who make the most of their 'bodyheartminding' (*xin* 心) realize their natural propensities (*xing* 性). And again, those who realize their natural propensities then realize *tian* 天." What is clear here is that such moral virtuosity is neither some characteristic pattern of behavior established by complying with external, antecedent principles, nor is it actualized from the reduplication of an erstwhile internal and innate human nature. Rather, such virtuosity is the product of a continuing collaboration between persons and their worlds. Again, these four inclinations are not only productive of a cultivated human efficacy (*shan* 善), but also provide the ground for the Mencian claim that everyone, given these initial conditions, can aspire to behave sagaciously in their conduct.

Just by way of clarification, the Mencian claim is not that each human being has some innate potential that can then be actualized to make every one of us a sage, but rather that the collaboration between our initial inclinations and our world can produce sagacious conduct. There is an important difference between saying that everyone has some inherent potential to become a sage, and that everyone who behaves like a sage is a sage. Sagacity is a quality of human virtuosity that allows for the full participation of exemplary human beings in guiding the workings of a flourishing cosmos.

There is much textual evidence that sagacity is the ultimate coalescence in the first-order *tianren* 天人 relationship. As we witness throughout the canonical Confucian texts, the vague notion of *tian* 天 takes on the visage of a particular human face as the texts repeatedly correlate these always unique sages with *tian* 天 by characterizing them metaphorically in grand, celestial terms. In this *Five Modes of Virtuosic Conduct* VII.12, for example, a common celestial vocabulary is used to correlate the excellence of the sage-king Wen (literally, King "Culture") as the paragon of human culture, with the way of *tian* 天:

聖者，禮樂之所由生，五行之所和也。和則樂，樂則有德，有德則邦家興。文王之見如此。文王在上也，於昭於天。此之謂也。

Sagacity and wisdom are whence propriety, and music arise, and are what

VII. THE *FIVE MODES OF VIRTUOSIC CONDUCT* (*WUXINGPIAN* 五行篇): THE INTERIM BETWEEN CONFUCIUS AND MENCIUS

bring harmony to the five modes of virtuosic conduct. Where there is such harmony, there is enjoyment, where enjoyment, then moral virtuosity, and where moral virtuosity, the nation and its families flourish. Such was the insight of King Wen. When the *Book of Songs* 235 states: "King Wen presiding above; he shines in the heavens," this is what it means.

The second portion of this passage takes "habituated concern" (*zhongxinzhiyou* 中心之憂) as the source of moral virtuosity. Here it seems to contradict the sentiments expressed with respect to the status of "concern" (*you* 憂) in the *Analects*, observing as the *Analects* does that 仁者不憂 "consummate persons are free of concerns" (9.29, 14.28) and 君子不憂不懼 "exemplary persons are neither concerned nor apprehensive" (12.4).

But with respect to "concern," the *Analects* in reference to moral virtuosity also states:

子曰:"德之不修,學之不講,聞義不能徙,不善不能改,是吾憂也。"
The Master said: "To fail to cultivate virtuosity in my conduct (*de* 德), to fail to practice what I have learned, to fail to follow through on what I know to be the most appropriate course of action (*yi* 義), and to fail to reform my misdeeds—these are the things that give me concern." (7.3)

and:

君子憂道不憂貧。
Exemplary persons concern themselves about the proper way, and not with poverty. (15.32)

Also *Mencius* 4B28 has the passage:

是故君子有終身之憂,無一朝之患也。
Thus, while exemplary persons are always concerned as a matter of temperament, they are not given to unexpected bouts of anxiety.

The expression "habituation" (*zhongxin* 中心) that features prominently in this chapter as an explanation of "taking shape within" (*xingyunei* 形於內) also occurs in the *Mencius* 2A3:

以德服人者，中心悦而誠服也。
Winning them over with moral virtuosity is because with habituated delight they will follow willingly.

and in 3A5:

夫泚也，非爲人泚，中心達於面目。
This perspiration, far from being for the sake of other people, was the physical expression of their habituated feelings.

Again, the appropriate correlation between "concern" (*you* 憂) and "enjoyment" (*le* 樂) is the main theme of *Mencius* 1B4:

樂民之樂者，民亦樂其樂；憂民之憂者，民亦憂其憂。樂以天下，憂以天下，然而不王者，未之有也。
When the ruler rejoices in the joy of the people, the people will also rejoice in his joy; when the ruler worries over the people's concerns, the people will also worry over his concerns. The ruler whose joy is shared by the world and whose concerns are those of the world is the definition of the True King.

VII.3: The Authentication of Moral Virtuosity in Action

五行皆形於内而時行之，謂之君子。士有志於君子道，謂之志士。善弗爲無近，德弗志不成，智弗思不得。思不精不察，思不長不得，思不輕[①] 不形，[不形則不安，] 不安 [則] 不樂，不樂 [則] 無德。

Those for whom all of the five modes of virtuosic conduct have taken shape within and who act upon them in a timely way are called exemplary persons (*junzi* 君子). Those scholar-officials (*shi* 士) whose intentions are set on the way of exemplary persons are called scholar-officials with purpose (*zhi* 志). With efficacy (*shan* 善), if one does not act upon it, there will be no progress; with moral virtuosity (*de* 德), if one is lacking in purpose, there will be no maturation; with wisdom (*zhi* 智) if there is no reflection, there will be no good outcome. Thinking that remains unfocused will not be insightful;

---

① In the Mawangdui version the text has "nimble" (*qing* 輕) rather than "lucid" (*qing* 清).

VII. THE *FIVE MODES OF VIRTUOSIC CONDUCT* (*WUXINGPIAN* 五行篇): THE INTERIM BETWEEN CONFUCIUS AND MENCIUS

thinking that is lacking resolve will not have a good outcome; thinking that is not nimble will not take shape. [If their thoughts do not take shape, they will be uneasy,] if they are uneasy, they find no enjoyment (*le* 樂), and if they find no enjoyment, they will be without moral virtuosity.

Comment: It is a commonplace to observe that the familiar dualisms separating theory from practice, and the formal from the informal, are anathema to the holistic, aesthetic cosmology that serves as interpretive context for these classical Confucian texts. Although the idea of authentication in practice is associated with Ming dynasty philosopher Wang Yangming 王陽明 and his mantra "the inseparability of knowing and doing" (*zhixingheyi* 知行合一), it is in fact one of the earliest tenets of the Confucian tradition. Whatever theorizing might mean, it does not reference some principle or body of principles we might associate with scientific reasoning proffered to explain phenomena in the abstract. Indeed, these Confucian canons challenge this more familiar understanding of theorizing by beginning from the primacy of practice and by taking theorizing as an intrinsic feature of practical activity itself. Indeed, to get the most out of our practical activities, we must be self-consciously critical and deliberate. Thus, erstwhile theoretical tools are generally introduced by philosophers in this tradition *in medias res*—that is, from the need to make their practices more productive and intelligent within the context of the practices themselves. This less familiar understanding of "theorizing" means we must "own" the project in the sense that our own practical narratives provide the concrete and inescapable context out of which our "theorizing" emerges.

VII.4: Consummate Conduct (*ren* 仁), Wisdom (*zhi* 智), and Sagacity (*sheng* 聖) as Necessary Conditions for Moral Suasion

不仁，思不能精。不智，思不能長。① ［不仁不智，］未見君子，憂心不能惙

---

① Literally, "long." *Huainanzi* 18/193/8 says: 聖人之思修，愚人之思叕 "The thinking of the sage is refined; that of a fool, 'short' (= shallow)."

悦;① 既見君子，心不能悦。②《詩》曰："[未見君子，憂心惙惙,]亦既見之，亦既觀之，我心則悦。" 此之謂也。不仁，思不能精。不聖，思不能輕。不仁不聖，未見君子，憂心不能忡忡；既見君子，心不能降。

Persons who are not consummate in their conduct (*ren* 仁) are not able to find focus in their thinking; persons who are not wise (*zhi* 智) are not able to have resolve in their thinking. When persons [who are neither consummate nor wise] have yet to encounter an exemplary person (*junzi* 君子), their concerned heartminds are not able to feel bad about it. And once they have encountered the exemplary person, their heartminds are not able to feel any delight in it. This is what it means when the *Book of Songs* 14 says, "[Not yet having met an exemplary person, my worried heartmind was full of sorrow,] but once I encountered this person and met with him, my heartmind was then full of delight."③

Persons who are not consummate in their conduct are not able to find focus in their thinking; persons who are not sagacious (*sheng* 聖) are not able to be agile in their thinking. When persons who are neither consummate nor sagacious have yet to encounter an exemplary person, their concerned heartminds are unable to feel their loss. And when they have encountered the exemplary person, their heartminds are not able to calm down.④

Comment: This passage alludes to the language of the *Book of Songs* 14 that states:

未見君子，憂心忡忡，亦既見止，亦既觀止，我心則降……未見君子，憂心惙惙，亦既見止，亦既觀止，我心則説……未見君子，我心傷悲，

---

① The Mawangdui text has "not able to be consolidated and resolved"(*bunengjingzhang* 不能精長) in the place of "not able to feel bad about it" (*bunengchuochuo* 不能惙惙).

② The Mawangdui text has "and since their thinking is not focused and resolved, they are not able to feel any delight in it (*sibujingchang, bunengyue* 思不精長，不能悦) in the place of 'once they have encountered the exemplary person,' their heartminds are not able to feel any delight in it" (*jijianjunzi, xinbunengyue* 既见君子，心不能悦).

③ Cf. Bernhard Karlgren (trans.), *The Book of Odes*, Stockholm: Bulletin of the Museum for Far Eastern Antiquities, 1950, pp. 8-9.

④ Note a similar passage in *Book of Songs* 168; cf. Legge, *Chinese Classics*, Vol. 4, p. 264, Karlgren, *Odes*, pp. 111-113. For *xiang* 降 Legge has "at rest" and Karlgren has "calms down."

VII. THE *FIVE MODES OF VIRTUOSIC CONDUCT* (*WUXINGPIAN* 五行篇): THE INTERIM BETWEEN CONFUCIUS AND MENCIUS

亦既見止，亦既覯止，我心則夷。
When I have not yet seen my lord (*junzi* 君子), my concerned heartmind is laden with anxiety, but having seen him, having met up with him, it then settles down.... When I have not yet seen my lord, my concerned heartmind is agitated, but having seen him, having met up with him, it is then delighted.... When I have not yet seen my lord, my concerned heartmind is hurting, but having seen him, having met up with him, it then calms down.

In this love song in the *Book of Songs*, a young maiden is pining after her lover. Such affect is elevated to be the attraction persons feel to the most morally exemplary among them. *Junzi* 君子 in this verse might best be translated as "my lord." But subsequent to the compilation of the *Songs*, *junzi* 君子 was appropriated by the Confucian texts as a key philosophical term with its meaning being extended from nobility of birth to nobility of conduct. Hence, I usually translate *junzi* 君子 as "exemplary persons" or "exemplary conduct," depending upon context. In this philosophical text, the *Songs* passage is being borrowed and retrofitted to make a philosophical point. A major tenet in the Confucian texts is to celebrate the suasive moral force of exemplary persons who have the power of transforming morally those who come into their orbit. The philosophical point being made here is that there are necessary conditions for the transformative force of exemplary persons to take effect. Herein we again find the correlation among consummate conduct (*ren* 仁), wisdom (*zhi* 智), and sagacity (*sheng* 聖) in that order as a strong theme throughout the text. These three of the five modes of virtuosic conduct seem to be a necessary condition for someone to become a candidate for moral suasion, with each of them seeming to be a precondition for the one that follows.

This passage has some resonance with *Analects* 7.26:

子曰："聖人，吾不得而見之矣；得見君子者，斯可矣。"子曰："善人，吾不得而見之矣；得見有恒者，斯可矣。亡而爲有，虛而爲盈，約而爲泰，難乎有恒矣。"

The Master said, "I will never get to meet a sage (*sheng* 聖)—I would be content to meet an exemplary person (*junzi* 君子)."

The Master said, "I will never get to meet a truly efficacious person (shanren 善人)①—I would be content to meet someone who is constant. It is difficult indeed for persons to be constant in a world where nothing is taken to be something, emptiness is taken to be fullness, and poverty is taken to be plenty."

VII.5-7: The Thinking of Consummate, Wise, and Sagacious Persons

仁之思也精，精則察，察則安，安則溫，溫則悅，悅則戚，戚則新（親），新（親）則愛，愛則玉色，② ［溫則見君子，見君子道則不憂，不憂則玉

---

① Confucius discusses "the efficacious person" (shanren 善人) several times: see also 11.20, 13.11, and 13.29.
② The expression "the radiance of jade" (yuse 玉色) has several meanings: "pure white, the unchanging color of jade, the appearance of resolve in one's conduct, and something that is superbly beautiful." The *Xunzi* provides commentary:

《荀子法行》子貢問於孔子曰："君子之所以貴玉而賤珉者，何也？爲夫玉之少而珉之多邪？"孔子曰："惡！賜！是何言也！夫君子豈多而賤之，少而貴之哉！夫玉者，君子比德焉。溫潤而澤，仁也；栗而理，知也；堅剛而不屈，義也；廉而不劌，行也；折而不撓，勇也；瑕適並見，情也；扣之，其聲清揚而遠聞，其止輟然，辭也。故雖有珉之雕雕，不若玉之章章。《詩》曰：'言念君子，溫其如玉。'此之謂也。"

Zigong posed a question to Confucius, saying: "Why is it that exemplary persons put great store in jade but have little interest in serpentine pseudo-jade? Is it because the former is rare while the latter is common?"

"My goodness, Zigong, how can you say such a thing? How could exemplary persons have little interest in something because it is common and put great store in something because it is rare? With respect to jade, exemplary persons make the comparison with moral virtuosity (de 德). Being warm, moist, and glossy, it is consummatory conduct (ren 仁); being solid and striated, it is wisdom (zhi 知); being hard, resilient, and unyielding, it is appropriateness (yi 義); being incorruptible and rounded, it is proper conduct; being split but yet unscratched, it is courage (yong 勇). Its flaws and its strengths are both manifest: the way things actually are. Striking it, the pure sound rings out and spreads, and can be heard far away. On ceasing, there is a sense of exhaustion and absence. Thus, even though serpentine lends itself to carving, it does not have the radiance of jade. When the *Book of Songs* 128 says: 'Thinking about my lord, he has the warmth of jade,' this is what it means."

VII. THE *FIVE MODES OF VIRTUOSIC CONDUCT* (*WUXINGPIAN* 五行篇): THE INTERIM BETWEEN CONFUCIUS AND MENCIUS

色,]① 玉色則形，形則仁。智之思也長，長則得，得則不忘，不忘則明，明則見賢人，見賢人則玉色，玉色則形，形則智。聖之思也輕，輕則形，形則不忘，不忘則聰，聰則聞君子道，聞君子道則玉音，玉音則形，形則聖。

The thinking of consummate persons (*ren* 仁) is focused; being focused, such persons are insightful; being insightful, they are at ease; being at ease, they are congenial; being congenial, they find delight; finding delight, they feel intimacy; feeling intimacy, they are affectionate towards their kin; being affectionate towards their kin, they are loving; being loving, they have the persistent radiance of jade; [being congenial, they encounter the exemplary person (*junzi* 君子); encountering the exemplary person, they are not concerned; unconcerned, they have the persistent radiance of jade;] having the unchanging radiance of jade, they take shape; taking shape, they are consummate in what they do.

The thinking of the wise (*zhi* 智) is prescient; being prescient, they succeed in what they do; being successful, they do not forget; not forgetting, they have acuity; having acuity, they discern worthy persons; discerning worthy persons, they have the persistent radiance of jade; having the persistent radiance of jade, they take shape; taking shape, there is wisdom in what they do.

The thinking of the sagacious (*sheng* 聖) is sharp; being sharp, it takes shape; taking shape, they do not forget; not forgetting, they are keen of hearing; being keen of hearing, they learn the way of exemplary persons; learning the way of exemplary persons, they spread the pure sounds of jade;② spreading the pure sounds of jade, they take shape; and taking shape, they are sagacious in what they do.

Comment: The causal-chain structure of the text is reminiscent of *Expansive Learning*, where each condition is necessary for the next. Each of the parallel passages, following the established order of consummate (*ren* 仁), wise (*zhi* 智), and sagacious (*sheng* 聖), move from focused, resolute and agile thinking respectively to a habituated mode of conduct. Each of them takes their way of thinking through that particular series of affective and

---

① This passage is inserted on the basis of the Mawangdui version.
② The Mawangdui text has "speak like kings" (*wangyan* 王言) while the Guodian text has "the pure sounds of jade" (*yuyin* 玉音)." The reference would seem to be the words that come from a worthy person.

cognitive capacities necessary in sum to consolidate this specified quality of thinking into an inner disposition for action. There are two ways in which this process resonates with Mencius. First, "thinking" (*si* 思) as the initial impetus that propels one toward habituation corresponds to Mencius's notion of prosocial "inclinations" (*duan* 端) that eventuate in efficacious conduct (*shan* 善). Again the tactile metaphor of the "persistent radiance of jade" (*yuse* 玉色) brings to mind the assumption in Mencius that a cultivated moral virtuosity is immediately manifested in a kind of radiant physicality. For example, in *Mencius* 7A21 it states that with these incipient modes of virtuosic conduct being rooted in the heartmind

其生色也睟然，見於面，盎於背，施於四體，四體不言而喻。
... the physical complexion that develops in this endeavor first glows radiantly on their faces, is further reflected in their carriage, and then extends throughout their extremities. Without their bodies having to say anything at all, everyone is keenly aware of this personal growth.

While the vocabulary of affection and intimacy is associated with consummate conduct, wisdom is defined in terms of visual discernment, and sagacity is keenness of hearing. Wise persons are discriminating, where their wisdom is made evident in their ability to recognize those who are worthy among us. And sagacious persons as virtuosic communicators have a profound capacity for listening where their keenness of listening is made evident in their ability to recognize the way of exemplary persons. On hearing of the way of exemplary persons, like the persistent ring of jade that has been struck, they spread its meaning to distant quarters.

VII.8: Consolidating Virtuosic Habits as an Inner Disposition for Action

"[鳲鳩在桑，其子七兮。] 淑人君子，其儀一兮。" 能爲一，然後能爲君子，慎其獨也。 "[燕燕於飛，差池其羽。之子於歸，遠送於野。] 瞻望弗及，泣涕如雨。" 能差池其羽，然後能至哀。君子慎其獨也。

"[The turtle dove is in the mulberry tree with her seven young;] good and exemplary persons (*junzi* 君子) are singular in their deportment." Only when persons are able to be singular in their conduct are they able to be exemplary. Thus, exemplary persons are ever concerned to consolidate their virtuosic

VII. THE *FIVE MODES OF VIRTUOSIC CONDUCT* (*WUXINGPIAN* 五行篇): THE INTERIM BETWEEN CONFUCIUS AND MENCIUS

habits as an inner disposition for action.

"[The swallows are flying; their wing feathers seem to be uneven in length. This young maid is going to her new husband's home; I send her far out into the wilderness.] I gaze vainly into the distance; my sobbing tears fall like rain." Only when I am able to see "the wing feathers to be uneven in length" am I able to experience the most profound grief. Exemplary persons are ever concerned to consolidate their virtuosic habits as an inner disposition for action.

Comment: The *Book of Songs* 152 reads:

鳲鳩在桑，其子七兮。淑人君子，其儀一兮。
The turtle-dove is in the mulberry tree with her seven young; this good man, our lord, in his comportment is beyond reproach.

(Cf. Legge, *Chinese Classics*, Vol. 4, p. 222; Karlgren, *Odes*, p. 95).
The *Book of Songs* 28 reads:

燕燕于飛，差池其羽。之子于歸，遠送于野。瞻望弗及，泣涕如雨。
The swallows are flying; their wing feathers seem to be uneven in length. This young maid is going to her new husband's home; I send her far out into the wilderness. I gaze vainly into the distance; my sobbing tears fall like rain.

(Cf. Karlgren, *Odes*, pp. 15-17. The passage is corrupt, and I have reconstructed it on the basis of the Guodian text.)

The key phrase here 慎其獨也 means to internalize and consolidate the five modes of virtuosic conduct as a habitual disposition for moral virtuosity.[①] Consolidating one's identity must be understood relationally and as an achievement. Such an identity is reflected in the uniqueness of one's own particular relations as they contribute to a flourishing community.

The expression *shendu* 慎獨 occurs also in *Xunzi* 7/3/30:

---

① See Liang Tao 梁涛, "Zhu Xi dui 'Shendu' de Wudu jiqi zai Jingxue Quanshi zhong de Yiyi 朱熹對"慎獨"的誤讀及其在經學詮釋中的意義, *Zhexue Yanjiu* 哲學研究 (2004), 第 3 期, pp. 48-54.

夫此順命，以慎其獨者也。善之爲道者，不誠則不獨，不獨則不形，不形則雖作於心，見於色，出於言，民猶若未從也；雖從必疑。
Exemplary persons accord with the propensity of things to consolidate their virtuosic habits as an inner disposition for action. For persons effective in advancing the way, if they do not have resolve, they will not achieve their uniqueness; if they do not achieve their uniqueness, they will not take on the proper form; if they do not take on the proper form, even though they were to initiate something in their heartmind that is then manifest in their countenance, and is again expressed in what they say, still the common people would not follow them, and even if they did follow them, they will certainly be suspicious.

This whole section of *Xunzi* uses the vocabulary of the *Focusing the Familiar*, and seems to be an elaboration upon it.

The other example of this expression *shenqidu* 慎其獨 is in the *Expansive Learning* (cf. Legge, *Chinese Classics*, Vol. 1, p. 367) which uses a vocabulary reminiscent of *Xunzi*:

此謂誠於中，形於外，故君子必慎其獨也。
This is what is meant by the saying: "Where there is resolve within it will take shape without." Thus, exemplary persons are necessarily concerned to consolidate their virtuosic habits as an inner disposition for action.

In *Zhuangzi* 17/6/41 (cf. A.C. Graham [trans.] *Chuang-tzu: The Inner Chapters*, London: George Allen & Unwin, 1981, p. 87; Burton Watson, *The Complete Works of Chuang Tzu*, New York, Columbia University Press, 1968, p. 83) there is the passage:

九日而後能外生；已外生矣，而後能朝徹；朝徹，而後能見獨；見獨，而後能無古今；無古今，而後能入於不死不生。
After nine days he was able to put life outside himself, and having put life outside himself, he was then able to attain the brightness of dawn; having attained the brightness of dawn, he was then able to see his own uniqueness; seeing his own uniqueness he was then able to set aside past and present; having set aside past and present, he was then able to enter a state of neither living nor dying.

VII. THE *FIVE MODES OF VIRTUOSIC CONDUCT (WUXINGPIAN* 五行篇): THE INTERIM BETWEEN CONFUCIUS AND MENCIUS

The use of *du* 獨 is often glossed as the consolidating of a personal identity that has "oneness" in the sense of a "uniqueness" (*yi* 一) achieved by the quality it has in the relations that give it context (*yiduobufen* 一多不分).

VII.9: The Inexhaustibility of the Habitude of Moral Virtuosity (*de* 德)

君子之爲善也，有與始，有與終也。君子之爲德也，有與始，無與終也。

While the conduct of the exemplary person (*junzi* 君子) being efficacious (*shan* 善) has its beginning and its end, exemplary persons having moral virtuosity (*de* 德) have their beginning, but have no end.

Comment: This passage repeats the contrast between efficacy (*shan* 善) and moral virtuosity (*de* 德) found in VII.2, where moral virtuosity is both an expression of the inner habituation of the five modes of virtuosic conduct, and the deep coalescence in the relationship between humans and *tian* 天 achieved in the person of the sage. While instances of the exemplary person's conduct deemed efficacious are determinate with a beginning and an end, the habitude of moral virtuosity itself as the source of such conduct is inexhaustible.

VII.10: Opening with Bells and Rallying Others with Jade Tubes

金聲而玉振之，有德者也。金聲，善也；玉音，聖也。善，人道也；德，天道也。唯有德者，然後能金聲而玉振之。

To open with bells and then rally others with jade tubes is to have moral virtuosity (*de* 德). The opening with bells is efficacy (*shan* 善) while the pure sound of jade tubes is sagacity (*sheng* 聖). Efficacy is the way-making of human beings (*rendao* 人道); moral virtuosity is the way-making of *tian* (*tiandao* 天道). It is only once one has moral virtuosity that they are able to "open with bells and rally others with jade tubes."

Comment: This metaphor of a musical performance that opens with bells and rallies others with jade tubes makes efficacious conduct preliminary to its habituation as moral virtuosity (*de* 德), and answers the question of how moral virtuosity "takes shape within." Moral virtuosity is ascribed both to the way-making of *tian* 天 and to those who by virtue of their sagacity are able to "open with bells and rally others with jade tubes." The depth of coalescence in the *tian*-human (*tianren* 天人) relationship is expressed in the Confucian texts through the celestial language used to describe the sages, giving the obscure notion of *tian* 天 a human face.

This passage is echoed in *Mencius* 5B1:

孟子曰:"伯夷,聖之清者也;伊尹,聖之任者也;柳下惠,聖之和者也;孔子,聖之時者也。孔子之謂集大成。集大成也者,金聲而玉振之也。金聲也者,始條理也;玉振之也者,終條理也。始條理者,智之事也;終條理者,聖之事也。智,譬則巧也;聖,譬則力也。由射於百步之外也,其至,爾力也;其中,非爾力也。"

Master Meng said: "Among the sages, Bo Yi was the unsullied sage, Yi Yin the highly responsible sage, Liu Xiahui the amiable and obliging sage, and Confucius the timely sage. It is Confucius who can be called the one who gathered up all of the great accomplishments. One who gathers up all of the great accomplishments is like a musical performance opening with bells and then following up with the jade tubes to bring it to a close. To open with striking the bells is a beginning that sets and modulates the tone; to close with jade tubes is an ending that continues and modulates the proper tone. To begin by setting the proper tone is the stuff of wisdom; to finish up by maintaining the proper tone is the stuff of sageliness. Wisdom can be compared to skill; sageliness to strength. It is like shooting an arrow from beyond a hundred paces. For the arrow to reach the target is a matter of strength; but for the arrow to hit the mark—this is more than merely strength."

In addition to the specific theme of correlating wisdom (*zhi* 智) and sagacity (*sheng* 聖) pervasive in *Five Modes of Virtuosic Conduct*, there is an obvious overlap in vocabulary and metaphor between this text and *Mencius*. Such resonance suggests that the Mencius here is a commentary elaborating upon this passage in the *Five Modes of Virtuosic Conduct*.

VII. THE *FIVE MODES OF VIRTUOSIC CONDUCT (WUXINGPIAN* 五行篇): THE INTERIM BETWEEN CONFUCIUS AND MENCIUS

VII.11-14: Vocabulary Clusters for Modes of Virtuosic Conduct

不聰不明，[不明不聖，] 不聖不智，不智不仁，不仁不安，不安不樂，不樂無德。不變不悅，不悅不戚，不戚不新（親），不新（親）不愛，不愛不仁。不直不肆，不肆不果，不果不簡，不簡不行，不行不義。不遠不敬，不敬不嚴，不嚴不尊，不尊不恭，不恭無禮。

To not be keen of hearing is to be lacking in acuity, [to not be acutely aware is to be lacking in sagacity (*sheng* 聖),] and to not be sagacious is to be lacking in wisdom (*zhi* 智). Lacking wisdom, one will not be consummate (*ren* 仁), and not being consummate, one will not be at ease. Not being at ease, one will not find enjoyment (*le* 樂), and not finding enjoyment, one will be lacking in moral virtuosity (*de* 德).

Not being attached,[①] one does not find delight; with no delight, one does not feel intimacy; with no feeling of intimacy, one does not have affection for one's kin; without affection for one's kin, one is not loving; without love, one is not consummate as a person.

Not being true, one will not be at ease; not being at ease, one will not be effective; not being effective, one will not see the big picture; not seeing the big picture, one will not do what is proper; not doing what is proper, one will not do what is most appropriate (*yi* 義).

If one does not keep the proper distance, one will not be respectful (*jing* 敬); in the absence of respect, there will be no dignity; without dignity, there will be no veneration; without veneration, there will be no reverence; without reverence, there will be no sense of propriety (*li* 禮).

Comment: The sequencing of a cluster of related terms here anticipates the structure of *Expansive Learning*. Each of these four statements, save the first one, provides a set of terms associated with one of the modes of virtuosic conduct. The first one as the exception states that keenness of hearing and acuity are necessary conditions for sagacity (*sheng* 聖) and wisdom (*zhi* 智). Clarity of sight and hearing enable sagacity and wisdom certainly, but they are also integral to the ease and enjoyment that come with a habituated inner disposition for virtuosic

---

① According to the "explanation" included in the MWD 10 text, *bian* 變 could be read as *lian* 戀 meaning "longing for, being attached to."

action. The text then provides the cluster of terms defining of moral virtuosity itself: consummate conduct (*ren* 仁), optimal appropriateness (*yi* 義), and a sense of propriety (*li* 禮). Consummate conduct (*ren* 仁) is an extension of love within the family. Doing what is most appropriate (*yi* 義) is being steadfast in doing what is proper in its broadest compass. Aspiring to propriety in one's roles and relations (*li* 禮) is expressed through a cluster of overlapping terms connoting a profound sense of deference.

VII.15-16: The Need for Sagacity and Wisdom in Recognizing the Way of Exemplary Persons

未嘗聞君子道，謂之不聰。未嘗見賢人，謂之不明。聞君子道而不知其君子道也，謂之不聖。見賢人而不知其有德也，謂之不智。見而知之，智也。聞而知之，聖也。明明，智也。虩虩，聖也。"明明在下，虩虩在上"，此之謂也。

Those who have not heard of the way (*dao* 道) of the exemplary person (*junzi* 君子) are said to be lacking in keenness of hearing; those who have not met the worthy person (*xianren* 賢人) are said to be lacking in acuity of sight. On hearing the way of the exemplary person, to fail to recognize it as such is to be lacking in sagacity (*sheng* 聖). On seeing worthy persons, to fail to recognize they have moral virtuosity (*de* 德) is to be lacking in wisdom (*zhi* 智). To recognize by sight is wisdom; to recognize it by ear is sagacity. To shine brilliantly is wisdom; to display majesty is sagacity. When the *Book of Songs* 236 observes: "shining its brightness below, displaying its majesty above," this is what it means.

Comment: Chen Lai would break the text at this point, making what has gone before the canonical text, and from this passage on, a commentary on the original document. He takes VII.11-VII.13 to be commentary on VII.1-VII.4 above with a focus on the theme of sagacity (*sheng* 聖) and wisdom (*zhi* 智).

Having acuity of sight defined in the language of "seeing" (*jian* 見) and seeing with "acuity" (*ming* 明) continues to be aligned with wisdom. And having keenness of hearing through "hearing" (*wen* 聞) and "keenness of hearing" (*cong* 聰) is aligned with sagacity. Such acuity is not simply clear-sightedness, but having the discernment necessary to recognize those

VII. THE *FIVE MODES OF VIRTUOSIC CONDUCT (WUXINGPIAN* 五行篇): THE INTERIM BETWEEN CONFUCIUS AND MENCIUS

who are worthy. And keenness of hearing is not simply having a sensitive ear, but having the capacity to hear and recognize the way of exemplary persons. Sagacity and wisdom are necessary conditions for learning and understanding the way of exemplary persons, and for being able to appreciate the moral virtuosity of worthy persons.

The passage cited from the *Book of Songs* 236 明明在下, 赫赫在上 "shining its brightness below, displaying its majesty above" is an allusion to *tian* 天, thus associating human wisdom and sagacity with *tian* 天. Cf. Karlgren, *Odes*, pp. 187-188.

VII.17: A Perceived Logic Among the Five Modes of Virtuosic Conduct

聞君子道, 聰也。聞而知之, 聖也。聖人知天道也。知而行之, 義也。① 行之而時, 德也。見賢人, 明也。見而知之, 智也。知而安之, 仁也。安而敬之, 禮也。聖智,② 禮樂之所由生也, 五行之所和也。和則樂, 樂則有德, 有德則邦家興。文王之見也如此。"文王在上也, 於昭於天", 此之謂也。

Hearing the way (*dao* 道) of the exemplary person (*junzi* 君子) is to be keen in hearing; hearing it and realizing what it is, is sagacity (*sheng* 聖). The sage realizes what the way of *tian* 天 is. Realizing what it is, to then act upon it is appropriateness (*yi* 義), and to act upon it at the proper time is moral virtuosity (*de* 德). Seeing worthy persons (*xianren* 賢人) is acuity. On seeing such persons to realize who they are is wisdom (*zhi* 智). Realizing who they are and being at ease with them is being consummate (*ren* 仁). Being at ease with them and showing them proper respect is propriety (*li* 禮).

Sagacity and wisdom are whence propriety and music (*yue* 樂) arise, and are what bring harmony (*he* 和) to the five modes of virtuosic conduct. Where there is such harmony, there is enjoyment (*le* 樂); where enjoyment, then moral virtuosity; and where moral virtuosity, the state and its families

---

① The Mawangdui version has "sagacity" (*sheng* 聖) rather than "appropriateness" (*yi* 義), but it does not seem to fit the context.

② The Mawangdui version is missing this sentence, but in its commentary on this passage it first cites this passage as 仁氣, 禮樂所由生也 "a consummatory ambiance is whence arise propriety and music" and then adds the comment: 言禮樂之生於仁義 "this states that propriety and music arise from consummatory and appropriate conduct."

flourish. Such was the insight of King Wen. When the *Book of Songs* 235 states: "King Wen presiding above; he shines in the heavens," this is what it means.

Comment: This is a key chapter revealing as it does a logic that obtains among the five modes of virtuosic conduct. The theme of sagacity (*sheng* 聖) and wisdom (*zhi* 智) continues, as does the theme of authentication in action leading to a cultivated habitude. The other three modes of moral virtuosity (*de* 德)—that is, appropriateness (*yi* 義), consummate conduct (*ren* 仁), and ritual propriety (*li* 禮)—are derived from sagacity and wisdom as completing the five-fold harmony that enables state and family to flourish. Although as we see in the *Expansive Learning* (*Daxue* 大學), personal cultivation is the root source of moral growth, the locus of such growth is in the relationships defining of social, political, and indeed cosmic order.

Once again, sagacity is associated with *tian* 天. In the first line, it declares "the sage knows what the way of *tian* 天 is," where acting upon this knowledge is the source of optimal appropriateness (*yi* 義). When what is appropriate is done in the most timely way, there is moral virtuosity (*de* 德). We saw in VII.2 that such virtuosity is seen both in "the way of *tian* 天" and in the conduct characteristic of the sage who has become such by habituating the five modes of virtuosic conduct. Of cosmic importance is such sagely conduct reflects deep coalescence (*du* 度) in the first-order *tian* 天-human relationship. Above in VII.4 we read:

五行皆形於內而時行之，謂之君子。
Those for whom all of the five modes of virtuosic conduct have taken shape within and who act upon them in a timely way are called exemplary persons.

When we compare what is said about exemplary persons in VII.4, there is a coincidence between the timely applications of such persons and the moral virtuosity ascribed to the sages.

The same association between the sage and *tian* 天 is reinforced metaphorically in the person and conduct of King Wen whose sagely rulership has made him a beacon in the heavens for the hundred generations that have followed him. Cf. Karlgren, *Odes*, pp. 185-186.

VII. THE *FIVE MODES OF VIRTUOSIC CONDUCT (WUXINGPIAN* 五行篇): THE INTERIM BETWEEN CONFUCIUS AND MENCIUS

VII.18: Efficacy (*shan* 善) as the Symbiosis of Four Modes of Virtuosic Conduct

見而知之，智也。知而安之，仁也。安而行之，義也。行而敬之，禮也。仁、義禮所由生也①，四行之所和也。和則同，同則善。

On seeing it, to realize what it is, is wisdom (*zhi* 智). Being wise, to find comfort in it is to be consummatory (*ren* 仁). Finding comfort in it, to act upon it is appropriateness (*yi* 義). On acting upon it, to show respect (*jing* 敬) is propriety (*li* 禮). Consummatory conduct is whence appropriateness and ritual propriety arise, and is what brings harmony (*he* 和) to the four modes of virtuosic conduct. Being harmonious, they function in unison, and being in unison, they are efficacious (*shan* 善).

Comment: There is a sequencing to these four modes of virtuosic conduct, with wisdom (*zhi* 智) coming first, consummate conduct (*ren* 仁) second, and with appropriateness (*yi* 義) and ritual propriety (*li* 禮) being derived from consummate conduct (*ren* 仁). At the same time, it is the symbiotic relationship that obtains among the application of these first four of the five modes of virtuosic conduct that produces harmony in practice and makes the consolidation of such conduct efficacious (*shan* 善). It is these four modalities of conduct specifically that constitute the prosocial "four inclinations" (*siduan* 四端) of Mencius. Such modes of conduct are thus better seen as interpenetrating aspects of moral virtuosity (*de* 德) than as exclusive categories. When we dispense with the distinctions that obtain among them, we have personal identity as the habituated disposition of the one heartmind.

VII.19: Consummate Conduct (*ren* 仁) and the Power of Human Feelings

顏色容貌溫變②也。以其中心與人交悅也，中心悅焉。遷於兄弟，戚也。戚而信之，新（親）也。新（親）而篤之，愛也。愛父，其繼愛人，仁也。

---

① The Mawangdui version has 仁義，禮智之所由生也 "consummate conduct and appropriateness is whence propriety and wisdom arise."
② The Mawangdui version has "and loving" (*lianlian* 戀戀) instead of "and changeable" (*bian* 變).

To be congenial and loving in both complexion and appearance in service to having delightful interactions with others in a habituated way, is to enjoy a real feeling of delight. To extend such delight to one's older and younger brothers is intimacy. Being intimate and living up to your word (*xin* 信) is family affection. To treat one's kin with affection and to be earnest in doing so is to be loving. To love one's father and then extend it to the loving of others is to be consummate in one's conduct (*ren* 仁).

Comment: A major theme in the Zisizi literature is the cosmic force of human feelings. The ultimate source of the five modes of virtuosic conduct is the earnest affection one is able to bring to the relations one has with others, beginning with intimate family bonds and then extending this consummate conduct outward. In VII.14, VII.15 and VII.16 we have a positive statement on consummate conduct (*ren* 仁), appropriateness (*yi* 義), and ritual propriety (*li* 禮) that was stated in negative terms in VII.10. Chen Lai suggests these three passages provide a basis for Mencius's doctrine of the "four inclinations" (*siduan* 四端) as the initial condition of the heartmind (*xin* 心), and can be directly correlated with the language Mencius uses to define each one of them.[①] *Mencius* 2A6, for example, states:

惻隱之心，仁之端也；羞惡之心，義之端也；辭讓之心，禮之端也；是非之心，智之端也。人之有是四端也，猶其有四體也。

Our heartmind in feeling pity at perceived suffering disposes it toward consummate conduct in our roles and relations (*ren* 仁); our heartmind in feeling shame at perceived crudeness disposes it toward appropriate conduct in our roles and relations (*yi* 義); our heartmind in its feelings of modesty and deference disposes it toward propriety in our roles and relations (*li* 禮); our heartmind in feeling a sense of discrimination disposes it toward wisdom in our roles and relations (*zhi* 智). Persons have these four inclinations (*siduan* 四端) just as they have their four limbs.

VII.20: Appropriateness (*yi* 義) Is Being Steadfast in Walking the Walk

中心辯然而正行之，直也。直而遂之，肆也。肆而不畏強御，果也。不以小

---

① Chen Lai 陳來, 竹帛《五行》與簡帛研究, pp. 136-137.

VII. THE *FIVE MODES OF VIRTUOSIC CONDUCT (WUXINGPIAN* 五行篇): THE INTERIM BETWEEN CONFUCIUS AND MENCIUS

道害大道，簡也。有大罪而大誅之，行也。貴貴，其等尊賢，義也。

To be habituated in one's power of discrimination and to act upon it properly is to be true in one's conduct. Being true, to stay the course is to be steadfast. Being steadfast, "to stand in awe neither of those who use coercion nor those who are contrary" is to be effective. To not let petty things get in the way of great accomplishments is to be broad-minded. To dispense severe punishments for heinous crimes is proper conduct. To revere the noble according to rank and to honor those who are worthy is appropriateness (*yi* 義).

Comment: The emphasis here is on making one's determinations, and then being steadfast in walking the walk. There is a strong phonetic and semantic association in the classical language between being true (*zhi* 直) in walking straight ahead, and moral virtuosity (*de* 德). The ancient pronunciation of the two characters is similar, and an early alternative form of the character moral virtuosity (*de* 德) is *de* 惪. To always do what is right within the broadest compass regardless of the circumstances is to do what is most appropriate (*yi* 義). In *Mencius* 5B3:

用下敬上，謂之貴貴；用上敬下，謂之尊賢。貴貴、尊賢，其義一也。

For those of lower status to show respect for their superiors is called revering the worthy; for those of higher status to show respect for those below them is called honoring the worthy. In doing what is most appropriate (*yi* 義) they are the same.

VII.21: Propriety (*li* 禮) Is Deference in Broad Compass

以其外心與人交，遠也。遠而莊之，敬也。敬而不懈，嚴也。嚴而畏之，尊也。尊而不驕，恭也。恭而博交，禮也。

Interacting with others in a reserved way is to be restrained. Restraint and strength is respect (*jing* 敬). Respect and resolve is dignity. Dignity and awe is veneration. Veneration without arrogance is reverence. Reverence in a broad field of relations is propriety (*li* 禮).

Comment: In service to how the modal term "propriety" (*li* 禮) is to be understood and expressed, this passage provides a vocabulary of deferential terms. Importantly, deference is collateral rather than beginning from any particular agency. Certainly, the younger members of a family defer to their elders. But to be effective in the intergenerational transmission of culture, elders must acknowledge the collaterality and defer as well to the always unique needs and the innovations of the succeeding generation.

VII.22-23: Seeing the Big Picture and Making Allowances

不簡，不行。不匿，不察於道。有大罪而大誅之，簡也。有小罪而赦之，匿也。有大罪而弗大誅也，不［行］也。有小罪而弗赦也，不察於道也。簡之爲言猶練也，大而晏者也。匿之爲言也猶匿匿也，小而防者也。簡，義之方也。匿，仁之方也。強，義之方。柔，仁之方也。"不競不絿，不剛不柔，"此之謂也。

To fail to see the big picture is to fail to act properly; to fail to make allowances is to fail to discern the proper way (*dao* 道). To punish heinous crimes with severity is to see the big picture; to respond to small infractions with leniency is to make allowances. To fail to punish heinous crimes with severity is to fail to act properly. To fail to make allowances for small infractions is to fail to discern the proper way. The expression "seeing the big picture" (*jian* 简) is like "experienced" (*lian* 练); it is a major undertaking and thus rarely seen. The expression "making allowances" (*ni* 匿) is like "glossing over" (*nini* 匿匿); it is a minor affair and thus everywhere. "Seeing the big picture" is the way to be appropriate (*yi* 義); "making allowances," is the way to be consummate (*ren* 仁). Being firm is the way to be appropriate; being lenient is the way to be consummate. When the *Book of Songs* 304 says "he was neither contentious nor insistent, neither firm nor lenient," this is what it means.

Comment: In this passage virtuosic conduct is correlated with proper governance, and is thus given a social and political context. It is only in being synoptic in one's view of things that the proper interests of all concerned can be taken into account (*yi* 義). Once what is proper has been determined, those in authority must act upon this judgment with resolve. Hence *yi* 義 entails firmness. At the same time, any particular situation requires the flexibility to set priorities, and to exercise compassion in overlooking minor infelicities. Proper governance thus requires both firmness and leniency. Given the particular circumstances, such capaciousness enables those with the responsibility for governance to be both firm and lenient at the same time. The *Book of Songs* 304 passage in describing Tang 湯, the

VII. THE *FIVE MODES OF VIRTUOSIC CONDUCT (WUXINGPIAN* 五行篇): THE INTERIM BETWEEN CONFUCIUS AND MENCIUS

sage-ruler of the Shang dynasty, states: 不競不絿，不剛不柔，敷政優優，百錄是遒 "being neither contentious nor insistent, neither firm nor lenient, he dispensed his policies with everyone in accord, and all good things came to him." Cf. Karlgren, *Odes*, pp. 264-265.

VII.24: Consolidating Great Accomplishments and Promoting the Worthy

君子集大成。能進之，爲君子，弗能進也，各止於其里。大而晏者，能有取焉。小而軫者，能有取焉。胥膚膚達諸君子道，謂之賢者。君子知而舉之，謂之尊賢；知而事之，謂之尊賢者也。前，王公之尊賢者也；後，士之尊賢者也。

Exemplary persons (*junzi* 君子) gather up all the great accomplishments. Being able to take these accomplishments further is what makes them exemplary persons; being unable to do so would limit them to their own place. Where these accomplishments are major and thus rarely seen, they are able to take something away from them; where these accomplishments are minor and thus common, they are also able to take something away from them. Xu Fufu in mastering the way of the exemplary person was called a worthy person (*xianzhe* 賢者). When exemplary persons recognize such people and promote them, they are said to hold the worthy in high esteem. When exemplary persons recognize them and put them into service, they are said to hold the worthy in high esteem. Early on, this practice was at first the former kings and dukes holding the worthy in high esteem, and more recently it has been scholars esteeming them as well.

Comment: The main message of this passage is that a primary responsibility of those with social and political authority is to promote the worthy and to put them into service. We can piece this practical imperative together by drawing on several passages from the *Mencius*. In *Mencius* 5B1 it uses similar language:

孔子之謂集大成。集大成也者，金聲而玉振之也。
It is Confucius who can be called the one who gathered up all of the great accomplishments. One who gathered up all of the great accomplishments is like a musical performance opening with bells and then following up with the jade tubes to bring it to a close.

In *Mencius* 5B6 in discussing Zisi's rejection of gifts from Duke Mu that were not coupled with the offer of a position, Mencius says:

> 悅賢不能舉，又不能養也，可謂悅賢乎？
>
> If in claiming to delight in worthy persons one is neither able to promote them nor to take care of them, can they really be said to delight in worthy persons?

This same 5B6 passage ends with 故曰：王公之尊賢者也 "Therefore it is said: 'This was the former dukes and kings holding the worthy in high esteem.'"

In *Mencius* 5B3 there is a distinction made that uses the same language as this passage. In describing Duke Ping of Jin's 晉平公 treatment of Hai Tang 亥唐, it says: 士之尊賢者也，非王公之尊賢也 "This is merely the case of a scholar esteeming the worthy; it is not the kings and dukes holding the worthy in high esteem."

Chen Lai takes VII.12 to VII.18 to be a subordinate commentary on various themes found in VII.5 to VII.9. Pang Pu has suggested that Xu Fufu 胥膚膚 here is Suolu Can 索盧參 who appears in the *Lüshichunqiu* 呂氏春秋孟夏記:①

> ……索盧參，東方之鉅狡也，學於禽滑黎。此六人者，刑戮死辱之人也，今非徒免於刑戮死辱也，由此為天下名士顯人，以終其壽，王公大人從而禮之，此得之於學也。
>
> ... Suolu Can was a well-known hustler from the eastern regions who studied with Qin Guli [perhaps a disciple of Mozi]. These six men were the kind of persons who were bound for the executioner's block and a disgraceful death, but not only did they avoid such an end, but went on to live out their long lives as world-famous scholars and persons of distinction. Kings, dukes, and high officials sought them out as teachers and treated them with high ritual proprieties. This is what they got from their education.

---

① Chen Lai 陳來，竹帛《五行》與簡帛研究, pp. 134-139. Pang Pu 龐樸, *Zhubo* "Wuxingpian" *Jiaozhu ji Yanjiu*, 竹帛《五行》篇校注及研究, Chutu Wenxian Yizhu Yanxi Congshu. Taipei, Wanjuanlou, 2000, p. 74.

VII. THE *FIVE MODES OF VIRTUOSIC CONDUCT (WUXINGPIAN* 五行篇): THE INTERIM BETWEEN CONFUCIUS AND MENCIUS

VII.25: A Symbiosis Among the Heartmind's (*xin* 心) Attendants

耳目鼻口手足六者，心之所役也。心曰唯，莫敢不唯；[心曰] ① 諾，莫敢不諾；[心曰] 進，莫敢不進；[心曰] 後②，莫敢不後；[心曰] 深，莫敢不深；[心曰] 淺，莫敢不淺。和則同，同則善。

The ears, eyes, nose, mouth, hands, and feet are the six attendants of the heartmind. When the heartmind says "yes," none dare but comply; when it says "agree," none dare but comply; when it says "advance," none dare but comply; when it says "withdraw," none dare but comply; when it says "with intensity," none dare but comply; when it says "casually," none dare but comply. Being harmonious (*he* 和), they act in unison, and acting in unison, they are efficacious (*shan* 善).

Comment: The heartmind holds sway over the functions of the other different elements of the body's sensorium, and coordinates their various activities into a single, efficacious unity. This theme of an efficacy achieved through a symbiosis in the activation of difference underlies all virtuosic conduct, and has physical as well as moral and political application. This kind of optimizing symbiosis is inclusive while at the same time having its own internal logic, with some aspects taking priority over others in different situations. This pattern of thinking is captured in the notion of "the inseparability and mutual entailment of one and many" (*yiduobufenguan* 一多不分觀) wherein the many are implicated in the one. While the heartmind "governs" the senses, far from being an external imposition, it is the guiding, reflective impetus within the physical sensorium itself.

There is a resonant passage in *Mencius* 6A7:

故曰：口之於味也，有同耆焉；耳之於聲也，有同聽焉；目之於色也，有同美焉。至於心，獨無所同然乎？心之所同然者何也？謂理也、義也。聖人先得我心之所同然耳。故理義之悅我心，猶芻豢之悅我口。

Thus it is said: In taste our palates are partial to the same flavors, in music our ears to the same sounds, and in beauty our eyes to the same forms. How could it be with respect to the heartmind (*xin* 心) alone we have

---

① Emending the passage on the basis of the Mawangdui version.
② The Mawangdui version has "withdraw" (*tui* 退) rather than "fall back" (*hou* 後).

nothing in common? What then do heartminds have in common? I would say it is a sense of coherence (*li* 理) and of appropriateness (*yi* 義). The sages were just the first among us to really grasp what our heartminds have in common. Thus, it is a sense of coherence and appropriateness are pleasing to my heartmind in the same way meat from livestock is pleasing to my palate.

The heartmind's sense of coherence and appropriateness enables it to bring a reflective and responsive intelligence to both the physical and intellectual aspects of the human experience.

This relationship between the heartmind and the senses is again the theme of *Mencius* 6A15:

耳目之官不思，而蔽於物，物交物，則引之而已矣。心之官則思，思則得之，不思則不得也。此天之所與我者，先立乎其大者，則其小者弗能奪也。此爲大人而已矣。

Our physical senses such as looking and listening are not reflective, and thus can be deceived by external things. When one thing is thus engaged by another, they do no more than distract each other. The office of the heartmind on the other hand is thinking and feeling. But it will only get what it is after if it actually thinks and feels. We have been given this as our native ability. If we begin by attending to these higher capacities, the inferior ones will not be able to wrest control from them. This is all there is to becoming a superior person.

When the physical sensorium is orchestrated by the thoughts and feelings of the heartmind, they function efficaciously and elevate the human experience to a higher level.

The Tang dynasty compendium *Yilin* 意林卷一子思子七卷 cites Zisizi as saying: 君子以心導耳目，小人以耳目導心 "Exemplary persons use the heartmind to guide the physical sensorium; petty persons do the opposite."

VII. THE *FIVE MODES OF VIRTUOSIC CONDUCT* (*WUXINGPIAN* 五行篇): THE INTERIM BETWEEN CONFUCIUS AND MENCIUS

VII.26: Correlative Methods for Advancing Knowledge

目而知之謂之進之。喻而知之，謂之進之。闢而知之，謂之進之。① 幾而知之，天也。"上帝臨汝，毋貳爾心"，此之謂也。

Knowing something as in witnessing it is called taking it further. Knowing by way of metaphor is called taking it further. Knowing by way of correlation is called taking it further. Knowing something by observing its inchoate beginnings is *tian* 天. When the *Book of Songs* 236 says "the high ancestors are watching over you; do not be of two minds," this is what it means.

Comment: These different ways of knowing in combination provide us with a window on a Confucian epistemology in which it is a panoramic view rather than any simple truth that is the highest form of knowing. Sagacious knowing is often associated with the prescience that sages have in anticipating what has yet to occur when it is still inchoate. It is this underdeterminacy in the human experience that serves as an opening for intervention and co-creativity, and just such prescience that thus links the sage with *tian* 天. *Shangdi* 上帝 like *tian* 天 is an anthropomorphic term for the numinous associated with ancestral and other sacrifices who in return for veneration provides its blessing. It is because of the comprehensive view of things and good will from these spiritual heights that the limits of human knowing can be overcome. Cf. Karlgren, *Odes*, pp. 188-189.

In this passage, there seems to be an allusion to the methods of advancing knowledge through the art of naming we find made explicit in the *Later Mohist Canons* in which *pi* 辟 and *mou* 侔 are defined as technical terms. Citing A.C. Graham:

辟也者，舉也，物而以明之。
"'Illustrating' is referring to other things in order to clarify one's case."
侔也者，比辭而俱行也。
"'Parallelising' is comparing propositions and letting all 'proceed'."②

This first passage with *pi* 辟 sheds light on how we might understand

---

① The order of these two sentences is reversed in the Mawangdui version.
② A.C. Graham, *Later Mohist Logic, Ethics and Science*, Hong Kong: Chinese University Press, 1978, pp. 482-483.

Analects 6.30:

能近取譬，可謂仁之方也已。
Being able to correlate one's conduct with those near at hand can be said to be the method of becoming consummate as a person.

VII.27: *Tian* 天 as a Guide in the *Tian*-Human (*tianren* 天人) Relation

天施諸其人，天也。其人施諸人，狎①也。(其人施諸人，不得其人不爲法。)
What *tian* 天 bestows on human beings is itself; what human beings bestow on other human beings is their humanity. (In what human beings bestow on other persons, they cannot serve as their object of emulation unless they are the right person.)

Comment: As expressed throughout these Confucian canons, *tian* 天 is the one great benefactor of human beings, providing the natural and cultural context in which persons can cultivate themselves as a creative force in cosmic flourishing. The parallel contrast here between *tian* 天 and undue "humanity" (*xia* 狎) (following the Mawangdui version) suggests that intimate relations among human beings needs to be guided by the higher demands made by *tian* 天. *Focusing the Familiar* 17 makes it clear that the largesse of *tian* 天 is in direct response to the moral virtuosity expressed by human beings in their conduct:

故大德必得其位，必得其祿，必得其名，必得其壽。故天之生物，必因其材而篤焉……故大德者必受命。
Thus, those of the greatest virtuosity (*dade* 大德) are certain to gain status, emoluments, reputation, and longevity. For the generosity of *tian* 天 in giving birth to and nurturing things is certain to be in response to the quality of the things themselves.... Those of the greatest virtuosity are thus certain to receive *tian*'s 天 charge.

---

① The Mawangdui version has "their human-beingness" (*ren* 人) as parallel with *tian* 天 instead of "their familiarity" (*xia* 狎).

VII.28: The Different Modes of Virtuosic Conduct as Different Responses to the Proper Way (*dao* 道)

聞道①而悅者，好仁者也。聞道而畏者，好義者也。聞道而恭者，好禮者也。聞道而樂者，好德者也。

Those who on hearing of the proper way (*dao* 道) of the exemplary person (*junzi* 君子) find delight in it are fond of consummate conduct (*ren* 仁); those who on hearing of this way stand in awe of it are fond of appropriate conduct (*yi* 義); those who on hearing of this way are reverent are fond of aspiring to ritual propriety (*li* 禮); those who on hearing of this way find enjoyment (*le* 樂) in it are fond of moral virtuosity (*de* 德).

Comment: Just learning of the way of exemplary persons is not enough. There is a complexity in the feelings that are stirred in persons who hear of it. Finding delight in this way is correlated with the kind of persons who are already consummate in their conduct; being awed by this way with persons who have a sense of optimal appropriateness; feeling reverence for this way with persons who live lives informed by ritual practices; and rejoicing in this way with persons who are models of moral virtuosity. But rather than understanding each of these responses in an exclusive sense, the expectation is that it is one and the same person who has consolidated these different modalities of moral conduct in their person to become who they are.

VIII. THE *MOZI* 墨子: ON DENOUNCING THE CONFUCIANS AND THEIR DOCTRINES

Mo Di 墨翟 or Master Mo (Mozi 墨子) as a historical figure is a shadowy presence in the classical philosophical literature born about the same time that Confucius left this earth (479 BCE). He is remembered by the metaphors he uses as a craftsman of some kind who works with his hands and employs tools such as the compass and set square. The text compiled around his name is comprised of several different evolving sections, and

---

① The Mawangdui version has "on hearing of the way of exemplary persons" (*wenjunzidao* 聞君子道) rather than "on hearing of the way" (*wendao* 聞道).

was edited together across the several centuries of the Warring States period (475-221 BCE). The *Mozi* serves as a good example of how respecting the interpretive context can make an important difference in our understanding of the early philosophical dialectic. Over the last generation in the publications of scholars such as Chris Fraser, Carine Defoort, Nicolas Standaert, David Wong, James Behuniak, Dan Robbins, Hui-chieh Loy, Ben Wong, and so on, they have done much to reinstate the *Mozi* as integral to the intellectual debates that flourished during the pre-Qin period, and to argue for a more robust understanding of a previously ignored and still much misunderstood text and tradition.①

From the Confucian canons—especially *Mencius* and *Xunzi*—and from other sources such as the *Zhuangzi*, we learn that the doctrines of the Mohists were a powerful intellectual force during this formative pre-Qin period. Indeed, where the Confucian texts rail against the lineages of Yang Zhu and Mozi as "YangMo" 楊墨, the *Zhuangzi* targets the Confucians and the Mohists as "RuMo" 儒墨. Even where the Mohists are not mentioned by name, a text such as *Focusing the Familiar* (*Zhongyong* 中庸) is arguably a deliberate response to the Mohist challenge to the Confucians on how to best understand the relationship between *tian* 天 and the human condition. In this early dialectic, the criticisms move in both directions.

Much of the representation of the Mohists in the Confucian texts is more polemic than it is fair criticism. In this respect, it is reminiscent of the Confucian response to Buddhism in the neo-Confucian literature. As should be clear from a quick survey of Mohist doctrines such as "personal cultivation" (*xiushen* 修身), "promoting the worthy" (*shangxian* 尚賢), "affection for scholar-officials" (*qinshi* 親士), "benefitting the whole world" (*litianxia* 利天下) and so on, there is much in Mohist philosophy that resonates with the tenets of classical Confucianism. At least on the surface, the Mohists promote what are decidedly key, family-centered Confucian values such as "family reverence" (*xiao* 孝), "consummate persons/conduct" (*ren*

---

① For a new and philosophically informed translation of this text, see Chris Fraser, *The Essential Mozi: Ethical, Political, and Dialectical Writings*, Oxford: Oxford University Press, 2020, and for a philosophical analysis, see his *The Philosophy of Mozi: The First Consequentialists*, New York: Columbia University Press, 2020. For the story of the evolution of the text itself, see *The Mozi as an Evolving Text: Different Voices in Early Chinese Thought*, ed. Carine Defoort and Nicolas Standaert, Leiden: Brill, 2013.

VIII. THE *MOZI* 墨子: ON DENOUNCING THE CONFUCIANS AND THEIR DOCTRINES

仁), and "optimal appropriateness" (*yi* 義). Indeed, as I will suggest below, the *Xunzi* as a syncretic text borrows quite freely from the Mohist teachings, particularly in his philosophy of language.

In the Confucian texts, there are strong reservations expressed about the Mohists, as we find in *Mencius* 3B9:

處士橫議, 楊朱、墨翟之言盈天下。天下之言, 不歸楊, 則歸墨。楊氏爲我, 是無君也; 墨氏兼愛, 是無父也。無父無君, 是禽獸也。

Unemployed scholar-officials make free with their opinions, and the doctrines of Yang Zhu and Mo Di fill the world. If the doctrines that prevail in the world are not those of Yang Zhu, then they come from Mo Di. Yang Zhu's doctrine of everyone for themselves amounts to the repudiation of one's sovereign lord, while Mo Di's doctrine of inclusive concern (*jian'ai* 兼愛) is a repudiation of the special affection one has for one's own father. To repudiate one's father and one's sovereign lord is to join the wild beasts of the field.

Of course, this is a most uncharitable reading of the Mohists who in fact take family reverence (*xiao* 孝) as a major tenet in their philosophy:

子墨子言曰: "仁者之爲天下度也, 辟之無以異乎孝子之爲親度也。今孝子之爲親度也, 將柰何哉? 曰: '親貧則從事乎富之, 人民寡則從事乎衆之, 衆亂則從事乎治之。' 當其於此也, 亦有力不足, 財不贍, 智不智, 然後已矣。無敢舍餘力, 隱謀遺利, 而不爲親爲之者矣。若三務者, 孝子之爲親度也, 既若此矣。雖仁者之爲天下度, 亦猶此也。" (Book 25 "Moderation in Burials" 節葬下)

Our Master Mo says: "A consummate ruler's concern for the world is analogous to and no different from a filial son's concern for his parents. How is the filial son's concern for his parents expressed? If his parents are poor, he engages in projects that will make them rich; if clan members are few, he engages in projects that will increase their numbers; if the clan is disorderly, he engages in projects that will bring about proper order. Of course, in carrying out these projects, he might find that his strength is not up to the task, that his resources are inadequate, and that he is lacking in the necessary wisdom. But he would not dare to give up working on behalf of his parents as long he has the last bit of strength, has any unlikely schemes, or has any remaining resources. The filial son's concern for his parents is expressed through carrying out these three tasks. And the same thing is true of the consummate ruler in his concern for the world."

Xunzi's critique of Mozi's extreme and indeed excessive austerity found in *Xunzi* 10 is a most compelling argument because it does reflect perhaps one of the most problematic assumptions in Mohist philosophy:

墨子之言昭昭然爲天下憂不足。夫不足非天下之公患也，特墨子之私憂過計也……天下之公患，亂傷之也。胡不嘗試相與求亂之者誰也？我以墨子之"非樂"也，則使天下亂；墨子之"節用"也，則使天下貧，非將墮之也，説不免焉。墨子大有天下，小有一國，將蹙然衣粗食惡，憂戚而非樂。

Throughout the teachings of Mozi there is this worry on behalf of the world that resources are inadequate. However such inadequacy is not a problem shared by the whole world, but is in fact a private worry that comes from his own miscalculations.... The problem shared by the world is the harm done to it by disorder. And who is it that is responsible for trying to bring about this disorder? I would say it is Mozi's "condemnation of music" that is a source of the world's disorder, and it is his "frugality in expenditures" that is the source of its poverty. It is not that I want to put him down, but his teachings leave me no choice. Were Mozi to rule the whole world or just a small state, he would reduce it to coarse clothes and bad food, all grief and worry, and no music or enjoyment.

When Mozi advocates for benefiting the whole world as his ultimate standard, it is the thinness of his definition of "benefit" that is and should be a legitimate concern for the Confucians. That is, the dour Mozi in condemning any expenditures other than those necessary for bare subsistence does not provide a philosophy that promises much by way of human flourishing or happiness. This criticism is perhaps best captured in Xunzi's characterization of Mozi: 墨子蔽於用而不知文 "Mozi being obsessed with usefulness had no sense of cultural refinement."

To give Mozi his due, we must remember that his ideas flourished during the widespread and protracted turmoil of the Warring States period when disposable resources were scarce. While the elite still had enough, the ordinary people had little or nothing. Indeed, it is under these dire circumstances that the Mohists formulate their criticisms of the Confucians

VIII. THE *MOZI* 墨子: ON DENOUNCING THE CONFUCIANS AND THEIR DOCTRINES

who they identify with the ruling elite.

We can make a summary list of the main tenets that the Mohist critique levels against the Confucians found in those excerpted passages from the *Mozi* translated below. The Mohists characterize the Confucians as 1) being impious in not believing in the powers of *tian* 天 and the divinity of the ghosts and spirits, 2) having extravagant burial practices that squander scarce resources and 3) having protracted mourning periods that are debilitating and again a waste of resources. 4) The Confucians rather than engaging in those productive activities that add to communal resources occupy themselves instead with the frivolous entertainments of song and dance. 5) The Confucian doctrine of a strong fatalism that would persuade people human effort makes no difference is a source of apathy and indolence that has the worst kind of economic and political consequences. 6) There is an illogic in Confucian practices where they are impious and yet spend so much time, effort, and resources on ritual ceremonies and sacrifices. 7) A close examination of their mourning practices shows that, contrary to their own rhetoric, they hypocritically put intimacy ahead of proper respect. 8) The Confucians are parasitic on the society, finding devious ways to satisfy their expensive tastes while doing absolutely no work to support themselves or others. 9) The Confucians in their speech and dress are antiquarians who take such superficial pomposity to be the substance of culture and high refinement. 10) Unwilling to brook innovation, Confucians are cultural conservatives and fundamentalists. 11) Never proffering an opinion unless asked, the Confucians do not respond to circumstances in sharing their counsel.

Perhaps the strongest complaint that the Confucians have against the Mohists is the populist power they derive from a committed following that "fills the world." And while we might cite chapter and verse from the canons to defend the Confucians against the Mohist charges, at the same time we must allow that Confucianism as a historical fact is often far from the espoused ideals of deference and interdependence. There has been a tendency historically for Confucian philosophy in practice to ossify, where family reverence (*xiao* 孝) becomes an oppressive patriarchical authoritarianism and ritual propriety becomes rigid and conservative rules of correct conduct. The celebration of intimate relations can lend itself to nepotism and corruption, and governance through role models and moral suasion can quickly lead to the worst kinds of self-deception and hypocrisy. Again, a commitment to the values of education and political influence can turn into arrogance, and the pursuit of cultural refinement into elitism.

VIII.1 Gongmeng (公孟)

48.14 子墨子謂程子曰:"儒之道足以喪天下者,四政焉。儒以天爲不明,以鬼爲不神,天鬼不説,此足以喪天下。又厚葬久喪,重爲棺槨,多爲衣衾,送死若徙,三年哭泣,扶後起,杖後行,耳無聞,目無見,此足以喪天下。又弦歌鼓舞,習爲聲樂,此足以喪天下。又以命爲有,貧富壽夭,治亂安危有極矣,不可損益也,爲上者行之,必不聽治矣;爲下者行之,必不從事矣,此足以喪天下。"程子曰:"甚矣!先生之毀儒也。"子墨子曰:"儒固無此若四政者,而我言之,則是毀也。今儒固有此四政者,而我言之,則非毀也,告聞也。"程子無辭而出。子墨子曰:"迷之!"反,後坐,進復曰:"鄉者先生之言有可聞者焉,若先生之言,則是不譽禹,不毀桀紂也。"子墨子曰:"不然,夫應孰辭,稱議而爲之,敏也。厚攻則厚吾,薄攻則薄吾。應孰辭而稱議,是猶荷轅而擊蛾也。"

Our Master Mo addressed Chengzi, saying: "There are four policies by way of the Confucians that are enough to bring ruin on the world. The Confucians hold *tian* 天 is unseeing and ghosts are not divine, offending both *tian* 天 and the ghosts. This is enough to bring ruin on the world.

"Again, they have extravagant burials and protracted periods of mourning, have layers of inner and outer coffins, have multiple coverings of burial shrouds, and send off the dead as though moving house. For three years they wail and weep, can only stand up when helped, and can only walk with a cane. Their ears hear nothing and their eyes see nothing. This is also enough to bring ruin on the world.

"Again, they strum and sing, drum and dance, and are engaged in every kind of music. This also is enough to bring ruin on the world.

"Again, the Confucians have a doctrine of fatalism where poverty or good fortune, longevity or an early demise, an orderly or disorderly world, security or danger, all have fixed limits and are irrevocable. If those in authority act upon this, they are certain to give up their governing and if the common run of people act upon it, they are certain to give up their occupations. This is also enough to bring ruin on the world."

Chengzi said: "You go too far, Sir, in accusing the Confucians!"

Our Master Mo replied: "If it is true that the Confucians do not hold these four policies and I say they do, then indeed I am accusing them. But since the Confucians do hold these four policies and I say as much, I am not

VIII. THE *MOZI* 墨子: ON DENOUNCING THE CONFUCIANS AND THEIR DOCTRINES

accusing them, but simply stating the way things are."
Chengzi unceremoniously withdrew.
Our Master Mo called to him to come back.
Chengzi after returning and seating himself, continued: "Are your words, Sir, worth listening to? According to what you have just said, we should neither be praising the Great Yu nor condemning the tyrants Jie and Zhou."
"Not so." said our Master Mo. "You are too quick in giving me your conventional and vacuous platitudes. When the attack is fierce, the defenses must be strong; when the attack is without consequence, defenses can be light. Responding to such platitudes is like shouldering a cart shaft to go after an ant."

Comment: Mozi summarizes for the Confucian Chengzi four criticisms the Mohists have of the Confucian way that they believe will bring ruin on the world: 1) the response of *tian* 天 and other divine entities to the Confucian lack of piety, 2) the expense in material and human resources squandered on unnecessarily extravagant burials and protracted mourning periods, 3) the expense in material and human resources fritted away on frivolous entertainments, and 4) the indolence, poverty, and disorder brought on by promoting a doctrine of strong fatalism that precludes the difference that real human effort can make.

When Chengzi responds by claiming that without Confucianism, there would be no basis for making a distinction between the historical sage-kings and tyrants. Mozi who takes himself to be a master of debate is decidedly unimpressed with the weakness of Chengzi's "argument," and replies with a humorous *ad hominin* that recalls the Mohist commitment to defensive warfare. For the Mohists, the several occupations of defensive warfare, defending logical premises and propositions, and being effective in debate all share in the value of protecting the integrity of specified boundaries.

48.9 公孟子曰："無鬼神。" 又曰："君子必學祭祀。" 子墨子曰："執無鬼而學祭禮，是猶無客而學客禮也，是猶無魚而爲魚罟也。"

Gongmengzi said: "There are no ghosts or spirits." And again he said: "Exemplary persons must learn about ceremonial sacrifices."

Our Master Mo said: "Learning the sacrificial rituals while holding that there are no ghosts is like learning proper etiquette when there are no guests, or making fishing nets when there are no fish."

Comment: An important criticism the Mohists make of the Confucians is that they are lacking in proper piety, believing as they do in neither *tian* 天 nor spirits and ghosts. The Mohists make much of what they perceive to be Confucian inconsistencies, where in spite of the Confucian lack of faith in the existence and power of such spiritual entities, they still commit themselves to learning all the minutia of sacrificial ceremonies.

VIII.2 Denouncing the Confucians (*feiruxia* 非儒下)

39.1 儒者曰:"親親有術,尊賢有等。"言親疏尊卑之異也。其禮曰:"喪父母三年,妻、後子三年,伯父叔父弟兄庶子其,戚族人五月。"若以親疏爲歲月之數,則親者多而疏者少矣,是妻後子與父同也。若以尊卑爲歲月數,則是尊其妻子與父母同,而親伯父宗兄而卑子也,逆孰大焉。……應之曰:"此誣言也,……爲欲厚所至私,輕所至重,豈非大姦也哉!"

    The Confucians say: "There are degrees of devotion due different kin and graduations of honor to be accorded different degrees of worthiness." They are here making their distinctions on the basis of the closeness of relatives, and on the degree people have of worthiness. In their code of rituals, it states: "The mourning period for father and mother is three years; for wife or eldest son, three years; for a paternal uncle, a brother, or other sons, a year; for other near close relatives, five months." If the number of years or months is a function of the closeness of the kin, then those who are closest should be more and the distant less, and yet the mourning period for a wife or eldest son is the same as the father. If the number of years or months is a function of the degree of worthiness, then the honor shown the wife and eldest son is the same as the parents, and devotion to paternal uncles and brothers is the same as the other sons. Could there be anything more perverse! ... We would reply to them by saying this is all a sham. ... This is showing partiality to those who are most intimate while slighting those who are most important. How could this be anything but utter deviance!

Comment: This passage resonates with a similar statement in *Focusing the Familiar* (*Zhongyong* 中庸) 20:

仁者人也,親親爲大;義者宜也,尊賢爲大。親親之殺,尊賢之等,禮所生也。

VIII. THE *MOZI* 墨子: ON DENOUNCING THE CONFUCIANS AND THEIR DOCTRINES

Becoming consummatory is becoming a person, wherein devotion to one's kin is what is most important. Being optimally appropriate is doing what is most fitting, wherein esteeming those who are most worthy is what is most important. The degree of devotion due different kin and the graduations of esteem accorded to different levels of worthiness is what gives rise to ritual propriety.

In *Mencius* 3B9 it levels an accusation against the Mohists: 墨氏兼愛，是無父也。無父無君，是禽獸也 "Mo Di's doctrine of inclusive concern (*jian-'ai* 兼愛) is a repudiation of the special affection one has for one's own father. To repudiate one's father and one's sovereign lord is to join the wild beasts of the field." But the Mohists, far from rejecting the special relationship persons have with members of their own family, take family reverence (*xiao* 孝) as a central tenet of their philosophy. The Mohist critique of the Confucians here as in most places is the inconsistency in their prescriptions for proper conduct. In their rhetoric the Confucians place honor above intimacy, but then violate this principle in their actual practices.

39.2 有强執有命以説議曰："壽夭貧富，安危治亂，固有天命，不可損益。窮達賞罰幸否有極，人之知力，不能爲焉。" 群吏信之，則怠於分職；庶人信之，則怠於從事。吏不治則亂，農事緩則貧，貧且亂政之本，而儒者以爲道教，是賊天下之人者也。

The Confucians hold tenaciously to a doctrine of fatalism, and in arguing for it say: "Longevity or an early demise, poverty or good fortune, security or danger, an orderly or disorderly world are all fixed and irrevocable as a matter of the mandate of *tian* (*tianming* 天命). Success or failure, reward or punishment, good fortune or adversity, have set limits. Human intelligence and fortitude can do nothing about it."

If the various officials put credence in this, they will be remiss in their assigned offices, and if the ordinary people believe it, they will be remiss in the conduct of their affairs. If the officials do not maintain proper order, there will be disorder, and if there is laxity in carrying out agricultural work, poverty will ensue. Poverty is the root of disorderly governance, and yet the Confucians take fatalism to be the teachings of the proper way. Such advocacy is to bring real harm to the world's peoples.

Comment: There are passages in the early Confucian texts that lend themselves to a kind of weak fatalism. For example, in *Mencius* 7A3:

孟子曰："求則得之，舍則失之，是求有益於得也，求在我者也。求之有道，得之有命，是求無益於得也，求在外者也。"

Mencius said: "Seek it and you shall find it, abandon it and you will suffer its loss. If this is so, then seeking has the advantage of acquiring something, and the outcome lies within oneself. But there is a proper way of seeking, and whether you are successful or not is beyond your control. Such being the case, seeking is of no advantage in acquiring something, and the outcome lies beyond oneself."

And the specific reference in this Mohist passage to the mandate of *tian* (*tianming* 天命) is the Confucian doctrine of political legitimization that lends itself to being misinterpreted as a kind of unilateral divine command.

But such examples are offset by the underlying Confucian commitment to the human capacity and responsibility to be co-creators with the heavens and the earth. Again, the Confucian doctrine of the mandate of *tian* 天 far from being the unilateral decree of *tian* 天 is the collateral synchronizing of the legitimacy of political authority with the virtuosity displayed by rulers in their governance of the people that provides the people with both moral education and material well-being.

Regardless of whether or not the charge of fatalism aligns with Confucian doctrine, the concern about how such deterministic assumptions would rob the human being of initiative and a sense of responsibility is certainly compelling. Such a doctrine precludes any confidence in human agency and the power of our actions to change the world.

39.3 且夫繁飾禮樂以淫人，久喪僞哀以謾親，立命緩貧而高浩居，倍本棄事而安怠傲，貪於飲食，惰於作務，陷於飢寒，危於凍餒，無以違之。是若人氣，鼸鼠藏，而羝羊視，賁彘起。君子笑之。怒曰："散人！焉知良儒。"夫夏乞麥禾，五穀既收，大喪是隨，子姓皆從，得厭飲食，畢治數喪，足以至矣。因人之家翠，以爲，恃人之野以爲尊，富人有喪，乃大說，喜曰："此衣食之端也。"

Moreover, the Confucians corrupt the people with their elaborate displays of rituals and music, and cheat their parents with protracted mourning and counterfeit grief. They advocate a doctrine of fatalism, are remiss on poverty alleviation, and revel in their own arrogance. They have turned their backs on what is fundamental, abandoned their responsibilities, and have found comfort in idleness and pride. They are greedy for food and drink, and

VIII. THE *MOZI* 墨子: ON DENOUNCING THE CONFUCIANS AND THEIR DOCTRINES

lazy when it comes to work. When besot with cold and hunger and threatened by freezing and starvation, they have no way of resolving their plight. They forage like beggars, stash away food like hamsters, have the stupid stare of a he-goat, and push their way in like castrated pigs. When exemplary persons laugh at them, they angrily reply: "How could a useless wretch like you know anything about a good Confucian?"

Come spring they beg for wheat, and summer, for barley. When the various grains have been harvested, they chase after big funerals with all of their children and grandchildren in tow. If everyone can get their fill of food and drink, and they can preside over a few funerals, they couldn't be more satisfied. They get fat on the families of others, and garner some respect by way of the fields that belong to others. When a wealthy family holds a funeral, they are delighted, saying with glee: "This is our chance to get food and clothing."

Comment: The Mohist grievance with the Confucians is that they are parasitic on the people, living high on the hog while contributing nothing themselves. Occupied with extravagant ceremonies and music funded from the public coffers, they add insult to injury with their arrogance and airs. Much in the language of the Mohist texts is flat, simple, and repetitive, and at times their "gotcha chop logic" is a bit tedious. But this passage is also not atypical in being full of satirical images painting a Dickensian picture of a shameless, well-bred elite with all of their high manners, living off of the hard work of honest people. It is not difficult to imagine how such attacks would garner support among the working classes and could get under the skin of the perhaps overly serious Confucians, especially when they would have to acknowledge a tendency in their doctrines and lifestyle that would justify just such a complaint.

39.4 儒者曰："君子必服古言然後仁。"應之曰："所謂古之言服者，皆嘗新矣，而古人言之，服之，則非君子也。然則必服非君子之服，言非君子之言，而後仁乎？

The Confucians say: "Exemplary persons can only be considered consummate in their conduct when they follow the ancients in their dress and speech."

We would reply to them by saying that what is now called ancient in dress and speech was all once new. If the ancients spoke and dressed in this way, then they were not exemplary persons. This being the case, can persons only be consummate in their conduct if they dress in the garments and speak in the manner of someone who is not exemplary?

Comment: The Mohists are quick to mock what the Confucians take to be the superior manners and refinements that come along with the performance of their ritualized roles and their education in the canonical texts. And the Mohists are not adverse to using their baby logic to find fault with such statements made by the Confucians. Of course, the Confucians might well answer them by saying that the ancients as moderns of another time would have undoubtedly found their refined manners in the conduct of their own ancients. The simple logical arguments found in some of these passages do not detract from the technical and sophisticated discussions we find in the Later Mohist Canons.

39.5 又曰:"君子循而不作。"應之曰:"古者羿作弓,伃作甲,奚仲作車,巧垂作舟,然則今之鮑函車匠皆君子也,而羿、伃、奚仲、巧垂皆小人邪?且其所循人必或作之,然則其所循皆小人道也?"

The Confucians also say: "Exemplary persons following the proper way, do not forge new paths."

We would reply to them saying in ancient times, Yi introduced the bow, Yu introduced armor, Xizhong introduced the carriage, and the tradesman Chui introduced the boat. Such being the case, are today's tanners, smiths, carriage-makers, and carpenters as followers all exemplary persons, and are Yi, Yu, Xizhong, and the tradesman Chui as innovators simply petty persons? Further, since whatever it is that the Confucians are following had to be introduced by someone, doesn't this mean that what they are in fact following are the ways of petty persons?

Comment: This passage is an allusion to *Analects* 7.1:

子曰:"述而不作,信而好古,竊比於我老彭。"
The Master said, "Following the proper way, I do not forge new paths; with confidence I cherish the ancients—in these respects I am comparable to Old Peng."

The logic of this Mohist criticism is impeccable if we take Confucius's self-description to be expository rather than as an expression of his profound deference to the cultural tradition, and again as a token of his personal modesty. And just such a Mohist criticism of Confucian traditionalism is alive and well in the commentarial tradition as it has continued down to the present day.

As we see in *Analects* 3.14, the self-understanding of Confucius in broad strokes is that he self-consciously sees himself as continuing an antique tradition reaching back into the second millennia BCE:

周監於二代，郁郁乎文哉！吾從周。
The Zhou dynasty looked back to the Xia and Shang dynasties. Such a wealth of culture! I follow the Zhou.①

This Zhou tradition was the compounding culture of the many generations that came before it. As the source of Confucius's education, it lives on in the lives of the people of his own day. *Analects* 9.5 remembers an incident when Confucius, traveling through the district of Kuang on his way from the state of Wei to Chen, is confronted by a perilous situation, and says:

文王既沒，文不在茲乎？天之將喪斯文也，後死者不得與於斯文也；天之未喪斯文也，匡人其如予何？
With King Wen (literally, King "Culture") long dead, does not our cultural heritage reside here in us? If *tian* 天 were going to destroy this cultural legacy, we latecomers would not have had access to it. If *tian* 天 is not

---

① See also *Analects* 8.20: "舜有臣五人而天下治。武王曰：'予有亂臣十人。'孔子曰：'才難，不其然乎？唐虞之際，於斯爲盛。有婦人焉，九人而已。三分天下有其二，以服事殷。周之德，其可謂至德也已矣。'" Shun had only five ministers and the world was properly governed. King Wu also said, "I have ten ministers who bring proper order to the world." Confucius said, "As the saying has it: 'Human talent is hard to come by.' Isn't it indeed the case. And it was at the transition from Yao to Shun that talented ministers were in greatest abundance. In King Wu's case with a woman, perhaps his wife, among them, there were really only nine ministers. The Zhou, with two thirds of the world in its possession, continued to submit to and serve the House of Yin. The excellence of Zhou can be said to be the highest excellence of all."

going to destroy this culture, what can the people of Kuang do to us!①

While Confucius was certainly a dedicated intermediary within a living Zhou tradition, he has also been singularly responsible for introducing, redefining, and elaborating upon a set of key terms as the authorized philosophical vocabulary for an evolving Confucianism: *ren* 仁 (aspiring to consummate conduct in one's roles and relations), *junzi* 君子 (exemplary persons), *yi* 義 (an optimizing appropriateness), and *li* 禮 (achieving propriety in one's roles and relations).

Again, it is Confucius who promotes personal cultivation as defining of the Confucian project, and who grounds Confucian role ethics and the vision of the consummate life in "family reverence" (*xiao* 孝). This being the case, it is not surprising that when Zhu Xi 朱熹 selects the *Four Books* as core texts representative of the tradition, he describes the *Expansive Learning* (*Daxue* 大學) as the most basic text. The *Expansive Learning* sets the Confucian project as a regimen of personal cultivation within the context of family and community relations. Zhu Xi then canonizes the *Analects* and the *Mencius* as the second and third of the *Four Books* respectively, with the explicit reason that these texts provide the fundamental vocabulary for this Confucian project, and in addition, offer the tradition role models for such personal cultivation in the persons of Confucius and Mencius.

Again, Zhu Xi celebrates the fourth of the *Four Books*, *Focusing the Familiar* (*Zhongyong* 中庸), as the highest and most exuberant statement of the Confucian project. This text remembers Confucius by centering its message of his own term "focusing the familiar" (*zhongyong* 中庸), and Mencius as well with his idiosyncratic use of the term "resolve" (*cheng* 誠). We find it is the person of Confucius himself who in *Focusing the Familiar* 30 is described as the very embodiment of the "massive transformations" that occur in the evolving cosmic order:

---

① According to the biography of Confucius, Confucius had left Wei and was on route to Chen when he passed through Kuang. The people of Kuang had recently been ravaged by Yang Huo, also from the state of Lu, and mistook Confucius for him. See Sima Qian 司馬遷, *Shiji* 史記 (*Records of the Grand Historian*), Beijing: Zhonghua Shuju, 1959, p. 1919. See also *Analects* 11.23.

VIII. THE *MOZI* 墨子: ON DENOUNCING THE CONFUCIANS AND THEIR DOCTRINES

仲尼祖述堯、舜，憲章文、武；上律天時，下襲水土。辟如天地之無不持載，無不覆幬，辟如四時之錯行，如日月之代明。萬物并育而不相害，道并行而不相悖，小德川流，大德敦化，此天地之所以爲大也。

Confucius revered Yao and Shun as his ancestors and carried on their ways; he emulated and made illustrious the way of Kings Wen and Wu. He modeled himself above on the rhythm of the turning seasons, and below he was attuned to the patterns of water and earth. He is comparable to the heavens and the earth, sheltering and supporting everything that is. He is comparable to the progress of the four seasons, and the alternating brightness of the sun and the moon. All things are nurtured together and do not cause injury to one another; the various ways are traveled together and are not conflicted. Their lesser virtuosity is to be seen as flowing streams; their greater virtuosity is to be seen as grand transformations. This is why the heavens and the earth are so grand.

39.7 又曰："君子若鍾，擊之則鳴，弗擊不鳴。"應之曰："夫仁人事上竭忠，事親得孝，務善則美，有過則諫，此爲人臣之道也。今擊之則鳴，弗擊不鳴，隱知豫力，恬漠待問而後對，雖有君親之大利，弗問不言，若將有大寇亂，盜賊將作，若機辟將發也，他人不知，己獨知之，雖其君親皆在，不問不言。是夫大亂之賊也！以是爲人臣不忠，爲子不孝，事兄不弟，交，遇人不貞良。……"

The Confucians also say: "Exemplary persons are like a bell. When struck it sounds, but if you do not strike it, it remains silent."

We would reply to them saying that consummate persons serve those above by doing their utmost and serve their parents with family reverence. When the affairs of lord and parents are felicitous, they offer their praises but where they stray from the path, they provide their remonstrance. This then is the proper way of the minister. But to only sound when struck and to otherwise remain silent is to conceal your knowledge and to conserve your strength, waiting dumbly and only answering when asked. Even though you might have on offer some major benefit for your lord or parents, you say nothing unless asked. Supposing like the trigger of a crossbow cocked and about to launch its bolt, there is a major rebellion about to rise up or bandits and villains about to descend upon us, and there is only you with nobody else in the know. Even though your lord and parents are right there, you won't say anything unless asked. This then is criminal behavior of the worst kind. In the conduct of a minister it is disloyal, in the conduct of a son it is unfilial, in the service to a brother it is unfaithful, and in relations with others it is lacking in integrity. . . .

Comment: Perhaps this criticism is directed specifically at *Xunzi* 1 where it states:

> 故不問而告謂之傲，問一而告二謂之囋。傲，非也，囋，非也；君子如嚮矣。
> To volunteer information without having been asked is arrogance; to volunteer two answers for one question is to be verbose. Since arrogance and verbosity are both to be denounced, exemplary persons instead have the responsiveness of an echo.

Otherwise, it is difficult to correlate the criticism in this passage that Confucians only speak when asked a question, with anything in the Confucian philosophical literature. It might possibly be an allusion to *Analects* 14.26 (also repeated in part in 8.14):

> 子曰："不在其位，不謀其政。"曾子曰："君子思不出其位。"
> The Master said, "Do not plan the policies of an office you do not hold." Master Zeng commented, "The thoughts of exemplary persons (*junzi* 君子) do not wander beyond their station."

But we simply need to recall chapter 15 in the *Classic of Family Reverence* (*Xiaojing* 孝經) in which Confucius insists honest and timely remonstrance with both parents and lord is not an option but a stern obligation. On the other hand, perhaps the practically-minded Mohists are criticizing a historical reality rather than a close reading of doctrinal texts. The important question is to what extent did Confucianism in practice fall short of its ideals.

IX. THE *XUNZI* 荀子: A SYNCRETIC CONFUCIAN PHILOSOPHY

In reading through the *Xunzi*, one gets a clear sense of this philosopher's self-understanding. Xunzi would have it that, in his focus on the immediate human experience and in the discipline he brings to personal cultivation, he is the legitimate heir to the legacy of Confucius. For the serious Xunzi (fl. 298-238 BCE), the education and refinement necessary to become a consummately moral person require resolute commitment and hard work. But for Xunzi, living some two centuries after the passing of Confucius and nearing the increasingly violent climax of the Warring States period, his world was defined by the drumbeat of a relentless march to empire. As just one measure of the magnitude of this chaos, the records report in a single battle in 260 BCE the famous Qin general Bai Qi 白起, "the human butcher" (*rentu* 人屠), put the 450,000-strong army of Zhao to the sword. Death in Xunzi's time had become a way of life, and what had become clear to all contestants at this juncture was the quest for hegemony was a zero-sum game. To lose the game of empire was to lose utterly.

In the last chapter of the *Xunzi*, a defense is mounted by one of his students as a eulogy to Xunzi in precisely these terms. In response to the observation that 孫卿不及孔子 "Xunzi was no Confucius," the student responds:

當是時也，知者不得慮，能者不得治，賢者不得使。故君上蔽而無睹，賢人距而不受。然則孫卿懷將聖之心，蒙佯狂之色，視天下以愚。《詩》曰："既明且哲，以保其身。"此之謂也。

In his time, the wise had no chance for deliberation, the able had no chance to govern properly, and the worthy had no chance to serve in office. The rulers above were blind and had no vision, and worthy persons being kept at bay held no sway. It was under such circumstances that Xunzi harboring the heartmind of a sage feigned madness to conceal his concerns and appeared to the world as a fool. This is what the *Book of Songs* 260 means when it says:

    So intelligent, he was also wise,
    He was just trying to stay alive.

Xunzi in his appropriation of the teachings of Confucius, had to adapt them to the turmoil of his times, and must be read with this in mind. Human beings as a matter of survival were distinguishing themselves by their rapaciousness and cruelty, and as a Confucian philosopher, Xunzi saw as his most important task the reinstatement and promotion of civility. Indeed, Confucius's own stern commitment to the rehabilitation of the Zhou ritual practices (*li* 禮) was inherited by Xunzi. The importance of ritual practices in Confucius is clear when we begin from his premise that persons are irreducibly social, and they can only be evaluated on the basis of the quality of the relationships they are able to effect with others in their families and communities (*ren* 仁). It is ritual action as a discourse in the broadest sense that enables persons to communicate effectively and to constitute themselves as a matrix of robust relations. Ritual practices are in one sense conservative. A community's memory, its culture, its values are reflected in this inherited repertoire of formalized actions and institutions, displaying as they do the cumulative investment of meaning and importance (*yi* 義) of its precursors in the cultural tradition. Ritual practices both preserve and transmit cultural significance. For this reason, the performance and embodiment of the ritual tradition not only socializes persons and makes them members of community, but it further refines, elevates, and enculturates them. Ritual informs persons of shared values and provides them with an elegant way of living conducive to the maintenance and enrichment of community life forms.

But for Confucius, while ritual practices provide standards of appropriateness sedimented within a cultural tradition that shapes its participants, such a way of life is not simply a given. Ritual practices also have a significant personal and creative dimension. What distinguishes ritual from law as a source of order is ritual action not only informs participants of what is proper, but is also performed by them in a way that expresses their own unique meanings. Rituals are formal structures that are personalized and reformulated to accommodate the uniqueness and the quality of each participant, enabling them to reform the community from their own inimitable perspective, and to leave their mark on the tradition. Where ritual practices are conduits of meaning to be appropriated by succeeding generations, they are also a reservoir that accumulates additional meaning from the intergenerational connector (*dao* 道) as it is being constructed and extended by the road-building of each generation. Ritual action is a necessary condition for Confucius's vision of social harmony because, by definition, it not only permits of, but actually requires personalization. For Confucius, a formal ceremony without personal commitment is a hollow, meaningless, and even antisocial parody of what should be a source of social cohesion and enjoyment. "Propriety" as a translation for ritual practice reflects the fact that the performance of ritual action is a "making it one's own" both in appropriating from and investing meaning in the continuing social and political order.

IX. THE *XUNZI* 荀子: A SYNCRETIC CONFUCIAN PHILOSOPHY

Ritual actions are unique not simply because they require personalization, but further because they express the achieved quality of the always particular performers. The significance of ritual action and its potential to produce social harmony is a direct function of the cultivated quality of its participants. Indeed, throughout the *Analects* the truly harmonious community, relying as it does upon its people to educate and refine themselves through ritual practice and to assume the internal and reflexive perspective entailed by a sense of shame, is defined as fundamentally self-ordering (2.3). Given the definition of the community as being constituted by an intrinsic network of interpersonal patterns of deference, ritualized life forms are immanent and emergent rather than imposed, with the ideal function of the "ruler" being to reign rather than to "rule" (15.5 and 2.1).

This self-ordering of community does not entail closure; it is neither compliance with some top-down decree nor the replication of some predefined ideal. It is instead a "middle-outward" project of disclosure. It is the coordination and mutual accommodation of members of community who, through ritual practices, pursue personal and sociopolitical realization simultaneously. Community thus defined exists neither as an immediate reality nor as a fixed ideal; it is programmatic and open-ended, a continuing aesthetic achievement, contingent upon the particular players and their moral imagination. Further, this demand of ritual action for personal signature, while promising to make the most of available diversity, means also that the achieved community will in some important respect always be "local," conditioned as it must be by the circumstances of its particular time and place, and by the aspirations and the imagination of its particular cultural leaders.

Such is Confucius's own understanding of ritual practices (*li* 禮) as a way of life. But is his understanding and that of Xunzi significantly different? For Confucius, there is an emphasis on the use of ritual to aestheticize the human experience where means and end are one and the same; we aspire to elegance in living to live elegantly. We might argue that in Xunzi, Confucius's own aesthetic emphasis is overwritten in important degree by his interpreting ritual practices as a means created by the sages to rationalize society in a way that lifts humanity out of its brutish state of nature, and makes human civilization a possibility.

In formulating his own theory of ritual practices, Xunzi begins from several premises that are elaborated upon in the representative passages I have selected below. *Tian* 天 as a value-neutral, and disenchanted amoral force provides the natural context for human beings whose native condition is basically an aggregate of base desires. Given that humankind by definition all share the same desires and aversions, and that their cumulative demand outweighs supply, the state of nature is a chaotic war of survival. Human beings do not have the option of avoiding such contest by withdrawing and living a solitary life because they are trapped by the pressure of their own desires, and because of the division of labor needed to best satisfy them. To resolve social strife and preclude its resurgence, the ancient sage-kings established conventions governing social and political status, and modes of conduct guaranteeing an orderly distribution of goods. Such conventions are the *li* 禮 or ritual practices, and being both contrived in their formal structures and natural in their appropriateness and efficacy, are a central component in Xunzi's vision of the moral life. Further, the fact that these conventions for conduct were formulated by sages in high antiquity at some considerable distance from the specific concerns of Xunzi's world is mitigated by Xunzi's conviction in the constancy of both the human condition and its continuing context:

君子位尊而志恭，心小而道大；所聽視者近，而所聞見者遠。是何邪？則操術然也。故千人萬人之情，一人之情也。天地始者，今日是也。百王之道，後王是也。君子審後王之道，而論百王之前，若端拜而議。推禮義之統，分是非之分，總天下之要，治海內之眾，若使一人。

Exemplary persons (*junzi* 君子) although having an exalted status are respectful in their purposes, recognizing their own thoughts and feelings are minor while the proper way is grand. But how is it that what they look at and listen to is near at hand, but what they are able to see and hear is so remote? It is because they have a firm grasp on how to parse experience. It is thus they see that the condition of all humankind is the same as any one of them, that the beginnings of the cosmos are still very much with us, and that the proper way of all kings is the same as the most recent king. Exemplary persons survey the proper way of the recent kings as their way of pronouncing on that of the kings of old, as though with hands raised in salute, they are expressing an opinion at court. As simple as looking at the situation of a single person, they discern the mainstay of ritual action and moral precepts, grasp the distinction between right and wrong, have a synoptic view of what is essential in the world, and bring proper order to the multitude.

IX. THE *XUNZI* 荀子: A SYNCRETIC CONFUCIAN PHILOSOPHY

Xunzi's attitude toward the tradition here is at obvious variance with that of Confucius. Confucius would know the present by a careful examination of the past, but Xunzi seems to recommend the converse:

故曰：欲觀聖王之迹，則於其粲然者矣，後王是也。彼後王者，天下之君也；舍後王而道上古，譬之是猶舍己之君，而事人之君也。故曰：欲觀千歲，則數今日；欲知億萬，則審一二；欲知上世，則審周道；欲審周道，則審其人所貴君子。故曰：以近知遠，以一知萬，以微知明，此之謂也。

Thus I would argue that if you want to examine the footprints of the sage-kings then look to where they are most obvious, that being those of the more recent kings. These latter-day kings were rulers over the entire world. To abandon the latter kings and talk about those of high antiquity is like abandoning your own lord in order to serve another. Thus I would say that if you want to examine a whole millennium then figure out today; if you want to understand millions just examine one or two; if you want to understand ancient ages just examine the way of the Zhou dynasty, and if you want to examine the Zhou, then examine the exemplary persons they honored most. There is a saying: Know what is remote from what is near at hand, know the many from the one, know the big picture from the smallest detail. This is my meaning.

For Confucius, exemplary persons not only understand the contours of the present situation by appeal to the relief and detail of historical models, but further can best address a future course of action by analogy with the past (2.11). It is particular historical persons and events as role models and sources of inspiration rather than abstract principles that are most helpful in charting a course. Xunzi, on the other hand, says repeatedly the 古今一也 "the ancient and the present are one" and 類不悖，雖久同理 "since classes of things do not contradict themselves, even though things are distant in time, they share in the same pattern."

With specific reference to ritual practices, Xunzi describes these *li* 禮 as markers on the proper way:

百王之無變，足以為道貫。一廢一起，應之以貫，理貫不亂。……水行者表深，表不明則陷。治民者表道，表不明則亂。禮者，表也。

What the Hundred Kings of old deemed to leave unchanged is taken as the continuous thread that runs through the proper way. Respond to all vicissitudes of life with this continuous thread, for where guided by this thread, there will be no disorder. . . . Watermen mark the depths, for where these markers are not clear, people will drown. To bring proper order to the common people, set markers on the proper way, for where these markers are not clear, there will be disorder. Ritual practices are just such markers.

For Xunzi, 夫道者體常而盡變 "as for this proper way, it embodies constancy and is the sum of all changes." His complaint against his Confucian predecessors such as Zisizi and Mencius is that they have only partial knowledge of the way and have thus failed to grasp the underlying unity provided by this vision of the moral life: 略法先王而不知其統 "they model themselves on the Former Kings only superficially but do not understand what unites these precursors." Xunzi's way of talking about the proper way contrasts rather sharply with the cumulative *dao* 道 of the *Analects*, where 人能弘道, 非道弘人 "it is persons who broaden the proper way, not the way that broadens persons" (15.29).

In this same vein, Henry Rosemont wants to give Xunzi his best argument. Rosemont challenges Karl Popper's condemnation of utopian states and offers Xunzi as a reasonable alternative to Popper's "open society." He defends what he calls Xunzi's "closed society" and its admittedly static nature by appeal to the prevailing economic circumstances of the time and by a sympathetic construal of what is possible within Xunzi's framework of minimum constraints. Xunzi's *li* 禮 serves as a state ideology that guarantees maximum security and a minimum well-being for all.[1]

But as we have seen, there seems to be an important distance between Xunzi and Confucius with respect to ritual practices. For Confucius, the *li* 禮 is meaning-invested and meaning-disclosing actions that are ultimately derived from the personal sense and expression of optimal appropriateness (*yi* 義). It is this grounding in personal appropriateness that makes *li* 禮 irreducibly participatory and makes the achievement of social harmony a "middle-outward" if not "bottom-up" communal responsibility that complements the authority of the tradition. Confucius in *Analects* 4.10 says

---

[1] Henry Rosemont, Jr., "State and Society in the *Hsün Tzu* [*Xunzi*]: A Philosophical Commentary," *Monumenta Serica*, Vol. 29 (1970-1971).

explicitly that *yi* 義 does not reduce to right and wrong or some generic principle:

子曰:"君子之於天下也, 無適也, 無莫也, 義之與比。"
The Master said, "Exemplary persons (*junzi* 君子) in making their way in the world are neither bent on nor against anything; rather, they go with what is most appropriate (*yi* 義)."

Xunzi, on the other hand, has departed from this Confucian understanding to an extent that has escaped the notice of few commentators. Derk Bodde, for example, with respect to Xunzi's understanding of *yi* 義, reports that

... in conjunction with the rules of proper conduct (*li* 禮) ... it [*yi* 義] seems to lose its sense of "righteousness" as practiced by the individual, and to become more general and impersonal, a thing possessed by society as a whole.①

In fact, Xunzi explicitly assimilates *yi* 義 to *li* 禮 to form a binomial expression *liyi* 禮義 in some 85 instances, more than one third of the occurrences of *li* 禮 in the entire text, with the effect of subordinating *yi* 義 to *li* 禮 and thus, in important degree, externalizing *yi* 義 as moral precepts. That there is this tendency for *yi* 義 to be externalized and made generic at the expense of its specific reference to individual instances of appropriateness is reflected in the rendering of *yi* 義 in the current English translations of the *Xunzi* as "justice," "just principles," "moral law," "moral principles," and "standards of righteousness."②

---

① Fung Yu-lan, *A History of Chinese Philosophy*, trans. D. Bodde, Princeton: Princeton University Press, 1952, Vol. 1, p. 287 footnote.

② See H. Dubs, *The Works of Hsüntze*, London: Probsthain, 1928; T.T. Ch'ü, *Law and Society in Traditional China*, Paris and The Hague: Mouton & Co., 1961; Joseph Needham, *Science and Civilisation in China*, Vol. II, Cambridge: Cambridge University Press, 1954; B. Watson (trans.), *Hsün Tzu: Basic Writings,* New York: Columbia University Press, 1963; Noah Fehl, *Li: Rites and Propriety in Literature and Life*, Hong Kong: Chinese University Press, 1971; J. Knoblock, *Xunzi: A Translation and Study of the Complete Works*, Stanford: Stanford University *(Continued on next page)*

The ramifications for *li* 禮 introduced by these altered implications of *yi* 義 are profound. The diminished importance of personal participation in the actual production of social harmony tends to transform *li* 禮 in important degree into an external, closed, and "top-down" set of prescriptions that dictates a regulatory order for society. Using Xunzi's own metaphors, the *li* 禮 are a plumbline, a pair of scales, a compass and set square, all of which can be applied to people to bring them to rule. *Li* 禮 provides a templet against which the people can be steamed and pressed into shape, and serves as a grindstone on which they can be whetted and brought to form:

> 故枸木必將待檃栝烝矯然後直；鈍金必將待礱厲然後利；今人之性惡，必將待師法然後正，得禮義然後治。
>
> Thus it is that warped wood can only be straightened by being steamed and bent into shape in a wood-press; blunt metal can only be sharpened by being whetted on a grindstone. And since the natural propensities (*xing* 性) of human beings are base, they can only be made proper through their teachers together with set norms, and can only be properly ordered through ritual practices and moral precepts (*liyi* 禮義).

There are several other signals in the *Xunzi* of the movement toward a more generic and objective conception of ritual practices. This perception is reinforced, for example, by the emergence of *li* 理—generally rendered "principle" or "reason"(perhaps better in *Xunzi* as "rationale")—as a central concept. Xunzi appeals to it for the authority that would rationalize both ritual practices (*li* 禮) and moral precepts (*yi* 義). There is the increasingly exalted status of the ruler to the extent that the issue of order versus chaos becomes focused in the effectiveness of the ruler at the top. As Hsiao Kung-chuan [Xiao Gongquan] 蕭公權 observes, the emphasis in Confucius and Mencius was on the moral quality of the ruler while the Legalist thinkers stressed the ruler's status and the power that issued from it.[1] In Xunzi as a latter-day Confucian and as the teacher of the leading

---

(Continued from previous page) Press, Vol. 1-3, 1988, 1990, 1994; Eric Hutton, *Readings in Classical Chinese Philosophy*, 2nd edition, ed. P.J. Ivanhoe and Bryan Van Norden, Indianapolis: Hackett Publishing Company, 2005.

[1] Hsiao Kung-chuan, *A History of Chinese Political Thought*, trans. F. Mote, Princeton: Princeton University Press, 1979, Vol. 1, p. 205.

Legalist philosophers Han Feizi and Li Si, there is real concern for both the ruler's moral quality and his exercise of power. Xunzi, with his idiosyncratic interpretation of the baseness of native human propensities, is inclined to rely on fear and awe in addition to deference as the best way to keep the people in line. His appropriation of "political purchase" (*shi* 勢) from the Militarists and Legalists, and the retrofitting of it as a Confucian concept together with the development of the "hegemon" (*ba* 霸) as an acceptable albeit inferior alternative to sagely government, are both indications of this inclination toward top-down, impositional order.

Corollary to the emphasis in Xunzi on the ruler as a source of order is the seemingly inflated importance accorded to the teacher and to set norms (*shifa* 師法). In the *Analects*, Confucius certainly includes teachers in his advocacy for moral exemplars, but he qualifies this tenet by emphasizing the centrality of one's own personal cultivation in the project inspired by them. In *Analects* 15.36, for example, Confucius makes just this important distinction between emulation and imitation, between inspiration and replication:

子曰："當仁，不讓於師。"
The Master said, "In striving to be consummate in your conduct (*ren* 仁), do not defer even to your teachers."

For Xunzi, by contrast, there is a stronger sense of imitation and replication that attends the concepts of both teacher and ritual practices:

禮者，所以正身也，師者，所以正禮也。無禮何以正身？無師吾安知禮之爲是也？禮然而然，則是情安禮也；師云而云，則是知若師也。……不是師法，而好自用，譬之是猶以盲辨色，以聾辨聲也，舍亂妄無爲也。故學也者，禮法也。夫師，以身爲正儀，而貴自安者也。《詩》云："不識不知，順帝之則。"此之謂也。

Ritual practices are the means to make oneself proper, and the teacher is the means to practice ritual properly. Without ritual practices, how am I to make myself proper? And if there is no teacher, how am I to know what should be done in ritual practices? When I do as the rituals prescribe, my feelings find their repose in these practices; when I speak as my teacher speaks, my wisdom will be like that of my teacher.... To do other than my teacher and the set norms because I want to do things in my own way is like the blindman trying to distinguish colors or the deaf person trying to distinguish different notes. It will occasion nothing but chaos. As for what is real learning, it is ritual and set norms. The teacher then is how I make myself proper and dignified, and how I honor the repose I find in myself. This is what the *Book of Songs* 241 means when it says: "Without need of intelligence or wisdom, accord with the model set by the ancestral spirits."

Admittedly, the portrait of Xunzi I have painted here stresses the "hardening of the categories" surrounding ritual practices into something more rigid and fixed than one finds in Confucius and the alternative Si-Meng lineage that follows from him. My failure so far to include and appreciate Xunzi's tireless exhortation to personal cultivation would certainly stir opposition from those commentators anxious to afford Xunzi a more liberal reading. Given that the philosophy offered in the *Xunzi* does contain an admixture of elements along a broad spectrum of ideas and that in Xunzi's own emphasis he vacillates rather broadly between extremes, it has been a relatively easy matter for interpreters of this text to choose passages that argue for his placement at very different positions on that spectrum.

Indeed, the decided tendency of Xunzi toward a rationalized Confucianism has lent itself to two very different interpretations. One strong reading of his insistence upon temporal and structural sameness relies upon the concept of sameness as strict identity. This realist interpretation is absolutist in the sense that it would eliminate any notion of change or evolution, and would thus deny any meaningful sense of history by asserting that from earliest times to the present, we basically have the same world and everything that is in it. Every person is identical with every other.

The weaker reading of Xunzi's rationalized Confucianism would appeal to the *Book of Changes* postulate of "continuity in change" (*biantong* 變通), and argue that sameness is a continuity in identity in a vital cosmology where one is many, many one (*yiduobufen* 一多不分). Xunzi's claims about sameness between past and present and between one and many are thus understood as an emphasis on a perceived continuity, not identity. Rather than entailing strict identity, this same cosmology with the primacy given to vital relationality is thus holographic, where the entire cosmic field resides within each focal detail, making the many one and the one, many.

What recommends this second interpretation over the first is that it has the virtue of reading Xunzi within his own interpretive context.

Kurtis Hagen with his "constructivist" interpretation of Xunzi's ritual practices belongs to this second historicist reading. He observes that for Xunzi, ritual practices

> ... have some naturalistic basis in that they are justified in terms of their efficacy in creating and maintaining social conditions conducive to human flourishing, and in this human nature cannot be ignored. Nevertheless, they are neither determinate nor exclusive, for they are dependent not only on nature but also on the contingencies of their historical development.[1]

Indeed, Hagen goes beyond ritual practices, as important as they are, to considering Xunzi's worldview broadly in mounting a full-on assault on the first of these two competing interpretations. He first reconstructs and then rejects what he describes as a strong "realist" position. On this reading

> ... Xunzi claims that the sages of old "gave birth" to a language that truly and uniquely describes the world and our roles and reciprocal obligations in it. On this view, the ritual patterns embodied by the sages are uniquely appropriate, and universally and eternally so. Moral categories expressed in language are real, and alternative interpretations are necessarily false and thus pernicious. There is no room for discussion, unorthodox doctrines are to be silenced and the crooked to be pressed straight in conformity with the true standard.[2]

Hagen in response to what he takes to be this impoverishing misreading of Xunzi, has advanced what he calls a more reasonable "constructivist" interpretation in which

---

[1] Kurtis Hagen, *The Philosophy of Xunzi: A Reconstruction*, La Salle, IL: Open Court, 2007, p. 85.
[2] Hagen, *The Philosophy of Xunzi*, pp. 2-3.

... the distinctions made by the sages have no absolute status. Rather, categories are judged according to values, such as harmony and social stability, which are in turn justified by the critical role in facilitating the satisfaction of a substantial number of our desires. Given that we humans are constituted the way we are, some sets of conceptions and social structures work better than others for providing what we find (or can find) satisfying. However, Xunzi's underlying worldview—informing everything from his philosophy of language to his understanding of the role of ritual propriety—suggests that there may be more than one way to achieve success in constructing a moral world.[1]

Xunzi is often touted as the most rationalistic of the classical Confucians. But it is because Xunzi's "rationalism" is grounded in history and culture without appeal to metaphysical determinants that he was instrumental in the persistence of what we might describe as a signature hybridic mode of Han thinking. In A.S. Cua's careful analysis of argumentation in Xunzi, he distinguishes Xunzi's "concrete" Confucian rationality from notions of abstract and impersonal reason familiar in classical Greek metaphysical thinking. Cua is concerned that the central role of retrospective history in the reasoning process be fully appreciated because it is this analogical historicist appeal that makes the exercise of Confucian rationality concrete and contingent. Cua states that

... the Confucian emphasis on the role of historical knowledge, given the backward-looking character of analogical projection, is a useful reminder that any piece of ethical reasoning, if it is to claim interpersonal significance, though itself occasioned by a present perplexity, must have some contact with the cultural-historical experience of the people. It is in culture and history that analogical projection finds its anchorage and not in rules and principles of *a priori* ratiocination. In this basic way, the prospective significance of analogical projection is rooted in retrospective ethical thinking.[2]

---

[1] Hagen, *The Philosophy of Xunzi*, pp. 8-9.
[2] A.S. Cua, *Ethical Argumentation: A Study in Hsün Tzu's Moral Epistemology*, Honolulu: University of Hawai'i Press, 1985, pp. 97-98. See also pp. 56-61.

For Xunzi, the functional approximation of what we would regard as valid reasoning involves the discovery and articulation of appropriate and efficacious historical instances of reasonableness. Erstwhile "reasoning" (*li* 理) and historical analogizing are inseparable. *Li* 理 reasoning that involves the mapping out of patterns can only operate on the basis of assumed classifications (*lei* 類). At the same time, it is the mapping operation of *li* 理, including or excluding membership on the basis of perceived similarities and differences, that establishes classifications (*lei* 類) in the first place.①

Perhaps Xunzi's greatest and most enduring influence came from the emphasis he placed on ritual practice as the instrument for socializing, enculturating, and humanizing the Confucian world. His description of the function of ritual in society is cited extensively in the histories and the many canons of ritual compiled during this period, and looms large in the syncretic philosophical literature that was to become the signature of the Han dynasty. With the emergence of a Confucian orthodoxy in the Han dynasty heavily indebted to the Xunzi branch of Confucianism, scholarly dispute was tempered by a fundamental commitment to deference and mutual respect. There is a general distaste for contentiousness and an active cultivation of what Xunzi calls *jianshu* 兼術 or "the art of accommodation."② Since rituals serve as patterns of deference that accommodate and harmonize differences in desires, attitudes, and actions, even in the exercise of criticism the ritual basis of order comes into play. Ideally, dispute is a cooperative exercise among responsible stake holders that leads to a search for alternatives upon which all can agree. After all, the ultimate goal of protest is not victory in dialectical contest that is necessarily divisive, but the strengthening of communal harmony.

In our several interpretive studies of Confucianism, I and my collaborators have made much of this ambiguity of order. We have invoked the Whiteheadian distinction between a holistic aesthetic order in which everything is relevant to anything, and a reductionistic logical or rational order in which one order is given originative and causal privilege. Logical construction entails an act of closure readily recognizable in those philosophical doctrines in which realization is the instantiation of some transcendent form or the actualization of some given potential. A further signal

---

① Cua, *Ethical Argumentation*, p. 54.
② Cua provides a detailed analysis of the "style" of argumentative engagement in late Zhou China. See *Ethical Argumentation*, esp. pp. 6-12.

of logical construction would be the articulation of fixed principles that allow for the organization and classification of the elements of experience without the principles themselves being affected in the process. Another signal would be the appeal to rational, moral, or aesthetic principles that can be advanced as independent evidence, and thus can stand as guarantee for a single-ordered cosmos applicable in all situations.

Aesthetic composition, by contrast, begins with the uniqueness of the one thing and the disclosure it affords the balanced complexity displayed in the totality of the effect. The meaning of this aesthetic order arises from the way in which a concrete, specific detail contributes itself as productive of a harmony expressed by a manifold of such details in their relationship to one another, and to the unsummed whole. We have used the language of first and second problematic thinking as a way of distinguishing this aesthetic from the logical sense of order.

I have suggested Xunzi's drift toward uniformities and a closed society is a movement away from Confucius's ideal of a self-ordering communal harmony in the direction of community regulated by a "top-down" system of norms and practices. This shift is discernible not only in Xunzi's emphasis on ritual practices (*li* 禮) and moral precepts (*yi* 義) as a relatively generic and persistent code of behaviors, but in several other variations on received Confucian doctrine. *Tian* 天 becomes a remote, seemingly objective and invariable order of nature. Xunzi introduces a constancy between past and present and between one and many, and the predictability that can be derived from this continuity. For Xunzi, the natural human condition is one of chaos that needs to be disciplined through the imposition of social distinctions and rational thinking.

Xunzi's apparent shift in the direction of a rationalizing order, however, can be and indeed has been grossly overstated. When we survey the historical circumstances leading up to the unification of the central states into one world, we see the ascendency of the Legalist thinkers and their appeal to a codified and public system of objective laws. Not only was political unification achieved, but a process of standardization affected society at every level: weights and measures for markets, axle widths for the repair and construction of roads, the standardization of written characters for official documents, the conjoining of walled fortifications into a Great Wall, the codification of ritual practices, the composition of texts such as the *Lüshichunqiu* and *Huainanzi* that aspire to a kind of encyclopedic knowledge, the compilation of comprehensive histories such as the *Records of the Grand Historian* (*Shiji* 史記), the classification of philosophers into philosophical lineages, the theorizing of disparate cultural mythologies and cosmologies into systematic narratives, and so on.

But this movement towards wholesale unification must be clearly distinguished from the second problematic notion of a single-ordered cosmos disciplined by antecedent first principles. Second problematic thinking is familiar in classical Greek metaphysics, but has little relevance for this early Confucian worldview. Instead, this Qin and Han syncretism is an example of a rationalizing and yet open-ended, evolving, and always hybridic order that, at the end of the day, remains fundamentally an inclusive, first problematic aesthetic order. Xunzi's singular contribution to the Confucianism that would emerge as state doctrine a century later in the Western Han dynasty was his transmission of an eclectic and fortified Confucianism—a Confucianism that aspired to the fullest degree of comprehensiveness (*quan* 全). He constructed an extended and amplified Confucianism—a more "comprehensive" Confucianism—by freely imbibing and digesting the doctrines of competing lineages of thought from within what is now in retrospect called the Hundred Schools of the pre-Qin period (*zhuzibaijia* 諸子百家), reshaping these same ideas to make them his own. And a fair argument can be made that the strength of Confucianism across the centuries has been this continuing porousness and characteristic hybridity. It has inspired a Confucian philosophy that, beyond those resources found within the tradition itself, has had and continues to have the capacity to absorb into itself those initially foreign doctrines that would compete with it, with the "Western learning" of Buddhism being one of its first encounters, and then later on and down to the present day, the many more iterations of "Western" learning from the Jesuits to Kant and Marx in our own time.

IX.1 Chapter 1: Exhortation to Learning (*quanxue* 勸學)

君子曰: 學不可以已。青，取之於藍，而青於藍; 冰，水爲之，而寒於水。木直中繩，輮以爲輪，其曲中規，雖有槁暴，不復挺者，輮使之然也。故木受繩則直，金就礪則利，君子博學而日參省乎己，則智明而行無過矣。故不登高山，不知天之高也; 不臨深谿，不知地之厚也; 不聞先王之遺言，不知學問之大也。干、越、夷、貉之子，生而同聲，長而異俗，教使之然也。《詩》曰: "嗟爾君子，無恒安息。靖共爾位，好是正直。神之聽之，介爾景福。"神莫大於化道，福莫長於無禍。吾嘗終日而思矣，不如須臾之所學也。吾嘗跂而望矣，不如登高之博見也。登高而招，臂非加長也，而見者遠；順風而呼，聲非加疾也，而聞者彰。假輿馬者，非利足也，而致千里；假舟楫者，非能水也，而絕江河。君子生非異也，善假於物也。

Exemplary persons (*junzi* 君子) say: Learning should never end. Although blue dye is extracted from the indigo plant, it is bluer than the plant itself. Although ice is formed from water, it is colder than the water itself. A piece of wood that is as straight as a plumbline can be bent to form a wheel such that its roundness matches the compass. The effect of the bending process is that even when cured, it will not return to its original shape. Thus it is that wood can be straightened with the plumbline and metal can be sharpened with the whetstone. When exemplary persons learn broadly and examine themselves daily, their intelligence will shine forth and their conduct will be beyond reproach.

Thus, if you do not climb a high mountain, you will not know the height of the heavens; if you do not peer into a deep river gorge you will not know the thickness of the earth; if you have not heard the transmitted teachings of the Former Kings, you will not know the profundity of their learning and knowledge. Even though the children of the Han, Yue, Yi, and Mo peoples have the same cry at birth, the fact that once grown they are following very different customs is a function of their education. The *Book of Songs* 207 says:

> Hey you fine fellows,
> Don't seek after a life of ease and comfort.
> Carry out the duties of your office
> And cherish those who are upright and honest.
> And should the spirits hear of this,
> The best of fortunes will be yours.

There is no wisdom greater than being transformed by the proper way, and no fortune more sustained than being free of disaster.

I once tried spending the entire day lost in thought only to find it was not worth a moment of learning. I once tried standing high on my tiptoes to gaze into the distance only to find it was not as good as the panoramic view available by climbing to a higher place. If you climb to a high place and wave your hands, even though your arms are not any longer, you can still be seen from a distance. If you give a shout from downwind, even though your voice is no louder, you can still be heard more clearly. It is not that persons who avail themselves of horse and carriage are faster afoot and thus can travel a thousand *li*; it is not that persons who avail themselves of a boat and oars are better as swimmers and thus can traverse the rivers and streams. It is not that exemplary persons are different from anyone else; they are just better at availing themselves of different things.

Comment: The Latin roots for education are *educare* and *educere*. The former *educare* references the familiar transmission of the fundamentals of a discipline from teachers to students, an important process that is a necessary condition for further education. *Educere*, on the other hand, is a conversation between teachers and students in which new knowledge is "educed" from students themselves. It is education as *educere* that the demanding teacher Confucius is referring to in *Analects* 7.8 when he says: 舉一隅不以三隅反，則不復也 "If on instructing students on one corner they do not come back to me with the other three, I will not repeat myself." Such education is not to be confused with any skill-set or training. For Confucius, at the end of the day, education is nothing less than the moral transformation of the students through a regimen of personal cultivation.[①] While such cultivation takes place within the matrix of relations that locates them squarely within their shared narratives, it still must be animated by personal resolve and commitment.

In this Xunzi passage, the metaphors used suggest that for him, education seems to be more *educare* than *educere*, and more external, instrumental, and functional than transformative. With the steaming of wood, the grinding of metal, the climbing up hills, and so on, the natural condition of something is being supplemented by an intervention that either enhances, refines, or replaces it, in order to enable it to do what it can do better. Carriages and boats are enhancement tools that take the place of our natural ability to run and swim. The conception of education here seems to focus on the ingenuity of exemplary persons in availing themselves of artificial technologies.

There is a clear allusion in this passage to *Analects* 15.31 that states:

子曰："吾嘗終日不食，終夜不寢，以思，無益，不如學也。"
The Master said, "Once, lost in my thoughts (*si* 思), I went a whole day

---

[①] John Dewey is remembered as having said: "Education is not preparation for life; it is life itself."

without eating and a whole night without sleeping. I got nothing out of it, and would have been better off devoting the time to learning (*xue* 學)."

But the specific point being made in this *Analects* passage with respect to the importance of learning has to be read in light of 2.15 that argues for the proper balance between learning and reflection when it says: 學而不思則罔, 思而不學則殆 "Learning (*xue* 學) without due reflection (*si* 思) leads to perplexity; reflection without learning leads to perilous circumstances."

積土成山, 風雨興焉; 積水成淵, 蛟龍生焉; 積善成德, 而神明自得, 聖心備焉。故不積跬步, 無以致千里; 不積小流, 無以成江海。騏驥一躍, 不能十步; 駑馬十駕, 功在不舍。鍥而舍之, 朽木不折; 鍥而不舍, 金石可鏤。螾無爪牙之利, 筋骨之強, 上食埃土, 下飲黃泉, 用心一也。蟹八跪而二螯, 非蛇蟺之穴, 無可寄托者, 用心躁也。是故無冥冥之志者, 無昭昭之明; 無惛惛之事者, 無赫赫之功。行衢道者不至, 事兩君者不容。目不能兩視而明, 耳不能兩聽而聰。螣蛇無足而飛, 梧鼠五技而窮。《詩》曰: "尸鳩在桑, 其子七兮。淑人君子, 其儀一兮。其儀一兮, 心如結兮。"故君子結於一也。

Amass enough earth to make a mountain and the rains and wind will swirl around it; dam up enough water to make a watery chasm and different kinds of dragons will appear within it; accumulate enough good deeds to become virtuosic in your conduct, and spiritual intelligence and sagely insight will be yours because of it. Thus it is that unless there is an accumulation of small steps there can be no journey that covers a thousand *li*; unless there is an accumulation of small streams there can be no confluence of them into the rivers and the seas. That the finest steed cannot cover ten paces in a single stride but that a worn-out nag can be harnessed for a ten-day journey is because achievement lies in not giving up. If in carving you give up along the way, you won't even get through a rotten piece of wood, but if you don't give up, you will be able to engrave metal and stone.

That earthworms without the benefit of sharp teeth and claws or the strength afforded by sinew and bone, are able to eat the soil when above ground and to drink spring water below is because they are single-minded in what they do. The fact that crabs with their eight legs and two claws in the absence of cavities left by eels or sea snakes have no safe place to conceal themselves is because they are scatterbrained. Thus it is that if there is no quiet, inexorable purpose, there will be no brilliant wisdom; if there is no single-hearted devotion, there will be no illustrious accomplishments. If you take the fork in the road, you will not get to where you are going, and if you

try to serve two masters, you will please neither. The eye cannot look at two things at the same time and see them clearly; the ear cannot listen to two things at the same time and hear them distinctly. The dragon has no feet and yet can fly; the mole cricket has all the tricks and can go nowhere. The *Book of Songs* 152 says:
> The turtle-dove is perched in the mulberry trees
> Teaching its seven young to fly.
> This good man, our lord,
> In his comportment he is beyond reproach
> Being beyond reproach in his comportment
> Is because he is single in his purposes.

Thus it is exemplary persons are disciplined of mind.

Comment: Xunzi follows Confucius (and Mencius as well, although Xunzi would deny this) in believing that becoming consummate as a human being requires unrelenting and assiduous effort. Throughout the *Xunzi* high value is placed on being disciplined, being single-minded in purpose, and being unflagging in one's efforts.

學惡乎始？惡乎終？曰：其數則始乎誦經，終乎讀禮；其義則始乎爲士，終乎爲聖人。真積力久則入。學至乎没而後止也。故學數有終，若其義則不可須臾舍也。爲之人也，舍之禽獸也。故書者，政事之紀也；詩者，中聲之所止也；禮者，法之大分，類之綱紀也。故學至乎禮而止矣。夫是之謂道德之極。禮之敬文也，樂之中和也，詩書之博也，春秋之微也，在天地之間者畢矣。君子之學也，入乎耳，著乎心，布乎四體，形乎動靜。端而言，蝡而動，一可以爲法則。小人之學也，入乎耳，出乎口；口耳之間，則四寸耳，曷足以美七尺之軀哉！古之學者爲己，今之學者爲人。君子之學也，以美其身；小人之學也，以爲禽犢。故不問而告謂之傲，問一而告二謂之囋。傲，非也，囋，非也；君子如嚮矣。學莫便乎近其人。禮樂法而不説，詩書故而不切，春秋約而不速。方其人之習君子之説，則尊以遍矣，周於世矣。故曰：學莫便乎近其人。學之經莫速乎好其人，隆禮次之。上不能好其人，下不能隆禮，安特將學雜識志，順詩書而已耳。則末世窮年，不免爲陋儒而已。將原先王，本仁義，則禮正其經緯蹊徑也。若挈裘領，詘五指而頓之，順者不可勝數也。不道禮憲，以詩書爲之，譬之猶以指測河也，以戈舂黍也，以錐餐壺也，不可以得之矣。故隆禮，雖未明，法士也；不隆禮，雖察辯，散儒也。

Where does learning begin and where does it end? I would say in proper sequence it begins in reciting the *Book of Documents* and ends with the reading of the *Record of Rituals*. As for its purpose, it begins in becoming a scholar-official (*shi* 士) and ends in becoming a sage (*shengren* 聖人). If persons genuinely invest their efforts over a long period of time, they will gain entry, and it is only with their death their learning will at last come to a close. In terms of sequence, learning has its proper end, but in terms of purpose, one can never give it up even for a second. To commit oneself to learning is to become a person; to give it up is to be a beast.

Thus it is that the *Book of Documents* is the record of political affairs, the *Book of Songs* sets the parameters on proper intonations, and the *Record of Rituals* establishes the important distinctions behind the proper norms and the structure underlying the various classifications. It is thus that true learning finds its terminus in the *Record of Rituals*, for it is only such learning that can be called the high point of all morality. The reverence and elegance of the *Record of Rituals*, the modulation and harmony of the *Book of Music*, the breadth of the *Book of Songs* and the *Book of Documents*, the detail of the *Spring and Autumn Annals*—it is these canons that bring completion to everything between the heavens and the earth.

The learning of exemplary persons (*junzi* 君子) enters the ear, is manifested in their thinking and feeling, pervades their physicality, and shapes their conduct in activity and repose. The candor of their words and the graciousness of their actions establish them as models for all. The learning of petty persons enters the ear and exits the mouth. With only four inches between ear and mouth, how is this enough to ennoble their entire persons from head to foot?

The ancients learned for the sake of themselves while people today learn for the sake of others. The learning of exemplary persons ennobles their persons while the learning of petty persons is made as an offering to others. To volunteer information without having been asked is arrogance; to volunteer two answers for one question is to be verbose. Since arrogance and verbosity are both to be denounced, exemplary persons instead have the responsiveness of an echo.

In learning, nothing is more felicitous than proximity to those who are learned. The *Record of Rituals* and the *Book of Music* provide us with norms but without explanation; the *Book of Songs* and the *Book of Documents* are ancient and not always relevant; the *Spring and Autumn Annals* is summary and its import is not easy to grasp. But when persons practice the teachings of the exemplary person, these teachings will be honored everywhere as they circulate throughout the world. Thus it is said that in learning, nothing is more felicitous than proximity to those who are learned, and on the pathway to learning nothing is more expeditious than to cherish such persons. And revering ritual practices is next. If you are not able to cherish such persons or revere ritual practices, how can you do anything but learn a mountain of trivia and blindly repeat the *Book of Songs* and the *Book of Documents*? Until the end of your days you will be nothing more than a shallow pedant.

But if you return to the Former Kings and root yourself in the values of consummate conduct (*ren* 仁) and moral precepts (*yi* 義), then ritual practices will guide you through all exigencies and along all byways. If in picking up a fur collar you use all five fingers to smooth it out, the hairs pressed down by the hand are innumerable. Not abiding by the tenets of ritual propriety in what you do but instead relying on the *Book of Songs* and the *Book of Documents* is like using your finger to measure the depth of a river, is like using a spear point to thrash the grain, or is like using an awl to eat from the supper pot. You are doomed to failure. Thus it is those who revere ritual practices even when lacking real insight can become model scholar-officials while those who fail to offer such reverence even when being persons of keen discrimination will be nothing but undisciplined pedants.

Comment: Xunzi reflects on the curriculum, and on the starting point and its end in the process of acquiring a proper Confucian education. In terms of the written texts, although he subordinates all of the other canons to the *Record of Rituals* as the highest statement of morality, each of these texts has its proper place and makes its contribution to the curriculum. Such an education is a lifetime project, and students must be unrelenting in their commitment. Xunzi sets a contrast between the learning of exemplary persons and that of petty persons. Where the learning of exemplary persons is transformative in every respect, petty persons are only able to acquire a superficial grasp of rote learning. Xunzi cites Confucius who observes that such people far from cultivating themselves to become consummate persons are more interested in the instrumental value learning has in making an impression on other people.

But unless a close reading of the texts is accompanied by a learned and exemplary teacher, rather than being true learning it becomes shallow and doctrinaire pedantry. For true learning, students must return to the teachings of the Former Kings, be firmly rooted in Confucian values, seek out exemplary persons, and must rely upon the guidance provided by ritual practices in all aspects of their lives.

百發失一，不足謂善射；千里蹞步不至，不足謂善御；倫類不通，仁義不一，不足謂善學。學也者，固學一之也。一出焉，一入焉，涂巷之人也；其善者少，不善者多，桀紂盜跖也；全之盡之，然後學者也。君子知夫不全不粹之不足以爲美也，故誦數以貫之，思索以通之，爲其人以處之，除其害者以持養之。使目非是無欲見也，使耳非是無欲聞也，使口非是無欲言也，使心非是無欲慮也。及至其致好之也，目好之五色，耳好之五聲，口好之五味，心利之有天下。是故權利不能傾也，群衆不能移也，天下不能蕩也。生乎由是，死乎由是，夫是之謂德操。德操然後能定，能定然後能應。能定能應，夫是之謂成人。天見其明，地見其光，君子貴其全也。

One who misses the target once in a hundred attempts does not deserve to be called an expert archer; one who fails to cover the last half pace after setting out on a journey of a thousand *li* does not deserve to be called an expert carriage driver; one who is not wholly conversant with the relations and categories around which things are organized and who fails to understand the continuity between consummate conduct (*ren* 仁) and moral precepts (*yi* 義) does not deserve to be called an expert scholar. What I mean by real scholars are those for whom everything coheres as one. Those who abandon one thing and come back with another are just the common rabble. With their incompetencies far outweighing their expertise, they are the likes of the despots Jie and Zhou and the Robber Zhi. Only those whose expertise is exhaustive qualify as real scholars.

Exemplary persons are keenly aware that what is lacking and impure does not deserve to be considered beautiful. It is for this reason that they use recitation and inquiry to bring their learning together, and then incisive probing and reflection to grasp it fully. As their way of applying it, they embody it in their persons, and in their cultivation of it they excise what is harmful. They discipline their eyes to abstain from seeing anything that is not right, their ears to abstain from hearing anything that is not right, their mouths to abstain from saying anything that is not right, and their heartminds to abstain from reflecting on anything that is not right. When they have truly come to cherish learning, their eyes will prefer it to the five colors, their ears to the five notes, their mouths to the five tastes, and their heartminds to holding sway over the whole world.

At this point, power and profit cannot deter them, cliques and popular opinion cannot dissuade them, and the whole world cannot affect them. In life they are like this and in death the same. Such a way of life is what is called having integrity. It is only when they have this kind of integrity that they are able to be resolute, and it is only when they are resolute that they are able to be responsive. Such as these then are what are meant by accomplished persons. Just as the heavens make manifest its brightness and the earth its vastness, exemplary persons treasure their completeness.

Comment: Throughout the *Xunzi*, there is this rationalization of the process of learning expressed as the pursuit of oneness and completeness. The question is whether Xunzi is a philosopher of closure or disclosure, a realist or a historicist, an absolutist or a constructivist, a rationalist or an advocate for rigor and coherence within a holistic aestheticism.

One way of reading Plato is as an abstract formist who provides an objective and universal answer, and thus closure. He is a metaphysical realist who understands the life of the philosopher as a theoretical and spiritual ascent from a world of appearance and mere opinion to that of Reality and the true intellectual knowledge of the unchanging Forms. The escape from the cave in the *Republic*, Diotima's introduction of Beauty-in-itself to a young Socrates in the *Symposium*, the escape of the soul from the body in the *Phaedo*, are all ways of conveying this intellectual journey and its certain end.

But a much more interesting reading of Plato is that he is an erotic ironist who advocates for philosophy as a continuing way of life. Philosophy is the process rather than an end. Plato on this reading is a poet and playwright, a purveyor of metaphor and a subversive artist, and has only been reduced to a metaphysical absolutist because of the melding of Greek philosophy with Christian dogma and twentieth century scientism.

Perhaps we ought to opt for the more interesting reading of Xunzi as well.

IX.2 Chapter 2: Personal Cultivation (*xiushen* 修身)

見善，修然必以自存也；見不善，愀然必以自省也。善在身，介然必以自好也；不善在身，菑然必以自惡也。故非我而當者，吾師也；是我而當者，吾友也；諂諛我者，吾賊也。故君子隆師而親友，以致惡其賊。好善無厭，受諫而能誡，雖欲無進，得乎哉！小人反是：致亂而惡人之非己也；致不肖而欲人之賢己也；心如虎狼，行如禽獸，而又惡人之賊己也。諂諛者親，諫爭者疏，修正爲笑，至忠爲賊，雖欲無滅亡，得乎哉！《詩》曰："潝潝訿訿，亦孔之哀。謀之其臧，則具是違；謀之不臧，則具是依。"此之謂也。

On witnessing efficacious conduct, one must examine one's own person

in earnest; on witnessing conduct that is perverse, one must look to oneself with trepidation. When one discovers such efficacy in one's own conduct one must staunchly affirm it; when one discovers such perversity in one's own conduct, one must loathe oneself as someone afflicted. Thus, those who would censure me for what is properly censured are my teachers, and those who would approve of me for what is properly approved of are my friends. But those who would flatter and curry favor with me are my malefactors. Thus it is that exemplary persons exalt their teachers and are intimate with their friends, but truly despise their malefactors. They cherish efficacious conduct without wavering, and on receiving remonstrance are able to be heedful in what they do. Even if they wanted to hold themselves back, how could they but get what they are after?

Base persons then are just the opposite. They bring on chaos and yet resent the reproaches of others; they do despicable things and yet expect others to consider them worthy persons. They have the heartmind of a wolf or tiger, conduct themselves like wild beasts, and yet hate it when others treat them as malefactors. They are intimate with those who would flatter and curry favor with them, and are estranged from those who would reprimand or remonstrate with them. Their cultivation of what is proper is farcical, and doing their utmost is only a source of harm. Even if they wanted to escape death and destruction, how could they but bring it on? This is what it means in the *Book of Songs* 195 when it says:

> They flock together and slander others,
> And I am filled with grief.
> When the counsel is sound,
> They all oppose it,
> And when it is not
> They all follow through on it.

Comment: The familiar contrast found throughout the *Analects* between the commitment to cultivation of exemplary persons and the lethargy of base persons is further elaborated upon here. Exemplary persons begin from vigilance in being self-critical of their own actions, and are also welcoming of the criticisms of others. They are glad to have the reproach of their teachers where appropriate, and the endorsement of their friends where it is deserved. They are able to learn from the sincere responses of teachers and friends to what they do, and are able to distinguish these voices from the sycophantic behavior of those who would make use of them.

Such models of conduct advance along the proper way. Base persons, on the other hand, exhibiting values precisely opposite to those of exemplary persons, make a farce of personal cultivation, and are hell-bent for ruin in everything they do.

志意修則驕富貴，道義重則輕王公；內省而外物輕矣。傳曰："君子役物，小人役於物。"此之謂矣。身勞而心安，爲之；利少而義多，爲之；事亂君而通，不如事窮君而順焉。故良農不爲水旱不耕，良賈不爲折閱不市，士君子不爲貧窮怠乎道。

If persons are well-disciplined in intentions and purpose, they can rise above wealth and honor; if they put great weight on the proper way and moral precepts, they can look askance at dukes and kings. When they pay attention to their inner disposition, they can look away from external things. This is what it means when the Commentary states: "Exemplary persons (*junzi* 君子) avail themselves of things while base persons are made use of by things."

Though it might tire the body, if the heartmind finds satisfaction in it, then do it. Though it might be of little advantage, if there is much meaning in it, then do it. Finding success in the service of a disorderly ruler is not as good as finding accord in the service of an impoverished one. Just as good farmers do not give up tilling the fields on account of flood or drought, and good merchants do not abandon their trade on account of sustaining a loss, so scholar-officials (*shi* 士) and exemplary persons do not neglect the proper way on account of their impoverished circumstances.

Comment: Xunzi continues a familiar theme from the *Analects*: that is, the aspirations of scholar-officials (*shi* 士) to become exemplary persons (*junzi* 君子) through a Confucian education that leads to public service. Confucius on several occasions exhorts his students to seek public office for the service and moral contribution one is able to make to the community rather than for the material benefits that come with office. The quality of the personal conduct of truly exemplary persons lifts them above any concern for wealth or power, and enables them to continue to act in exemplary ways regardless of their material conditions. They labor in service to the proper way regardless of personal comfort or benefit.

體恭敬而心忠信，術禮義而情愛人；橫行天下，雖困四夷，人莫不貴。勞苦之事則爭先，饒樂之事則能讓，端愨誠信，拘守而詳；橫行天下，雖困四夷，人莫不任。體倨固而心埶詐，術順墨而精雜汙；橫行天下，雖達四方，人莫不賤。勞苦之事則偷儒轉脫，饒樂之事則佞兌而不曲，辟違而不慤，程役而不錄；橫行天下，雖達四方，人莫不棄。

If in physical comportment you are reverent and respectful, in mental disposition you do your utmost and live up to your word, in conduct you accord with ritual practices and moral precepts, and in your sentiments you love other people, then in traversing the world even if you are reduced to living among the barbarians, there is no one who will not honor you. If in difficult circumstances you struggle to take the lead, but amid riches and plenty you are able to yield to others, if you are upright, sincere, live up to your word, and are restrained and meticulous in your conduct, then in traversing the world even if you are reduced to living among the barbarians, there is no one who will not retain your services.

If in physical comportment you are haughty and stubborn, and in mental disposition you are cunning and deceitful, in conduct you follow dark ways and in your feelings you are shady and corrupt, then in traversing the world even if you are reduced to living among the barbarians, everyone will still look on you with contempt. If in difficult circumstances you shrink back and are evasive, but amid riches and plenty you are fawning and unrestrained, if you are deceitful and imprudent, and do not carry out the duties of your charge, then in traversing the world even if you are reduced to living among the barbarians, everyone will still look to throwing you out.

Comment: Those Confucians who aspire to office do so for the difference they can make to the lives of the people rather than for personal profit. Such a commitment is evidenced in their deportment and conduct. A contrast is set between those whose way of life is grounded solidly in the norms set by ritual practices and moral precepts, and those who act wantonly and with abandon. Such a moral bearing is respected everywhere. Those who exhibit such values and moral conduct, wherever they go in the world, will be honored and employed. But those whose conduct is lacking in such a moral compass and who are given to vice, wherever they go in the world, will not only be viewed with contempt, but will be rejected outright.

好法而行，士也；篤志而體，君子也；齊明而不竭，聖人也。人無法，則倀倀然；有法而無志其義，則渠渠然；依乎法，而又深其類，然後溫溫然。

Persons who cherish norms and put them into practice are scholar-officials (*shi* 士); those who are earnest in their purposes and embody these norms are exemplary persons (*junzi* 君子); those who have keen insight into these norms and are unrelenting in their application are sages (*shengren* 聖人). Persons without norms are wild and unruly; those who observe norms but cannot fathom their meaning are anxious and at a loss as to what to do; it is only those who have confidence in the norms and have a deep understanding of what they mean who are temperate and affable.

Comment: The term translated as "norms" in this passage is *fa* 法. It is a term frequently associated with a doctrinal lineage, the Legalists (*fajia* 法家), that begins a few generations earlier than Xunzi with Shang Yang 商鞅, and that includes two of Xunzi's students, Han Fei 韓非 and Li Si 李斯. The majority of the occurrences of the character *fa* 法 in the early texts would indicate that prior to the rise of the Legalist tradition, this term was used to convey the meaning of "model, standard, norm" in the broadest sense. Only well into the Warring States period when the Legalist theorists had appropriated this character as a technical term and injected it with their own meaning did it come to connote "penal law." Prior to this evolution, penal law was expressed by the character *xing* 刑 that meant first "punishments," and then by extension, "penal law."

端愨順弟，則可謂善少者矣；加好學遜敏焉，則有鈞無上，可以爲君子者矣。偷儒憚事，無廉恥而嗜乎飲食，則可謂惡少者矣；加惕悍而不順，險賊而不弟焉，則可謂不詳少者矣，雖陷刑戮可也。老老而壯者歸焉，不窮窮而通者積焉，行乎冥冥而施乎無報，而賢不肖一焉。人有此三行，雖有大過，天其不遂乎！

Those who are upright, amiable, and deferential to elders can be called fine young persons. If you add to this a love of learning, modesty, and agility, they can be deemed exemplary persons (*junzi* 君子).

Those who shrink back and are evasive, who are lacking in modesty and a sense of shame, and who have an inordinate taste for food and drink, can be called despicable young persons. If you add to this recklessness, disobedience, belligerence, and impudence, they can be called ill-fated young persons, and it will only be well-deserved if they end up on the executioner's block.

Those who revere the aged will be sought out by the strong and able, those who do not distress the oppressed will have the company of those who are well-off, and those who do good things without thought of reward will be pursued by the worthy and unworthy alike. For those associated with these three kinds of conduct, even if some great disaster is about to befall them, won't the fates see them through?

Comment: The values advocated by Xunzi continue the family-centered prime moral imperative of "family reverence." The younger generation is encouraged to embrace such values, and as they put these values into practice, to live exemplary lives.

君子之求利也略，其遠害也早，其避辱也懼，其行道理也勇。君子貧窮而志廣，富貴而體恭，安燕而血氣不惰，勞倦而容貌不枯，怒不過奪，喜不過予。君子貧窮而志廣，隆仁也；富貴而體恭，殺埶也；安燕而血氣不衰，柬理也；勞倦而容貌不枯，好交也；怒不過奪，喜不過予，是法勝私也。《書》曰："無有作好，遵王之道。無有作惡，遵王之路。"此言君子之能以公義勝私欲也。

Exemplary persons (*junzi* 君子) have little interest in seeking after personal profit, but are quick to keep harm at bay. They are overcautious in avoiding disgrace, but are courageous in practicing the tenets of the proper way (*dao* 道). In the face of hardship and poverty, exemplary persons are broad in their purposes, and amid wealth and honor they are the embodiment of gentility. When in repose, they do not become lethargic, and when tired and spent, they maintain appearances. They do not become aggressive in their anger nor extravagant in their joy.

That exemplary persons are broad in their purposes in the face of hardship and poverty is because they extoll consummate conduct (*ren* 仁). That amid riches and honor they are the embodiment of gentility is because they do not take advantage of their privileged life. That in repose they do not become lethargic is because they have a sense of structure. That they maintain appearances when tired and spent is because they appreciate good form. That they do not become aggressive in their anger nor extravagant in their joy is because decorum prevails over personal desires.

The *Book of Documents* states: "Do not have things you covet, but follow the way of the True King; do not have things you despise, but follow the path of the True King." This explains how it is that exemplary persons are able to put the public good before personal desires.

Comment: Xunzi provides a definition of exemplary persons that echoes many of the expectations expressed in the *Analects*: having the courage of one's convictions, maintaining integrity in the face of hardship and poverty, maintaining decorum even when exhausted, and expressing modesty and gentility as the proper response to wealth and privilege.

IX.3 Chapter 8: Confucian Achievements (*ruxiao* 儒效)

秦昭王問孫卿子曰:"儒無益於人之國。"孫卿子曰:"儒者法先王,隆禮義,謹乎臣子而致貴其上者也。人主用之,則埶在本朝而宜;不用,則退編百姓而愨;必爲順下矣。雖窮困凍餧,必不以邪道爲貪。無置錐之地,而明於持社稷之大義。嗚呼而莫之能應,然而通乎財萬物,養百姓之經紀。埶在人上,則王公之材也;在人下,則社稷之臣,國君之寶也;雖隱於窮閻漏屋,人莫不貴之,道誠存也。"

King Zhao of Qin asked Master Xun: "Do the Confucians in fact have nothing on offer that would improve my state?"

Master Xun replied: "The Confucians emulate the Former Kings, place high value in ritual propriety (*li* 禮) and moral precepts (*yi* 義), and observe faithfully the roles of minister and son in extending the utmost honor to their benefactors. When the ruler drafts them into service, in discharging their duties everything is done right. If the ruler does not employ them, in returning to their role as members of the community they behave properly, and are certain to be compliant subjects.

"Even when in dire straits beleaguered by hunger and cold, they will never seek out some nefarious scheme for their own benefit. Without a scrap of land to call their own, they are still clear in their grasp of the profound meaning of the altars to the soil and grain. Even when no one is able to respond to their desperate entreaties, they are still clear on the sanctions that govern things and the proper guidelines for providing for the welfare of the people. When raised above others, they have the talent needed to assist a king or duke, and when not given such status, they are still able ministers to the altars of soil and grain and a treasure to the ruler. Even when they are secluded in some leaky and run-down shack, that there is no one who does not show them honor is because they embody the proper way (*dao* 道) with the utmost sincerity."

Comment: Xunzi gives a profile of Confucians who are properly educated in Confucian values, and as such, how they have enormous worth to the ruler and the state. Underscoring the isomorphism between family and state, Xunzi makes the point that their service to their lord is not dependent upon the status given to them within the hierarchy. Drafted into service or not, properly compensated or otherwise, these Confucians have an unwavering commitment to the institutions of state power and to the welfare of the people.

我欲賤而貴，愚而智，貧而富，可乎？曰：其唯學乎。彼學者，行之，曰士也；敦慕焉，君子也；知之，聖人也。上爲聖人，下爲士、君子，孰禁我哉！鄉也混然涂之人也，俄而並乎堯禹，豈不賤而貴矣哉！鄉也效門室之辨，混然曾不能決也，俄而原仁義，分是非，圓回天下於掌上，而辯黑白，豈不愚而知矣哉！鄉也胥靡之人，俄而治天下之大器舉在此，豈不貧而富矣哉！

"Is it possible for someone like me to ascend from humble station to a place of honor, from obtuseness to wisdom, from poverty to wealth?" asked the King.

"It is simply a matter of education." said Master Xun. Those who put their learning into practice are called scholar-officials (*shi* 士), those who are assiduous in their studies become exemplary persons (*junzi* 君子), and those who really understand such learning become sages (*shengren* 聖人). At best education leads to becoming a sage, and at worst a scholar-official or an exemplary person—who is there to stop them?

"In the first instance someone is just a person on the street and then suddenly they are on a par with a Yao or a Yu—is this not a case of ascending from humble station to a place of honor? In the first instance someone is so muddled they cannot tell the difference between the house and its door. And then suddenly they understand the origins of consummate conduct (*ren* 仁) and moral precepts (*yi* 義), can make appropriate discriminations, and can turn the whole world over in the palm of their hand as easily as telling white from black—is this not a case of ascending from obtuseness to wisdom? In the first instance someone is penniless with nothing to their name, and then suddenly they hold the reins of power over the whole world—is this not ascending from poverty to wealth?"

Comment: Throughout his writings, Xunzi places enormous store in the transformative force of education. Here the question is how does one achieve political status, wisdom, and wealth? For Xunzi, a proper course of learning is sufficient to transform an unremarkable person into a sage-ruler, into someone with the wisdom that comes with morality, and into someone who holds sway over the whole world. As with Confucius, Xunzi is a person who "cherishes learning" (*haoxue* 好學) above all else. And believing that the substance of education is moral virtuosity, Xunzi like Confucius is a most demanding teacher. For both of them, becoming moral requires unrelenting effort.

IX.4 Chapter 9: Regulations of a True King (*wangzhi* 王制)

請問爲政？曰：賢能不待次而舉，罷不能不待須而廢，元惡不待教而誅，中庸雜民不待政而化。分未定也，則有昭繆也。雖王公士大夫之子孫也，不能屬於禮義，則歸之庶人。雖庶人之子孫也，積文學，正身行，能屬於禮義，則歸之卿相士大夫。故姦言，姦說，姦事，姦能，遁逃反側之民，職而教之，須而待之，勉之以慶賞，懲之以刑罰。安職則畜，不安職則棄。五疾，上收而養之，材而事之，官施而衣食之，兼覆無遺。才行反時者死無赦。夫是之謂天德，是王者之政也。

May I ask after proper governing?

I replied: Raise up the worthy and capable without waiting on seniority, and get rid of the weak and incompetent without any hesitation. Execute the incorrigibly criminal without trying to rehabilitate them, and transform the common run of people without imposing regulations on them. Even before ranks have been fixed, there is an obvious order among people. Though persons might be the progeny of royalty and high officials, if they are not able to observe ritual practices and moral precepts, send them back to the commoners. And though they might be the offspring of commoners, if they are highly educated, upright in their conduct, and able to observe ritual practices and moral precepts, raise them up to be high ministers and officials.

Among the common people, there are those who make heretical pronouncements, subscribe to heretical doctrines, do heretical things, have heretical skills, and who are evasive and perverse. Give them a post, teach them, and show them some patience. Encourage them with commendations and rewards, admonish them with fines and punishments. If they perform well in office, cultivate them; if they do not, get rid of them.

With respect to the disabled, those in authority should take them in, care for them, and put them to work according to their abilities. Give them official duties to enable them to feed and clothe themselves, and make sure all are taken care of without remainder. But if any of these persons in their talents or conduct offend against the tenor of the times, then show no mercy in putting them to death.

This then is what is called godlike virtuosity, and is the proper governing of the True King.

Comment: There is much that is modern here in Xunzi's political philosophy. Throughout his doctrines, we see a strong emphasis on hierarchical structures as well as on the transformative force of proper education. As with Confucius before him, Xunzi in his emphasis on distinctions of rank and status is liberal as an advocate of social mobility based upon character and conduct rather than bloodline. A persistent standard he invokes is whether or not people comport themselves according to ritual practices and moral precepts. With respect to persons already in office, a firm hand is needed in promoting those who perform their duties properly and for getting rid of the incompetent. With respect to those corrupt few who would undermine the system, they are to be dealt with severely.

Of particular notice is Xunzi's attitude toward the common people. He is not patronizing, and is open to the possibility that through effort and education, they might make their way up to the highest ranks in government. And even when they have a rough beginning, they are deserving of training, patience, and opportunity for advancement. Again, if under such conditions they fail to perform, they are not to be tolerated.

Most remarkable is the system he prescribes for dealing with the handicapped and disabled. He gives them the dignity of appropriate employment rather than simply providing for them. To the extent they are able, they should be given work and should earn their own keep. He is generous in making sure every single person is included in his welfare scheme, but is unforgiving in the severity with which he deals with even the disabled if they take advantage of this generosity.

凡聽：威嚴猛厲，而不好假道人，則下畏恐而不親，周閉而不竭。若是，則大事殆乎弛，小事殆乎遂。和解調通，好假道人，而無所凝止之，則姦言並至，嘗試之說鋒起。若是，則聽大事煩，是又傷之也。故法而不議，則法之所不至者必廢。職而不通，則職之所不及者必隊。故法而議，職而通，無隱謀，無遺善，而百事無過，非君子莫能。故公平者，聽之衡也；中和者，聽之繩也。其有法者以法行，無法者以類舉，聽之盡也。偏黨而不經，聽之辟也。故有良法而亂者，有之矣，有君子而亂者，自古及今，未嘗聞也。傳曰："治生乎君子，亂生乎小人。"此之謂也。

If in general the ruler in listening to counsel is stern and severe and has no taste for drawing upon others and taking their advice, his subordinates will be disaffected and become afraid of him. They will simply close up and withhold their thoughts. Such being the case, important matters will be neglected and even minor affairs will go awry.

If on the other hand the ruler is too affable and conciliatory, delights in drawing upon others and seeking their advice, and has no sense of where this all ends, he will be inundated with perverse ideas, and every kind of speculation will be pressed upon him. Such being the case, in seeking counsel on important matters, he will be so mired in minor details it will undermine good governance.

Hence, when laws are not attended to by proper deliberation, anything lying outside of an official's immediate compass will go unanswered. When responsibilities of office are not fully understood, any matters lying outside of their immediate purview are certain to be overlooked. Hence laws must receive proper deliberation, and responsibilities of office must be fully understood. When there are no hidden agendas and no opportunities lost, there will be no failures in the various affairs of government. None but exemplary persons (*junzi* 君子) are capable of this.

Thus, fairness is the scale on which counsel is to be weighed, and its capacity to effect a flourishing state is its proper measure. Best practice in taking counsel is that where there are laws then apply them, and where there are none, proceed according to precedent. Worst practice in taking counsel is to be partisan and not be guided by constant standards. There have certainly been cases of disorder even when good laws are in place, but from time immemorial there has never been disorder when an exemplary person is ruler. This is what it means when the traditional adage says: "Proper governance is born of exemplary persons; disorder of petty persons."

Comment: Xunzi here is providing advice to rulers on how to take advice. Extremes in the attitude of the ruler toward ministers in either severity or license are to be avoided. Xunzi is an advocate of structure, regulation, and social distinctions, and with his emphasis upon ritual practices and moral precepts, it gives the institutions of governance a strong moral aspect. Laws and careful deliberation as well as promoting a synoptic understanding of the responsibilities that attend official position are necessary conditions for effective governance, but at the end of the day, for Xunzi, there is no guarantee save for the exemplary quality of the ruler himself.

分均則不偏，埶齊則不壹，眾齊則不使。有天有地，而上下有差；明王始立，而處國有制。夫兩貴之不能相事，兩賤之不能相使，是天數也。埶位齊，而欲惡同，物不能澹則必爭；爭則必亂，亂則窮矣。先王惡其亂也，故制禮義以分之，使有貧富貴賤之等，足以相兼臨者，是養天下之本也。《書》曰："維齊非齊。" 此之謂也。

Where everyone is of the same rank, there will be no staffing available;

where everyone has the same authority, there will be no uniting around any one of them; and when the multitude is all on the same level, there will be no one to do the work. Just as with the heavens and the earth, there is the distinction between high and low. It was only when enlightened kings came to the throne that they handled their affairs of state through regulations.

That two equally esteemed persons are not able to serve each other and two equally lowly persons cannot work for each other is in the nature of things. When rank and authority are on a par and preferences are the same, the fact that there is not enough to go around will necessarily incite quarrels. Where there is quarrelling there is disorder, and where disorder, straitened circumstances.

It was because the Former Kings detested such chaos that they regulated affairs through ritual practices and moral precepts and thus made distinctions among people. It is because establishing differences in wealth and station can determine who supervises whom that it is the root that nourishes the world. When the *Book of Documents* says "If there is equality then there must be inequality," this is what it means.

Comment: Simple egalitarianism leads to anarchy because it precludes any locus of authority. Hierarchical relations within any society and its institutions are necessary for it to function effectively. It is a recognition of such hierarchy as a natural fact in the world around us that gave rise to political ranks and distinctions, and to the implementation of regulatory measures to organize the distribution of goods. Just as making the distinction "this" gives rise to a "that," so equality itself brings along with it the possibility of inequality. Xunzi would be impatient with any uncritical endorsement of equality, and even more so with any blanket condemnation of hierarchies. Throughout the *Xunzi*, a major theme is making sure these necessary hierarchies are properly served by promoting the most worthy and talented.

馬駭輿，則君子不安輿；庶人駭政，則君子不安位。馬駭輿，則莫若靜之；庶人駭政，則莫若惠之。選賢良，舉篤敬，興孝弟，收孤寡，補貧窮。如是，則庶人安政矣。庶人安政，然後君子安位。傳曰："君者，舟也，庶人者，水也；水則載舟，水則覆舟。" 此之謂也。故君人者，欲安，則莫若平政愛民矣；欲榮，則莫若隆禮敬士矣；欲立功名，則莫若尚賢使能矣。是人君之大節也。三節者當，則其餘莫不當矣。三節者不當，則其餘雖曲當，猶將無益也。孔子曰："大節是也，小節是也，上君也；大節是也，小節一出焉，一入焉，中君也；大節非也，小節雖是也，吾無觀其餘矣。"

If horses are spooked when pulling a carriage, the ruler who is riding in it will not be safe; if the common people are spooked in the administering of governance, the ruler who is dispensing it will not be secure in his position. If horses are spooked when pulling a carriage, there is nothing better than settling them down; if the common people are spooked in the administering of governance, there is nothing better than treating them with kindness. Select the best and the worthy, promote earnestness and respect, encourage family reverence and deference to elders (*xiaoti* 孝弟), gather in the orphaned and widowed, lend assistance to the poor and destitute. If you do this, once the common people are secure under your governance, the ruler will find safety in his position. This is what the traditional adage means when it says "The ruler is the boat and the common people the water; just as the water floats the boat, it can also capsize it."

Thus, if the ruler desires safety, then nothing works as well as governing fairly and loving the common people. If he desires honor, then nothing works as well as exalting ritual practices and showing respect to his scholar-officials. If he desires to be accomplished and make a name for himself, nothing works as well as promoting the worthy and employing the able. These then are the obligations the ruler has in governing the people. When these three obligations are met, all other responsibilities will be taken care of as a matter of course. But if they are not met, even if the ruler finds some way to meet his other obligations, it will be of no avail. Confucius said: "If the major obligations are met and the minor ones as well, this is the best kind of ruler. If the major obligations are met but the minor ones are hit or miss, this is the mediocre ruler. If the ruler fails to meet the major obligations, even where the minor obligations are all taken care of, I would not want to see anything more of him."

Comment: There is a symbiotic relationship that obtains between ruler and ruled that the ruler must respect. The security of his position as ruler is dependent upon the support of the people, and the support of the people requires compassionate governance inclusive of all. A suppressed premise is the isomorphism between family and state. Xunzi summarizes the ruler's duty to the people in terms of three major obligations upon which their support depends: love and care for the people, observance of ritual practices and respect for his officials, and the promotion of the worthy and able. Of course, there are many obligations beyond these three, and the best of rulers seek to take care of them all. But if the ruler at the end of the day fails to live up to these three, all is lost.

王奪之人，霸奪之與，強奪之地。奪之人者臣諸侯，奪之與者友諸侯，奪之地者敵諸侯。臣諸侯者王，友諸侯者霸，敵諸侯者危。用強者，人之城守，人之出戰，而我以力勝之也，則傷人之民必甚矣；傷人之民甚，則人之民必惡我甚矣；人之民惡我甚，則日欲與我鬥。人之城守，人之出戰，而我以力勝之，則傷吾民必甚矣；傷吾民甚，則吾民之惡我甚矣；吾民之惡我甚，則日不欲爲我鬥。人之民日欲與我鬥，吾民日不欲爲我鬥，是強者之所以反弱也。地來而民去，累多而功少，雖守者益，所以守者損，是以大者之所以反削也。諸侯莫不懷交接怨，而不忘其敵，伺強大之間，承強大之敝，此強大之殆時也。知強大者不務強也，慮以王命，全其力，凝其德。力全則諸侯不能弱也，德凝則諸侯不能削也，天下無王霸主，則常勝矣。是知強道者也。

The True King wins over the people, the hegemon wins over his allies, and those who use force win more territory. He who wins over the people has the vassal lords as his ministers and he who establishes alliances is befriended by them, but he who occupies more land incurs the enmity of the vassal lords. He who has the vassal lords as his ministers is the True King, he who is befriended by the vassal lords is a hegemon, and he who incurs the enmity of the vassal lords is in real danger.

If I am a ruler who would use force, wanting to exercise my might in defeating the people of another state who are defending their fortified cities, and thus routing those who are being sent out to engage me in battle, the toll I am inflicting upon those people is severe indeed. Where the toll inflicted upon the people of another state is severe, the hatred of these people directed toward me will be fierce, and with this hatred being fierce, their desire to go to battle against me will increase daily.

With the people of other states defending their own cities and being sent out to do battle with me, the toll I am inflicting on my own people will be severe indeed. Where the toll inflicted on my own people is severe, the hatred of my own people directed toward me will be fierce, and with this hatred being fierce, their desire to go to battle for me will decrease daily. It is the daily growth in the desire of the people of other states to go to battle against me, and the daily decrease in the desire of my own people to go to battle for me, that undermines someone who like me would use force.

More land is taken but the people flee from it; my worries increase but my achievements are minimal. Even though what is to be protected has increased, those available to protect it have diminished. This is how what has become great is pared away. There are none among the feudal lords who, harboring resentment and wanting revenge, ever forget their enmity towards me. With all of them biding their time to find an opening to take advantage of some weakness in the great and mighty, the moment of greatest peril is upon me.

Those who really understand the use of force do not rely upon it. They figure out how to use the mandate of the king to keep their strength intact and to consolidate their moral authority (*de* 德). With their strength intact, the vassal lords cannot weaken them, and with their moral authority consolidated the vassal lords cannot pare it away. If there is no True King or hegemon ruling the world, such rulers will be constant in their victories. This then is understanding the way of using force.

Comment: The paradoxes of territorial imperialism and the lessons learned from the fall of empires are timeless, and have as much relevance today as they did during the Warring States period. Xunzi provides a logical analysis of how the use of force is self-defeating. The use of force to conquer and occupy foreign lands is a double-bind in that it ultimately exhausts one's own resources while creating enemies of everyone, both foreign and domestic, friend and foe. To the extent that the use of force produces enmity everywhere, rather than increasing one's power and influence, it has the opposite effect.

王者之人：飾動以禮義，聽斷以類，明振毫末，舉措應變而不窮，夫是之謂有原。是王者之人也。
On the Person of the True King: He appeals to ritual practices and moral precepts in conducting his affairs, applies proper protocols in hearing counsel and making his decisions, and acts intelligently down to the finest detail. In his decision-making and in his response to changing circumstances, he is never at a loss. This is what is called having full control of the fundamentals. This then is the person of the True King.

王者之制：道不過三代，法不二後王；道過三代謂之蕩，法二後王謂之不雅。衣服有制，宮室有度，人徒有數，喪祭械用皆有等宜。聲，則非雅聲者舉廢；色，則凡非舊文者舉息；械用，則凡非舊器者舉毀。夫是之謂復古，是王者之制也。
On the Regulations of the True King: His methods are not drawn from times earlier than the Three Dynasties, and his norms are not at odds with the later kings. Methods that are antecedent to the Three Dynasties can be described

as precarious, and norms at odds with the later kings can be described as inelegant. There are regulations governing dress and attire, there is proper measure governing palace buildings, and there are set limits governing personal attendants. The articles in use for funerals and sacrifices are all dispensed according to the appropriate status. Any music lacking in traditional elegance should be abandoned; any patterns not consistent with classical designs should be prohibited; any funerary or sacrificial articles that do not accord with established forms should be discarded. This is what is called reviving antiquity. These then are the regulations of the True King.

王者之論：無德不貴，無能不官，無功不賞，無罪不罰。朝無幸位，民無幸生。尚賢使能，而等位不遺；析愿禁悍，而刑罰不過。百姓曉然皆知夫爲善於家，而取賞於朝也；爲不善於幽，而蒙刑於顯也。夫是之謂定論。是王者之論也。

On the Precepts of the True King: Only those with virtuosity shall be honored; only the able shall hold office; only the accomplished shall be rewarded; only the guilty shall be punished. No one at court shall find their post as a matter of mere chance and no one among the common people shall receive their livelihood as a matter of mere chance. Promote the worthy and employ the able, with each of them being given the proper rank without exception. Chasten reprobates and prohibit violence but do not use penal law and punishments in excess. All of the people will know clearly anything good that is done in the privacy of the home will be commended at court, and anything bad done in secret will be met with punishment in public view. This is what is called laying down one's precepts. These then are the precepts of the True King.

王者之法：等賦、政事、財萬物，所以養萬民也。田野什一，關市幾而不征，山林澤梁，以時禁發而不稅。相地而衰政。理道之遠近而致貢。通流財物粟米，無有滯留，使相歸移也，四海之內若一家。故近者不隱其能，遠者不疾其勞，無幽閒隱僻之國，莫不趨使而安樂之。夫是之爲人師。是王者之法也。

On the Legal System of the True King: Through tax regulation, government policy, and maintaining material well-being, he takes care of all of the people. The tax on land use is one part in ten, and at check points and markets there are inspections, but no further taxes. Again, the resources from the woodlands and wetlands are regulated according to season, but no taxes are levied. The fertility of the land is assessed and fees calibrated accordingly. Transportation distances are calculated in determining tribute amounts. The

IX. THE *XUNZI* 荀子: A SYNCRETIC CONFUCIAN PHILOSOPHY

flow of commodities and foodstuffs is not hampered or obstructed and goods come and go freely so that all within the four seas are as one family. For this reason, those states close at hand do not conceal what they have on offer and those at some distance do not begrudge their labors. Even with the remote and secluded states, they all hasten to contribute their services, and find peace and enjoyment in doing so. This is to be a leader among the people. This then is the legal system of the True King.

Comment: Xunzi lays out the several conditions needed in order to rule as a True King beginning first and foremost with the moral quality of the person of the king. To this is added the appropriate regulations drawn from traditional sources, the precepts to be followed, and a comprehensive and inclusive legal system that is fair in the taxes levied on the lands. As with Mencius, there is great thought put into a systematic way of governing that respects the symbiosis between providing for the ruled and the success and security of those who would rule.

北海則有走馬吠犬焉，然而中國得而畜使之。南海則有羽翮、齒革、曾青、丹干焉，然而中國得而財之。東海則有紫紶、魚鹽焉，然而中國得而衣食之。西海則有皮革、文旄焉，然而中國得而用之。故澤人足乎木，山人足乎魚，農夫不斲削、不陶冶而足械用，工賈不耕田而足菽粟。故虎豹爲猛矣，然君子剝而用之。故天之所覆，地之所載，莫不盡其美，致其用，上以飾賢良，下以養百姓而安樂之。夫是之謂大神。《詩》曰："天作高山，大王煌之。彼作矣，文王康之。" 此之謂也。

In the far northern reaches they have fleet-footed horses and barking dogs. But the central states having imported them, they breed these animals and put them to work. In the far southern reaches they have varieties of feathers, tusks and hides, copper, and cinnabar. But the central states having imported them, they make use of them in the things they produce. In the far eastern reaches they have indigo plants, fabrics, fish, and salt. But the central states having imported them, they make them into clothing and foodstuffs. In the western reaches they have skins, hides and colorful yak tails. But the central states having imported them, they put them to good use.

It is in this way that those who live in the wetlands have enough lumber and those who live in the mountains have enough fish. The farmers need not do any chiseling or carving, casting or forging, and yet they have all of the implements they need. Tradesmen and merchants need not till the fields and yet have all of the foodstuffs they need. Hence it is that although tigers and leopards are ferocious animals, exemplary persons (*junzi* 君子) can skin them and make good use of them.

Thus, within all that the heavens cover and on all that the earth supports, there is nothing that cannot be made the most of and turned to good use. Such things adorn the lives of the worthy and the meritorious above, and below they provide sustenance for the people who find comfort and enjoyment in them. This is what is called godly intelligence. This is what it means in the *Book of Songs* 270 when it says:

> Nature provided the high hills
> King Tai finding them grand
> Established his capital there
> And King Wen lived there in health and happiness.

Comment: This passage tells the story of how the central states have pursued civilization through the production of culture, material and otherwise. In the first phase of development, raw goods are imported into the central states from distant lands, and these resources are then transformed through human ingenuity into the accoutrements of a cultured civilization. In the second phase, a division of labor is established in the central states, and everyone is able to acquire what they need to live good lives. Nature provides the materials and humankind is able to "appreciate" them in all of the different senses of this word. The *Book of Songs* celebrates the collaboration between nature and humankind with the ultimate product being the health and happiness that comes with the cultural refinement symbolized here by King Wen (or King "Culture").

以類行雜，以一行萬。始則終，終則始，若環之無端也，舍是而天下以衰矣。天地者，生之始也；禮義者，治之始也；君子者，禮義之始也；爲之，貫之，積重之，致好之者，君子之始也。故天地生君子，君子理天地；君子者，天地之參也，萬物之摠也，民之父母也。無君子，則天地不理，禮義無統，上無君師，下無父子、夫婦，是之謂至亂。君臣、父子、兄弟、夫婦，始則終，終則始，與天地同理，與萬世同久，夫是之謂大本。故喪祭、朝聘、師旅一也；貴賤、殺生、與奪一也；君君、臣臣、父父、子子、兄兄、弟弟一也；農農、士士、工工、商商一也。

Use categories to organize complexity, and unity to organize multiplicity. The beginning is the end, the end the beginning, just as a circle has no terminus. Neglect this insight, and the whole world will fall apart. The heavens and earth are where life begins, ritual practices and moral precepts are where proper order begins, and exemplary persons (*junzi* 君子) are where ritual practices and moral precepts themselves begin. Acting upon them, linking them all together, piling them up again and again, and cherishing them; this is where exemplary persons begin.

It is thus that the heavens and the earth engender exemplary persons, and exemplary persons bring coherence to the heavens and the earth. Exemplary persons form a trinity with the heavens and the earth, are the steward of the myriad things, and are the father and mother of the common people. Without exemplary persons, there would be no order in the world, and ritual practices and moral precepts would have no unity. Above there would be no lord or leader, and below there would be no relationship between father and son, husband and wife. This then would be the worst kind of disorder.

In the relationships between ruler and minister, father and son, older and younger brother, and husband and wife, the beginning is the end, the end the beginning. These relations have the same coherent pattern as the heavens and the earth, and are as old as history itself. It is what is called the great root. Thus it is that funeral rites and sacrifices, court ceremonies, and the deployment of the military are all one; honoring and humiliating, pardoning and executing, giving and taking away are all one. The ruler ruling, ministers ministering, fathers fathering, sons son-ing, brothers brothering are all one. Farmers farming, officials official-ing, tradesmen trading, and merchants merchanting are all one.

Comment: Xunzi speaks here to the relationship between the one and the many, and continuity and multiplicity, arguing that there is a coherence that emerges out of the complexity of all things to bring them together as one. Were it otherwise, everything would fall apart. Xunzi here is rehearsing an early version of the dynamic cosmological postulate formulated by contemporary philosopher Tang Junyi: one is many, many one (*yiduobufenguan* 一多不分觀). The emergence of such a unifying order runs through all aspects of the human experience: the natural order of things, the moral fabric of society, the institutions of governance, social and political roles and relations, and the various occupations that define society. Importantly, this "one" is not a dominant, independent, and rationalizing order such as God or impersonal reason that makes of the world a *kosmos* or universe. Rather, this order is an aestheticism: the unsummed totality of all orders. Just as every unique detail in the *Mona Lisa* is integral to it in making its contribution to the totality of the one aesthetic effect, each of the myriad things (*wanwu* 萬物) contributes to the cosmic order called *dao* 道. And just as each detail in the *Mona Lisa* is an aspectual window in construing the masterpiece from its own unique perspective, each of the myriad things is focal in its construal of its field called *dao* 道. *Dao* 道 then is the unsummed totality of all orders, the many as one.

水火有氣而無生，草木有生而無知，禽獸有知而無義，人有氣、有生、有知，亦且有義，故最爲天下貴也。力不若牛，走不若馬，而牛馬爲用，何也？曰：人能群，彼不能群也。人何以能群？曰：分。分何以能行？曰：義。故義以分則和，和則一，一則多力，多力則強，強則勝物；故宮室可得而居也。故序四時，裁萬物，兼利天下，無它故焉，得之分義也。

Fire and water have *qi* 氣 but no life, the grasses and trees have life but no awareness, birds and animals have awareness but no sense of moral precepts (*yi* 義). Human beings then have *qi* 氣, life, awareness, and also a sense of moral precepts, and are thus the noblest of creatures in the world. How is it that without the strength of an ox or the speed of a horse, that human beings can make use of both of these animals? I would say that it is because human beings are able to constitute community while these other animals cannot. How is it that human beings can constitute community? I would say that it is because they discriminate. What then is the basis on which they discriminate? I would say that it is their moral precepts.

Thus, if moral precepts are the basis of discrimination there is harmony (*he* 和), where there is harmony, there is unity, where there is unity, there is a concentration of strength, where there is a concentration of strength, there is power, and where there is power, all things can be overcome. It is thus that human beings can live happily in the palaces and buildings they construct. The fact that they accord with the four seasons, exercise control over everything, and bring benefit to all things in the world is for no other reason than they have the capacity to discriminate and a sense of moral precepts.

Comment: What is distinctively human is the capacity to make distinctions on the basis of their moral precepts (*yi* 義). It is this capacity that makes human community possible and provides it with its tensile strength. It both elevates human beings over all other creatures in the world and enables them to exercise their benign influence in benefitting all things. The question that arises is how to square the description of human beings in this passage with Xunzi's assessment of the native human propensities (*xing* 性) he describes as base, and that seem to be lacking in moral compass.

What then is the relationship that obtains among Xunzi's cluster of moral terms: ritual practices (*li* 禮), moral precepts (*yi* 義), rationale (*li* 理) and *dao* 道? Where do moral precepts come from, and what is the basis of their authority? We might cite A.S. Cua for clarification:

> For Hsün Tzu [Xunzi], the *li* are the formal prescriptions for proper conduct. They are clear "markers of *tao* [*dao*]" that owe to the accumulated ethical experiences of the sages. But it is *i* [*yi*], the sense of what is fitting and appropriate that enables the agent to follow its guidance, that is, to do what he deems reasonable to do in an occurrent situation. The *li*, so to speak, present only the "highlights" of the ethical knowledge and experience of the sages. But their relevance to concrete situations depends on the exercise of *i* or the sense of what is fitting and appropriate.①

What is important in understanding Xunzi's vision of moral precepts is the collaborative role of subjectivity and objectivity in determining proper conduct:

> There are no fixed rules in ethical thinking in exigent situations. And that means there are no definitive starting points for analogical projections as a form of reasoning. The prospective significance of an analogical projection is always subject to defeat in new circumstances that call for a renewed exercise of *i* [*yi*]. This exercise of *i* is a matter of agency, of personal judgment as to what is right and fitting, but what it aims at is the objectively right act in an exigent situation. . . . *Li* [rationale 理] does not speak with a single voice.

In this collaborative role of subjectivity and objectivity, we once again see the relevance of Tang Junyi's cosmological postulate: one is many, many one (*yiduobufenguan* 一多不分觀). *Yi* 義 as moral precepts even in Xunzi's more rationalized Confucianism is not a single, universal standard, but is rather what emerges as most fitting in any particular situation. However conservative Xunzi becomes in parsing this moral vocabulary and however

---

① Cua, *Ethical Argumentation*, p. 98.

conventionalized moral precepts become, *yi* 義 does not depart entirely from this original meaning of appropriateness.

故人生不能無群，群而無分則爭，爭則亂，亂則離，離則弱，弱則不能勝物；故宮室不可得而居也，不可少頃舍禮義之謂也。能以事親謂之孝，能以事兄謂之弟，能以事上謂之順，能以使下謂之君。

Thus, humankind in seeking their livelihood must organize themselves in community. But community without social distinctions will lead to dissension. Where there is dissension, there is discord, where there is discord, there is estrangement, where there is estrangement there is weakness, and where there is weakness, people are unable to succeed in what they do. They will thus be unable to live happily in the palaces and buildings they construct. This is what I mean when I say ritual practices and moral precepts (*liyi* 禮義) cannot be neglected even for a moment.

To accord with ritual practices and moral precepts in serving one's kin is called family reverence (*xiao* 孝), in serving one's elder brothers it is called fraternity (*ti* 弟), in serving those above it is called deference, and in serving those below it is called rulership.

Comment: Community can only function effectively on the basis of hierarchical distinctions and the patterns of deference they occasion. These distinctions rooted in family relations are integral to the moral imperatives defining of life in family and community, and are galvanized through ritual practice and accordance with moral precepts.

君者，善群也。群道當，則萬物皆得其宜，六畜皆得其長，群生皆得其命。故養長時，則六畜育；殺生時，則草木殖；政令時，則百姓一，賢良服。聖主之制也：草木榮華滋碩之時，則斧斤不入山林，不夭其生，不絕其長也。黿鼉魚鱉鰍鱣孕別之時，罔罟毒藥不入澤，不夭其生，不絕其長也。春耕、夏耘、秋收、冬藏，四者不失時，故五穀不絕，而百姓有餘食也。汙池淵沼川澤，謹其時禁，故魚鱉優多，而百姓有餘用也。斬伐養長不失其時，故山林不童，而百姓有餘材也。聖王之用也：上察於天，下錯於地，塞備天地之間，加施萬物之上，微而明，短而長，狹而廣，神明博大以至約。故曰：一與一是為人者，謂之聖人也。

A ruler is the person adept at gathering people around him. When the way of gathering people together is followed as it should be, everything will find its proper place, the six domestic animals will all breed and thrive, and all sentient beings will live out their allotted life spans. When raised in a timely way, the six animals will proliferate; when pruned in a timely way, all plant life will flourish; when governed in a timely way, the people will act as one, and the worthy and meritorious among them will offer their services.

As for the regulations of a sagacious lord: when the plants and trees are blossoming and bursting with new life, no axes or machetes that would interfere with their growth and arrest it prematurely are allowed in the mountains and woodlands. When the various fishes and water creatures are spawning and laying their eggs, no nets or toxins that would interfere with gestation and arrest growth prematurely are allowed in the wetlands. By plowing, weeding, harvesting, and storing up in the proper season, the grain will flow and the people will have more than enough to eat. By regulating access to the ponds, lakes, streams and marshlands according to the proper season, the fishes and turtles will be abundant and the people will have more than they can consume. It is because felling and healthy growth have their proper seasons that the mountains and woodlands are not denuded and people have more than enough lumber.

As for the activities of the sagacious king: he surveys the heavens above and makes a grid of the earth below. He fills up all between the heavens and the earth and attends to everything in due course. Subtle yet brilliant, concise yet extended, precise yet vast, the breadth and compass of his intelligence renders everything utterly simple. Thus it is said: The person who can make everything one on behalf of others, is what it means to be a sage.

Comment: This passage begins with a paronomastic pun on "ruler" (*jun* 君) and "gathering" (*qun* 群), a mode of definition by semantic and phonetic association familiar in the classical canons. This notion of "gathering" is writ large by including not only the people, but all of props that make up the human drama as well. The passage is then given over to the responsibility of the ruler to serve his people by respecting the seasonal cycle and thus optimizing nature's bounty for all. The ruler must establish and enforce those ecological regulations that would allow nature to fulfill its own promise as the giver of life in the plant world, in the animal world, and in the world of human beings as well. Given the interdependence of all things within what is ultimately a single ecology, the ruler's service to the people requires coordinating the human experience in such a way as to enable humankind to become an important contributor to a single optimizing symbiosis. This responsibility of attending judiciously to the different yet continuous phases in an endless natural cycle is correlated with Xunzi's understanding of sagacity as being the capacity to make the complex simple and the multifarious one. This capacity of the sage to make the many one reflects an epistemology of compass and comprehensiveness that serves as the counterpart to the Greek quest for a single, abstract truth.

殷之日，案以中立，無有所偏，而爲縱橫之事，偃然案兵無動，以觀夫暴國之相卒也。案平政教，審節奏，砥礪百姓，爲是之日，而兵劍天下之勁矣。案然修仁義，伉隆高，正法則，選賢良，養百姓，爲是之日，而名聲劍天下之美矣。權者重之，兵者勁之，名聲者美之。夫堯舜者一天下也，不能加毫末於是矣。

At a time when the ruler's state is flourishing, he should take a neutral stand, not leaning one way or the other. In the game of empire, he should patiently hold his troops in abeyance to watch as his belligerent neighbors lay waste to each other.

By governing fairly, observing ritual formalities, and disciplining his people, there will come the day when in military prowess he will stand alone in the world. By practicing consummate conduct (*ren* 仁), acting according to moral precepts (*yi* 義), making every effort to elevate what is noble, acting justly through the laws and standards, selecting out the most worthy and meritorious, and taking good care of the people, there will come a day when in name and reputation he will stand alone in the world. With his authority secure, his military prowess formidable, and his reputation second to none, even a Yao or a Shun would have nothing to add to this ruler in bringing unity to the world.

Comment: Military prowess and the weight of fine reputation are not gained by aggressive action mounted against powerful neighbors abroad. Instead, these capabilities are won by taking care of business at home. Observing the proper ritual protocols, governing fairly according to the laws of the land, living up to the highest moral standards, elevating the most worthy to high office, and taking care of the needs of the people—it is only the ruler who observes such a regimen that can emerge as the model leader to unite the world.

權謀傾覆之人退，則賢良知聖之士案自進矣。刑政平，百姓和，國俗節，則兵勁城固，敵國案自詘矣。務本事，積財物，而勿忘棲遲薛越也，是使群臣百姓皆以制度行，則財物積，國家案自富矣。三者體此而天下服，暴國之君案自不能用其兵矣。何則？彼無與至也。彼其所與至者，必其民也。其民之

IX. THE *XUNZI* 荀子: A SYNCRETIC CONFUCIAN PHILOSOPHY

親我也，歡若父母，好我芳如芝蘭，反顧其上則若灼黥，若仇讎；彼人之情性也雖桀跖，豈有肯爲其所惡，賊其所好者哉！彼以奪矣。故古之人，有以一國取天下者，非往行之也，修政其所，莫不願，如是而可以誅暴禁悍矣。故周公南征而北國怨，曰："何獨不來也！"東征而西國怨，曰："何獨後我也！"孰能有與是鬭者與？安以其國爲是者王。

When plotters and schemers who would subvert the state are removed from the court, officials who are worthy and sagacious will come forward of their own accord. When laws and punishments are just, the people harmonious, and the customs of the state modest, the military will be strong, the walled-fortifications secure, and enemy states will yield on their own initiative. If the ruler attends to the agrarian base, amasses wealth, does not forget the cost of incompetence, and gets all of the ministers and people to act according to regulation, then wealth will accumulate and the state will grow prosperous of its own making.

When these three conditions are met, the whole world will submit and the rulers of aggressive states will be unable to marshal their own troops against me. Why is this? Because none of their troops will join in their invasion. Those who they are going to send to invade us must be their own people. But their own people love me and extend this love to me as to their own mother and father, as though savoring the fragrance of the iris and orchid. And in looking back at their own ruler, they see him as wielding a branding iron and as their own sworn enemy. Even if their people had the disposition of the despot Jie or the Robber Zhi, how could they be willing to take up arms for the sake of someone they hate in order to do harm to someone they love? The battle has already been won.

Thus it was with the ancients who with just one state were able to acquire the whole world. They did not march out to accomplish this, but rather cultivated their own best policies so that everyone wanted to serve them. This was the way they were able to punish the bellicose and to arrest their violence. It was thus when the Duke of Zhou marched south, the states in the north all complained "Why does he forsake us?" And when he marched east, the states in the west all complained "Why does he leave us to last?" Who could contest with someone like this? Anyone who is able to govern his state in this way is a True King.

Comment: A suppressed premise in Xunzi's political philosophy that reflects his times is that the relentless march to empire is a winner-take-all, zero-sum game. During the Warring States period in which international relations amounted to little more than the constant threat of war, Xunzi's counsel is that the best strategy for bringing unity to the empire is governing your own state in such a manner that your model of moral governance wins over the people of the competing states. Other states will yield to your leadership because it is in their own best interest to do so. This strategy of ruling by making your rule serve the best interests of everyone concerned is the conception of the "All-under-Heaven" political system (*tianxiatixi* 天下體系) associated with the establishment of the Zhou dynasty.

IX.5 Chapter 12: The Way of the Ruler (*jundao* 君道)

有亂君，無亂國；有治人，無治法。羿之法非亡也，而羿不世中；禹之法猶存，而夏不世王。故法不能獨立，類不能自行；得其人則存，失其人則亡。法者，治之端也；君子者，法之原也。故有君子，則法雖省，足以遍矣；無君子，則法雖具，失先後之施，不能應事之變，足以亂矣。不知法之義，而正法之數者，雖博臨事必亂。故明主急得其人，而闇主急得其執。急得其人，則身佚而國治，功大而名美，上可以王，下可以霸；不急得其人，而急得其執，則身勞而國亂，功廢而名辱，社稷必危。故君人者，勞於索之，而休於使之。《書》曰：「惟文王敬忌，一人以擇。」此之謂也。

Just as there are disorderly rulers but no such thing as disorderly states, so there are persons who effect proper order but no such thing as laws (*fa* 法) that can accomplish it. The technique (*fa* 法) of Archer Yi has not been lost, but such a one as Yi did not appear in the succeeding generations. The model (*fa* 法) of the Great Yu even now survives, but the Xia dynasty did not produce a True King like him in the generations that followed. Thus, the law or the technique or the model cannot stand on its own, nor can categories of things operate on their own. Where there is the right person, they survive; where the right person cannot be found, they are lost. Laws (techniques, models) are the beginning of proper order, but exemplary rulers (*junzi* 君子) are their source.

Thus, where there are exemplary rulers, even if the laws have been whittled away they will still be enough to meet all contingencies. Where there are no exemplary rulers, even though there is a full complement of laws, they will not be applied at the right time, they will not be responsive to changing circumstances, and they will only result in disorder. Absent an understanding of the moral import behind the laws, those who try to work on the basis of the explicit formulation of them, even when they have a broad view of things, will end in certain disaster.

Hence the enlightened ruler is keen to find the right person while the benighted ruler is keen to gain political power and advantage (*shi* 勢). For those keen to find the right person, they will be personally at ease, their state will be well-ordered, their accomplishments substantial, and their reputations raised high. The best among them can become True Kings while even those at a lower level can become hegemons. For those who are keen to gain power and advantage rather than the right person, they will personally be drained, their country in disorder, their accomplishments nil, their names disgraced, and the altars of their state certain to be imperiled.

Thus, those who would rule over others expend their energy in seeking after the talented and able, and find their leisure in employing them. This is what it means when in the *Book of Documents* it says "It was only King Wen who was on high alert, and who personally selected the one right person."

Comment: In the examples given here, we can see that most of the occurrences of this term *fa* 法 in the early texts prior to the rise of the Legalist tradition had the broad connotations of "norm, model, technique, standard." Only well into the Warring States period when the Legalist theorists had taken over this character as a technical term and injected it with their own meaning did it come to reference penal law.

Where Confucius and Mencius, committed as they were to the primacy of moral education, could afford to deal with penal law in a more perfunctory manner, the emergence and subsequent strength of the Legalist challenge to Confucianism made it imperative that Xunzi define this term more carefully. Perhaps the assumption that locates him squarely in the Confucian camp is the importance he invests in exemplary persons as the innovators, interpreters, and executors of the law, and the ancillary role accorded to the laws themselves. He is certainly adamant that laws are an essential element in a well-governed state, but at the same time, he is also emphatic in subordinating the laws themselves to the persons who interpret and apply them. Laws in themselves are no guarantee of effective rule, and can lead to either order or disorder. The laws were devised by mortals and require competent trustees to uphold and apply them. The priority of people over law is a recurring theme throughout the text.

Xunzi appropriates the notion of "purchase or advantage" (*shi* 勢) first made popular in the Militarist texts and then later given a Legalist reformulation as "political purchase." Xunzi's primary objection to the Legalist conception of *shi* 勢 is where they regard *shi* 勢 itself to be a sufficient condition for political control, Xunzi as a Confucian is convinced that *shi* 勢 without the popular support of the people is ultimately untenable. And the people can only be won over by the actions of a morally superior ruler who is devoted to the public good—that is, the True King. The contrast between the Confucians and the Legalists is expressed here as the Confucians being keen on seeking the right persons where the Legalists would rely upon accruing political power through the application of law.

There is another characteristic of Xunzi's attitude toward law that, although perhaps implicit in traditional Confucian teachings, was not really made explicit until Xunzi. In confronting the positivistic attitudes of the Legalists, Xunzi draws a sharp distinction between the spirit and moral import of the law on the one hand, and the letter and detail of the law on the other. While the Confucians saw law as a repository of the moral accomplishments of the inherited tradition and insisted that an understanding of moral precepts must stand behind the application of abstract law, the Legalists argued that in order for laws to function effectively they must be made public, and must be objective and automatic. Laws must remain free of the human element to the extent that the ruler himself must not interfere in the mechanical operations of the Legalist state.

請問爲國? 曰: 聞修身, 未嘗聞爲國也。君者儀也, 民者景也, 儀正而景正。君者槃也, 民者水也, 槃圓而水圓。君者盂也, 盂方而水方。君射則臣決。楚莊王好細腰, 故朝有餓人。故曰: 聞修身, 未嘗聞爲國也。

May I ask about how to govern a state properly?

I replied: I have heard about cultivating one's own person, but never about how to govern a state properly. The ruler is a pillar and the common people are his shadow. Where the pillar is upright, so is the shadow. The ruler is a basin and the common people are the water. Where the basin is round, so is the water. The ruler is a broad-mouthed jar. Where the jar is square the water is square. If the ruler is an arrow, his ministers are his thumb ring. It was because King Zhuang of Chu was fond of thin waists that his court was full of people starving themselves. Thus I say: I have heard about cultivating one's own person, but never about how to govern a state properly.

Comment: The theme of the ruler serving as a moral role model who thus educates and transforms the people is a familiar one in the political philosophy of *Xunzi* and the other classical Confucian texts. It is in having this power of personal suasion that the ruler is able to reign rather than rule the state, and to preside over rather than administer the government.

故人主欲彊固安樂，則莫若反之民；欲附下一民，則莫若反之政；欲修政美俗，則莫若求其人。彼或蓄積而得之者不世絕。彼其人者，生乎今之世，而志乎古之道。以天下之王公莫好之也，然而是子獨好之；以天下之民莫爲之也，然而是子獨爲之。好之者貧，爲之者窮，然而是子猶將爲之也，不爲少頃輟焉。曉然獨明於先王之所以得之，所以失之，知國之安危臧否，若別白黑。是其人也，大用之，則天下爲一，諸侯爲臣；小用之，則威行鄰敵；縱不能用，使無去其疆域，則國終身無故。故君人者，愛民而安，好士而榮，兩者無一焉而亡。《詩》曰："介人維藩，大師爲垣。" 此之謂也。

If the ruler of the people wants to be strong, secure, and happy, there is no better way than getting back to his people; if he wants to be able to rely on his ministers and unify his people, there is no better way than reverting to proper governance; if he wants to cultivate proper governance and elevate the culture, there is no better way than seeking out the right people.

The accumulation and selection of the right people has continued generation after generation. If such persons being born in the present age have their purposes fixed on the way of the ancients, in spite of the fact that there is not one king or duke in the world that cherishes this way, they alone would advocate for it. In spite of the fact that among the world's people there are none who would act upon this way, they alone would put it into practice. In spite of the fact that those who cherish the way of the ancients are impoverished and those who act upon it are in dire straits, they would still of their own accord put it into practice without a moment's hesitation. They alone have a full comprehension of the successes and failures of the Former Kings. And as easily as telling white from black, they understand the difference between state security and danger, between what is in the state's interest and otherwise.

With this quality of people, if you make substantial use of them, the world will be as one and the vassal lords will all submit; if you only make use of them in lesser degree, the dignity of their conduct will impress neighboring and rival states; and even if you are not able to make any use of them at all, as long as they remain within your territorial boundaries, the state will forever be without incident. Thus, for the ruler of the people, in loving the common people he brings security to the state, and in cherishing the scholar-officials (*shi* 士) he enables the state to flourish. But where he does neither of these things, the state will perish. This is what is meant when the *Book of*

Songs 254 says that "Good persons are a protective barrier for the state, and its teeming population its wall."

Comment: Xunzi emphasizes the fact that in the proper governance of the ruler, there must be a recognition of the importance of selecting the right persons and of cherishing the common people. What distinguishes the right persons in any generation is that, regardless of prevailing conditions and regardless of their own professional fortunes, they have an unwavering commitment to the way of the ancients. The employment of such persons in any degree at all vouchsafes the security and the prosperity of the state.

爲人主者，莫不欲強而惡弱，欲安而惡危，欲榮而惡辱，是禹桀之所同也。要此三欲，辟此三惡，果何道而便？曰：在慎取相，道莫徑是矣。故知而不仁，不可；仁而不知，不可；既知且仁，是人主之寶也，王霸之佐也。不急得，不知；得而不用，不仁。無其人而幸有其功，愚莫大焉。今人主有大患：使賢者爲之，則與不肖者規之；使知者慮之，則與愚者論之；使修士行之，則與汙邪之人疑之，雖欲成功，得乎哉！譬之，是猶立直木而恐其景之枉也，惑莫大焉！語曰：好女之色，惡者之孽也；公正之士，衆人之痤也；修道之人，汙邪之賊也。今使汙邪之人，論其怨賊，而求其無偏，得乎哉！譬之，是猶立枉木而求其景之直也，亂莫大焉。

For those who would be rulers of the people, there are none who would trade strength for weakness, security for danger, or honor for disgrace. In this respect the Great Yu and the despot Jie are one and the same. What is the way then that can make it easy for them to satisfy these three desirables and avoid the three that are not? I would say that there is no more direct way than being circumspect in choosing a prime minister.

Since it would not work to appoint someone who is wise (*zhi* 知) but not consummate in their conduct (*ren* 仁), or vice versa, it has to be someone who is both wise and consummate. This would be a person whom the ruler of the people could treasure, and who would be of great assistance to either the True King or the hegemon. To not be keen on going after such a person is to be lacking in wisdom, and to get such a person but not put him to good use is to fail to be consummate. There can be no greater foolishness than to think in the absence of such a person, you can still by some stroke of luck have all of his accomplishments.

These days those who would be rulers have a great infirmity. When they appoint worthy persons to carry out the government, they then admonish them together with those who are not worthy. When they appoint those with the wisdom to think things through, they then criticize them along with those who are obtuse. When they appoint cultivated scholar-officials (*shi* 士) to do things, they are as suspicious of them as those who are vile and perverse. Even though they are hoping for real accomplishments, are they really going to succeed?

To use a metaphor, it is like planting a perfectly erect tree and then being afraid that it will cast a crooked shadow. Could anything be more muddle-headed? There is an old saying: "A woman's beauty is a disaster for one who is ugly; the upright scholar-official is an ulcer for the commonest of people; persons who have cultivated the proper way are traitors to those who are vile and perverse." If you appoint those who are vile and perverse to be critical of those who they hate and resent as traitors, and then expect an unbiased opinion from them, do you think you will get it? This is like planting a gnarly and crooked tree and hoping it will cast an upright shadow. Can there be anything more absurd?

Comment: As throughout the *Analects*, the two terms "wisdom" or "living wisely" (*zhi* 知) and "consummate conduct" or "living consummately" (*ren* 仁) are discussed in tandem, with neither one of them being sufficient without the other. Again, there is the emphasis on the quality of the people over institutions when it comes to advancing proper governance, beginning from the top with both the ruler himself and his prime minister. A critical responsibility of the ruler is to conduct himself in such a way as to optimize the talents of the right people. Another familiar theme here is the suasive power of moral role models: as the wind blows the grass will bend.

A constant refrain in Xunzi is meritocracy: the power of discrimination in governance enabled by seeing the big picture. His epistemology of comprehensiveness means that for the ruler, it is only the panoramic view that one can trust. In the hierarchy, this is a view from the top with the ruler and prime minister presumably having the greatest purview. Having found the right person for prime minister, further discrimination on the part of the ruler requires that worthy officials are not simply grouped together with those who are much less so, and then treated according to the same measures.

人主欲得善射遠中微者，縣貴爵重賞以招致之。內不可以阿子弟，外不可以隱遠人，能中是者取之；是豈不必得之之道也哉！雖聖人不能易也。欲得善馭及速致遠者，一日而千里，縣貴爵重賞以招致之。內不可以阿子弟，外不可以隱遠人，能致是者取之；是豈不必得之之道也哉！……古有萬國，今有十數焉，是無它故，莫不失之是也。故明主有私人以金石珠玉，無私人以官職事業，是何也？曰：本不利於所私也。彼不能而主使之，則是主闇也；臣不能而諛能，則是臣詐也。主闇於上，臣詐於下，滅亡無日，俱害之道也。夫文王非無貴戚也，非無子弟也，非無便嬖也，偶然乃舉太公於州人而用之，豈私之也哉！以爲親邪？則周姬姓也，而彼姜姓也；以爲故邪？則未嘗相識也；以爲好麗邪？則夫人行年七十有二，齫然兩齒墮矣。然而用之者，夫文王欲立貴道，欲白貴名，以惠天下，而不可以獨也。非于是子莫足以舉之，故舉是子而用之。

Where the ruler of the people wants to retain expert archers who can shoot from a distance and hit a small target, he should dangle high rank and handsome rewards in order to recruit them. At court he cannot pander to his own children or younger brothers, and outside the court he cannot ignore those who are coming from afar. If they can hit the target then enlist them—is this not the only way to recruit them? Even the sages could not do better.

Where the ruler of the people wants to retain expert charioteers who can drive fast and go far, and who in one day can traverse a thousand *li*, he should dangle high rank and handsome rewards in order to recruit them. At court he cannot pander to his own children or younger brothers, and outside the court he cannot ignore those who are coming from afar. If they can cover the distance then enlist them—is this not the only way to recruit them? . . .

In ancient times there were innumerable states but today there are only about ten. This is for no other reason than the fact that impartiality has been abandoned. Hence, the enlightened ruler enriches those for whom he has personal affection with gold, precious stones, pearls, and jade, but would never think of appointing them to office or enlisting them in important affairs. Why is this?

I would say that as a fundamental principle the enlightened ruler does not show partiality for those for whom he has personal affection. Any ruler who would appoint those who are not capable is a benighted ruler. And an incompetent minister who feigns competence is a fraud. With a benighted ruler on the throne and fraudulent ministers serving him, the day of reckoning is not far off. This is the way to bring on injury all around.

Now it wasn't that King Wen had no noble relatives, no sons and younger brothers, and no favorites among his ministers. Taking the long and broad view, he selected the Grand Duke from among the fishermen and gave him office. How could this be a matter of personal affection? Was it because he was a relative? But the surname of the House of Zhou was Ji while the

Duke's surname was Jiang. Was it because they had a history? But they had never met before. Was it because the Duke was a handsome man? But the Duke was already seventy-two and did not have a tooth in his head. The reason King Wen gave him office was that he wanted to establish a noble way and to achieve noble reputation as his means of showing his beneficence to the whole world, but he could not do this alone. Other than the Duke, there were none worthy of the office, and so King Wen appointed him prime minister and made good use of him.

Comment: In recruiting the best people to assist him in governing the state, the ruler must be impartial, and look to competence rather than personal affection. While personal affection can be expressed through opulent gifts, it can never take the form of political favors. Nepotism is anathema to proper governance, and is the reason most of the many states that historically made up the House of Zhou have all collapsed. Xunzi gives the example of how King Wen in setting up his administration recruited Jiang Ziya 姜子牙, a former minister of the Shang dynasty who had abandoned the corrupt court and become a fisherman. After his appointment, Jiang Ziya known as the Grand Duke achieved great reputation as prime minister and wise counselor to the House of Zhou.

墙之外，目不見也；里之前，耳不聞也；而人主之守司，遠者天下，近者境內，不可不略知也。天下之變，境內之事，有弛易齵差者矣，而人主無由知之，則是拘脅蔽塞之端也。耳目之明，如是其狹也；人主之守司，如是其廣也；其中不可以不知也，如是其危也。然則人主將何以知之？曰：便嬖左右者，人主之所以窺遠收衆之門戶牖嚮也，不可不早具也。故人主必將有便嬖左右足信者，然後可。其知惠足使規物，其端誠足使定物，然後可；夫是之謂國具。……故人主無便嬖左右足信者，謂之闇；無卿相輔佐足任使者，謂之獨；所使於四鄰諸侯者非其人，謂之孤；孤獨而晻，謂之危。國雖若存，古之人曰亡矣。《詩》曰："濟濟多士，文王以寧。"此之謂也。

　　His eyes cannot see beyond the wall and his ears cannot hear things from half a mile away, and yet the political responsibilities of the ruler are such that he must have a passing knowledge of what goes on both within the borders of his state and the world at large. In a changing world, the affairs within the borders of the state can become lax and erratic, and if the ruler has no avenue for understanding what is going on, it can be the beginning of limitations and obstruction. The perception of the ruler's eyes and ears is so very narrow, yet his political responsibilities are so broad. Between these two conditions he simply must acquire the necessary knowledge, or there is real danger.

My answer is this: The preferred ministers who surround him are his resource to see into what is far off, and to learn what is going on within the doors and windows of the multitude. It is never too early to take advantage of them. Thus it is that only when the ruler has full trust in his circle of preferred ministers that he is viable. It is only when these ministers have enough wisdom to manage things and enough integrity to stabilize things that he is viable. These ministers can be called the state apparatus. . . .

Thus it is that a ruler who lacks a circle of preferred ministers whom he can trust fully is called benighted; the ruler who is lacking high officials and administrators whom he can rely upon fully to carry out their duties is called a lonely soul; and when the ministers he dispatches to the neighboring vassal lords are not his own people he is called orphaned. To thus be orphaned, all alone, and benighted is called being imperiled. Even though his state might still exist, the ancients would pronounce it doomed. This is what the *Book of Songs* 235 means when it says "The many scholar-officials (*shi* 士) so imposing and dignified, King Wen can rest easy."

Comment: Rulers who have political responsibilities that require of them panoramic vision and synoptic understanding must confront the simple fact that they are only one person. To rely upon his own insight to carry out his duties is quite literally to be benighted, orphaned, and alone. The alternative is for the ruler to depend on trusted ministers to be his eyes and ears, and to thereby extend his powers of perception to penetrate all corners of the state and beyond. It is only by relying on trusted ministers who have integrity in carrying out the affairs of state that he can be secure in his position and his state can flourish.

Although the starting point is the same, this Confucian response stands in stark contrast to the Legalists. For the Legalists too, the ruler must be cognizant of the fact that he has the limitations of being a single person. If he seeks to exercise control on the basis of these personal capacities rather than taking advantage of the political purchase (*shi* 勢) afforded him by the leverage of his position as ruler, he pits himself against the world. To rely exclusively on his own faculties for maintaining control is not nearly as effective as tapping the collective power of the empire made available to him as a function of his status as ruler. By controlling the handles on the political machine and manipulating the *gravitas* of rulership, even a person of very average parts can run the state effectively. The people do the work required of them by the sovereign not for any love he may show them, but because the generous rewards and severe punishments on offer make this course of action to their own best advantage.

IX.6 Chapter 15: Debating Military Affairs (*yibing* 議兵)

臨武君與孫卿子議兵於趙孝成王前，王曰："請問兵要？"臨武君對曰："上得天時，下得地利，觀敵之變動，後之發，先之至，此用兵之要術也。"孫卿子曰："不然！臣所聞古之道，凡用兵攻戰之本，在乎壹民。弓矢不調，則羿不能以中微；六馬不和，則造父不能以致遠；士民不親附，則湯武不能以必勝也。故善附民者，是乃善用兵者也。故兵要在乎善附民而已。"臨武君曰："不然。兵之所貴者埶利也，所行者變詐也。善用兵者，感忽悠闇，莫知其所從出。孫吳用之無敵於天下，豈必待附民哉！"

The Lord of Linwu and Xunzi had a debate on military affairs in the presence of King Xiao of Zhao. The King said: "May I ask what is most essential in military affairs?"

The Lord of Linwu replied: "Overhead make sure you have the weather on your side, and underfoot the advantage of the terrain. Watch the movements of the enemy closely, and marching out after he does, get there before him. These then are the essential techniques in deploying the military."

"I disagree," announced Xunzi. "From what I have heard about the ways of the ancients, the root of deploying the military and mounting the attack lies in winning over the people. If the bow and arrow were not synchronized, even the Archer Yi would be unable to hit the mark. If the six horses were not brought into accord, even the legendary charioteer Zaofu would be unable to reach distant places. If scholar-officials (*shi* 士) and the people were not devoted to them, even a Tang or Wu would be unable to achieve certain victory. Those good at winning the hearts and minds of the people are most expert in deploying the military. What is most essential in military affairs is nothing more than excelling in winning the devotion of the people."

"I would beg to differ," said the Lord of Linwu. "What is most highly valued in deploying the military is strategic advantage (*shi* 勢) and favorable conditions, and adaptability and deception in your movements. Those most expert in deploying the military respond quickly and secretly so that no one knows whence they came. Sun Wu and Wu Qi in using these techniques were unmatched in the world. Why is it necessary to rely on the devotion of the people?"

Comment: The *Xunzi* is one of the most critical and cogently argued texts of the pre-Qin period. Xunzi offers a Confucian rebuttal to the Militarist assertion that "strategic advantage" (*shi* 勢) should be considered the most essential condition for victory on the battlefield, and the subsequent Legalist assertion that *shi* 勢 as "political" strategic advantage is the primary consideration in effecting political order and control. In the appropriation of this concept of *shi* 勢 in the *Xunzi*, the question Xunzi raises is what actually constitutes advantage on the battlefield: honed military tactics, irontight political control, or the unwavering support of the people? This chapter opens with a rejection of what is presented as the Militarist school's amoral attitude toward the use of arms. For Xunzi, Confucian moral precepts are as applicable to the administration of military undertakings as they are to the administration of the state.

孫卿子曰："不然。臣之所道，仁者之兵，王者之志也。君之所貴，權謀埶利也；所行，攻奪變詐也；諸侯之事也。仁人之兵，不可詐也；彼可詐者，怠慢者也，路亶者也，君臣上下之間，渙然有離德者也。故以桀詐桀，猶巧拙有幸焉。以桀詐堯，譬之：若以卵投石，以指撓沸；若赴水火，入焉焦沒耳。故仁人上下，百將一心，三軍同力；臣之於君也，下之於上也，若子之事父，弟之事兄，若手臂之扞頭目而覆胸腹也，詐而襲之，與先驚而後擊之，一也。且仁人之用十里之國，則將有百里之聽；用百里之國，則將有千里之聽；用千里之國，則將有四海之聽，必將聰明警戒和傳而一。故仁人之兵，聚則成卒，散則成列，延則若莫邪之長刃，嬰之者斷；兌則若莫邪之利鋒，當之者潰。圜居而方止，則若盤石然。觸之者角摧，案角鹿埵隴種東籠而退耳。且夫暴國之君，將誰與至哉？彼其所與至者，必其民也，而其民之親我歡若父母，其好我芬若椒蘭，彼反顧其上，則若灼黥，若讎仇；人之情，雖桀跖，豈又肯爲其所惡，賊其所好者哉！是猶使人之子孫自賊其父母也，彼必將來告之，夫又何可詐也！故仁人用國日明，諸侯先順者安，後順者危，慮敵之者削，反之者亡。《詩》曰：'武王載發，有虔秉鉞；如火烈烈，則莫我敢遏。'此之謂也。"

"Not so," said Xunzi. "What I am talking about is the deployment of the military by the consummate person (*ren* 仁) who has the intentions of a True King. What my lord values most highly is 'calibration' (*quan* 權), 'planning' (*mou* 謀), 'strategic advantage' (*shi* 勢), and 'favorable conditions' (*li* 利), and the way you would prosecute the battle is 'attack' (*gong* 攻), 'seizure' (*duo* 奪), 'adaptability' (*bian* 變), and 'deception' (*zha* 詐). These tactics are the business of the vassal lords.

"In the deployment of the military by the consummate person, there can be no deception. Those who can be deceived are the negligent, the remiss, and the worn down. Deception happens where there is estrangement between ruler and ministers and where there is divisiveness in the ranks. It is thus that a despot Jie can deceive another Jie, where the degree of his cunning will determine success. If we want a metaphor for Jie trying to deceive the sage-king Yao, it is like hurling an egg at a boulder, or using your finger to stir boiling water. It would be the same as Jie's rushing into fire or water to be wholly consumed or drowned.

"Within the ranks under the consummate person, all of the commanders are of one mind, and the three divisions are one concerted force. In the relations between ministers and ruler, between subordinates and their superiors, it is like a son serving his father or a younger brother serving his older brother. It is like the hands and arms shielding the face and eyes, or covering the breast and stomach. To use deception in ambushing such troops would be the same as first giving them fair warning and then attacking them.

"Moreover, when the consummate person is in charge of a state ten *li* square, the people of a hundred *li* square will be his eyes and ears. Where it is a hundred *li* square, the people of a thousand *li* square will be his eyes and ears. Where the state is a thousand *li* square and with the whole world serving as his eyes and ears, the intelligence he receives that provides him this advance warning will be consolidated as one voice. In the deployment of the military by the consummate person, when assembled they form a company, and when dispatched they march out in formation. When extended they are like the long blade of the Moye sword where anything that comes into contact with them will be severed. When thrust forward, they are like the sharp point of the Moye sword where anything it strikes will be run through. When drawn up in a round or square formation, they are like a huge boulder where anything that strikes against it will be shattered, or having been split wide open, will have to withdraw.

"As for the ruler of a belligerent state, who is he going to get to join him in the invasion? Those who would join him must be his own people. But his own people love me, and extend this love to me as their own mother and father, as though savoring the fragrance of the pepper plant and orchid. But in looking back at their own ruler, they see him as wielding a branding iron and as their own sworn enemy. Even if they had the disposition of the despot Jie or the Robber Zhi, how could they be willing to take up arms for the sake of someone they hate in order to do harm to someone they love? This is like sending someone's children to harm their own mother and father. Of course, they are certain to betray him. Wherein could there be any deception?

"Thus, every day the consummate person is in charge of a state, it gets brighter. Those among the vassal lords who are first to seek accord with him are secure while those who lag behind are in danger; those who would oppose him will have their lands pared away while those who turn against him will perish. This is what the *Book of Songs* 304 means when it says:

With the martial king Tang unfurling his banners
And reverently grasping his battle-ax
He was like a blazing fire.
Who then could withstand us?"

Comment: Xunzi's foil here is the Lord of Linwu, and the vocabulary he uses echoes the technical vocabulary of the Militarists in the canonical texts, the *Sunzi* and the *Sun Bin*. It was undoubtedly meant to have just such an association for the reader. Xunzi himself also appeals to some of the metaphors used in these same *Art of Warfare* texts. The principles of war announced by the Lord of Linwu and then summarily rejected by Xunzi are meant to give the impression that they are statements of basic Militarist theory. Xunzi for example dismisses the Militarist tactical interpretation of strategic advantage (*shi* 勢) in military engagements and subordinates it to the suasive power of the moral ruler and the popular support of the people it garners. Xunzi argues that the actual purchase provided by *shi* 勢 is the by-product of moral governance. The ultimate outcome of war is not dependent upon temporary military advantages such as provisioning, planning, and favorable terrain, but is determined by the concerted and overwhelming support of the people.

In this passage, the unifying theme is the ineffectiveness of the Militarist tactic of deception (*zha* 詐) against those who embrace a Confucian moral regimen. Deception can only work in a competition among deceitful rulers themselves. But even then when such rulers try to employ deception, their own people will come to despise them. And with the villain's own people enamored of those who dispense moral governance, no one will be willing to raise a sword to fight on his behalf.

"秦人其生民也陿阸，其使民也酷烈，劫之以執，隱之以阸，忸之以慶賞，酋之以刑罰，使天下之民，所以要利於上者，非鬥無由也。阸而用之，得而後功之，功賞相長也，五甲首而隸五家，是最爲衆強長久，多地以正，故四世有勝，非幸也，數也。"

"The Qin rulers provide for their people within a narrow and limited territory. They exploit the people with their cruelty and harshness, and coerce them with the weight of their authority. They oppress them with privation, entice them with rewards, and trample on them with their punishments. They make it so the single pathway to benefit for their subordinates is found on the battlefield. They deprive their people by exploiting them, and only give them a semblance of benefit when the people can show some specific achievement. Rewards are commensurate with accomplishments. Five heads taken from enemy soldiers will earn a person the labor of five families.

"This strategy is the best way to sustain a strong and populous state for an extended time and to get a lot of taxes from the land. That for four generations they have been victorious is not a matter of luck, but because of their policies."

Comment: Among the states playing the zero-sum game for empire, Xunzi shows some respect for the effectiveness of the strict policies of Qin that have made them strong and rich. But he is also prescient in anticipating that political power won at the expense of exploiting the people is ultimately unsustainable. Although shortly after Xunzi's death Qin's militaristic policies do lead them to victory, their failures in the kind of proper governance advocated by the Confucians bring on the collapse of the newly established empire within less than one generation. And again, it is the eclectic and hybridic Confucian philosophy advocated by Xunzi and the generations of scholars who follow in his wake that within a century of the fall of Qin becomes the basis of a state orthodoxy that will last for two millennia.

"王者有誅而無戰，城守不攻，兵格不擊，上下相喜則慶之，不屠城，不潛軍，不留衆，師不越時。故亂者樂其政，不安其上，欲其至也。"臨武君曰："善！"陳囂問孫卿子曰："先生議兵，常以仁義爲本；仁者愛人，義者循理，然則又何以兵爲？凡所爲有兵者，爲爭奪也。"孫卿子曰："非汝所知也！彼仁者愛人，愛人故惡人之害之也；義者循理，循理故惡人之亂之也。彼兵者所以禁暴除害也，非爭奪也。故仁者之兵，所存者神，所過者化，若時雨之降，莫不説喜。是以堯伐驩兜，舜伐有苗，禹伐共工，湯伐有夏，文王伐崇，武王伐紂，此四帝兩王，皆以仁義之兵，行於天下也。故近者親其善，遠方慕其德，兵不血刃，遠邇來服，德盛於此，施及四極。《詩》曰：'淑人君子，其儀不忒。' 此之謂也。"

"The True King leads punitive expeditions but never goes to war. When the walled fortifications are strongly defended he does not attack. When the enemy's troops show resistance, he does not engage them. When the rulers and the people of a state are happy with each other, congratulations to them are in order. He does not massacre the inhabitants of a fortified city, does not ambush the enemy's troops, does not keep his army in the field for extended periods, and does not allow a campaign to go beyond its season. Thus, the people of states in turmoil admire his policies, and being unhappy with their own leadership, long for his arrival."

The Lord of Linwu said: "This is very good."

Chen Xiao inquired of Xunzi: "You, Sir, in debating the deployment of the military always take consummate conduct (*ren* 仁) and moral precepts (*yi* 義) as your basis. Since consummate conduct is loving the people, and moral precepts are according with what is right, what does this have to do with deploying the military? Generally speaking, those who want to take up arms are out to fight and plunder."

"This is not something you will understand." said Xunzi. "Those who are consummate do love the people, and it is because they love them that they hate it when harm befalls them. Moral precepts are according with what is right, and it is because they are according with what is right that they hate it when people make trouble for others. Their deploying the military is to arrest violence and to forestall harm; it is not to fight and plunder. Thus, with consummate persons deploying the military, wherever they billet is raised up, and whatever they pass is transformed. Just as with the falling of the seasonal rains, everyone rejoices in them.

"It is for this reason that when Yao led a punitive expedition against Huan Dou, when Shun led an expedition against the rulers of the You Miao, when the Great Yu led an expedition against the ruler Gong Gong, when Tang led an expedition against the ruler of the Xia, when King Wen led an expedition against the Chong, and when King Wu led an expedition against the despot Jie, these four emperors and two kings all marched across the world with a military committed to consummate conduct and to doing what is right. It is thus that those near at hand had great affection for their goodness and those at a distance pined for their moral virtuosity. Without their swords drawing blood, those far and near came to submit to them, and with their moral virtuosity flourishing in one place, it spread out to the distant quarters. This is what the *Book of Songs* 152 means when it says:

This good man, our lord,
In his comportment he is beyond reproach."

Comment: Xunzi makes a distinction between "punitive expeditions" and making "war" on the basis of whether such actions are motivated by ethical considerations or personal benefit respectively. We have here an early version of a doctrine of righteous war, a Confucian just war theory based on the love of the ruler for the people. According to Xunzi, the campaigns undertaken by the sage-kings and cultural heroes were all motivated by their commitment to consummate conduct (*ren* 仁) and moral precepts (*yi* 義). Warfare undertaken in service to these Confucian values means that the ruler goes into battle only when the prosecution of war serves the interests of the people, both his own people and those who are suffering the oppression of failed governance. As a secondary consideration, Xunzi's argument is based on the primacy of vital relations, and means simply that if the people do better, so does the ruler. The only way for the state to flourish is for the ruler to be committed to the welfare of the people, and the happier the people, the stronger the state.

李斯問孫卿子曰:"秦四世有勝,兵強海內,威行諸侯,非以仁義爲之也,以便從事而已。"孫卿子曰:"非汝所知也! 汝所謂便者,不便之便也;吾所謂仁義者,大便之便也。彼仁義者,所以修政者也;政修則民親其上,樂其君,而輕爲之死。故曰:凡在於軍,將率末事也。秦四世有勝,諰諰然常恐天下之一合而軋己也,此所謂末世之兵,未有本統也。故湯之放桀也,非其逐之鳴條之時也;武王之誅紂也,非以甲子之朝而後勝之也。皆前行素修也,所謂仁義之兵也。今女不求之於本,而索之於末,此世之所以亂也。"

Li Si inquired of Xunzi, saying: "The state of Qin has been victorious for four generations with its military being the strongest in the world and its authority holding sway over the other vassal lords. This success is not the outcome of consummate conduct (*ren* 仁) and moral precepts (*yi* 義), but simply because of expedience in taking advantage of their opportunities."

"This is not something you will understand." said Xunzi. "What you are calling expedience is not real expedience. What I am referring to as consummate conduct and moral precepts is in fact the greatest expedience of all. The values of consummate conduct and moral precepts in the way of cultivating good governance means that when governance is thus cultivated, the people love those in authority, find pleasure in their ruler, and think nothing of dying on his behalf.

"As I have said, with respect to military affairs in general, commanders leading their troops into war is a minor affair. The four generations of Qin victories are the consequence of their having lived in constant terror that the world will become united and trample them underfoot. They are what you might call a military reflecting the worst of times in its service to a state that has not grasped the basic principles of governance. It is thus that Tang's expelling the tyrant Jie did not just happen when he chased him to Mingtiao, and King Wu's punishing the tyrant Zhou was not just because of his victory on the morning after the *jiazi* day. In both cases it was because of what Tang and Wu had done prior and their unrelenting personal cultivation. They led what is called a military committed to consummate conduct and doing what is right. The reason we are living in a chaotic age is because we are probing the surface rather than getting to the root of the matter."

Comment: Li Si who served as the Prime Minister of the state of Qin for forty years was first a student of Xunzi. He moved from the state of Chu to Qin to seek out an opportunity for political advancement. It is not clear from this passage at what point in time this exchange between student and teacher took place. But Xunzi does not think that the record of Qin victories can be sustained without grounding both governance and the deployment of the military in Confucian moral values. Again, the argument is for the symbiotic relationship between a strong and secure government and the welfare of its people.

An interesting issue in this passage that might illuminate some important underlying philosophical assumptions is the appeal to the notion of "expedience" (*bian* 便). Li Si introduces this term to establish a contrast between Qin's use of military power and opportunity in their achieving political success, and Xunzi's appeal to morality as the ultimate source of the flourishing state. Xunzi challenges Li in claiming it is in fact consummate conduct (*ren* 仁) and moral precepts (*yi* 義) rather than mere military and political power that are what is most expedient by way of conduct. Xunzi's argument is that if expedience does in fact describe the most efficient means of achieving a goal, it is morality rather than military prowess that does the job when the goal is effective governance.

Perhaps something can be learned about how Xunzi's assumptions regarding the expedience of Confucian moral values differ from those that ground ethical theory in a foundational individualism if we ask: Whence arises the decidedly negative connotations "expedience" has in Western

IX. THE *XUNZI* 荀子: A SYNCRETIC CONFUCIAN PHILOSOPHY

ethical theory? The term "expedience" as it is used in common parlance generally refers to one side of an exclusive self-other, means-end dualism. Expedience is understood as promoting one's own interest at the expense of others, and as being driven by a concern for self-interest rather than for principle. Further, expedience is often assumed to advocate for any means to a desired end that serves the urgency of one's needs. The term "expedience" in Western ethical discourse has largely pejorative implications because it generally assumes the end justifies the means, and thus anything goes.

But the "self-other" and "means-end" distinctions that would thus qualify the use of "expedience in conduct" in fact have little relevance for the Confucian values of consummate conduct and moral precepts. From the Confucian perspective in which persons are constituted by their relations and in which the goal is optimizing the interests of all concerned, these self-other and means-end distinctions have no purchase. That is, on a personal level, if the other who is constitutive of my own person does better, I do better as well. The teacher and the student become consummate teacher and student together, or not at all. The same inclusive holism would obtain at a political level in which the ruler does better if the people do better.

And further, the Confucian would claim that erstwhile "principles" are posterior as cultural generalizations drawn from efficacious actions rather than antecedent, self-sufficient rules that can be applied as regulative standards to adjudicate conduct. This being so, expedient conduct itself is the ultimate and continuing source of principles rather than an offence against them. With respect to means and ends, in the Confucian tradition in which both the method and the ultimate purpose is consummatory conduct at a personal and political level, means and ends are inseparable and mutually entailing. We seek to act consummately in order to live consummately. With these qualifications in hand, we can better understand Xunzi's claim that these basic Confucian values are indeed the expedient in the way of acting.

"凡人之動也，爲賞慶爲之，則見害傷焉止矣。故賞慶、刑罰、埶詐，不足以盡人之力，致人之死。爲人主上者也，其所以接下之百姓者，無禮義忠信，焉慮率用賞慶、刑罰、埶詐，除陁其下，獲其功用而已矣。大寇則至，使之持危城則必畔，遇敵處戰則必北，勞苦煩辱則必奔，霍焉離耳，下反制其上。故賞慶、刑罰、埶詐之爲道者，傭徒鬻賣之道也，不足以合大衆，美國家，故古之人羞而不道也。故厚德音以先之，明禮義以道之，致忠信以愛之，尚賢使能以次之，爵服慶賞以申之，時其事，輕其任，以調齊之，長養之，如保赤子。政令以定，風俗以一，有離俗不順其上，則百姓莫不敦惡，莫不毒孽，若祓不祥；然後刑於是起矣。是大刑之所加也，辱孰大焉！將以爲利邪？則大刑加焉，身苟不狂惑戇陋，誰睹是而不改也哉！"

"Generally speaking, when the activities of the people are undertaken for the sake of reward and profit, on seeing any possibility of injury in such affairs, they cease and desist. It is for this reason that policies such as reward and profit, punishments and fines, and strategic advantage and deception are not enough to get the most out of people to the extent that they will risk their lives for the state. If the rulers and those in authority do not engage their subordinates and the people with ritual practices (*li* 禮), moral precepts (*yi* 義), conscientiousness (*zhong* 忠), and credibility (*xin* 信), but instead attempt to use reward and profit, punishment and fines, and strategic advantage and deception, they will oppress the people, and at the end of the day, will only get a modicum of work and product out of them. In the face of a major invasion, if you send the people to defend the city walls against imminent danger, they are sure to defect. If you send them into battle in the enemy's territory, they are sure to turn and flee. If you ask of them toil and hardship, they are sure to bolt. Subordinates within the government will revolt and wield control over their superiors. Thus, using reward and profit, punishment and fines, and strategic advantage and deception are methods used for hired laborers and shopkeepers, and are inadequate to the task of unifying the people and bringing glory to the state. It was for this reason the ancients saw only shame in turning to such ways.

"Hence lead the people with the music of true virtuosity (*de* 德) in governance, show them the way by clarifying ritual practices and moral precepts, demonstrate your love for them with your conscientiousness and credibility, effect proper rank and status by promoting the worthy and employing the able, and use official robes, titles, and other rewards to win them over. Employ them according to the proper season and lighten their duties to bring proper order to their ranks. Nourish and care for the people as you would in looking after an infant.

"Once the policies and norms of government have been fixed and the popular customs made uniform, if there are those who offend against such customs or act contrary to the powers that be, everyone without exception will revile and loathe them as though purging some inauspicious influence. It is only under such circumstances that punishments should be enforced. What can be a greater disgrace than to suffer capital punishment? If they know that seeking illicit benefit is going to result in capital punishment who but a madman or imbecile would not reform their conduct?"

Comment: Although Xunzi is critical of what he would interpret as the Militarist emphasis on strategic advantage (*shi* 勢) and deception (*zha* 詐) as the most important factors in waging war and winning battles, his critique of using rewards and punishments is directed more at the Legalists who he sees as having turned proper governance into a kind of martial law. Xunzi is arguing against the primacy given to the political application of strategic advantage in Legalist philosophy that rejects the Confucian reliance upon political exemplars and moral suasion. Where the Confucians place their faith in the transforming influence of the ruler as a consummate *person*, the Legalists stress the objective conditions of his *position* that enables the manipulation of political purchase and his rule by intimidation. Moral and intellectual superiority in the administration of government must take precedence over the manipulation of political advantage.

When social and political order has been effected by enlightened governance and the moral transformation of the people, the people themselves will have internalized the shared values of the state to the extent that they will join the rulers in common cause in approving appropriate punishments for miscreants and ne'er-do-wells.

"凡兼人者有三術：有以德兼人者，有以力兼人者，有以富兼人者。彼貴我名聲，美我德行，欲爲我民，故辟門除涂，以迎吾入。因其民，襲其處，而百姓皆安。立法施令，莫不順比。是故得地而權彌重，兼人而兵俞強：是以德兼人者也。非貴我名聲也，非美我德行也，彼畏我威，劫我執，故民雖有離心，不敢有畔慮，若是則戎甲俞衆，奉養必費。是故得地而權彌輕，兼人而兵俞弱：是以力兼人者也。非貴我名聲也，非美我德行也，用貧求富，用飢求飽，虛腹張口，來歸我食。若是，則必發夫掌窌之粟以食之，委之財貨以富之，立良有司以接之，已期三年，然後民可信也。是故得地而權彌輕，兼人而國俞貧：是以富兼人者也。故曰：以德兼人者王，以力兼人者弱，以富兼人者貧，古今一也。"

"Generally speaking, there are three ways to annex a population: through virtuosity, by force, and with wealth. If they respect my name and reputation, admire my virtuosic conduct, and want to be my people, they will open the gates and clear the roadways in order to invite me in. If I accommodate the people, and allow them to remain in their homes, the people will be content. In establishing laws and issuing edicts, no one will be opposed. This is how to get more territory and consolidate my power, and to unify the people and strengthen the military. This then is the way of using virtuosity to annex a population.

"With no need to have my name and reputation revered or to win admiration for my virtuosic conduct, if the people stand in awe of my authority and bow to my might, even were they inclined to resist, they would give no thought to rebellion. In such a case I will need to augment the military, and the costs for provisioning them are certain to increase. For such reasons, in acquiring territory my authority will be diminished, and in annexing the population my military prowess will be weakened. This then is the way of using force to annex a population.

"With no need to have my name and reputation revered or to win admiration for my virtuosic conduct, but relying on the fact that those impoverished will seek wealth and those starving will seek sustenance, with empty stomachs and gaping mouths they will come to me simply to eat. In such a case, I will have to dispense grain from my granaries to feed them, provision them with chattel and goods by way of wealth, and appoint responsible officials to take care of them. And even so, it will take a good three years to win their trust. For these reasons, in acquiring territory my authority will be diminished, and in annexing the population my state will be impoverished. This then is the way of using wealth to annex a population.

"It is for this reason I would say that those who would use virtuosity to annex a population are True Kings, those who would use force are weakened in doing so, and those who would use wealth are impoverished in the process. This is as true today as it was in ancient times."

Comment: A familiar Legalist slogan is "strengthen the military and enrich the state" (*qiangbingfuguo* 强兵福國). Imperialist logic would have it that gaining additional territory and increasing one's population is synonymous with enriching one's state. Xunzi argues that this in fact is not so. The irony is that gaining land and appropriating an additional population either through force or with wealth levies a cost on the state in terms of military and civilian expenditures. It is only in winning over a population through the virtuosity of one's governance that as more territory is gained, one's authority is enhanced, and one's military prowess is strengthened. There is a logic in Xunzi's advocacy of virtuosic governance.

IX.7 Chapter 17: On Nature (*tianlun* 天論)

不爲而成，不求而得，夫是之謂天職。如是者，雖深，其人不加慮焉；雖大，不加能焉；雖精，不加察焉，夫是之謂不與天爭職。天有其時，地有其財，人有其治，夫是之謂能參。舍其所以參，而願其所參，則惑矣。列星隨旋，日月遞炤，四時代御，陰陽大化，風雨博施，萬物各得其和以生，各得其養以成，不見其事，而見其功，夫是之謂神。皆知其所以成，莫知其無形，夫是之謂天功。唯聖人爲不求知天。

Completing without doing and gaining without seeking—these then are the workings of nature (*tian* 天). In matters such as these, even though they are profound, they are not something human beings should ponder; even though broad in compass, they are not something human beings should address; even though tempting, they are not something human beings should delve into. This is what is called refraining from competing with nature in its work. Nature has its seasons, the earth its bounty, and human beings their proper governance. This is what is meant by forming a trinity with the other two. But for human beings to abandon what entitles them to be part of the trinity in wanting to take on what their partners do is to muddle things up.

The constellations of stars turn in the heavens, the sun and moon succeed each other in illuminating the world, the four seasons follow in their progression, *yin* 陰 and *yang* 陽 underwrite the grand transformations, the winds and rains reach everywhere, and each of the myriad things gets what it needs to grow and flourish. That we do not see their operations but do see their results is what is called their mystery. That everyone knows what nature produces and yet none know the formless forces behind it is what is called its bounty. It is only the sage (*shengren* 聖人) who does not seek to understand nature.

Comment: The vague concept of *tian* 天 conventionally translated "Heaven" is sometimes in the early literature associated with ancestors as a numinous, anthropomorphic force. In other Confucian texts the trinity of heaven, earth, and humankind as the "three forces" (*sancai* 三才) requires a collaboration among them to establish and sustain a cosmic moral order and to guarantee cosmic flourishing for all. In *Focusing the Familiar* 1, for example, human feelings and the meaning they produce are integral to cosmic flourishing:

中也者，天下之大本也；和也者，天下之達道也。致中和，天地位焉，萬物育焉。

This notion of equilibrium is the great root of the world; an optimizing harmony then is the advancing of way-making in the world. When equilibrium is sustained and an optimizing harmony is fully realized, the heavens and the earth maintain their proper places and all things flourish in the world.

We have seen Xunzi in his political philosophy makes the argument that proper social and political order emerges from the human capacity to introduce distinctions and to reinforce the hierarchical social structure through ritual practices. There is a natural tension that emerges in human society between our desires and the competition for their satisfaction. Xunzi defines ritual practices as a strategy developed by the ancient sages to provide satisfaction of these desires and to thus prevent disorder.

Xunzi introduces an understanding of *tian* 天 that in many ways is the logical outcome of a historical evolution. Early on, *tian* 天 is the numinous object of human reverence that seems to hold sway over human affairs, and needs to be propitiated with regular sacrificial offerings. Over time, we witness growing confidence within the human world that *tian* 天 functions on the basis of a shared cosmic morality, and thus that human beings can control their own affairs through the cultivation of moral conduct. In *Xunzi*, *tian* 天 is further disenchanted by becoming the impersonal and yet complex operations of nature. Xunzi's perception that discriminations are essential for proper order would seem to encourage this further human independence from *tian* 天. Xunzi in his understanding of the trinity departs from the other early texts by introducing boundaries among the three forces that allow each to find its realization without encroaching upon the other two. To be clear, Xunzi does allow human beings should be engaged with nature to the extent that the human world can make the most of its bounty. But rather than seeing their relationship as one of mutual contribution to a shared symbiosis, Xunzi tends to construe nature as an objective, mechanical process that provides the forum for human realization, and expresses real concern that the subtle and complex workings of nature can be compromised if they suffer from human interference. At the end of the day, while Xunzi certainly allows that human beings should exercise their wits in collaborating with nature and taking full advantage of its copious bounty, it is the speculative, metaphysical questions about nature he thinks we do well to abjure.

故大巧在所不爲，大智在所不慮。所志於天者，已其見象之可以期者矣；所志於地者，已其見宜之可以息者矣：所志於四時者，已其見數之可以事者矣；所志於陰陽者，已其見和之可以治者矣。官人守天，而自爲守道也。

The greatest cleverness lies in what one refuses to do, and the greatest wisdom (*zhi* 智) lies in what one refuses to ponder. When the sages turn their attention to nature, what they see is only those phenomena that have relevance to their lives. When they turn their attention to earth, what they see is only its fittingness in allowing things to grow. When they turn their attention to the four seasons, what they see is only those operations that have to do with their own affairs. When they turn their attention to the dynamics of *yin* 陰 and *yang* 陽, what they see is only the harmony (*he* 和) that can enable them to achieve proper social and political order. While the functionaries of sagely rulers attend to matters of nature, the rulers themselves give their full attention to the proper way (*dao* 道).

Comment: Xunzi's epistemology of comprehensiveness begins from the claim that the most panoramic and synoptic view is the best view. Emerging from practice as something done, this epistemic view certainly has a cognitive aspect, but it also includes all of the other elements necessary to "realize" a world in the sense of making it real. This epistemology in which "knowing is doing" is the Confucian alternative to the contemplative, spectator notion familiar in classical Greek philosophy where there is a single, abstract and objective truth to be derived from the reality-appearance dualism. The question we are left with here in Xunzi is whether his attitude towards coordinating the human experience with nature without seeking to fully understand it is consistent with his search for the most synoptic appreciation of the human experience. We might ask: Does humankind not have to incorporate a knowledge of nature into its practices? We find that Xunzi is critical of Zhuangzi in saying 莊子蔽於天而不知人 "Zhuangzi being obsessed with nature had no sense of human beings," but perhaps this criticism could be reversed with respect to Xunzi to describe his own limitations.

治亂，天邪？曰：日月星辰瑞曆，是禹桀之所同也，禹以治，桀以亂；治亂非天也。時邪？曰：繁啟蕃長於春夏，畜積收臧於秋冬，是禹桀之所同也，禹以治，桀以亂；治亂非時也。地邪？曰：得地則生，失地則死，是又禹桀之所同也，禹以治，桀以亂；治亂非地也。《詩》曰："天作高山，大王荒之。彼作矣，文王康之。"此之謂也。

Are proper order and disorder in the human world brought about by nature (*tian* 天)? I would say that the sun, moon, stars, and the solar periods are something the Great Yu and the despot Jie shared in common. With Yu there was proper order, with Jie disorder. Proper order and disorder are not due to nature.

Are they due to the seasons then? That the crops flourish and grow in the spring and summer and are harvested and stored up in the fall and winter were something the Great Yu and Jie shared in common. With Yu there was proper order, with Jie disorder. Proper order and disorder are not due to the seasons.

Are they due to the land then? I would say that if you have land you live, and if you don't you die. This again was something the Great Yu and Jie shared in common. With Yu there was proper order, with Jie disorder. Proper order and disorder are not due to the land.

This is what it means when in the *Book of Songs* 270 it says:
Nature provided the high hills
King Tai finding them grand
Established his capital there
And King Wen lived there in health and happiness.

Comment: For Xunzi, natural conditions are constant, and are unrelated to order and disorder in the human world. Within a process cosmology that begins from the interdependence of all things, his position is not only novel, but perhaps even counterintuitive. The prevailing assumption throughout most of the other Confucian texts is that disorder in the natural world such as earthquakes, floods, fires as well as sightings of unnatural omens are nothing less than nature's indictment of the human political world for its failures in proper governance. These natural disasters are portents in the sense that they portend continuing calamities until the political order is set right. The rationalist Xunzi in this respect anticipates the Han dynasty philosopher, Wang Chong 王充 (27-97 CE), who held similar views about the independence of the natural order of things, and condemned superstitious beliefs about either natural or supernatural aberrations having some causal relationship with the human experience.

天不爲人之惡寒也輟冬，地不爲人之惡遼遠也輟廣，君子不爲小人之匈匈也輟行。天有常道矣，地有常數矣，君子有常體矣。君子道其常，而小人計其功。《詩》曰："禮義之不愆，何恤人之言兮！" 此之謂也。

Nature (*tian* 天) does not suspend winter because human beings have an antipathy for the cold. The earth does not suspend its vast reaches because human beings have an antipathy to travel to remote and distant places. Exemplary persons (*junzi* 君子) do not suspend what they do because of the clamor of petty persons. Nature has its constant operations, the earth has its constant logistics, and exemplary persons have their constant comportment. While exemplary persons are constant in their conduct, petty persons weigh up their advantages. This is what the *Book of Songs* means when it says "If you have not offended against ritual practices (*li* 禮) and moral precepts (*yi* 義), why worry about what others have to say?"

Comment: Xunzi insists that the operations of nature and the conditions provided by the earth are constant, and stand independent of human likes and dislikes. He finds analogy between the constancy of nature and the conduct of exemplary persons who also remain unaffected by the dissonance of petty persons.

星隊木鳴，國人皆恐。曰：是何也？曰：無何也！是天地之變，陰陽之化，物之罕至者也。怪之，可也；而畏之，非也。夫日月之有食，風雨之不時，怪星之黨見，是無世而不常有之。上明而政平，則是雖並世起，無傷也；上闇而政險，則是雖無一至者，無益也。夫星之隊，木之鳴，是天地之變，陰陽之化，物之罕至者也；怪之，可也；而畏之，非也。

When stars fall from the sky and trees howl in the wind, the whole population of the state quakes with fear, saying how can this be happening? I would say there is no reason. These are only rare occurrences that happen because of the changes that take place in our natural environment and the transformations brought on by *yin* 陰 and *yang* 陽. Wonder at them you may, but fear them you mustn't.

The sun and moon have their eclipses, the wind and the rains are not always seasonal, and strange stars are occasionally seen in the sky. There has never been a time when such things did not occur. With an enlightened ruler and government that is fair, even if such events were to occur all at the same time, there would be nothing amiss. But if the ruler is benighted and the government malicious, even if no such events occur, it would not make them any better.

When stars fall from the sky and trees howl in the wind, these are only rare occurrences that happen because of the changes that take place in our natural environment and the transformations brought on by *yin* 陰 and *yang* 陽. Wonder at them you may, but fear them you mustn't.

Comment: Commonsense during Xunzi's time was that strange occurrences in nature are omens that indicate problems in governance in the human world. Xunzi takes exception to such beliefs, dismissing them as so much superstition. For Xunzi, anomalies are themselves an integral part of the natural order, and their occurrences have no more meaning than just that: natural anomalies.

物之已至者，人祅則可畏也。楛耕傷稼，耘耨失薉，政險失民；田薉稼惡，糴貴民飢，道路有死人：夫是之謂人祅。政令不明，舉錯不時，本事不理：夫是之謂人祅。勉力不時，則牛馬相生，六畜作祅，禮義不修，內外無別，男女淫亂，則父子相疑，上下乖離，寇難並至：夫是之謂人祅。祅是生於亂。三者錯，無安國。其說甚爾，其菑甚慘。可怪也，而亦可畏也。傳曰："萬物之怪書不說。"無用之辯，不急之察，棄而不治。若夫君臣之義，父子之親，夫婦之別，則日切瑳而不舍也。

Among the strange things that have occurred, what should be feared are those portents of a human making. Plowing done badly will do harm to the crops, hoeing and weeding done badly will diminish the harvest, government that is malevolent will lose its people.

Fields overgrown and crops that are meager, crop seed that is expensive and people starving, dead bodies lying on the roadways—these then are what are called human portents.

Political policies that are uninformed, public works that are unseasonal, basic occupations that are not properly overseen—these then are what are called human portents.

Corvée labor demanded at the wrong time so that horses and cows crossbreed and the six domestic animals produce mutants, ritual practices (*li* 禮) and moral precepts (*yi* 義) not being observed, family and public business not being properly discriminated, men and women carousing wantonly so that fathers and sons don't know each other, superiors and their subordinates being estranged in their relations, and marauding bandits and calamities arriving in tandem—these then are what are called human portents.

Such human portents are born of disorder, and when all of them occur at the same time, there is no security for the state. Although the explanation for them lies close at hand, the calamities they occasion are catastrophic. They are not only to be wondered at, but to be feared as well.

There is the traditional saying: "Strange phenomena that occur in the world of things are not explained in the *Book of Documents*." Useless debates over these events and superficial investigations into them can be dispensed with altogether. But the moral precepts (*yi* 義) governing the relationship between lord and ministers, the affection felt between father and son, the distinctions proper to husband and wife—these then must be worked at and polished every day, and must never be abandoned.

Comment: Xunzi introduces a clear distinction between strange but harmless omens in nature that occur as a matter of course, and those portents traceable to human maleficence, and that thus announce imminent disaster. The former may be a source of wonder, but they are not to be feared; the latter are truly terrible, and should quite properly be treated as a source of human peril. Rather than investing energies in investigating and trying to make sense of strange phenomena, human beings do better to pay attention to those moral imperatives that govern the institutions of family, community, and state.

雩而雨，何也？曰：無何也，猶不雩而雨也。日月食而救之，天旱而雩，卜筮然後決大事，非以爲得求也，以文之也。故君子以爲文，而百姓以爲神。以爲文則吉，以爲神則凶也。

What is the reason that when you pray for rain, it rains? I would say there is none. It is the same as when you don't pray for rain and it rains. The sun and moon suffer an eclipse and we try to save them, the fields experience drought and we pray for rain, and again important matters are only decided upon after we perform divination. It is not because in doing such things we get what we want—such practices are just for the sake of ceremony. Hence, exemplary persons (*junzi* 君子) take such practices to be ceremonial while the common people take them to be supernatural. To regard them as ceremonial is auspicious; to regard them as supernatural is unfortunate.

Comment: There are popular practices that ornament events in the human experience, and they should be embraced as proper ceremony. But from Xunzi's perspective, it is most unfortunate to construe exercises such as prayer and divination as invoking the supernatural and thus as in some way having causal efficacy. The wise among us see them for what they are: merely a matter of ceremony. The foolish on the other hand assume there are supernatural powers behind them.

大天而思之,孰與物畜而制之! 從天而頌之,孰與制天命而用之! 望時而待之,孰與應時而使之! 因物而多之,孰與騁能而化之! 思物而物之,孰與理物而勿失之也! 願於物之所以生,孰與有物之所以成! 故錯人而思天,則失萬物之情。

Rather than extolling nature (*tian* 天) and reflecting on its operations, isn't it better to nourish and properly regulate things? Rather than subjugating ourselves to nature and singing its praises, isn't it better to regulate what nature has mandated and make fair use of it? Rather than yearning for the right time and waiting for it to arrive, isn't it better to be responsive to the times and spur things along? Rather than letting things proliferate of their own accord, isn't it better to develop our capacity to transform them? Rather than reflecting on things and making objects out of them, isn't it better to manage them and not miss the opportunities they provide? Rather than longing after the source from which things grow, isn't it better to assist them in their process of maturation? Thus, if you are obsessed with nature and don't take care of what belongs to mankind, you will lose sight of what things actually are.

Comment: Xunzi recommends a certain pragmatic modesty with respect to the world in which we live. Instead of pursuing the big theoretical questions about what nature is and the big ethico-religious questions about how to exalt and serve it, we do better to attend to the practical issues of how to develop our own capacities to assist nature in optimizing the opportunities it provides for us. Rather than establishing a severe dichotomy between nature and mankind, Xunzi tries to draw a line between being obsessed with the grand, speculative, and seductive questions the answers to which do not make any real difference, and being properly responsive to those operations of nature that affect the human experience in a way in which we can contribute productively. An ill child is ill whether or not there is a God, and time spent speculating on how a perfect God could allow this to happen is perhaps not as good an investment of our time as figuring out a cure for what ails the child.

百王之無變,足以爲道貫。一廢一起,應之以貫,理貫不亂。不知貫,不知應變。貫之大體未嘗亡也。亂生其差,治盡其詳。故道之所善,中則可從,畸則不可爲,匿則大惑。

IX. THE *XUNZI* 荀子: A SYNCRETIC CONFUCIAN PHILOSOPHY

What the Hundred Kings of old deemed to leave unchanged is properly taken to be the continuous thread that runs through the proper way. Respond to all vicissitudes of life with this continuous thread, for where guided by this thread, there will be no disorder. To lack an understanding of this continuous thread is to lack an understanding of how to respond to change. The substance of this continuous thread has always been with us. Disorder is born from falling short of it; proper order is applying it in every detail. With respect to what is most efficacious along the proper way, in staying centered on it, we have our bearings, departing from it in one direction or another should be resisted, and running contrary to it is a muddled mind at its worst.

Comment: Xunzi perceives a continuity between the ways of old and the present day. For Xunzi, it is a recognition of this continuous thread that enables us to stay centered and respond effectively to an always changing world. There is an important difference between something that persists in change as a thread that runs through it, and something that is permanent and stands outside of change altogether. Xunzi's commitment is importantly to the former rather than the latter.

萬物爲道一偏，一物爲萬物一偏。愚者爲一物一偏，而自以爲知道，無知也。慎子有見於後，無見於先。老子有見於詘，無見於信。墨子有見於齊，無見於畸。宋子有見於少，無見於多。有後而無先，則群衆無門。有詘而無信，則貴賤不分。有齊而無畸，則政令不施，有少而無多，則群衆不化。《書》曰："無有作好，遵王之道；無有作惡，遵王之路。" 此之謂也。

The myriad things are but one aspect of the proper way (*dao* 道), and any one thing is but one aspect of the myriad things. Obtuse persons are but one aspect of one kind of thing, so that when they think they have grasped the proper way, they are foolish indeed. Shen Dao had some insight into holding back but did not understand moving ahead. Laozi had some insight into contraction, but did not understand what it means to extend. Mozi had some insight into uniformity, but did not understand the value of diversity. Song Jian had insight into reduction, but did not understand what it means to increase.

Where there is just holding back and no moving ahead the multitude has no way forward. Where there is contraction but no extending there is no distinction between noble and base. Where there is uniformity and no diversity, government policies cannot be carried into action. Where there is reduction but no increase, the multitude will not be transformed.

This is what it means when in the *Book of Documents* it says "Do not have things you covet, but follow the way of the True King; do not have things you despise, but follow the path of the True King."

Comment: Xunzi often invokes an epistemology of comprehensiveness rather than appealing to some given truth. In any of the correlations made in *yinyang* 陰陽 "imagistic thinking," comprehensiveness requires that both binaries being correlated be understood and included: contraction and extension, for example. Xunzi's criticism of the doctrines of competing philosophers usually takes the form of their having an understanding of only one side and not the other, and thus a biased rather than a synoptic view of things. For Xunzi, it is the way of the True King that is truly inclusive.

IX.8 Chapter 19: On Ritual Practices (*lilun* 禮論)

禮起於何也？曰：人生而有欲，欲而不得，則不能無求。求而無度量分界，則不能不爭；爭則亂，亂則窮。先王惡其亂也，故制禮義以分之，以養人之欲，給人之求。使欲必不窮乎物，物必不屈於欲。兩者相持而長，是禮之所起也。故禮者養也。芻豢稻粱，五味調香，所以養口也；椒蘭芬苾，所以養鼻也；雕琢刻鏤，黼黻文章，所以養目也；鐘鼓管磬，琴瑟竽笙，所以養耳也；疏房檖貌，越席床第几筵，所以養體也。故禮者養也。君子既得其養，又好其別。曷謂別？曰：貴賤有等，長幼有差，貧富輕重皆有稱者也。……人苟生之為見，若者必死；苟利之為見，若者必害；苟怠惰偷懦之為安，若者必危；苟情說之為樂，若者必滅。故人一之於禮義，則兩得之矣；一之於情性，則兩喪之矣。故儒者將使人兩得之者也，墨者將使人兩喪之者也，是儒墨之分也。

What is the origin of ritual propriety (*li* 禮)? I would reply that human beings at birth have desires. And until these desires are satisfied, human beings cannot but seek the means to do so. When in the search for satisfaction there is neither proper measure nor limit, they cannot but quarrel among themselves. Quarrelling leads to disorder, and disorder to impoverishment. The Former Kings hated such disorder, and thus formulated ritual practices (*li* 禮) and moral precepts (*yi* 義) as a way of making distinctions clear, of guaranteeing a proper range of desires, and of giving people a pathway to satisfaction. They made it so that desires did not exhaust the means to satisfy them, and that goods were sufficient to meet the desires. Taking care to promote a balance between proper desires and the goods needed to satisfy them was the origin of ritual propriety.

IX. THE *XUNZI* 荀子: A SYNCRETIC CONFUCIAN PHILOSOPHY

Ritual propriety is about satisfaction. The meat from domesticated animals, the various grains, and the spices needed to season them are how we satisfy the palate. Aromatic grasses and woods, and sweet-smelling fragrances are how we satisfy our sense of smell. Inlaid gemstones and incised metal, embroidery and finely woven patterns are how we satisfy our eyes. Bells and drums, zithers and flutes are how we satisfy our ears. Spacious rooms, hideaway chambers, plaited straw mats, couches, armrests, bamboo beds, and floor mats are how we satisfy our bodies. Thus, ritual propriety is about satisfaction.

While exemplary persons (*junzi* 君子) are concerned about their satisfaction, they also pay attention to the distinctions that should be observed. What then are the distinctions? There are graduations between noble and base; there is status that separates elders from their juniors. Rich and poor, the important and the trivial all have their proper place. . . .

If persons are obsessed with all that life has to offer, they are sure to die. If they are obsessed with what will benefit them, they are sure to suffer harm. If they think they will find security in indolence and timidity, danger awaits them. If they think enjoyment lies in simply satisfying their natural emotions, they will perish utterly.

Thus, if persons are focused on both ritual propriety and moral precepts, they will satisfy both their desires and the requirements of ritual propriety. But if they are focused solely on their emotions and desires, all will be lost. It is thus the difference between Confucian and Mohist doctrines is that the former will bring about the satisfaction of both desires and the demands of ritual propriety, while the latter will fail on both counts.

Comment: Xunzi provides a naturalistic rather than an aesthetic account of how the conventions defining ritual propriety have come about. An imbalance between human desires and the goods needed to satisfy them necessarily results in social disorder. Xunzi thus traces ritualized practices back to the formulation of an enlightened strategy for balancing the quantum of desires and the available goods needed to satisfy them. Indeed, Xunzi takes the substance and function of ritual propriety to be the acquisition of the necessary kinds of things needed to satisfy the physical sensorium: taste, smell, sight, hearing, and bodily comforts, with the proviso that such satisfactions must be regulated by the various hierarchical distinctions defining of a functioning society.

A proper balance must be sought in the tension that obtains among things. To be preoccupied with all that life has to offer, for example, will bring about a premature death. It is this proper balance sought in the Confucian doctrines that guarantees satisfaction of both desires and ritual demands. By contrast, the preoccupation with only one side of things (emotions and desires) at the expense of the other (ritual demands) advocated by the Mohists will bring about certain disaster.

禮有三本：天地者，生之本也；先祖者，類之本也；君師者，治之本也。無天地，惡生？無先祖，惡出？無君師，惡治？三者偏亡，焉無安人。故禮上事天，下事地，尊先祖，而隆君師。是禮之三本也。故王者天太祖，諸侯不敢壞，大夫士有常宗，所以別貴始；貴始得之本也。郊止乎天子，而社止於諸侯，道及士大夫，所以別尊者事尊，卑者事卑，宜大者巨，宜小者小也。

Ritual propriety (*li* 禮) has three roots. The heavens and the earth are the root of life; the ancestors are the root of the family lineage; rulers and political leaders are the root of proper order. If there were no heavens and earth, how could there be life? If there were no ancestors, how could there be a family genealogy? If there were no rulers and political leaders, how could there be proper order? If even one of these roots is lost, there can be no security for humankind. Thus, ritual propriety serves the heavens above and earth below, honors the ancestors, and exalts the rulers and political leaders. These are the three roots of ritual propriety.

It is for this reason that the king places his first ancestor on a par with *tian* 天, that the vassal lords would not dare to allow the ancestral hall to become dilapidated, and that the high ministers and officials are constant in their devotion to clan lineages. This is how they make distinctions in their noble beginnings, where honoring such beginnings is the root of their moral authority. The *jiao* 郊 sacrifice to the altar of *tian* 天 can only be performed by the emperor, but the *she* 社 sacrifice to the altar of the earth can be performed by everyone from vassal lords down to the high ministers and officials. This is the distinction that the noble should serve the noble, the humble the humble, while the great is reserved for the great, and the small for the small.

Comment: In celebrating the cosmic importance of ritual propriety, Xunzi traces its beginnings back to the fact of life itself, the "zoetological" ground of this process cosmology, and "the art of living" that issues from it. Zhao Tingyang 趙汀陽 in reflecting on this *Book of Changes* cosmology underscores the importance of two metaphors: "setting the root" (*zhagen* 扎根) and "growth" (*shengzhang* 生長). Zhao reflects on how first setting the root, and then on that basis, pursuing growth is the beginning and the projected end in the Confucian way of becoming consummately human:

> The primary issue for the human way is that of generation and regeneration, and the first step herein is growth. This is the starting point for the evolutionary thread of Chinese thought. The "doing" of growth must seek what a thing relies upon to be "deeply rooted and firmly planted" in its growth. Therefore, growth first of all requires putting down roots. The two metaphors of growth and putting down roots set out the path for Chinese thought.[①]

The root is set and the tradition grown through the ritual observances that punctuate the intergenerational transmission of a living civilization. The organization of the continuing cultural genealogy is expressed through ritual practices that reflect both the natural and the human order with all of their distinctions and persistent hierarchies.

凡禮，始乎梲，成乎文，終乎悦校。故至備，情文俱盡；其次，情文代勝；其下復情以歸大一也。天地以合，日月以明，四時以序，星辰以行，江河以流，萬物以昌，好惡以節，喜怒以當，以爲下則順，以爲上則明，萬變不亂，貳之則喪也。禮豈不至矣哉！立隆以爲極，而天下莫之能損益也。本末相順，終始相應，至文以有別，至察以有説，天下從之者治，不從者亂，從之者安，不從者危，從之者存，不從者亡，小人不能測也。

All ritual practices (*li* 禮) begin with simplicity, are consummated with elegance, and end in transformative education. They reach their apogee when both feelings and elegance are fully expressed. The next level is when feelings and elegance succeed each other in turn, and the nadir is when feelings revert to their lowest common denominator. These practices are how the heavens and the earth collaborate, how the sun and the moon shine, how the seasons turn, how the stars and constellations move across the night sky, how the rivers and streams flow, and how all things flourish. They moderate our likes and dislikes and make joy and anger appropriate to the occasion. They

---

① Zhao Tingyang, *The Making and Becoming of China* 惠此中國, pp. 148-149 人道問題首先正是 "生生"，而 "生生" 的第一步便是生長，這正是中國思想演化綫索的始發點。生長之事，必求生長之物 "深根固柢" 而使存在獲得生長的依據，因此生長首先要縶根。"生長" 和 "縶根" 這兩個隱喻表示了中國思想的行徑。

are what brings those below into accord and gives those above their wisdom. With all of the myriad changes following in their proper order, it is only in turning against ritual practices that all is lost.

How could these ritual practices be anything but the ultimate norms? When they are exalted as the highest standards, no one in the world is able to detract from them. What is most basic complements what is most peripheral, and beginning and end are in proper sequence. In their superlative elegance, they embody all distinctions, and in their circumspection, they make sense of everything. Petty persons cannot fathom the fact that when the world is in accord with ritual practices there is proper order, but when it is not, only chaos; that when the world is in accord with these practices there is peace, but when it is not, only danger; that when the world is in accord with these practices there is life, but when it is not, only annihilation.

Comment: Ritual practices are described herein as a kind of cosmic grammar that when expressive of both feelings and elegance, they enable all of the operations of the cosmos including the human experience to complement each other and to thus achieve their full musicality. Such elegant life practices provide the formal structures necessary for continuing refinement, and as such, are the ultimate source of meaning. Implicated in these normative practices are the proper distinctions necessary for everything at its proper time to make its proper contribution. These practices in enabling human beings to coordinate their life experience with the cosmic order, are thus the difference between human flourishing and chaos.

故繩墨誠陳矣，則不可欺以曲直；衡誠縣矣，則不可欺以輕重；規矩誠設矣，則不可欺以方圓；君子審於禮，則不可欺以詐偽。故繩者，直之至；衡者，平之至；規矩者，方圓之至；禮者，人道之極也。然而不法禮，不足禮，謂之無方之民；法禮，足禮，謂之有方之士。禮之中焉能思索，謂之能慮；禮之中焉能勿易，謂之能固。能慮、能固，加好者焉，斯聖人矣。故天者，高之極也；地者，下之極也；無窮者，廣之極也；聖人者，道之極也。故學者，固學爲聖人也，非特學無方之民也。

When the blackening plumbline is set to provide a true measure, there can be no deception in what is straight and what is crooked. When the scales are properly suspended to provide a true measure, there can be no deception in weighing things up. When the compass and set square are properly laid out to provide a true measure, there can be no deception in what is round and what is square. When exemplary persons (*junzi* 君子) are fully conversant with ritual practices (*li* 禮), there can be no deception with respect to what is specious and what is a matter of conscious effort. Thus it is that the plumbline is the ultimate norm for determining what is true, the scales for what is fair, the compass and set square for what is round and square, and ritual practice for what is the acme of the proper human way (*dao* 道).

It is for this reason that those who do not take ritual practices as their norm and thus fail to find their satisfaction in them can be called wayward people, while those who take them as their norm and do find their source of satisfaction in them are called scholar-officials (*shi* 士) who know where they are going. Being able to think within the context of ritual practices can be called being deliberate; being unwavering within ritual practices can be called being steadfast. If delight in ritual practice is added to being deliberate and steadfast—this then is the sage (*shengren* 聖人). Thus, just as the heavens are the ultimate in height, the earth in depth, and the boundless in compass, so the sages are the acme of the proper human way. Thus it is that true learning lies in the aspiration to become a sage, and does not lie in merely becoming one of these wayward people.

Comment: In the first paragraph of this passage, the association between ritual practices and the various tradesmen's tools fixes and rationalizes these practices in a way that we have not seen in the other Confucian texts. Such an understanding of ritual practices is qualified by the paragraph that follows introducing not only deliberation and steadfastness into the picture, but also the delight to be had in walking the proper way. And there is a hierarchy among those who are committed to this ritualized way of life, from the scholar-officials up to the sages as the highest order of humanity.

禮者，以財物爲用，以貴賤爲文，以多少爲異，以隆殺爲要。文理繁，情用省，是禮之隆也。文理省，情用繁，是禮之殺也。文理情用相爲内外表墨，並行而雜，是禮之中流也。故君子上致其隆，下盡其殺，而中處其中。步驟馳騁厲騖不外是矣。是君子之壇宇宮廷也。人有是，士君子也；外是，民也；於是其中焉，方皇周挾，曲得其次序，是聖人也。故厚者，禮之積也；大者，禮之廣也；高者，禮之隆也；明者，禮之盡也。《詩》曰："禮儀卒度，笑語卒獲。" 此之謂也。

Ritual practices (*li* 禮) make use of material goods in their various functions, follow a pattern of noble and base in their formalities, make use of more or less in respecting differences in status, and use degrees of reverence to denote standing. When the form and pattern are made optimal and feeling and function are minimized, ritual practices are at their most ornate; when the opposite, then ritual practices are at their simplest. When form and pattern, feeling and function, are the outside and the inside, the surface and the core, and are then mixed together in carrying out the practices, this is ritual practice at its proper mean.

It is for this reason that exemplary persons (*junzi* 君子) making the most of the ornateness and getting the most out of the simplicity dwell at this proper mean, and whether walking to and fro, or bustling about in haste, never depart from it. This mean in ritual practices is their altar and their sanctuary. Those who attain this mean are scholar-officials (*shi* 士) and exemplary persons; those who do not are common people. Those who dwell within it, move slowly about and traverse it all to bring every corner of it into accord—these then are the sages (*shengren* 聖人). Their generosity is the capaciousness of ritual, their greatness is the vastness of ritual, their grandeur is the majesty of ritual, their brilliance is their mastery of ritual.

This is what it means in the *Book of Songs* 209 when it says:
Ritual practice and comportment in their proper measure;
Talk and laughter with proper decorum.

Comment: Throughout Xunzi in all aspects of his philosophy, from personal cultivation to his epistemology to the proper performance of ritual practices, high value is accorded the attainment of a capacious and comprehensive inclusiveness. Ritual practices are material and spiritual, and are expressive of human values and institutionalized hierarchies. In their formal ornament and trappings, they are awesome and humbling, and in the informal feelings and activities they evoke, they give rise to sincerity and solemnity. Ritual practices are holistic in the sense that a proper mean must be sought between these informal and formal aspects as they are integral to the proper performance of them. When form and feeling are present in proper measure, they are complementary of each other and productive of ritual in its highest form. Those who are able to realize this synergy are exemplary in their conduct, while those who are able to draw upon this synergy and make the most of it are able to attain the status of sagehood.

禮者，斷長續短，損有餘，益不足，達愛敬之文，而滋成行義之美者也。故文飾、粗惡、聲樂、哭泣、恬愉、憂戚，是反也；然而禮兼而用之，時舉而代御。故文飾、聲樂、恬愉，所以持平奉吉也；粗惡、哭泣、憂戚，所以持險奉凶也。故其立文飾也，不至於窕冶；其立粗惡也，不至於瘠棄；其立聲樂、恬愉也，不至於流淫、惰慢；其立哭泣、哀戚也，不至於隘懾傷生，是禮之中流也。

Ritual practices (*li* 禮) shorten what is too long and lengthen what is too short, reduce what is in excess and make up deficiencies. They express the formal aspects of love (*ai* 愛) and respect (*jing* 敬) and nurture what is most beautiful in moral conduct (*yi* 義). Refined adornment and coarseness, music and wailing, happiness and anxiety are all opposites, and yet ritual practices bring them all together and make use of them, drawing upon each of them in sequence and at the proper time. Thus, refined adornment, music (*yue* 樂), and happiness bring with them the peace and tranquility needed on auspicious occasions, while coarseness, wailing, and anxiety bring with them the tensions needed on inauspicious occasions.

The proper mean in ritual practices is the use of refined adornment that does not degenerate into the sensual and seductive, is the use of coarseness that does not degenerate into emaciation and neglect, is the use of music and happiness that does not degenerate into lewdness and license, or rudeness and indolence, and is the use of wailing and grief that does not degenerate into despondency and injury to life.

Comment: Here again is the theme of comprehensiveness. Ritual practices are what enable us to modulate and make the necessary adjustments within the complexity and the contradictions of the human experience. These practices are comprehensive in drawing upon the full complement of the many elements and activities that together constitute a human life, using each one of them in the right measure and at the right time. Within these ritual practices there is always a proper mean to be sustained that precludes taking any particular modality of experience to an untoward extreme, and thus allowing it to degenerate into immoral conduct.

故曰：性者，本始材朴也；偽者，文理隆盛也。無性則偽之無所加，無偽則性不能自美。性偽合，然後成聖人之名，一天下之功於是就也。故曰：天地合而萬物生，陰陽接而變化起，性偽合而天下治。天能生物，不能辨物也，地能載人，不能治人也；宇中萬物生人之屬，待聖人然後分也。《詩》曰："懷柔百神，及河喬嶽。" 此之謂也。

Thus it is said that native human tendencies (*xing* 性) are the basic materials we begin from, and conscious effort (*wei* 偽) is the flourishing of cultural forms and rationales. If there were no native tendencies then conscious effort would have nothing on which to work, and if there was no conscious effort, native tendencies would not be able to refine themselves. It is only in the collaboration between native tendencies and conscious effort that the concept of the sage (*shengren* 聖人) emerges and such persons succeed in their achievement of bringing coherence to the world.

Hence it is said that with the collaboration of the heavens and the earth, the myriad things are born; with the intercourse between *yin* 陰 and *yang* 陽, the process of transformation is activated; and with the collaboration of native tendencies and conscious effort, proper order in the world is achieved. Nature is able to give birth to things but not to differentiate among them; the earth is able to give support to human beings, but is not able to bring them proper governance. All of the myriad things under the canopy of the heavens that are integral to the human experience can only assume their proper station with the arrival of the sages. This is what the *Book of Songs* 273 means when it says:

> They have embraced and brought respite to the myriad spirits,
> Even those spirits of the rivers and the highest mountains.

Comment: This passage is important in clarifying the perceived collaborative relationship between the technical terms "native human tendencies" (*xing* 性) and "conscious effort" (*wei* 偽), a clarification that precludes conventional descriptions such as "evil" for the former and "artifice" for the latter. For Xunzi, native tendencies are the raw and as yet unrefined materials defining of human beginnings that conscious effort must then elevate and refine. In parsing this relationship, we must resist the nature/nurture dualism inherited out of the substance ontology of the classical Greeks. "Native tendencies" and "conscious effort" are correlative categories such as *yin* 陰 and *yang* 陽 or the heavens and the earth that can only be understood in a symbiotic reference to each other. And like these categories, their collaboration is a natural one. We might think of *wei* 偽 as the continuing historical evolution in human development described by contemporary philosopher Li Zehou 李澤厚 as a process of cultural "sedimentation" (*jidian* 積澱).

Also important here is how to understand the role of the sages. At some point in this generative collaboration between raw materials and conscious effort, the category of the sage emerges with their project of both discriminating and classifying things, thereby bringing coherence to the relationships that obtain among them in their physical and their moral aspects. The unbounded holism in these correlative relationships makes the occupation of the sages a fundamentally aesthetic project.

凡禮，事生，飾歡也；送死，飾哀也；祭祀，飾敬也；師旅，飾威也。是百王之所同，古今之所一也，未有知其所由來者也。……三年之喪，二十五月而畢，哀痛未盡，思慕未忘，然而禮以是斷之者，豈不以送死有已，復生有節也哉！……故三年以爲隆，緦麻、小功以爲殺，期、九月以爲間。上取象於天，下取象於地，中取則於人，人所以群居和一之理盡矣。故三年之喪，人道之至文者也，夫是之謂至隆。是百王之所同也，古今之所一也。

Generally speaking, ritual practices (*li* 禮) in their service to those being born is putting on a display of joy, in sending the dead on their way is putting on a display of grief, in performing the sacrificial rites to the ancestors is putting on a display of respect, and in marshalling the troops is putting on a display of might and grandeur. Such was the way shared in by the Hundred Kings, and it is the constant that continues from antiquity down to the present day, although we do not know its origins. . . .

The three-year period of mourning comes to an end in the twenty-fifth month. Even though the grief and the pain of loss have not yet subsided, and we still have the longing for those who have passed very much in mind, still ritual practice must in this way make an end to the period of mourning. Otherwise, how would we be able to bring closure to our service to the departed and at some determinate time return to our daily lives? . . .

Thus it is that the three-year period of mourning is considered the highest degree of reverence, with the three-month "linen and hemp mourning dress" period and the five-month "*xiaogong* garment" period being the lowest, and the nine-month period falling in between. The highest degree of reverence takes its inspiration from the heavens and the lowest from the earth with that in between being modeled on mankind. This sets the ideal wherein people come together and dwell in unity and harmony. Thus it is that the custom of the three-year mourning period is the ultimate formal ceremony, and can be said to express the highest degree of reverence. Such was the way shared in by the Hundred Kings, and it is the constant that continues from antiquity down to the present day.

Comment: Ritual practices cover all aspects of the human experience from birth to death, and from the reverence for ancestors to the serious business of war. Among these practices, it is the three-year mourning period that expresses the highest degree of reverence. We know these customs have been passed down consistently from high antiquity, although we do not know their ultimate origins. In these practices, the periods vary according to the honor appropriate to the status of the person being mourned, with the hierarchy itself being inspired by the cosmic order in which the high heavens are lofty and the humble earth is underfoot. It is thus these ritual practices provide the framework that allows for human beings to dwell together in harmony and peace.

祭者，志意思慕之情也。愓詭唈優而不能無時至焉。故人之歡欣和合之時，則夫忠臣孝子亦愓詭而有所至矣。彼其所至者，甚大動也；案屈然已，則其於志意之情者惆然不嗛，其於禮節者闕然不具。故先王案爲之立文，尊尊親親之義至矣。故曰：祭者，志意思慕之情也。忠信愛敬之至矣，禮節文貌之盛矣，苟非聖人，莫之能知也。聖人明知之，士君子安行之，官人以爲守，百姓以成俗；其在君子以爲人道也，其在百姓以爲鬼事也。……卜筮視日、齋戒、修涂、几筵、饋薦、告祝，如或饗之。物取而皆祭之，如或嘗之。毋利舉爵，主人有尊，如或觴之。賓出，主人拜送，反易服，即位而哭，如或去之。哀夫！敬夫！事死如事生，事亡如事存，狀乎無形，影然而成文。

Sacrificial rites (*ji* 祭) are the authentic expression of the longing for the departed that pervades all thoughts and purposes. It is inevitable that we are visited by feelings of disquietude, palpitations, and despondence. Even while participating in shared convivialities, loyal ministers and filial sons will be affected by these feelings. When beset with such feelings and sorely moved by them, if there is no outlet, then the authentic expression of the longing for the departed that pervades all thoughts and purposes will be frustrated and the proper ritual observances will be incomplete. It was for this reason that the Former Kings established these formalities whereby the full meaning of honor for the honored and affection for loved ones could be expressed.

It is for this reason I say sacrificial rites are the authentic expression of the longing for the departed that pervades all thoughts and purposes. As the highest expression of the Confucian values of conscientiousness (*zhong* 忠), living up to one's word (*xin* 信), love (*ai* 愛), and respect (*jing* 敬), and the flowering of ritual observances (*li* 禮) and proper comportment, if it were not for the sages (*shengren* 聖人), there would be no one who could understand them. The sages have full comprehension of them, the scholar-officials (*shi* 士) and exemplary persons (*junzi* 君子) find comfort in performing them, the officials maintain them, and the ordinary people carry them on as a matter of custom. For exemplary persons, such rites are the way of being fully human; for the ordinary people they are the way of serving the spirits. . . .

In performing sacrificial rites, there is divination to identify an auspicious

IX. THE *XUNZI* 荀子: A SYNCRETIC CONFUCIAN PHILOSOPHY

day, fasting and purification, and there are offerings to be laid out on the tables and mats. The invocator is informed as though the spirit of the dead is there to enjoy the ceremony. Each of the offerings is taken up and sacrificed as though the spirit of the dead is there to taste them. It is the master of ceremony and no one else who has the honor of raising the wine goblet as though the spirit of the dead is there to drink from it. When the guests are to depart, the master of ceremony escorts them out with proper decorum, comes back to change out of his funeral garments, and then returning to his original place, weeps as though the spirit of the dead had left with them. Such grief! Such reverence! It is in serving the dead as though serving the living, serving the departed as though serving those present, and thus giving substance to that which is without form, that these formalities find their consummation.

Comment: As the solemn practices that set the root for the cultural genealogy, we must not underestimate the importance of sacrificial rites in the evolution of Confucian philosophy. Animal sacrifice is fundamental in this Confucian "zoetology" or "art of living." The solemn liberating of the life of the sacrificial animal and the sharing of its meat is the sanctification and celebration of life itself. Such regularized discursive practices are replete with personal, social, political, and religious meaning. The importance of this tradition is reflected in the fact that the complex oracle bone writing system with some five thousand characters had its origins in these same practices. This writing system was then subsequently used in the compilation of the canonical texts that have served as the axis for a cultural identity and the continuing intergenerational transmission of a living civilization.

Such sacrificial rites are grounded in the natural feelings that arise as this generation succeeds the one before to continue a lineage that reaches back into the mists of history. The succeeding generation's very identity is derived from this process of transmission and embodiment, with the sacrificial rites being not only the most concrete way of expressing the debt owed to those who have come before, but also a necessary cathartic for giving expression to the most authentic of human feelings. The most profound value grounding all Confucian conduct is the feelings of deference that serve as a catalyst for personal and communal growth. The formulation of these ritual practices is associated with the early sages who understood clearly the continuing human need to have an outlet for both their grief and their gratitude.

Xunzi discounts the supernatural implications of such rites by contrasting the understanding of these practices by exemplary persons with those of the common people. Exemplary persons see such rites as being integral to the way of becoming fully human that might well include a human-centered spiritual dimension, while the common people associate such practices with ghosts and spirits. Even so, this chapter on ritual practices concludes with a vivid image of how these sacrificial rites with all of their formal accoutrements, however they might be interpreted, provide the master of ceremony with a seemingly intimate séance with the spirit of the departed.

IX.9 Chapter 21: Dispelling Obsessions (*jiebi* 解蔽)

凡人之患，蔽於一曲，而闇於大理。治則復經，兩疑則惑矣。天下無二道，聖人無兩心。今諸侯異政，百家異説，則必或是或非，或治或亂。亂國之君，亂家之人，此其誠心，莫不求正而以自爲也。妒繆於道，而人誘其所迨也。私其所積，唯恐聞其惡也。倚其所私，以觀異術，唯恐聞其美也。是以與治雖走，而是己不輟也。豈不蔽於一曲，而失正求也哉！心不使焉，則白黑在前而目不見，雷鼓在側而耳不聞，況於使者乎？德道之人，亂國之君非之上，亂家之人非之下，豈不哀哉！故爲蔽：欲爲蔽，惡爲蔽，始爲蔽，終爲蔽，遠爲蔽，近爲蔽，博爲蔽，淺爲蔽，古爲蔽，今爲蔽。凡萬物異則莫不相爲蔽，此心術之公患也。

The affliction most people have is that they are obsessed with one corner and cannot see the big picture. If they can cure this problem, they can get back to the straight and narrow, but if they go in two different directions, they will lose their way. There are not two proper ways in the world, and sages are not of two minds. Since in these times the vassal lords have different ways of governing and the various schools of thought have different teachings, it must be the case that some are right and some wrong, that some bring order and others disorder.

Even the rulers of a disorderly state and the followers of perverse doctrines search in all sincerity for what is proper, and think that they have found it. They behave contrary to the proper way, and others entice them with their promises. Given what they have learned, they are loath to hear others speak ill of it. And entertaining alternative ways of thinking through the lens of their own prejudices, they are loath to hear others sing the praises of these different ideas. It is thus that even though they are moving farther away from the proper way, they never give up the conviction that they are right. How could this be other than being obsessed with one corner while failing in their search for the proper way?

If they are not thinking, then even with black and white before their eyes they do not see it, and even with the pounding of a large drum right beside them, they do not hear it. How much more so is the case of persons who are obsessed? At the same time, is it not a shame that those who have found the proper way are denounced by the rulers of disorderly states above, and by the followers of perverse doctrines below.

Where do such obsessions come from? Wanting or despising things can become an obsession, or the beginning or the end of things, or the nearness or distance of things, or the breadth or shallowness of things, or the antiquity or contemporaneousness of things. It is because everything is different that any one of them can become an obsession. This is a common affliction in our way of thinking.

Comment: One often remarked upon characteristic of these early Confucian texts is the absence of the notion of "truth" in the sense of a correspondence between idea and reality. Instead of the analytic exercise of "grasping" some reality behind what is less so, there is the challenge of gaining as synoptic view of any particular situation as possible. The metaphor behind this early Confucian epistemology is a comprehensive mapping of the way forward directed at moving straight ahead. Hence the criticism made of other philosophers is seldom one of right and wrong, but rather one of seeing only one part of the picture while being ignorant of the rest. The image of the frog in the well speaks to the limitations and the dangers of insularity in our thinking.

This distinction between "way-seeking" and "truth-seeking" is key to understanding Xunzi's epistemology of comprehensiveness. This passage can lend itself to a serious misunderstanding when it claims that "there are not two proper ways in the world, and sages are not of two minds." Rather than asserting the existence of some universal, objective, and unchanging standard, it is instead making the familiar Confucian claim that "one is many, many one" (*yiduobufen* 一多不分): that is, the one proper way and the single-mindedness of the sages emerge from seeing the big picture and taking all of the various ways into account, for good and for bad. This way of understanding the proper way is made clear in the paragraphs that follow and in its association with the person of Confucius.

昔賓孟之蔽者，亂家是也。墨子蔽於用而不知文。宋子蔽於欲而不知得。慎子蔽於法而不知賢。申子蔽於埶而不知知。惠子蔽於辭而不知實。莊子蔽於天而不知人。故由用謂之道，盡利矣。由欲謂之道，盡嗛矣。由法謂之道，盡數矣。由埶謂之道，盡便矣。由辭謂之道，盡論矣。由天謂之道，盡因矣。此數具者，皆道之一隅也。夫道者體常而盡變，一隅不足以舉之。曲知之人，觀於道之一隅，而未之能識也。故以爲足而飾之，內以自亂，外以惑人，上以蔽下，下以蔽上，此蔽塞之禍也。孔子仁知且不蔽，故學亂術足以爲先王者也。一家得周道，舉而用之，不蔽於成積也。故德與周公齊，名與三王並，此不蔽之福也。

Of old among the itinerant philosophers there are examples of purveyors of perverse doctrines. Mozi being obsessed with usefulness, had no sense of cultural refinement. Song Jian being obsessed with wanting, did not know what to do with what he got. Shen Dao being obsessed with law, had no appreciation of those who were worthy. Shen Buhai being obsessed with expedience, had no understanding of the role of wisdom. Hui Shi being obsessed with rhetoric, had no grasp on actuality. Zhuangzi being obsessed with nature, had no sense of human beings.

It is thus that those who take usefulness as the proper way know nothing but benefit; those who take wanting as the proper way know nothing but satisfaction; those who take law as the proper way know nothing but procedures; those who take expedience as the proper way know nothing but convenience; those who take rhetoric as the proper way know nothing but debate; those who take nature as the proper way know nothing but following its dictates.

Each of these various doctrines has only grasped one corner of the proper way (*dao* 道). As for the proper way, since it is the embodiment of constancy and exhausts all possible changes, it is not possible that one corner can do it justice. Such biased people in seeing only one corner of the proper way are never able to acknowledge it as such. They take it to be good enough and simply dress it up, muddling their own minds and deluding the minds of others. Those above impose their obsessions on those below, and those below impose them on those above, thus occasioning the disaster that comes with obsession and insularity.

Confucius by contrast was a person of consummate conduct (*ren* 仁) and wisdom (*zhi* 知), and wholly free of obsessions. Thus, in studying the whole corpus of the various doctrines he was on a par to be counted among the Former Kings. In his own lineage he embraced the most comprehensive way, and demonstrated it in his practices without any obsession over old habits of thinking. Thus it was that in his virtuosity he stood shoulder to shoulder with the Duke of Zhou and in name he joined the pantheon of the Three Kings. Such is the good fortune that comes with staying free of obsessions.

Comment: Xunzi in criticizing the cohort of competing philosophers by using their own language and alluding to the strongest suit by which they are popularly known, gives himself real credibility. For example, the language of utility and practicality is ubiquitous throughout the *Mozi*, and if there is any attention given to cultural refinements in the life of the people it is to denounce them as unnecessary and wasteful extravagances. Xunzi then continues to make his case by appealing to perhaps the central term in Mohist doctrine, "benefit" (*li* 利), claiming such an obsession construes benefit for the whole world in the thinnest of terms. With Mozi at least, Xunzi's critique has some merit.

Xunzi then turns to Confucius as the alternative to philosophers who can only see one corner of the big picture. From the *Analects* and throughout the Confucian canons, the praise of Confucius and his proper way is repeatedly couched in the language of flexibility and the capaciousness that follows from such inclusivity and accommodation. For Xunzi, Confucius is master of all doctrines, and although having the stature of the hoary sages of old, far from being constrained by old habits, his single lineage is both open and catholic in its thinking and practices.

萬物莫形而不見，莫見而不論，莫論而失位。坐於室而見四海，處於今而論久遠。疏觀萬物而知其情，參稽治亂而通其度，經緯天地而材官萬物，制割大理而宇宙裏矣。恢恢廣廣，孰知其極？睪睪廣廣，孰知其德？涫涫紛紛，孰知其形？明參日月，大滿八極，夫是之謂大人。夫惡有蔽矣哉！

None of the myriad things that has form goes unperceived, nothing that is perceived is without its sequence, and nothing that is in sequence loses its place. Persons who embody the proper way (*dao* 道) can dwell in their own homes and yet see the four seas; they can live in the present and yet discourse on things remote in time and place. With a penetrating insight into all things, they understand what they really are. Surveying the phenomenon of order and disorder, they are clear on its measure. Taking the warp and woof of the heavens and the earth, they are in control of the myriad things, and holding sway over their operations, blanket the entire cosmos.

So synoptic in their vision, who knows their limits? So brilliant and illuminating, who knows their virtuosity (*de* 德)? So roiling and profuse, who knows their form? In their brilliance, they are a match for the sun and moon, and in their compass they span the eight directions. These then are what are called truly great persons. How could they possibly have any obsessions!

Comment: Xunzi with truly (and uncharacteristic) cosmic hyperbole paints a portrait of those persons who embody the proper way. Important here is the holography. Implicated in such truly great persons is the entire cosmos, and all falls under their virtuosic sway. In *Focusing the Familiar* 30 Confucius specifically is described in such grand cosmic terms:

仲尼……上律天時，下襲水土。辟如天地之無不持載，無不覆幬，辟如四時之錯行，如日月之代明。

Confucius . . . modeled himself above on the rhythm of the turning seasons, and below he was attuned to the patterns of water and earth. He is comparable to the heavens and the earth, sheltering and supporting everything that is. He is comparable to the progress of the four seasons, and the alternating brightness of the sun and moon.

Such sages are elevated to a celestial plane in which they become the face of the natural operations of the cosmos. The optimal depth (*du* 度) of the relation between the cosmos and the sages as the highest order of humanity that is captured in the mantra "the continuity between and inseparability of the human and the cosmic orders" (*tianrenheyi* 天人合一) is the humanization of the cosmos and the naturalization of humankind.

農精於田，而不可以爲田師；賈精於市，而不可以爲市師；工精於器，而不可以爲器師。有人也，不能此三技，而可使治三官。曰：精於道者也。精於物者也。精於物者以物物，精於道者兼物物。故君子壹於道，而以贊稽物。壹於道則正，以贊稽物則察；以正志行察論，則萬物官矣。

The farmer is proficient in planting his crops, but does not have the capability of being the minister of agriculture. The merchant is proficient in marketing his wares, but does not have the capability of being the minister of commerce. The tradesman is proficient in doing his job, but does not have the capability of being minister of works. But there are people who though not proficient in these three occupations can be appointed to the offices that oversee them. That is but to say that there are people who are proficient in the way of things, and that there are those who are only proficient in doing things. Those who are proficient in doing things do them, while those who are proficient in the way of things have a synoptic understanding of them.

Thus it is that exemplary persons (*junzi* 君子) concentrate on the proper way (*dao* 道), and use it to assist in their examination into things. With those who concentrate on the proper way of doing things, things are done right; with those who use this way to assist in their examination into things, they are circumspect in their oversight of them. When the investigation and deliberation is carried out with the proper attitude, all things will function as they should.

Comment: There is an important distinction to be made between having the skills to do some occupation well, and having the ability to locate this particular occupation and oversee it within the broader scheme of things. What makes persons exemplary and worthy of high office is not only a synoptic understanding of the important occupations that enable the community to function, but the capacity to integrate everything within the life of the community in such a way that it is able to flourish. Perhaps the most essential quality is being able to lead others by moral example. Important here too is the flexibility needed for promoting the proper way, and that can be appealed to in making necessary adjustments for optimal results.

凡以知，人之性也；可以知，物之理也。以可以知人之性，求可以知物之理，而無所疑止之，則没世窮年不能徧也。其所以貫理焉雖億萬，已不足浹萬物之變，與愚者若一。學，老身長子，而與愚者若一，猶不知錯，夫是之謂妄人。故學也者，固學止之也。惡乎止之？曰：止諸至足。曷謂至足？曰：聖王。聖也者，盡倫者也；王也者，盡制者也；兩盡者，足以爲天下極矣。故學者以聖王爲師，案以聖王之制爲法，法其法以求其統類，以務象效其人。嚮是而務，士也；類是而幾，君子也；知之，聖人也。……爲之無益於成也，求之無益於得也，憂戚之無益於幾也，則廣焉能棄之矣，不以自妨也，不少頃干之胸中。不慕往，不閔來，無邑憐之心，當時則動，物至而應，事起而辨，治亂可否，昭然明矣。

Generally speaking, the capacity for knowing (*zhi* 知) is integral to our natural human propensities (*xing* 性). And what can be known is the coherence (*li* 理) that obtains among things. So you take this natural propensity for knowing and seek to understand the coherence that obtains among things. But if no boundary is set, your lifetime will slip away on you and you will exhaust your years without being able to understand all there is to know. Even though you try countless different ways to trace out this pattern of coherence, in the end you will still not be able to fathom the complete cycle of the changes that all things undergo, and will just be a fool for trying. In your studies you grow old and your children grow up, and you are still the fool for not giving it up. This then is what is called a ludicrous person.

Thus, as for real learning, it must have its terminus. Wherein lies this terminus? I would say that it is when you have reached full competence. What then can be called full competence? I would say it is captured in the expression "sage-king." Sagacity (*sheng* 聖) lies in having an exhaustive understanding of human relations; kingliness lies in having an exhaustive understanding of governance. Those who have an exhaustive understanding of both have the substance to set the highest standard for the world. It is for this reason scholars should take the sage-king as their mentor, and the governance of the sage-king as their norm. They should emulate the norms of the sage-king in seeking after the grasp that such persons have had of the big picture, and must model themselves on their very persons. Those who exert themselves in seeking after this ideal are scholar-officials (*shi* 士), those who are of the same kind and almost there are exemplary persons (*junzi* 君子), and those who actually realize it are sages (*shengren* 聖人)....

If what you are doing does not contribute to your success, if what you are seeking does not help you get what you need, if worry and distress add nothing to the outcome, then put real distance between yourself and such distractions. Don't let such things become self-impairing and don't give them a moment of your time. Do not yearn for what is past, do not be anxious over what has yet to come, and do not be troubled in your thoughts. If you act at the right time, respond when things happen, deal with things as they occur, then whether or not they will be propitious will become abundantly clear.

Comment: The desire to know is natural to the human condition, but the cosmos and its various operations will not yield up its many complex mysteries to the human mind. To try to know everything without setting the proper limits on your studies is to squander your life by being drawn away from what is important, and to thus wander into foolishness. What then is the proper boundary for learning? The suppressed pragmatic premises in this text are the inseparability of knowing and doing and the need to authenticate what is known in practice. Xunzi like William James is asking "What difference does it make?" And if it doesn't make a difference, time is better spent on something that does.

Xunzi like Confucius before him is not interested in either speculation or knowledge for its own sake. In a cosmos of boundless complexity, priorities must be set. Both Confucius and Xunzi look to the art of living provided by historical role models as the inspiration for having a full and satisfying life. The sage-kings are paradigmatic figures who have achieved the highest order of humanity. They laid the foundation for the norms necessary for understanding human relations and proper governance. To set out inspired by this ideal is to become a scholar-official, to approximate it is to become an exemplary person, and to actually realize it is to become a sage yourself.

Xunzi is keenly aware of how we waste a lot of our time on things that don't make any difference. He is also mindful of the fact that ninety-five percent of things we worry about never happen, and the other five percent are inevitable, and thus will happen regardless. In overcoming these untoward habits, we do well to avoid such distractions and simply deal with things as they come.

IX.10 Chapter 22: On Using Names Properly (*zhengming* 正名)

後王之成名：刑名從商，爵名從周，文名從禮，散名之加於萬物者，則從諸夏之成俗，曲期遠方異俗之鄉，則因之而爲通。

The Later Kings fixed the reference of names (*ming* 名) as follows: For the names of punishments, they followed the Shang dynasty. For the names of ranks and titles, they followed the Zhou dynasty. For the names of formal ceremonies, they followed ritual practices (*li* 禮). For the miscellaneous names they used for the myriad things, they followed the established customs of the various Huaxia (proto-Chinese) states, enabling those living where winding roads converge in distant places with all of their different customs, to make allowances and communicate with each other.

Comment: This notion of *zhengming* 正名 has conventionally been translated as "the rectification of names," suggesting that in our conduct we need to satisfy the stipulated definition of names and ranks. And this requisite is certainly part of the story. For Confucius, for example, there is an immediate association between using political titles of office strictly, and the integrity of the state. In the *Zuo Commentary on the Spring and Autumn Annals* there is an account of a person who in being rewarded for saving a prominent man's life declines the offer of a city and asks instead to be allowed to use the dress and accoutrements of a prince:

> 仲尼聞之日，惜也，不如多與之邑，唯器與名，不可以假人，君之所司也，名以出信，信以守器，器以藏禮，禮以行義，義以生利，利以平民，政之大節也，若以假人，與人政也，政亡，則國家從之，弗可止也已。
>
> Confucius on hearing about this said: "What a pity! It would have been better to give him many cities. It is insignias of office and titles alone that cannot be conceded to pretenders—they must be managed by the ruler. Proper titles give rise to confidence (*xin* 信), and confidence is what protects the insignias of office. It is insignias in which the meaning of ritual propriety is invested, and it is ritual propriety (*li* 禮) that carries appropriate conduct (*yi* 義) into practice; appropriate conduct is what gives rise to benefit, and it is benefit that brings equanimity to the people. Such things are what structure government, and if you concede them to pretenders, you concede the government along with them. If the government is lost, the state will follow, and there can be no stopping it."[1]

Confucius here denounces this charade bitterly in language reminiscent of the locus classicus for the doctrine of *zhengming* 正名, *Analects* 13.3. A major theme running through the *Analects* is Confucius's insistence that unrelenting attention must be given to retaining a strict correspondence between formal ritual practices and the ranks of office, with the risk of political collapse being the consequence of doing otherwise.[2] More specifically, Confucius was repeatedly chagrined at the powerful Ji family's usurpation of practices and privileges appropriate to the royal house.[3]

Xunzi in his elaboration on Confucius's doctrine of *zhengming* 正名

---

[1] The *Zuo Commentary to the Spring and Autumn Annals* Duke Cheng 2. Cf. Legge, *Chinese Classics*, Vol. 5, p. 344. The *Hanshi Waizhuan* records a story in which again Confucius in attendance on Ji Sun (see *Analects* 14.36) worries over the appropriate use of names. See D.C. Lau and Chen Fong Ching, *A Concordance to the Hanshi Waizhuan*, Hong Kong: The Commercial Press, 1992, 5.34/41/19.

[2] See for example *Analects* 3.10, 3.22, 11.6, 11.17.

[3] See for example *Analects* 3.1, 3.2, 3.6.

IX. THE *XUNZI* 荀子: A SYNCRETIC CONFUCIAN PHILOSOPHY

also has a deep and abiding respect for the function of language to convey the aggregated social, political, and cosmic order from generation to generation, and from dynasty to dynasty, and thus to provide a civilizational solidarity.

散名之在人者：生之所以然者謂之性；性之和所生，精合感應，不事而自然謂之性。性之好、惡、喜、怒、哀、樂謂之情。情然而心爲之擇謂之慮。心慮而能爲之動謂之僞；慮積焉，能習焉，而後成謂之僞。

As for the miscellaneous names (*ming* 名) of those things that lie within the human experience, that which is what it is at birth is called native human tendencies (*xing* 性). That which is harmonious (*he* 和) from birth, and being effortlessly responsive and naturally spontaneous, is called native human tendencies. The capacity of these native human tendencies for liking and disliking, for delight and anger, and for grief and pleasure are what are called feelings. Having feelings such as these, the heartmind in choosing from among them is called thinking. With the heartmind thinking, being able to act upon its thoughts is called conscious effort (*wei* 僞). When thinking accumulates and can be habituated to succeed in what it attempts, this is called conscious effort (*wei* 僞).

Comment: In this passage, Xunzi is again referencing a specific set of terms used in describing human affairs that have been established and put into practice. Indeed, it is on the basis of these terms having an established usage that Xunzi criticizes Mencius:

> 孟子曰："人之學者，其性善。"曰：是不然。是不及知人之性，而不察乎人之性僞之分者也。……不可學，不可事，而在人者，謂之性。
> Mencius says that "since human beings can be educated, their *xing* 性 is good." I would argue that this is not so. Mencius in his lack of understanding of the human *xing* 性, is unable to discern the distinction between *xing* 性 itself and deliberate activity (*wei* 僞).... What cannot be learned and cannot be acquired but is simply inherent in persons is what is called *xing* 性.

In criticizing Mencius, Xunzi begins by assuming his own understanding of *xing* 性 as being an unlearned "given" is incontrovertibly what *xing* 性 actually means. Such being the case, according to Xunzi's logic, when

Mencius says *xing* 性 enables us to be good, Mencius is at the same time asserting that being good is unlearned and does not require deliberate effort. Being good is as easy as simply being and acting human. Of course, this naturalistic interpretation of *xing* 性 that Xunzi is imputing to Mencius—what you are born with makes you good—is explicitly rejected in *Mencius* 6A3 by Mencius as a *reductio ad absurdum* when it is proposed by Mencius's contemporary, Master Gao. Even though Xunzi treats *xing* 性 as a native tendency, we must resist the uncritical assumption that he is making some ontological claim about an essential and causal nature familiar in classical Greek philosophy.

故王者之制名，名定而實辨，道行而志通，則慎率民而一焉。故析辭擅作名，以亂正名，使民疑惑，人多辨訟，則謂之大姦。其罪猶爲符節度量之罪也。

Thus, for the kings in institutionalizing their names (*ming* 名), if the name is settled and actual situations are distinguished, thereby enabling them to promote the proper way (*dao* 道) and realize what they intend to do, then these kings can be circumspect in leading the people and in bringing consistency to their lives. Hence, those logic choppers who arrogate to themselves the creation of names and throw the proper use of language into confusion, and in so doing, sow doubt and delusion among the people and instigate countless disputes—these are despicable villains. Their crime is no different from those who would tamper with tallies or rig weights and measures.

Comment: Again, established practices in the use of names are essential for proper governance and social order, bringing consistency and coherence to the everyday lives of ordinary people. Those who would wantonly offend against the customary use of language for their own gain are a serious source of disruption. Significantly, the analogy Xunzi appeals to for the proper use of language is the established convention governing contractual tallies, and weights and measures.

A full explanation of this doctrine of *zhengming* 正名, in addition to reflecting an appreciation of the way in which language conveys past realizations of the world, must provide some account of how naming (*ming* 名) can be used creatively to command (*ming* 命) new worlds into being, enabling us thereby to optimize emerging circumstances. Naming is a performance ("a making of form") that is similar to ritual practices (*li* 禮). One aspect of both naming and ritual practice is the way in which they as formal structures capture and convey not only meaning, but moral meaning (*yi* 義). Using a name or performing a ritual action is the analogical correlation of past and present circumstances to evoke this invested meaning. An important characteristic of both name and ritual practice is that they are also informal, and thus context-specific, always qualified by a unique set of circumstances. Their meaning cannot be exhausted by a genetic analysis that only accounts for what they mean in themselves, but must also have recourse to an explanation that reveals their relationship and meaning for their particular and ever-changing context.

A given name or ritual action, although describable at an abstract formal level, is truly meaningful only as a particular and personal disclosure of meaning. When we translate ritual practice (*li* 禮) as "propriety," and when we aspire to using language "properly," we appeal to L. *proprius* in its primitive sense of "making one's own." Thus, "appropriate" ritual actions that conduce to an achieved "propriety" in roles and relations and the "proper" use of language require a personalization within an always specific situation.

The challenge that this fluidity of names and their patternings represent to a purely logical, referential explanation of *zhengming* 正名 is reinforced by the performative force of naming. Ritual practices are not only performed *by* people, but because they also evoke a certain kind of response, in an important sense they *perform* people as well. Similarly, names not only describe actual situations, but also propel such situations toward one realization as opposed to another.

然則何緣而以同異？曰：緣天官。凡同類同情者，其天官之意物也同。故比方之疑似而通，是所以共其約名以相期也。……五官簿之而不知，心徵知而無說，則人莫不然謂之不知。此所緣而以同異也。然後隨而命之，同則同之，異則異之。

On what basis then do we distinguish what is the same from what is different? I would say we rely on our natural senses. Generally speaking, when things are of the same kind and have the same characteristics, our senses also perceive them as being the same. Hence, we make comparisons among things that seem similar and group them together. This is how we come to the general name (*ming* 名) they share for inclusive stipulation.... When the senses take note of something but it is not understood, or where the heartmind has some understanding but cannot explain it, then everyone is going to say that they simply do not understand it. This then is the basis whereby sameness and difference are discriminated. When subsequently we name something, the same things should have the same name, and what is different, a different name.

Comment: Rather than advancing doctrines as universal principles or organizing experience around a taxonomy of natural kinds grounded in some notion of strict identity, Confucian philosophy proceeds from analogy with, and always provisional generalizations derived from, those *particular* historical instances of things.

We might take "persons" as an example of sameness. With substance ontology informing our best intuitions, the self-same reduplicative essence or form (*eidos*) defining each person and the species as a whole, means that all members of a class are fundamentally and essentially the same, and only incidentally different. We might also remember in Aristotle's time, such categorical thinking essentialized and naturalized differences in race and gender producing a discriminatory consciousness that has persisted until modern times, for good and for bad. On the one hand, it can be invoked to insist upon the sanctity of human life, and on the other, to demarcate erstwhile fixed racial and gender differences.

While our commonsense might have this specific referent, this same ontological notion of strict identity carries over in a contemporary, more liberated dress: for example, into the legal status of all persons in the courtroom, where the convention is that all individuals regardless of the contingencies of gender, generation, race, religion, class, and so on, are ostensibly equal before the law. Justice is blind. To argue thusly that our many differences are at best contingent attributes grounded in a shared and essential sameness, offers us a much-truncated version of unique identity and personal integrity. And whether or not discounting our difference serves the interests of justice is not always clear.

By contrast, the relationally-constituted model of persons assumed in Confucian philosophy asserts that each of us is an inimitable matrix of vital, concrete relations all the way down, without any assumed shared essence. On that basis, it would further claim the commonalities of our class membership are dependent upon overlapping relations and complex analogies rather than any notion of strict identity, and in so doing, would advance a conception of persons that while seemingly more defused, in fact brings with it a much stronger sense of unique identity. The enhanced uniqueness of relationally-constituted persons was not lost on the classical pragmatists such as William James, John Dewey, and George Herbert Mead.

IX. THE *XUNZI* 荀子: A SYNCRETIC CONFUCIAN PHILOSOPHY

知異實者之異名也，故使異實者莫不異名也，不可亂也，猶使同實者莫不同名也。故萬物雖衆，有時而欲無舉之，故謂之物；物也者，大共名也。推而共之，共則有共，至於無共然後止。有時而欲徧舉之，故謂之鳥獸。鳥獸也者，大別名也。推而別之，別則有別，至於無別然後止。名無固宜，約之以命，約定俗成謂之宜，異於約則謂之不宜。名無固實，約之以命實，約定俗成，謂之實名。名有固善，徑易而不拂，謂之善名。

Because we know different situations require different names (*ming* 名), in order to avoid confusion, we make sure this is so in all cases. It is like making sure that all of the same situations have the same name. Hence, even though the myriad things are so diverse, on occasion we want to refer to them collectively, and thus call them "things." "Things" then is the broadest generic term. We extend in generality from the general to the more general, and only stop when there is nothing more generic. On other occasions, we want to refer to specific kinds of things, and thus call them "birds" and "beasts." Birds and beasts then are more specific terms. We contract in specificity from the specific to the more specific, and only stop when there is nothing more specific.

Names are not fixed in their appropriateness, but become so by mutual agreement. When there is mutual agreement and the name becomes customary in its usage, it is then said to be appropriate. When used in a way different from what has been agreed upon, it is then said to be used inappropriately. Names are not fixed in their reference, but become so by mutual agreement. When there is mutual agreement and the reference becomes customary, it is said to be the referent. Names can be stable in their efficacy; when direct, easy to use, and not at odds with the phenomenon, they are said to be efficacious names.

Comment: Xunzi's understanding of the doctrine of "using language properly" (*zhengming* 正名) is for the most part consistent with that of Confucius. For both of them, their starting point is the importance of the felicitous use of language within the human community as it is ambient in the ordinary affairs of the day.

This Confucian insight that language as an activity is performative and perlocutionary—it does something—has become familiar to us in J.L. Austin and the later work of Ludwig Wittgenstein. Indeed, Wittgenstein has an understanding of how language functions that resonates with the prospective expectations expressed by Confucius and Xunzi. Introducing his notions of "language games" and "family resemblances," Wittgenstein is keenly aware that language and life are two aspects of the same experience. He challenges realist assumptions that language is somehow separate, and by mapping it onto the world, it comes to "correspond" to reality in some referential and representational way. Wittgenstein uses the term "language-games" to highlight "the fact that the speaking of language is part of an activity, or a form of life," (PI 23), where such games consist "of language and the actions into which it is woven" (PI 7).

Wittgenstein has a keen awareness of the underdeterminedness of language, allowing room for the prospective activation of the ambiguities and equivocations always present to increase its meaning and effect. He argues that concepts do not need to be clearly defined to be meaningful and to precipitate change in the world. Wittgenstein uses the analogy of "family resemblances" to describe how the same word is used in many different ways without any ultimately final or essential meaning, and to underscore the lack of any formal boundaries or necessary precision in the different applications of one and the same concept. Such an understanding of language highlights the allusiveness and the productive ambiguity that attend the imaginative use of language.

Early Chinese concepts, says Angus Graham, often "tend to be more dynamic than their closest Western equivalents, and that English translation freezes them into immobility."[1] It is only recently over the past century with the insights of contemporaries such as Wittgenstein and more recently George Lakoff and Mark Johnson, that we have called into question the assumption that concepts can serve us as a univocal currency to guarantee the cogency of our arguments. Indeed, we have now largely abandoned the expectation that concepts can be a source of univocity, and the certainty that would attend it. Graham remarks on this recent transition:

> We are losing the faith, except in logic and mathematics, that a concept can be established by precise definitions which free the word from the analogies which guide its ordinary usage.[2]

Instead, given the perceived inseparability of language and action in our

---

[1] Graham, *Studies in Chinese Philosophy*, p. 8.
[2] Graham, *Disputers of the Tao*, p. 120.

"language games," we have come to understand language as being irreducibly interdependent with an always evolving practical context that at best offers us "family resemblances" among the categories we might appeal to in our attempts to best theorize our experience. In our search for cultural equivalencies in comparative philosophy, we might speculate that our earlier essentialist assumptions about the univocal nature of concepts themselves might have arisen from a substance ontology that naturalizes form and stasis and thus favors the more stable, decontextualizing noun as making available to us the unchanging object of knowledge. Such assumptions contrast rather clearly with any attempt to theorize a dynamic process cosmology committed to the inseparability of a rhythmic, contrapuntal forming and functioning (*tiyong* 體用) and thus favors the contextualizing gerund (or verbal noun), not as the object of knowledge per se, but as the source from which we can draw the best reconnoitering information we will require to advance most expeditiously on our prospective journey.

實不喻，然後命，命不喻，然後期，期不喻，然後說，說不喻，然後辨。故期命辨說也者，用之大文也，而王業之始也。名聞而實喻，名之用也。累而成文，名之麗也。用麗俱得，謂之知名。名也者，所以期累實也。辭也者，兼異實之名以論一意也。辨說也者，不異實名以喻動靜之道也。期命也者，辨說之用也。辨說也者，心之象道也。心也者，道之工宰也。道也者，治之經理也。心合於道，說合於心，辭合於說。正名而期，質請而喻，辨異而不過，推類而不悖。聽則合文，辨則盡故。以正道而辨姦，猶引繩以持曲直。是故邪說不能亂，百家無所竄。有兼聽之明，而無矜奮之容；有兼覆之厚，而無伐德之色。說行則天下正，說不行則白道而冥窮。是聖人之辨說也。《詩》曰："顒顒卬卬，如圭如璋，令聞令望。豈弟君子，四方為綱。" 此之謂也。

A name (*ming* 名) is assigned when an actual situation is not understood. It is further stipulated when the name is not understood. It is then given explanation when what is stipulated is not understood. And further distinctions are introduced when the explanation is not understood. Thus, stipulating, naming, making distinctions, and explaining are the important patterns characteristic of our practices and where the undertakings of the king begin.

The function of a name is to allow for the actual situation to be understood when the name is heard. Accruing and completing these patterns is the aesthetic of naming. Getting both their practical function and the aesthetic is called understanding naming. As for names, they are how we stipulate an aggregation of situations. As for phrases, they are how we combine the names for different situations to give expression to one single meaning. As for making distinctions and explaining, they bring coherence to the relationship between situation and name to provide an understanding in our modalities of action. As for stipulating and naming, they are how the making of distinctions and explaining work. As for making distinctions and explaining, they are how the heartmind conjures up the proper way (*dao* 道). As for the heartmind, it is both craftsman and supervisor of the proper way. And as for the proper way, it is what guides and informs good governance.

When the heartmind is in accord with the proper way, when explanations are in accord with the heartmind, and when phrases are in accord with their explanation, then names being used properly are stipulated as such. What is really going on is understood, distinctions and differences are not overstated, and analogical correlations do not bring with them contradictions. What is heard is then in accord with the pattern of events, and distinctions are made that provide an exhaustive account of things.

Using the proper way to circumscribe perversity is like stretching out the plumbline to distinguish the crooked from the straight. In this way, heretical doctrines will not be able to occasion disorder, and the various schools of thought will not be able to falsify its meaning. The sages (*shengren* 聖人) have the clarity of having heard it all, and yet are without the demeanor of arrogance and pride. Their generosity is everywhere and yet they do not parade their moral qualities. When their doctrines prevail, the whole world is properly ordered, but when they do not, even in the midst of their obscurity and poverty, they try to make the proper way clear. These then are the distinctions and explanations made by the sages. This is what the *Book of Songs* 252 means when it says:

So dignified and majestic
Like a jade scepter and mace.
A person heard of and looked up to, far and wide,
Our happy lord brings his guidance to the four quarters.

Comment: Certainly, living language is informed by a history of usage that allows for its content to be stipulated, and in this sense, is retrospective in its meaning. But the need to *zhengming* 正名 does not end here. It is also prospective. That is, it is a living language and has to be used in a way sensitive to the specifics of the always changing context and in a way that respects the uniqueness of the persons involved in the conversation.

We might take a concrete Confucian example of how language is both

IX. THE *XUNZI* 荀子: A SYNCRETIC CONFUCIAN PHILOSOPHY

persistent and evolving within the lived and generative relationships that constitute human narratives. It is because Confucius himself introduces and develops the notion of "consummate persons or conduct" (*ren* 仁) as a key philosophical idea that his students ask him repeatedly to clarify what he means by this term. And he in turn provides each of them with an explanation— an explanation tailored specifically to the different needs of the different students. Indeed, it is often remarked upon that in the *Analects* on six different occasions Confucius is reported to have been asked by his protégés about the meaning of *ren* 仁 or "consummate conduct," and on each of these occasions he gives a different answer. This is because an impoverished, reticent, respectful, and conscientious Yan Hui would need a different understanding of what it means to become consummate in his conduct from a wealthy, self-possessed, assertive, and sometimes self-serving Zigong. We might reflect on the fact that language has syntactical and morphological implications as well as semantic force, and as such, requires a sensitivity to positioning and place (*wei* 位) as integral to its meaning. It is not just what one says that conveys meaning, but where, when, and to whom one is speaking.

One day, recounts the *Xunzi*, the Master is holding court with his protégées, and quizzes each of them to evaluate their current understanding of his neologism, *ren* 仁.① The older, passionate, but less capable student, Zilu, demonstrates some degree of insight in his response. He insists that *ren* 仁 means raising the self-esteem of others and making them feel good about themselves—that is, "causing others to love themselves" (*shiren'aiji* 使人愛己). Indeed, persons who accomplish this, says Confucius, have achieved a degree of refinement, and might be called scholar-officials (*shi* 士). His more imaginative student, Zigong, in replying to Confucius's question about the meaning of *ren* 仁, reverses the force of *ren* 仁 from enabling others to be self-regarding, to be other-regarding oneself, and thus asserts that *ren* 仁 is a kind of altruism—"loving others" (*airen* 愛人). Confucius allows such persons in loving others have indeed attained a higher degree of refinement, and might be called not only scholar-officials

---

① *Xunzi* 105.29.28-31: 子路入，子曰："由！知者若何？仁者若何？"子路對曰："知者使人知己，仁者使人愛己。"子曰："可謂士矣。"子貢入，子曰："賜！知者若何？仁者若何？"子貢對曰："知者知人，仁者愛人。"子曰："可謂士君子矣。"顏淵入，子曰："回！知者若何？仁者若何？"顏淵對曰："知者自知，仁者自愛。"子曰："可謂明君子矣。"

but also exemplary in their persons (*shijunzi* 士君子).

Then Confucius's favorite student, Yan Hui steps up to take his turn, and states flatly that *ren* 仁 means "self-loving" (*ziai* 自愛). Confucius is delighted with what he takes to be a most concise and penetrating understanding of *ren* 仁, describing those given to such self-regarding as exemplary persons who are truly enlightened (*mingjunzi* 明君子). Of course, among discrete "human beings," it would be hard to see how "self-loving" by itself would lead to consummatory conduct. *Ren* 仁 so defined might even be construed as a self-regarding narcissism that would hardly lead to excellence in one's relations. The difference that makes a difference in the case of Confucian "human becomings," however, lies in an alternative understanding of "self" as an evolving configuration of relationships. Yan Hui's point in this passage is that, given the irreducible collaterality of the "human becomings," "self-loving" is neither the self-directed egoism assumed when one encourages others to love themselves nor the other-directed altruism of loving other people. Indeed, for the person comprised of intrinsic rather than extrinsic relations in constitutive rather than contingent roles, such a self-regarding love with its embedded sense of "me" is bi-directional; it is at once reflexive and inclusive. That is, "self-loving" would mean to cherish those specific roles and relationships I am committed to nourishing as the very source and substance of my own personal realization—it is an inclusive "loving me" in my relationship with my spouse, my children, my students, my colleagues, and so on.

This use of a reflexive binomial such as "self-loving" (*ziai* 自愛) found in the *Xunzi* that locates one within one's relationships is quite common in the early Confucian texts. Indeed, Herbert Fingarette suggests that in translating the Confucian philosophical literature which includes terms such as *zixing* 自省, we do better to use the reflexive prefix form of "self-" as in "self-examining" or the postfix "-self" as in "examining myself" as a deliberate strategy for avoiding the entification of a substantial, superordinate self.[①] Fingarette would have us avoid altogether the independent noun "self" as in "examining the self:"

> Why should we reify "self" by giving it the independent noun form in English, and thus impute to Confucius the notion of some inner entity, some

---

[①] See *Analects* 4.17.

core of one's being—whether egoistic or ideal. . . . [W]e ought to make it a point to avoid speaking of "the self" in Confucius. We ought to speak of a person as acting, but not suggesting by "person" this notion of an Actor who somehow embraces inwardly a moral or psychic core which is then expressed in action. On the contrary, the fundamental moral-human reality is . . . the social nexus, and persons along with many other things received their specific, humanly relevant nature, as well as their humanly relevant location, by reference to and as a result of the communal lifeforms. "Person" is an abstraction, a set of complex attributes conceptually abstracted from the social reality; social reality on the other hand is not an abstraction but is the concrete reality.①

辭讓之節得矣，長少之理順矣；忌諱不稱，袄辭不出。以仁心說，以學心聽，以公心辨。不動乎眾人之非譽，不治觀者之耳目，不賂貴者之權埶，不利傳辟者之辭。故能處道而不貳，咄而不奪，利而不流，貴公正而賤鄙爭，是士君子之辨說也。《詩》曰："長夜漫兮，永思騫兮，大古之不慢兮，禮義之不愆兮，人之言兮！"此之謂也。君子之言，涉然而精，俛然而類，差差然而齊。彼正其名，當其辭，以務白其志義者也。彼名辭也者，志義之使也，足以相通，則舍之矣。苟之，姦也。故名足以指實，辭足以見極，則舍之矣。

Exemplary persons (*junzi* 君子) and scholar-officials (*shi* 士) show proper measure in their deference to others, and accord with the ethics of seniority. They are not given to talking about improper things, nor do they give expression to the strange and uncanny. In their explanations they show compassion, they listen with intelligence, and they make their arguments with impartiality. They are not moved by the praise or blame of the many; they don't play to the eyes and ears of those watching on; they can't be bought by the power and privilege of those with high status; and they find no profit in popular lore. It is for this reason that they are able to proceed along the proper way without being sidetracked, can be flexible but not coerced, and can be receptive but not compromised. They honor what is just and proper while despising the mean and the quarrelsome. Such then are the judgments and expositions of exemplary persons and scholar officials. This is what the *Book of Songs* means when it says:

---

① Herbert Fingarette, "Reason, Spontaneity, and the *Li*," *Chinese Texts and Philosophical Contexts: Essays Dedicated to Angus C. Graham*, ed. Henry Rosemont, Jr., La Salle, IL: Open Court, 1991, pp. 198-199.

Slowly moves the long night,
And I am preoccupied with my many failings.
But I have not betrayed high antiquity
And I do not offend against ritual practices (*li* 禮) and moral precepts (*yi* 義).
What worry do I have over what others have to say?

The words of exemplary persons are plain and simple but precise and to the point, and while understated, are appropriate. They go in different directions and yet have their logic. Exemplary persons use names properly and are precise in their phraseology in service to the clarity of their intentions and meaning. For them, these names and this phraseology are the bearers of their intended meaning. Being sufficient for effective communication, they take them no further. To be careless with their words would be immoral. This is the reason that, with names doing justice to the actual situation and their phraseology sufficient to make their point, they take them no further.

Comment: The efficacy of what exemplary persons say not only influences the immediate community, but also has profound and lasting consequences for the world broadly. In the *Book of Changes* that makes explicit a shared cosmology, exemplary persons as the source of effective speech and action are described as being catalytic within a pattern of circumstances that then precipitates a desirable course of events:

君子居其室，出其言，善則千里之外應之，況其邇者乎，居其室，出其言不善，則千里之外違之，況其邇者乎，言出乎身，加乎民，行發乎邇，見乎遠。言行君子之樞機，樞機之發，榮辱之主也。言行，君子之所以動天地也，可不慎乎。

If what exemplary persons (*junzi* 君子) say even while remaining at home is felicitous, those in distant quarters will respond to it; how much more so those near at hand. If what is said is not felicitous, those in distant quarters will oppose it; how much more so those near at hand. What is said comes from one's person but has an effect on the people; actions arise near at hand but are seen from a distance. Words and actions are the hinge and trigger of exemplary persons. And the operations of the hinge and trigger control honor and disgrace. Since it is with words and actions exemplary persons move the heavens and the earth, how could they be but circumspect with respect to them?[①]

The quality of discourse evidenced by exemplary persons is measured by its degree of appropriateness and meaning (*yi* 義), and this sense of appropriateness is whence the feelings of genuine commitment to meaningful relations emerge. Indeed, it is the quality of genuineness within the discourse that is the ground of effective communication, and that distinguishes an emerging consensus from manipulation, inclusive remonstrance from exclusive condemnation, ethical exhortation from indoctrination, and a liberating intimacy from taking liberties and thus invading someone's privacy.

IX.11 Chapter 23: Native Human Propensities Are Base (*xing'e* 性惡)

人之性惡，其善者偽也。今人之性，生而有好利焉，順是，故爭奪生而辭讓亡焉；生而有疾惡焉，順是，故殘賊生而忠信亡焉；生而有耳目之欲，有好聲色焉，順是，故淫亂生而禮義文理亡焉。然則從人之性，順人之情，必出於爭奪，合於犯分亂理，而歸於暴。故必將有師法之化，禮義之道，然後出於辭讓，合於文理，而歸於治。用此觀之，人之性惡明矣，其善者偽也。

The native tendencies (*xing* 性) of human beings are base; that they can become good is a matter of conscious effort (*wei* 偽).

Now with respect to these native tendencies, at birth there is a fondness for personal advantage inherent in them. And when acted upon, these tendencies give rise to aggression and conflict at the expense of any inclination toward courtesy and deference. At birth there are feelings of envy and hatred inherent in them. And when acted upon, these tendencies give rise to violence and cruelty at the expense of any inclination to doing one's best and living up to one's word. At birth there are sensual desires and a fondness for music and beauty inherent in them. And when acted upon, these tendencies give rise to license and wantonness at the expense of any inclination to observe ritual practices (*li* 禮), moral precepts (*yi* 義), and proper formalities.

It is for this reason that indulging these native human tendencies and acting upon such feelings will inevitably give rise to aggression and conflict accompanied by the violation of social roles and the disruption of right

---

① "Great Commentary" A8.

thinking, leading ultimately to violence. Again, it is only when these tendencies are transformed through the influence of teachers and norms and the way of ritual practices and moral precepts that they will occasion conduct inspired by courtesy and deference together with the observance of cultural formalities, and will lead ultimately to proper governance.

Viewing the human condition from this perspective, it is clear our native tendencies are base and they can become good only as a matter of conscious effort.

Comment: Xunzi makes a distinction between native human tendencies (*xing* 性) and the outcomes of conscious effort (*wei* 偽) seen in the "On Ritual" chapter described in the following terms:

> 性者，本始材朴也；偽者，文理隆盛也。無性則偽之無所加，無偽則性不能自美。
> Native human tendencies (*xing* 性) are the basic materials we begin from, and conscious effort (*wei* 偽) is the flourishing of cultural forms and structures. If there were no native tendencies then conscious effort would have nothing on which to work, and if there was no conscious effort, native tendencies would not be able to refine themselves.

This generative process is the historical aestheticization of the human experience that occurs in the contrapuntal relationship between natural tendencies and conscious effort.

Although Xunzi is making a distinction between what we are born with and what is deliberately acquired, we must resist translating Xunzi's naturalism into a metaphysical claim that would align Xunzi with the dualistic realism of a Plato or an Aristotle. Xunzi is not introducing some self-same and immutable "form" or *eidos* "inherent in persons" that propels them to satisfy their final cause or *telos*, thereby separating human beings from their world.

Angus Graham in insisting on distinguishing between Greek substance ontology and Chinese process cosmology, uses the example of the Mencian notion of "person" specifically (that can also be extended to Xunzi) in his insistence that the projection of such foreign teleological assumptions in our translating the term *xing* 性 as "human nature" has led to a profound and persistent misreading of Mencius. Allowing Graham to speak for himself, he says that when we ascribe a theory of "human nature" to Mencius, the very "translation of *xing* 性 by 'nature' predisposes us to mistake it for a transcendent origin, which in Mencian doctrine would also be a transcendent end."[1]

With such teleology and idealism shaping our own commonsense, reading *xing* 性 as "human nature" suggests to us that human "beings" have a universal human essence that is invariant in all times and places, including a human *telos* or end as their erstwhile final cause. Indeed, it is precisely this kind of essentialism that has now become a standard reading of Mencius and Xunzi in the commentarial literature, a persistent teleological misreading that Graham over his long career first endorsed, returned to repeatedly for further reflection, and then ultimately rejected.[2]

孟子曰："今人之性善，將皆失喪其性故也。"曰：若是則過矣。今人之性，生而離其朴，離其資，必失而喪之。用此觀之，然則人之性惡明矣。所謂性善者，不離其朴而美之，不離其資而利之也。使夫資朴之於美，心意之於善，若夫可以見之明不離目，可以聽之聰不離耳，故曰目明而耳聰也。今人之性，飢而欲飽，寒而欲煖，勞而欲休，此人之情性也。今人見長而不敢先食者，將有所讓也；勞而不敢求息者，將有所代也。夫子之讓乎父，弟之讓乎兄，子之代乎父，弟之代乎兄，此二行者，皆反於性而悖於情也；然而孝子之道，禮義之文理也。故順情性則不辭讓矣，辭讓則悖於情性矣。用此觀之，人之性惡明矣，其善者偽也。

Mencius said: "Now the native tendencies (*xing* 性) of mankind are good (*shan* 善), so the cause of their baseness is that they have abandoned and lost such tendencies." I would say this statement is mistaken. With respect to these native tendencies, if at birth persons are already moving away from their simplicity and their basic material, then they are necessarily losing and abandoning such tendencies. From this perspective, it is clear that the native tendencies of human beings are base (*e* 惡). Those who would say the native

---

[1] A.C. Graham, "Replies" in Henry Rosemont Jr. (ed.), *Chinese Texts and Philosophical Contexts: Essays Dedicated to Angus C. Graham*, La Salle, IL: Open Court, 1991, p. 287.

[2] For the history of this revisionist reading, see my "Reconstructing A.C. Graham's Reading of *Mencius* on *xing* 性: A Coda to 'The Background of the Mencian Theory of Human Nature' (1967)," *Having a Word with Angus Graham: At Twenty-five Years into His Immortality,* ed. Carine Defoort and Roger T. Ames, Albany: State University of New York Press, 2018.

tendencies are good are making what is simple into something beautiful and what is basic material into something that has benefit (*li* 利). Their ascribing beauty to what is simple and what is just basic, and goodness to the intentions of the heartmind, is like saying clarity of vision is inseparable from the eyes and acuteness of hearing is inseparable from the ears. The beauty and goodness of the native tendencies is just like the clarity of the eye's vision and the acuteness of the ear's hearing.

Now the native tendencies of human beings are wanting a full stomach when they are hungry, wanting warmth when they are cold, and wanting rest when they are tired. These are the natural feelings and native tendencies of human beings. And yet that persons in the presence of their elders would not dare to eat first is because they want to show them deference. Persons who though tired do not seek their own repose is because they want to give others relief. For sons to defer to their fathers, and younger brothers to their elder brothers, for sons to give relief to their fathers, and younger brothers to their elder brothers—this kind of conduct runs contrary to their native tendencies and is counter to their natural feelings. Such being the case, the way of family reverence (*xiao* 孝) is an expression of the cultural formalities of ritual practices (*li* 禮) and moral precepts (*yi* 義). Thus, to act upon the natural feelings and native tendencies is to show neither courtesy nor deference because showing such courtesy and deference is in fact acting contrary to them.

Looking at it from this perspective, native tendencies are clearly base, and they can become good only as a matter of conscious effort (*wei* 偽).

Comment: Xunzi offers a polemical reading of Mencius. For him, Mencius is claiming that native human tendencies are in the first instance good, and for humans to act otherwise is to lose this propensity. For Xunzi, this assumption is to ascribe a cultivated beauty to what is basic and simple. It is to make the mistake of equating native tendencies with the acquired keenness of our senses.

Xunzi's own position is that our native tendencies and our natural emotions are simply driven by desires and their satisfaction. Cultural forms such as ritual practices and the moral imperatives of family reverence are the product of the conscious effort invested in sublimating these desires into activities that are refined and elegant. Importantly, the relationship that Xunzi sees between native tendencies and conscious effort is collaborative and symbiotic, and as a continuing historical process, has given us our sages and the social and political institutions that define human morality.

問者曰:"人之性惡,則禮義惡生?" 應之曰: 凡禮義者,是生於聖人之僞,非故生於人之性也。故陶人埏埴而爲器,然則器生於陶人之僞,非故生於人之性也。故工人斲木而成器,然則器生於工人之僞,非故生於人之性也。聖人積思慮,習僞故,以生禮義而起法度,然則禮義法度者,是生於聖人之僞,非故生於人之性也。若夫目好色,耳好聽,口好味,心好利,骨體膚理好愉佚,是皆生於人之情性者也;感而自然,不待事而後生之者也。夫感而不能然,必且待事而後然者,謂之生於僞。是性僞之所生,其不同之徵也。

Someone may ask: If native human tendencies (*xing* 性) are in fact base (*e* 惡), how then did ritual practices (*li* 禮) and moral precepts (*yi* 義) arise in the first place?

I would respond to them by saying that, generally speaking, ritual practices and moral precepts arose from the conscious effort (*wei* 僞) of the sages (*shengren* 聖人), and did not arise from something in their native human tendencies. Thus it is that when potters throw their clay to make a vessel, the vessel is the product of the conscious effort of the potters and is not something that comes from their native tendencies. Similarly, when carpenters carve their wood to make a utensil, the utensil is the product of the conscious effort of the carpenters, and is not something that comes from their native tendencies. The sages over time gathered up their different ideas, and through conscious effort tried them out. In so doing they have produced ritual practices and moral precepts, and have generated their norms and standards. These institutions are the product of the conscious effort of the sages, and are not something that comes from their native tendencies.

Now the eye's fondness for beauty, the ear's for fine music, the mouth's for delicious foods, the heartmind's for what is of benefit, and the body's for pleasure and repose all arise from our natural feelings and native tendencies. They are spontaneous impulses and not the product of something we have done. Those things that do not happen as a matter of spontaneous impulse but require us to do something before they can occur are said to be a matter of conscious effort. This then is fair evidence that what is produced as a matter of native tendencies and of conscious effort are indeed different.

Comment: Xunzi is anticipating a question that is sure to arise with regard to his perhaps overly severe distinction between native tendencies and conscious effort. If native tendencies come first, how do human beings in the first instance emerge from the state of nature and their seeming animality, to become cultured and moral persons? Perhaps the answer lies in the perceived nature of the relationship that obtains between *xing* 性 and *wei* 偽. Consistent with the cosmology that provides Xunzi an interpretive context, these categories are correlative and symbiotic rather than dualistic and exclusive, and are historicist rather than ontological. Thus it is that the accumulation of ideas and experimentation in them over time enables particular persons to emerge as sages, and enables them as sages to generate the social and political institutions what are distinctively human. This story of the emergence of both human technologies and institutions is recounted in the *Book of Changes*. The specific sages can be read as historical figures whose names have come to represent a particular epoch in which certain advances were made. That human geniuses in our own era such as a Nietzsche or an Einstein are both historical figures and at the same time, are representative of epochal changes, is not a fact that diminishes them as cultural heroes.

故聖人化性而起偽，偽起而生禮義，禮義生而制法度；然則禮義法度者，是聖人之所生也。故聖人之所以同於眾，其不異於眾者，性也；所以異而過眾者，偽也。夫好利而欲得者，此人之情性也。假之有弟兄資財而分者，且順情性，好利而欲得，若是，則兄弟相拂奪矣；且化禮義之文理，若是，則讓乎國人矣。故順情性則弟兄爭矣，化禮義則讓乎國人矣。

Hence the sages (*shengren* 聖人) applied their conscious effort (*wei* 偽) to transform these native tendencies (*xing* 性). Through conscious effort they were able to generate ritual practices (*li* 禮) and moral precepts (*yi* 義), and to institutionalize their norms and standards. In this way, ritual practices, moral precepts, norms and standards are what have been produced by the sages. Hence the way in which the sages are the same as and no different from the multitude, is in their native tendencies. Where they are different from and excel beyond the multitude, is in their conscious effort.

Now being fond of what will profit us and our desire to acquire it are an expression of our natural feelings and native tendencies. Suppose there is a case wherein a younger and older brother are to proportion out some property and goods. If they act upon their natural feelings and native tendencies—that is, their fondness for what will profit them and their desire to acquire it—they will surely fight over the goods and quarrel with each other. Now were these tendencies to be transformed through the cultural forms of ritual practices and moral precepts, in such a case, they would defer even to a stranger. Hence where we act upon our natural feelings and native tendencies, even brothers will fall to bickering, but where these tendencies have been transformed through ritual practices and moral precepts, we will defer even to a stranger.

Comment: Human cultural forms and institutions have been developed by the sages as the highest order of human beings to transform the untoward consequences of acting upon our natural feelings and native tendencies into a refined and elegant way of life. What is important here is that these initial tendencies have been transformed and sublimated rather than being simply eliminated. Just as this historical process of enculturation has elevated the human experience, it has in its unfolding over time generated a category of cultural heroes called sages. The sages emerge as integral to the continuing process rather than standing outside of it and then acting upon it.

故善言古者，必有節於今；善言天者，必有徵於人。凡論者貴其有辨合，有符驗。故坐而言之，起而可設，張而可施行。今孟子曰："人之性善。"無辨合符驗，坐而言之，起而不可設，張而不可施行，豈不過甚矣哉！故性善則去聖王，息禮義矣。性惡則與聖王，貴禮義矣。故隱栝之生，爲枸木也；繩墨之起，爲不直也；立君上，明禮義，爲性惡也。用此觀之，然則人之性惡明矣，其善者僞也。

Hence those who are good at expounding on antiquity are surely able to show how past events tally with the present day. And those who are good at expounding on nature (*tian* 天) are surely able to produce evidence drawn from the human experience. In such discussions high value is placed on what is consistent with the facts and what is empirically sound. Hence, sitting on their mats they expound their theories, standing up they work them out, and then applying them, they are able to put them into practice.

Now when Mencius says our native tendencies (*xing* 性) are good (*shan* 善), it is neither consistent with the facts nor is it empirically sound. Sitting on his mat he expounds this theory, but standing up he is not able to work it out, and applying it, he is unable to put such a theory into practice. How could he be more mistaken?

If in fact native human tendencies were good, we would have no need of sage-kings (*shengwang* 聖王) and could dispense altogether with ritual practices (*li* 禮) and moral precepts (*yi* 義). But these native tendencies being base (*e* 惡), we must join with the sage-kings and honor ritual practices (*li* 禮) and moral precepts (*yi* 義). The origin of the wood press is the need to straighten what is warped, and the source of the plumbline is the need to true what is crooked. That rulers are set up and illuminate ritual practices and moral precepts is because native tendencies are base. Looking at it from this perspective, native tendencies are clearly base, and they can become good only as a matter of conscious effort (*wei* 偽).

Comment: Xunzi's sustained argument against his (mis-)interpretation of Mencius is that Mencius's claim that native human tendencies are good does not comport with the facts and is empirically false. He thus accuses Mencius of formulating a theory that cannot be authenticated in practice. On Xunzi's reckoning, if our native tendencies are an unlearned given and they are good (a naturalistic position Mencius explicitly rejects in 6A3), we would have a flourishing world with no need for sages or their contrived morality.

Mencius's actual position, however, is that our natural tendencies are prosocial inclinations, and if we cultivate them, they will produce socially efficacious results that are desirable (*keyu* 可欲) and hence what we call "good" (*shan* 善). We have the capacity within the initial conditions of a human narrative to become morally competent persons, but if we do not act upon this capacity, we will lose it.

True to Xunzi's commitment to an epistemology of comprehensiveness, he insists expertise can only be claimed when theory and practice are co-incident. In arguing our native tendencies need to be disciplined, Xunzi's appeal to craftsmen metaphors such as straightening what is bent suggests that the natural condition of wood is that it needs to be worked. And the aesthetics of cabinetmaking is to work such raw and warped materials into a magnificent piece of furniture. Xunzi's own position does not assume some strong "human nature" teleology as a suppressed premise, but rather takes human culture as a fundamentally aesthetic achievement on the part of the moral artisans we designate as our sages because they have been able to accomplish this.

凡人之性者，堯舜之與桀跖，其性一也；君子之與小人，其性一也。今將以禮義積偽爲人之性邪？然則有曷貴堯禹，曷貴君子矣哉！凡貴堯禹君子者，能化性，能起偽，偽起而生禮義。然則聖人之於禮義積偽也，亦猶陶埏而爲之也。用此觀之，然則禮義積偽者，豈人之性也哉！所賤於桀跖小人者，從其性，順其情，安恣睢，以出乎貪利爭奪。故人之性惡明矣，其善者偽也。

Speaking in general terms, as far as native human tendencies (*xing* 性) are concerned, they are the same for the sages Yao and Yu as they are for the despot Jie and the robber Zhi, and they are again the same for exemplary persons (*junzi* 君子) and those who are petty-minded. Can we then still maintain that ritual practices (*li* 禮), moral precepts (*yi* 義), and concerted conscious effort (*wei* 偽) are all integral to our natural tendencies?

If this were the case, then how is it that we honor Yao and Yu, and again how is it that we honor exemplary persons? In fact, that we honor Yao, Yu, and exemplary persons is because they are able to transform their native tendencies and are able to apply conscious effort in doing so. It is through this same conscious effort that they have produced ritual practices and moral precepts. That these sages (*shengren* 聖人) have produced ritual practices and moral precepts through concerted conscious effort is just like potters throwing their pots. Looking at it from this perspective, how could ritual practices, moral precepts, and concerted conscious effort be integral to our native tendencies?

The fact that we look on the despot Jie, the robber Zhi, and petty-minded persons with contempt is because they give free rein to their native tendencies and act upon their natural feelings. Indulging their desires and their ferocity, they are greedy and contentious. Looking at it from this perspective, native tendencies are clearly base (*e* 惡), and they can become good (*shan* 善) only as a matter of conscious effort.

Comment: There are at least two different ways to evaluate the claim that the native tendencies of the sage and the despot are one and the same. A teleological reading would have it that everyone has the potential to become a sage, and that while some realize this potential, others fall far short. An alternative reading would see sages as emerging in the historical process of human enculturation and would thus take this observation in a more aesthetic direction. The potential for persons to become sages lies in and emerges out of the activities that constitute a human narrative. Those ordinary persons who in their own lives achieve *real* significance are sages. And given our initial conditions and our cultural resources, all of us have the opportunity to live such significant lives.

"塗之人可以爲禹。" 曷謂也? 曰：凡禹之所以爲禹者，以其爲仁義法正也。然則仁義法正有可知可能之理。然而塗之人也，皆有可以知仁義法正之質，皆有可以能仁義法正之具，然則其可以爲禹明矣。今以仁義法正爲固無可知可能之理邪？然則唯禹不知仁義法正，不能仁義法正也。將使塗之人固無可以知仁義法正之質，而固無可以能仁義法正之具邪？然則塗之人也，且內不可以知父子之義，外不可以知君臣之正。今不然。塗之人者，皆內可以知父子之義，外可以知君臣之正，然則其可以知之質，可以能之具，其在塗之人明矣。今使塗之人者，以其可以知之質，可以能之具，本夫仁義法正之可知可能之理，可能之具，然則其可以爲禹明矣。今使塗之人伏術爲學，專心一志，思索孰察，加日縣久，積善而不息，則通於神明，參於天地矣。故聖人者，人之所積而致矣。

What does it mean when it is said "any person off the street has the capability to become a sage Yu?"

I would say what makes a Yu a Yu is that he was consummate in his conduct (*ren* 仁), accorded with moral precepts (*yi* 義), and acted according to the norms and what is proper. Moreover, consummate conduct, moral precepts, norms, and propriety have a rationale (*li* 理) by which they can be known and practiced. Since any and all persons off the street have the capability to understand consummate conduct, moral precepts, norms, and propriety, and all have the ability to put them into practice, it is clear then that they all could become a Yu.

Now were we to surmise that there is no rationale by which consummate conduct, moral precepts, norms, and propriety can be known and practiced, then even Yu himself would not be able to know or practice them. Were we to surmise that persons off the street have neither the capability to understand them nor the ability to put them into practice, then at home they would not be able to understand the moral imperative governing the relationship between father and son, and in the public square they would be unable to understand the proper relationship governing ruler and minister.

But this is not the case. Since at home persons off the street do understand the moral imperative governing the relationship between father and son, and in the public sphere do under understand the proper relationship between ruler and minister, it is clear that they have the capability to understand consummate conduct, moral precepts, norms, and propriety, and the ability to put them into practice. And since they have the capacity and the ability, were they to apply themselves to understanding them and practicing them, it is clear that they could become a Yu.

Now if persons off the street were to master the skills and commit themselves to a regimen of study, were they to become single-minded in their purpose, to think through things deeply and carefully, and after an extended period of application, to thus unrelentingly and without respite accrue merit, they could aspire to this quality of brilliance and could form a trinity with the heavens and the earth. As for the sages (*shengren* 聖人), they are simply persons who did as much and reached these heights.

Comment: The Confucian claim "everyone can become a sage" is often read essentialistically as an assertion that the sage is some universally given potential in human nature. When this potential is actualized it provides a person with those extraordinary talents through which to affect the world in some incomparable way. Some interpreters in searching for democratic elements in classical Confucianism have latched on to this universalizing claim as a ground for an egalitarianism. For Xunzi and for Mencius too, it is important to understand that human beings are not "potentially" sages by virtue of some self-same, innate trait defining of all members of humankind who then, by virtue of it, reduplicatively become sages. The claim "everyone can become a sage" is an assertion that the spontaneous emergence of real significance in the ordinary business of the day is itself the meaning and content of sagely virtuosity. Given our initial conditions and our cultural resources, all of us have the opportunity to live such significant lives.

There is an important difference between saying everyone has some inherent potential for becoming a sage, and everyone who through assiduous effort and unrelenting commitment behaves like a sage is in fact a sage. The potential for sagehood lies not *within* individuals exclusive of their worlds, but when sages do appear, they have emerged *pari passu* in the collaborative and transactional careers of human becomings that constitute the substance of a human life. The potential to become a sage emerges over time within the increasingly distinguished narratives of those persons who become most authoritatively human. When the best among us behave habitually and consistently with sagacity in their conduct, they are then sages. Said simply, sages are what sages do.

曰：＂聖可積而致，然而皆不可積，何也？＂曰：可以而不可使也。故小人可以爲君子，而不肯爲君子；君子可以爲小人，而不肯爲小人。小人君子者，未嘗不可以相爲也，然而不相爲者，可以而不可使也。故塗之人可以爲禹，則然；塗之人能爲禹，則未必然也。雖不能爲禹，無害可以爲禹。足可以遍行天下，然而未嘗有遍行天下者也。夫工匠農賈，未嘗不可以相爲事也，然而未嘗能相爲事也。用此觀之，然則可以爲，未必能也；雖不能，無害可以爲。然則能不能之與可不可，其不同遠矣，其不可以相爲明矣。

You might ask: Why is it that sages (*sheng* 聖) can accrue this merit and reach such heights, while everyone else cannot?

I would reply: Although everyone has the capability, they cannot be made to do so. Hence, petty-minded persons are capable of becoming exemplary persons (*junzi* 君子), but they are not willing to do so, and likewise exemplary persons are capable of becoming petty-minded persons but again they are not willing to do so. While they have always been capable of changing places with each other, that they do not do so is what I mean when I say they are capable of doing it, but they cannot be made to do so.

Hence persons off the street are capable of becoming a Yu, but it is not necessarily the case that they are able to do so. Even though they are unable to become a Yu, this does not take away from the fact that they have the capability to do so. We are capable of traversing the globe on foot, but there is no one who has yet to do so.

Now tradesmen, carpenters, farmers, and merchants have always had the capability to do the work of each other's occupations, but they have never done so. Looking at it from this perspective, just because they have the capability does not necessarily mean they are able to do it. And even if they are not able, it does not take away from the fact that they have the capability to do so. Indeed, the difference between capability and ability is huge. That they have always had the capability to trade occupations is clear.[1]

Comment: Xunzi makes an important distinction here between "capability" (*keyi* 可以) and "ability" (*neng* 能) in explanation of the fact that only a few of us become sages. Kwong-loi Shun undertakes a careful analysis of how these two expressions are used in the early philosophical literature, and I take the language of the contrast between "capability" and "ability" from him.[2] Shun demonstrates that a person is "capable" (*keyi* 可以) of doing something only when certain conditions are met: *Analects* 4.2: 不仁者不可以久處約 "Those who are not consummate in their conduct are not capable of enduring hardships for long." The condition of being consummate must be met before hardships can be endured.

Neng 能 on the other hand is simply having the ability to do something,

---

[1] I have emended the text by adding *weichang* 未嘗 in order to continue the parallel structure of the passage.

[2] See Kwong-loi Shun, *Mencius and Early Chinese Thought*, Stanford: Stanford University Press, 1997, pp. 216-218.

but not necessarily doing it. When Mencius is discussing ethical conduct, the conditions for both *keyi* 可以 and *neng* 能 seem to be an emotional disposition to behave in a certain way. Given Mencius's doctrine of the "four inclinations" (*siduan* 四端), the distinction between *keyi* 可以 and *neng* 能 as the ability to do something thus seems moot, and he at times uses the expressions interchangeably.

Xunzi, on the other, is critical of Mencius for precisely the assumption that such an emotional disposition is integral to our native propensities, and so maintains a distinction between "capability" (*keyi* 可以) that requires these emotional conditions first be met before doing something, and *neng* 能 as the ability to do it.

繁弱、鉅黍古之良弓也；然而不得排檠則不能自正。桓公之葱，太公之闕，文王之錄，莊君之曶，闔閭之干將、莫邪、鉅闕、辟閭，此皆古之良劍也；然而不加砥厲則不能利，不得人力則不能斷。驊騮、騹驥、纖離、綠耳，此皆古之良馬也；然而必前有銜轡之制，後有鞭策之威，加之以造父之馭，然後一日而致千里也。夫人雖有性質美而心辯知，必將求賢師而事之，擇良友而友之。得賢師而事之，則所聞者堯舜禹湯之道也；得良友而友之，則所見者忠信敬讓之行也。身日進於仁義而不自知也者，靡使然也。今與不善人處，則所聞者欺誣詐偽也，所見者汙漫淫邪貪利之行也，身且加於刑戮而不自知者，靡使然也。傳曰："不知其子視其友，不知其君視其左右。"靡而已矣！靡而已矣！

Fanruo and Jushu are two famous bows from antiquity. But if they had not been pressed into shape with the bow-press, they would not have been able to true themselves. The Cong of Duke Huan, the Que of the Grand Duke, the Lu of King Wen, the Hu of Lord Zhuang, and King Helü's Ganjiang, Moye, Juque, and Bilü are all famous swords from antiquity. But if they had not been honed on the whetstone, they would not have been able to achieve their sharpness, and if they were not wielded with human strength, they would not have been able to cut into anything. Hualiu, Qiji, Xianli, and Lü'er are all famous steeds from antiquity. But before they could journey a thousand *li* in a single day it was necessary to restrain them with the bit and bridle in front, to coax them on with a horse whip from behind, and in addition, to have them driven by the legendary Zaofu.

Now even if there are persons who are exceptional by nature and who have a discriminating mind, it is essential that they seek out a worthy teacher to work under, and select out the best of companions as their friends. If they can work under a worthy teacher, then what they will learn will be the ways (*dao* 道) of Yao, Shun, Yu, and Tang. And if they can associate with the best of companions, then what they will experience will be conduct that is conscientious (*zhong* 忠), has integrity (*xin* 信), is respectful (*jing* 敬), and shows deference. Every day without even being aware of it, they will be making progress in the moral quality of their conduct because they will be molded by their environment.

Now if such persons dwell together with bad people, then what they will learn is cheating, deceit, fraud, and hypocrisy, and what they will experience will be conduct that is indolent, wanton, depraved, and insatiable. They will in their persons without even being aware of it, be moving ever closer to the severest of punishments because they will be molded by their environment. There is a traditional saying: "If you do not know someone, look to their friends; if you do not know a ruler, look to his attendants." It is the environment, just the environment.

Comment: For Xunzi, given his interpretive context, nothing is what it is simply by virtue of some intrinsic value. Rather, the legendary examples of excellence have all been shaped and been made what they are by contextualizing influences. Since this is as true of persons as it is of bows, swords, and horses, it is incumbent upon persons regardless of their native talents to seek out the most worthy teachers and the most admirable of friends. Such an attitude is consistent with the Confucian precept that the substance of morality is growth in one's roles and relations through the internalization of the fecund social, natural, and cultural resources that would conduce to such flourishing.

BIBLIOGRAPHY OF WORKS CITED

Ames, Roger T. (2022). "Unloading the Essentialism Charge: Reflections on Methodology in Doing Philosophy of Culture," in *Comparative Philosophy and Method: Contemporary Practices and Future Possibilities*, ed. Steven Burik, Robert Smid, and Ralph Weber. London: Bloomsbury Academic Press.

—— (2021). *Human Becomings: Theorizing Persons for Confucian Role Ethics*. Albany: State University of New York Press.

—— (2018). "Reconstructing A.C. Graham's Reading of Mencius on *xing* 性: A Coda to 'The Background of the Mencian Theory of Human Nature' (1967)," in *Having a Word with Angus Graham: At Twenty-five Years into His Immortality*, ed. Carine Defoort and Roger T. Ames. Albany: State University of New York Press.

—— (2016). "On Teaching and Learning (*Xueji* 學記): Setting the Root in Confucian Education," in *Chinese Philosophy on Teaching and Learning: Xueji* 學記 *in the Twenty-First Century*, ed. Xu Di and Hunter McEwan. Albany: State University of New York Press.

—— (2016). "Philosophizing with Canonical Chinese Texts: Seeking an Interpretive Context," in *The Bloomsbury Research Handbook of Chinese Philosophy Methodologies*, ed. Sor-hoon Tan. London: Bloomsbury Press.

—— (2011). "War, Death and Ancient Chinese Cosmology: Thinking Through the Thickness of Culture," in *Mortality in Traditional Chinese Thought*, ed. Amy Olberding and Philip J. Ivanhoe. Albany: State University of New York Press.

—— (2011). *Confucian Role Ethics: A Vocabulary*. Honolulu and Hong Kong: University of Hawai'i and Chinese University Press joint publication. Reprinted (2020). Albany: State University of New York Press.

—— (1991). "Pluralism and Protest: The Chinese Experience," in *China Report* 27(2).

Ames, Roger T. and David L. Hall (trans.) (2001). *Focusing the Familiar: A Translation and Philosophical Interpretation of the* Zhongyong. Honolulu: University of Hawai'i Press.

Barnes, Johnathan (ed.) (1984). *The Complete Works of Aristotle: The Revised Oxford Translation*. Princeton: Princeton University Press.

Behuniak, James, Jr. (2005). *Mencius on Becoming Human*. Albany: State University of New York Press.

Berthrong, John (1998). *Concerning Creativity: A Comparison of Chu Hsi, Whitehead, and Neville*. Albany: State University of New York Press.

Chan Wing-tsit (1963). *A Source Book in Chinese Philosophy*. Princeton: Princeton University Press.

Chang Kwang-chih (1964). "Some Dualistic Phenomena in Shang Society," in *Journal of Asian Studies* 24(1).

Cheever, Susan (2007). *American Bloomsbury: Louisa May Alcott, Ralph Waldo Emerson, Margaret Fuller, Nathaniel Hawthorne, and Henry David Thoreau: Their Lives, Their Loves, Their Work*. New York: Simon and Schuster.

Chen Lai 陳來 (2009). 竹帛《五行》與簡帛研究. Beijing: SDX Joint Publishing Company.

Ch'ü, T.T. (1961). *Law and Society in Traditional China*. Paris and The Hague: Mouton & Co.

Cua, A.S. (1985). *Ethical Argumentation: A Study in Hsün Tzu's Moral Epistemology*. Honolulu: University of Hawai'i Press.

Defoort, Carine and Nicolas Standaert (ed.) (2013). *The Mozi as an Evolving Text: Different Voices in Early Chinese Thought*. Leiden: Brill.

Dewey, John (2009). *The Correspondence of John Dewey, 1871-2007 (I-IV)*, Electronic Edition, Vol. 1, 1871-1918, 1891.03.14 (00453) John Dewey to Thomas Davidson, ed. Larry Hickman. Virginia: InteLex Corporation.

—— (2008). *The Middle Works of John Dewey*, Vol. 4, ed. Jo Ann Boydston. Carbondale: Southern Illinois University Press.

—— (1985). *The Later Works of John Dewey* (1925-1953), Vols. 1 and 14, ed. Jo Ann Boydston. Carbondale: Southern Illinois University Press.

—— (1934). *Art as Experience*. New York: Penguin.

Dubs, Homer H. (1928). *The Works of Hsüntze*. London: Probsthain.

Elvin, Mark (1985). "Between Earth and Heaven: Conceptions of the Self in China," in *The Category of the Person: Anthropology, Philosophy, History*, ed. Michael Carrithers, Steven Collins, and Steven Lukas. Cambridge: Cambridge University Press.

Emerson, Ralph Waldo (1862). "American Civilization," in *Atlantic Monthly* 9.

Farquhar, Judith (1999). "Technologies of Everyday Life: The Economy of Impotence in Reform China," in *Cultural Anthropology* 14(2).

—— (1994). *Knowing Practice: The Clinical Encounter of Chinese Medicine*. Boulder: Westview Press.

—— (1991). "Objects, Processes, and Female Infertility in Chinese Medicine," in *Medical Anthropology Quarterly* (NS) 5(4).

Fehl, Noah (1971). *Li: Rites and Propriety in Literature and Life*. Hong Kong: Chinese University Press.

Fingarette, Herbert (1991). "Reason, Spontaneity, and the *Li*," in *Chinese Texts and Philosophical Contexts: Essays Dedicated to Angus C. Graham*, ed. Henry Rosemont Jr. La Salle, IL: Open Court.

—— (1983). "The Music of Humanity in the *Conversations of Confucius*," in *Journal of Chinese Philosophy* 10(4).

Fraser, Chris (2020). *The Essential Mozi: Ethical, Political, and Dialectical Writings*. Oxford: Oxford University Press.

—— (2016). *The Philosophy of the Mozi: The First Consequentialists*. New York: Columbia University Press.

—— (2010). "Mohism," in *The Stanford Encyclopedia of Philosophy (Fall 2012 Edition)*, ed. Edward N. Zalta. http://plato.stanford.edu/archives/fall2012/entries/mohism/.

Fung Yu-lan (1952). *A History of Chinese Philosophy*, trans. D. Bodde. Princeton: Princeton University Press.

Gao Heng 高亨 (1979). 周易大傳今注. Jinan: Qilu Shushe.

Geaney, Jane (2002). *On the Epistemology of the Senses in Early Chinese Thought*. Honolulu: University of Hawai'i Press.

Graham, A.C. (1991). "Replies," in *Chinese Texts and Philosophical Context: Essays Dedicated to Angus C. Graham*, ed. Henry Rosemont Jr. La Salle, IL: Open Court.

—— (1990). *Studies in Chinese Philosophy and Philosophical Literature*. Albany: State University of New York Press.

—— (1989). *Disputers of the Tao: Philosophical Argument in Ancient China*. La Salle, IL: Open Court.

—— (1978). *Later Mohist Logic, Ethics and Science*. Hong Kong: Chinese University Press.

Granet, Marcel (1977). "Right and Left in China," in *Right and Left: Essays on Dual Symbolic Classification*, ed. Rodney Needham. Chicago: University of Chicago Press.

—— (1934). *La pensée chinoise*. Paris: Editions Albin Michel.

Hagen, Kurtis (2007). *The Philosophy of Xunzi: A Reconstruction*. La Salle, IL: Open Court.

Hall, David L. (1982). *Eros and Irony: A Prelude to Philosophical Anarchism*. Albany: State University of New York.

Hall, David L. and Roger T. Ames (1998). *Thinking from the Han: Self, Truth, and Transcendence in Chinese and Western Culture*. Albany: State University of New York Press.

—— (1995). *Anticipating China: Thinking Through the Narratives of Chinese and Western Culture*. Albany: State University of New York Press.

—— (1987). *Thinking Through Confucius*. Albany: State University of New York Press.

Hamilton, Gary G. and Wang Zheng (trans.) (1992). *From the Soil: The Foundations of Chinese Society, A Translation of Fei Xiaotong's Xiangtu Zhongguo* 鄉土中國. Berkeley: University of California Press.

Hansen, Chad (1992). *A Daoist Theory of Chinese Thought*. Hong Kong: Oxford University Press.

Hay, John (1994). "The Persistent Dragon (lung [long])," in *The Power of Culture*, ed.

W. Peterson, A. Plaks, and Y.S. Yü. Hong Kong: Chinese University Press.

Hoyt, Sarah F. (1912). "The Etymology of Religion," in *Journal of the American Oriental Society* 32(2).

Hsiao Kung-chuan (1979). *A History of Chinese Political Thought*, trans. Frederick W. Mote. Princeton: Princeton University Press.

Hutton, Eric (2005). *Readings in Classical Chinese Philosophy*, 2nd edition, ed. P.J. Ivanhoe and Bryan Van Norden. Indianapolis: Hackett Publishing Company.

Ivanhoe, P.J. (1990). *Ethics in the Confucian Tradition*. Atlanta: Scholars Press.

James, William (1981). *The Varieties of Religious Experience: A Study in Human Nature*. New York: Penguin.

—— (1984). *William James: The Essential Writings*, ed. Bruce W. Wilshire. Albany: State University of New York Press.

Jiang Tao (2006). "Intimate Authority: The Rule of Ritual in Classical Confucian Political Discourse," in *Confucian Cultures of Authority*, ed. Peter D. Hershock and Roger T. Ames. Albany: State University of New York Press.

Johnson, Mark (1987). *The Body in the Mind: The Bodily Basis of Meaning, Imagination, and Reason*. Chicago: University of Chicago Press.

Johnston, Ian (2010). *The Mozi: A Complete Translation*. Hong Kong and New York: Chinese University Press and Columbia University Press joint publication.

Johnston, Ian and Wang Ping (trans.) (2012). *Daxue and Zhongyong: Bilingual Edition*. Hong Kong: Chinese University Press.

Jullien, François (trans.) (2016). *The Book of Beginnings*. New Haven: Yale University Press.

Karlgren, Bernhard (trans.) (1950). *The Book of Odes*. Stockholm: Bulletin of the Museum for Far Eastern Antiquities.

Keightley, David (1990). "Early Civilization in China: Reflections on How it Became Chinese," in *Heritage of China: Contemporary Perspectives on Chinese Civilization*, ed. Paul S. Ropp. Berkeley: University of California Press.

—— (1988). "Shang Divination and Metaphysics," in *Philosophy East and West* 38(4).

Kim, Myeong-seok (2014). "Is There No Distinction Between Reason and Emotion in *Mengzi*?" in *Philosophy East and West* 64(1).

Knoblock, J. (1988, 1990, 1994). *Xunzi: A Translation and Study of the Complete Works*, Vols. 1-3. Stanford: Stanford University Press.

Kwan Tze-wan. "Multi-function Character Database," at http://humanum.arts.cuhk.edu.hk/Lexis/lexi-mf/.

Lau, D.C. (trans.) (1984). *Mencius: A Bilingual Edition*. Hong Kong: Chinese University Press.

—— (trans.) (1983). *Confucius: The Analects (Lunyu)*. Hong Kong: Chinese University Press.

—— (trans.) (1970). *Mencius*. London: Penguin.

Lau, D.C. and Chen Fong Ching (1992). *A Concordance to the Hanshi Waizhuan*. Hong Kong: The Commercial Press.

—— (1992). *A Concordance to the Huainanzi*. Hong Kong: The Commercial Press.

Legge, James (trans.) (1960 rep.). *The Chinese Classics*, 5 Volumes. Hong Kong: University of Hong Kong Press.

Leibniz, G.W. (1998). *Writings on China*, trans. Daniel J. Cook and Henry Rosemont Jr. La Salle, IL: Open Court.

Li Zehou 李澤厚 (2018). "An Explanation of the Summary Chart on Ethics" 關於"倫理學總覽表"的説明, in *Zhongguo Wenhua* 中國文化 1.

Liang Tao 梁涛 (2004). "Zhu Xi dui 'Shendu' de Wudu jiqi zai Jingxue Quanshi zhong de Yiyi" 朱熹對"慎獨"的誤讀及其在經學詮釋中的意義, in *Zhexue Yanjiu* 哲學研究 3.

Loewe, Michael (1982). *Chinese Ideas of Life and Death: Faith, Myth and Reason in the Han Period* (202BC-220AD). London: Allen and Unwin.

Major, John (1993). *Heaven and Earth in Early Han Thought*. Albany: State University of New York Press.

—— (1977). "Reply to Richard Kunst's Comments on *hsiu* and *wu hsing*," in *Early China* 3.

—— (1976). "A Note on the Translation of Two Technical Terms in Chinese Science: *wu-hsing* and *hsiu*," in *Early China* 2.

Makeham, John (1996). "The Formation of *Lunyu* as a Book," in *Monumenta Serica* 44.

Mote, Frederick (1972). "The Cosmological Gulf Between China and the West," in *Transition and Permanence: Chinese History and Culture*, ed. David C. Buxbaum and Frederick W. Mote. Hong Kong: Cathay Press.

Munro, Donald (1979). *Concept of Man in Contemporary China*. Ann Arbor: University of Michigan Press.

—— (1979). "The Shape of Chinese Values in the Eye of an American Philosopher," in *The China Difference*, ed. Ross Terrill. New York: Harper & Row.

Needham, Joseph (1956). *Science and Civilisation in China*, Vol. II. Cambridge: Cambridge University Press.

Ni Peimin (trans.) (2017). *Understanding the Analects of Confucius: A New Translation of* Lunyu *with Annotations*. Albany: State University of New York Press.

Nylan, Michael (2011). *Yang Xiong and the Pleasures of Reading and Classical Learning in China*. New Haven: American Oriental Society.

Olberding, Amy (2019). *The Wrong of Rudeness: Learning Modern Civility from Ancient Chinese Philosophy*. New York: Oxford University Press.

Palsson, Gisli, et al. (2013). "Reconceptualizing the 'Anthropos' in the Anthropocene: Integrating the Social Sciences and Humanities in Global Environmental Change Research," in *Environmental Science & Policy* 28.

Pang Pu 龐樸 (2000). Zhubo "Wuxingpian" Jiaozhu ji Yanjiu 竹帛《五行》篇校注及研究. Taipei: Wanjuanlou.

—— (1999). "Yizhong Youji de Yuzhou Shengcheng Tushi: Jieshao Chujian *Taiyi Shengshui* 一種有機的宇宙生成圖式：介紹楚簡《太一生水》," in *Daojia Wenhua Yanjiu* 道家文化研究 17.

Peerenboom, Randell P. (1998). "Confucian Harmony and Freedom of Thought: The Right to Think Versus Right Thinking," in *Confucianism and Human Rights*, ed. Wm. T. de Bary and Tu Wei-ming. New York: Columbia University Press.

Perkins, Franklin (2004). *Leibniz and China*. Cambridge: Cambridge University Press.

Peters, F.E. (1967). *Greek Philosophical Terms: A Historical Lexicon*. New York: New York University Press.

Peterson, Willard J. (1982). "Making Connections: Commentary on the Attached Verbalizations of the *Book of Change*," in *Harvard Journal of Asiatic Studies* 42(1).

Reding, Jean-Paul (2004). "Words for Atoms, Atoms for Words—Comparative Considerations on the Origins of Atomism in Ancient Greece and the Absence of Atomism in Ancient China," in *Comparative Essays in Greek and Chinese Rational Thinking*. Aldershot: Ashgate.

Rosemont, Henry, Jr. (2015). *Against Individualism: A Confucian Rethinking of the Foundations of Morality, Politics, Family and Religion*. Idaho Falls: Lexington Books.

—— (1970). "State and Society in the *Hsün Tzu* [*Xunzi*]: A Philosophical Commentary," in *Monumenta Serica* 29.

Rosemont, Henry, Jr. and Roger T. Ames (2008). "Family Reverence (*xiao*) as the Source of Consummatory Conduct (*ren*)," in *Dao: A Journal of Comparative Philosophy* 7(1).

—— (trans.) (1998). *The Analects of Confucius: A Philosophical Translation*. New York: Ballantine.

Sandel, Michael (1982). *Liberalism and the Limits of Justice*. Cambridge: Cambridge University Press.

Schilpp, Paul (ed.) (1941). *The Philosophy of Alfred North Whitehead*. New York: Tudor.

Schipper, Kristofer (1978). "The Taoist Body," in *History of Religions* 17(3/4).

Schleiermacher, Friedrich (1999). *The Christian Faith*, ed. H.R. Mackintosh and J.S. Stewart. London: T & T Clark.

Schwartz, Benjamin (1985). *The World of Thought in Ancient China*. Cambridge, MA: Harvard University Press.

Shaughnessy, Edward L. (trans.) (1997). *I Ching: The Classic of Changes*. New York: Ballantine.

Shun Kwong-loi (1997). *Mencius and Early Chinese Thought*. Stanford: Stanford University Press.

Shusterman, Richard (2008). *Body Consciousness: A Philosophy of Mindfulness and Somaesthetics*. Cambridge: Cambridge University Press.

Sima Qian 司馬遷 (1959). *Shiji* 史記 (*Records of the Grand Historian*). Beijing:

Zhonghua Shuju.

Sivin, Nathan (1995). *Medicine, Philosophy and Religion in Ancient China: Researches and Reflections*. Aldershot: Variorum.

—— (1974). Foreword to Manfred Porkert, *The Theoretical Foundations of Chinese Medicine*. Cambridge, MA: MIT Press.

Slingerland, Edward (trans.) (2003). *Analects: With Selections from Traditional Commentaries*. Indianapolis: Hackett Publishing.

Sommer, Deborah (2008). "Boundaries of the Tǐ Body," in *Asia Major* Third Series 11.

Tang Junyi 唐君毅 (1991). *The Complete Works of Tang Junyi* 唐君毅全集, Vols. 4, 5, 11 and 13. Taipei: Xuesheng Shuju.

—— (1953). *The Spiritual Value of Chinese Culture* 中國文化之精神價值. Taipei: Zhengzhong Shuju.

—— (1943). *Collected Studies on a Comparison of Chinese and Western Philosophical Thinking* 中西哲學思想之比較研究集. Taipei: Zhengzhong Shuju.

Taylor, Charles (2016). *The Language Animal: The Full Shape of the Human Linguistic Capacity*. Cambridge, MA: Harvard University Press.

—— (1989). *Sources of the Self: The Making of the Modern Identity*. Cambridge, MA: Harvard University Press.

Tredennick, Hugh (trans.) (1954). *The Last Days of Socrates*. New York: Penguin.

Tredennick, Hugh and Harold Tarrant (trans.) (1993). *Plato: The Last Days of Socrates*. London: Penguin.

Tu Wei-ming (1997). "Chinese Philosophy: A Synopsis," in *A Companion to World Philosophies*, ed. Eliot Deutsch and Ron Bontekoe. Oxford: Blackwell.

—— (1989). *Centrality and Commonality: An Essay on Confucian Religiousness*. Albany: State University of New York Press.

Waley, Arthur (trans.) (1937). *The Book of Songs*. London: Grove Press.

Wang Aihe (2000). *Cosmology and Political Culture in Early China*. Cambridge: Cambridge University Press.

Watson, Burton (trans.) (1963). *Hsün Tzu: Basic Writings*. New York: Columbia University Press.

Whitehead, A.N. (1985). *Process and Reality: An Essay in Cosmology*, Donald Sherburne Corrected Edition. New York: Free Press.

—— (1938). *Modes of Thought*. New York: Macmillan.

Williams, Bernard (1981). *Moral Luck: Philosophical Papers 1973-1980*. New York: Cambridge University Press.

Wong, David B. (1991). "Is There a Distinction Between Reason and Emotion in Mencius?" in *Philosophy East and West* 41(1).

Xu Weiyu 許維遹 (ed.) (1955). *Lüshichunqiu Jishi* 呂氏春秋集釋. Beijing: Wenxue Guji Kanxingshe.

Yang Bojun 楊伯峻 (1960). 孟子譯注. Beijing: Zhonghua Shuju.

Yu Jiyuan (2007). *The Ethics of Confucius and Aristotle: Mirrors of Virtue*. New York: Routledge.

Zhang Xianglong 張祥龍 (2008). "概念化思維與象思維 (Conceptualizing Thinking and Imagistic Thinking)," in *Journal of Hangzhou Normal University* 5.

Zhao Tingyang 趙汀陽 (2016). 惠此中國 (*The Making and Becoming of China*). Zhongxin Chubanshe (CITIC Press Group).

Zhou Zhongling 周鍾靈, Shi Xiaoshi 施孝適, and Xu Weixian 許惟賢 (ed.) (1982). *Hanfeizi Suoyin* 韓非子索引. Beijing: Zhonghua Shuju.

Zhou Yiqun (2010). *Festival, Feasts, and Gender Relations in Ancient China and Greece*. New York: Cambridge University Press.

Zhuangzi 莊子 (1947). *Zhuangzi Yinde* 莊子引得 (*A Concordance to Chuang Tzu*), Harvard-Yenching Institute Sinological Index Series, Supp. 20, ed. Hong Ye. Peking: Harvard Yenching Institute.